Wiley CMA™ Exam Review
STUDY
GUIDE

2023

Part 1: Financial Planning, Performance, and Analytics

Wiley CMA™ Exam Review

STUDY GUIDE

2023

Part 1: Financial Planning, Performance, and Analytics

Cassy Budd
Kip Holderness
Kari Olsen
Monte Swain
Marjorie Yuschak
Tamara Phelan

Cover design: Wiley
Cover image: © shuoshu/Getty Images

For general information on our other products and services or for technical support, please contact our Customer Care Department within the United States at (800) 762-2974, outside the United States at (317) 572-3993 or fax (317) 572-4002.

Wiley publishes in a variety of print and electronic formats and by print-on-demand. Some material included with standard print versions of this book may not be included in e-books or in print-on-demand. If this book refers to media such as a CD or DVD that is not included in the version you purchased, you may download this material at http://booksupport.wiley.com. For more information about Wiley products, visit www.wiley.com.

Library of Congress Publication Data:

ISBN 978-1-394-15182-0 (print)
ISBN 978-1-394-15184-4 (ePDF)
ISBN 978-1-394-15186-8 (ePub)

Printed in the United States of America.

SKY10036195_092922

Contents

About the Instructors

Cassy Budd, MAcc, B.S.
Cassy Budd is a Teaching Professor at Brigham Young University in the Accountancy School. She has more than 10 years of experience in public accounting (with PricewaterhouseCoopers) and 16 years of experience teaching accounting at the University level (3 years at USU and 13 years at BYU). Through the years, she has been honored to win the Norm and Cindy Nemrow Excellence in Teaching Professorship (2017), Advisor of the Year at Utah State University School Of Accountancy (2004), the Service Learning Engaged Scholar award (2004), the Mark Chain/FSA 2016 Innovation Graduate Teaching Award (2016), the Teaching Excellence Award from the Marriott School of Management (2015), and the Dean Fairbanks Teaching and Learning Faculty Fellowship at Brigham Young University (2012).

She speaks Italian and has a wonderful husband of 30 years, 4 amazing children, and a darling grandson. Together, they love to spend time outdoors hiking, biking, skiing and simply enjoying nature. Cassy currently serves as the President of the Teaching, Learning and Curriculum section of the American Accounting Association.

Cassy wrote and lectures Part 1, Section A, "External Financial Reporting Decisions."

Kip Holderness, Ph.D., CMA
Kip Holderness is an Assistant Professor and Accounting Ph.D. Coordinator at West Virginia University, where he has taught since 2013. Prior to this, he has experience teaching accounting at Brigham Young University. He teaches managerial and forensic accounting and works extensively with doctoral students conducting various research projects. Kip teaches internal controls, as well as the technology and analytics sections of the CMA exam. His research focuses primarily on the impact of fraud and employee deviance on organizations. He has received numerous research grants from the Institute for Fraud Prevention and the Institute of Management Accountants. In his spare time, Kip enjoys cabinetry and beekeeping.

Kip wrote and lectures the following:

- Part 1, Section E, "Internal Controls"

- Part 1, Section F, "Technology and Analytics"

Kari Joseph Olsen, Ph.D., CPA, CMA
Kari Joseph Olsen is the Associate Professor of Accounting at Utah Valley University and has published research on management control systems and personality characteristics in the *Journal of Management Accounting Research, Journal of the America Taxation Association*, and in *Issues in Accounting Education*. He received his Ph.D. in accounting from the University of Southern California in 2015, and he received his M.S. and B.S. in accounting from BYU in 2009. He teaches management accounting, and his research interests are in management control systems, performance feedback, and personality characteristics. Through his years of teaching, he has received various awards, including the UVU MBA Outstanding Faculty award (2019), the USC Mary Pickford Foundation Doctoral Teaching Award (2014), and the USC Marshall Ph.D. Teaching Award (2013).

Kari wrote and lectures the following:

- Part 2, Section B, "Corporate Finance"

- Part 2, Section D, "Risk Management"

Monte Swain, Ph.D., CPA, CMA, CGMA

Monte Swain is the Deloitte Professor in the School of Accounting at Brigham Young University. Since graduating from Michigan State University in 1991, he has researched and taught management accounting at Brigham Young University. He offers advanced instruction and research in management accounting and strategic performance measures. His specialties include behavioral issues in decision support systems, activity-based costing, and activity-based management, among others. Through his career, he been the recipient of a number of teaching awards, including the Brummet Distinguished Award for Management Accounting Educators from the Institute of Management Accountants (2016) and the Faculty Mentoring Award from the BYU Executive MBA Program (2015). Additionally, he is a licensed CPA and Certified Management Accountant.

As the lead lecturer on Wiley CMA™ Review Course, Monte wrote and lectures the following sections:

- Part 1, Section B, "Planning, Budgeting, and Forecasting"
- Part 1, Section C, "Performance Management"
- Part 1, Section D, "Cost Management"
- Part 2, Section C, "Decision Analysis"
- Part 2, Section E, "Investment Decisions"
- Part 2, Section F, "Professional Ethics"

Marjorie Yuschak, MBA, CMA

Marjorie Yuschak is an adjunct professor at The College of New Jersey. She teaches Financial Accounting and Managerial Accounting courses and leverages her 20+ years of experience as a former finance manager to help train executives to effectively present ideas that positively influence business outcomes. She began her career at Johnson & Johnson developing an expertise in cost/managerial accounting, financial reporting, and employee stock option programs. Marj also facilitates the CMA review classes for Villanova University and runs a consulting business that provides coaching for accounting, communication skills, and small business management. She is a member of the Raritan Valley Chapter of the IMA in New Jersey.

Marj wrote and lectures Part 2, Section A, "Financial Statement Analysis."

Tamara Phelan, MBA, CPA, CMA

Tamara Phelan is an Instructor in the Department of Accountancy at Northern Illinois University, and she received her MM from Northwestern University in Finance and Marketing.

Tamara wrote and lectures the lesson "Integrated Reporting," which appears in Part 1, Section A, "External Financial Reporting Decisions."

About the Exam

CMA Exam Procedures and Registration

Becoming a Certified Management Accountant requires time and effort — but the opportunities for career advancement are worth it.

Meet These Requirements

Maintain membership in IMA. If you aren't a member, join IMA now at www.imanet.org/membership.

- Hold a bachelor's degree from an accredited college/university or a related professional certification. Please refer to the IMA's CMA Requirements section at www.imanet.org/cma-certifcation/getting-started

- Have at least two continuous years of professional experience in management accounting or financial management.

- Enter into the CMA program. Visit www.cmacertifcation.org for more information.

- Complete and pass Parts 1 and 2 of the CMA Exam.

- Abide by the IMA's Statement of Ethical Professional Practice, found at www.imanet.org/insights-and-trends/business-leadership-and-ethics/ima-statement-of-ethical-professional-practice

Don't meet the educational or professional experience requirements and want to get certified? There is an option for every situation. IMA offers a seven-year grace period for candidates in this situation. You can sit for the exam and then finish your bachelor's degree or two years of professional experience within the next seven years from the date of the exam. Once you do, you'll automatically become an active CMA.

Take the CMA Exam

The CMA exam is broken into two parts, which are both computer-based and administered in hundreds of testing facilities worldwide. With three two-month testing windows each year, you can sit for each exam part at a time and place convenient for you.

Examination Windows:
Exams are offered only during these two-month periods:

1. January and February

2. May and June

3. September and October

> **Note**
> While the testing windows here are typical, Covid-19 has affected test windows, with some windows expanding to accommodate disruptions in testing. For example, the May and June window in 2021 was expanded to April, May, and June. Check for updated dates and other testing news at https://www.prometric.com/test-takers/search/icma

Register for the CMA Exam

Follow these easy steps to fulfill the examination requirement for your CMA certification:

Step 1: Register for the exam at www.imanet.org/cma-certifcation/

Step 2: Receive confirmation of your registration, which provides your authorization number(s), testing window(s), and the Instructions for Candidates.

Step 3: Schedule your exam appointment(s) with Prometric, IMA's testing partner: www.prometric.com.

Step 4: Show up for your scheduled exam appointment(s) with the required identification documents.

> **Tip**
> Be sure to schedule your appointment as soon as possible. Your authorization number is only valid for the testing window you selected. You can't postpone your exams.

Exams are administered via Prometric Testing Centers throughout the world and are available in accordance with local customs. To locate a Testing Center and schedule exam appointments, visit www.prometric.com/ICMA

Exam Fees

Professional Member Fees

Non-refundable CMA Entrance Fee: $250*

Exam Fee: $415 per part

Rescheduling Fee**: $50

Student/Academic Member Fees

Non-refundable CMA Entrance Fee: $188*

Exam Fee: $311 per part

Rescheduling Fee**: $50

Total Cost to Earn Your CMA with No Exam Retakes:

Non-Student/Professional: $1080

Student (still in school): $810

*The CMA Entrance Fee covers:

- Credential review for educational qualification
- Credential review for experience qualification
- SIx months access to the CMA Exam Support package, which includes printable practice questions
- Final Score Report
- Performance feedback reports for candidates who do not pass
- Personalized, numbered certificate for office display
- Congratulatory notification to employer or others, if desired[1]

CMA Exam Scoring

The CMA Exam has a unique scoring system that can sometimes be confusing for candidates. Here's everything you need to know to correctly interpret your CMA Exam score.

Release of CMA Exam Scores

Essays are graded offline by the ICMA, the certifying body of IMA, so do not expect to see your results the day of your exam. Instead, the ICMA will e-mail your exam results to you approximately six weeks from the end of the month in which you've taken your test.

---

*Please note there are no official, set score release dates.
**You must reschedule your exam more than 30 days prior to your scheduled appointment. You can only move the date to a later date within the same two-month testing window.

At the time grades are released, results are also available online in your myIMA Dashboard.

Exam Window	Score Release Window
January and February	3rd week of February – 1st week of April
May and June	3rd week of June – 2nd week of August
September and October	3rd week of October – 2nd week of December

Weighting of the CMA Exam

- The multiple-choice questions section is worth 75% of the total score.

- Essays are worth 25% of the total score.

- To be able to take the essay section, you must score at least 50% on the multiple-choice section.

CMA Exam Scoring Scale

Parts 1 and 2 of the CMA Exam are scored on a scale of 0 to 500.

In order to equate all scores for all forms of the exam, the scores for each part are placed on a scale from 0 to 500. On this scale, a score of 360 represents the minimum passing scaled score. The scaled score allows candidates to know how they performed in relation to the passing standard of 360. (Source: IMA)

Your Performance Report

Performance Reports are sent via e-mail from Prometric to all candidates who take an exam part.

The performance reports are e-mailed approximately 14 days after exam results are posted to the candidate's profile.

Candidates who do not pass the exam will receive a report that indicates their performance on each of the key topic areas in the multiple-choice section as well as their overall performance on the essay section of the exam. There are three performance ratings: Satisfactory, Marginal, and Unsatisfactory.

Introduction

Welcome to Part 1, "Financial Planning, Performance, and Analytics." The study text aligns perfectly with your Wiley CMA™ Exam Review Course so that you can follow along and make notes as you review the lectures. To test yourself after your study, take a lesson or session assessment; practice questions in the comprehensive test bank; or take a practice exam to get the test-day experience and hone your skills.

This study guide covers the following sections from the Institute of Certified Management Accountants (ICMA®) Content Specification Outline, which you will find in Appendix.

Section A, "External Financial Reporting Decisions" (15%)

Section B, "Planning, Budgeting, and Forecasting" (20%)

Section C, "Performance Management" (20%)

Section D, "Cost Management" (15%)

Section E, "Internal Controls" (15%)

Section F, "Technology and Analytics" (15%)

Section A. External Financial Reporting Decisions

Topic 1. Financial Statements

Overview of Financial Statements and Income Statement

After studying this lesson, you should be able to:

- Identify users of the balance sheet, income statement, statement of changes in equity, and the statement of cash flows and their needs (1.A.1.a).

- Demonstrate an understanding of the purposes and uses of each statement (1.A.1.b).

- Identify the limitations of each financial statement (1.A.1.d).

- Identify how various financial transactions affect the elements of each of the financial statements and determine the proper classification of the transaction (1.A.1.e).

- Identify the major components and classifications of [the income] statement (1.A.1.c).

- Demonstrate an understanding of how [an income statement] is prepared (1.A.1.g).

- Demonstrate an understanding of expense recognition practices (1.A.2.cc).

- Define gains and losses and indicate the proper financial statement presentation (1.A.2.aa).

- Identify the correct treatment of discontinued operations (1.A.2.ee).

- Define and calculate comprehensive income (1.A.2.dd).

> Financial statements are used by a variety of stakeholders both inside and outside an organization to determine the financial position of the organization. Financial statements do have some inherent limitations which are discussed in this lesson. There are four main financial statements used by stakeholders: income statement, statement of changes in equity, balance sheet, and cash flow statement. This lesson will discuss the income statement including other comprehensive income. The other three financial statements will be covered in subsequent lessons.

I. A variety of users, or stakeholders, depend on financial statements to determine the financial position and health of organizations. These may be parties within the organization, or outside of the organization.

   A. Internal users:

      1. Managers use financial statements to determine whether the organization is utilizing resources in the most cost-effective manner and to make key investment and financing decisions.

      2. Employees analyze financial statements for their own job security and to determine the impact of profit-based compensation.

   B. External users:

      1. Shareholders and prospective investors use financial statements to determine whether they can receive an appropriate return on investment.

      2. Financial institutions assess the ability of organizations to comply with debt covenants and to repay loans or other debt through financial statement analysis.

      3. Suppliers use financial statements to assess the ability of their customers to pay bills on time.

      4. Customers use financial statements to assess whether their suppliers will remain in business to provide an ongoing supply of goods and services.

5. Competitors compare their performance to others in their industry or area using financial statements.

6. Regulators review financial statements to assess whether public organizations have adhered to statutory reporting requirements and to determine if additional rules are necessary for other stakeholders to be fully informed.

II. While the financial statements are useful for a variety of purposes noted above, they contain some inherent limitations. Some of these items require additional disclosure in the notes to the financial statements to enable stakeholders to make fully informed decisions.

    A. *Periodicity*: Monthly, quarterly, and annual reporting periods are generally not good indicators of the natural business cycle. Users should be aware of this issue as it relates to the specific organization in order to properly interpret the financial statements.

    B. *Historical information*: Because the financial statements are issued several weeks after the close of a fiscal period, the information contained therein is purely historical in nature and may not be directly relevant to ongoing operations. Organizations generally present two to three years of financial information together to enable users to better project future results using trend analysis. Still, the historical nature of the information presented must be considered together with any additional information known about the current status of the organization in order to maximize usefulness of the financial statements.

    C. *Valuation*: A variety of measures are used for financial statement elements. Organizations are required to disclose their policies for significant accounting estimates and measurements in the notes to the financial statements.

        1. *Historical cost*: Some non-monetary accounts use historical cost because it is objectively measured, but it is less relevant as time passes (i.e., Inventory, Property and Equipment).

        2. *Estimates*: Some accounts are based on management estimates and judgements. These estimates introduce an element of uncertainty in the financial information (i.e., Warranty Reserves, Allowance for Doubtful Accounts).

        3. *Fair value*: Accounts with objective market prices are often recorded at market value (i.e., Marketable Securities, Bonds).

    D. *Accounting Methods*: Organizations often have a choice in accounting methods for various accounts and transactions. These choices may create difficulty when comparing the results of two different organizations (i.e., depreciation methods, inventory cost flow assumptions). Organizations are required to disclose their significant accounting policy choices in the notes to the financial statements.

    E. *Omissions*: Several relevant items are omitted from the financial statements. For example, organizations are not permitted to include the value of their workforce, customer base, or internally developed intangibles, such as reputation, in the assets on the balance sheet. In addition, certain non-cash investing and financing transactions are omitted from the cash flow statement. For example, a purchase of a building through the issuance of stock would not appear on the cash flow statement, but would be included in the notes to the financial statements.

III. Organizations use four main financial statements to communicate financial information to stakeholders.

    A. The income statement shows the organization's sources of revenues, gains, expenses, and losses for the period presented which result in the net income or loss for that period.

        1. Revenues and expenses generally result from the primary operations of the organization.

        2. Gains and losses result from peripheral activities of the organization.

        3. Elements on the income statement are recorded on an accrual basis. Revenues are recorded when earned and realized or realizable and expenses are recorded when incurred, regardless of when cash or other consideration is exchanged.

4. The income statement is often combined with a presentation of Other Comprehensive Income items. These items are not considered part of net income, but represent additional changes to the organization's economic position during the period presented. When this information is included, the financial statement is called the Statement of Comprehensive Income.

B. The statement of changes in equity presents the organization's detailed changes in each equity account over the course of the period presented. The accounts typically presented in the statement of changes in equity include the following:

1. *Preferred Stock*: Contributed capital for non-voting stock which generally carries a stated dividend rate that will be paid first in the event the organization declares a dividend.

2. *Common Stock* (at par value, if applicable): Contributed capital for voting stock with no specified return, whether through growth or through dividends.

3. *Additional Paid-In Capital*: Contributed capital in excess of par values.

4. *Treasury Stock*: A contra equity account for recording stock repurchased by the organization.

5. *Retained Earnings*: Accumulated net income earned by the organization from inception less any dividends declared during that same time.

6. *Accumulated Other Comprehensive Income*: Accumulated other comprehensive income items not included in the calculation of net income.

C. The balance sheet shows the organization's classification of assets, liabilities, and owners' equity as of the end of the period presented.

1. Assets represent the resources available to the organization for carrying out its purpose such as cash, accounts receivable, inventory, or property and equipment.

2. Liabilities represent third-party claims to the assets of the organization. Liabilities are the amounts owed by the organization to third parties, such as debt, accounts payable, or wages payable.

3. Equities represent owner claims to the assets of the organization. Equity can arise through contributions from owners (i.e., common stock) or through the operations of the organization (i.e., retained earnings).

D. The Statement of Cash Flows explains the overall change to the organization's cash position over the course of the period presented. This change is broken down into three categories of cash flows, the combination of which equal the total change in cash for the period presented:

1. *Operating Cash Flow*: The cash flows from the central operations of the organization. Generally, this would include cash inflows from customers, cash outflows to employees and suppliers, and cash flows for interest and taxes.

2. *Investing Cash Flow*: The cash flows associated with longer term investing activities of the organization. Generally, this would include cash outflows for purchases of property and equipment and other investments, and cash inflows from the sale of these same items.

3. *Financing Cash Flow*: The cash flows associated with the financing strategy of the company. Generally, this would include cash inflows from borrowings (bank or bond), cash inflows from the sale of stock (common or preferred), cash outflows from the principal repayments on debt, cash outflows from purchasing treasury stock, and cash payment of dividends to owners.

IV. The income statement may be presented using one of two methods.

    A. The single-step method shows the organization's total revenues and gains compared to total expenses and losses. Net income is simply the difference between these two amounts.

    B. Illustration of single-step income statement: ABC Co. has the following revenues, expenses, gains, and losses in 20X2:

Sales Revenue	$3,000,000
Dividend Revenue	20,000
Gain on Sale of Equipment	40,000
Cost of Goods Sold	1,900,000
Wage Expence	380,000
Administrative Expenses	360,000
Interest Expense	20,000
Income Tax Expense	150,000
Loss on Sale of Securities	10,000

The following income statement presents ABC's results of operations for 20X2 using the single-step method:

ABC Co.		
Income Statement for the year ended December 31, 20X2		
Sales Revenue	$3,000,000	
Dividend Revenue	20,000	
Gain on Sale of Equipment	40,000	
Total Revenues and Gains		$3,060,000
Cost of Goods Sold	1,900,000	
Wage Expense	380,000	
Administrative Expenses	360,000	
Interest Expense	20,000	
Loss on Sale of Securities	10,000	
Income Tax Expense	150,000	
Total Expenses and Losses		2,820,000
Net Income		$240,000

    C. A multi-step income statement shows how an organization's revenue, gains, expenses, and losses are split into operating and non-operating activities. This type of income statement provides a more detailed look at how an organization's primary business operations are performing compared to peripheral activities.

    D. Illustration of multi-step income statement: Using the same information for ABC Co. above, the following income statement presents ABC's results of operations for 20X2 using the multiple-step method:

ABC Co.		
Income Statement for the year ended December 31, 20X2		
Sales Revenue	$3,000,000	
Cost of Goods Sold	1,900,000	
Gross Profit		$1,100,000
Wage Expense	380,000	
Administrative Expenses	360,000	
Operating Expenses		740,000
Operating Income		360,000
Dividend Revenue	20,000	
Gain on Sale of Equipment	40,000	
Other Revenues and Gains		60,000
Interest Expense	20,000	
Loss on Sale of Securities	10,000	
Other Expenses and Losses		30,000
Income Before Tax		390,000
Income Tax Expense		150,000
Net Income		$240,000

    E. Earnings per common share are required to be shown on the face of the income statement for public companies.

V. Discontinued operations are shown separately after the results from continuing operations in the income statement.

    A. Discontinued operations result when an organization disposes of a component of a business and those operations and cash flows are clearly distinguishable from other operations of the organization.

    B. Gains or losses from discontinued operations are shown net of their tax impact.

    C. If a public company has discontinued operations, earnings per common share is required to be shown for income from continuing operations, discontinued operations, and net income.

Practice Question

LMNO Company is a well-diversified company. They decided to discontinue the paint-producing division of their company. During year 20X5, the paint-producing division lost $150,000 (net of tax). At the end of the year, LMNO sold the paint-producing division for a loss of $60,000 (net of tax). Aside from the paint-producing division, LMNO had the following additional activity during year 20X5.

Sales Revenue	$7,000,000
Dividend Revenue	35,000
Gain on Sale of Equipment	5,000
Cost of Goods Sold	3,200,000
Wage Expense	960,000
Administrative Expenses	770,000
Interest Expense	65,000
Income Tax Expense for Continuing Operations	807,200
Loss on Sale of Securities	27,000

Produce a multi-step income statement in good form.

Continues...

Answer

LMNO Co.		
Income Statement for the year ended December 31, 20X5		
Sales Revenue	$7,000,000	
Cost of Goods Sold	3,200,000	
Gross Profit		$3,800,000
Wage Expense	960,000	
Administrative Expenses	770,000	
Operating Expenses		1,730,000
Operating Income		2,070,000
Dividend Revenue	35,000	
Gain on Sale of Equipment	5,000	
Other Revenues and Gains		40,000
Interest Expense	65,000	
Loss on Sale of Securities	27,000	
Other Expense and Losses		92,000
Income Before Tax		$2,018,000
Income Tax Expense		807,200
Income from Continuing Operations		1,210,800
Discontinued Operations		
Loss from discontinued paint-producing division (net of tax)	150,000	
Loss from disposal of paint-producing division (net of tax)	60,000	
		210,000
Net Income		1,000,800

VI. Other Comprehensive Income (OCI) is made up of economic gains and losses that are not defined as part of net income.

A. Common components of OCI include the following:

1. Unrealized holding gains and losses on available-for-sale (AFS) securities

2. Gains and losses on cash flow hedges

3. Increases and decreases in equity due to foreign currency translation adjustments arising from the translation of foreign subsidiaries into U.S. dollars

4. Certain gains and losses related to defined benefit pensions

B. OCI can be presented in one of two ways:

1. In a combined Statement of Income and Comprehensive Income, which begins with the individual components of the income statement presented first followed by the individual components of OCI and ending with total Comprehensive Income (Net Income plus OCI) for the period presented.

2. In a separate fifth financial statement titled Statement of Comprehensive Income, which begins with net income as the first line followed by the individual components of OCI and ending with total Comprehensive Income for the period presented.

3. OCI amounts are accumulated in equity through Accumulated Other Comprehensive Income (AOCI) in a manner similar to the way revenues, expenses, gains, losses, and dividends are accumulated in equity through Retained Earnings.

C. Illustration: Continuing the ABC Co. example from above, ABC has a $5,000 (net of tax) unrealized holding loss on AFS securities during 20X2. ABC's combined Statement of Comprehensive Income would appear as follows:

ABC Co.		
Statement of Income and Comprehensive Income for the year ended December 31, 20X2		
Sales Revenue	$3,000,000	
Cost of Goods Sold	1,900,000	
Gross Profit		$1,100,000
Wage Expense	380,000	
Administrative Expenses	360,000	
Operating Expenses		740,000
Operating Income		360,000
Dividend Revenue	20,000	
Gain on Sale of Equipment	40,000	
Other Revenues and Gains		60,000
Interest Expense	20,000	
Loss on Sale of Securities	10,000	
Other Expenses and Losses		30,000
Income Before Tax		390,000
Income Tax Expense		150,000
Net Income		240,000
Unrealized Holding Loss (net of tax)		5,000
Comprehensive Income		$235,000

Practice Question

Gregory Corporation uses a multi-step format on a combined Statement of Income and Comprehensive Income to report its results of operations each year. During 20X3, Gregory Corporation reported the following selected information on that statement:

Comprehensive Income	$ 64,000
Gross Profit	$382,000
Operating Expenses	$261,000
Sales Revenue	$596,000
Net Income	$ 60,000
Income Before Tax	$100,000

What are the total amounts Gregory Corporation reported for Cost of Goods Sold, Other Losses, Income Tax Expense, and Other Comprehensive Income (net of tax) in 20X3?

Answer

Amounts can be derived by recreating a combined Statement of Income and Comprehensive Income for Gregory Corporation and deriving the required amounts from those given in the problem data.

Continues...

Gregory Corporation	
Statement of Income and Comprehensive Income for the year ended December 31, 20X3	
Sales Revenue	$596,000
Cost of Goods Sold	?
Gross Profit	382,000
Operating Expenses	261,000
Operating Income	
Other Losses	?
Income Before Tax	100,000
Income Tax Expense	?
Net Income	60,000
Other Comprehensive Income (net of tax)	?
Comprehensive Income	$64,000

- Cost of Goods Sold = Sales Revenue less Gross Profit ($596,000 – $382,000) or $214,000

- Other Losses = difference between Income Before Tax and Operating Income. Operating Income of $121,000 can be derived from the given information ($382,000 – $261,000), so Other Losses is $21,000 ($100,000 – $121,000).

- Income Tax Expense = Income Before Tax less Net Income ($100,000 – $60,000) or $40,000

- Other Comprehensive Income (net of tax) = Comprehensive Income less Net Income ($64,000 – $60,000) or $4,000

Gregory Corporation	
Statement of Income and Comprehensive Income for the year ended December 31, 20X3	
Sales Revenue	$596,000
Cost of Goods Sold	214,000
Gross Profit	382,000
Operating Expenses	261,000
Operating Income	121,000
Other Losses	21,000
Income Before Tax	100,000
Income Tax Expense	40,000
Net Income	60,000
Other Comprehensive Income (net of tax)	4,000
Comprehensive Income	$64,000

Summary
Stakeholders both inside and outside an organization use financial statements to better understand the financial position and health of an organization. Financial statements have inherent limitations, some of which are addressed in the notes to the financial statements. It is important to understand other inherent limitations as well. The first financial statement is the income statement and can be presented using a single-step method or multi-step method. Both methods for preparing the income statement should be understood. Additionally, you should understand other comprehensive income, which is made up of economic gains and losses that are not defined as part of net income. The other three financial statements will be discussed in subsequent lessons.

Statement of Changes in Equity and Balance Sheet

After studying this lesson, you should be able to:

- Identify the major components and classifications of [the statement of changes in equity] (1.A.1.c).

- Demonstrate an understanding of how [a statement of changes in equity] is prepared (1.A.1.g).

- Identify transactions that affect paid-in capital and those that affect retained earnings (1.A.2.v).

- Determine the effect on shareholders' equity of large and small stock dividends (1.A.2.w).

- Identify the major components and classifications of [the balance sheet] (1.A.1.c).

- Demonstrate an understanding of how [a balance sheet] is prepared (1.A.1.g).

The previous lesson gave an introduction to the financial statements as well as discussed the income statement in greater depth. This lesson will focus on the next two financial statements: the statement of changes in equity and the balance sheet.

I. The statement of changes in equity presents the organization's detailed changes in each equity account over the course of the period presented. The accounts typically presented in the statement of changes in equity include the following:

   A. Preferred Stock: Contributed capital for non-voting stock which generally carries a stated dividend rate that will be paid first in the event the organization declares a dividend.

      1. Generally non-voting stock ownership.

      2. Generally carries a specified dividend rate stated as a percentage of par value. For example, a $100 par 8% preferred share would be entitled to an $8 dividend annually if the organization declared dividends. Preferred Stock dividends must be paid before any common shareholders receive dividends from the organization.

      3. May be convertible into common stock at a specified conversion ratio.

      4. May be callable at a specified price at the option of the organization.

      5. Behind company creditors, but ahead of common shareholders for preference in the case of bankruptcy or other liquidation of the organization.

   B. Common Stock

      1. Usually carried at par value unless the stock is "no par" stock, in which case the entire amount paid for the stock is classified as common stock.

      2. Dividends are not predetermined like preferred stock and are only paid when declared and only then, after the preferred shareholders receive their stated dividend.

      3. Last in line for preference in the case of bankruptcy or other liquidation.

   C. Additional Paid-In Capital

      1. Amount received by the organization for stock over the par value of the shares.

      2. Can be affected by various equity transactions, including stock dividends, resales of treasury stock, and issuance of options and warrants.

   D. Treasury Stock

      1. Amount paid by the organization to repurchase its own stock

      2. Shown as contra equity, or a reduction to the equity section

E. Retained Earnings

   1. Net income or loss for the organization is ultimately recorded in retained earnings.

   2. Dividends declared are a reduction to retained earnings.

F. Accumulated Other Comprehensive Income

   1. Other comprehensive income or loss for the organization is ultimately recorded in Accumulated Other Comprehensive Income.

   2. Items accumulated here are not part of the calculation of net income.

G. Non-Controlling Interest

   1. When an organization has a controlling interest in another entity, but not complete ownership, 100% of the assets and liabilities of the subsidiary are included in the balance sheet of the organization and the portion of the subsidiary that is owned by third parties is segregated as a separate component of equity.

II. Several common transactions affect the equity accounts.

A. Sale of new shares: Generally sold for an amount above par value. Cash received is recorded and the common stock/preferred stock account is increased for the par value and the additional paid-in capital account is increased for the balance.

B. Issuance of options: Usually issued as a form of compensation and recorded as part of additional paid-in capital as compensation expense is recognized.

   1. Total compensation expense is valued at the fair value of the options on the date they are granted.

   2. Compensation expense is recognized over the service period required for the employee to become vested in the options.

C. Dividends: Retained earnings is reduced when a cash dividend is declared. If payment of the dividend is delayed, a payable is also recorded and then reduced when the payment is later made.

D. Net Income/Loss: Increases/Decreases retained earnings each year.

E. Other Comprehensive Income Items: Increase/Decrease accumulated other comprehensive income each year.

F. Repurchase of treasury stock: Treasury stock is increased (which is a reduction to equity) for the cost of the treasury shares.

G. Resale of treasury stock.

   1. When sold for an amount in excess of the repurchase price, the cost is taken out of treasury stock and the excess is added to additional paid-in capital.

   2. When sold for an amount below the repurchase price, the cost is taken out of treasury stock and the difference is taken from additional paid-in capital to the extent it was previously increased for treasury stock transactions. If no additional paid-in capital from treasury stock transactions exists, the difference is taken from retained earnings.

H. Stock split: Generally has no impact on any of the equity accounts as long as the par value is also changed to reflect the new share size. For example, if 100 shares of $1 par common stock undergo a 2-for-1 stock split, the result would be 200 shares of $0.50 par common stock. Common stock is $100 before the split (100 × $1) and is still $100 after the split (200 × $0.50) so no journal entry is needed.

I. Stock dividends: A stock dividend occurs when an organization distributes additional shares of stock to existing stockholders as a dividend rather than paying them cash.

   1. Small stock dividend: Less than 20–25% of the number of shares outstanding. Retained earnings is reduced for the fair value of the stock being issued, common stock is increased for the par value of the stock issued, and the difference is included in additional paid-in capital.

2. Large stock dividend: Greater than 20–25% of the number of shares outstanding. Retained earnings is reduced for the par value of the stock being issued and common stock is increased for the same amount. No impact on additional paid-in capital, similar to a stock split.

Practice Question

Jolley, Inc. has 100,000 common shares outstanding with a $1 par value and a market value of $8. Jolley declares a 22% stock dividend.

What is the impact on the various equity accounts if the transaction is considered a small stock dividend?

What is the impact on the various equity accounts if the transaction is considered a large stock dividend?

Answer

1. A small stock dividend is recorded at fair value. 22,000 new shares are issued (100,000 × 22%) and the fair value of $176,000 is taken from retained earnings (22,000 × $8), common stock is increased by $22,000 (22,000 × $1) to reflect the par value of the new shares and the balance of $154,000 ($176,000 – $22,000) is recorded as an increase to additional paid-in capital.

2. A large stock dividend is recorded at par value. 22,000 new shares are issued (100,000 × 22%) and the par value of $22,000 is taken from retained earnings (22,000 × $1) and common stock is increased for the same amount.

III. Illustration: The basic format for the statement of changes in equity is illustrated using ABC Co. information for 20X2.

ABC Co. Statement of Changes in Equity for the year ended December 31, 20X2						
	Common Stock	**APIC**	**Treasury Stock**	**Retained Earnings**	**AOCI**	**Total Equity**
December 31, 20X1	$100,000	$220,000	($10,000)	$210,000	$7,000	$527,000
Purchase of Treasury Stock			(5,000)			(5,000)
Issuance of New Common Shares	10,000	35,000				45,000
Net Income				240,000		240,000
Other Comprehensive Income					(5,000)	(5,000)
December 31, 20X2	$110,000	$255,000	($15,000)	$450,000	$2,000	$802,000

IV. The balance sheet shows the organization's assets, liabilities, and owners' equity as of the end of the period presented. The balance sheet is the only one of the four main financials statements that presents information as of a point in time, rather than over a period of time. The classic accounting equation "assets = liabilities + equity" is illustrated through the balance sheet.

A. Assets represent the resources available to the organization for carrying out its purpose. Assets are presented in order of liquidity within two general categories, current or non-current, based upon the period of time the assets are expected to convert to cash.

1. Cash, accounts receivable, inventory, prepaid assets, and other items expected to be realized within one year (or the operating cycle if longer) are classified as current.

2. Property and equipment, intangible assets, and other assets expected to benefit the company for longer than one year (or the operating cycle if longer) are classified as non-current.

B. Liabilities represent third party claims to the assets of the organization. Liabilities are the amounts owed by the organization to third parties, such as debt, accounts payable, or wages payable. Liabilities are presented in the order they come due within two general categories, current or non-current, based upon the period of time before assets or other resources of the company will be utilized to satisfy the liability.

1. Accounts payable, accrued expenses (wages, utilities, rent, etc.), deferred revenue, principal portions of long-term debt due in the coming year, and other liabilities expected to be settled with cash or other current assets within one year (or the operating cycle if longer) are classified as current.

2. Liabilities due after one year (or the operating cycle if longer), such as bonds or bank debt, are classified as long-term. In addition, deferred tax liabilities are considered long-term liabilities by definition.

C. Equities represent owner claims to the assets of the organization. These accounts were explained in part I of this lesson.

1. Equity accounts are generally presented in order of liquidation preference with preferred stock first, followed by common stock and additional paid-in capital. Retained earnings and accumulated other comprehensive income are generally presented last in the equity section.

D. The balance sheet is incomplete without the additional disclosures in the notes to the financial statements. These disclosures help investors understand the key assumptions and methods of accounting used so they can more effectively compare prior periods and assist with comparisons with other companies. Key disclosures include the following items.

1. Significant accounting policies, including the following:

    a. Any securities classified as cash equivalents

    b. Inventory valuation method and cost flow assumptions

    c. Method of depreciation

2. Significant estimates made within the accounts

3. Amounts within major classes of inventory (i.e., raw materials, work in process, finished goods)

4. Gross amounts within major classes of property and equipment (i.e. furniture, equipment, buildings, land) and accumulated depreciation for each

5. Components of deferred tax assets and liabilities

6. Expected annual principal payments on debt for the next five years and all amounts due thereafter

7. Sinking fund provisions for bonds

8. Par values and contractual provisions for preferred stock and common stock

9. Details about employee stock compensation programs

10. Significant commitments or contingencies not recorded in the balance sheet

11. Other information as may be needed for a full understanding of the items reported in the balance sheet

V. Illustration: The basic format for the balance sheet is illustrated using ABC Co. information for 20X2.

ABC Co. Balance Sheet as of December 31, 20X1 end 20X2		
	20X1	**20X2**
Cash	$30,000	$100,000
Accounts Receivable	155,000	225,000
Inventory	200,000	450,000
AFS Investments	90,000	67,000
Property and Equipment	480,000	450,000
Total Assets	$955,000	$1,292,000
Accounts Payable	$213.000	$270,000
Accrued Wages	15,000	20,000
Long-Term Debt	200,000	200,000
Total Liabilities	428,000	490,000
Common Stock	100,000	110,000
Additional Paid-In Capital	220,000	255,000
Treasury Stock	(10,000)	(15,000)
Retained Earnings	210,000	450,000
Accumulated Other Comprehensive Income	7,000	2,000
Total Equity	527,000	802,000
Total Liabilities and Equity	$955,000	$1,292,000

Practice Question

Jolley, Inc. is preparing its 20X1 balance sheet and needs some assistance with properly classifying some of its liabilities. Jolley's operating cycle is approximately 90 to 120 days. Identify whether the following items should be current or non-current on the balance sheet.

1. Debt of $10,000 payable over 5 years at a rate of $2,000 per year plus interest.

2. Bonds of $100,000 due in full in 15 years. Interest of $6,000 is payable on the bonds each year and the full amount of the interest was already recorded and paid for 20X1. Accordingly, no interest payable was recorded at the end of the year.

3. Deferred Tax Liability of $3,000 expected to reverse entirely within the next year.

4. Accrued Warranty of $12,000 expected to be paid out evenly over the next three years.

5. Accounts Payable of $38,000 generally due between 30 and 90 days.

Answer

1. Because $2,000 is due in the coming year and the remainder is due thereafter, this debt should be classified as current for $2,000 and non-current for $8,000.

2. Because the principal portion of the bonds is not due for 15 years, the entire amount should be classified as non-current. Jolley has fully paid its interest for the year, so they have no need for a payable associated with the interest. Classification of the interest is not relevant.

3. By definition, Deferred Tax Liabilities are non-current liabilities.

Continues…

4. The accrued warranty should be split as current and non-current based on the expected payments related to the warranty. $4,000 would be current and $8,000 would be non-current.

5. Because the amount is expected to be paid within the next year, the entire amount is current.

Summary

The statement of changes in equity presents the organization's detailed changes in each equity account over the course of the period presented. The accounts typically presented in this financial statement include: preferred stock, common stock, additional paid-in capital, treasury stock, retained earnings, accumulated other comprehensive income, and non-controlling interest. You should be familiar with the common transactions that affect equity accounts. The balance sheet shows the organization's assets, liabilities, and owner's equity as of the end of the period presented. Assets represent the resources available for carrying out the organization's purpose and can be current or non-current. Liabilities represent third-party claims to the organization's assets and are also represented as current or non-current. Equities represent owner claims to the organization's assets. It is also important to know the key disclosures related to the balance sheet.

Statement of Cash Flows and Financial Statement Articulation

After studying this lesson, you should be able to:

- Identify the major components and classifications of [the statement of cash flows] (1.A.1.c).

- Demonstrate an understanding of how [a statement of cash flows] is prepared (1.A.1.g).

- Demonstrate an understanding of the relationship among the financial statements (1.A.1.f).

The previous two lessons have addressed the income statement, statement of changes in equity, and balance sheet. The last financial statement is the statement of cash flows. This lesson will focus on the statement of cash flows as well as show how the four financial statements, when properly prepared, connect to each other through various accounts.

I. The statement of cash flows reconciles the overall change to the organization's cash position over the course of the period presented. Because the other financial statements are prepared using accrual accounting, the statement of cash flows is useful for understanding cash resources and needs of the organization. On the cash flow statement, the change in cash is broken down into three categories of cash flows, the combination of which equal the total change in cash for the period presented:

   A. Operating Cash Flow: The cash flows from the central operations of the organization. Generally, this would include cash inflows from customers, cash outflows to employees and suppliers, and cash flows for interest and taxes. Two methods are used to present the operating section of the cash flow statement, the indirect method and the direct method.

   1. Indirect method: This is the most common method used. It begins with net income, then reconciles to operating cash flow by adjusting from accrual accounting to cash basis accounting. Common adjustments to net income to arrive at operating cash flow are:

      a. Add back non-cash expenses such as depreciation, amortization, and stock compensation.

      b. Remove non-operating gains (subtract) and losses (add) such as gains and losses on investments or property and equipment.

      c. Adjust for the changes in operating assets and liabilities such as accounts receivable, inventory, prepaid assets, accounts payable, accrued liabilities, interest payable, and taxes payable.

         i. Increases in operating assets AND decreases in operating liabilities are subtracted.

         ii. Decreases in operating assets AND increases in operating liabilities are added.

      d. Illustration: The operating section of the 20X2 cash flow statement for ABC Co., prepared using the indirect method, is presented below:

Net Income	$240,000
Adjustments for non-cash items:	
Gain on Sale of Equipment	($40,000)
Loss on Sale of Securities	10,000
Depreciation Expense	50,000
Adjustments for changes in balance sheet accounts:	
Increase in Accounts Receivable	(70,000)
Increase in inventory	(250,000)
Increase in Accounts Payable	57,000

Increase in Wages Payable	5,000
Total adjustments to Net Income	(238,000)
Net Cash Inflow from Operating Activities	$2,000

2. **Direct method:** This method shows actual gross cash inflows from their sources derived (from customers, from interest) and gross cash outflow for each purpose (to suppliers, for wages, for interest, for taxes). The FASB has stated a preference for this method, but it is rarely used. If the direct method is used, the organization is also required to show the reconciliation of net income to cash flows from operations, effectively requiring both methods to be disclosed.

   a. Illustration: The operating section of the 20X2 cash flow statement for ABC Co., prepared using the direct method, is presented below:

Cash received from customers	$2,930,000
Cash paid to suppliers	(2,093,000)
Cash paid for wages	(375,000)
Cash paid for administrative expenses	(310,000)
Cash received from dividends	20,000
Cash paid for interest	(20,000)
Cash paid for taxes	(150,000)
Net Cash Inflow from Operating Activities	$2,000

B. Investing Cash Flow: The cash flows associated with longer term investing activities of the organization. Generally, this would include cash outflows for purchases of property and equipment and other investments, and cash inflows from the sale of these same items.

   1. The non-operating assets, usually long-term assets, of the organization should be analyzed to support the preparation of the investing section.

   2. Illustration: The investing section of the 20X2 cash flow statement for ABC Co. is presented below:

Purchase of PPE	$(60,000)
Sale of PPE	80,000
Purchase of AFS Secutities	(32,000)
Sale of AFS Secutities	40,000
Net Cash Inflow from Investing Activities	$28,000

C. Financing Cash Flow: The cash flows associated with the financing strategy of the company. Generally, this would include cash inflows from borrowings (bank or bond), cash inflows from the sale of stock (common or preferred), cash outflows from the principal repayments on debt, cash outflows from purchasing treasury stock, and cash payment of dividends to owners.

   1. The non-operating liabilities, usually long-term liabilities, and equity accounts of the organization should be analyzed to support the preparation of the financing section. The statement of changes in equity is particularly helpful in preparing part of this section as it relates to the equity accounts.

   2. Illustration: The financing section of the 20X2 cash flow statement for ABC Co. is presented below:

Issuance of Common Shares	$45,000
Repurchase of Treasury Stock	(5,000)
Net Cash Inflow from Financing Activities	$40,000

D. Supplemental disclosures are required for the cash flow statement.

    1. Cash paid for interest

    2. Cash paid for taxes

    3. Significant non-cash investing and financing transactions (e.g., the issuance of bonds for the purchase of a building)

Practice Question

Classify each of the following items as either operating cash flow, investing cash flow, financing cash flow, or non-cash flow. If the item is non-cash, explain whether and how it would appear on the cash flow statement.

a. Payments received from customers

b. Loss on the sale of available-for-sale securities

c. Interest payments received

d. Cash received from the issuance of bonds

e. Dividends paid to preferred shareholders

f. Depreciation expense

g. Cash received from the sale of property and equipment

h. Cash payment on a mortgage loan (part interest and part principal)

i. Issuance of stock to acquire another organization

Answer

a. Operating

b. Non-cash: would be a reconciling item in the operating section of the statement of cash flows if the indirect method is used

c. Operating

d. Financing

e. Financing

f. Non-cash: would be a reconciling item in the operating section of the statement of cash flows if the indirect method is used

g. Investing

h. Part operating (interest), part financing (principal)

i. Non-cash: would be disclosed as a significant non-cash financing (new stock) and investing (acquisition) activity

---

I. The four main financial statements articulate, or connect, to each other through various accounts when properly prepared.

    A. Net income (and other comprehensive income) from the income statement (or from the combined statement of income and comprehensive income) will appear in the statement of changes in equity.

    B. The beginning and ending balances of each equity account on the statement of changes in equity will equal the balances in the equity accounts on the balance sheet from the previous year (beginning equity balances) and the current year (ending equity balances).

C. Net income from the income statement will flow to the top line of the statement of cash flows when the indirect method (operating section) is used.

D. Non cash gains and losses from the income statement will flow to the statement of cash flows when the indirect method (operating section) is used.

E. The beginning cash balance and the ending cash balance from the balance sheet will flow to the statement of cash flows.

F. The changes in the beginning and ending balances of operating assets and liabilities on the balance sheet will flow to the cash flow statements when the indirect method is used (operating section).

G. Illustration: A full set of ABC Co. financial statements for the year ended 20X2 follow. The amounts noted above have been color coded to illustrate the articulation between the statements as outlined above.

ABC Co.
Statement of Income and Comprehensive Income
for the year ended December 31, 20X2

Sales Revenue	$3,000,000	
Cost of Goods Sold	1,900,000	
Gross Profit		$1,100,000
Wage Expense	380,000	
Administrative Expenses	360,000	
Operating Expenses		740,000
Operating Income		360,000
Dividend Revenue	20,000	
Gain on Sale of Equipment	40,000	
Other Revenues and Gains		60,000
Interest Expense	20,000	
Loss on Sale of Securities	10,000	
Other Expenses and Losses		30,000
Income Before Tax		390,000
Income Tax Expense		150,000
Net Income		240,000
Unrealized Holding Loss (net of tax)		5,000
Comprehensive Income		$235,000

ABC Co.
Statement of Changes in Equity
for the year ended December 31, 20X2

	Common Stock	APIC	Treasury Stock	Retained Earnings	AOCI	Total Equity
December 31, 20X1	$100,000	$220,000	($10,000)	$210,000	$7,000	$527,000
Purchase of Treasury Stock			(5,000)			(5,000)
Issuance of New Common Shares	10,000	35,000				45,000
Net Income				240,000		240,000
Other Comprehensive Income					(5,000)	(5,000)
December 31, 20X2	$110,000	$255,000	($15,000)	$450,000	$2,000	$802,000

ABC Co. Balance Sheet as of December 31, 20X1 and 20X2		
	20X1	**20X2**
Cash	$30,000	$100,000
Accounts Receivable	155,000	225,000
Inventory	200,000	450,000
AFS Investments	90,000	67,000
Property and Equipment	480,000	450,000
Total Assets	$955,000	$1,292,000
Accounts Payable	$213,000	$270,000
Accrued Wages	15,000	20,000
Long-Term Debt	200,000	200,000
Total Liabilities	428,000	490,000
Common Stock	100,000	110,000
Additional Paid-In Capital	220,000	255,000
Treasury Stock	(10,000)	(15,000)
Retained Earnings	210,000	450,000
Accumulated Other Comprehensive Income	7,000	2,000
Total Equity	527,000	802,000
Total Liabilities and Equity	$955,000	$1,292,000

ABC Co. Statement of Cash Flows for the year ended December 31, 20X2		
Net Income		$240,000
Adjustment for non-cash items:		
Gain on Sale of Equipment	($40,000)	
Loss on Sale of Securities	10,000	
Depreciation Expense	50,000	
Adjustments for changes in balance sheet accounts:		
Increase in Accounts Receivable	(70,000)	
Increase in Inventory	(250,000)	
Increase in Accounts Payable	57,000	
Increase in Wages Payable	5,000	
Total adjustments to Net Income		(238,000)
Net Cash Inflow from Operating Activities		2,000
Investing Activities:		
Purchase of PPE	(60,000)	
Sale of PPE	80,000	
Purchase of AFS Securities	(32,000)	
Sale of AFS Securities	40,000	
Net Cash Inflow from Investing Activities		28,000
Financing Activities:		
Issuance of Common Shares	45,000	

ABC Co. Statement of Cash Flows for the year ended December 31, 20X2		
Repurchase of Treasury stock	(5,000)	
Net Cash Inflow from Financing Activities		40,000
Increase in Cash		70,000
Beginning Cash Balance		30,000
Ending Cash Balance		$100,000
Cash paid for interest	$ 20,000	
Cash paid for taxes	$150,000	

Practice Question

List the financial statement(s) that would include the following amounts.

a. Net Income

b. Cash balance

c. Increase in Accounts Receivable

d. Equity account balances

e. Gain on Sale of Equipment

f. Other Comprehensive Income

Answer

All of the major financial statements articulate with each other. Some items that are included on one financial statement are used in other places on other statements. If they are all prepared correctly, they will connect with each other. The items listed above would be included in the following financial statements:

a. Income Statement

  Statement of Changes in Equity

  Statement of Cash Flows (when the indirect method is used for the operating section)

b. Balance Sheet

  Statement of Cash Flows

c. Statement of Cash Flows

d. Balance Sheet

  Statement of Changes in Equity

e. Income Statement

  Statement of Cash Flows

f. Combined Statement of Income and Comprehensive Income OR

  Statement of Comprehensive Income

  Statement of Changes in Equity

Summary

The statement of cash flows is useful for understanding cash resources and needs of the organization because it reconciles the overall changes to the organization's cash position over the course of the period presented. Cash flows are broken down into three categories: operating, investing, and financing. Operating cash flows are from the central operations of the organization and can be presented using the indirect method or the direct method. Investing cash flows are related to longer term investing activities. Financing cash flows are associated with the financing strategy of the organization. You should also be familiar with the accounts that connect the financial statements together.

Integrated Reporting

After studying this lesson, you should be able to:

- Define integrated reporting (IR), integrated thinking, and the integrated report and demonstrate an understanding of the relationship between them (1.A.1.h).

- Identify the primary purpose of IR (1.A.1.i).

- Explain the fundamental concepts of value creation, the six capitals, and the value creation process (1.A.1.j).

- Identify elements of an integrated report: i.e., organizational overview and external environment, governance, business model, risks and opportunities, strategy and resource allocation, performance, outlook, basis of preparation and presentation (1.A.1.k).

- Identify and explain the benefits and challenges of adopting IR (1.A.1.l).

Integrated Reporting is a relatively new method of reflecting an organization's financial and nonfinancial information. This concept was developed in the United Kingdom and has slowly grown in popularity since a framework was published in 2013. The output of Integrated Reporting is an Integrated Report: a voluntary, non-audited view of an organization's value chain which is directed to stakeholders outside of the organization. This lesson will introduce Integrated Reports, including the fundamental concepts, the elements, and the benefits and challenges of Integrated Reports.

I. Defining Integrated Reporting

    A. Integrated reporting is a process founded on integrated thinking that results in a periodic integrated report by an organization about value creation over time and related communications regarding aspects of value creation. (Copyright © December 2013 by the International Integrated Reporting Council ("the IIRC"). All rights reserved. Used with permission of the IIRC. Contact the IIRC (info@theiirc.org) for permission to reproduce, store, transmit or make other uses of this document.)

    B. The definition of integrated reporting is found in the "International IR Framework" published in 2013 by the International Integrated Reporting Council (IIRC), a global coalition of regulators, investors, companies, standard setters, and accounting professionals.

    C. The Integrated Reporting Council uses the symbol <IR> to abbreviate the name of this topic. The use of the less-than symbol and the greater-than symbol in the icon are noteworthy:

        1. The use of the less-than symbol is interesting because an integrated report should be concise, or short and "to the point." The <IR> Framework explains that the integrated report "Expresses concepts clearly and in as few words as possible." As such, an integrated report is "less than" an entire annual report or 10-K.

        2. That said, the integrated report encompasses six capitals: financial, manufactured, intellectual, human, social and relationship, and natural. As such, an integrated report is "greater than" a traditional financially oriented annual report because it has a much broader scope.

    D. To summarize, <IR> is both "less than" and "greater than" traditional financial reporting.

    E. <IR> is a process or a series of activities that people inside an organization will perform. As such, the Framework is a methodology for this process.

        1. The adoption of <IR> is also a process. An organization would typically start by exploring how to use <IR> by obtaining education and training and then perhaps piloting <IR> in a single division or with a single product line.

    2. In this way, <IR> is like a systems development effort:

        a. The words "integrated thinking" are used in the <IR> definition. In this context, "integrated thinking" is very similar to "cross-functional," meaning that people from different areas of an organization work together as a team.

        b. The output of the <IR> process is an integrated report, produced or published on a periodic basis.

        c. The main topic, or focus, of an integrated report is value creation. Value creation is considered at a very high level:

            i. The process that results in increases, decreases, or transformations of the capitals caused by the organization's business activities and outputs. In short, value creation is the sum of the organization's activities which, in theory, aims to increase the overall stock of capitals.

            ii. For example, an organization's financial capital is increased when it makes a profit, and the quality of its human capital is improved when employees become better trained.

II. Why You Haven't Heard of Integrated Reporting

    A. Integrated reporting is a relatively new term or label to describe advanced performance reporting. The <IR> Framework was developed in the United Kingdom and was published in 2013.

    B. This topic was likely not covered in the Managerial Accounting textbook(s) you used in college. Even if the textbook included this topic, it was likely discussed in one of the later chapters of the book, which not all Accounting professors have time to teach.

    C. This topic will appear on the CMA Exam for the first time in 2020 and has been grouped with External Financial Reporting Decisions, which encompasses about 15% of the CMA exam Part 1.

    D. Other forms of "Advanced Performance Reporting" have been developed and discussed over the past 25 years; these forms are Cost of Quality, Triple Bottom-Line Reporting, and Sustainability Reporting. Common elements to all these "flavors" of reporting include:

        1. They are not required.

        2. They are not audited by professional accountants.

        3. They involve participation and cooperation of nonfinancial members of the organization.

        4. They measure data far beyond financial metrics.

III. Value Creation and the Six Capitals

    A. Value creation is the process that results in increases, decreases, or transformations of the capitals caused by the organization's business activities and outputs.

    B. An organization creates value for:

        1. The organization itself, which enables financial returns to the providers of financial capital

        2. Others outside of the organization (i.e., stakeholders and society at large)

C. The <IR> Framework includes a diagram that illustrates the value creation process:

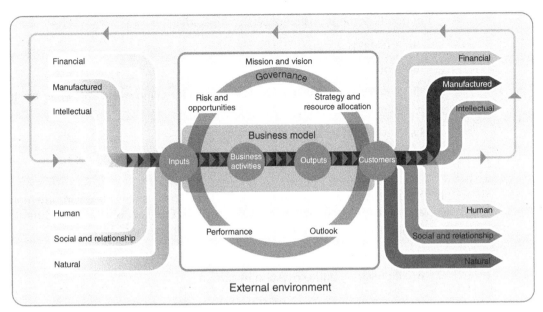

Value creation (preservation, diminution) over time

1. The diagram begins on the left-hand side with the six capitals. The six capitals come together in the center of the diagram into the organization's business model. The business model takes inputs, performs business activities, generates outputs, and creates outcomes. The right-hand side of the diagram again illustrates the six capitals, but now the colorization, or shading, of each capital is darker or bolder, to reflect improvement or enhancement.

The six capitals which are central to <IR> are the following:

Financial

Intellectual

Social and relationship

Human

Manufactured

Natural

    a. Financial capital is the pool of funds that has the following characteristics:

        i. It is available to an organization for use in the production of goods or the provision of services.

        ii. It is obtained through financing, such as debt, equity, or grants, or generated through operations or investments.

    b. Intellectual capital is organizational, knowledge-based intangibles, including:

        i. Intellectual property, such as patents, copyrights, software, rights, and licenses

        ii. Organizational capital such as tacit knowledge, systems, procedures, and protocols

    c. Social and relationship capital includes:

        i. Shared norms, common values, and behaviors

        ii. Key stakeholder relationships

    d. Human capital is people's competencies, capabilities, and experience, and their motivations to innovate.

e. Manufactured capital is defined as manufactured physical objects (as distinct from natural physical objects) that are available to an organization for use in the production of goods or the provision of services, including:

    i. Buildings

    ii. Equipment

    iii. Infrastructure (such as roads, ports, bridges, and waste and water treatment plants)

    iv. Inventory

    v. Tools, patterns, and molds that a company would make and use in its production process

f. Natural capital is defined as all renewable and non-renewable environmental resources and processes that provide goods or services that support the past, current, or future prosperity of an organization. It includes the following:

    i. Air, water, land, minerals, and forests

    ii. Biodiversity and ecosystem health

A tool to help remember the six capitals is the mnemonic FISHMAN:

Financial

Intellectual

Social and relationship

Human

Manufactured

and

Natural

IV. The Integrated Report

A. An integrated report is a concise communication about how an organization's strategy, governance, performance, and prospects, in the context of its external environment, lead to the creation of value over the short, medium, and long term.

B. An integrated report includes eight Content Elements, which answer the question posed below for each.

1. Organizational overview and external environment:

What does the organization do and what are the circumstances under which it operates?

2. Governance:

How does the organization's governance structure support its ability to create value in the short, medium, and long term?

3. Business model:

What is the organization's business model?

4. Risks and opportunities:

What are the specific risks and opportunities that affect the organization's ability to create value over the short, medium, and long term, and how is the organization dealing with them?

5. Strategy and resource allocation:

Where does the organization want to go and how does it intend to get there?

6. Performance:

To what extent has the organization achieved its strategic objectives for the period and what are its outcomes in terms of effects on the capitals?

7. Outlook:

What challenges and uncertainties is the organization likely to encounter in pursuing its strategy, and what are the potential implications for its business model and future performance?

8. Basis of preparation and presentation:

How does the organization determine what matters to include in the integrated report and how are such matters quantified or evaluated?

These Content Elements can be remembered using the mnemonic GROOMPOPS:

Governance

Risks and opportunities

Organizational **O**verview and external environment

business **M**odel

Performance

Outlook

Preparation and presentation basis

Strategy and resource allocation

V. Benefits and Challenges of Adopting <IR>

A. Benefits—The developers of <IR> have identified the elements of an organization which are most important to stakeholders outside the organization, especially providers of financial capital.

1. This approach provides a clear, condensed version of an organization's annual financial report, guidance, mission, vision, and governance in a single place.

2. This approach provides a more cohesive and efficient approach to corporate reporting When most major organizations adopt <IR>, comparing one entity to another will be more straightforward, resulting in a more efficient allocation of financial capital.

B. Challenges—Implementation of <IR> will be:

1. Complex for organizations with multiple divisions, subsidiaries, and operations. A separate Integrated Report, with a unique value chain diagram, would be required for each business model.

2. Burdensome for small- and medium-sized organizations. Unless <IR> is allowed to replace any portion of a 10-K or a statement regarding Internal Controls, <IR> will become an additional, incremental work effort.

3. No reporting standards: Judgment must be used in determining how much to report, which could result in inconsistencies between Integrated Report formats for similar organizations. Such inconsistency would appear to negate the benefits of common, comparable Reports.

4. Additional cost for no quantifiable benefits. The benefits described in the <IR> framework are qualitative: no headcount reductions, no production improvements will occur as a result of adoption of <IR>.

5. Forward-looking content elements may breed litigation risk. Providing information regarding the opportunities which may lie ahead for an organization in the short, medium, and long term and explaining how the organization will deal with them may be seen by some stakeholders as predictions or promises of future benefits. If the opportunities do not come to fruition, some stakeholders may resort to litigation.

Summary

Integrated Reporting is being used by entities around the world; the number of users has grown each year since 2013. An Integrated Report contains information about six different capitals which an organization uses and generates as it goes about its business. The Integrated Reporting framework lists eight Content Elements which, ideally, are included in an Integrated Report. While complete inclusion of all eight Content Elements may not occur for all users, there has been a trend toward dissemination of more nonfinancial information to stakeholders. Adoption of Integrated Reporting is typically a multiyear process, and many organizations will use a phased approach to implementation. Collection, coordination, and reporting of both financial and nonfinancial information as it relates to an organization's value chain has long been the domain of management accountants. Integrated Reporting is an important development within the accounting profession and wise management accountants should be conversant on this topic.

Topic 2.1 Recognition, Measurement, Valuation and Disclosure – Assets

Receivables

After studying this lesson, you should be able to:

- Identify issues related to the valuation of accounts receivable, including timing of recognition and estimation of the allowance for credit losses (1.A.2.a).

- Distinguish between receivables sold (factoring) on a with-recourse basis and those sold on a without-recourse basis, and determine the effect on the balance sheet (1.A.2.b).

Many organizations sell to customers without collecting cash at the time of sale. When this happens, an asset called accounts receivable is used to keep track of the amount owed. Every organization that uses accounts receivables also carries the risk that a customer will not pay the organization. As a result, the organization must have methods for accounting for uncollectible accounts receivable. This lesson will discuss the accounting methods associated with both recording accounts receivable and the accounting for credit losses, or bad debts, due to non-payment of accounts receivable. In addition, this lesson will address accounting for factoring, the transaction that occurs when an organization sells its accounts receivable to third parties.

I. Generally, when organizations sell to customers without collecting cash at the time of sale, an account receivable is created. The customer is expected to pay the organization at some point in the future.

II. When non-cash sales are made, accounts receivable are recorded at the time revenue is recognized in accordance with revenue recognition under U.S. GAAP. [See the lesson Revenue Recognition in Part 1, Section A, Topic 2.3 for a review of revenue recognition and special considerations for when the typical pattern of recognition is disrupted.]

    A. Following is the standard accounts receivable entry for a $100 sale made on account. Note that if the sale was for inventory, a corresponding entry to cost of goods sold and inventory would also be required.

Accounts Receivable	100	
Revenue		100

To record a sale on account.

    B. When the $100 cash is collected, the entity records the following entry.

Cash	100	
Accounts Receivable		100

To record cash collected on account.

III. Credit risk, also known as default risk, measures the risk that a customer will not ultimately pay the organization as promised at the time of sale.

    A. A customer failing to pay an accounts receivable results in an uncollectible account, or bad debt, to the selling entity.

    B. Organizations must balance the desire for increased sales from selling on credit with the risk of incurring credit losses related to its customers uncollectible accounts.

IV. Organizations account for credit losses, or bad debts, in one of two ways.

A. Allowance method—The organization estimates the amount of bad debt it will incur and records the expense in the same period as the related sales using an allowance account called Allowance for Credit Losses, or Allowance for Uncollectible Accounts.

Bad Debt Expense	1,000	
Allowance for Uncollectible Accts		1,000

To record estimated bad debt expense and allowance for uncollectible accounts.

1. Recording an allowance helps an organization match expenses associated with uncollectible accounts to related revenues.

2. The organization assumes some amount of receivables will not be collected for purposes of estimating bad debt expense.

3. Under the allowance method, the organization is reducing accounts receivable without knowing which specific customers will not pay their debts in the future. The use of a separate account for the estimate of uncollectible receivables will allow the sum of the subsidiary (individual customer) ledgers to reconcile to the account receivable balance.

4. The allowance for uncollectible accounts is subtracted from accounts receivable when preparing the balance sheet. The financial statements, therefore, will reflect only the amount that is expected to be collected, or Net Realizable Value (NRV) of Accounts Receivable. This amount is commonly referred to as Net Accounts Receivable.

Accounts Receivable	$100,000
Less: Allowance for Uncollectible Accounts	($10,000)
Equals: Net Accounts Receivable	$90,000

5. When a specific customer account is identified as uncollectible, the organization can write off the amount by reducing both the allowance for uncollectible accounts and accounts receivable. This adjustment does not change the amount of Net Accounts Receivable reflected on the balance sheet. The entry to write off the sale noted above would be:

Allowance for Uncollectible Accts	100	
Accounts Receivable		100

To write off a specific customer account as uncollectible.

6. Organizations use two approaches for estimating uncollectible receivables under the allowance method.

   a. Percentage of receivables or balance sheet approach—The organization assumes a percentage of existing accounts receivable will not be collectible and adjusts the allowance account to reflect that percentage each time the financial statements are prepared.

   i. Because this method is based on a percentage of accounts receivable, a balance sheet account, it is often referred to as the balance sheet approach.

   ii. The accounts receivable aging is often used to estimate the total amount of uncollectible accounts at the end of the period. The estimated amount is compared to the amount remaining in the allowance account and the necessary adjustment is recorded.

- If the allowance for uncollectible accounts is too small, bad debt expense is increased and income goes down.

- If the allowance for uncollectible accounts is too large, bad debt expense is decreased and income goes up.

b. Illustration: An organization has the following accounts receivable aging and estimates for expected uncollectible percentages at the end of Year 1.

	0–30 days	31–60 days	61–90 days	> 90 days	Total
Amount	$295,000	$87,000	$15,000	$3,000	$400,000
% Uncollectible	3%	5%	10%	60%	
Allowance needed	$8,850	$4,350	$1,500	$1,800	$16,500

If the current balance in the allowance account is $15,000, the organization makes the following entry:

Bad Debt Expense	1,500	
Allowance for Uncollectible Accounts		1,500

To adjust allowance for uncollectible accounts at end of Year 1.

If, on the other hand, the current balance in the allowance account is $17,000, the organization makes the following entry:

Allowance for Uncollectible Accounts	500	
Bad Debt Expense		500

To adjust allowance for uncollectible accounts at end of Year 1.

c. Percentage of revenues or income statement approach—The organization assumes a certain percentage of sales are uncollectible and records bad debt expense based on that percentage of revenue in a given period.

  i. Because this method is based on a percentage of revenue, an income statement account, this is often referred to as the income statement approach.

  ii. Periodically, an organization will review its allowance for uncollectible accounts to ensure that it is sufficient to cover uncollectible amounts and adjust the balance as needed. Regular large adjustments to the allowance would indicate that the percentage of sales being used for the estimate should be adjusted going forward.

d. Illustration: An organization has $100,000 of revenues each month and assumes 1% of all revenues are uncollectible. The organization makes the following entry each month:

Bad Debt Expense	1,000	
Allowance for Uncollectible Accounts		1,000

To record monthly bad debt expense.

If, at the end of the year, the balance in the allowance account is $10,500 (after write-offs during the year), and a review of the accounts receivable aging indicates the need for a $16,500 allowance, the organization would adjust the allowance by recording an additional $6,000 in bad debt expense. In addition, the organization would likely increase its percentage of sales used for recording bad debt expense from 1% to 1.5% going forward.

B. Direct write-off method—The organization waits until a specific account is identified as not collectible and removes the accounts receivable with an offsetting entry to bad debt expense.

Bad Debt Expense	100	
Accounts Receivable		100

To write off an uncollectible account receivable.

1. Under U.S. tax laws, bad debts are only recorded using the direct write-off method.

2. The direct write-off method is the simplest method to use.

3. A disadvantage of using the direct write-off method is that the expense for bad debt is not matched to the revenue associated with the sale.

4. Generally, the direct write-off method is not acceptable for U.S. GAAP reporting purposes unless the uncollectible amounts are clearly immaterial or there is no reasonable basis for estimating bad debts.

Practice Question

Company X has the following accounts receivable aging and estimates for expected uncollectible percentages at the end of Year 1.

	0–30 days	31–60 days	61–90 days	> 90 days	Total
Amount	$398,000	$187,000	$55,000	$10,000	$650,000
% Uncollectible	2%	4%	8%	50%	

Company X has a current credit balance in its allowance for uncollectible accounts of $22,000 and bad debt expense of $62,000 before adjusting entries.

1. What is the necessary amount of the adjustment to bad debt expense?

2. What is the Net Accounts Receivable that will be reflected in the balance sheet after the adjustment is made?

Answer

1. Allowance for uncollectible accounts needs to be adjusted by $2,840 and bad debt expense will increase by that amount:

	Amount		Percentage		Estimate
0–30 days	398,000	×	.02	=	7,960
31–60 days	187,000	×	.04	=	7,480
61–90 days	55,000	×	.08	=	4,400
> 90 days	10,000	×	.50	=	5,000
					24,840

Current credit balance in the allowance for uncollectible accounts before adjustment is $22,000 so it must increase by $2,840 to bring the allowance to the required balance of $24,840.

2. After the adjustment, the Net Accounts receivable balance shown in the balance sheet is $625,160, calculated as follows:

Accounts Receivable	$650,000
Less: Allowance for Uncollectible Accounts	($24,840)
Equals: Net Accounts Receivable	$625,160

V. Organizations can sell, or factor, accounts receivable to third parties and receive a percentage of the receivables immediately as cash.

    A. There are several advantages and disadvantages to factoring receivables.

        1. Advantages

            a. It is a quick source of cash.

            b. Fees are usually based on the credit quality of the organization's customers, *not* the organization itself.

            c. The organization can raise cash without incurring any additional debt.

            d. The organization does not have to secure financing with existing assets.

        2. Disadvantages

            a. It is a short-term cash solution.

            b. Investors and creditors could perceive factoring as a sign of financial difficulty.

            c. Fees and expenses can be very high.

    B. Factoring can be done either with recourse or without recourse.

        1. With recourse means the organization selling accounts receivable bears the risk of loss relative to collecting the customers' balances.

            a. Fees are generally lower when factoring with recourse than without recourse.

            b. If the customer does not pay its accounts receivable, the selling organization is required to compensate the factor for the loss.

            c. The selling organization must estimate the amount of the recourse obligation and record it at the time of the factoring.

            d. Illustration: Company A sells $100,000 of accounts receivable to Company B with recourse. Company B, the factor, assesses a 2% finance charge and withholds an additional 5% to cover possible uncollectible amounts. Company A estimates the recourse obligation to be $3,500. Company A makes the following entry to record the factoring:

Cash	93,000	
Due from Factor	5,000	
Loss on Factoring	5,500	
Accounts Receivable		100,000
Recourse Obligation		3,500

To record factoring of receivables and recognition of recourse obligation.

The loss on the factoring transaction is the sum of the 2% finance charge and the estimated recourse obligation ($2,000 + $3,500). The Due from Factor and Recourse Obligation accounts will be settled once both parties agree that all collection efforts have been exhausted and the amount of uncollectible accounts is known.

        2. Without recourse means the factor (the organization purchasing the accounts receivable from the selling organization) bears the risk of loss relative to collecting the customers' balances.

            a. The organization selling the accounts receivable will generally receive less cash when factoring without recourse to compensate for the increased risk to the factor.

            b. If the customer does not pay its accounts receivable, the selling organization is not impacted by this nonpayment.

c. Illustration: Company A sells $100,000 of accounts receivable to Company B without recourse. Company B, the factor, assesses a 5% finance charge and withholds an additional 4% to cover late-paying customers. Company A makes the following entry to record the factoring:

Cash	91,000	
Due from Factor	4,000	
Loss on Factoring	5,000	
Accounts Receivable		100,000

To record factoring of receivables without recourse.

In this case, the loss on the factoring transaction is simply the 5% finance charge as there is no estimated recourse obligation. The Due from Factor will be settled once all money has been collected from customers or both parties agree that all collection efforts have been exhausted.

Practice Question

Company Y sells $150,000 of accounts receivable to Company Z with recourse. Company Z, the factor, assesses a 4% finance charge and withholds an additional 3% to cover possible uncollectible amounts. Company Y estimates the recourse obligation to be $7,000.

1. What is the amount of the loss on factoring that Company Y will record upon the sale of these receivables to Company Z?

2. Assume Company Y wishes to renegotiate the sale of receivables to be without recourse instead. Is the amount of the finance charge likely to be greater than or less than 4%? Why?

Answer

1. The loss on factoring will include both the finance charge and the amount of the recourse obligation:

Finance Charge ($150,000 × .04)	$ 6,000
Recourse Obligation	7,000
Total Loss on Factoring	$13,000

2. The finance charge is likely to be greater than 4% as Company Z will want compensation for taking on the risk of loss associated with collectability of the accounts if the sale is without recourse.

Summary

According to revenue recognition principles under U.S. GAAP, when non-cash sales are made, accounts receivable are recorded at the time revenue is recognized. Credit risk, or default risk, is the risk that a customer will ultimately not pay the organization as promised. There are two methods of accounting for credit losses, also known as bad debts. The first is the allowance method, which is when the organization estimates the amount of bad debt it will incur and records the expense in the same period as the related sales using an allowance account. The second method is the direct write-off method, which is when an organization waits until a specific account is identified as not collectible to remove the account receivable using an offsetting entry to bad debt expense. Organizations sometimes factor, or sell, their accounts receivable to a third party in order to receive a percentage of the receivables immediately as cash.

Inventory

After studying this lesson, you should be able to:

- Identify issues in inventory valuation, including which goods to include, what costs to include, and which cost assumption to use (1.A.2.c).

- Identify and compare cost flow assumptions used in accounting for inventories (1.A.2.d).

- Calculate the effect on income and on assets of using different inventory methods (1.A.2.f).

- Identify advantages and disadvantages of the different inventory methods (1.A.2.h).

- Recommend the inventory method and cost flow assumption that should be used for a firm given a set of facts (1.A.2.i).

- Demonstrate an understanding of the lower of cost or market rule for LIFO and the retail inventory method and the lower of cost and net realizable value rule for all other inventory methods (1.A.2.e).

- Analyze the effects of inventory errors (1.A.2.g).

Most organizations that deliver goods to their customers must carry inventory. When accounting for inventory an organization must consider which costs to include in the inventory as well as which cost flow assumptions to use. This lesson will discuss many issues related to inventory including: costs to be included in inventory, periodic vs. perpetual inventory systems, the four most common cost flow assumptions, accounting for declines in inventory value, inventory errors, and changes to inventory costing methods.

I. Many organizations, including manufacturing and construction firms, carry inventory to deliver goods to their customers.

    A. Organizations must consider a variety of factors to determine the proper accounting for their inventory.

        1. Which goods and related costs should be included in inventory?

            a. Costs to get the items ready for sale are included in inventory and are expensed as costs of sales when the inventory is sold.

            b. Costs not included in inventory (selling costs, shipping to the customer, etc.) are expensed as operating expenses when incurred.

            c. The inclusion or exclusion of costs in inventory can have a significant impact on an organization's gross profit.

        2. Which inventory costing assumption should the organization use?

            a. Depending on cost behavior, different inventory methods (described below) can have a material effect on an organization's gross profit.

            b. Organizations should select the inventory method which best reflects its economic reality.

    B. Organizations can use either the periodic or the perpetual method to account for inventory.

        1. Periodic method: The organization's beginning inventory balance is reflected on the balance sheet throughout the year.

            a. Purchases on account are recorded in a Purchases account separate from inventory with the offsetting entry to Accounts Payable.

            b. Sales to customers during the period do not affect the inventory accounts in real time.

c. During the period, the organization tracks transactions like transportation in, purchase discounts, and purchase returns (not sales returns) in separate accounts for each type of transaction.

d. At the end of each period, the organization will count its inventory and calculate cost of goods sold using the amounts from all of the inventory-related accounts:

Beginning Inventory	XX,XXX
Plus: Transportation In	XXX
Purchases	XXX,XXX
Less: Purchase Returns and Allowances	(X,XXX)
Purchase Discounts	(X,XXX)
Goods Available for Sale	XXX,XXX
Less: Ending Inventory	(XX,XXX)
Cost of Goods Sold	XXX,XXX

e. An adjusting entry is then made to accomplish the following:

   i. Remove the beginning inventory balance

   ii. Record the correct ending inventory balance

   iii. Close various inventory related accounts used during the year (Purchases, Transportation in, Purchase Returns and Allowances, Purchase Discounts)

   iv. Record cost of sales for the period (this is the amount needed to balance the entry)

   An example of this entry is shown below.

Merchandise Inventory (Ending)	XX	
Purchase Returns and Allowances	XX	
Purchase Discounts	XX	
Cost of Goods Sold	XX	
Merchandise Inventory (Beginning)		XX
Purchases		XX
Transportation In		XX

To correct inventory balance and record cost of goods sold.

2. Perpetual method: The organization records costs associated with inventory purchases and cost of sales directly to the merchandise inventory account as transactions (purchases, sales, returns, discounts) take place throughout the year.

a. The perpetual method allows organizations to match cost of sales and inventory transactions more closely with their sales and cash expenditures during the year.

b. A moving average costing system requires a perpetual inventory method.

C. Organizations should include the following items in their inventories:

1. All goods available for sale. Examples for certain industries include the following:

a. Manufacturing organizations—All components that are part of the final product.

   i. Components

   ii. Assemblies

   iii. Freight required to transport these materials

   iv. Handling associated with preparing the materials for eventual manufacturing

    b. Retail organizations—Cost of goods purchased for resale.

    c. Construction organizations—The cost of building supplies to be part of the finished project.

  2. All freight, import duties, and related transportation costs required to bring goods for sale to the organization.

  3. All direct labor associated with turning purchased components and supplies into finished products.

    a. Labor associated with machining or cutting raw material into components usable for production.

    b. Labor associated with assembling components into goods available for sale.

  4. All manufacturing overhead expenses required to support the process of manufacturing or construction. Examples include:

    a. Labor costs associated with factory maintenance and other functions that are not associated directly with producing goods for sale.

    b. Costs of machinery required for manufacturing.

    c. Utility costs for manufacturing facilities.

    d. Office and administrative expenses supporting the manufacture of goods.

D. For manufacturing organizations, inventory will consist of three categories.

  1. Raw materials, which are the purchased goods not yet placed into production and all related inbound transportation costs.

  2. Work in process, which accounts for all costs of goods in production but not yet completed.

  3. Finished goods, which are products available for sale.

E. Retail or merchandising organizations generally only have Finished Goods inventory.

F. Service organizations often use Work-in-Process accounts to account for the work professionals perform directly related to revenue-producing projects. The accounting is very similar to that of manufacturing accounting.

Practice Question

Jazz Note Corporation had the following information about inventory transactions during the year 20X4:

Beginning Inventory	120 units @ $5
Purchases	850 units @ $5
Sales	670 units @ $10
Ending Inventory	300 units @ $5

Prepare the journal entries and calculate cost of goods sold and ending inventory using:

1. The perpetual inventory method.

2. The periodic inventory method.

Answer

1. Perpetual Inventory Method:

Beginning Inventory: No entry needed. The Inventory account shows the inventory on hand at $600.

Continues…

Purchase of 850 units at $5:

Inventory	4,250	
Accounts Payable		4,250
Purchase 850 units at $5/unit		

Sale of 670 units @ $10:

Accounts Receivable	6,700	
Sales Revenue		6,700
Cost of Goods Sold	3,350	
Inventory		3,350
Sell 670 units at $10/unit and record associated cost of goods sold at $5/unit		

Ending Inventory of 300 units @ $5: No entry needed because the inventory account already reflects the ending balance as shown below:

	Inventory		
Beginning Inventory	600		
Purchases	4,250	3,350	Sales
Ending Inventory	1,500		

2. Periodic Inventory Method:

Beginning Inventory: No entry needed. The inventory account shows the inventory on hand at $600.

Purchase of 850 units @ $5:

Purchases	4,250	
Accounts Payable		4,250
Purchase 850 units at $5/unit		

Sale of 670 units @ $10: Remember that there is no entry to record the cost of inventory at the time .of sale.

Accounts Receivable	6,700	
Sales Revenue		6,700
Sell 670 units at $10/unit		

Ending Inventory of 300 units @ $5:

Inventory*	1,500	
Cost of Goods Sold**	3,350	
Purchase		4,250
Inventory (beginning)		600
To adjust ending inventory to 300 units observed at the physical count at $5/unit, to close out the purchases account, and to recognize cost of goods sold for the period.		
*Ending Inventory is calculated as 300 × $5 = $1,500.		
**Cost of Goods Sold = Beginning Inventory + Purchases − Ending Inventory.		

Cost of Goods Sold = $600 + $4,250 − $1,500 = $3,350.

II. Retail and manufacturing organizations can use one of four common methods to account for the cost of raw materials and merchandise inventory.

   A. Specific identification method—Common in organizations with highly customized or unique finished goods, the specific identification method assigns actual costs to specific goods. When the goods are sold, the organization records cost of goods sold associated with the specific item being sold. This is the only costing method in which the cost flow matches the actual physical flow of goods exactly. The remaining three methods require cost flow assumptions to be made that may not reflect the actual physical flow of the goods all the time.

   B. First-in, First-out (FIFO)—The costs of the oldest goods in inventory (the goods purchased first) are expensed as cost of sales first.

   C. Last-in, First-out (LIFO)—The costs of the newest goods in inventory (the goods purchased last) are expensed as cost of sales first.

   D. Average cost—As goods are purchased or moved from raw material to merchandise inventory, average unit costs are recalculated. Cost of goods sold is based on a moving average cost per unit.

   1. An organization will recompute average cost after each purchase.

   2. Accounting software, such as QuickBooks, will generally compute average costs under the average cost inventory method.

   E. Illustration: Company A has purchased a widget for the following prices on the following dates.

Purchase Date	Units	Cost/unit	Total cost
1/1/20X5	100	$10	$1,000
2/1/20X5	100	$12	$1,200
3/1/20X5	100	$15	$1,500
Total			$3,700

On 3/2/20X5, Company A sells 125 units of the widget.

   1. FIFO will record cost of sales starting with the oldest inventory first.

   a. Cost of sales = (100 units × $10/unit) + (25 units × $12/unit) = $1,000 + $300 = $1,300

   b. Ending inventory = (75 units × $12/unit) + (100 units × $15/unit) = $900 + $1,500 = $2,400

   2. LIFO will record cost of sales starting with the newest inventory first.

   a. Cost of sales = (100 units × $15/unit) + (25 units × $12/unit) = $1,500 + $300 = $1,800

   b. Ending inventory = (75 units × $12/unit) + (100 units × $10/unit) = $900 + $1,000 = $1,900

   3. Average cost will record cost of sales and inventory based on an average cost of the units in inventory.

   a. Average cost/unit = $3,700 ÷ 300 units = $12.33/unit

   b. Cost of sales = (125 units × $12.33) = $1,542

   c. Ending inventory = (175 units × $12.33) = $2,158

Practice Question

Company B sells broomsticks. They purchase inventory on the following dates in January 20X6:

Date of Transaction	# of Broomsticks Purchased	Cost per Broomstick	Total Cost
1/1/20X6	125	$11.00	$1,375.00
1/9/20X6	75	$11.50	$862.50
1/19/20X6	100	$9.50	$950.00
1/30/20X6	50	$13.00	$650.00
Total	**350**		**$3,837.50**

Company B also sold 250 broomsticks during January 20X6.

Calculate (a) the cost of goods sold for January, and (b) the ending inventory under the following methods:

1. FIFO Inventory Method

2. LIFO Inventory Method

3. Weighted-Average Cost Inventory Method

Answer

1. *FIFO Inventory Method*: Record the cost of goods sold using the oldest inventory first.

   a. Cost of Goods Sold = (125 units × $11.00) + (75 units × $11.50) + (50 units × $9.50) = **$2,712.50**

   b. Ending Inventory = (50 units × $9.50) + (50 units × $13.00) = **$1,125.00**

2. *LIFO Inventory Method:* Record the cost of goods sold using the newest inventory first.

   a. Cost of Goods Sold = (50 units × $13.00) + (100 units × $9.50) + (75 units × $11.50) + (25 units × $11.00) = **$2,737.50**

   b. Ending Inventory = (100 units × $11.00) = **$1,100.00**

3. *Weighted-average Cost Inventory Method:* The Cost of Goods Sold and Inventory is based on an average cost of the units in inventory.

   Average cost/unit = $3,837.50 ÷ 350 units = $10.96/unit

   a. Cost of Goods Sold = 250 units × $10.96 = **$2,740.00**

   b. Ending Inventory = 100 units × $10.96 = **$1,096.00**

III. The following factors influence the choice of method for inventory costing.

   A. FIFO will generally better reflect the actual physical flow of goods as most organizations will sell goods purchased first to minimize spoilage and obsolescence costs.

   B. LIFO is not allowed under International Financial Reporting Standards (IFRS). Only specific identification, FIFO, and average cost methods are allowed.

   C. If prices are rising (inflationary environment), LIFO will produce higher cost of sales.

      1. Gross margins and net income for organizations using LIFO will be lower than organizations using average costing or FIFO.

      2. Income tax liability will be lower for organizations using LIFO, meaning the organization will generally pay less in cash income taxes than organizations using FIFO or average cost.

   D. If prices are falling (deflationary environment), LIFO will produce lower cost of sales.

1. Gross margins and net income for organizations using LIFO will be higher than organizations using average costing or FIFO.

2. Income tax liability will be higher for organizations using LIFO, meaning the organization will generally pay more in cash income taxes than organizations using FIFO or average cost.

IV. The market value of inventory may decrease because of any number of factors.

A. New technology makes inventory obsolete.

B. Fire or other natural disaster can damage or destroy inventory.

C. Under most inventory cost flow assumptions (all except the LIFO and Retail Methods), when an organization determines the net realizable value (NRV) of inventory is less than the historical cost of inventory, then it must reduce the value of inventory to NRV. This is called the lower of cost or NRV principle. This new written-down value becomes "cost" for future evaluation.

D. Net realizable value (NRV)—The value an organization would expect to receive for the inventory in the current environment less any costs associated with selling the inventory.

E. Losses recognized for NRV write-downs are recorded as part of Cost of Goods Sold in the period of the write-down. Illustration: Company Q has inventory with a historical cost of $10,000 that has declined in value and is not expected to recover. Current NRV is determined to be $9,000, so Company Q records the following entry:

Cost of Goods Sold	1,000	
Inventory		1,000

To record a $1,000 loss on NRV write-down of inventory.

The impact is to reduce the value of inventory and record an additional expense because of the inventory's lost value.

F. Illustration:

Lower of Cost or NRV

		Product A	Product B	Product C
(a)	Cost	$40	$50	$50
(b)	Expected Selling Price	60	45	55
(c)	Expected Selling/Disposal Costs	6	10	8
(b) – (c)	NRV—Selling Price Less Selling Costs	54	35	47
	Lower of Cost or NRV	40	35	47

G. When an organization uses either the LIFO or Retail Method cost flow assumptions, inventory should be written down to market using the Lower of Cost or Market (LCM) principle.

1. Replacement cost – The cost the organization would incur to purchase a similar type of inventory at current costs, including the costs associated with transporting and handling the inventory.

2. Net realizable value (NRV) - The value an organization would expect to receive for the inventory in the current environment less any costs associated with selling the inventory

3. Normal profit – The profit an organization would receive for the inventory if sold at its "regular" market price (i.e., the market price in an environment where the organization is experiencing normal business conditions)

4. The inventory's market value is generally the replacement cost as defined above, but can be no higher than the ceiling and no lower than the floor.

a. Ceiling – The NRV of the inventory item

b. Floor – The NRV of the inventory less the normal profit of the inventory

H. Illustration: Lower of Cost or Market

		Product A	Product B	Product C	Product D	Product E
a)	Cost	40	50	50	40	60
b)	Replacement Cost	43	52	48	50	55
c)	Expected Selling Price	60	45	80	65	50
d)	Expected Selling/Disposal Costs	6	5	5	8	10
e)	Normal Profit (20% Margin)	12	9	16	13	10
	CEILING: NRV = Selling Price – Selling Costs (c – d)	54	40	75	57	40
	FLOOR: NRV – Profit Maring (c – d – e)	42	31	59	44	30
	Replacement Costs (b)	43	52	48	50	55
	Market Value	43	40	59	50	40
	Cost (a)	40	50	50	40	60
	Lower of Cost or Market (LCM)	40	40	50	40	40

1. Product A

   a. The replacement cost of 43 is between the ceiling of 54 and the floor of 42, so the market value is replacement cost of 43.

   b. The cost of 40 is lower than the market of 43, so LCM values inventory at 40.

2. Product B

   a. The replacement cost of 52 is higher than the NRV ceiling of 40, so the market value is 40.

   b. The market value of 40 is lower than cost of 50, so LCM values inventory at 40.

3. Product C

   a. The replacement cost of 48 is lower than the floor of 59, so market value is 59.

   b. The cost of 50 is lower than market value of 59, so LCM values inventory at 50.

4. Product D

   a. The replacement cost of 50 is between the ceiling of 57 and the floor of 44, so the market value is the replacement cost of 50.

   b. The cost of 40 is lower than market value of 50, so LCM values inventory at 40.

5. Product E

   a. The replacement cost of 55 is higher than the ceiling of 40, so the market value is NRV of 40.

   b. The market value of 40 is less than the cost of 60, so LCM values the inventory at 40.

V. Many organizations conduct inventory counts either at year-end or at various times during the year. Inventory counting errors affect the organization's asset value and income depending on the nature of the inventory errors.

   A. If inventory has been under-counted (real inventory value > counted inventory value), the following impact occurs.

1. Ending inventory is adjusted to below actual.

Cost of Goods Sold	XXX	
Inventory		XXX

To record the book to physical count adjustment for inventory.

2. Cost of sales is higher than actual.

3. Net income will be lower than actual.

4. The entry to correct for under-counted inventory before the books are closed is shown below.

Inventory	XX	
Cost of Goods Sold		XX

To correct inventory for current year under-count.

B. If inventory is over-counted (counted inventory value > real inventory value), the following impact occurs.

1. Ending inventory is adjusted to above actual.

Inventory	XX	
Cost of Goods Sold		XX

To record the book to physical count adjustment for inventory.

2. Cost of sales is lower than actual.

3. Net income will be higher than actual.

4. The entry to correct for over-counted inventory before the books are closed is shown below.

Cost of Goods Sold	XX	
Inventory		XX

To correct inventory for current year over-count.

C. In the event that an inventory error is discovered after the organization's books are closed for a given year, the error correction becomes a prior-period adjustment.

1. Prior-period adjustments replace the Cost of Goods Sold account with Retained Earnings since any balances in Cost of Goods Sold are ultimately closed to Retained Earnings as part of the closing process.

2. The entry to correct for previously under-counted inventory is shown below.

Inventory	XX	
Retained Earnings		XX

To correct inventory for previous year under-count.

3. The entry to correct for previously over-counted inventory is shown below.

Retained Earnings	XXX	
Inventory		XXX

To correct inventory for previous year over-count.

VI. Changing inventory costing methods is a significant accounting change.

   A. If an organization changes its inventory costing method, it will be required to disclose the change and restate prior-period financial statements to reflect the change as of the beginning of the period presented.

   B. Organizations constantly changing accounting methods are generally considered to have lower quality of earnings and will see their value discounted by investors who are not as trusting of financial results.

Practice Question

T Company has discovered an inventory error that needs to be adjusted. List the journal entries that should be made to correct the error under the following unrelated circumstances:

1. In April 20X3, T Company discovers that inventory was overstated by $10,000 on the 20X2 books. This error was found after the 20X2 books were already closed.

2. Prior to the closing of the 20X2 books, T Company discovers that their 20X2 Inventory was overstated by $8,000 due to a counting error.

Answer

1. This is an example of a prior-period adjustment. Prior-period adjustments are not made directly to Cost of Goods Sold; rather the adjustment is made to Retained Earnings. In this case, inventory for 20X2 was overstated. If inventory was overstated, Cost of Goods Sold would have been understated and net income would have been overstated. The following entry is needed to correct the error:

Retained Earnings	10,000	
Inventory		10,000

To record a prior-period adjustment to correct overstated 20X2 inventory.

2. Because the books have not been closed for the year, this adjustment can be made directly to the Cost of Goods Sold account to correct it. If the Inventory balance was over-counted, the Cost of Goods Sold account would need to be increased; otherwise the Net Income would be overstated. These accounts can be corrected with the following entry:

Cost of Goods Sold	8,000	
Inventory		8,000

To correct overstated 20X2 inventory.

Summary

Many organizations carry inventory to deliver goods to their customers. These organizations will evaluate all costs associated with inventory and decide whether to include it as inventory or to expense as an operating expense. Additionally, when accounting for inventories, organizations must decide whether to use a periodic system (costs associated with inventory are not recorded to inventory until the end of the period) or a perpetual system (costs associated with inventory are recorded continuously throughout the year). There are four common methods to account for inventory: specific identification; first-in, first-out; last-in, first-out; and average cost. Decreasing market value, physical inventory counts, and a change in inventory costing methods can all have an impact on inventory and must be accounted for when such instances occur.

Accounting for Investments in Other Entities

After studying this lesson, you should be able to:

- Demonstrate an understanding of the following debt security types: trading, available-for-sale, and held-to-maturity (1.A.2.j).

- Demonstrate an understanding of the valuation of debt and equity securities (1.A.2.k).

> When organizations have idle cash that is not currently needed for operations, they must find ways to invest this cash. The most common investments are to purchase debt or equity positions in other organizations. This lesson will discuss the various classifications of marketable securities and how to account for each type as well as the various accounting methods for equity purchases.

I. Organizations often hold marketable securities as a way to invest idle cash before it is needed for business operations.

   A. These securities allow the organization to maintain sufficient cash liquidity while still allowing the opportunity to earn additional income.

   B. Organizations must classify these securities in one of three ways. The classification is based on the organization's intent related to the debt securities at the time of purchase.

   1. Trading—The organization's intent is to resell these debt securities in the near term.

      a. Bonds issued by another entity with intent to be sold by the organization in the short term are examples of trading securities at the balance sheet date.

      b. The balance sheet will reflect quoted market value of trading securities.

      c. Changes in market value for trading securities are recognized in income.

      d. Interest on trading securities is recognized in income when earned.

   2. Held-to-maturity—The organization has the ability and intent to hold the debt security until it matures (becomes due).

      a. The balance sheet will reflect amortized cost for the debt security.

         i. If the security was purchased at a discount to par value (i.e., less than the security's par value as stated on the security's documentation), a contra-asset account called "Discount on Bond" will be recorded to reduce the bond's carrying value relative to par value.

         ii. If the security was purchased at a premium to par value (i.e., more than the security's par value as stated on the security's documentation), an adjunct account called "Premium on Bond" will be recorded to increase the bond's carrying value relative to par value.

      b. The organization will record interest revenue as a function of the bond's carrying value and market rate of interest at the time of the purchase. The discount or premium associated with the bond will be amortized as interest is recognized over the life of the bond.

      c. The carrying value of the bond changes with the amortization of the discount or premium and changes in market value are not recorded.

   3. Available-for-sale (AFS) securities are any debt securities not specifically designated as trading or held-to-maturity.

      a. Illustration: An organization holds a bond that it may sell if the bond's market price is favorably impacted by changes in interest rates but it has no plans to sell the bond in the short term. Since the organization does not intend to hold the bond to maturity, nor does it intend to sell the bond in the short term, the security is neither held-to-maturity nor trading. The proper classification is AFS.

b. The balance sheet will reflect quoted market value of AFS securities.

c. Changes in market value for AFS securities are recognized directly to equity in Other Comprehensive Income (OCI), which is *not* a part of net income.

d. Amounts accumulated in OCI remain there until gains and losses are realized through the sale of the security.

e. Realized gains and losses from the sale of AFS securities flow through income. Realized gains and losses are the difference between what was paid for the security and the amount received upon sale.

f. Interest on AFS securities is recognized in income when earned.

g. Illustration: Company A purchases 10 of Company Z bonds at a par value of $1,000 each on 1/1/20X5. Company A classifies the security as AFS. Company Z's bond value on 12/31/20X5 is $800 per bond. Company A sells all of the Company Z bonds for $900 each on 2/1/20X6. Entries for this security follow:

1/1/20X5		
Available-for-Sale Securities	10,000	
Cash		10,000

To record the purchase of Company Z bond.

12/31/20X5		
Other Comprehensive Income	2,000	
Available-for-Sale Securities		2,000

To record the decrease in value of Company Z bond.

2/1/20X6		
Cash	9,000	
Realized Loss on AFS Securities	1,000	
Available-for-Sale Securities		8,000
Other Comprehensive Income		2,000

To record the sale and realized loss on Company Z bond.

C. Alternatively, an organization may elect the fair value option for investments in debt securities and account for them in a manner similar to Trading Securities discussed above.

Practice Question

Y Corporation invests its idle cash in investment securities. During 20X5, the following events occurred in connection with their investment activities:

• Purchased 70 T Corporation bonds at $1,000 par value on 1/3/20X5.

• Sold 30 T Corporation bonds for $1,050 per bond on 5/1/20X5.

• The remaining T Corporation bonds had a fair value of $925 per bond on 12/31/20X5.

Continues…

What effect will these events have on Y Corporation's Net Income and Other Comprehensive Income (OCI) if the securities are classified as:

1. Trading

2. Available-for-Sale

Answer

1. *Trading*: Changes in the market value for trading securities are recognized in income as realized gains upon the sale of securities.

   5/1/20X5: Y Corporation will recognize a gain of $1,500 for the sale of 30 securities. This is calculated as follows: (Market Value at time of sale – Cost of Bonds) × Number of Bonds: ($1,050 – $1,000) × 30 bonds = $1,500.

   12/31/20X5: Y Corporation will recognize a loss of $3,000 in Income for the change in market value. This is calculated as (Current Market Value – Previous Market Value) × Number of Bonds: ($925 – $1,000) × 40 = ($3,000).

   Net Income: $1,500 decrease ($1,500 – $3,000)

   OCI: No Impact on OCI because the unrealized loss on market value flows through Net Income for trading securities.

2. *Available-for-Sale*: Changes in the market value of available-for-sale securities are recognized in OCI, which is *not* a part of Net Income. Dividends and realized gains upon the sale of securities are recognized in Net Income.

   5/1/20X5: Y Corporation will recognize a gain of $1,500 for the sale of 30 securities. This is calculated as follows: (Market Value at time of sale – Cost of Bonds) × Number of Bonds: ($1,050 – $1,000) × 30 bonds = $1,500.

   12/31/20X5: Y Corporation will recognize a decrease of $3,000 in Other Comprehensive Income for the change in market value. This is calculated as (Current Market Value – Previous Market Value) × Number of Bonds: ($925 – $1,000) × 40 = ($3,000).

   Net Income: $1,500 increase from the realized gain on the sale of securities.

   OCI: $3,000 decrease because the unrealized loss on market value flows through OCI for AFS securities.

II. Organizations often purchase equity shares in other organizations for a variety of purposes. There are three methods of accounting for equity investments.

   A. The fair value method is used when the organization owns a small amount of stock in another company and cannot significantly influence the investee's operations. The resulting accounting under the fair value method is the same as the accounting for debt securities classified as Trading.

      1. The balance sheet will reflect quoted market value of these securities.

      2. Changes in market value for these securities are recognized in income.

      3. Dividends on these securities are recognized in income when earned.

   B. Organizations will use the equity method of accounting for an equity investment in another company when it can exert significant influence, but not control, over the investee's operations.

      1. Generally, ownership between 20% and 50% is presumed to create significant influence.

      2. An organization may exert significant influence over its investee even where they own less than 20%.

         a. Investor has a representative on the board of directors.

         b. Common management between the investor and investee.

   c. Material intercompany transactions between the investor and investee.

   d. The investee uses much of the investor's technology.

   e. The investor's share of ownership is greater than other ownership shares in the investee (i.e., investor owns 15% and no other owner has more than 5%).

3. The equity method requires the following accounting transactions:

   a. The original investment in the investee is recorded at cost.

   b. The investor's pro-rata share of the investee's net income(loss) is recorded as an increase (decrease) to the investment account and the investor's income.

   c. Any dividends paid to the investor reduce the amount in the investor's investment account.

   d. Illustration: On 1/1/20X5, Company A purchases 30% of the shares in Company B for $100,000 and obtains significant influence. On 12/31/20X5, Company B reports $50,000 of net income. On 3/31/20X6, Company B declares $10,000 in dividends. Entries for this investment follow:

1/1/20X5		
Equity Investment—Company B	100,000	
Cash		100,000

To record the purchase of Company B stock.

12/31/20X5		
Equity Investment—Company B	15,000	
Other Income		15,000

To record the investor share of Company B income. ($50,000 × 30%)

3/31/20X6		
Cash	3,000	
Equity Investment—Company B		3,000

To record receipt of dividends from Company B. ($10,000 × 30%)

   e. Alternatively, an organization may elect the fair value option for investments in equity securities with significant influence and account for them in a manner similar to the fair value method discussed above.

C. Organizations will use the consolidation method of accounting for an investment in another company when it can exert control over the investee's operations.

1. Generally, ownership above 50% is presumed to create control.

2. Under consolidation accounting, the investor will present financial statements as though it is one company, with the subsidiary's assets, liabilities, and results of operations included in the investor's financial statements. Assets and liabilities of the subsidiary will be recognized in the consolidated financial statements at fair value at the time of purchase.

3. Goodwill, the amount by which the value of the entire subsidiary exceeds the value of its identifiable assets, is included in the consolidated financial statements.

4. Only the equity of the parent company will appear in the consolidated financial statements, since the subsidiary entity is controlled by the parent.

5. For any amount of subsidiary ownership not held by the investor, a non-controlling interest will be reflected in the financial statements.

6. Illustration: Company A purchases 70% of Company B for $700,000. The remaining 30% interest in Company B is valued at $300,000. Company B's net identifiable assets are appraised at a fair value of $800,000, but are recorded on Company B's records at $700,000. The $100,000 difference in fair value of the net identifiable assets is attributed to land held by Company B. The calculation of Goodwill and the consolidated balance sheet immediately after the purchase are shown below.

Company A's purchase price	$ 700,000
Value of non-controlling interest	300,000
Fair value of Company B	1,000,000
Fair value of Company B's identifiable assets	(800,000)
Goodwill	$ 200,000

	Company A	Company B	Adjustments		Consolidated AB
Assets	$3,300,000	$ 800,000	(a)	100,000	$4,200,000
Investment in B	700,000	-	(b)	(700,000)	-
Goodwill	-	-	(c)	200,000	200,000
Total Assets	**4,000,000**	**800,000**			**4,400,000**
Liabilities	1,000,000	100,000			1,100,000
Equity	3,000,000	700,000	(d)	(700,000)	3,000,000
Non-Controlling Interest	-	-	(e)	300,000	300,000
Total Liabilities and Equity	**$4,000,000**	**$ 800,000**			**$4,400,000**

a. To increase assets to reflect the fair value of the land held by Company B at the time of the purchase.

b. To remove the investment in B from the consolidated records because a company should not show an investment in itself.

c. To record the value of Goodwill at the time of purchase.

d. To remove the equity of Company B since it is controlled by Company A.

e. To reflect the non-controlling ownership interest in Company B.

As Company B earns net income, Company A will account for the entire amount on its financial statements, with the non-controlling interest share of income (30% in this case) going to increase the non-controlling interest account.

Practice Question

Y Corporation invests their idle cash in investment securities. During 20X5, the following events occurred in connection with their investment activities:

- Purchased 700 shares of T Corporation's stock at $12.50 per share on 1/3/20X5.

- Sold 300 shares of T Corporation's stock for $13.00 per share on 5/1/20X5.

- T Corporation declared a dividend of $0.75 per share on 6/1/20X5.

- The remaining shares of T Corporation's stock had a fair value of $10.25 per share on 12/31/20X5.

What effect will these events have on Y Corporation's Net Income and Other Comprehensive Income (OCI) if Y Corporation cannot exercise any influence over T Corporation as a result of the investment in T Corporation stock?

Continues...

Answer

When an investor cannot exercise influence over the investee, changes in the market value for equity securities are recognized in income as are the dividends when they are earned and realized gains upon the sale of securities.

5/1/20X5: Y Corporation will recognize a gain of $150 for the sale of 300 securities. This is calculated as follows: (Market Value at time of sale – Cost of Shares) × Number of Shares. ($13.00 – $12.50) × 300 shares = $150.

6/1/20X5: Y Corporation will recognize income of $300 for the dividend on the 400 shares they still hold (700 - 300). This is calculated as follows: Dividend × Number of Shares. $0.75 × 400 = $300.

12/31/20X5: Y Corporation will recognize a loss of $900 for the change in market value. This is calculated as (Current Market Value – Previous Market Value) × Number of Shares. ($10.25 – $12.50) × 400 = ($900).

Net Income: $450 decrease ($150 + $300 - $900)

OCI: No Impact on OCI because the unrealized loss on market value flows through Net Income for trading securities.

Practice Question

On 1/1/20X7, First Place Company purchases 45% of Second Place Company's outstanding stock for $550,000. During 20X7 First Place Company and Second Place Company recorded net income of $700,000 and $450,000 respectively. First Place Company declared dividends of $100,000 and Second Place Company declared dividends of $65,000.

1. What is the amount of income First Place will recognize during 20X7 relative to its investment in Second Place?

2. What is the value of the Investment in Second Place after all appropriate entries have been recorded by First Place in 20X7?

Answer

Because First Place Company owns 45% of Second Place Company's stock, they are presumed to exercise significant influence; consequently, First Place will record the investment using the equity method.

1. To find First Place Company's portion of the Net Income under the equity method, multiply Second Company Net Income by the First Place investment percentage. In this case: $450,000 × 45% = **$202,500**.

2. To find First Place Company's investment value at the end of 20X7 under the equity method, begin with the initial investment, add First Place Company's income from the investment, and subtract the dividends from the investment:

Purchase of 45% of Second Place Company's stock	$550,000
+ Income from Second Place (calculated above)	202,500
– Dividends from Second Place*	(29,250)
Total Investment value at the end of 20X7	**$723,250**

* To find First Place Company's portion of the declared dividend, multiply the declared dividend by the investment percentage. In this case: $65,000 × 45% = $29,250.

Continues...

Journal entries for First Place in 20X7 relative to this investment follow (not required):

1/1/20X7		
Equity Investment—Second Place Company	550,000	
Cash		550,000

To record initial investment in Second Place.

12/31/20X7		
Equity Investment—Second Place Company	202,500	
Other Income		202,500

To record 45% portion of Second Place Company's Net Income.

12/31/20X7		
Cash	29,250	
Equity Investment—Second Place Company		29,250

To record Second Place Company dividend.

Summary

Organizations invest in marketable securities as a way of maintaining sufficient cash liquidity while still earning additional income. Organizations that invest in debt securities must classify these securities as trading, held-to-maturity, or available-for-sale. The classification is determined based upon the organization's intent at the time of purchase. When purchasing equity shares in other organizations, there are three levels of influence. Based upon its amount of influence and ability to control the investee, an organization will use either the fair value method, the equity method, or the consolidation method.

Long-Term Assets

After studying this lesson, you should be able to:

- Recommend a depreciation method for a given set of data (1.A.2.m).

- Determine the effect on the financial statements of using different depreciation methods (1.A.2.l).

- Demonstrate an understanding of the accounting for impairment of long-term assets and intangible assets, including goodwill (1.A.2.n).

- Demonstrate an understanding of the treatment of gain or loss on the disposal of fixed assets (1.A.2.bb).

Most organizations purchase long-term assets that they use for an extended period of time. Organizations use depreciation to spread the cost of these assets over the period that they provide benefit to the organization. This lesson will discuss the various facets of tangible and intangible long-term assets, including managerial judgments, depreciation methods, the effects of depreciation method on the financial statements, impairment of assets, and sale of assets.

I. Tangible assets

   A. Organizations recognize depreciation on fixed or long-term assets purchased to spread the cost of the assets over the period they will provide benefit to the organization. Depreciation calculations require various judgments to be made by management.

      1. The cost of the asset includes all costs of acquisition, shipping, installation, or other costs associated with getting the asset ready for its intended use.

      2. Expected useful life of the asset, or the period over which the asset is expected to provide benefit to the organization, must be estimated.

      3. Expected salvage value at the end of the asset's useful life must be estimated. The amount depreciated for the asset should reflect the estimated cost to the entity for use of the asset during its useful life. The asset should not be depreciated below salvage value as it is the amount the entity expects to receive for the asset upon disposal and is, therefore, not a cost to the entity of using the asset.

      4. Depreciation method must be selected by management and should reflect the usage pattern of the asset.

   B. Organizations can select from a number of different depreciation methods.

      1. Straight-line depreciation recognizes an equal amount of depreciation over the asset's useful life.

         a. Illustration: An organization purchases a vehicle for $25,000 and expects to sell the car for $5,000 at the end of five years. The organization will depreciate $4,000 each year [($25,000 − $5,000) ÷ 5] = $4,000. At the end of five years, the net asset value ($25,000 less accumulated depreciation) will be $5,000.

      2. Sum of the year's digits (SOYD) depreciation assumes that an asset is more productive and provides more benefit earlier in its life than later in life. SOYD depreciation records more depreciation in early years than in the later years of an asset's life and is often called an accelerated depreciation method as a result.

         a. SOYD multiplies the depreciable amount (cost less salvage value) by a unique fraction each year of the asset's life to calculate the amount of depreciation to be recorded.

            i. The numerator of the fraction is the number of years remaining in the asset's life at the beginning of the year for which the calculation is made.

    ii. The denominator of the fraction is the sum of the year's digits (hence the name) for the asset's useful life.

  b. Illustration: An organization purchases a vehicle for $25,000 and expects to sell the car for $5,000 at the end of four years. The depreciable amount is $20,000 (cost of $25,000 less the salvage value of $5,000). For year 1, the numerator in the unique fraction is 4 because there are four years remaining in the asset's life at the beginning of that year. The denominator is the sum of the year's digits, or 10 (1 + 2 + 3 + 4). Depreciation in the first year is $8,000 ($20,000 × 4/10). Each year's depreciation is shown in the table below.

Year	Depreciable Amount		Fraction		Depreciation for the Year
1	20,000	×	4/10	=	8,000
2	20,000	×	3/10	=	6,000
3	20,000	×	2/10	=	4,000
4	20,000	×	1/10	=	2,000*

*Note that after 4 years, the organization has recognized the full depreciable amount of $20,000 for the car.

3. The double declining balance (DDB) method is another accelerated depreciation method.

  a. DDB calculates annual depreciation by multiplying the book value of the asset (cost less accumulated depreciation) by $2 \div n$, where n = number of years in the asset's useful life.

  b. The calculation is repeated each year until the asset has been depreciated down to its salvage value.

  c. Illustration: An organization purchases a vehicle for $25,000 and expects to sell the car for $5,000 at the end of five years. The book value will be multiplied by 40% (2/5) each year to find the depreciation expense for that year until the asset has been reduced to its salvage value. Each year's depreciation is shown in the following table.

Year	Beg. Book Value (a)		Percent		Depreciation for the Year (b)	End Book Value (a) − (b)
1	25,000	×	40%	=	10,000	15,000
2	15,000	×	40%	=	6,000	9,000
3	9,000	×	40%	=	3,600	5,400
4	5,400	×	40%*		400	5,000
5	5,000	×	*		0	5,000

*Note that in Year 4, the asset would be depreciated below its salvage value if the full percentage was applied. For this reason, only the amount needed to reduce the asset to its salvage value is expensed. In addition, no deprecation is taken in Year 5 because DDB reduces the asset's book value to its salvage value in Year 4.

4. Units of production (UOP) depreciation recognizes that some assets have an expected number of units they will produce during the expected life.

  a. UOP calculates depreciation expense by spreading the depreciable cost evenly over the number of units used up during the asset's life.

  b. Depreciable cost is divided by the total number of units expected to be produced to find cost per unit.

  c. Each year the cost per unit is multiplied by the number of units produced that year to find depreciation expense.

  d. The asset is not depreciated below its salvage value.

  e. Illustration: An organization purchases a vehicle for $25,000 and expects to sell the car for $5,000 at the end of four years. At the date of purchase, the vehicle is expected to be driven 100,000 miles in the four-year period of operation. The resulting expected cost per mile is $0.20 [(25,000–5,000) ÷ 100,000]. Depreciation expense for each year is shown in the table below, assuming the actual miles driven each are as follows:

Year	Actual Miles Driven		Cost per Mile		Depreciation for the Year
1	25,000	×	0.20	=	5,000
2	30,000	×	0.20	=	6,000
3	27,000	×	0.20	=	5,400
4	26,000	×	0.20*		3,600

*Note that in Year 4, depreciation expense is reduced from the $0.20/mile estimate to ensure that the asset is not depreciated below its salvage value.

C. Accumulated depreciation is a contra-asset account that reduces the amount of fixed assets. Each asset is recorded on the financial records at cost, and all depreciation is recorded in the Accumulated Depreciation account. Organizations record depreciation expense with the following general accounting entry:

Depreciation Expense	XXX	
Accumulated Depreciation		XXX

To record depreciation expense.

D. Recognizing the impact of different depreciation methods.

    1. Because depreciation is an expense, different depreciation methods result in different effects on the balance sheet and net income.

        a. Accelerated depreciation methods, such as the double-declining balance method, result in higher depreciation expense earlier in the asset's life. Higher expenses reduce net income and the value of the asset on the balance sheet will decline more quickly under an accelerated depreciation method.

        b. Organizations looking to show higher net income during a period of high investment will use the straight-line depreciation method to show lower depreciation expenses and higher net income in early years.

    2. Organizations utilize different depreciation methods for book and tax purposes, resulting in deferred tax assets and liabilities [discussed in more detail in Part 1, Section A, Topic 2.3 Accounting for Income Taxes].

        a. Organizations seeking to lower income tax payments may want to use an accelerated depreciation method for tax purposes to maximize after-tax cash flow as early as possible to invest in other projects.

            i. Higher depreciation expenses will lower taxable income, reducing tax payments early in the asset's life.

            ii. During later years, the organization will record higher taxable income and pay more in income taxes than it would using the straight-line method.

E. Impairment of tangible assets: Periodically, management will review fixed assets for impairment losses. The process for calculating impairment losses requires two steps.

    1. *Step 1 Recoverability test:* The sum of the future undiscounted cash flows expected to come from the asset is compared to the book value (cost less accumulated depreciation) of the asset.

        a. If the future cash flows exceed the book value of the asset, the asset is considered recoverable and no impairment exists. In this case, the second step need not be performed.

        b. If the future cash flows are less than the book value of the asset, the asset is considered unrecoverable and impairment loss must be calculated and recognized. In this case, the second step is required.

2. *Step 2 Impairment loss:* If the asset is unrecoverable, management must estimate the fair value of the asset, which will be less than the book value. The impairment loss to be recognized is the difference between the book value of the asset and the fair value of the asset. This step can be referred to as an impairment test or a fair value test.

    a. Several methods for estimating fair value may be used.

        i. Quoted market prices for similar assets, if available

        ii. Outside appraisal

        iii. Discounting the future cash flows used in step 1

        iv. Internal appraisal based on expert knowledge of the industry and the specific assets in question

    b. The impairment loss is recorded in the period that the loss is identified.

    c. After an impairment loss is recognized, future annual depreciation on the asset should be recalculated to reflect the newly revised value and any updated estimates of remaining useful life and salvage value.

3. Illustration: Company Z owns an aging factory with a book value of $250,000 and expected future undiscounted cash flows of $175,000. The fair value of the factory is estimated to be $160,000. *Step 1:* The future undiscounted cash flows are less than the book value of the factory, so it fails the recoverability test. *Step 2:* The impairment loss is $90,000 ($250,000 book value less $160,000 fair value) and will be recorded with the following entry:

Loss on Impairment	90,000	
Factory		90,000

To record impairment loss on the factory.

F. Sales of tangible assets

1. When a fixed asset is sold, gains or losses will be recognized by the organization.

    a. Depreciation should be brought current before calculation of any gain or loss on the sale of a long-term asset.

    b. The historical cost of an asset as well as all related accumulated depreciation should be removed from the organization's records at the time of sale.

    c. If the asset is sold for more than its book value at the time of sale, a gain is recorded.

    d. If the asset is sold for less than its book value at the time of sale, a loss is recorded.

2. Illustration: An organization sells a vehicle with a historical cost of $25,000 and accumulated depreciation of $20,000. The vehicle is sold for $6,000 and depreciation is current at the time of sale. The organization realizes a $1,000 gain on the sale of the vehicle, calculated as the difference between the selling price of $6,000 and the book value of $5,000 (25,000 – 20,000).

Practice Question

Company Q purchases a widget maker for $120,000 and expects to use it for the next 10 years when the salvage value of the machine is expected to be $20,000. The company expects the machine to produce 400,000 widgets in the 10 years it uses the machine. Actual widgets produced in years 1, 2, and 3 are 30,000, 35,000, and 50,000. Calculate what depreciation expense for years 1, 2, and 3 would be using each of the following depreciation methods:

a. Straight-line

b. Sum of the year's digits

Continues...

c. Double declining balance

d. Units of production

Answer

a. Straight-line depreciation is $10,000 each year [($120,000 – $20,000) ÷ 10].

b. Sum of the year's digits denominator is 55 (10 + 9 + 8 + 7 + 6 + 5 + 4 + 3 + 2 + 1). The depreciable amount is $100,000 (120,000 – 20,000). The following table shows the calculation for depreciation expense using SOYD in years 1, 2, and 3.

Year	Depreciable Amount		Fraction		Depreciation for the Year
1	100,000	×	10/55	=	18,182
2	100,000	×	9/55	=	16,364
3	100,000	×	8/55	=	14,545

c. Double declining balance percentage is 20% (2/10). The following table shows the calculation for depreciation expense using DDB in years 1, 2, and 3.

Year	Beg. Book Value (a)		Percent		Depreciation for the Year (b)	End Book Value (a) – (b)
1	120,000	×	20%	=	24,000	96,000
2	96,000	×	20%	=	19,200	76,800
3	76,800	×	20%	=	15,360	61,440

d. Units of production estimated cost per widget is $0.25/widget [(120,000 – 20,000)/400,000]. The following table shows the calculation for depreciation using UOP in years 1, 2, and 3.

Year	Actual Widgets Made		Cost per Widget		Depreciation for the Year
1	30,000	×	0.25	=	7,500
2	35,000	×	0.25	=	8,750
3	50,000	×	0.25	=	12,500

II. Intangible assets

    A. Intangible assets with a finite life

        1. Amortized in a manner similar to the depreciation of tangible assets. Generally, straight line amortization is used and salvage values are often zero.

        2. Impairment of finite life intangible assets follows the same two-step process as tangible asset impairment discussed above.

    B. Intangible assets with an indefinite life

        1. Not amortized.

        2. Carried at cost and reviewed for impairment when circumstances indicate a possible problem and at least annually.

        3. Impairment test is one step: compare recorded value to fair value and recognize impairment losses when fair value is lower.

    C. Goodwill

        1. Only recorded when a business is acquired for more than the fair value of the net identifiable assets of the business.

2. Reviewed for impairment using a one-step process.

   a. Compare the fair value of the reporting unit to which goodwill belongs to the recorded value of the reporting unit.

      i. If the fair value of the reporting unit exceeds the book value of the reporting unit, goodwill is not impaired.

      ii. If the fair value of the reporting unit is less than the book value of the reporting unit, the goodwill is impaired and the impairment loss is equal to the amount of the difference. The impairment loss cannot, however, exceed the amount of goodwill recorded.

   b. Illustration: Company P has a subsidiary, Company S with a recorded value of $200,000, which includes goodwill of $40,000. The fair value of Company S is $180,000. Because the fair value of Company S is less than its recorded value, Company P has determined that Company S goodwill is impaired by the amount of the difference, or $20,000 ($180,000 – $200,000). Because the impairment loss is less than the amount of recorded goodwill ($40,000), the Company will record the entire amount of the loss with the following entry:

Loss on Impairment	20,000	
Goodwill		20,000

To record impairment loss on Company S goodwill.

Practice Question

Red Peppermint Co. purchases a customer list for $5,500,000 on 1/1/20X2. This database has information such as names, contact history, and order history. Red Peppermint Co. believes that this list will provide a benefit to them for four years. At the end of the four years, it is expected that this database will have no salvage value. Red Peppermint Co. uses the straight-line method to calculate amortization expense of intangible assets. Provide the journal entries for 20X2 for:

a. The purchase of the customer list

b. Amortization Expense

Answer

a. The purchase of the customer list

This asset is initially recorded at the purchase price.

Customer List	5,500,000	
Cash		5,500,000

To record the purchase of the customer list.

b. Amortization Expense

Amortization expense for intangible assets is calculated in a similar manner as depreciation expense for tangible assets. The calculation of amortization expense using the straight-line method is as follows:

(Purchase Price – Salvage Value) ÷ Years of Useful Life

The amortization expense for this example is calculated as:

($5,500,000 – 0) ÷ 4 years = **$1,375,000/year**

Continues...

Amortization Expense	1,375,000	
Accumulated Amortization–Customer Lists		1,375,000

To record the first year of amortization for the customer list.

Summary

Depreciation is used to spread the cost of long-term assets (less their salvage value) over the expected useful life of the asset. There are several deprecation methods to choose from, including straight-line, sum of the year's digits, double declining balance, and units of production. The method of depreciation used will impact the organization's financial statements and taxes. If a long-term asset becomes impaired, an organization must record a loss and update depreciation estimates. When a long-term asset is sold, gains or losses will be recognized and the asset and related depreciation accounts will be removed from the financial records. Intangible assets with a finite life are amortized similar to tangible assets. Intangible assets with an infinite life and goodwill must be tested for impairment and losses recorded if impairment occurs.

Topic 2.2 Recognition, Measurement, Valuation and Disclosure – Liabilities

General Liabilities

After studying this lesson, you should be able to:

- Identify the classification issues of short-term debt expected to be refinanced (1.A.2.o).

- Compare the effect on financial statements when using either the assurance warranty approach or the service warranty approach for accounting for warranties (1.A.2.p).

> In the normal course of business, organizations incur liabilities that are probable future sacrifices of economic benefits that arise from a present obligation to transfer assets or provide services to other entities and result from past transactions or events. Liabilities must be recorded in the balance sheet as either current or non-current based on when they are expected to be satisfied. This lesson will further discuss liabilities and when to classify them as current or non-current as well as how to account for warranties.

I. A liability includes three important characteristics:

    A. Probable future sacrifices of economic benefits

    B. Arises from a present obligation to transfer assets or provide services to other entities

    C. Resulting from past transactions or events

II. Liabilities are recorded in the balance sheet as either current or long term based on when they are expected to be satisfied.

    A. Current: A liability that will be settled with current assets (i.e., cash, accounts receivable, inventory) or efforts of the company (services) within a year or the operating cycle, whichever is longer.

        1. The operating cycle is the time it takes for an organization to go from a cash investment in inventory, to sale of that inventory, to collection of cash for that sale.

            a. Most companies have operating cycles less than one year so current liabilities will be those settled within one year.

            b. A few industries have operating cycles more than one year so current liabilities will be those settled within the operating cycle. Some examples of industries with operating cycles longer than one year are wine makers, large equipment manufacturers (i.e., Boeing), and tree growers.

    B. Non-Current: A liability that has a due date beyond one year or the operating cycle, whichever is longer.

    C. Because liquidity ratios are important to many organizations, they prefer to classify liabilities as non-current where possible. In order for an organization to classify an existing current liability as non-current at the balance sheet date, the following criteria must be met:

        1. The organization must have the intent to refinance the liability into a non-current liability. This intent must be documented, usually in board or executive committee meeting minutes.

        2. The organization must have the ability to refinance the liability into a non-current liability. This ability can be demonstrated in one of the following ways:

            a. The short-term liability is refinanced into a long-term liability or equity after the balance sheet date, but before the financial statements are issued.

    b. The organization has entered into a financing agreement that clearly permits the organization to refinance the short-term liability on a long-term basis.

III. Warranties are accounted for in two ways depending upon the type of warranty or the purpose of the accounting.

    A. Assurance Warranty Approach: The organization accounts for warranties that are automatically attached to the sale of a product, for which there is no additional revenue received, by expensing the warranty cost at the time of sale. This approach is generally required for GAAP purposes.

        1. Assurance warranty expense is estimated and accrued as a liability in the year of sale for the underlying product.

        2. Assurance warranty costs incurred during the warranty period will reduce the assurance warranty liability as paid.

        3. Any difference between the original estimate and the amount expended is used to inform future assurance warranty estimates, which are increased or decreased as needed.

        4. Illustration: Company A sells $800 Flat Screen TVs with a 2-year assurance warranty. Company A estimates that the average cost of assurance warranty-related repairs for each Flat Screen sold is $20. In year 1, Company A sells 1,000 TV's and spends $7,000 on warranty repairs related to these sales.

        The warranty expense for year 1 is $20,000 (1,000 × $20) and the liability for warranties is $13,000 ($20,000 – $7,000) at the end of year 1. This liability will be further reduced in the future as Flat Screens are repaired under warranty.

    B. Service Warranty Approach: GAAP approach to accounting for extended warranties that are sold separately from the product.

        1. Revenue from the sale of the extended service warranty is deferred as a liability and recognized as revenue over the extended warranty period.

        2. Costs to repair products under an extended service warranty are expensed as incurred during the extended service warranty period.

        3. Illustration: Company A sells $800 Flat Screen TVs with a 2-year assurance warranty. Company A estimates that the average cost of assurance warranty related repairs for each Flat Screen sold is $20. In addition to the assurance warranty, Company A offers a 2-year extended service warranty (for years 3 and 4) for an additional $50 if purchased at the time of sale. The original sale for one Flat Screen with an assurance *and* extended service warranty is recorded as follows:

Cash	850	
Sales Revenue		800
Deferred Service Warranty Rev		50

To record the sale of 1 Flat Screen with an Extended Warranty.

Assurance Warranty Expense	20	
Assurance Warranty Liability		20

To accrue warranty expense for assurance warranty on 1 Flat Screen.

The assurance warranty is accounted for as noted above. The deferred extended service warranty revenue account will remain on the records for years 1 and 2. At the end of years 3 and 4, the following entry will be made:

Deferred Service Warranty Rev	25	
Service Warranty Revenue		25

To record the recognition of service warranty revenue.

In addition, the expenses related to fulfilling extended service warranties during years 3 and 4 will be expensed to Service Warranty Expense as incurred.

Practice Question

KME Company creates security equipment. In 20X3 KME Company sells 250 systems for $6,750 each. All sales are cash only, no sales on account. Each system has a one-year assurance warranty included with the purchase. Based on prior experience, KME estimates that the average assurance warranty cost will be $350 per unit. Because of the service and replacement costs in connection with these sales, KME incurs $52,500 in assurance warranty costs in 20X3 and $35,000 in 20X4. Answer the following questions in relation to this problem:

1. What amount of Sales Revenue is recognized during 20X3?

2. What is the amount of Assurance Warranty Expense recognized in 20X3 and 20X4 related to the 20X3 sales?

3. What is the balance, if any, of the Assurance Warranty Liability account at the end of 20X3 and 20X4 related to the 20X3 sales?

Answer

1. Sales Revenue will be recognized for the number of systems sold × the purchase price for each system. In this case: 250 systems × $6,750 = **$1,687,500**.

2. The estimated assurance warranty expense to be recorded in 20X3 is the number of units sold × estimated assurance warranty cost per unit. In this case: 250 Units × $350 average cost per unit = **$87,500**. This amount would be accrued as an Assurance Warranty Expense and an Assurance Warranty Liability would be recorded at the time of sale in 20X3. No expense would need to be recorded in 20X4 related to the 20X3 sales unless the estimate of the liability needed to be adjusted. In this case, the total amount paid out in both years equals the estimate, so no additional expense will be recorded in 20X4.

3. The Assurance Warranty Liability account would decrease for any amounts paid out during 20X3. The assurance warranty costs paid out during 20X3 equals $52,500; consequently, the amount of the Assurance Warranty Liability equals $87,500 – $52,500 or **$35,000**.

Journal entries for KME Company during 20X3 relative to this sale follow (not required):

January–December 20X3:		
Cash	1,687,500	
Sales Revenue		1,687,500

To recognize revenue for the sale of security systems during 20X3.

January–December 20X3:		
Assurance Warranty Expense	87,500	
Assurance Warranty Liability		87,500

To recognize the estimated assurance warranty expense for 20X3 sales.

January–December 20X3:		
Assurance Warranty Liability	52,500	
Cash*		52,500

*The credit could be to anything associated with the expense including inventory, payables, cash, etc.

To recognize the payment of warranty costs during 20X3.

Continues…

January – December 20X4:		
Assurance Warranty Liability	35,000	
Cash**		35,000

**The credit could be to anything associated with the
expense including inventory, payables, cash, etc.

To recognize the payment of assurance warranty costs during 20X4.

Practice Question

Broad Company produces refrigerators. They sell refrigerators that cost $800 to produce for $1,500 with a 2-year assurance warranty. Broad Company estimates that the average assurance warranty repair cost for each refrigerator is $80 within the first two years and $50 for years 3–5. Broad also offers an extended 3-year service warranty for an additional $120 if it is purchased at the time of sale.

1. How much revenue is recognized for each unit at the time of sale and how much, if any, revenue is deferred?

2. What revenue, if any, should be recorded in years 1–5 for the extended service warranty?

3. When will Broad Company record expenses associated with the assurance warranty?

4. When will Broad Company record expenses associated with the extended service warranty?

Answer

1. $1,500 of revenue is recognized at the time the sale for each unit. The $120 that is paid for the extended service warranty is deferred.

2. Broad Company will recognize revenue ratably over the three-year period beginning in year 3 for the extended service warranty. Therefore, Broad will recognize $40 ($120 ÷ 3 years) of revenue in each of years 3, 4, and 5.

3. Broad Company will record $80 in assurance warranty expense at the time of sale for each unit. This amount is the expense associated with the assurance warranty and should be accrued at the time of sale.

4. Broad company will expense costs associated with fulfilling the extended service warranty as incurred during years 3–5.

Summary

Liabilities include three important characteristics: probable future sacrifices of economic benefits, arises from a present obligation to transfer assets or provide services to other entities, and results from past transactions or events. An organization must decide whether to classify liabilities as current or non-current. Current liabilities will be settled within one year or the operating cycle while long-term liabilities will be settled beyond one year or the operating cycle. Warranties are accounted for in two different ways: assurance warranty approach and service warranty approach. It is important to understand the difference between these two approaches and when it is appropriate to use them.

Leases

After studying this lesson, you should be able to:

- Distinguish between operating and finance leases (1.A.2.t).
- Recognize the correct financial statement presentation of operating and finance leases (1.A.2.u).

Rather than owning assets outright, sometimes organizations will lease assets from the legal owner. A lease is a legal contract in which the legal owner, or lessor, grants the lessee the right to use an asset during a specified period of time for a specified series of payments. Depending on the terms of the contract, leases can be classified as either finance or operating and this classification determines the method of accounting. This lesson will define the two different types of leases as well as describe how to account for each type of lease.

I. A lease is a legal contract in which the legal owner of an asset (the lessor) grants the counterparty to the contract (the lessee) the right to use an asset (leased item) over a specified period of time (the lease term) for a specified series of payments (minimum lease payments). Organizations use leases to acquire the use of various assets as an alternative to owning them outright.

   A. Lessees will classify leases as one of two types:

      1. Finance Lease—The lessor transfers some of the rights and benefits of ownership to the lessee.

         a. A lease for a specialized piece of machinery where the lessee is responsible for repairs, insurance, or other activities traditionally considered part of ownership is an example of a finance lease.

      2. Operating Lease—The lessor transfers only the right to use the property to the lessee and the lessor/owner retains most of the risks and benefits of ownership.

         a. An apartment lease is an example of an operating lease, as the landlord pays for all repairs and other costs of ownership. In addition, the apartment lease is generally for a relatively short period of time when compared to the life of the asset.

   B. The accounting for leases is dependent upon the classification of the lease as finance or operating.

      1. Finance Lease—Treat the arrangement as a borrowing and a purchase.

         a. Borrowing: The lessee records a liability for the present value of the minimum lease payments and amortizes the liability as payments are made, similar to amortizing typical mortgage debt with equal payments.

         b. Purchase: The lessee records the property as a right-of-use (ROU) asset and recognizes depreciation expense on its income statement.

      2. Operating Lease—The lessee records a liability for the present value of the minimum lease payments and amortizes the liability as payments are made. An ROU asset is recorded at lease signing and the lessee amortizes the ROU asset to allow for total lease expense (interest plus ROU asset amortization) to be recognized on a straight-line basis over the life of the lease.

II. The Financial Accounting Standards Board (FASB) has documented five criteria to determine if a lease should be recorded as a finance lease:

   A. There is a transfer of ownership to the lessee at the end of the lease term.

   B. There is an option to purchase the asset at a price significantly below expected market value at the end of the lease term (a "bargain purchase option").

   C. The lease term is for a major part of the remaining economic life of the underlying asset. While no bright line exists here, the FASB has given a guideline of 75% of the expected useful life of the asset when determining whether the lease term is for a "major" part of the asset's life.

   D. The present value of the minimum lease payments exceeds substantially all of the fair value of the underlying asset. While no bright line exists here, the FASB has given a guideline of 90% of the fair market value of the asset when determining whether the minimum lease payments are for "substantially all" of the asset's value.

      1. The discount rate used for the present value calculation should be:

         a. The lessor's interest rate implicit in the lease (if known to the lessee), or

         b. The lessee's incremental borrowing rate

   E. The underlying asset is so specialized for the lessee that it is expected to have no alternative future use to the lessor at the end of the lease term.

   F. *Only one* of the preceding five criteria must be met to record the lease as a finance lease.

III. Illustration 1: On January 1, Company A (lessor) leases a car to Company B (lessee) for 5 years with annual payments of $2,000 due at the time of signing and annually beginning on December 31 thereafter. The useful life of the car is 10 years and there is no bargain purchase option available or automatic title transfer to Company B at the conclusion of the lease agreement. The fair value of the car at the time of lease signing is $9,000. Company B's incremental borrowing rate is 8% and the rate implicit in the lease is not known to Company B. The present value factor for an annuity due of $1 at 8% for 5 periods is 4.31213.

   A. Lease Classification: Finance as determined specifically by the fourth criterion below.

      1. Bargain purchase option? NO

      2. 2 Title transfer? NO

      3. 75% test? NO [5-year lease term divided by 10-year life = 50% < 75%]

      4. 90% test? YES [($2,000 × 4.31213) ÷ 9,000 = 96% > 90%]

      5. Specialization? NO [car]

   B. A finance lease is recorded in a manner similar to purchasing the car with debt.

      1. At lease signing, Company B will record the present value of the minimum lease payments as an asset on the balance sheet with a corresponding liability. In addition, Company B will record the initial payment on the lease due at lease signing.

ROU Asset	8,624	
Lease Liability		8,624

To record the lease signing.

Lease Liability	2,000	
Cash		2,000

To record the initial lease payment on car lease due at lease signing.

2. At the end of each lease year, Company B will record amortization on the ROU asset similar to depreciation expense on an asset owned outright.

Amortization Expense	1,725	
ROU Asset		1,725

To record the lease amortization for the first year (8,624 ÷ 5).

3. When the next lease payment is made on December 31, Company B will split the lease payment into interest expense (based on their 8% incremental borrowing rate because the implicit rate is not known) and a reduction of the capital lease payable liability, similar to a level-payment mortgage loan.

Interest Expense	530	
Lease Liability	1,470	
Cash		2,000

To record the 2nd annual lease payment.
[Interest = (8,624 – 2,000) × 8%] [Lease liability reduction = 2,000 payment – 530 interest]

4. Interest will decline for each of the next three payments as the amount of the liability decreases with each payment, similar to a level-payment mortgage loan.

Practice Question

A Company is planning on leasing construction equipment from C Company starting on January 2, 20X8. The terms of the lease require annual payments of $43,000 for seven years. The implicit interest rate is 11%. The first payment is due on the first day of the lease and subsequent payments are due on December 31 of each year beginning in 20X8. The equipment has a useful life of nine years, there is no bargain purchase option included in the contract, and the title will not transfer from C Company to A Company at the end of the lease term. The fair value of the equipment at the time of the lease signing is $275,000.

1. Which of the five FASB lease classification criteria cause the lease to be classified as finance?

2. What is the amount of the ROU asset balance at the end of the 2nd year of the lease (after lease amortization is recorded)?

3. What is the amount of the lease liability immediately following the 3rd payment?

Answer

1. The lease would be classified as finance because it meets the 3rd criterion below:

    - Bargain purchase option? NO

    - Title transfer? NO

    - 75% test? YES [7-year lease term divided by the 9-year life of the equipment = 78% > 75%]

    - 90% test? NO [Divide the present value of the minimum lease payments by the fair value of the equipment. The present value of the minimum lease payments is $224,913. $224,913 ÷ $275,000 = 82% < 90%. To find the present value of the minimum lease payments, use the following values: Years (N): 7, Interest Rate (I): 11, Payment (P): $43,000, Solve for Present Value (PV). Make sure that your calculator is in Begin mode because the first payment is due at the beginning of the lease term.]

    - Specialization? NO [construction equipment]

2. ROU Asset balance at the end of the 2nd year = $160,653. Annual Amortization Expense = Present Value of the leased equipment ÷ term of lease = $224,913 ÷ 7 = $32,130.

Continues…

3. The remaining amount for the lease liability following the 3rd payment is $133,405. The beginning of the amortization schedule is shown below.

Payment	Date	Amount	Interest	Principal	Balance
					$224,913
1	January 1, 20X8	43,000	0	43,000	181,913
2	December 31, 20X8	43,000	20,010	22,990	158,923
3	December 31, 20X9	43,000	17,482	25,518	133,405

IV. Illustration 2: On January 1, Company A (lessor) leases a typical binding machine to Company B (lessee) for 5 years with annual payments of $2,000 due at the time of signing and annually on January 1 thereafter. The useful life of the machine is 10 years and there is no bargain purchase option available or automatic title transfer to Company B at the conclusion of the lease agreement. The fair value of the machine at the time of lease signing is $15,000. Company B's incremental borrowing rate is 8% and the rate implicit in the lease is not known to Company B. The present value factor for an annuity due of $1 at 8% for 5 periods is 4.31213.

A. Lease Classification: Operating as determined by the criteria below.

1. Bargain purchase option? NO

2. Title transfer? NO

3. 75% test? NO [5-year lease term divided by 10-year machine life = 50% < 75%]

4. 90% test? NO [($2,000 × 4.31213) ÷ 15,000 = 57% < 90%]

5. Specialization? NO [typical binding machine]

B. The lessee must record a ROU asset and a lease liability for the present value of the minimum lease payments at lease signing. Because this is an operating lease, lease expense will be recognized on a straight-line basis and will include both interest expense on the liability and amortization of the ROU asset.

C. Interest in the first year is $530. [(PV $8,624 less $2,000 first advance payment) × 8%]

D. Amortization of the ROU asset in the first year is $1,470. [$2,000 annual straight-line lease expense less $530 interest]

E. Example journal entries follow.

January 1, Year 1		
ROU Asset	8,624	
Lease Liability		6,624
Cash		2,000

To record the lease and initial lease payment on machine lease at lease signing.

December 31, Year 1		
Lease Expense	2,000	
Lease Liability		530
ROU Asset		1,470

To record first year of expense for machine lease.
Interest portion: $530 [(PV $8,624 – $2,000 first advance payment) × 8%]
Amortization of ROU portion: $1,470 [$2,000 annual straight-line lease expense – $530 interest]

January 1, Year 2		
Lease Liability	2,000	
Cash		2,000

To record the second lease payment.

December 31, Year 2		
Lease Expense	2,000	
Lease Liability		412
ROU Asset		1,588

To record second year of expense for machine lease.

Interest portion: $412 [(PV $6,624 + $530 interest – $2,000 second payment) × 8%]

Amortization of ROU portion: $1,588 [$2,000 annual straight-line lease expense – $530 interest]

Practice Question

Jake Company plans to lease standard back hoe equipment on January 1, 20X4. The terms of the lease require annual payments of $15,000 for three years. The implicit interest rate is 8% and the present value of the lease payments is $41,749. The first payment is due on January 1, 20X4 and future payments are due on December 31. The terms of the lease do not include a bargain purchase option and the title does not transfer at the end of the lease. The equipment has a useful life of 15 years and a fair value of $250,000 at the time of signing.

1. Using the five FASB lease classification criteria, how will this lease be classified?

2. Would your answer to the first question change if the lease agreement specifies that the lessee has the option to buy the asset for $1 at the conclusion of the lease? Why? Why not?

Answer

1. The lease would be classified as operating because it does not meet any of the following lease criteria:

   - Bargain purchase option? NO

   - Title transfer? NO

   - 75% test? NO [3-year lease term divided by the 15-year life of the equipment = 20% < 75%]

   - 90% test? NO [Divide the present value of the minimum lease payments by the fair value of the equipment. The present value of minimum lease payments = $41,749. $41,749 ÷ $250,000 = 17% < 90%]

   - Specialization? NO [standard back hoe]

2. The lease would be classified as finance because the lessee has the option to buy the asset for $1, a bargain, at the conclusion of the lease. This satisfies the first lease classification criterion, and only one of the five criteria must be satisfied in order to classify the lease as finance.

Summary

A lease is a legal contract between the lessee and the lessor in which the lessee agrees to pay a specified minimum lease payment for a specified amount of time in exchange for the right to use an asset owned by the lessor. Operating leases transfer only the right to use the asset to the lessee while the lessor retains legal ownership. With operating leases, the lessee records a ROU asset and lease liability at lease signing. The interest on the liability and the amortization of the ROU asset are combined and reported as lease expense on a straight-line basis each year. A finance lease transfers some of the rights and benefits of ownership to the lessee and the arrangement is treated as a borrowing and a purchase with assets and liabilities recorded on the lessee's balance sheet. The FASB has documented five criteria to determine if a lease should be recorded as a finance lease. It is important to understand when a lease must be recorded as a finance lease as well as to understand the accounting for both types of leases.

Topic 2.3 Accounting for Income Taxes and Revenue Recognition

Accounting for Income Taxes

After studying this lesson, you should be able to:

- Differentiate between temporary differences and permanent differences and identify examples of each (1.A.2.s).

- Distinguish between deferred tax liabilities and deferred tax assets (1.A.2.r).

- Demonstrate an understanding of interperiod tax allocation/deferred income taxes (1.A.2.q).

Taxable income can often differ from net income reported under GAAP or IFRS due to different rules from government taxing authorities. As such, companies will define the differences as either temporary or permanent depending on why these differences occur. This lesson will define permanent and temporary differences in book and taxable income as well as give examples and illustrations of these differences.

I. Net income under U.S. generally accepted accounting principles (GAAP) or International Financial Reporting Standards (IFRS) can differ from taxable income reported to government taxing authorities such as the United States Internal Revenue Service (IRS).

    A. Differences are defined as either temporary or permanent depending on the reasons why the GAAP to Tax accounting differences occur.

        1. Permanent differences occur when GAAP revenues are not taxable or GAAP expenses are not deductible under the tax law. These differences will never reconcile because the underlying definition of what constitutes income and deductions for tax differ from the definition of what constitutes GAAP revenue and expense.

            a. Examples of non-taxable revenues:

                i. Interest received from investments in bonds issued by state and municipal governments

                ii. Life insurance proceeds on the death of an insured executive

                iii. Portion of dividends received from U.S. corporations that is not taxable due to the dividends received deduction

            b. Examples of non-deductible expenses:

                i. Investment expenses incurred to obtain tax-exempt income

                ii. Premiums paid for life insurance policies when the payer is the beneficiary

                iii. Compensation expense pertaining to some employee stock option plans

                iv. Fines or penalties due to violations of the law

                v. 50% of meals and entertainment expenses

            c. Permanent differences do not result in deferred tax assets or liabilities, because the book to tax differences will never be reconciled in future periods.

            d. Illustration: X Company reported $200,000 in pretax book income, which included $15,000 of municipal bond interest and $10,000 in expenses for environmental fines paid by the company. No other book to tax differences exist in the organization's results and the tax rate is 40%. Income tax expense for X Company is $78,000 [($200,000 − $15,000 + $10,000) × 40%].

2. Temporary differences occur when revenue or expenses are recorded in different periods for book purposes compared to tax purposes.

   a. Examples of temporary differences:

      i. Long-term construction contracts or other revenue arrangements (i.e. installment sales, cash received in advance of service) are recognized on a modified cash basis for tax and an accrual basis for GAAP

      ii. Estimated expenses (i.e., warranties, bad debts, contingencies) not deducted until paid for tax but accrued under GAAP

      iii. Depreciation usually accelerated for tax but often straight line for books

      iv. Deferred compensation deducted when paid for tax but accrued over the employee service period for GAAP

      v. Investment gains and losses recognized when realized (sold) for tax but recognized using fair value measurement during the holding period for GAAP

   b. Taxable income recognized before book income generally results in a Deferred Tax Asset: Company A sells 2-year magazine subscriptions. For book purposes, Company A records unearned revenue when received and recognizes revenue over the subscription period. For tax purposes the subscription is recognized as revenue when it is received (wherewithal-to-pay concept). In the year the cash is received, Company A will pay tax and record a Deferred Tax Asset (DTA). The DTA will be consumed and expensed as Deferred Tax Expense (DTE) in future periods as the subscription revenue is recognized in book earnings.

   c. Book income recognized before taxable income generally results in a Deferred Tax Liability: Company B records depreciation on a straight-line method for book purposes but uses a statutorily required accelerated depreciation method for tax purposes. At the start of the depreciation period, expenses for tax purposes will exceed book expenses because Company B records a higher depreciation expense for tax purposes. Book income will exceed taxable income during this time. At the end of the depreciation period, book expenses will be greater than expenses for tax purposes. Taxable income will exceed book income later in the life of the asset.

   d. DTA Illustration: Company C receives a $1,200 payment in December 20X4 for a 20X5 subscription. The tax rate is 30%. For book purposes, Company C will record $100 of revenue per month ($1,200 ÷ 12 months) beginning in January 20X5. For tax purposes, $1,200 is recognized as taxable income when it is received in 20X4. This results in a tax payable of $360 ($1,200 × 30%) and a DTA of the same amount. Essentially, Company C has prepaid its tax on revenue that will be recognized for GAAP purposes in the following year. The following entry will be recorded in 20X4:

Deferred Tax Asset	360	
Deferred Tax Benefit		360
Current Tax Expense	360	
Tax Payable		360

To recognize a deferred tax asset for subscription revenue received before it is earned.

In 20X5, Company C will recognize $1,200 of revenue for the subscription, but will have no tax payable because the income was already taxed in 20X4. Because the revenue is included in 20X5 books, Company C will show book tax expense of $360 resulting from the utilization (reduction) of the DTA with the following entry:

Deferred Tax Expense	360	
Deferred Tax Asset		360

To record tax expense and the reduction of the DTA for subscription revenue recognized in the current year.

e. DTL Illustration: Company D has pretax income before depreciation expense of $200,000. An asset acquired during the year has book depreciation of $50,000 and tax depreciation of $100,000 and Company D has no other book to tax differences. Company D has a 30% tax rate. Pretax book income is $150,000 ($200,000 – $50,000) so book tax expense is $45,000 ($150,000 × 30%). However, taxable income is $100,000 ($200,000 – $100,000), so Company D has a tax payable of only $30,000 ($100,000 × 30%) in tax for the year. Because this is the first year of the asset's life, the difference between these two amounts results in the creation of a Deferred Tax Liability (DTL), which represents tax that will be paid in a future year when the book depreciation exceeds the tax depreciation on the asset. The resulting entry for the first year is noted below:

Current Tax Expense	30,000	
Deferred Tax Expense	15,000	
Tax Payable		30,000
Deferred Tax Liability		15,000

To record book tax expense for the year and recognize a deferred tax liability.

In a future year, Company D has pretax income before depreciation expense of $300,000. Company D records $50,000 in book depreciation and $10,000 in tax depreciation and Company D still has a 30% tax rate and no other book to tax differences. Pretax book income is $250,000 ($300,000 – $50,000) so book tax expense is $75,000 ($250,000 × 30%). However, taxable income is $290,000 ($300,000 – $10,000), so Company D has a tax payable of $87,000 ($290,000 × 30%) in tax for the year. The $12,000 difference ($87,000 – $75,000) would be a reduction of the existing DTL in the following entry:

Current Tax Expense	87,000	
Deferred Tax Liability	12,000	
Current Tax Payable		87,000
Deferred Tax Benefit		12,000

To record book tax expense for the year and recognize a reduction to the deferred tax liability.

f. DTAs and DTLs are calculated using enacted tax rates from the future periods in which the timing differences are expected to reverse.

g. Total Tax Expense is a combination of Current Tax Expense, the amount of tax liability on the organization's current-year tax return, and Deferred Tax Expense, the change in the organization's DTAs and DTLs.

h. DTAs and DTLs are netted together and, depending upon the net value, the amount is presented in *either* the long-term assets *or* long-term liabilities on the balance sheet.

i. If the realizable value of a DTA is questionable because there may not be future taxable income to offset the future reduction of taxable income represented by the DTA, a valuation allowance will be recorded to reduce the value of the DTA. Recording a valuation allowance (a credit) will increase tax expense for the period (a debit).

Practice Question

Autonomous Automobiles (Auto), a manufacturer of self-driving vehicles, had pretax financial income of $30 billion for the year 20X1, its first year of operations. Auto has a current tax rate of 24% and a future enacted tax rate of 21%. The following differences between financial and taxable income were reported by Auto for the current year (all numbers in millions):

- Excess of tax depreciation over book depreciation………..............................$11,500
- Interest revenue on municipal bonds…..1,600
- Estimated warranty expense over actual expenditures.........................9,000
- Fines paid…...6,400
- Unrealized gains on marketable securities recognized for financial reporting.............3,000

1. Calculate Auto's taxable income and current tax payable.

2. Calculate Auto's deferred tax asset or liability.

3. Prepare the journal entry needed to record Auto's total tax expense for the year. What is Auto's total tax expense for the year?

Answer

1. Auto's taxable income and current tax expense is calculated as follows (in millions):

Pretax Financial Income	$30,000
Permanent Differences:	
Interest Revenue Municipal Bonds	(1,600)
Fines Paid	6,400
Temporary Differences:	
Depreciation	(11,500)
Warranty Expense	9,000
Unrealized Gain	(3,000)
Taxable Income	$29,300
Tax ($29,300 × 24%)	$7,032

2. Auto's net deferred tax liability is calculated as follows:

Temporary Differences	Balance	Tax Rate	DTA/(DTL)
Depreciation	$(11,500)	21%	$(2,415)
Warranty Expense	9,000	21%	1,890
Unrealized Gain	(3,000)	21%	(630)
Deferred Tax Asset (Liability)			$(1,155)

3. The journal entry to record the total tax expense and deferred tax liability is as follows:

Current Tax Expense	7,032	
Deferred Tax Expense	1,155	
Current Tax Payable		7,032
Deferred Tax Liability		1,155

To record book tax expense for the year and recognize a deferred tax liability.

Total Tax Expense on the income statement for the year is $8,187 ($7,032 + $1,155).

Summary

Tax accounting rules are often different than book accounting rules. As such, taxable income often differs from book income. These differences are defined as either temporary or permanent depending on the underlying reasons for the difference. Permanent differences occur when GAAP revenues are not taxable or GAAP expenses are not deductible under the tax law and these differences will never reconcile. Temporary differences occur when revenue or expenses are recorded in different periods for book purposes compared to tax purposes. Temporary differences are recognized in the financial statements through deferred tax assets (DTAs) or deferred tax liabilities (DTLs).

Revenue Recognition

After studying this lesson, you should be able to:

- Apply revenue recognition principles to various types of transactions (1.A.2.x).

- Demonstrate an understanding of revenue recognition for contracts with customers using the five steps required to recognize revenue (1.A.2.y).

- Demonstrate an understanding of the matching principle with respect to revenues and expenses and be able to apply it to a specific situation (1.A.2.z).

As part of the overall accounting and financial statement preparation process, organizations provide goods and services and record revenue. Revenue is recorded as or when performance obligations under contracts with customers are completed. This lesson will discuss the FASB's five-step model for revenue recognition: (1) Identify the contract with a customer, (2) identify separate performance obligations in the contract, (3) determine the transaction price, (4) allocate the transaction price to the performance obligation(s) identified in the contract, and (5) recognize revenue for each performance obligation.

I. Revenue Recognition, New Standard

   A. As part of the Convergence Project, the Financial Accounting Standards Board (FASB) and the International Accounting Standards Board (IASB) released a converged standard for recognizing revenue from contracts with customers. The standard is effective for all companies for fiscal periods beginning after December 15, 2018, and no significant differences in revenue recognition between U.S. GAAP and IFRS will remain.

   B. The converged standard requires organizations to recognize revenue using the following steps:

      1. Identify the contract with a customer.

      2. Identify separate performance obligations in the contract.

      3. Determine the transaction price.

      4. Allocate the transaction price to the performance obligation(s) identified in the contract.

      5. Recognize revenue for each performance obligation.

   C. Each of these five steps must be considered before proper revenue recognition can take place.

II. Identify the Contract with a Customer

   Before revenue can be recognized, the organization must determine if a contract exists. The following should be considered in identifying a contract with a customer.

   A. The contract must be approved by all parties and can be written, oral, or simply implied by normal business practice.

   B. Relevant rights and obligations of each party (generally the seller's performance obligations and the buyer's payment terms) are clear.

   C. The contract has commercial substance.

   D. Some situations may indicate that no contract exists for purposes of revenue recognition. In these cases, revenue would not be recognized before it is determined that a contract does exist.

      1. If each party has the unilateral right to terminate the contract without compensating the other party, then no contract exists until either

         a. The entity has transferred goods or services to the customer.

         b. The entity has received or is entitled to receive consideration for goods or services.

2. If collectability of substantially all of the consideration for goods or services is not probable, then no contract exists, and revenue would not be recognized until nonrefundable consideration is received and the organization has satisfied its performance obligations.

Practice Question

Property Partners Group (PPG) signed a contract with Danny's Development, Inc. (DDI) on January 1 in which PPG agreed to install water mains to 10 newly partitioned residential lots. The contract allowed each party to terminate the agreement at any time before construction began. PPG received $100,000 from DDI on February 1 as a deposit toward the contracted work, and PPG began processing the appropriate permits for construction. PPG began construction on the water mains on March 1. At what point does a contract exist for purposes of revenue recognition?

Answer

February 1. No contract exists at January 1 due to the cancellation clause. On February 1, a revenue contract exists because PPG has received consideration for the project. Depending upon the evaluation of the remaining revenue recognition steps, however, PPG still might not be able to recognize revenue until later.

III. Identify Separate Performance Obligations in the Contract

    A. A performance obligation is a promise to transfer distinct goods and/or services to the customer.

    B. Identification of performance obligations should be done from the perspective of the customer. As a result, performance obligations could be explicit in the contract or simply implied by normal business practices if those practices create reasonable expectation on the part of the customer.

    C. Contracts may contain more than one performance obligation.

        1. Illustration: An organization sells equipment with installation and an attached warranty agreement; the selling organization would recognize revenue independently for the three distinct performance obligations:

            a. Delivery of the equipment

            b. Installation of the equipment

            c. Fulfillment of the warranty obligation

    D. Organizations are not required to identify separate performance obligations that are immaterial. Materiality for this purpose is determined by reference to the individual contract, not the organization as a whole.

        1. Illustration: An organization sells equipment and provides a technician to set up the machine; the setup may or may not be deemed a separate performance obligation based on materiality.

            a. If the machine price is $2,000 and the cost of sending out a technician is $200, the setup is likely to be considered material in the context of the contract and would be considered a separate performance obligation.

            b. If the machine price is $2,000,000 and the cost of sending out a technician is $200, the setup is likely to be considered immaterial in the context of the contract and the contract would have a single performance obligation: delivery of the machine.

Practice Question

Manny's Machinery Corp. (MMC) sells commercial floor-buffing machines and are known for their superior customer service. A typical sales contract explicitly includes the floor buffer, access to an online training program, and a six-year warranty that covers all repair costs. A separate six-year monthly maintenance contract may be purchased at the option of the customer.

Continues...

MMC has learned through experience that monthly tune-ups for the buffers during the first 6 months of use dramatically increases the longevity of the buffers because the equipment needs to properly "season" during that early usage. As a result, MMC regularly sends technicians to service new machines during those first 6 months regardless of whether the customer has purchased the optional maintenance contract.

Jerry's Janitors (JJ) has recently signed a contract for the purchase of two buffing machines with the warranty. JJ declined to purchase the optional maintenance contract. What are MMC's performance obligations in the sales contract with JJ?

Answer

MMC would have the following performance obligations in the contract with JJ:

1. Delivery of the buffing machines (explicit in the contract)

2. 6-year repair warranty (explicit in the contract)

3. 6-month maintenance (reasonable expectation by JJ because it is implied by MMC's normal business practice)

The online training program could possibly be considered a performance obligation if MMC determined that it was material in the context of the contract.

IV. Determine the Transaction Price

    A. The transaction price is the amount of consideration the organization expects to receive.

    B. If a customer pays noncash consideration (goods, services, stock, etc.), the fair value of the noncash consideration is included in the transaction price.

    C. If the contract contains a provision for variable consideration, the organization must estimate the amount of consideration it expects to receive under the contract. Variable consideration can come from

        1. Cash discounts: Generally considered a reduction of the initial transaction price

        2. Volume discounts: The organization should estimate the number of units that will be sold and calculate the average per unit selling price based on the contract pricing schedule at that volume. The transaction price would be based on this estimate.

        3. Rebates: Generally considered a reduction of the initial transaction price; however, if the rebate is given in return for something from the customer (i.e., marketing), the rebate would not impact the transaction price and would be recorded as an expense.

            a. Illustration: Company Z sells Product A for $100 each to all customers. Company Z gives a $5 rebate on Product A to any customer who refers another purchasing customer to Company Z. The rebate would likely be considered a marketing expense rather than a reduction of the transaction price because Company Z is receiving a marketing service in return for the rebate.

        4. Right of return: Returns should be estimated, and the transaction price should be reduced for this estimate. Similar contracts can be aggregated for purposes of this estimation.

            a. Illustration: Company Z sells Product A for $100 each to all customers with a 30-day return policy. Historical information indicates that approximately 1% of Product A sales are returned in the 30-day window. During the month of October, Company Z sold 4,000 units of Product A. Because the contracts for Product A are all similar, Company Z may aggregate them for purposes of estimating the returns. As a result, the transaction price for the sales in October, after considering the 1% average return rate, would be $396,000 (4,000 × $100 × 99%).

Practice Question

Walley's Wheel Factory (WWF) produces bicycle wheels. WWF normally sells its wheels to small bike shops, but has recently been attracting the attention of a few large bicycle manufacturers because of their superior quality. WWF signed a contract to supply wheels to Bike Builders Corp (BBC) for their winter production season from November through February. The contract requires a minimum purchase of 1,000 wheels over the four-month period and contract price per wheel during the same period is as follows:

First 1,000 wheels	$22/wheel
Next 500 wheels	$20/wheel
Additional wheels beyond 1,500	$18/wheel

WWF expects a 20% probability that BBC will purchase the minimum 1,000 wheels, a 60% probability that BBC will purchase 1,500 wheels, and a 20% probability that BBC will purchase 1,800 wheels. If BBC purchases 400 wheels in November and remits $8,800 (400 × $22) to WWF upon delivery, what is the transaction price per wheel that WWF should use for the purchase?

Answer

The transaction price should be based upon the expected weighted average revenue per wheel after considering the likely volume discount.

1. Probability weighted expected volume under the contract is 1,460 wheels [(20% × 1,000) + (60% × 1,500) + (20% × 1,800)].

2. Total revenue expected under the contract using weighed average volume is $31,200 [(1,000 × $22) + (460 × $20)].

3. The estimated transaction price per wheel is $21.37 [$31,200 ÷ 1,460] so the aggregate transaction price for the November sale to BBC is $8,548 [$21.37 × 400 wheels] and would be recorded as revenue. The difference between revenue and the amount received from BBC, $252 ($8,800 − $8,548), would be recorded as a contract liability to be released in later months when the volume discount kicks in for BBC.

V. Allocate the Transaction Price to the Performance Obligation(s) Identified in the Contract

    A. Where multiple goods or services are included in the same contract, the transaction price is allocated to each performance obligation based on their relative individual selling prices.

    B. Individual selling prices should be based upon observable stand-alone selling prices used when the organization sells the item separately. When stand-alone selling prices are not observable, individual selling prices can be estimated using the following methods.

        1. Adjusted market price: The price that the market is willing to pay for the good or service. Can be estimated by reference to the observable price of a similar competitor product and then adjusting for differences as needed.

        2. Expected cost plus margin: The estimated cost of producing the good or providing the service plus an amount for reasonable margin.

        3. Residual approach: The amount left over after subtracting observable stand-alone prices for other performance obligations in the contract from the total transaction price. This method can only be used if

            a. The organization sells the good or service at highly varied prices or

            b. The organization does not have an established price for that good or service and the good or service has not been previously sold individually.

Practice Question

Carlotta Corp (CC) has recently signed a contract with a customer that includes three separate products (performance obligations). The total transaction price is $48,000 and CC has gathered the following information related to the performance obligations:

Product	Observable Stand-alone Price	Adjusted Market Price Estimate	Expected Cost plus Margin Estimate
1	$40,000	$41,000	Not available
2	Not available	$4,000	$10,000
3	$6,000	$10,000	Not available

1. How would CC allocate the transaction price to each of the products if they determine that Adjusted Market Price is a better estimate than Expected Cost plus Margin, where available?

2. How would CC allocate the transaction price to each of the products if they determine that Expected Cost plus Margin, where available, is a better estimate than Adjusted Market Price?

Answer

CC should use Observable Stand-alone Prices when available, so only Product 2 would require a price estimate for purposes of allocating the transaction price.

1.

Product	Stand-alone Price	% of Total Value	Allocation of Transaction Price
1	$40,000	80%	$38,400
2	4,000	8%	3,840
3	6,000	12%	5,760
Total	$50,000	100%	$48,000

2.

Product	Stand-alone Price	% of Total Value	Allocation of Transaction Price
1	$40,000	71%	$34,080
2	10,000	18%	8,640
3	6,000	11%	5,280
Total	$56,000	100%	$48,000

VI. Recognize Revenue for Each Performance Obligation

   A. Revenue should be recognized when, or as, each performance obligation is satisfied by transferring control of the good or service to the customer.

   B. Each performance obligation is reviewed to determine if the control over the good or service is transferred over time or at a point in time.

   C. If the transfer of control of the good or service happens over time, revenue is recognized over the same period. Control is transferred over time if

   1. The customer simultaneously receives and consumes the benefit of the performance obligation.

   2. The satisfaction of the performance obligation creates or enhances an asset already controlled by the customer.

3. The good or service has no alternative future use to the selling organization and the organization has a right to payment for work completed.

D. For all contracts that are executed over a period of time, revenue is recognized by measuring the progress toward completion. This measurement can be determined using output methods or input methods, but the method chosen must be appropriate for the circumstances of the contract.

    1. Output methods measure the results actually achieved or value actually transferred to a customer.

        a. The organization must first estimate the amount of output needed to satisfy the performance obligation.

        b. The progress toward completion ratio is determined by measuring the outputs to date divided by the total output needed to satisfy the contract.

        c. The amount of revenue recognized to date should be the completion ratio times the transaction price for the performance obligation.

        d. Units completed, milestones reached, units delivered, or passage of time could be output measures.

    2. Input methods measure how much effort or cost has been expended to satisfy a performance obligation.

        a. The organization must first estimate the amount of input needed to satisfy the performance obligation.

        b. The progress toward completion ratio is determined by measuring the inputs to date divided by the total input needed to satisfy the contract.

        c. The amount of revenue recognized to date should be the completion ratio times the transaction price for the performance obligation.

        d. Hours worked, costs incurred, machine hours, or passage of time could be input measures.

E. If the transfer of control does not happen over time, revenue is recognized at a point in time. The following are some factors that may indicate the proper point in time at which control has transferred and at which revenue should be recognized.

    1. The entity has an enforceable right to payment.

    2. Title to the asset has transferred to the customer.

    3. Physical possession of the asset has transferred to the customer.

    4. Risks and rewards of ownership have transferred to the customer.

    5. The customer has formally accepted the good or service.

Practice Question

Nice New Buildings Team (NNBT) specializes in building luxury resorts. NNBT is finalizing a contract with Great Hotels (GH), a notable luxury resort group, to build a new ski resort in Park City, Utah. NNBT is charging GH $60 million for the project, which will cost NNBT $50 million to build. The project is considered a single performance obligation and NNBT appropriately uses an input method based on total costs to recognize revenue over time. The project will take four years to complete. Below is a table of costs that occurred during the project:

Year	Costs	Cumulative Costs
1	$10,000,000	$10,000,000
2	15,000,000	25,000,000

Continues…

Year	Costs	Cumulative Costs
3	15,000,000	40,000,000
4	10,000,000	50,000,000

How much revenue should NNBT record in each year?

Answer

The input method recognizes revenue throughout the life of the contract based on the estimated percentage of the overall project completion by reference to project costs. NNBT will calculate the percent complete as total contract costs incurred to date divided by total estimated cost of the contract. Then NNBT will calculate cumulative revenue by multiplying expected revenue by percent complete and calculate yearly revenue to be recorded by subtracting previously recorded revenue from cumulative revenue. The table below shows the amount of revenue NNBT would record for each year of the project:

Year	Yearly Costs (a)	Cumulative Costs (b)	Percent Complete (c) (b ÷ 50,000,000)	Cumulative Revenue (d) (60,000,000 × c)	Yearly Revenue (e) (d – Previously Recorded Revenue)
1	$10,000,000	$10,000,000	20%	$12,000,000	$12,000,000
2	15,000,000	25,000,000	50%	$30,000,000	$18,000,000
3	15,000,000	40,000,000	80%	$48,000,000	$18,000,000
4	10,000,000	50,000,000	100%	$60,000,000	$12,000,000

Summary
Organizations use the five-step model for revenue recognition. It is important to analyze each step of the model before recognizing revenue. Organizations must first determine if there is a contract with a customer for purposes of revenue recognition. If there is a contract, then the remaining revenue recognition steps should be reviewed. Organizations should then identify the performance obligations in the contract, calculate the transaction price, allocate the transaction price to the performance obligations, and finally recognize revenue. Revenue is recognized either over time or at a point in time depending upon how the performance obligations are satisfied. If revenue is recognized over time, the organization may use an input method or an output method for determining the amount of revenue to be recognized each period.

Topic 4. IFRS Differences

IFRS Differences in Accounting

After studying this lesson, you should be able to:

- Identify and describe the following differences between U.S. GAAP and IFRS: (i) expense recognition, with respect to share-based payments and employee benefits; (ii) intangible assets, with respect to development costs and revaluation; (iii) inventories, with respect to costing methods, valuation, and write-downs (e.g., LIFO); (iv) leases, with respect to lessee operating and finance leases; (v) long-lived assets, with respect to revaluation, depreciation, and capitalization of borrowing costs; and (vi) impairment of assets, with respect to determination, calculation, and reversal of loss (1.A.2.ff).

The two most common accounting standards used throughout the world are U.S. Generally Accepted Accounting Principles (U.S. GAAP) and International Financial Reporting Standards (IFRS). Up to this point, the lessons in Section A have used U.S. GAAP rules. In many cases these two sets of standards are very similar, but in some cases, there are significant differences. This lesson will describe the main differences between these two sets of accounting standards.

I. Expense Recognition, with Respect to Share-Based Payments and Employee Benefits

    A. In most cases, expense recognition under IFRS is similar to U.S. GAAP.

    B. There are a small number of key exceptions.

        1. All share-based compensation, such as stock options, must be measured using a fair value approach.

            a. Total compensation expense is measured at grant date by multiplying the number of options granted by their fair value at grant date.

            b. Fair value is generally found using pricing models such as Black-Scholes.

            c. The intrinsic value method [(Market Price – Strike Price) × Number of Shares] of measuring share-based compensation is used in limited situations under U.S. GAAP, but is prohibited under IFRS.

        2. Total compensation expense is spread over the service period using the accelerated method under IFRS in equity awards with graded vesting.

            a. Straight-line method for recognizing compensation expense may be elected for U.S. GAAP, but no such election is available under IFRS.

            b. Illustration: Lots of Stock Company offered $90,000 of stock-based compensation to its employees, which will vest in equal amounts at the end of each of the next three years.

                i. Under U.S. GAAP, Lots of Stock Company elects the straight-line method and the compensation expense will be allocated evenly over the three vesting years. This results in a $30,000 ($90,000 ÷ 3) compensation expense each year.

                ii. Under IFRS, using the accelerated method because no straight-line election is available, the $90,000 of stock-based compensation will be treated like three different grants, one vesting each year. This accelerates the rate at which the entire compensation expense is recorded.

                Year 1: The compensation expense in the first year is $55,000 calculated as follows: [$30,000 × (1 year ÷ 1 year)] + [$30,000 × (1 year ÷ 2 years)] + [$30,000 × (1 year ÷ 3 years)].

Year 2: The compensation expense in the second year is $25,000, calculated as follows: [$30,000 × (1 year ÷ 2 years)] + [$30,000 × (1 year ÷ 3 years)].

Year 3: The compensation expense in the third year is $10,000, calculated as follows: [$30,000 × (1 year ÷ 3 years)].

II. Intangible Assets

A. Revaluation

1. Under U.S. GAAP, intangible assets are carried at amortized cost.

2. Under IFRS, intangible assets may be carried at amortized cost (the cost model) or revalued to fair value (the revaluation model) if there is an active market for the asset.

B. Research and Development Costs

1. Under both U.S. GAAP and IFRS, research costs are expensed as incurred.

2. Under IFRS, development costs for internally developed intangible assets may be capitalized once the technological feasibility of the project has been established and the following conditions are met:

   a. The organization can demonstrate how the asset will generate future economic benefits.

   b. The organization can demonstrate that it will use or sell the asset.

   c. The organization has both the intent and the ability (i.e., financial and human resources) to complete the development.

   d. The organization can measure the costs of development.

3. Under U.S. GAAP, all development costs are expensed as incurred, except for software development, which follows a process similar to IFRS described above.

III. Inventory

A. IFRS does not allow the use of the last-in, first-out (LIFO) inventory method.

B. Inventory previously written down for lower of cost or net realizable value issues can be written back up to original cost if there is a recovery. U.S. GAAP does not allow write-up of inventory previously written down unless both the write down and the recovery occur within the same fiscal year (i.e., Q2 write-down and Q3 recovery).

IV. Leases, with Respect to Lessee Operating and Finance Leases

A. IFRS leases are not classified as operating vs. finance like they are under U.S. GAAP. Rather, under IFRS, leases are accounted for similar to finance leases under U.S. GAAP.

B. Lease accounting does not apply to assets with low values (immaterial) or to leases with a term shorter than 12 months. The payments made under these lease agreements would be expensed as incurred and no asset or liability would be recognized upon lease signing.

V. Long-Lived Tangible Assets

A. Under IFRS, assets that can be separated into component parts must be separated for purposes of depreciation. U.S GAAP does not require separation and would generally treat each asset as one item to be depreciated.

B. Under IFRS, organizations may elect to carry property, plant and equipment (PP&E) at depreciated cost similar to U.S. GAAP (the cost model) or at fair value under the revaluation model after initial acquisition.

1. If the cost model is used, organizations may use a variety of depreciation methods similar to those available under U.S. GAAP.

2. Only PP&E whose fair value can be reliably estimated can be carried at a revalued amount.

3. PP&E is depreciated as normal, and revaluation gains and losses are calculated by comparing the book value to the estimated fair value upon revaluation.

4. Depreciation after a revaluation is recalculated using the revalued amount and the remaining useful life of the PP&E.

5. Gains on revaluation are recorded in other comprehensive income (directly to equity) unless they are a reversal of a loss on revaluation previously recorded in income, in which case they are recorded in income until the entire loss is reversed.

6. Losses on revaluation are recorded in income unless they are a reversal of a previous revaluation surplus recorded in other comprehensive income, in which case they are recorded in other comprehensive income until the entire previous surplus is consumed.

C. Capitalization of interest when an organization is preparing a long-lived asset for its intended use differs between U.S. GAAP and IFRS.

1. IFRS requires capitalization of interest that is directly attributable to the construction or production of the asset.

2. U.S. GAAP requires capitalization of interest that could have been avoided if the project had not been undertaken. This could include capitalization of interest from loans for general corporate purposes that are not directly attributable to the asset and often requires an estimate of a weighted average interest rate from various corporate obligations to be used.

Practice Question

Fancy Dishes (FD), a company that manufactures and sells glassware to supermarkets, follows IFRS. On January 1, 20X1, FD purchased a $750,000 machine that creates gold-edged glassware. The fair value of the machine can be reliably estimated and FD elected to carry the machine at fair value under the revaluation model. The machine will be depreciated straight-line over the next 20 years. On December 31, 20X1, FD determined that the estimated fair value of the machine was $760,000. On December 31, 20X2, FD determined that the estimated fair value of the machine was $660,000.

1. What is the revaluation gain or loss in Year 1 and where is the amount recorded?

2. What is the revaluation gain or loss in Year 2 and where is the amount recorded?

Answer

1. At December 31, 20X1, the machine was depreciated by $37,500 ($750,000 ÷ 20 years), to arrive at a book value of $712,500 ($750,000 – $37,500). The machine was then revalued to $760,000. Gains on revaluation are recorded in other comprehensive income unless they are a reversal of a loss on revaluation previously recorded in income, in which case they are recorded in income until the entire loss is reversed. In this situation, the revaluation gain of $47,500 ($760,000 – $712,500) in Year 1 will be recorded in other comprehensive income.

2. Once a revaluation occurs, the new depreciation expense is calculated based on the new value of the asset divided by the remaining life. At December 31, 20X2, the machine was depreciated by another $40,000 ($760,000 ÷ 19 years), to arrive at a book value of $720,000 ($760,000 – $40,000). The machine was then revalued to $660,000. Losses on revaluation are recorded in income unless they are a reversal of a previous revaluation surplus recorded in other comprehensive income, in which case they are recorded in other comprehensive income until the entire previous surplus is consumed. In this situation, $47,500 of the $60,000 ($720,000 – $660,000) revaluation loss in Year 2 offset the surplus of $47,500 in other comprehensive income from Year 1 while the remaining $12,500 ($60,000 – $47,500) revaluation loss is recorded in income.

VI. Impairment of Assets, with Respect to Determination, Calculation, and Reversal of Loss

A. Under U.S. GAAP, impairment is reviewed at the individual asset level. Under IFRS, an organization should review for impairment at the cash-generation unit (CGU) level.

1. A CGU is the smallest level of assets that generate cash independent of other assets in the organization. A CGU is usually made up of more than one asset.

2. The largest CGU an organization has is an operating segment, such as a division of a business.

B. Under IFRS, a one-step impairment test is used rather than the two-step model used for U.S. GAAP. The single step compares the recoverable amount of the CGU to the carrying amount of the CGU and losses are recorded when the recoverable amount is lower. The recoverable amount is the greater of the

1. Fair value of the CGU less selling costs (net realizable value)

2. Value of the CGU in use (discounted cash flow analysis)

C. Recognizing reversals of prior impairment losses is prohibited under U.S. GAAP, but allowed under IFRS.

1. If the cost model is used for the assets, recovery of loss for long-lived fixed assets and for intangible assets with a finite life is allowed up to the point of the initial carrying cost less an adjustment for depreciation/amortization.

2. If the cost model is used for indefinite-lived intangible assets, recovery of past losses is allowed up to the original carrying amount of the intangible asset.

Summary

In the global world that we live in today, it is important to understand the difference between U.S. GAAP and IFRS accounting standards. Expense recognition is largely the same between the two standards but you should understand the differences for share-based payments and employee benefits. In addition, you should be familiar with the U.S. GAAP and IFRS differences in regards to intangible assets, inventory, leases, long-lived tangible assets, and impairment of assets.

aq.rec.002_1802

1. When the allowance method of recognizing bad debt expense is used, the allowance for doubtful accounts would decrease when a(n):

    A. Specific account receivable is collected.
    B. Bad Debt Expense is recorded using the balance sheet approach.
    C. Bad Debt Expense is recorded using the income statement approach.
    D. Specific uncollectible account is written off.

aq.gen.liab.001_1802

2. A company has the following liabilities at year-end:

Mortgage note payable; $16,000 due within 12 months	$355,000
Short-term debt that the company has refinanced with long-term debt shortly after year-end but prior to the issuance of the financial statements	$175,000
Deferred tax liability arising from book and tax differences in depreciation	$25,000

    What amount should the company include in the current liability section of the balance sheet?

    A. $0
    B. $ 16,000
    C. $ 41,000
    D. $191,000

aq.cf.fsa.002_1802

3. In its cash flow statement for the current year, Ness Co. reported cash paid for interest of $70,000. Ness did not capitalize any interest during the current year. Changes occurred in several balance sheet accounts as follows:

Accrued interest payable	17,000 decrease
Prepaid interest	23,000 decrease

    In its income statement for the current year, what amount would Ness have reported as interest expense?

    A. $ 76,000
    B. $ 30,000
    C. $ 64,000
    D. $110,000

aq.inv.oe.008_1802

4. If a company uses the equity method to account for an investment in another company, which of the following is true?

    A. Income to the investing company consists only of actual dividends, interest, or capital gains.
    B. All of the investee's income is included in the investor's income except for income relating to intra-entity transactions.
    C. A proportionate share of the investee's net income is included in the investor's income statement.
    D. Income of the investee is included in the investor's income but reduced by any dividends paid to the investor.

aq.leases.002_1904

5. Lease A does not contain a bargain purchase option, but the lease term is for a major part of the remaining economic life of the underlying asset. Lease B does not transfer ownership of the property to the lessee by the end of the lease term, but the present value of the minimum lease payments exceeds

substantially all of the fair value of the underlying asset. How should the lessee classify these leases? (Answers are in form of: Lease A, Lease B)

A. Finance lease, Finance lease
B. Finance lease, Operating lease
C. Operating lease, Finance lease
D. Operating lease, Operating lease

aq.cf.fsa.004_1802

6. In a company's statement of cash flows, interest paid is:

A. part of the investing section
B. part of the financing section
C. part of the operating section
D. part of the debt service section

aq.lta.002_1802

7. Zulu Corp.'s (Zulu) comparative balance sheet at December 31, Year 6 and Year 5, reported accumulated depreciation balances of $800,000 and $600,000, respectively. Property with a cost of $50,000 and a carrying amount of $40,000 was the only property sold in Year 6. How much depreciation was charged to Zulu's operations in Year 6?

A. $190,000
B. $200,000
C. $220,000
D. $210,000

aq.lta.004_1802

8. This information pertains to equipment owned by Brigade Company.

- Cost of equipment: $10,000

- Estimated residual value: $2,000

- Estimated useful life: 5 years

- Depreciation method: Straight-line

The accumulated depreciation at the end of year 3 is:

A. $4,800.
B. $1,600.
C. $6,000.
D. $5,200.

aq.acc.inc.tax.009_1802

9. Sandy Inc. prepares financial statements under IFRS. At December 31, Year 4, Sandy's income for financial (book) purposes equaled $100,000 and Sandy's only temporary difference related to depreciation. For financial (book) purposes, depreciation equaled $10,000 and for tax purposes, depreciation equaled $15,000. The difference is expected to reverse evenly over the next two years. The enacted tax rate for the current year, Year 4, is 30% and the enacted tax rate for all future years is 40%. In its year-end balance sheet, what amount should Sandy report as a deferred tax asset (liability)?

A. $1,500 deferred tax asset
B. $1,500 deferred tax liability
C. $2,000 deferred tax asset
D. $2,000 deferred tax liability

aq.inv.oe.003_1802

10. Shelton Devin Corp. has two stock investments in which they own 30% of the outstanding stock. The CEO of the company is not in favor of presenting consolidated financial statements. Based on the information, which of the following is **most likely** true?

A. The decision of the CEO is correct as companies are required to issue consolidated statements only when the ownership exceeds 50%.

B. The decision of the CEO is wrong as companies are required to issue consolidated statements when the ownership exceeds 20%.

C. The decision of the CEO is wrong as companies are required to issue consolidated statements only if they hold more than ten subsidiaries.

D. The decision of the CEO is correct as companies are required to issue consolidated statements only when they have three or more subsidiaries.

aq.ifrs.001_1802

11. Simply Pharmaceutical (SP) is a company that specializes in (1) research and development of new medications and (2) acquisition of patents for new medications. SP follows IFRS accounting standards. In SP's situation, which of the following statements about the treatment of intangible assets is correct?

A. Intangible assets must be measured using the cost model.

B. Intangible assets with indefinite lives must be amortized annually.

C. Intangible assets may be revalued to fair value if there is an active market for the asset.

D. Research and development costs are expensed as incurred, except for software development.

aq.rev.rec.014_1809

12. All of the following are steps of the five recognition steps to recognizing revenue **except**:

A. Select an output method for estimating stand-alone selling price.

B. Identify the contract with a customer.

C. Determine the transaction price.

D. Identify separate performance obligations in the contract.

aq.rec.003_1802

13. A method of estimating bad debts that focuses on the income statement rather than the balance sheet is the allowance method based on:

A. Direct write-off.

B. Aging the trade receivable accounts.

C. Credit sales.

D. The balance in the trade receivable accounts.

AQ.int.repo.003_1904

14. Manufactured capital, as defined under Integrated Reporting, includes all of the following items **except**:

A. Work-in-process inventory

B. Patents and trademarks

C. Custom-made tools and patterns used in the manufacturing process

D. Roads and bridges

aq.rev.rec.001_1809

15. In November and December Year 1, Dorr Co., a newly organized magazine publisher, received $72,000 for 1,000 3-year subscriptions at $24 per year, starting with the January Year 2 issue. Dorr elected to include the entire $72,000 in its Year 1 income tax return. What amount should Dorr report in its Year 1 income statement for subscriptions revenue?

A. $0

B. $ 4,000

C. $24,000

D. $72,000

Section B. Planning, Budgeting, and Forecasting

Topic 1. Strategic Planning

Strategy and SWOT

After studying this lesson, you should be able to:

- Discuss how strategic planning determines the path an organization chooses for attaining its long-term goals, vision, and mission, and distinguish between vision and mission (1.B.1.a).

- Identify the time frame appropriate for a strategic plan (1.B.1.b).

- Identify the external factors that should be analyzed during the strategic planning process and understand how this analysis leads to recognition of organizational opportunities, limitations, and threats (1.B.1.c).

- Identify the internal factors that should be analyzed during the strategic planning process and explain how this analysis leads to recognition of organizational strengths, weaknesses, and competitive advantages (1.B.1.d).

This first lesson in strategic planning demonstrates the difference between an organization's vision statement and mission statement, both of which then inform the organization's specific strategy. Before actually designing the strategy, management must first scan the environment, which is a process of gathering data and evaluating all critical environmental factors—both outside of and within the organization. SWOT analysis (Strengths, Weaknesses, Opportunities, Threats) is a well-known strategy tool to help organizations perform environmental scanning. SWOT can also be used subsequently to help focus the organization's strategy.

I. What Is Strategy?

    A. Strategy is the long-term planning and work of the organization.

        1. Strategy work is not the day-to-day operations work of the organization, but strategy does guide that daily work in the organization.

        2. Strategy provides a framework and feedback mechanism to evaluate the long-term effects of daily work on the future of the organization.

    B. Strategy work can be basically separated into design and implementation. More specifically, the strategic planning process can be outlined with the following diagram.

The Strategic Planning Process

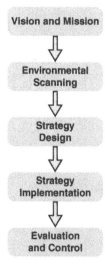

The three lessons in Topic 1 focus on the first three steps of the Strategic Planning Process: Visions and Mission, Environmental Scanning, and Strategy Design. The remaining topics in Section B focus on Strategy Implementation. Evaluation and Control is the focus of Section C.

    C. Strategy design and strategy implementation:

        1. It is important to distinguish between strategy design and strategy implementation.

        2. Typically, boards of directors or advisory councils work with the chief executive officers to design the strategy.

        3. Once the strategy is designed, then it becomes the job of the organization's top management team, including the chief executive officers, to implement the strategy.

        4. Strategy design and implementation is an iterative feedback loop. The process of implementing strategy provides feedback to adjust and clarify strategy while the evolving strategy design provides assessment and guidance to the implementation process.

II. Vision versus Mission

    A. Whether or not the employees and directors realize it, all for-profit companies and not-for-profit organizations—even community associations and government entities—are guided by a strategy.

        1. Strategy represents the core values that are currently being pursued by the organization, regardless of whether the employees are consciously aware of their organization's values.

        2. The current strategy of an organization can be observed by the choices it makes in the process of investing its resources and spending its money.

    B. An organization that intentionally identifies its values in the process of designing and implementing strategy should then base its vision and mission on those values. The vision and mission for an organization should be clearly and concisely laid out as a set of two separate statements.

        1. The vision statement describes what the organization intends to **be** or **become**. The vision statement answers the question, "Who are we?" The vision statement guides subsequently the development of the mission statement.

        2. The mission statement describes what the organization is committed to **do** or how it will **act**. The mission statement answers the question, "What do we do?" The mission statement should be specific enough that the organization can identify whether it is progressing toward an ultimate measurable goal.

        3. The organization's actual strategy is *not* the vision statement and mission statement. The organization's strategy is a much more detailed set of evolving objectives that establishes how the organization will successfully implement its mission in a competitive environment.

III. Environmental Scanning

    A. Strategy must be designed to work effectively in the environment in which the organization operates. Environmental scanning is a systematic process of gathering data and insights about the setting in which the organization will deploy its strategy.

    B. The research work in environmental scanning can employ surveys, interviews, publications, focus groups, consultants, retreats, conferences, or any other resource that provides insight to the organization.

    C. The organization's "environment" includes the following aspects:

        1. The world in which the organization operates, which involves economic trends, government and legal mandates, and demographic factors

        2. The organization's competitors, both current and potential

3. The organization's customers, both current and potential

4. Suppliers and other stakeholders who may partner with the organization, including local governments and community groups

5. The organization's internal structure, comprising employees, physical assets, financial resources, intellectual property, etc.

D. The first four aspects of the environment are "external factors" and the last factor comprises the "internal factors." These factors need to be carefully considered in the design of the organization's strategy.

IV. Environmental Scanning with SWOT

A. There are a number of tools available to help perform environmental scanning and to help design strategy. One well-known tool that can be used for both environmental scanning and designing strategy is SWOT (Strengths, Weaknesses, Opportunities, Threats). The diagram shown here demonstrates how SWOT can be used to scan the organization's environment.

SWOT ANALYSIS

Strengths
Internal <u>Positive</u> Factors:
Human skills
Financial resources
Physical assets
Reputation and Brand

Weaknesses
Internal <u>Negative</u> Factors:
Human skills
Financial resources
Physical assets
Reputation and Brand

Opportunities
External <u>Positive</u> Factors:
Future trends
The economy
Demographics
Competitive forces

Threats
External <u>Negative</u> Factors:
Future trends
The economy
Demographics
Competitive forces

B. Note that SWOT analysis separates factors into internal factors and external factors. Internal factors are divided into strengths and weaknesses.

1. Four examples of internal factors are provided in this diagram: human skills, financial resources, physical assets, and reputation and brand. There are, of course, many types of internal factors that an organization may possess.

2. Internal factors can represent either a strength or a weakness, depending on whether the factor is desirable or undesirable, and whether the organization possesses it or not.

C. Four examples of external factors are also provided, and these factors can represent either opportunities or threats to the organization. Of course, there can be many other types of opportunities and threats besides future trends, the economy, demographics, and competitive forces.

V. Designing Strategy with SWOT

A. SWOT can also be used to support the work of strategy design. With the environmental scanning complete, the SWOT tool can be reconfigured slightly to help managers focus more clearly on the type of strategy they intend to pursue, as illustrated in the diagram shown here.

SWOT MATRIX

B. Organizations must manage both the strengths and weaknesses inherent in their organization. They should adjust to take advantage of opportunities as well as guard against threats in their industry.

C. It is *not* the objective of the SWOT matrix for organizations to design their strategy to be equally focused across all types of strategic objectives above (e.g., S-O strategies, W-O strategies, etc.).

1. Instead, a successful strategy should be designed to emphasize one area of the SWOT matrix while paying adequate attention to the other three areas.

2. Strategy is as much about what the organization chooses to *not emphasize* as it is about what the organization does emphasize!

Practice Question

Cade's Last Decade Clothes is an online business that sells hard-to-find vintage clothing representing unique styles and brands that are at least ten years old. Cade is a college student who has an eye for vintage fashion. He works with two other colleagues to constantly peruse thrift shops, charity stores, and yard sales. There is a surprisingly high demand among 15- to 30-year olds for this type of clothing, and business is growing to a point where Cade is considering a new strategy to significantly expand the business with a training program to quickly identify and train at least 20 more buyers across three different geographic regions. A significant investment in technology will be required to manage inventory, order fulfillment, and online payments. At this point, there doesn't appear to be any other online retailer that competes with a similar purchase and resale model for this type of clothing.

Use a SWOT analysis to identify at least two possible strengths, two possible weaknesses, two possible opportunities, and two possible threats that Cade should consider as he begins the work of designing a new strategy for his business.

Answer

See the analysis below that describes possible environmental factors for the SWOT model. Other factors are certainly possible. Be sure that your solution clearly positions internal factors as either strengths or weaknesses, and external factors as either opportunities or threats.

Continues…

Internal Factors

Strengths:

Early mover in this new clothing retail space.

Established talent to identify desirable clothing available to purchase.

Low capital requirements mean that business is inexpensive to locate in other markets.

Weaknesses:

Does Cade have the management skill to manage a significantly larger organization?

Can purchasing talent be developed across many employees in distant markets?

Will sufficient financing be available for the technology needed to expand the business?

External Factors

Opportunities:

Traditional clothing retailers are not likely to compete in a used clothing market.

If the economy slows down, the market for used clothing may actually increase.

The market for used clothing could possibly extend to young kids and older adults.

Threats:

Competitive barriers are low—other smaller retailers in this market could appear.

The market taste for vintage clothing from last decade could suddenly disappear.

Used vintage clothing is a "scarce resource"—can enough be purchased to support a growing business?

Summary

Strategy work involves planning for the long-term success of the organization. Strategic planning is basically separated into design work versus implementation work. Effective strategy design determines the organization's vision ("Who are we?") and mission ("What do we do?") based on its values, and then establishes specific strategic objectives that represent its vision and mission. Environmental scanning is a necessary aspect of strategy design since strategic objectives must be launched in a context of internal and external factors that determine what the organization actually can and should do. SWOT analysis is one of a number of strategic tools available to managers. SWOT separates environmental *internal* factors into **S**trengths and **W**eaknesses. SWOT also separates environmental *external* factors into **O**pportunities and **T**hreats. SWOT can also be used to guide strategy design as a choice process to emphasize different combinations of internal strengths and weaknesses to pursue external opportunities or guard against external threats.

Strategic Objectives and Generic Strategy

After studying this lesson, you should be able to:

- Demonstrate an understanding of how the mission leads to the formulation of long-term business objectives such as business diversification, the addition or deletion of product lines, or the penetration of new markets (1.B.1.e).

- Explain why short-term objectives, tactics for achieving these objectives, and operational planning (master budget) must be congruent with the strategic plan and contribute to the achievement of long-term strategic goals (1.B.1.f).

- Identify the characteristics of successful strategic plans (1.B.1.g).

- Describe Porter's generic strategies, including cost leadership, differentiation, and focus (1.B.1.h).

This lesson introduces Porter's generic strategies, which provide an overall framework for strategy design. Organizations that intend to compete effectively in the long run need to design their strategy to deliver on cost leadership, product differentiation, or a market segment focus. This lesson also discusses specific characteristics of a successful strategic plan.

I. Porter's Generic Strategies

   A. Michael Porter is a famed Harvard professor who has established several important strategy design models. Porter's generic strategies describe the basic choices an organization has in order to compete successfully in the marketplace. His generic strategies are modeled here.

Competitive Scope	Competitive Advantage	
	Lower Cost	**Differentiation**
Broad (Industry)	1. Cost Leadership Strategy	2. Differentiation Strategy
Narrow (Segment)	3a. Focus Strategy (Lower Cost)	3b. Focus Strategy (Differentiation)

   B. There are three fundamental strategic approaches to sustaining a competitive advantage that can result in above-average profits over the long run.

      1. A cost leadership strategy involves establishing a position across the industry as a lower-cost producer (or lower-cost provider if the product is a service) by developing certain cost advantages.

      2. In a differentiation strategy, the organization identifies what customers in the industry value with respect to unique product or service characteristics, and then establishes a position to provide those unique needs.

      3. A focus strategy is based on identifying a certain segment or niche within the industry, and then establishing either a lower cost advantage or a differentiation advantage in serving that particular industry segment.

C. Cost Leadership Strategy

    1. Cost leadership focuses on the organization's ability to sell a high volume of lower-cost products or services. In order to be able to implement this strategy, the organization should have high levels of productivity and efficiency, as well as access to extensive distribution resources.

    2. Additional factors affecting the successful implementation of a cost leadership strategy include proprietary production technology, control of low-cost production inputs (raw materials, labor, etc.), and access to low-cost financial capital.

D. Differentiation Strategy

    1. A differentiated product or service is perceived to offer unique features or benefits to the customer (e.g., gasoline that contains special additives to improve engine longevity). In general, differentiated products inspire higher levels of brand loyalty in customers, making them less sensitive to price differences among products.

    2. In order to support a strategy of product differentiation, the organization must foster continued product innovation and improvement through investment in research and development, and must effectively market the product to maintain the brand.

E. Focus Strategy

    1. Segmentation of the marketplace is essential for a focus strategy (also referred to as niche marketing). Segments (or niches) may be based on geographic regions, population demographics, or a variety of special interests or needs.

    2. The competitive advantage is gained by customizing the product to meet the needs of the specialized market segment. Competition within market segments can be based either on lower costs or on product differentiation.

II. Long-Run and Short-Run Strategy Planning

A. Remember that strategies are specific action plans of the organization that are (hopefully) derived from a unified mission and vision. When discussing the time frame of a strategy, the focus is time frame of a strategy, the focus is typically on the long run.

B. Porter's generic strategies point out that the organization's overall long-run strategy should be based on cost leadership, product differentiation, or a segment (niche) focus.

C. With the longer-run strategy in place, the organization can then concentrate on shorter, more specific time frames for programs and initiatives (i.e., sub-strategies) involving marketing campaigns, personnel development, or operation investments, etc.

    1. To establish long-term success, the organization's short-term operating objectives must be in line with the overall strategic approach; otherwise, strategy planning and implementation will be ineffective.

    2. Similarly, the goals of lower-level managers must be consistent with top management's goals to avoid goal incongruence and performance misalignment.

III. Characteristics of Successful Strategic Plans

A. Characteristics of successful strategic plans include the following:

    1. The strategic plan is based on a clear statement of the organization's vision and mission.

    2. The strategic plan is based on realities in the environment (both external and internal).

    3. The process of building the strategic plan is inclusive such that managers and employees feel collective ownership.

    4. The strategic plan serves as a reference point for decision-making in the organization.

    5. The plan compels managers to align their own planning and decision making with the longer-term goals and strategy of the organization.

6. The plan improves communication and aids coordination among managers by helping them align their goals with the overall strategy.

7. Performance evaluation and incentive compensation can be tied clearly to the strategic plan.

B. Successful strategic plans are never perfect and need to be reviewed and updated periodically as the organization's environment shifts and managers learn better how to compete successfully.

Practice Question

Warren Cycles is a manufacturing and distribution company that competes worldwide in the motorcycle industry. It is a highly competitive consumer marketplace. Warren has struggled over the years to establish an ongoing position with adequate profit, and is now working through a complete review and redesign of its strategy. It is considering four possible strategic approaches, as listed ahead.

1. Establish an international brand for lower priced, good quality motorcycles. Invest in large-scale manufacturing operations to mass produce the motorcycles with an eye on economies of scale.

2. Focus on the market in Southeast Asia with an extremely low-priced, rugged bike. The design includes an extended seat length for carrying more than two riders. This design keeps the product from penetrating the traditional market.

3. Compete in the high-end motorcycle market with a designer motorcycle that provided the client with the opportunity to individually "compose" the product as their own custom bike before it goes to production. When complete, the bike is personally delivered to the client in a small celebration event.

4. Target the narrow, but very visible, older customer segment (generally more than 60 years old) to design and deliver a three-wheeled motorcycle (sometimes called a "trike") to address demand in this segment for improved road tour riding and stabilized standing and parking performance.

Evaluate each of these four possible strategies and categorize them using Porter's general strategies model.

Answer

Strategy 1 is a cost leadership strategy that is deployed across the entire industry market.

Strategy 2 is a market (segment) focus strategy that emphasizes low-cost characteristics.

Strategy 3 is a differentiation strategy that is deployed across the entire industry market.

Strategy 4 is a market (segment) focus strategy that emphasizes differentiation characteristics.

Summary

Porter's generic strategies serve as an overall framework to help organizations identify their basic strategic position. Strategic plans for organizations should fall within one of three categories: cost leadership, product differentiation, or market segment focus. With a well-designed strategy in place for the long run, divisions and managers in the organization can then build shorter sub-strategies to pursue specific plans and initiatives. Successful strategic planning can be described across seven specific characteristics. In general, successful strategic plans are based on a clear vision, mission, and assessment of the environment. Further, successful strategic planning provides clarity and incentives across the organization to align planning, control, and evaluation of decisions and performance.

Specific Strategy Tools

After studying this lesson, you should be able to:

- Demonstrate an understanding of the following planning tools and techniques: SWOT analysis, Porter's Five forces, situational analysis, PEST analysis, scenario planning, competitive analysis, contingency planning, and the BCG Growth-Share Matrix (1.B.1.i).

There are a number of tools that have been developed over the years to help organizations evaluate their markets and beginning designing strategy. In this lesson we'll learn about the BCG Growth-Share Matrix, scenario analysis and contingency planning, PEST and PESTLE analysis, and Porter's Five Forces model of competitive factors.

I. BCG Growth-Share Matrix

    A. Boston Consulting Group (BCG) developed a strategy planning tool that visually represents an organization's products or services across two market dimensions: the overall growth of the market, and the organization's share of the market. By distinguishing business units as one of four types, organizations can use the BCG Matrix to make resource allocation decisions. The matrix is depicted here.

BCG Growth-Share Matrix

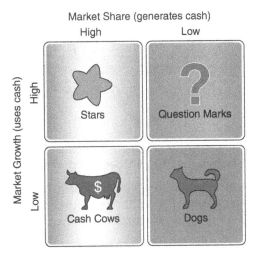

    B. Cash cows are products, services, or business units that have a large share of an established (slow growth) market. Cash cows require little investment and can generate a lot of cash that can be used in other business units. Organizations usually design **harvest strategies** for this kind of business.

    C. Stars have a high share of a fast-growing market. The organization typically needs to spend significant resources in order to maintain its share of this market. If the organization can hold onto its share, this business can turn into a cash cow when the market stabilizes. Organizations usually design **invest strategies** for this kind of business.

    D. Question marks are also in a fast-growing market. By holding a small share of the market, these products or services have a lot of potential to do well, but have yet to actually deliver strong results. There is significant risk that the business may turn into a dog, though the hope is that it evolves into a star. Organizations usually design **explore strategies** for this kind of business.

    E. Dogs are obviously an undesirable business. A small share of a market that isn't growing may not require much cash to maintain, but there is often significant capital resources and valuable management attention tied up in these businesses. Unless there is an important purpose to remain in this market, organizations usually design **divest strategies** for this kind of business and recover some cash.

II. Situational Analysis

    A. The BCG Matrix helps organizations use their market, and their position in the market, to design strategy. To be effective with this tool, managers need to clearly understand their markets. This requires a careful examination of the organization's internal and external environment, which was described in an earlier lesson as environmental scanning (and is also known as situational analysis). There are two specific types of situational analysis, known as scenario analysis and contingency planning.

    B. Scenario analysis, popular in military organizations, helps companies consider the complexities of an uncertain business environment with many factors that interact with each other. By carefully modeling how different scenarios might interact to impact the organization's market and business, managers can do better strategy planning. Typically, scenario analysis begins by grouping possible events or factors into two categories: (1) factors the organization has some knowledge about or ability to affect and (2) factors that are entirely uncertain and uncontrollable.

    C. Contingency planning often follows the scenario analysis. Contingency planning involves developing alternative strategies in order to be prepared for unexpected conditions or outcomes. Good contingency planning can minimize the negative effect of surprising events, as well as optimize opportunities that may unexpectedly present themselves.

III. PEST and PESTLE

    A. One very specific tool used to analyze external factors and conditions is PEST analysis. The PEST model is an acronym for Politics, Economy, Social, and Technology factors, and is illustrated here.

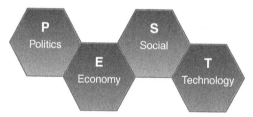

    1. Politics factors include regulation issues, political stability, legal environment, tax policies, etc. Essentially, these factors describe all aspects of government intervention into the economy.

    2. Economy factors include inflation, unemployment, quality of labor force, stability of currency, economic growth rate, etc. Both macroeconomic (e.g., policy) and microeconomic (e.g., market behavior) factors are considered here.

    3. Social factors include demographics, culture, education levels, leisure interests, attitudes toward environment, social responsibility, etc. These factors are important to understanding what drives consumer behavior.

    4. Technology factors include manufacturing, computers, communication, transportation, medical, etc. Not only do these factors determine the kind of products and services that are or will be available, but also they impact how products and services are distributed and subsequently supported.

    B. PEST analysis is often expanded to include two more factors, environment and legal, which forms the PESTLE analysis model, as illustrated here.

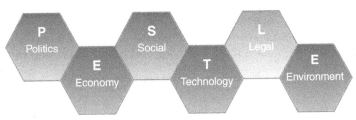

1. Legal factors include regulations governing consumer and employee safety, intellectual property, competition fairness, product warranties, etc.

2. Environment factors include scarcity of raw materials, pollution impacts, weather patterns, geography, etc.

IV. Competitive Analysis and Porter's Five Forces

A. Assessing the nature of competition in the market should be based on four key aspects of current and potential competitors: (1) competitors' objectives, (2) competitors' assumptions, (3) competitors' capabilities, and (4) competitors' strategies.

B. The analysis can include a comparative assessment of each competitor by identifying the key success factors in the market, and then rating each competitor on their strength in each factor.

C. Michael Porter models the competitive forces in an industry across five dimensions, as illustrated here.

Porter's Five Forces

Threat of Substitute Products

Supplier Power

Intensity of Competition

Customer Power

Threat of New Entrants

1. Suppliers, if powerful, can pressure the industry with higher prices, which moves profit out of the industry to the suppliers. When there are few suppliers, or the cost to switch suppliers is high, then suppliers are more powerful.

2. Customers can also have more or less buying power. Similar to suppliers, fewer customers results in more powerful customers. More flexibility to switch across competitors also creates more power for customers.

3. Substitute products are products in other industries. The more viable those substitute products are, the higher the threat. More alternatives for customers puts pressure on prices.

4. The threat of new entrants is determined by the nature of barriers to enter the market. Government restrictions, patents and proprietary knowledge, and capital investment requirements all contribute to market entry barriers.

5. The intensity of competition is affected by the other four forces. In addition, it is a function of specific competitive issues such as the number of competitors in the industry (more creates higher intensity), rate of market growth (slow creates more intensity), product differentiation (low creates more intensity), and exit barriers (high create more intensity).

Practice Question

Identifying business units within the BCG Growth-Share Matrix can help managers design more specific strategies. Align each of the following strategies with each of the four types of business units in the BCG matrix.

Strategy 1: Invest in new technologies to increase share of the market.

Strategy 2: Divest out of the market before it begins declining quickly.

Strategy 3: Research evolving customer preferences to determine how much to invest into the market.

Strategy 4: Continually improve cost efficiencies to defend position with incremental price decreases.

Answer

Strategy 1 would be most appropriate for a **Star** business unit.

Strategy 2 would be most appropriate for a **Dog** business unit.

Strategy 3 would be most appropriate for a **Question Mark** business unit.

Strategy 4 would be most appropriate for a **Cash Cow** business unit.

Practice Question

Analyzing competition is complex. Porter's Five Forces model helps identify clear factors involved in the competitive landscape of an industry. Identify which of the following industry factors best represents each competitive force in Porter's model.

Factor 1: Industry is crowded with many competitors (i.e., rivals).

Factor 2: Industry is crowded with lots of suppliers (i.e., sources to purchase raw materials).

Factor 3: Customers are large institutions that are beginning to expand across the industry (i.e., buying out rival firms in the industry).

Factor 4: Local government has recently deregulated the industry, opening up opportunity for new competitors.

Factor 5: Advances in technology are creating alternative solutions to customer needs.

Answer

Factor 1 represents the **Intensity of Competition** in Porter's Five Forces.

Factor 2 represents the **Power of Suppliers** in Porter's Five Forces.

Factor 3 represents the **Power of Customers** (buying power) in Porter's Five Forces.

Factor 4 represents the **Threat of New Entrants** in Porter's Five Forces.

Factor 5 represents the **Threat of Substitute Products** in Porter's Five Forces.

Summary

The BCG Growth-Share Matrix describes business units (products, services, etc.) on two dimensions, overall market growth and share of the market, which results in four classifications: cash cow, star, question mark, and dog. These four classifications suggest possible strategy designs. Understanding how to effectively compete using a particular strategy design requires careful, intelligent understanding of market conditions. A number of tools can help in that regard. Scenario analysis and contingency planning helps managers think carefully about different scenarios that may happen, how those scenarios can interact, and what plans can be put in place to adjust to evolving scenarios. PEST(LE) analysis identifies four (six) different environment conditions to evaluate: politics, economy, social, technology (legal, environment). Porter's Five Forces can be used to assess the competitive landscape. The Five Forces include the power of customers and suppliers, the threat of new entrants and substitute products, and the intensity of competition in the industry.

Topic 2. Budgeting Concepts

Strategy Implementation and Budgeting

After studying this lesson, you should be able to:

- Describe the role that budgeting plays in the overall planning and performance evaluation process of an organization (1.B.2.a).

- Explain the interrelationships between economic conditions, industry situation, and a firm's plans and budgets (1.B.2.b).

- Identify the role that budgeting plays in formulating short-term objectives and planning and controlling operations to meet those objectives (1.B.2.c).

- Demonstrate an understanding of the role that budgets play in measuring performance against established goals (1.B.2.d).

- Identify the characteristics that define successful budgeting processes (1.B.2.e).

- Explain the role of budgets in monitoring and controlling expenditures to meet strategic objectives (1.B.2.r).

A well-designed strategy needs to be carried forward into an effective operational plan. This is the budgeting process in the organization. A successful budgeting system is aligned with the strategy and focuses the organization's resources, is responsive to the organization's environment, is informative and motivating for employees, and provides a feedback learning loop in the organization to strengthen future processes.

I. The Role of Budgeting in Strategy Implementation

    A. Spending money and investing resources represents the organization's strategy.

        1. To the extent that spending and investing decisions are not supporting the strategic position and role in the strategic plan, the organization is not effectively implementing its strategy.

        2. Hence, effective budgeting should focus on spending and investing that clearly ties to the organization's strategic objectives.

        3. Budgeting is the natural translation of strategy into quantifiable terms!

    B. Strategy implementation by the organization's managers follows the strategy design by the organization's leaders.

        1. Strategy implementation involves identifying short-term objectives and then establishing processes to achieve those objectives.

        2. Short-term objectives and processes must be constantly evaluated and adjusted to ensure alignment with the organization's long-term objectives and overall strategy. This is particularly important as the organization's strategy evolves to address new economic and competitive conditions.

II. Responsive Budgeting

    A. A good budget must be both firm and flexible. Employees, departments, and divisions should be able to depend on a budget that makes firm commitments on resources that will be available, and that firmly establishes expectations on performance.

B. On the other hand, a good budget must have the flexibility to respond appropriately to changing conditions. While budgets should not be constantly adjusted, when the occasion warrants change, the budget needs to flex.

    1. For example, when conditions in the organization's setting make a significant shift, the budget should likely respond. Remember that the PESTLE analysis tool (politics, economy, social, technology, legal, and environment) represents different conditions that can affect the budget.

    2. As another example, competitive conditions can also shift, necessitating a change to the budget. Porter's Five Forces provides a useful tool for assessing competitive conditions. These forces include the power of customers and suppliers, the threat of new entrants and substitute products, and the intensity of competition in the industry.

III. Aligning the Organization

    A. Managers work to implement strategy by establishing operational objectives. Achieving the operational objectives is a decision-making and management process that involves planning, controlling, and evaluating operations in the organization. This process is a feedback loop that can be illustrated here.

    B. Operational planning is where the strategy is defined into operational objectives, performance measures are set, and resources are committed. This is the budgeting process for the organization.

    C. Controlling operational processes requires that expectations are established and incentivized, results are gathered and reported, and variances from the budget are computed.

    D. Evaluating the operations involves rewarding performance, analyzing results to understand why objectives were met or not, and using the insight gained to complete the feedback loop and inform the planning stage for the upcoming operational cycle.

IV. Characteristics of Successful Budgeting

    A. There are a number of important characteristics of successful budgeting. This lesson has already emphasized two of those characteristics. The first characteristic is that the budget clearly connects to and supports the organization's strategy.

B. The second characteristic of successful budgeting is an intelligent balance between firmness and flexibility. As stated earlier, employees depend on the budget to represent resources, measures, and incentives that won't change unless there is a compelling need for the budget to respond to significant shifts in the market.

C. The budget should accurately represent forecasts of the overall business environment (external factors) as well as represent realities of the organization's own environment (internal factors). Accountants tend to favor conservatism, but conservatism is not nearly as valuable a characteristic in budgeting as is accuracy.

D. Everyone in the organization needs to clearly understand and strongly commit themselves to the budget. These qualities are present when everyone feels ownership of the budget, which results from the opportunity to participate in building the budget.

E. The budget should be motivating for everyone in the organization. Budgets effectively represent goals and performance standards. When budget incentives are appropriate and budget expectations are reachable with effort (i.e., stretch targets), then the budget will exhibit motivational characteristics.

F. Finally, as seen in the diagram above, budgeting is a learning feedback process. Every budgeting cycle should be assessed to understand what was unanticipated or misunderstood, and that insight should then inform and improve the next budgeting cycle.

Practice Question

Name at least five important elements of a successful budgeting process.

Answer

The following are a number of important elements of a successful budgeting process:

- Strongly representative and supportive of the organization's strategy

- Focuses the spending of money and the investing of resources on the organization's strategy

- Based on short-term operational objectives that align with the organization's strategy

- Balances firmness so that employees can depend on resources and expectation with the occasional need to flexibly adjust to changing circumstances in the organization's environment

- Prioritizes accurate forecasts and expectations rather than conservative estimate of needs and performance

- Provides the opportunity for employees to have a voice in the budget, which results in ownership of the budget across the organization

- Uses appropriate incentives and stretch targets in order to be motivational for employees

- Continuously improves by gathering insights on current budgeting successes and failures to improve future budgeting process

---

Summary

A great strategy isn't worth much if it can't be translated into an effective operational budget for the organization. Good budgets are aligned with the strategy and are based on short-term operational objectives that guide the deployment of resources across the organization. The realities of environmental factors must also guide budgets, and budgets need to be responsive (flexible) to significant shifts in the environment. Employees should feel ownership of, and be motivated by, the budget in order for it to be effective in implementing strategy. Budgeting is part of an overall decision-making and management process that involves planning, controlling, and evaluating processes. These processes connect together as a feedback learning cycle.

The Budgeting Process

After studying this lesson, you should be able to:

- Explain how the budgeting process facilitates communication among organizational units and enhances coordination of organizational activities (1.B.2.f).

- Describe the concept of a controllable cost as it relates to both budgeting and performance evaluation (1.B.2.g).

- Explain how the efficient allocation of organizational resources is planned during the budgeting process (1.B.2.h).

- Identify the appropriate time frame for various types of budgets (1.B.2.i).

- Identify who should participate in the budgeting process for optimum success (1.B.2.j).

- Describe the role of top management in successful budgeting (1.B.2.k).

- Identify best practice guidelines for the budget process (1.B.2.l).

Budgets are how strategy is deployed across the organization. Effective budgets establish communication, coordination, and motivation to achieve a long-run strategy by executing on short-run plans. You'll learn in this lesson that successfully creating an effective budget entails clear objectives and an open process of participation across the organization.

I. Allocating Resources

    A. Strategy defines how the organization spends money and allocates resources. In fact, the organization's strategy (intentional or not) can be observed in how it spends its money and allocates its resources (i.e., positions its assets).

    B. That said, the real work of spending money and positioning assets is carried out in the day-to-day decisions taking place during the organization's period of operations. These decisions are planned, controlled, and evaluated as a core aspect of budgeting.

II. Budgeting Time Frames

    A. Budgets are built working backwards from a long-run view based on the organization's strategy. Conversely, budgets are achieved working forwards using a short-run focus on operations.

        1. Beginning with the three-to-five year focus of the strategy plan, budgets are typically designed by working backwards from the strategy to design one-to-three-year targets, followed by quarterly targets, monthly targets, and perhaps weekly targets.

        2. When actually operating with the budget, performance is achieved by focusing on short-run operations (weekly or monthly), and working forward to achieve more long-run objectives in the quarterly and annual budgets.

        3. As organizations work through each operating period, the budget is continuously built forward to always maintain a one-to-three-year operating plan. This is the process of a "rolling" budget.

    B. Remember, the time frame of operating budgets always needs to tie back to the long-run focus of the organization's strategy, which will be closer to the three-to-five-year time span.

III. Communication and Performance Evaluation

    A. Budgeting should be one of the key tools in the organization to facilitate communication and coordination between individuals and divisions within the organization.

        1. The bigger and more complex the organization, the more crucial it is to develop clear budgets to support communication and coordination.

        2. Budgets help divisions know what resources they can expect to receive, and what deliverables they are expected to provide.

    B. Budgets serve multiple purposes, and sometimes those purposes can conflict. Another key deliverable of budgets is to support performance evaluation.

        1. When evaluating performance by comparing actual results to the planned budget, the concept of controllable costs is crucial.

        2. Successful budgeting requires accurate estimates of costs, which managers help provide. However, some planned costs are not controllable (e.g., property taxes, certain salaries, etc.). Managers should be responsible to help accurately plan (i.e., forecast) all costs, but their performance should be evaluated only on costs they can control.

        3. When managers are held responsible for costs they cannot control, the incentive is strong to overestimate costs in order to build slack into these cost estimates. Budgetary slack provides cushion for the manager in the event uncontrollable costs are higher. However, budgetary slack reduces the accuracy and usefulness of budget plans for the whole organization.

IV. Roles in the Budgeting Process

    A. The diagram shown below illustrates the traditional budgeting cycle.

        1. The process begins with the formation of a budget committee. In some organizations, the committee is not limited to executive leadership, but will also involve directors of selected strategic business units (SBUs) and other managers.

        2. Budget guidelines are established by the budget committee and include strategic objectives, major organization goals, and incentives.

        3. To the extent the organization values significant participation in the budgeting process by lower-level managers, initial budget proposals are submitted "bottom up" by managers (rather than "top down" by executives).

        4. As budget proposals are submitted across the organization, an iterative process of negotiation and revision begins as the organization works out expectations and the sharing of limited resources between divisions across the organization.

        5. The negotiation and revision continues in the final step as the budget committee reviews and provides feedback. Eventually, the budget is completed and presented to the organization's leadership (executives, board of directors, etc.).

The Budget Process

Form Budget Committee
{ • CFO
• Controller
• Key SBU Directors

Establish Budget Guidelines
{ • Strategic Objectives
• Major Goals
• Incentives

Submit Budget Proposals
{ Submitted by each SBU director

Revisions

Negotiate Budget Proposals
{ Negotiate resources shared between SBU directors

Revisions

Review & Approve the Final Budget
{ Committee approves, then reports back to organization execs

B. The actual process of building a budget will illustrate a key aspect of the organization's culture—employee participation.

   1. Organizations make important choices regarding the extent of top-down versus bottom-up budgeting, which effectively describe how different levels of employees will participate in the management of the organization.

   2. Bottom-up (participating) budgeting involves more time and resources, but results in a more informed budget with higher ownership by the employees.

   3. Top-down (authoritative) budgeting takes less time and resources and doesn't exhaust the employees as much, but the budget may have blind spots and may be resisted by the employees.

V. Best Practice Guidelines

   A. Link the budget to strategy. This linkage is critical since budgets determine how resources will be allocated and what measures will be used to evaluate progress.

   B. Design budgeting processes that allocate resources strategically. Every business unit needs funding for both capital investment and operating expenses, and funding needs usually exceed available resources. Hence, competition for resources within the organization is inevitable. Tradeoff decisions must be based on long-run strategy.

   C. Establish budget targets based on realistic expectations *and* based on stretch goals. Budgets are used for both planning purposes and motivation purposes, and these purposes can conflict. Budgets needs to carefully balance these two purposes.

   D. Reduce budget complexity and budget cycle time. Organizations need to constantly strive to reduce budget complexity and streamline budgeting procedures. Overly complex budgets that take too much time and resources to complete will disrupt the organization's core activities.

   E. Develop flexible budgets that accommodate change. Organizations should review budgets regularly and make adjustments if needed. Knowing that budgets have some flexibility frees managers from the need to build slack into budget estimates to cover unexpected and uncontrollable developments.

Practice Question

Assume that you've been employed as a consultant to help a growing organization establish an effective budgeting process. Describe for the executive team an effective budgeting process that involves department managers throughout the organization. Indicate important qualities that will be demonstrated by a successful master budget.

Answer

An effective budgeting process begins with guidance from a budget committee that represents both executive leaders and division managers. That guidance should establish the strategic objectives, primary goals, and employee incentives that need to be incorporated into each department budget. Each department manager then prepares and submits an initial budget. To the extent these budgets need to coordinate and share resources across departments, the managers should negotiate these issues with each other. Once all of the department budgets are revised and reconciled, then the set of budgets are submitted back to the budget committee for feedback, and likely more revision. Eventually, the budgets are approved, and the master budget plan is presented to the organization's executive leadership (and board of directors, if relevant).

A successful master budget needs to clearly connect to and support the organization's strategy by effectively allocating scarce resources to accomplish the strategy over the long run. The budget should balance realistic expectations with stretch goals that motivate employees. The budgeting process itself should be efficient in order to not use too much time and exhaust participants. Once deployed, the budget should be periodically reviewed and adjusted if necessary to accommodate changing circumstances.

Summary

Budgets are, hopefully, an intentionally strategic effort to tie short-run spending and asset deployment decisions to long-run strategy. The time frame of an operational budget typically rolls out across weeks, months, quarters, and then years. Effective budgets are used by employees and divisions to communicate and coordinate with each other. When budgets are also used to motivate performance, it is important that only controllable costs are used in the evaluation process. The budget process traditionally follows a cycle of budget proposals that are submitted, negotiated, and revised until the final budget is established and approved by the organization's leadership. Best practices in the budget process include clear linkage to the organization's strategy, budget targets that are realistic and stretch the employees, budget processes that are fast and efficient, and periodic reviews to adjust budgets as needed based on changing circumstances.

Building Budget Standards

After studying this lesson, you should be able to:

- Demonstrate an understanding of the use of cost standards in budgeting (1.B.2.l).

- Differentiate between ideal (theoretical) standards and currently attainable (practical) standards (1.B.2.m).

- Differentiate between authoritative standards and participative standards (1.B.2.n).

- Identify the steps to be taken in developing standards for both direct material and direct labor (1.B.2.o).

- Demonstrate an understanding of the techniques that are used to develop standards such as activity analysis and the use of historical data (1.B.2.p).

- Discuss the importance of a policy that allows budget revisions that accommodate the impact of significant changes in budget assumptions (1.B.2.q).

- Define budgetary slack and discuss its impact on goal congruence (1.B.2.s).

Cost standards form the basis of the organization's budget. Costs are based on two inputs: quantity × price. Once the standard costs are formed for direct materials, direct labor, and production overhead, they can be combined to establish the total standard cost for the product or service. You'll learn in this lesson how standard costs are developed, and important budgeting concepts that affect these cost standards and how they're used by managers.

I. Cost Standards

    A. Companies use cost standards throughout the management process of planning, controlling, and evaluating costs in the organization.

    B. A standard cost sheet is, essentially, a "recipe card" that specifies standard prices and standard quantities to build a single product or service, as demonstrated below

Standard Cost Sheet

	Input Quantity	Cost per Input	Cost per Unit
Direct Materials	0.70 pounds	$12.50 per pound	$8.75
Direct Labor	2.20 hours	$23.00 per hours	$50.60
Variable Overhead	2.20 hours	$8.50 per DL hours	$18.70
Fixed Overhead	2.20 hours	$14.60 per DL hours	$32.12
Total Product Cost			**$110.17**

    Note that the input quantity multiplied by the cost per input equals cost per unit. Also note in this example that overhead costs are being allocated on the basis of direct labor (DL) hours.

    C. These standards are used for both planning and evaluation purposes. A fundamental issue to be addressed in the budgeting process is whether to use *ideal* (i.e., theoretical) *cost standards* or *attainable* (i.e., practical) *cost standards*.

        1. Ideal standards represent the expected cost per input and input quantity based on an assumption that prices paid for materials, labor, and overhead are at the absolute lowest possible level, and assuming that the use of materials, labor, and overhead is absolutely efficient without any waste or error. When ideal standards are used in the organization, they are generally created in a top-down budgeting approach.

2. Actual results are not likely to attain the ideal standards, and certainly won't be better than ideal. However, these standards are consistent and less likely than attainable standards to be biased in the standard-setting process.

3. Attainable standards are based on more reasonable expectations about average prices and usage. These standards are generally created in a bottom-up budgeting approach.

4. Actual results may be higher or lower than the attainable standards. The challenge in setting attainable standards is the higher likelihood of error or bias that may be built into the numbers by managers.

D. Remember from the previous lesson that the budget process may be based on an authoritative (top-down) or based on a participative (bottom-up) process. There is an important balance between these two approaches that should be considered when setting cost standards.

1. Authoritative cost standards are not likely to be biased by lower-level managers who will subsequently be evaluated based on the standards.

2. On the other hand, participative cost standards will incorporate more of the lower-level managers' knowledge and experience, which should reduce error in the forecast of cost standards.

II. Developing Standards

A. Computing the standard quantity of direct materials for one unit of finished output involves identifying the amount of material content designed for the finished unit. This content then needs to be adjusted for normal expectations (e.g., allowances) regarding scrap or quality rejects, as exhibited below.

Quantity Standard — Aluminum Material	Pounds per Unit
Aluminum content per unit	0.62
Normal scrap	0.05
Allowance for rejected units	0.03
Standard Quantity per unit	**0.70**

B. In addition to determining the standard quantity used, the standard price of the direct material must also be computed. The price needs to include all expected (e.g., average) costs of receiving the raw material and preparing it for production, as exhibited below.

Price Standard — Aluminum Material	Price per Pound
Price for Grade A Aluminum	$ 11.00
Freight-in Shipping	.75
Handling Expense	1.20
Total	$ 12.95
Less discount	(.45)
Standard Price per Pound	**$ 12.50**

C. Similarly, the standard quantity and standard price of direct labor costs are determined by considering all costs of labor, and accommodating for normal expectations of scrap and rejected output, as exhibited below.

Quantity Standard — Direct Labor	Hours per Unit
Calculated time per unit	1.90
Allowance for scheduled breaks	0.15
Allowance for down time	0.10
Allowance for rejected units	0.05
Standard Quantity per Unit	**2.20**

Price Standard — Direct Labor	Price per Hour
Hourly wage rate (average)	$ 17.00
Payroll taxes (13.2%)	2.25
Fringe benefits (22.0%)	3.75
Standard Price per Hour	**$ 23.00**

D. Computing the standard costs for variable and fixed production overhead costs is traditionally approached by simply dividing the budgeted quantity of overhead costs by the budgeted quantity of the activity used to allocate overhead (e.g., direct labor hours). However, this approach is often a gross simplification of complex overhead costs. In a later lesson, we'll examine the challenges of building and using overhead cost allocation rates.

III. Capturing Data for Standards

A. Where do the data come from that are used to build standard prices and standard quantities? Often, the organization will begin by pulling historical data from its own records to compute averages. This is a reasonable way to begin the analysis, but managers need to forecast what may change in the future with respect to prices of materials and labor, as well as quantities of materials and labor used in production.

B. Of the two cost inputs used for standards, prices and quantities, the most difficult standard to accurately compute is quantities. The production process in most organizations is complex, involving many activities that support and impact the direct labor that forms the final product or service.

1. Due to this complexity, managers and cost accountants often engage in a careful analysis of all activities involved in producing or supporting the final product or service.

2. This activity analysis is the basis of activity-based costing (ABC), which will be examined in a later lesson.

IV. Budgetary Slack and Goal Congruence

A. Most organizations choose to follow a participative, rather than authoritative, approach to budgeting. This bottom-up approach that involves lower-level managers has a number of advantages that we've examined in an earlier lesson.

B. However, the bottom-up (participative) approach to budgeting assumes that everyone involved in establishing cost standards share the same goals and objectives. This important concept is called *goal congruence*.

1. When the performance of managers is evaluated using the same cost standards that go into the budget, these managers are personally at risk from outside factors that can create unfavorable results that are outside of their control. In this situation, the organization will not have a high level of goal congruence.

2. When the performance evaluation and compensation of managers who help to establish cost standards are at risk, then managers are tempted to build slack into their estimates.

Budgetary slack has been mentioned in an earlier lesson, but this crucial concept is clearer in the context of setting cost standards as we've discussed in this lesson.

C. Reducing budgetary slack in the budgeting process is handled by (1) limiting performance evaluation to controllable costs, and by (2) periodically reviewing and adjusting the budget when outside factors cause the original cost standards to become less representative or irrelevant.

Practice Question

Interpretive Dimensions provides sign language interpreters for major business conferences. A typical business conference day involves six hours of presentations with four half-hour breaks. Providing sign language support generally requires two interpreters each working in 15-minute shifts while the other interpreter rests. Set-up time (coordinating with conference hosts and setting up the physical space) at the beginning of each day requires about an hour. Interpreters are paid an hourly rate of $30. Fringe benefits are estimated to be 30% of wages, and payroll taxes amount to 10% of wages.

Determine the standard cost of sign language labor to support a business conference day.

Answer

Quantity Standard — Sign Language Interpreters	Hours per Day
Presentation time	6.00
Allowed time for breaks (4 × .5)	2.00
Set-up time	1.00
Time per Interpreter	9.00
Number of interpreter	× 2
Standard Quantity per Unit	**18.00**

Price Standard — Sign Language Interpreters	Price per Hour
Hourly wage rate	$ 30.00
Fringe benefits (30%)	9.00
Payroll taxes (10%)	3.00
Standard Price per Hour	**$ 42.00**

Standard Cost Sheet

	Input Quantity	Cost per Input	Cost per Day
Total Labor Cost per Conference Day	18.0 hours	$42.00 per hour	**$756.00**

Summary

Standard costs can be developed and reported using an approach that approximates a "recipe card." Standard costs are developed by determining expected quantity of inputs used, and then multiplying that quantity by the expected price of each input. In setting these standard quantities and standard prices, organizations choose to use ideal (theoretical) standards or attainable (practical) standards. Ideal standards are generally created in top-down budgeting and are less prone to error and bias than attainable standards that are created in bottom-up budgeting. Using the insight and information held by involved employees, attainable standards are based on more reasonable assumptions. However, attainable standards will often have some amount of budgetary slack built into the quantity and price estimates by managers who are subsequently evaluated based on their ability to achieve the budget.

Topic 3. Forecasting Techniques

Regression Analysis

After studying this lesson, you should be able to:

- Demonstrate an understanding of a simple regression equation (1.B.3.a).

- Define a multiple regression equation and recognize when multiple regression is an appropriate tool to use for forecasting (1.B.3.b).

- Calculate the result of a simple regression equation (1.B.3.c).

Forecasting is a crucial aspect of budget planning. Regression analysis is a popular tool to evaluate past cost data in order to identify possible cost drivers that can be used to forecast (estimate) future costs. This lesson will provide an overview of how to use the results of a regression analysis to estimate variable and fixed costs, and to build a cost equation to forecast a range of future costs.

I. Forecasting

    A. Budgeting is about planning for the future. Managers need to forecast many variables when planning for the future, including costs, prices, production, demand, etc.

    B. Forecasting is not the same as budget planning. Budgets, however, should be based on accurate forecasts.

    C. Accountants value conservatism in making estimates and measuring value. However, this does not mean that a conservative approach should be reflected in the budget. Accurate forecasts, not conservative forecasts, are key to successful budgeting.

II. Simple Regression Analysis

    A. Regression analysis tools can be useful when forecasting costs. Regression analysis is a statistical tool used to highlight patterns in historical cost data. Managers can then use insights gathered from the analysis of past data to forecast future costs.

    B. Consider the data below for eight quarters of production at a windsurfing board manufacturing plant.

Seabreeze, Inc.

Quarter	Boards	Cost
1	105	$111,300
2	128	$168,750
3	185	$159,000
4	245	$210,145
5	211	$226,200
6	152	$235,250
7	129	$105,700
8	168	$241,500

    Simple regression analysis (sometimes called single linear regression analysis) can be used to explore these data to see if there is a relationship between the production of boards and the costs in the manufacturing plant.

    C. Before computing the regression analysis, a scatterplot can be used to visually inspect the data. Plotting the manufacturing costs on the y-axis and the volume of boards produced on the x-axis, the scatterplot shown below demonstrates a cost relationship.

123

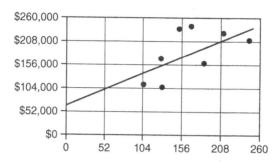

Notice that a line has been drawn through the data points. The line is "fitted" to minimize the average squared distance between each of the data points. The purpose of the line is to represent the relationship, on average, between costs and boards.

D. In fact, the line in the scatterplot above was fitted using a regression analysis tool in Excel™. The regression analysis result is displayed below.

Simple Regression Results

	Coefficients	Standard Error	t Stat	P-value	Lower 95%	Upper 95%	Lower 80%	Upper 80%
Intercept	$66,049	$64,422	1.03	0.34	($91,585)	$223,683	($26,702)	$158,801
Boards	$703	$377	1.87	0.11	($219)	$1,624	$160	$1,245

E. The first column in the regression results above, Coefficients, reports the intercept and the slope (based on the volume of boards) for the regression line in the scatterplot displayed earlier. Remember the traditional equation for a straight line?

$$y = mx + b$$

The intercept (b) represents the total fixed costs in the data, and the slope (m) represents the variable costs per board. The equation above can be used to represent an equation for total costs in the manufacturing plant as follows.

Total costs = Variable cost rate(Boards) + Total fixed costs

Total costs = $703(Boards) + $66,049

III. Statistical Significance

A. The simple regression results, which provide a total cost equation for the board manufacturer, are not at all precise. That is, the variable cost rate is not exactly $703, and total fixed costs are not exactly $66,049. Note that the simple regression results reported above include a statistical analysis of the cost estimates.

B. Total fixed costs (the regression intercept) has a standard error of $64,422. Assuming these are normally distributed data, this means that there is approximately a 68% probability that the actual fixed costs in this dataset fall within $64,422 of the original estimate of $66,049. In other words, the actual cost is somewhere between $1,627 and $130,471 ($66,049 ± $64,422). That's a very wide cost estimate range—probably too wide to be useful for budget planning purposes. And note that there is approximately a 32% probability (100% – 68%) that the actual fixed cost is outside of this wide range!

C. The regression analysis estimate for total fixed costs in this example is not very precise, as seen in the very large standard error of $64,422. This imprecision is also demonstrated in the t-Stat and P-value of 1.03 and 0.34, respectively. Acceptable statistical significance, which relates to the precision, traditionally demands a t-Stat above 2 (above 3 is preferred) and a P-value below 0.10 (below 0.05 is preferred).

D. The simple regression results also provide a set of confidence intervals. In the results reported above, there is a 95% probability that actual fixed costs are between *negative* $91,585 and *positive* $223,683. In other words, we can't say with 95% confidence that there actually exist any fixed costs in this organization! Similarly, the 80% confidence interval is crossing into the negative range, indicating that we don't have even 80% confidence in the existence of fixed costs for this organization (based on these eight quarters of data).

E. The statistical report on the $703 variable cost rate is better than the statistical report on the total fixed costs, though not much better. The standard error at $377, compared to the $703 estimate, is more precise than the total fixed cost error. The t-stat (1.87) and p-value (0.11) are getting close to the minimum 2.0 and 0.10, respectively. However, we can't say with 95% confidence that there is a variable cost rate in these data (based on the lower 95% estimate that crosses over to a negative number). We can say with 80% confidence that the variable cost rate is between $160 and $1,245 per board. Again, though, that range is probably too wide to be useful in budget planning.

IV. Practical Significance

A. The regression analysis tool in Excel™ provides additional statistics we can use to evaluate the usefulness of the overall data analysis. Even though the individual cost measures (variable cost rate and total fixed costs) are not very precise, the total cost equation may still be useful for forecasting total costs. Remember the total cost equation for the board manufacturer is:

Total costs = $703(Boards) + $66,049

B. The report on regression statistics below provides three measures that indicate the practical usefulness, sometimes called the practical significance, of the total cost equation for the board manufacturer.

Regression Statistics

Multiple R	0.61
R Square	0.37
Adjusted R Square	0.26
Standard Error	$46,665
Observations	8

1. The Multiple R statistic of 0.61 is the simple correlation of total costs and volume of boards. In other words, there is a 61% correlation between these two numbers. In this dataset, for example, when the volume of boards goes up 10%, then the total costs goes up 6.1% (10% × 61%). However, this correlation is limited to the dataset. It doesn't mean that *future* manufacturing costs and the volume of board production will have a 61% correlation.

2. The R Square of 0.37 indicates how much we understand about total costs in the dataset based on the volume of board production in the dataset. The 0.37 statistic means that variance (change) in the board production explains 37% of the variance (change) in manufacturing costs. Conversely, 63% (100% − 37%) of the cost variance can't be explained. Further, the Adjusted R Square of 0.26 is actually a more appropriate measure to use when explaining variance in the cost data. This statistic essentially adjusts the results for the size of the dataset. Remember that we only have eight quarters of data in this set, which isn't a lot of data.

3. Finally, the $46,665 reported above is the Standard Error for the total cost equation. This is similar to the standard error for the intercept (total fixed costs) and for the slope (variable cost rate), but this standard error relates to the total cost that managers forecast using the total cost equation. For example, if managers plan to produce 175 boards in the next quarter, then the total costs would be forecast as follows:

Total costs = $703(175 Boards) + $66,049 = $189,074

Again, remember that this solution can't be used precisely. It needs to be adjusted based on the standard error. Hence, based on a plan to produce 175 boards, managers would forecast total costs between \$142,409 and \$235,739 (\$189,074 ± \$46,665), but only with about 68% confidence. That's not very precise.

V. Using Multiple Regression Analysis

A. The simple regression analysis results above are not going to be very useful for accurate forecasting of costs. It's important that managers understand the wide variance in the cost estimates for the board manufacturer, and not over-rely on the numbers for budget planning. Otherwise, the budget is not going to be helpful to plan, control, and evaluate operations.

B. What's needed to improve the forecast is more data and better data about what drives cost for this organization. In most organizations, costs are impacted by many different activities. Simple regression analysis, however, uses only one activity to predict costs. Conversely, multiple regression analysis can use many activities to help managers understand and forecast costs.

C. Consider the dataset below for a new regression analysis example. These data represent 24 semesters of activities and costs for a university (most of the data are not displayed in order to save room in the exhibit).

Montgomery University

Semester	Students Enrolled	Sections Taught	Courses Listed	Total University Costs
Fall 06	28,874	7,065	2,670	\$117,160,456
Spring 07	29,091	6,775	2,670	\$117,352,268
Fall 07	28,621	6,232	2,628	\$115,928,777
Spring 08	27,310	6,833	2,678	\$116,889,599
⋮	⋮	⋮	⋮	⋮
Fall 16	29,374	7,521	3,030	\$127,352,245
Spring 17	32,227	7,258	2,820	\$128,577,777
Fall 17	31,263	7,249	2,817	\$128,408,000
Spring 18	29,197	7,142	2,876	\$129,436,179

D. In the exhibit above we have data on the number of students enrolled, the number of sections taught, and the number of courses listed and available in the general catalog for the university. We also have the total costs semester-by-semester at this university. Which of these activities is driving costs? Of course, it is very likely all three of these activities are cost drivers for the university, but we can use statistics to explore these three cost relationships.

E. Using the regression analysis tool in Excel™, a multiple regression analysis of the data above is provided below.

Multiple Regression Results

	Coefficients	Standard Error	t Stat	P-value	Lower 95%	Upper 95%	Lower 80%	Upper 80%
Intercept	\$19,464,902	\$18,869,075	1.03	0.31	(\$19,895,299)	\$58,825,103	(\$5,543,051)	\$44,472,855
Students Enrolled	\$1,045	\$596	1.75	0.09	(\$198)	\$2,287	\$255	\$1,834
Sections Taught	\$4,159	\$1,451	2.87	0.01	\$1,132	\$7,186	\$2,236	\$6,082
Courses Listed	\$15,778	\$5,529	2.85	0.01	\$4,245	\$27,311	\$8,451	\$23,106

Based on the Coefficients displayed in the first column above, the total cost equation for the university is:

Total costs = \$1,045(Students) + \$4,159(Sections) + \$15,778(Courses) + \$19,464,902

F. Compared to the board manufacturing example, these regression analysis results are generally more precise, which is better for forecasting purposes. However, the total fixed costs estimate (the Intercept) is not at all precise with a standard error ($18,869,075) that is nearly as large as the cost estimate itself ($19,464,902). The t-Stat for fixed costs is much less than 2, and the P-value is much more than 0.10. As well, the confidence intervals at both 95% and 80% are crossing into the negative range.

G. On the other hand, the estimates for the three variable cost rates are better, though somewhat weak in precision for the variable cost per student enrolled ($1,045).

H. Taken all together, the cost estimates form a useful total cost equation, based on the regression statistics reported below.

Regression Statistics

Multiple R	0.83
R Square	0.68
Adjusted R Square	0.64
Standard Error	$2,698,662
Observations	24

With an Adjusted R Square statistic of 0.64, the cost estimates in the analysis are explaining 64% of the variance in total costs in the dataset.

I. Finally, managers can use the Standard Error ($2,698,662) to forecast total costs. For example, if the university budget is planned next semester for 29,500 enrolled students, to teach 7,100 sections, and to have 2,800 courses available for students, the total cost equation would be:

$$\text{Total costs} = \$1,045(29,500) + \$4,159(7,100) + \$15,778(2,800) + \$19,464,902$$
$$= \$123,999,702$$

1. Based on the $2,698,662 Standard Error, budget managers could predict the total costs to range from $121,301,040 to $126,698,364 (= $123,999,702 ± $2,698,662). They should be approximately 68% confident in forecasting that the actual costs next semester will fall within that range.

2. It is likely that budget managers want higher confidence in forecasting a budgeted cost range than 68%. Using statistics, a different confidence interval can be established, but it requires a wider range for the forecast. The formula to adjust the confidence range precisely is beyond the scope of this lesson. However, if it can be assumed that the activity and cost data follow a normal distribution pattern, then simply doubling the Standard Error will provide a confidence interval with approximately 95% probability.

$$95\% \text{ Confidence Interval} = \$123,999,702 \pm (2 \times \$2,698,662)$$
$$= \$118,602,378 \text{ to } \$129,397,026$$

Practice Question

Press Publishing Corporation has two major magazines: *Star Life* and *Weekly News*. The budgeting team needs to forecast monthly production costs for next year based on the volume of magazines produced and sold. A simple regression analysis was performed on last year's monthly data for each magazine, and is reported below.

Continues...

Regression Analysis for *Star Life* Magazine

	Coefficients	Standard Error	t Stat	P-value	Lower 95%	Upper 95%	Lower 80%	Upper 80%
Intercept	$70,966	$4,711	15.07	0.00	$60,471	$81,462	$64,503	$77,430
Copies	$0.26	$0.02	14.47	0.00	$0.22	$0.30	$0.24	$0.29

Multiple R	0.98
Adjusted R Square	0.95
Standard Error	$4,621
Observations	12

Regression Analysis for *Weekly News* Magazine

	Coefficients	Standard Error	t Stat	P-value	Lower 95%	Upper 95%	Lower 80%	Upper 80%
Intercept	$44,917	$4,016	11.18	0.00	$35,969	$53,866	$39,406	$50,428
Copies	$0.42	$0.02	19.27	0.00	$0.38	$0.47	$0.39	$0.45

Multiple R	0.99
Adjusted R Square	0.97
Standard Error	$3,898
Observations	12

What is the total cost equation for each magazine, and how much of the cost variance is being explained by the volume of magazine copies produced?

Answer

Star Life Magazine: Total costs = $0.26(Copies) + $70,966 per month

95% of the variance in production costs is explained by the volume of magazine copies.

Weekly News Magazine: Total costs = $0.42(Copies) + $44,917 per month

97% of the variance in production costs is explained by the volume of magazine copies.

Summary

Managers need to make forecasts of future costs in order to build the budget. Regression analysis is one useful tool for analyzing past costs and related activity (i.e., cost drivers) to identify variable cost and fixed cost estimates. There are a number of statistical tools that can be used to perform regression analysis, including the regression analysis tool in Excel™. A regression analysis will produce coefficients (estimates) of the intercept (total fixed costs) and slope (variable cost rate) for a line that is fitted to past data. However, while the initial coefficients are precise numbers, these estimates need to be evaluated for statistical significance and adjusted for standard errors to establish a forecast range of cost estimates.

Expected Value Computations and Learning Curve Analysis

After studying this lesson, you should be able to:

- Calculate the expected value of random variables (1.B.3.g).

- Identify the benefits and shortcomings of expected value techniques (1.B.3.h).

- Use probability values to estimate future cash flows (1.B.3.i).

- Demonstrate an understanding of learning curve analysis (1.B.3.d).

- Calculate the results under a cumulative average-time learning model (1.B.3.e).

- List the benefits and shortcomings of regression analysis and learning curve analysis (1.B.3.f).

Regression analysis is focused on *past* data to identify cost patterns for managers to use in forecasting the future. In this lesson, we'll learn about two alternative tools that directly focus on *future* expectations, which can be even more useful to managers for forecasting purposes. Expected value computations combine several possible future outcomes to forecast an expected future value of all possible outcomes. Learning curve analysis captures expected learning improvements in the organization's processes and costs to forecast a moving average of future costs.

I. Probability and Uncertainty

    A. Budgeting is about planning for the future, and the future is uncertain. Managing and making decisions in an uncertain environment is a fundamental fact of business.

    B. Uncertainty is particularly an issue when forecasting. In previous lessons, we have discussed outside factors that create uncertainty in the organization's environment. These factors include:

        1. External opportunities and threats as represented in SWOT analysis

        2. Uncontrollable factors involving politics, the economy, social trends, technology, legal developments, and environment issues as represented in PESTLE analysis

        3. Competitive forces such as supplier power, customer power, threat of entrants and substitute products in the competitive space, and the overall intensity of competition as represented in Porter's Five Forces

II. Expected Value Computations

    A. Regression analysis explores past data to identify possible trends in costs or in any other factors that need to be forecasted for budget planning. However, the result of regression analysis on costs, for example, is limited in that it represents a forecast of a single set of cost data.

    B. When managers are facing multiple possible future outcomes, it's risky to forecast and base the budget on a single possible outcome. Alternatively, managers can mathematically "combine" several outcomes to form an "expected value" based on all possible outcomes, weighted by their respective probabilities.

    C. The formula for the expected value of a set of possible outcomes is:

$$EV = \sum (rp)$$

    where r = result of the outcome, and p = probability of the outcome. (Remember that the Greek sign $\sum$ represents "sum up.")

    D. For example, in a budget planning process it is estimated that the fixed costs next year for a division will be $200,000. However, there is a 10% probability the fixed costs could be as low as

$150,000. There is also a 20% probability that fixed costs would be as high as $300,000. The expected value of fixed costs next year would be computed as follows:

Expected Value Computation

Outcome	Result	Probability	Weighted Value
1	$200,000	70%	$140,000
2	$150,000	10%	$15,000
3	$300,000	20%	$60,000
Expected Value =		100%	$215,000

Note that the total probability must add up to 100%. Hence, if there is a 10% probability of Outcome 2 and a 20% probability of Outcome 3, then the original forecast (Outcome 1) must have a 70% probability.

E. In the example above, the expected value of fixed costs next year is $215,000. This amount represents a rational combination of management expectations, and can be used as the forecast for next year.

III. Benefits and Shortcomings of Expected Value Computations

    A. There are several benefits of expected value computations.

        1. Expected value computations that incorporate multiple possibilities are generally more representative of an uncertain future compared to forecasts of a single possible outcome.

        2. Further, the expected value computation reduces multiple outcomes down to a single value, which is easily understood and can be entered into a budget plan.

    B. On the other hand, expected value computations have some shortcomings.

        1. While the EV formula itself is an unbiased and rational combination of alternative outcomes, the underlying probabilities used in the formula are usually based on subjective judgments.

        2. The result of the EV formula is *not* the most likely outcome in the future. It is a weighted average of the possible results used in the computation. This shortcoming is particularly important if the possible outcomes are discrete events (rather than a continuous range of possibilities).

Practice Question

Marokov Corporation is trying to forecast the effect of an upcoming environmental regulation on the variable costs of one of their key products. The regulation is still being debated in the legislature. There is a 50% chance that the regulation will not be released in time to affect next year's variable costs. Marokov management expects that the regulation, when it is released, is equally likely to increase variable costs by either 5% or 10%. Currently, the product's variable costs are $140 per unit.

Based on these expectations, what is the expected variable cost for Marokov's key product next year?

Answer

There are three possible outcomes in this forecast analysis. There is a 50% probability that regulation will not be released in time and the costs next year will be unchanged at $140 per unit. And there is a 50% probability that the regulation will be released in time to change next year's variable costs. Since the regulation is equally likely (50:50 probability) to increase costs by either 5% or 10%, then there is a 25% probability (50% × 50%) the variable costs will be $147 per unit ($140 × 1.05), and a 25% probability that the variable costs will be $154 per unit ($140 × 1.10). As computed below, the expected value of these three possible outcomes is $145.25.

Continues...

Expected Value Computation

Outcome	Result	Probability	Weighted Value
Unchanged	$140,000	50%	$70,000
5% Increase	$147,000	25%	$36,000
10% Increase	$154,000	25%	$38,000
Expected Value =		**100%**	**$145,000**

IV. Learning Curve Analysis

    A. Not only are there uncertain outcomes in the organization's external environment, but its internal workplace is dynamic and changing as well. As the organization's workforce gains experience with products and processes, both individuals and the organization learn how to work better (faster throughput, higher quality, etc.).

    B. Learning improvements in the organization take place based on individual training and experience, improved process methods, more advanced tools and technology, innovations on product design, and better supervision. As a result, productivity will improve and costs will reduce over time.

    C. The nature of learning is that it "curves." That is, learning results in the biggest improvements in the beginning, and then learning (and improvement) becomes smaller over time until learning is essentially "flat."

    D. One common approach to learning curves is defined in terms of cumulative averages of time or cost that reduce by a constant percentage over time. The key factor to understand is that the analysis is focused on improvements in *cumulative averages* rather than on the individual improvement for each unit of output.

    E. The concept is that as output doubles, the cumulative average time or cost of the total output is reduced by a constant percentage. For example, assume that a newly hired employee in a bicycle shop can produce her first bike in 3 hours, but gets faster as shown in the production chart below.

Production Chart

Total Quantity	Average Hours per Bike	Total Time
1 bike	3.00 hours	3.0 hours
2 bikes	2.40 hours	4.8 hours
4 bikes	1.92 hours	7.7 hours
8 bikes	1.54 hours	12.3 hours

Note that as the total quantity of production doubles, the average hours per bike is reduced by 20%. This pattern is called an 80% cumulative learning trend since the cumulative average hours per bicycle for any production quantity level can be multiplied by 80% to establish the employee's cumulative average when the production quantity is doubled.

F. The cumulative learning rate in the example can be illustrated as a learning curve, as shown below.

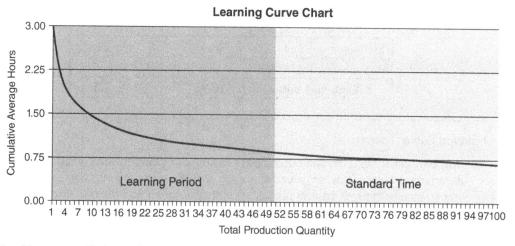

1. Managers will determine a point in the learning curve when the rate of learning is basically flattened out. At that point, a constant standard cost can be set. Before that point, the organization must anticipate a declining rate of change in the cost standard across a range of production. This range is called the "learning period."

2. In the learning curve above, the rate of learning for this employee has flattened out at a volume level of about 50 total bicycles produced. At this point, budget planners can establish a standard time of approximately 45 minutes (0.75 hours) per bike. This will become the standard quantity of time per bike once the employee has produced 50 or more bikes.

G. Computing the cumulative average is done with a short but somewhat complicated formula.

$$Y = aX^b$$

where Y = cumulative average per unit

a = time required for first unit

X = cumulative number of units

b = ln learning curve % ÷ ln 2

(*Note*: "ln" indicates the natural log.)

H. Computing the cumulative average per unit can also be easily calculated by hand, *but only at production levels that double from the previous production level*, as demonstrated in the chart below.

80% Cumulative Average Time Computation

Total Quantity	80% Computation	Cumulative Average Hours per Bike	Total Time
1 bike		3.00 hours	3.0 hrs
2 bikes	3.00 × 80% =	2.40 hours	4.8 hrs
3 bikes	?	? hours	? hrs
4 bikes	2.40 × 80% =	1.92 hours	7.7 hrs
5 bikes	?	? hours	? hrs
6 bikes	?	? hours	? hrs
7 bikes	?	? hours	? hrs
8 bikes	1.92 × 80% =	1.54 hours	12.3 hrs

As can be seen above, this shortcut method can only compute the cumulative average hours at production levels where total quantity produced has doubled from the previous level. Also note that Total Time (total production time) is computed as follows: Total Quantity × Cumulative Average Hours per Bike.

I. The learning curve discussion so far has focused on forecasting improvements to production time. Remember that budgets must eventually measure costs. Standard costs per unit of output are a function of input quantity multiplied by input price. Hence, if production time (i.e., labor quantity) is forecasted to improve, then the standard labor cost per unit of output should be reduced over time.

J. Learning curve analysis can also be applied to other organization factors besides production time, such as production defect rates, levels of product or service quality, etc.

V. Benefits and Shortcomings of Learning Curve Analysis

A. When forecasting costs, learning curve analysis provides several benefits versus regression analysis.

1. Regression analysis searches for cost patterns in past data. But learning curve analysis is anticipating movement in future costs by recognizing that the organization is learning and becoming more efficient with its processes.

2. By anticipating where costs are moving, organizations can establish more relevant budgets with appropriate stretch targets. Organizations can also predict and set more aggressive market pricing based on expected learning curves.

B. On the other hand, learning curve analysis has some shortcomings.

1. A fundamental assumption of learning curve analysis is that the learning rate is assumed to be constant. This may or may not be true. In particular, outside factors as depicted in SWOT and PESTLE analysis, as well as in Porter's Five Forces, can create sudden and significant shifts in human learning and behavior inside the organization.

2. Learning curve analysis is focused on human learning and behavior. Hence, learning curve analysis may not be relevant to more machine-intensive processes.

Practice Question

The budget planning team at the Fancy Furniture Company decided to start a new product line of dining chairs. When the production line started, it took 10 hours to make the first batch of six chairs. The learning rate is estimated to be 90%.

Forecast the cumulative average time per batch to make the first four batches of chairs. What will be the total production time to make these four batches of chairs?

Answer

Using the formula $Y = aX^b$

$a = 10$ hours

$X = 4$ batches

$b = \ln 90\% \div \ln 2 = -0.152$

$10(4^{-0.152}) = 8.1$ cumulative average hours per batch for the first four batches

4 batches × 8.1 hours = 32.4 total hours for all four batches

Alternatively, using the short-cut approach:

90% Cumulative Average Time Computation

Total Quantity	90% Computation	Cumulative Average Hours per Batch	Total Time
1 batch		10.0 hours	10.0 hrs
2 batches	10.0 × 90% =	9.0 hours	18.0 hrs
4 batches	**9.0 × 90% =**	**8.1 hours**	**32.4 hrs**

Summary

Managers are challenged in the budget planning process to make forecasts about the future. Regression analysis explores past data to identify a single cost pattern that may or may exist in the future. On the other hand, expected value computations can explore and combine several possible future outcomes by determining the cost result of each outcome and multiplying that outcome by its expected probability. The formula for the expected value computation is $EV = \Sigma(rp)$. Learning curve analysis provides a more sophisticated approach to anticipating cost patterns in the future. Learning curve analysis establishes a learning rate that provides managers with a method to predict cost efficiencies as the organization gains experience working with internal processes. The formula for learning curve analysis provides the cumulative average input quantity (e.g., labor time) for the total production to date. The formula is $Y = aX^b$. As a shortcut, learning curve analysis can be approximated by multiplying the cumulative average input quantity by the learning curve rate to determine the new cumulative average input quantity, but only at production levels where the output doubles.

Topic 5. Annual Profit Plan and Supporting Schedules

Sales Budgets and Production Budgets

After studying this lesson, you should be able to:

- Explain the role of the sales budget in the development of an annual profit plan (1.B.5.a).

- Identify the factors that should be considered when preparing a sales forecast (1.B.5.b).

- Identify the components of a sales budget and prepare a sales budget (1.B.5.c).

- Explain the relationship between the sales budget and the production budget (1.B.5.d).

- Identify the role that inventory levels play in the preparation of a production budget and define other factors that should be considered when preparing a production budget (1.B.5.e).

- Prepare a production budget (1.B.5.f).

Note that we are delaying our discussion of Topic 4 involving specific budgeting tools and methodologies until after we've established the purpose and process of the traditional master budgeting system here in Topic 5.

This lesson introduces the "big picture" that is the master budget for the organization. This master budget demonstrates the relationship between strategy and budget schedules. The core of the master budget is the operational budget, which is driven by the sales budget schedule. In this lesson, we focus on the specifics of building a sales budget, followed by the production budget.

I. Budgeting is Personal

   A. Good budgeting skills are important. Organizations that are good at operational budgeting have similar characteristics as individuals who are good at personal budgeting.

      1. These characteristics include being disciplined, organized, flexible, proactive, and goal orientated.

      2. Strong communication skills are also paramount when the budget is used to guide an organization, whether it be a company or a household.

   B. Successful budgeting is a function of having both good budgeting skills and a good budgeting system. Beginning with this lesson, we will work on defining the structure of good budgeting systems.

II. The Master Budget System

   A. Operational budgeting involves the creation and coordination of many interrelated budget schedules. Keeping track of these schedules and how they work together to support short-term operating objectives and long-term strategic objectives requires seeing the "big picture" of the master budget system.

   B. The exhibit below illustrates the master budget system. This exhibit will be very important to understanding the budget schedules and pro forma statements described in this lesson, as well as the next several subsequent lessons. Be sure to refer to this exhibit as the "big picture" view here, and for the next several lessons.

THE MASTER BUDGET

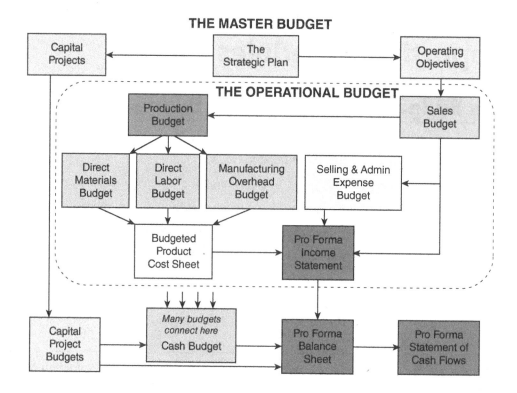

C. At the top of the master budget is the organization's strategic plan. That plan, as we've discussed in previous lessons, drives both the strategy-focused allocation of resources to long-term capital projects, and the strategy-focused deployment of spending and employees to short-term operating objectives.

D. Beginning with the sales budget schedule, the operational budget establishes an operational path to the pro forma income statement. (Note that *pro forma* essentially means *budgeted*.) The sales budget is the key driving force for the overall operational budget.

E. If the company is a manufacturing or service organization, the next schedule in the operational budget is the production budget, which then determines the three product cost budgets for direct materials, direct labor, and manufacturing (production) overhead.

1. Remember that the cost structure for service organizations is very similar to manufacturing organizations. The "product" is a service for the client that is produced using labor and overhead, as well as, for certain service organizations, some materials or supplies.

2. Merchandising organizations do not create the product they sell. Instead of a production budget, these organizations will use a purchasing budget, which does *not* subsequently lead to budgets for direct materials, direct labor, and manufacturing overhead.

F. A budgeted product cost sheet, which specifies the standard input costs (quantity and price) for each product, summarizes the product costs used to establish cost of goods sold for the pro forma income statement.

G. In addition to budgeted product costs, the pro forma income statement also needs budgeted selling and administrative expenses (sometimes called selling, general, and administrative expenses). The selling and administrative expense budget is driven directly by the sales budget.

H. The pro forma income statement, sometimes called the budgeted statement of operations, completes the overall operational budget. The pro forma balance sheet and pro forma statement of cash flows then follow (and flow from) the pro forma income statement.

I. The cash budget is different from the pro forma statement of cash flows. We'll discuss these differences in a later lesson. Overall, the statement of cash flows is used to "translate" accrual accounting into cash flows while the cash budget is focused more directly on cash management.

J. The capital projects budget is where the long-term strategic spending is planned and managed. These investment expenditures are carried forward into the organization's cash budget.

K. Beginning with the sales budget, the structure of each budget will be demonstrated using the example of a manufacturer of custom wood-built rowboats called the Sunbird Boat Company.

III. The Sales Budget

A. Remember that accurate forecasting is crucial to successful budgeting. The most challenging forecasting work in the organization is done for the sales budget (also called the revenue budget).

B. The sales budget itself looks fairly straightforward. As demonstrated in the budget below for the Sunbird Boat Company, the sales budget is a simple composition of volume × price.

Sales Budget

	Q1	Q2	Q3	Q4	Total
Sales Volume	20 boats	60 boats	40 boats	30 boats	150 boats
× Price	$4,200	$4,200	$4,200	$4,200	$4,200
Revenue	$84,000	$252,000	$168,000	$126,000	$630,000

1. However, volume and price measures (statistics) are not independent. This fact complicates the forecast work since sales volume and sales price interact with each other (and, for some industries, interact very strongly).

2. Depending on the nature of the price economics in the boat industry in this example operational budget, increasing prices can actually shift sales volumes either up or down. [*Note*: The economics of sale price management is explored in a separate lesson in Part 2 Section C.]

C. Organizations generally have more ability to control expenses compared to controlling revenue. Hence, sales volumes and prices that make up revenue need to be carefully forecasted. Sales prices and sales volumes are impacted significantly by many external factors that have been described in earlier lessons using models like SWOT, PESTLE, and Porter's Five Forces.

D. Organizations invest significant time and resources researching the market industry, economic environment, and competitive landscape to reduce the uncertainty around the sales forecast. Common tools employed include:

1. Cross-functional research teams

2. External consultants

3. Market surveys

4. Customer-focus groups

5. Leading economic indicators

6. Test markets in controlled (or isolated) regions and customer groups

7. Sophisticated analysis of large internal and external data sets (sometimes called big data analytics)

IV. The Production Budget

A. For some organizations, the production budget may be relatively simple to assemble once the sales budget is complete. Whatever is needed for the budgeted sales volume is then scheduled to be produced.

B. However, inventory complicates the relationship between these two budgets. Organizations typically use inventory as a "cushion" against unexpected or uncontrollable sales or production events. When organizations must hold inventory, the result is that the budgeted sales volume will *not* equal the budgeted production volume.

C. When inventory is present in the budget, the relationship between sales volume and production volume is:

Sales volume + Ending inventory − Beginning inventory = Production volume

Remember that one production period's ending inventory level becomes the next production period's beginning inventory level. Inventory levels are established according to budget policy.

D. Consider the production budget below for the Sunbird Boat Company.

Production Budget

	Q1	Q2	Q3	Q4	Total
Sales Volume	20 boats	60 boats	40 boats	30 boats	150 boats
Planned Ending Inventory	24 boats	16 boats	12 boats	16 boats	16 boats
Boats Needed	44 boats	76 boats	52 boats	46 boats	166 boats
Less Beginning Inventory	(10 boats)	(24 boats)	(16 boats)	(12 boats)	(10 boats)
Production Volume	34 boats	52 boats	36 boats	34 boats	156 boats

1. Note that sales volume in the first row has been carried forward from the sales budget.

2. Sunbird management has a budget policy of planning for ending inventory levels equal to 40% of the following quarter's sales volume needs. This pattern is demonstrated above in the second row. Since the planned ending inventory for Q4 (Quarter 4) is 16 boats, management must be forecasting the following year's Q1 sales volume to be 40 boats (16 boats ÷ 40%).

3. The sales volume plus ending inventory determines the number of boats needed for the quarter. To determine the budgeted production volume, the number of boats needed is reduced by the boats on hand at the beginning of the quarter (the beginning inventory level). It is important to see that the beginning inventory level in one quarter is the ending inventory level in the previous quarter. Since the planned beginning inventory for upcoming Q1 is 10 boats, management must be planning to end the current year with 10 boats on hand.

E. Be sure to take the time you need to understand how inventory levels are adjusting Sunbird's budgeted sales volume to determine its budgeted production volume.

F. Finally, note that the bottom line of the production budget is *not* a dollar amount. It is stated in terms of production units. The organization can't simply multiply the budgeted production volume by a cost per unit (as is done with the budgeted sales volume multiplied by price per unit). There are three types of costs involved in the production process, each requiring its own budget (direct materials, direct labor, and manufacturing overhead). We'll study these budgets in the next lesson.

Practice Question

The sales forecast for birdhouses built by Ryan Enterprises is provided below.

Sales Forecast

	Q1	Q2	Q3	Q4	Total
Volume	10,000	30,000	35,000	50,000	125,000

The company uses a budget policy of maintaining an ending inventory of 20% of the next quarter's sales. Due to some unexpected events, the production manager expects to end the current year with an inventory of 10,000 birdhouses.

Prepare a quarterly production budget. Assume that the sales forecast for the first quarter of the following year is the same as the first-quarter forecast for this upcoming year.

Continues…

Answer

Production Budget

	Q1	Q2	Q3	Q4	Total
Sales Volume	10,000	30,000	35,000	50,000	125,000
Planned End. Inventory	6,000	7,000	10,000	2,000	2,000
Units Needed	16,000	37,000	45,000	52,000	127,000
Less Beg. Inventory	(10,000)	(6,000)	(7,000)	(10,000)	(10,000)
Production Volume	6,000	31,000	38,000	42,000	117,000

Summary

The master budget is introduced in this lesson, which is effectively a "big picture map" of the organization's entire budgeting system. Be sure to study this master budget diagram to understand how the individual budget schedules interconnect together to support the organization's strategy. A crucial subset of the master budget is the operational budget, which is driven by the sales budget schedule. The sales budget requires significant forecasting effort to determine the expected sales volume and sales price that then determine budgeted sales revenue. Following the sales budget is the production budget schedule. Most organizations plan to maintain inventory levels. When they do, the production budget formula is: sales volume + ending inventory – beginning inventory = production volume.

Budgeting for Production Costs

After studying this lesson, you should be able to:

- Demonstrate an understanding of the relationship between the direct materials budget, the direct labor budget, and the production budget (1.B.5.g).
- Explain how inventory levels and procurement policies affect the direct materials budget (1.B.5.h).
- Prepare direct materials and direct labor budgets based on relevant information and evaluate the feasibility of achieving production goals on the basis of these budgets (1.B.5.i).
- Demonstrate an understanding of the relationship between the overhead budget and the production budget (1.B.5.j).
- Separate costs into their fixed and variable components (1.B.5.k).
- Prepare an overhead budget (1.B.5.l).

This lesson continues the Sunbird Boat Company example from the previous lesson to describe how to build cost budgets for direct materials, direct labor, and manufacturing overhead.

I. The Master Budget "Big Picture"

    A. This lesson continues the example from the previous lesson on Sunbird Boat Company's operational budget. This lesson focuses on building the production cost budgets that eventually form budgeted cost of goods sold for the pro forma income statement.

    B. Typically, the production cost budgets represent the three product costs: direct materials, direct labor, and manufacturing overhead. Be sure to keep in mind the position of these three budgets within the big picture of the overall master budget. You can visually position these three budgets in the illustration below.

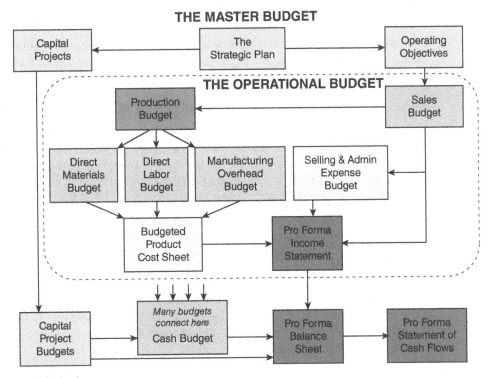

THE MASTER BUDGET

II. Direct Materials Budget

    A. The direct materials budget, like all of the production cost budgets, is a function of the production budget. The direct materials budget can be described in three parts.

1. First, beginning with budgeted production volume, the direct materials budget uses the standard input quantity to determine the total direct materials needed to support production.

2. Second, if the organization maintains an inventory of direct materials, then the budgeted production needs will *not* equal the quantity of direct materials that will need to be purchased. As a result, the relationship between production needs and materials to be purchased is:

Production needs + Ending inventory − Beginning inventory = Materials to purchase

3. Finally, by multiplying the materials to be purchased by the standard price of materials, the cost budget for direct materials purchases can be established.

B. Let's carry forward from the previous lesson the budgeting example for the Sunbird Boat Company. In the previous lesson, we determined a budget for quarterly production of custom wood-built rowboats. That production volume is used below to build the direct materials budget for Sunbird based on a standard quantity of 80 board feet of wood per boat and a standard price of $10 per board foot.

Direct Materials Budget

	Q1	Q2	Q3	Q4	Total
Production Volume	34 boats	52 boats	36 boats	34 boats	156 boats
× Standard Feet per Boat	80 ft	80 ft	80 ft	80 ft	80 ft
Material Needs for Production	2,720 ft	4,160 ft	2,880 ft	2,720 ft	12,480 ft
Planned Ending Inventory	1,248 ft	864 ft	816 ft	960 ft	960 ft
Total Material Needed	3,968 ft	5,024 ft	3,696 ft	3,680 ft	13,440 ft
Less Beginning Inventory	(600) ft	(1,248) ft	(864) ft	(816) ft	(600) ft
Total Material to Purchase	3,368 ft	3,776 ft	2,832 ft	2,864 ft	12,840 ft
× Standard Price	$10.00	$10.00	$10.00	$10.00	$10.00
Direct Material Purchases	**$33,680**	**$37,760**	**$28,320**	**$28,640**	**$128,400**

1. Sunbird's budget policy follows a practice of maintaining inventory equal to 30% of next quarter's production needs. Hence, the Q1 planned ending inventory of 1,248 feet is computed by the 4,160 feet needed for Q2 production multiplied by 30%. Note that the 960 feet of inventory planned for the end of Q4 indicates that Sunbird management plans to produce 40 boats in the following quarter (40 boats × 80 feet × 30% = 960 feet).

2. Notice that the beginning inventory planned for Q1 is 600 feet. This amount is different from Sunbird's 30% budget policy, which would be 816 feet (Q1 production needs 2,720 feet × 30%). Please understand that this budget is following the final *results* of the current year. It appears that while Sunbird may have originally planned to end the current year with 816 feet of wood in inventory, it is *actually* ending the year with 600 feet.

3. After the materials needed for production are adjusted by Sunbird's inventory policy, the budgeted quantity of wood to be purchased each quarter is multiplied by the standard price to determine the final direct material purchases budget.

III. Direct Labor Budget

A. The direct labor budget is obviously uncomplicated by any kind of inventory policy. The budgeted production volume is multiplied by the standard quantity of hours (which for Sunbird Boat Company is 50 hours per boat) to establish the direct labor hours needed to support production.

The direct labor hours needed to support production are multiplied by the standard price (i.e., wage rate) for labor to determine the budgeted direct labor payroll. Using Sunbird's standard wage rate of $28 per hour, the organization's direct labor budget is presented below.

Direct Labor Budget

	Q1	Q2	Q3	Q4	Total
Production Volume	34 boats	52 boats	36 boats	34 boats	156 boats
× Standard Hours per Boat	50 hrs	50 hrs	50 hrs	50 hrs	50 hrs
Direct Labor Hours	1,700 hrs	2,600 hrs	1,800 hrs	1,700 hrs	7,800 hrs
× Standard Price	$28.00	$28.00	$28.00	$28.00	$28.00
Direct Labor Payroll	**$47,600**	**$72,800**	**$50,400**	**$47,600**	**$218,400**

IV. Manufacturing Overhead Budgets

    A. Manufacturing overhead (sometimes called production overhead, factory overhead, or plant overhead) is composed of many different kinds of costs necessary for the organization's production process.

        1. In the budgeting process, manufacturing overhead is separated into variable costs and fixed costs. This distinction is important since variable costs have a constant cost rate per unit that results in a varying **total cost** based on changing levels of production volume. Conversely, fixed costs are fixed at the total amount, but will have a varying **cost rate** based on changing levels of production volume.

        2. Note that direct materials and direct labor costs are traditionally assumed to be variable (though this may or may not be the case for particular organizations). On the other hand, the manufacturing overhead budget is effectively managing two different types of costs, variable costs and fixed costs.

    B. In the Sunbird Boat Company example, management has identified three sources of variable manufacturing overhead costs (indirect materials, indirect labor, and utilities). Management has also identified four sources of fixed manufacturing overhead costs (property taxes, insurance, depreciation, and supervisor's salary). The budgeted costs for each quarter are presented in the MOH budget below.

Manufacturing Overhead (MOH) Budget

	Q1	Q2	Q3	Q4	Total
Indirect materials	$3,400	$5,200	$3,600	$3,400	$15,600
Indirect labor	7,650	11,700	8,100	7,650	35,100
Utilities	1,700	2,600	1,800	1,700	7,800
Total Variable MOH	**$12,750**	**$19,500**	**$13,500**	**$12,750**	**$58,500**
Property taxes	$1,000	$1,000	$1,000	$1,000	$4,000
Insurance	900	900	900	900	3,600
Depreciation – plant	5,000	5,000	5,000	5,000	20,000
Supervisor's salary	12,600	12,600	12,600	12,600	50,400
Total Fixed MOH	**$19,500**	**$19,500**	**$19,500**	**$19,500**	**$78,000**
Total MOH Expense	**$32,250**	**$39,000**	**$33,000**	**$32,250**	**$136,500**
less Depreciation	$ (5,000)	$ (5,000)	$ (5,000)	$ (5,000)	$(20,000)
MOH Payments	**$27,250**	**$34,000**	**$28,000**	**$27,250**	**$116,500**

    C. Building the MOH budget involves two aspects. The first aspect of this budgeting process is determining MOH costs. Note that the depreciation of plant assets is included in MOH costs. However, remember that depreciation is a non-cash expense, which is why depreciation expense needs to be deducted to determine the budgeted MOH payments. (We'll come back to MOH payments in a later lesson on cash budgets.)

D. The second aspect is building standard cost rates in order to apply MOH costs to units produced. This is necessary in order to establish the budgeted cost of goods sold for the pro forma income statement (which we'll cover in the next lesson). The math involved in budgeted overhead application rates is simple:

Overhead allocation rate = Budgeted annual MOH costs ÷ Budgeted annual activity volume

1. The standard MOH cost rates for Sunbird are computed below.

Manufacturing Overhead Application Rates

Variable MOH	Total	Fixed MOH	Total
Indirect materials	$15,600	Property taxes	$4,000
Indirect labor	35,100	Insurance	3,600
Utilities	7,800	Depreciation – plant	20,000
Total Variable MOH	**$ 58,500**	Supervisor's salary	50,400
÷ Production Labor	7,800 hrs	**Total Fixed MOH**	**$ 78,000**
Variable MOH per Direct Labor Hour	**$ 7.50**	÷ Production Labor	7,800 hrs
		Fixed MOH per Direct Labor Hour	**$10.00**

2. It must, however, be understood that it is a significant challenge for management to build these rates accurately based on the appropriate activity volume or volumes. [You'll study this important topic in Section D, Topic 1.]

3. In our example, Sunbird is using direct labor hours as the activity basis to allocate overhead costs. If it turns out that direct labor hours are not the right cost driver for these overhead costs, the MOH budget is not going to be accurate for planning, controlling, and evaluation purposes.

V. The Budgeted Standard Cost Sheet

A. With the production cost budgets completed and standard cost rates established, the standard cost sheet can be developed. This cost sheet is necessary for the pro forma income statement (i.e., budgeting operating statement). It is also a valuable management tool for building cost variances in order to control and evaluate performance in the organization. [You'll study this important topic in Section C, Topic 1.]

B. The Sunbird Boat Company standard cost sheet is provided below. Note that this cost sheet stipulates the standard input quantity and standard input price of each production cost for a single boat product.

Sunbird Boat Company Standard Cost Sheet

	Input Quantity	Price per Input	Cost per Boat
Direct Materials	80 feet	$10.00 per foot	**$800.00**
Direct Labor	50 hours	$28.00 per DL hour	**1,400.00**
Variable Overhead	50 hours	$7.50 per DL hour	**375.00**
Fixed Overhead	50 hours	$10.00 per DL hour	**500.00**
Total Product Cost			**$3,075.00**

C. This standard cost sheet carries forward into the pro forma income statement, which we will study in the next lesson.

Practice Question

Jordan Auto has developed the following production plan for its new auto part.

Production Budget

	January	February	March	April
Production Volume (parts)	12,000	8,000	13,000	15,000

Each part contains four pounds of raw material at a standard price of $16 per pound. The desired raw materials ending inventory is 40% of the next month's production needs plus an additional 100 pounds.

Prepare the direct materials purchases budget for each of the first three months of the coming year. Jordon Auto management is planning on the beginning inventory for January to be in compliance with its inventory policy of 40% needed to support production that month.

Answer

Direct Materials Budget

	January	February	March	April
Production Volume	12,000	8,000	13,000	15,000
× Standard Pounds per Part	4	4	4	4
Material Needs for Production	48,000	32,000	52,000	60,000
Planned Ending Inventory	12,900	20,900	24,100	
Total Material Needed	60,900	52,900	76,100	
Less Beginning Inventory	(19,300)	(12,900)	(20,900)	
Total Material to Purchase	41,600	40,000	55,200	
× Standard Price	$16.00	$16.00	$16.00	
Direct material Purchases	**$665,600**	**$640,000**	**$883,200**	

Note that January beginning inventory = January production needs 48,000 parts × 40% + 100 = 19,300 pounds.

Practice Question

Annecy Chocolate Company makes and sells two kinds of candy: chocolate peanut bars and caramel bars. The second-quarter production budget for each of the bars is as follows:

Production Budget

	April	May	June
Chocolate Peanut Bars	640	1,000	860
Caramel Bars	750	500	700

From experience, Annecy's management knows that it takes approximately 15 minutes to make a box of chocolate peanut bars and 30 minutes to make a box of caramel bars. Annecy pays its direct labor employees $14 per hour.

Prepare a direct labor budget for each of the two products for second quarter of the year.

Continues…

Answer

Direct Labor Budget

Chocolate Peanut Bars	April	May	June	Total
Production Volume	640	1,000	860	2,500
× Standard Hours per Box	0.25	0.25	0.25	0.25
Direct Labor Hours	160	250	215	625
Caramel Bars				
Production Volume	750	500	700	1,950
× Standard Hours per Box	0.5	0.5	0.5	0.5
Direct Labor Hours	375	250	350	975
Total Direct Labor Hours	**535**	**500**	**565**	**1,600**
× Standard Price	$14.00	$14.00	$14.00	$14.00
Direct Labor Payroll	**$7,490**	**$7,000**	**$7,910**	**$22,400**

Practice Question

Sanchez Sleep Systems manufactures nylon mesh hammocks for a chain of retail outlets located throughout the Southeast. The company plans to manufacture and sell 30,000 hammocks during the fourth quarter. Overhead costs are expected to include:

Variable Overhead Costs

Indirect Materials	$4.25 per hammock
Indirect Labor	$11.50 per hammock
Other Overhead	$3.25 per hammock

Fixed Overhead Costs

Salaries	$60,000 per quarter
Insurance	$5,000 per quarter
Depreciation	$25,000 per quarter

Compute Sanchez's overhead cost rates per hammock and prepare the manufacturing overhead budget for the fourth quarter.

Answer

Variable Overhead Costs

Indirect Materials	$ 4.25	per hammock
Indirect Labor	11.50	per hammock
Other Overhead	3.25	per hammock
Variable OH Rate	$19.00	per hammock
× Production Volume	30,000	hammocks
Total Variable OH Cost	**$570,000**	**per quarter**

Continues...

Fixed Overhead Costs

Salaries	$60,000	per quarter
Insurance	5,000	per quarter
Depreciation	25,000	per quarter
Total Fixed OH Cost	$90,000	per quarter
÷ Production Volume	30,000	hammocks
Fixed OH Rate	**$3.00**	**per hammock**

Manufacturing Overhead Budget

	Rate per Hammock	Total per Quarter
Variable Overhead	$19.00	$570,000
Fixed Overhead	3.00	90,000
Total Overhead	**$22.00**	**$660,000**

Note that depreciation expense ($25,000) is included here in the total fixed overhead costs of $90,000. This is because Sanchez is building a *cost* rate for its overhead cost budget. Later, when Sanchez is building a cash budget, this depreciation expense won't be included.

Summary
Once the production budget has been built, the budgets for all the production costs can commence. Traditionally, there are three basic production cost budgets: direct materials, direct labor, and manufacturing overhead. Remember that the direct materials budget will need to be adjusted based on the organization's inventory management policies. On the other hand, the direct labor budget simply combines the standard input quantities and standard input prices to compute the labor costs that need to be scheduled for production. The manufacturing overhead (MOH) budget should be separated into its variable cost and fixed cost components. Once the MOH budget has been built, it can be used to establish the standard MOH costs per unit of output, which are needed to build budgeted costs of goods sold.

Wrapping Up Operational Budgeting

After studying this lesson, you should be able to:

- Identify the components of the cost of goods sold budget and prepare a cost of goods sold budget (1.B.5.m).

- Demonstrate an understanding of contribution margin per unit and total contribution margin, identify the appropriate use of these concepts, and calculate both unit and total contribution margin (1.B.5.n).

- Identify the components of the selling and administrative expense budget (1.B.5.o).

- Explain how specific components of the selling and administrative expense budget may affect the contribution margin (1.B.5.p).

- Prepare an operational (operating) budget (1.B.5.q).

This lesson continues the Sunbird Boat Company example from the previous two lessons. In this lesson, we build the budgeted statement of operations, which is the foundation of the pro forma income statement. We also explore how to build a budgeted contribution margin statement. Reconciling these two statements (statement of operations and contribution margin statement) requires working with inventory and the fixed manufacturing overhead cost rate.

I. The Statement of Operations and the Income Statement

    A. When managers refer to the income statement in the budgeting process, they'll often describe it as the "statement of operations" or the "operating statement." However, this description isn't referencing the entire income statement as stipulated by financial reporting regulation.

    B. The operating statement is focused on the profit generated by the organization's primary business. It reports on the product cost (i.e., cost of goods sold) and period costs (i.e., selling and administrative expense), but it does not include the non-operating expenses such as interest and taxes. The operating statement and the income statement are compared below.

Operating Statement	Income Statement
Sales Revenue	Sales Revenue
Cost of Goods Sold	Cost of Goods Sold
Gross Margin	Gross Margin
Selling & Admin Expense	Selling & Admin Expense
Operating Income	Operating Income
	Interest Expense
	Net Income
	Tax Expense
	Net Income After Tax

II. Computing Cost of Goods Sold

    A. Computing the budget for cost of goods sold can be done using the traditional income statement formula, which is used below to depict the computation for our continuing example of budgeting operations for the Sunbird Boat Company.

Sunbird's Budgeted Cost of Goods Sold

Direct Material Purchases	$128,400
plus Beginning Direct Materials Inventory	6,000
less Ending direct Materials Inventory	(9,600)
Direct Materials Production Costs	$124,800
Direct Labor Production Costs	218,400
Manufacturing Overhead Production Costs	136,500
Total Production Costs	$479,700
plus Beginning Finished Goods Inventory	30,750
less Ending Finished Goods Inventory	(49,200)
Cost of Goods Sold	**$461,250**

1. The traditional cost of goods sold (COGS) formula begins with direct materials purchases, which are adjusted for beginning and ending inventory to compute the cost of direct materials used in production. This cost is combined with direct labor and manufacturing overhead costs used in production. The total production costs (i.e., total manufacturing costs) are adjusted for the beginning and ending inventory of finished goods to determine the COGS computation.

2. You can work through the past two lessons to pull the numbers needed to build this budget, but there are easier approaches to computing budgeted cost of goods sold using the production budget and the standard cost sheet we created for Sunbird's custom wood-built rowboats.

B. Total production costs, finished goods inventory levels, and cost of goods sold can all be computed directly from the volumes and inventory levels for finished goods using the total standard cost per boat. Consider the final COGS computation in the budget above. Pulling forward the standard cost sheet and production budget from the last two lessons, we can compute all the key COGS numbers as shown below.

Sunbird's Budgeted Cost of Goods Sold

Total Production Costs	$479,700
plus Beginning Finished Goods Inventory	30,750
less Ending Finished Goods Inventory	(49,200)
Cost of Goods Sold	**$461,250**

Standard Cost Sheet

This Year's Budget	Cost per Boat
Direct Materials	**$800**
Direct Labor	**1,400**
Variable Overhead	**375**
Fixed Overhead	**500**
Total Product Cost	**$3,075**

Production Budget

Finished Goods Inventory	Total	
Sales Volume	150 boats	× $3,075 = **$461,250**
Planned Ending Inventory	16 boats	× $3,075 = $49,200
Boats Needed	166 boats	
Less Beginning Inventory	(10 boats)	× $3,075 = $30,750
Production Volume	156 boats	× $3,075 = $479,700

1. Based on a standard cost of $3,075 per boat, Sunbird management should be able to compute the budgeted cost of total production by multiplying the production volume by the standard cost (156 × $3,075 = $479,700). The cost of beginning and ending inventory can be computed in a similar manner, which provides all the numbers needed to compute budgeted COGS.

2. However, there is a shortcut computation available. Notice above that budgeted COGS can be computed more directly by simply multiplying the *sales* volume by the standard cost (150 × $3,075 = $461,250).

3. It is important you realize that a crucial assumption is being made in putting together the budgeted COGS for Sunbird Boat Company. The crucial assumption is that total standard costs ($3,075) are the same for the upcoming year being budgeted *and* for the current year of operations. This is important because beginning inventory is coming from the current year while production volume and ending inventory is being planned for the upcoming year. As a result, sales volume will contain boats from both years. If standard costs shift between these two operating years, then Sunbird must separately compute the effect of beginning inventory and ending inventory. In other words, using the shortcut computation above depends on standard costs to be unchanged between the two years.

III. Completing the Statement of Operations

A. With the budgeted amount of cost of goods sold in hand, we can return to the operating statement to compute gross margin (sales revenue – cost of goods sold).

B. Before completing the operating statement, we need to budget for selling and administrative expense. Hence, in the exhibit below we are introducing some new numbers for our Sunbird Boat Company example.

Variable Selling & Admin Expense			Fixed Selling & Admin Expense		
Delivery	$100	per boat	Salaries	$96,000	per year
Commissions	110	per boat	Depreciation	4,400	per year
Total	**$210**	**per boat**	Advertising	5,200	per year
× Boats Sold	150	boats	**Total Budget**	**$105,600**	
Total Budget	**$31,500**	**this year**			

Total S&A Budget

Variable	$31,500
Fixed	105,600
Total Budget	**$137,100**

Budgeted Operating Statement

Sales Revenue	$630,000
Cost of Goods Sold	(461,250)
Gross Margin	$168,750
Selling & Admin Expense	(137,100)
Operating Income	**$31,650**

1. Selling and administrative (S&A) expense is another form of overhead for the organization. And like manufacturing overhead, these expenses typically have variable and fixed cost components. Sunbird Boat Company has two variable S&A expenses, which are the costs of delivering boats ($100 per boat), and the sales commissions paid ($110 per boat). Based on budgeted sales of 150 boats, Sunbird expects to spend $31,500 for these S&A expenses.

2. There are also fixed S&A expenses at Sunbird. These yearly fixed expenses include an executive salary ($96,000), depreciation on non-production assets ($4,400), and advertising

($5,200). Hence, regardless of the number of boats sold, Sunbird is planning to spend $105,600 for fixed S&A expenses.

3. The budgeted variable and fixed S&A expense totals to $137,100. When combined with the $461,250 in cost of goods sold, Sunbird's budgeted operating income can be established as $31,650. Later, when Sunbird management has prepared estimates for interest expense and tax expense, the complete pro forma income statement can be prepared using this budgeted operating statement.

IV. The Contribution Margin Statement

A. It is important that managers are able to budget for operating income in a manner that allows preparation of pro forma income statements based on financial reporting requirements such as Generally Accepted Accounting Principles (GAAP) or International Financial Reporting Standards (IFRS). However, an operating statement structured according to GAAP or IFRS is not always how managers want to use their budget to manage operations.

B. For many kinds of decisions, managers need to understand the *contribution margin* provided by operations. Contribution margin represents the difference between revenue and *all* variable costs (both variable production costs and variable S&A expense). The exhibit below contrasts the operating statement with the contribution margin statement.

Operating Statement	Contribution Margin Statement
Sales Revenue	Sales Revenue
Cost of Goods Sold	Variable Costs
Gross Margin	Contribution Margin
Selling & Admin Expense	Fixed Costs
Operating Income	Operating Income

1. The main difference between the two statements is the repositioning of costs above and below the "margin" line. All product costs (material, labor, overhead) are positioned above the *gross* margin line in the operating statement, and non-production costs (selling and administrative) are below. In contrast, all variable costs (whether related to production or to sales and administration) are above the *contribution* margin line in the contribution margin statement.

2. For organizations that do not maintain inventory, the operating income for these two statements will be the same. However, for organizations that hold inventory, there is one other important difference between these two statements. To the extent that inventory levels or fixed production costs fluctuate from year to year, the total costs on these two statements will vary. We'll work through a reconciliation between the two operating incomes below that demonstrates this difference.

C. While building the operational budget for Sunbird Boat Company, we have been classifying production costs and S&A expenses as variable or fixed according to the volume of sales activity. This classification allows us to build a budgeted contribution margin statement for Sunbird, as shown below.

Variable Production Costs			Fixed Production Costs		
Direct Mat.	$800	per boat	Property taxes	$4,000	per year
Direct Labor	1,400	per boat	Insurance	3,600	per year
MOH	375	per boat	Depreciation–plant	20,000	per year
Total	**$2,575**	**per boat**	Supervisor's salary	50,400	per year
× Boats Sold	150	boats	**Total**	**$78,000**	**per year**
Total Budget	**$386,250**	**this year**			

Total S&A Budget		Total Cost Budget	
Variable	$31,500	Variable	$417,750
Fixed	105,600	Fixed	183,600
Total Budget	**$137,100**	**Total Budget**	**$601,350**

Budgeted CM Statement

Sales Revenue	$630,000
Variable Costs	(417,750)
Contribution Margin	$212,250
Fixed Costs	(183,600)
Operating Income	**$28,650**

1. The original standard cost sheet includes four separate cost calculations for direct materials, direct labor, variable overhead (manufacturing overhead), and fixed overhead. The variable production costs include only the first three cost items, which total up to $2,575 per boat. When multiplied by 150 boats planned to be sold, the budgeted variable production costs for the year are $386,250. When combined with the variable S&A expense ($31,500), total variable costs at Sunbird are budgeted to be $417,750.

2. In the previous lesson, we identified the fixed production costs that the Sunbird management team is budgeting for the year. These four costs (property taxes, insurance, depreciation, and the supervisor's salary) total $78,000. Combined with the fixed S&A expense ($105,600), Sunbird's total fixed costs are budgeted to be $183,600.

D. As an alternative view of operating profit, the contribution margin statement supports a number of important management decision processes, including cost-volume-profit analysis (i.e., break-even analysis), relevant cost analysis for operating decisions, and pricing analysis.

V. Reconciling the Operating Statement and the Contribution Margin Statement

A. With all budgeted costs classified according to their behavior (variable vs. fixed), Sunbird is budgeting its operating income to be $28,650. This operating income from the contribution margin statement is different from budgeting operating income based on a traditional financial reporting view that separates costs into product and period expense classifications, and computes the operating income to be $31,650. The two statements are compared below. Why is there a $3,000 difference in operating income?

Budgeted Operating Statement		Budgeted CM Statement	
Sales Revenue	$630,000	Sales Revenue	$360,000
Cost of Goods Sold	(461,250)	Variable Costs	(417,750)
Gross Margin	$168,750	Contribution Margin	$212,250
Selling & Admin Expense	(137,100)	Fixed Costs	(183,600)
Operating Income	**$31,650**	**Operating Income**	**$28,650**

B. Reconciling operating income on the operating statement with operating income on the contribution margin statement is a function of the change in inventory and the allocated fixed costs of production. Recall from the previous lesson that total fixed manufacturing overhead ($78,000) was divided by total budgeted production volume (156 boats) to establish a fixed overhead rate of $500 per boat, and was included as a cost item in Sunbird's standard cost sheet. This cost rate will be used to allocate fixed manufacturing overhead cost to each boat produced. If inventory is budgeted to increase at Sunbird (which it is), then some of the fixed manufacturing overhead will not be expensed to the traditional operating statement, but will be instead listed an increase to inventory on the pro forma budget sheet.

C. As shown in the exhibit below, this fixed manufacturing cost per unit can be combined with the increase in inventory to explain why the operating statement is budgeted to be $3,000 higher than the contribution margin statement.

Standard Cost Sheet

This Year's Budget	Cost per Boat
Direct Materials	$800
Direct Labor	1,400
Variable Overhead	375
Fixed Overhead	500
Total Product Costs	**$3,075**

Income Difference	$3,000
Beginning Inventory	10
Ending Inventory	16
Inventory Increase	6
× Fixed MOH Rate	$500
Reconciliation	**$3,000**

1. Recall at the beginning of this lesson, when we were computing the shortcut for budgeted cost of goods sold, that we assumed that standard costs per unit at Sunbird are the same for the upcoming year as for the current year. We're making the same assumption here.

2. If the standard cost per unit for fixed manufacturing overhead is different between the two years, then the reconciliation for operating income is a little more involved. Specially, the beginning inventory would need to be multiplied by the current year's standard cost per unit, and ending inventory multiplied by next year's standard cost per unit, to complete the reconciliation between the two statements.

Practice Question
Bingham Sports is launching a new line of snowboards. Production and sales begin in November. The sales and production budgets for the first two months are provided below, along with the standard cost sheets for each month.

Budgeted	November	December
Production Volume	625 boards	800 boards
Sales Volume	600 boards	750 boards
Ending Inventory	25 boards	75 boards

Budgeted	November	December
Sales Price	$400.0	$400.0

Standard Costs per Unit	November	December
Variable Production Costs	$195.00	$195.00
Fixed Production Costs	64.00	50.00
Total Production Costs	**$259.00**	**$245.00**

Continues...

Budgeted	November	December
Selling & Admin Expense	$75,000	$75,000

Note that there will be 75 snowboards in inventory at the end of December (25 snowboard surplus in November plus the 50 snowboard surplus in December).

Due to the increased volume of production planned for December, the fixed production cost per unit is budgeted to decrease from $64 to $50 per snowboard.

The selling price is budgeted to be $400 per snowboard. Selling and administrative expense is composed entirely of fixed costs and is budgeted to be $75,000 per month.

For the month of December, compute the COGS budget, the budgeted operating statement, and the budgeted contribution margin statement. Finally, reconcile the difference in operating income between the two statements.

Answer

COGS Budgets	December
Variable Production Costs	$156,000
Fixed Production Costs	40,000
Total Production Costs	$196,000
plus Beginning Inventory	6,475
less Ending Inventory	(18,375)
Cost of Goods Sold	$184,100

Operating Statement	December
Revenue	$300,000
less COGS	(184,100)
Gross Margin	$115,900
less Selling & Admin Exp	(75,000)
Operating Income	$40,900

CM Statement	December
Revenue	$300,000
less Variable Costs	(146,250)
Contribution Margin	$153,750
less Fixed Costs	(115,000)
Operating Income	$38,750

Income Difference	$2,150
Fixed Production Costs in Beginning Inventory	$(1,600)
Fixed Production Costs in Ending Inventory	$3,750
Reconciliation	$2,150

Beginning with the budget for cost of goods sold (COGS), note that the production volume is combined with standard costs per unit to compute budgeted total costs. For example, 800 snowboards × $195 = $156,000 variable production costs. Also note that total costs for beginning inventory in December is based on the standard total production costs per unit for *November*: 25 snowboards × $259 = $6,475. On the other hand, ending inventory in December is based on standard costs for *December*: 75 snowboards × $245 = $18,375.

Continues...

With budgeted COGS completed, the operating statement can be assembled, resulting in $40,900 budgeted operating income.

The budgeted contribution margin (CM) statement uses variable cost to compute contribution margin. Note that since this computation is for the income statement, the total variable costs is based on the volume of *units sold*: 750 snowboards × $195 = $146,250. Fixed costs on the CM statement includes both all fixed in December, including all fixed production costs and all fixed S&A expenses (in this question, S&A expenses are fixed). Because the contribution margin approach expenses all fixed costs to the income statement, the total fixed production costs is based on the volume of units produced in December. Hence, budgeted fixed costs are computed as 800 snowboards × $50 + $75,000 = $115,000.

The $2,150 difference in operating income between the two statements is reconciled by computing the November fixed costs that are released to the operating statement when the 25 snowboards produced in November are sold in December (25 snowboards × $64), and by computing the December fixed costs that remain on the balance sheet representing the 75 boards remaining unsold from December production (75 snowboards × $50).

Summary

The traditional operating statement is the foundation of the pro forma income statement. The operating statement reports only cost of goods sold along with selling and administrative expense. The pro forma income statement includes other expense items not related to the organization's operation. When computing cost of goods sold for the operating statement, the standard cost per unit at the organization can be multiplied by the budgeted sales volume (so long as standard costs per unit are constant between years). Revenue minus cost of goods sold is gross margin. Reducing gross margin by planned selling and administrative expense provides the budgeted operating income. Managers can also use a contribution margin approach to compute operating income. This approach entails separating all budgeted costs into variable or fixed costs, subtracting variable costs from revenue to compute contribution margin, and then subtracting fixed costs to compute operating income. Reconciling income on the operating statement with income on the contribution margin statement is a function of the change in inventory multiplied by the fixed manufacturing cost per unit.

Capital Expenditures and Cash Budgets

After studying this lesson, you should be able to:

- Prepare a capital expenditure budget (1.B.5.r).

- Demonstrate an understanding of the relationship between the capital expenditure budget, the cash budget, and the pro forma financial statements (1.B.5.s).

- Define the purposes of the cash budget and describe the relationship between the cash budget and all other budgets (1.B.5.t).

- Demonstrate an understanding of the relationship between credit policies and purchasing (payables) policies and the cash budget (1.B.5.u).

- Prepare a cash budget (1.B.5.v).

This lesson focuses on the impact of long-term capital projects and short-term operational budgeting on the organization's cash budget.

I. Capital Project Budgets

    A. Let's return back to the "big picture" of the master budget as illustrated below.

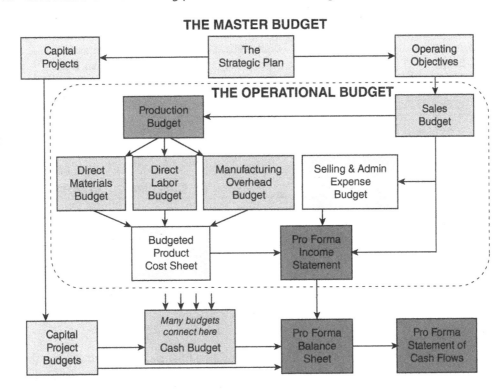

THE MASTER BUDGET

    B. The master budget represents how the organization's strategy is implemented. The strategic plan is used to establish short-term operating objectives that then guide the operating budget. We've spent the last three lessons working through the details of the operating budget.

    C. The strategic plan is also used to identify long-term capital projects that either strengthen the organization's current business position or help the organization move or expand into a new business position. In contrast to smaller spending decisions that involve less risk, capital projects are extensive investments requiring significant financial, management, and labor capital over lengthy periods of time.

D. Capital projects typically start with a particular proposal and approval process that is often described in terms of "capital budgeting." The capital budgeting process, for most organizations, involves three key facets. [See Part 2 Section C for an extensive lesson series on the capital budget process.]

    1. Financial analysis of capital budgeting projects often uses traditional evaluation tools such as net present value (NPV), internal rate of return (IRR), payback, and return on investment (ROI).

    2. Risk analysis of capital budgeting projects involves assessing uncertainty with respect to inputs and outcomes. Sophisticated analytical tools can illustrate the range of possible results that encompass a capital project proposal.

    3. Qualitative analysis is crucial to keep capital project decisions focused on non-quantitative characteristics that can address core strategic objectives for the organizations. These core objectives often involve issues related to quality, culture, brand, environment, and ethics.

E. Once the capital project planning is complete for a master budget cycle and resources have been committed, each project's development and launch must be carefully controlled and evaluated by management. Depending on the scale and scope of the project, any number of budgets, schedules, and stewardship procedures can be established to control and evaluate project progress.

F. Below is one example of a capital project schedule for Phase 1 of a long-term project that tracks actual completion and spending levels as compared to budget across the Phase 1 six-month timeline.

Capital Project Schedule — Phase 1

Date	Planned Completion Stage	Actual Completion Stage	Completion Variance	Budget Cost to Date	Actual Cost to Date	Cost Variance
1-Feb	10%	20%	100% F	$ 25,000	$ 32,000	28% U
1-Mar	23%	23%	0%	$ 56,000	$ 45,000	20% F
1-Apr	35%	31%	11% U	$ 98,000	$ 73,000	26% F
1-May	61%	56%	8% U	$126,000	$ 92,000	27% F
1-Jun	81%	68%	16% U	$153,000	$113,000	26% F
1-Jul	**100%**	**85%**	15% U	**$185,000**	**$144,000**	22% F

Note in this schedule that Phase 1 is behind on planned completion (15% behind schedule), but is 22% ahead of planned spending. Hence, it appears that the organization might be slowing down the project to save costs. Hopefully, this is an intentional management decision.

G. Capital project costs factor into the organization's cash budget. As you can observe in the master budget exhibit at the beginning of this lesson, the cash budget serves as a connecting bridge between capital projects and operating objectives.

II. The Cash Budget

A. The statement of cash flows is regulated as a published financial statement to have three sections: cash from operations, cash from investing, and cash from financing. Similarly, cash budgets in organizations can also be divided into three sections, but with different themes. For most organizations, cash budgets focus explicitly on cash receipts, cash disbursements, and financing.

B. Returning to the Sunbird Boat Company example, consider how it is budgeting for cash receipts. As Sunbird closes out its current year, management is planning on a $60,000 ending balance in accounts receivable from customers. Further, Sunbird's budget policy assumes that 80% of sales will be collected in the current quarter, and the remaining 20% collected in the subsequent quarter. The cash receipts schedule below begins with the budgeted revenue we established in an earlier lesson.

Sales Revenue Budget

	Q1	Q2	Q3	Q4	Total
Revenue	$ 84,000	$252,000	$168,000	$126,000	$360,000
Current Quarter Collections	$ 67,200	$201,600	$134,400	$100,800	$504,000
Past Quarter Collections	60,000	16,800	50,400	33,600	160,800
Total Sales Collections	**$127,200**	**$218,400**	**$184,800**	**$134,400**	**$664,800**

Note for Q1 that cash collections for the current quarter is budgeted to be $84,000 × 80% = $67,200. Cash collections in Q1 for the past quarter will be the $60,000 in Sunbird's ending accounts receivable for the current year. For Q2, current-quarter collections are budgeted to be $252,000 × 80% = $201,600. Past-quarter collections in Q2 will be the remaining sales uncollected from Q1, or $84,000 – $67,200 = $16,800. This number can be computed more directly as $84,000 × 20% = $16,800.

C. In the last two lessons, we worked through cost budgets for direct materials, direct labor, manufacturing overhead, and selling & administrative expense for Sunbird.

1. The first line in the schedule below is the budget for direct materials purchases that we've previously computed. Sunbird purchases all direct materials on account, and has $11,650 in accounts payable as the current year concludes. We'll assume that the Sunbird budget policy stipulates to pay 60% of purchases in the current quarter, and the remaining 40% in the next quarter. Its cash payments schedule for direct material purchases is provided below.

Direct Materials Budget

	Q1	Q2	Q3	Q4	Total
Direct Material Purchases	$33,680	$37,760	$28,320	$28,640	$128,400
Current Quarter Payments	$20,208	$22,656	$16,992	$17,184	$ 77,040
Past Quarter Payments	11,650	13,472	15,104	11,328	51,554
Total DM Payments	**$31,858**	**$36,128**	**$32,096**	**$28,512**	**$128,594**

Similar to Sunbird's approach for cash collections, the cash payments for each quarter is 60% of current-quarter purchases and 40% of previous-quarter purchases.

2. The result of the direct labor payroll budget that we put together previously is provided below. We'll assume that Sunbird pays out all payroll costs in the quarter incurred. Hence, direct labor costs and cash paid for direct labor each quarter is projected to be the same.

Direct Labor Budget

	Q1	Q2	Q3	Q4	Total
Direct Labor Payroll	$47,600	$72,800	$50,400	$47,600	$218,400

3. We also completed budgets for manufacturing overhead (MOH) and selling & administrative expense (S&A) in the last two lessons. You may remember we noted at that time that depreciation expense in these budgets does not represent a cash payment. Hence, depreciation is subtracted from these budgets to determine the cash paid.

Manufacturing Overhead (MOH) Budget

	Q1	Q2	Q3	Q4	Total
Total MOH Expense	$32,250	$39,000	$33,000	$32,250	$136,500
less Depreciation	$(5,000)	$(5,000)	$(5,000)	$(5,000)	$(20,000)
MOH Payments	**$27,250**	**$34,000**	**$28,000**	**$27,250**	**$116,500**

Selling & Administrative (S&A) Budget

	Q1	Q2	Q3	Q4	Total
Total S&A Expense	$30,600	$39,000	$34,800	$32,700	$137,100
less Depreciation	$(1,100)	$(1,100)	$(1,100)	$(1,100)	$ (4,400)
S&A Payments	**$29,500**	**$37,900**	**$33,700**	**$31,600**	**$132,700**

While it is certainly possible that Sunbird could have a budget policy to defer payments on some of these cash expenses, we're assuming here that management expects to fully pay these expenses in each quarter incurred.

4. In preparation for the cash budget, all four cash payments schedules are listed in the disbursements schedule below.

Disbursements for Operations

	Q1	Q2	Q3	Q4	Total
DM Payments	$31,858	$36,128	$32,096	$28,512	$128,594
DL Payroll	47,600	72,800	50,400	47,600	218,400
MOH Payments	27,250	34,000	28,000	27,250	116,500
S&A Payments	29,500	37,900	33,700	31,600	132,700
Operating Disbursements	**$136,208**	**$180,828**	**$144,196**	**$134,962**	**$596,194**

Note that bringing forward the production and administrative cost budgets into the cash budget is basically a matter of determining the payment policy on each of these types of costs. The timing of cash payments may be more or less complicated than we have established for the Sunbird Boat Company. The key is to understand clearly each organization's budget policy with respect to cash payments.

D. Remember that there are typically three sections in an organization's cash budget: receipts, disbursements, and financing. Sunbird's cash budget is presented below.

Cash Budget

	Q1	Q2	Q3	Q4	Total
Beginning Cash	$100,000	$100,000	$109,754	$130,358	$100,000
Receipts	127,200	218,400	184,800	134,400	664,800
Cash Available	**$227,200**	**$318,400**	**$294,554**	**$264,758**	**$764,800**
Disbursements:					
Operations	$136,208	$180,828	$144,196	$134,962	$596,194
Interest (12%)		810			810
Income Tax	18,000				18,000
Dividends			20,000		20,000
Equipment				95,000	95,000
Cash Used	**$154,208**	**$181,638**	**$164,196**	**$229,962**	**$730,004**
Minimum Cash	100,000	100,000	100,000	100,000	100,000
Excess Cash Financing:	**$(27,008)**	**$ 36,762**	**$ 30,358**	**$(65,204)**	**$(65,204)**
Borrowings	27,008			65,204	92,212
Repayments		(27,008)			(27,008)
Ending Cash	**$100,000**	**$109,754**	**$130,358**	**$100,000**	**$100,000**

1. Note the budget begins with the expected cash balance for each quarter. Then the cash receipts from collections on sales are provided. Following the receipts is the disbursements section, which begins with the line summarizing all payments for Sunbird's operations.

2. Following the stream of payments for operations are four planned disbursement events for the budget year. Sunbird has $18,000 in income tax that is owed from the previous year, and expects to make that payment in Q1. In Q2 you see a planned payment for $810 in interest expense. We'll discuss that computation below when we put together the financing section of the cash budget. A $20,000 dividend payment is planned for Q3, and Sunbird expects to purchase $95,000 in capital equipment in Q4.

3. Finally, the financing section of the cash budget demonstrates how Sunbird will manage its available cash level from quarter to quarter. Sunbird has established a policy of maintaining a minimum of $100,000 cash on hand for operations. You can see in Q1 that Sunbird has cash available of $227,200. After cash disbursements planned for Q1 ($154,208), Sunbird will dip to $72,992, which is $27,008 below its minimum cash policy. Therefore, Sunbird needs to borrow the difference, likely using an established line of credit it maintains with a bank. In Q2, Sunbird has excess cash of $36,762. Therefore, Sunbird can pay off the line of credit from Q1. Assuming a 12% annual interest, Sunbird will also need to pay $810 in interest costs in Q2 ($27,008 × 12% × ¼ year = $810.24). Subsequently, in Q4, Sunbird will have another cash shortfall of $65,204 and will need to borrow money again to be paid back the following year.

E. Be sure you understand all of the computations involved in building Sunbird's cash budget. There are a number of computations, but all of them are reasonably simple. What's most important is that you can follow the line of operating budgets that connect to the cash budget, each of which impacts the cash budget in one way or another.

F. With the cash budget in hand, managers can consider the impact of how collections and disbursements might affect the organization's ability to manage operations and prepare for unexpected events. If it appears that there won't be sufficient cash in the organization at key points in the future, managers have three overall approaches to solving the cash need.

1. Two of the approaches to improve cash levels are quite visible in the cash budget. First, the organization can improve its operating cash flow by increasing the amount of cash generated by operations or reducing the amount of cash used in operations. Second, the organization can take out short-term operating loans.

2. The third approach is not as obvious in the cash budget, but it can be a highly effective management device. In our example, Sunbird extends credit to its customer, and by virtue of its credit policy, is able to collect 80% of sales in the current quarter. Its credit policy is a combination of establishing clear deadlines with its customers for payment and encouraging payment with fees or discounts. A stricter credit policy will accelerate cash collections, but perhaps at the expense of losing some sales. Hence, Sunbird will need to balance the impact of its credit policy on faster cash collections versus high volumes of sales.

3. Similarly, Sunbird has a credit relationship with its suppliers. Sunbird's purchasing and payables policy may pressure its supplier to accept payments on a slower basis. However, if Sunbird puts too much pressure on its suppliers to accept delayed payments, it may lose favorable pricing terms, or even lose entirely some key supplier relationships. Again, management needs to carefully balance slower cash payments with better supply prices and availability.

Practice Question

Rocky Peak Company uses the following budget policy to plan for cash receipts on sales:

Budget Policy — Cash Collections

Collected in month of sale	70%
Collected in the first month after sale	15%
Collected in the second month after sale	10%
Collected in the third month after sale	4%
Uncollectible	1%

Sales Budget

July	$60,000
August	$70,000
September	$80,000
October	$90,000
November	$100,000
December	$85,000

Budgeted sales for the last six months of the upcoming budget year are also shown above.

What are the budgeted total cash collections during October?

What is the expected year-end balance in accounts receivable, net of allowance for uncollectible accounts?

Answer

October Collections Budget

Month	Sales	Percent	Collected
July	$60,000	4%	$2,400
August	70,000	10%	7,000
September	80,000	15%	12,000
October	90,000	70%	63,000
		Total	**$84,400**

Solving for total cash collections in October requires working backward to identify previous months' sales that are subsequently collected in October.

Budgeted Accounts Receivable Balance

Month	Sales	Percent	Collected
October	$90,000	4%	$3,600
November	100,000	10% + 4%	14,000
December	85,000	15% + 10% + 4%	24,650
		Total at Year End	**$42,250**

Solving for the year-end accounts receivable balance requires evaluating how much sales revenue remains from the last three months of the year that can still be collected. Note, for example, that 70% of December sales are collected in December. However, that doesn't mean that 30% of December sales exist in the net balance of accounts receivable because 1% of December sales is not expected to be collected.

Practice Question

The following information is available for Laurel Company, a wholesale company:

Sales Budget

October	6,200 units
November	6,700 units
December	7,100 units

Inventory Data

Accounts Payable Balance, Oct 1	$55,000
Beginning inventory, Oct 1	2,000 units
Desired Ending Inventory, Dec 31	1,800 units

Additional information:

- Desired inventory at the end of each month is 20% of next month's sales.

- The purchase price of inventory is $45 per unit.

- Each month 70% of purchases is paid by the end of the month. The remaining 30% is paid in the following month.

Prepare the inventory purchase payments schedule for October, November, and December.

Answer

Inventory Purchase Payments Schedule

	October	November	December
Sales Volume (units)	**6,200**	**6,700**	**7,100**
Planned Ending Inventory	1,340	1,420	1,800
less Beginning Inventory	(2,000)	(1,340)	(1,420)
Purchase Volume (units)	**5,540**	**6,780**	**7,480**
× Price	$45	$45	$45
Budgeted Purchases	**$249,300**	**$305,100**	**$336,600**
Current Month Purchase Pmts	$174,510	$213,570	$235,620
Past Month Purchase Pmts	55,000	74,790	91,530
Total Purchase Payments	**$229,510**	**$288,360**	**$327,150**

This solution requires first determining how much inventory needs to be purchased to support the budgeted sales volume. The budgeted purchases are then evaluated with respect to the payment policy for Laurel Company to determine budgeted purchase payments.

Summary

Strategy drives both long-term capital project spending (investments) and short-term operational objectives and goals. Organizations use capital budgeting techniques to evaluate and select projects to fund. Organizations then establish careful budgets and schedules to control and evaluate spending, completion, and other key performance indicators as the project moves forward. Eventually, both long-term project budgets and short-term operational budgets come together to impact the organization's cash budget. Typically, cash budgets are designed to explicitly track cash collections, cash disbursements, and financing needs to accommodate shortfalls in certain periods, and to repay previous operational financing loans. Organizations manage their cash needs by improving operations (more revenue, less expense), obtaining short-term loans, and establishing credit and payment policies with customers and suppliers.

Topic 4. Budget Methodologies

Comparing Flexible, Rolling, Activity-Based, Zero-Based, and Project Budgeting

After studying this lesson, you should be able to:

- For each tool or method, define its purpose, appropriate use, and time frame (1.B.4.a).
- Identify the budget components and explain the interrelationships among the components (1.B.4.b).
- Demonstrate an understanding of how the budget is developed (1.B.4.c).
- Compare and contrast the benefits and limitations of the budget system (1.B.4.d).
- Evaluate a business situation and recommend the appropriate budget solution (1.B.4.e).
- Prepare budgets on the basis of information presented (1.B.4.f).
- Calculate the impact of incremental changes to budgets (1.B.4.g).

Notice that this lesson, representing Topic 4, is placed after the Topic 5 lessons. The purpose of this ordering is to first establish the purpose and process of the traditional master budgeting system (Topic 5), and then contrast the master budgeting system with some specific budgeting tools and methodologies (Topic 4).

Now that we've worked through the details of each budget schedule in the master budget system, this lesson explores some specific tools and methodologies that managers can use to guide their master budget planning.

I. The Master Budget

    A. To review, the master budget structure is displayed below.

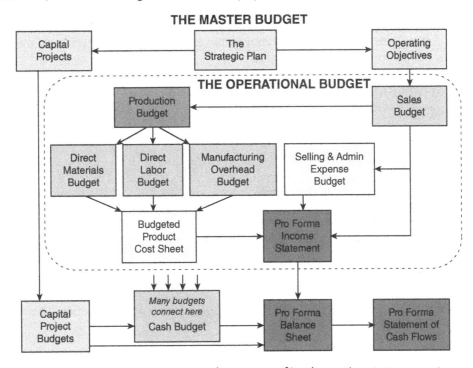

    B. The master budget structure represents the process of implementing strategy as a two-pronged process.

165

1. Remember that one side of the master budget involves periodic planning for long-term capital investing to establish the organization's strategic position in its environment and competitive space. This management work is project budgeting.

2. The other side of the master budget comprises the constant planning for short-term operational spending to achieve strategic objectives. This management work is operational budgeting.

C. The master budget structure is, in fact, a basic configuration within which managers choose to implement specific budgeting tools and methods. In this lesson we will discuss two specific budgeting tools (rolling budgets and flexible budgets) and two specific budgeting methods (activity-based budgeting and zero-based budgeting). Any combination of these tools and methods can be applied to the master budgeting process to guide both operational budgets and capital project budgets.

II. Continuous Rolling Budgets

A. A continuous rolling budget, sometimes simply called a rolling budget, is used to establish and maintain a constant number of operating periods moving forward in the master budget.

B. Organizations generally have long-running budget plans with more detailed operating periods early on in the budget plan (e.g., weekly, monthly) and more general operating periods later in the plan (semiannual, annual). For example, consider the three-year budget plan below.

The Continuous Rolling Budget

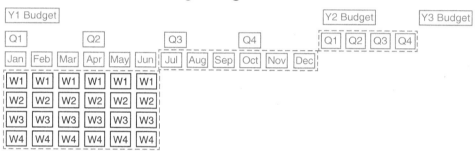

1. This budget plan establishes six months of weekly budgets, followed by a half year of monthly budgets, followed by a year of quarterly budgets, and finally at the third year the plan concludes with an annual budget.

2. As each month of operations concludes, the budget team rolls forward the budget plan to maintain this same structure. As shown below, with January operations for Year 1 (Y1) completed, the organization has rolled forward the budget plan to build the monthly budget for January in Year 2 (Y2).

The Continuous Rolling Budget

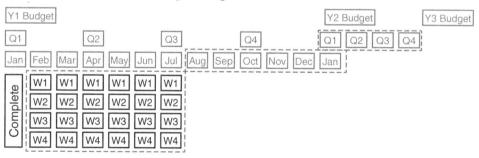

3. When the March operations are complete in Year 1, which will complete the first quarter (Q1), the organization will roll forward the budget plan to build the quarterly budget for Q1 in Year 3.

C. Using a rolling budget tool in the master budget plan provides a number of benefits, including the following:

1. Once the master budget plan is established, the rolling budget tool breaks the budget process down into more manageable monthly processes rather than a lengthier annual process.

2. In the three-year rolling budget example above, managers are effectively planning each month to look forward three years into the future. Managers who are constantly viewing the long-run future of the organization will tend to be more strategic in the work they do and the decisions they make.

3. The rolling budget approach should improve the relevancy of data and perspective used in the master budget process as current data, perspective, and experience are incorporated each month into the budget plan.

D. The obvious cost of using rolling budgets is the commitment across the organization to be in continuous budgeting mode. Despite the benefits listed above, the time and resources spent in the budgeting effort still represents time and resources *not* being invested in day-to-day operations. Hence, it's critical that the monthly budgeting process is designed to be as efficient as possible. Hopefully, the rolling budget is incorporated into the constant management process of planning, controlling, and evaluating operations.

E. To summarize, rolling budgets are particularly helpful to organizations that want to avoid an annual master budget planning event that can consume a large block of management time. More importantly, a rolling budget process helps keep everyone constantly focused on the organization's strategy and how it is moving forward into the future.

III. Flexible Budgets

A. Flexible budgets are used to examine possible future scenarios in sales volume. In addition, flexible budgets are crucial for computing variances in order to evaluate past operating results based on relevant costs. [We'll explore this crucial purpose of flexible budgets in the lessons on variance analysis in Section C.]

B. Returning again to our example with the Sunbird Boat Company, remember that we've been building a master budget based on budgeted sales of 150 boats in the upcoming year. The budgeted operating statement below provides the data we compiled on budgeted sales of 150 boats.

Budgeted Operating Statement

Sales Volume	150 boats	160 boats	140 boats
Sales Revenue	$630,000	$672,000	$588,000
Cost of Goods Sold	(461,250)	?	?
Gross Margin	$168,750	?	?
Selling & Admin Expense	(137,100)	?	?
Operating Income	$31,650	?	?
Price per boat = $4,200			

Production Costs

	per Boat
Direct Materials	$800
Direct Labor	1,400
Variable MOH	375
Fixed MOH	500
Total Product Costs	$3,075

Selling & Admin Expense

	per Boat
Delivery	$100
Commissions	110
Fixed S&A OH	704
Total S&A Expense	$914

1. The operating statement for 150 boats is based on the price and cost data above. Revenue and expenses are computed as follows

   The sales revenue = $4,200 × 150 boats = $630,000
   Cost of goods sold = $3,075 × 150 boats = $461,250
   Sell & Admin Exp = $914 × 150 boats = $137,100

2. These computations make sense, *but only for a sales volume level of 150 boats*. Note that Sunbird management isn't able to use these costs to build operating budgets at sales volumes other than 150 boats. The problem is that the cost rates for fixed MOH at $500 per boat and for fixed S&A at $704 boat will not remain constant at the 160-boat and 140-boat sales volumes.

3. The reason the fixed cost rates won't remain constant is that these are costs that are only constant in total. The fixed MOH cost rates were computed originally based on the budgeted production of 156 boats (based on work we completed in an earlier lesson). The fixed S&A costs were computed based on the budgeted sales volume of 150 boats. The total fixed costs can be recomputed as follows.

   Total Fixed MOH = $500 × 156 boats = $78,000
   Total Fixed S&A = $704 × 150 boats = $105,600

4. On the other hand, if Sunbird used a contribution margin format that separately tracks variable and fixed costs, then it can budget for operating income based on multiple projections on sales volume. The exhibit below demonstrates Sunbird's flexible budgeting tool.

Budgeted Contribution Margin Statement

Sales Volume	150 boats	160 boats	140 boats
Sales Revenue	$360,000	$672,000	$588,000
Variable COGS	(386,250)	(412,000)	(360,500)
Variable S&A	(31,500)	(33,600)	(29,400)
Contribution Margin	$212,250	$226,400	$198,100
Fixed COGS	(78,000)	(78,000)	(78,000)
Fixed S&A	(105,600)	(105,600)	(105,600)
Operating Income	$28,650	$42,800	$14,500

Production Costs

VC per Boat	$2,575
Total Fixed MOH	$78,000

Selling & Admin Expense

VC per Boat	$210
Total Fixed S&A	$105,600

5. In the three contribution margin statements above, Sunbird is tracking variable costs as a rate per boat, but managing fixed costs in total. Based on a clear separation of variable and fixed costs, Sunbird can effectively build flexible budgets based on multiple future scenarios.

6. Note that operating income at 150 boats in the contribution margin statement above ($28,650) is different from operating income in the previous operating statement ($31,650). We've discussed this difference in a previous lesson that involved reconciling these two types of profit statements.

C. Flexible budgets provide a valuable view that supports the management process of planning, controlling, and evaluating costs. In particular, flexible budgets handle costs in a manner consistent with the total cost formula:

$$\text{Total costs} = \text{Variable cost rate}(\text{Activity}) + \text{Total fixed costs}$$

With a clear view on cost behavior, managers are able to build "what-if" budgets based on different sales volume scenarios. Further, managers are better able to plan budgeted costs and evaluate actual results with a clear view on cost behavior (variable versus fixed).

D. The challenge with using flexible budgets that separate costs into variable cost and fixed cost behaviors is that this is not the same approach used for external financial statements. External financial statements are required to separate costs into product costs and period costs in order to compute costs of goods sold, as well as selling and administrative expense.

    1. As pointed out earlier, the operating income numbers are different for the operating statement versus the contribution margin statement. This difference is due to the allocation of fixed manufacturing overhead costs to Sunbird's inventory as required for the operating statement that is eventually used to build the pro forma income statement.

    2. Hence, in order to use flexible budgeting tools, organizations will need to manage fixed manufacturing overhead costs differently for pro forma income statements used to communicate with external investors and creditors.

E. To summarize, flexible budgets are particularly helpful to organizations that need to plan for multiple possible sales outcomes in the future. Further, with its separate focus on variable costs versus fixed costs, flexible budgets are also important to organizations working to control costs and evaluate cost performance.

IV. Activity-Based Budgeting

A. Rolling budgets and flexible budgets are specific types of tools in the master budget plan. Most sophisticated organizations use both rolling and flexible budget tools in their master budget planning. At a more conceptual level, organizations also make important management choices about the particular methodology used in the budgeting process. Activity-based budgeting is a detailed budget methodology that results in a more sophisticated and detailed view of the many activities that drive costs in most organizations.

B. Traditional budget methodologies follow a fairly simple cost allocation approach that groups costs by departments and then allocates costs based on unit measures such as direct labor hours, headcount, or square feet of space. The traditional cost allocation model is represented below.

Cost Drivers in Traditional Budgeting

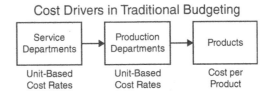

Conversely, activity-based budgeting methods focus on identifying and using core activities throughout the organization to establish activity cost rates in order to assign costs to products, customers, and other business targets based on actual consumption relationships.

Cost Drivers in Activity-Based Budgeting

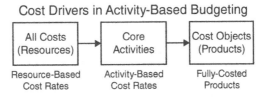

Organizations that practice activity-based budgeting will have a much larger and more diversified mix of cost driver rates in the master budget system. It is particularly important to note that activity-based budgeting methods result in significantly more cost rates compared to traditional budgeting methods.

C. Activity-based budgeting methodologies generally provide much more accurate cost planning, control, and evaluation results for management use. Further, by concentrating on core activities, activity-based budgeting methods are better focused on identifying and supporting value-added processes in the organization. The improvement in the accuracy of cost measurement and better focus on value-added processes is a major incentive for organizations to pursue activity-based budgeting methods. [*Note*: Activity-based budgeting is a key feature in activity-based cost (ABC) systems, which are studied extensively in lessons located in Section D.]

D. Activity-based budgeting is neither simple nor cheap. In terms of both time and financial costs, this budgeting methodology requires significant resources to design and implement. Organizations need to carefully consider the costs and benefits involved in the complexity of management systems that focus on activities rather than on departments in the process of budgeting costs.

E. When cost management is critical to the organization, particularly in highly competitive markets where profit margins can be very tight, the enhanced insight and cost control that results from activity-based budgeting systems may be well worth the effort required to implement.

V. Zero-Based Budgeting

A. A simplified approach to budgeting is to essentially begin with the previous year's budget, determine what conditions or costs have changed, and then make incremental adjustments to the old budget in order to establish the new budget. This incremental approach to budgeting is in direct contrast to the much more rigorous zero-based budgeting methodology that assumes nothing from previous years.

B. Zero-based budgeting takes a very structured approach to regularly (e.g., annually) demand that all budgeting choices (spending, processes, priorities, etc.) are taken back to a "blank page" to be fully evaluated and, if approved, put into the master budget plan. Nothing is assumed to carry forward to the next year's budget without working through a complete evaluation and approval process.

    1. In theory, the zero-based budgeting method begins by evaluating all current and proposed projects in the organization, and prioritizing projects based on relationship to the organization's evolving strategy. Benefits and costs of each project are also considered in establishing what projects are cut or reduced, and what projects are implemented or expanded.

    2. The evaluation of projects becomes the core of the negotiations that encompass most budget processes in the organization. These negotiations then determine how resources are committed and shared across the organization to support priority projects.

    3. With the organization's project list re-determined, and decisions made about next year's investments and spending, the detailed work of building sales, production, and cost schedules can then begin.

C. Zero-based budgeting is extremely rigorous, and strongly supports efficiency in the organization. Compared to the results of more incremental budgeting methods wherein assumptions about operations and processes are carried forward each year, the zero-based budgeting methodology is much more effective at controlling and reducing budgetary slack.

D. This rigorous approach to budgeting is clearly more time-consuming and more costly than incremental budgeting methods that carry forward processes and assumptions year to year. In fact, the demands of zero-based budgeting can be so severe that some organizations will entirely avoid it, or try to move so quickly through the process that key research and dialogue is skipped over. One way to mitigate the costs of this methodology is to rotate the zero-based system across the organization over time. For example, the organization may choose to use zero-based budgeting procedures in one third of the organization each year, rotating the procedure across the organization over a three-year period of time. In off years, a more incremental budgeting approach is used in non-focused areas of the organization.

E. The zero-based methodology was originally developed for government organizations to help discipline what was perceived to be runaway spending. For organizations willing to invest in the rigor, zero-based budgeting methodology continues to be useful for organizations that need significant discipline to focus back on strategy and to reduce inefficient spending.

VI. Project Budgets

A. Recall that project budgets and the operational budget are both part of the master budget plan (see the beginning exhibit). Project budgets generally represent strategy-focused investments made by the organization to strengthen or shift its competitive position.

B. Like the operational budget, project budgets can use any of the budgeting tools and methodologies described here in this lesson. For example, let's assume that the Sunbird Boat Company has made a strategic decision to build a new manufacturing facility.

1. In the capital project budget for the construction of the new facility, Sunbird would be well advised to use a continuous rolling budget that establishes monthly (or even weekly) schedules for the near future, and longer-term schedules (quarterly and semiannually) later in the project's timeline. As each month of construction is concluded, Sunbird would roll forward the project plan to update and maintain a constant minimum of detailed budget periods in the overall project plan.

2. Sunbird will likely also choose to identify variable costs and fixed costs in the project budget in order to establish several budget scenarios based on, for example, decisions to expand or reduce the size of the facility during the construction process. A flexible budget tool like this can quickly facilitate "what-if" questions in the planning process.

3. With respect to the budget methodologies we've reviewed in this lesson, Sunbird might make a deep commitment to understand and manage project costs by identifying key activities and establishing a large number of activity cost rates in the construction project budget. This activity-based budgeting method would be used rather than working with a smaller set of standard cost rates provided by the departments that are involved in the project.

4. If Sunbird decides to pursue a zero-based budgeting methodology, then managers in charge of building and updating the budgeting will avoid carrying forward assumptions about costs and processes from previous project budgets. Instead, the project budget will be built entirely from scratch based on a rigorous consideration of the importance of each construction activity and the specific costs and benefits expected to be associated with the activity.

C. Remember that operational budgets and project budgets alike can use any combination of the tools and methodologies described in this lesson. To that point, Sunbird's manufacturing facility construction project could be built using a rolling budget that distinguishes variable and fixed costs in order to flexibly explore different budgets based on possible adjustments to the size of the finished facility. The construction project could also involve activity-based budgeting methods and be based on the initial assumption that no cost measures or processes can be carried forward from previous projects (i.e., a zero-based budgeting approach).

Practice Question
Zack Johnson is the controller for the small company he works for. He needs to build a flexible budget to plan for and control key overhead costs in the organization. After concluding an analysis of overhead costs in the company, he established the following cost formulas for variable costs per machine hour and monthly fixed costs.

Continues...

Cost per Month	Formula
Plant utilities	$15(MH) + $5,000
Equipment maintenance	$5(MH) + $12,000
Equipment depreciation	$45(MH)
Rent on production plant	$23,000

The normal production budget is based on 1,920 machine hours for the month. Actual production could be 10% lower or 20% higher. Build a flexible budget for manufacturing overhead costs.

Answer

Manufacturing Overhead Flexible Budget

	Normal	−10%	+20%
Machine Hours	1,920	1,728	2,304
Variable Costs:			
Utilities	$28,800	$25,920	$34,560
Maintenance	9,600	8,640	11,520
Depreciation	86,400	77,760	103,680
Total Variable Costs	$124,800	$112,320	$149,760
Fixed Costs:			
Utilities	$5,000	$5,000	$5,000
Maintenance	12,000	12,000	12,000
Rent	23,000	23,000	23,000
Total Fixed Costs	$40,000	$40,000	$40,000
Total Manufacturing Overhead	**$164,800**	**$152,320**	**$189,760**

Practice Question

Smith Machining makes three products. The company's annual budget includes $1,000,000 of manufacturing overhead. In the past, the company has allocated overhead costs based on normal capacity of 40,000 direct labor hours. Management at Smith would like to explore activity-based budgeting, and has determined that overhead costs can be broken into four overhead pools: order processing, setups, milling, and shipping. The following is a summary of budgeted costs and activities:

Activity	Budgeted Cost	Expected Level
Order processing	$175,000	10,000 orders
Setups	160,000	4,000 setups
Milling	410,000	20,500 machine hours
Shipping	255,000	25,000 shipments
Total	$1,000,000	

Calculate the budgeted overhead rate based on the traditional methodology of direct labor hours.

Calculate the budgeted overhead rates based on activity-based budgeting methodology.

Continues...

Answer

Traditional	Overhead Rate
Direct labor hours	$25.00 per direct labor hour

Activity	Overhead Rate
Order processing	$17.50 per order
Setups	$40.00 per setup
Milling	$20.00 per machine hour
Shipping	$10.20 per shipment

Summary

The master budget diagram provided at the beginning of this lesson depicts an overall flow of budget schedules that form the organization's operational budget and its capital project budgets. This lesson describes two specific tools that can be used to design either an operational budget or a project budget. The tools are rolling budgets and flexible budgets. This lesson also describes two specific budget methodologies that can guide how an operational budget or project budget is developed. These methods include activity-based budgeting or zero-based budgeting. None of these tools or methods is exclusive of the others. That is, managers can choose to use any combination of these four resources when planning the master budget.

Topic 6. Top-level Planning and Analysis

Pro Forma Financial Statements

After studying this lesson, you should be able to:

- Define the purpose of a pro forma income statement, a pro forma balance sheet, and a pro forma statement of cash flows, and demonstrate an understanding of the relationship among these statements and all other budgets (1.B.6.a).

- Prepare pro forma income statements based on several revenue and cost assumptions (1. B.6.b).

- Evaluate whether a company has achieved strategic objectives based on pro forma income statements (1.B.6.c).

- Use financial projections to prepare a pro forma balance sheet and a pro forma statement of cash flows (1.B.6.d).

- Identify the factors required to prepare medium- and long-term cash forecasts (1.B.6.e).

- Use financial projections to determine required outside financing and dividend policy (1.B.6.f).

The end result of the master budgeting process is the pro forma financial statements (income statement, balance sheet, and statement of cash flows). However, as part of initial strategy planning, managers will often project pro forma financial statements based on key assumptions and performance goals, and then use those pro forma financial statements to subsequently guide the master budgeting process. This final lesson in this section demonstrates the process of building projected pro forma financial statements *in advance* of the master budgeting process.

I. Closing the Strategic Loop

    A. In this final lesson, we come back once more to the overall view of the master budget (below). All the detailed schedules comprising the operational budget are collapsed together in this diagram in order to focus on the end result—the pro forma financial statements.

THE MASTER BUDGET

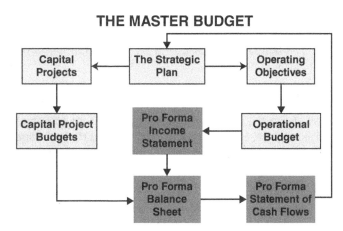

    B. The term *pro forma* essentially means "as a matter of form." Pro forma financial statements provide a view of the organization's future financial performance based on current financial statements and anticipated future actions. Pro forma financial statements are designed to demonstrate the "form" the organization will take as its strategy plan advances forward.

    C. The comparison of pro forma financial statements with results reported in actual financial statements are a key measure of the success of the organization's strategic work. This is why the pro forma financial statements are demonstrated to link back to the strategic plan as a feedback evaluation loop, as shown above.

II. Building the Pro Forma Income Statement

    A. Throughout the last several lessons we've been building a detailed operational budget for the Sunbird Boat Company, beginning with the sales budget and painstakingly working through the details of each subsequent budget schedule.

    B. With these detailed budgets now completed, the pro forma financial statements can finally be assembled. However, when designing strategy, executives and directors will often create pro forma statements as an end goal that *precedes* the work of the detailed operational budgeting process.

    C. Typically, this kind of pro forma work begins by targeting some measure of sales growth based on a specific strategy. Managers can then use a "percentage-of-sales method" to establish certain types of expenses and balance sheet accounts that are normally impacted by sales revenue.

    D. To demonstrate the percent-of-sales method, we'll start with Sunbird's current (actual) income statement, and we'll assume that Sunbird's management team is designing a strategy that they expect will provide a 15% compound annual growth rate (CAGR) on revenue. The expected CAGR on sales becomes the starting point for Sunbird's pro forma income statement, as shown below.

Current Income Statement			Pro Forma
Sales volume	130 boats	(1)	150 boats
Sales revenue	$ 550,000	(1)	$ 632,500
Cost of goods sold	(396,000)	72.0%	(455,400)
Gross margin	$ 154,000	28.0%	$ 177,100
Selling & admin expense	(110,000)	20.0%	(126,500)
Operating profit	$ 44,000	8.0%	$ 50,600
Interest expense	(2,200)	(2)	(3,530)
Net income before tax	$ 41,800	7.6%	$ 47,070
Income tax	(18,000)	(3)	(18,828)
Net income after tax	$ 23,800		$ 28,242

(1) 15% compound annual growth rate (CAGR)
(2) 0.4% of revenue plus $1,000
(3) 40% average tax rate

    E. Based on the planned CAGR of 15%, sales for the pro forma income statement are set at 150 boats and $632,500 in revenue.

    F. Expenses are then evaluated to identify which expenses are a function of sales, and what percentage of sales should be used to establish the expense for the pro forma income statement. In the analysis above, the sales percentages that represent cost of goods sold, as well as selling & administrative expense, are assumed to carry forward to the budget year (72% and 20%, respectively). For interest expense, management expects to carry forward the current interest cost percentage (0.4% of revenue), plus an additional $1,000 based on expected additional debt. Income tax expense is based on Sunbird's average tax rate (40%).

    G. Percentages used in this method do not need to be based on the current income statement. The goal for management is to establish targeted expenses based on realistic expectations or stretch goals representing the organization's strategy.

III. Building the Pro Forma Balance Sheet

    A. The percent-of-sales method can also be used to guide the development of the pro forma balance sheet. Similar to the income statement analysis, Sunbird management evaluates the current balance sheet to determine accounts that have a "natural" relationship to sales revenue, that is, accounts that would be expected to increase or decrease based on the size of the business related to sales. Sunbird's approach to its pro forma balance sheet is presented below.

Current Assets			
Cash	$100,000	18.2%	$115,115
Accounts receivable	60,000	10.9%	68,943
Inventory	36,750	6.7%	42,378
Long-term Assets			
Land	250,000	(1)	250,000
Building and equipment	700,000	(2)	800,000
Less accum depreciation	(120,000)	(3)	(145,000)
Total Assets	**$1,026,750**		**$1,131,436**
Current Liabilities			
Accounts payable	$11,650	2.1%	$13,283
Income taxes payable	18,000	(4)	18,828
Bank line of credit	100,000	(5)	Balance entry
Stockholders' Equity			
Common stock	718,000	(6)	718,000
Retained earnings	179,100	(7)	187,342
Total Liabilities & Equity	**$1,026,750**		**$1,131,436**
Current Revenue = $550,000 Target Revenue = $632,500			

(1) Unchanged
(2) Plus $100,000
(3) Plus $25,000
(4) From income stmt
(5) Adjust to balance!
(6) Unchanged
(7) Beg R/E
+ Income $28,242
− Dividend $20,000

B. The balance sheet accounts most likely to respond proportionally to growth in sales are cash, accounts receivable, inventory, and accounts payable. Sunbird management has evaluated the percentage relationship between these four accounts and the $550,000 sales revenue for the current year, and then has chosen to use those same percentages to project these same accounts for the pro forma balance sheet based on the projected (target) sales of $632,500.

C. The management team then makes individual projections on the remaining accounts for the pro forma balance sheet. There is no plan to increase the land asset during the budget year, but Sunbird will purchase $100,000 in equipment assets. There is $25,000 in depreciation expense to be recognized. Income taxes payable will reflect the tax expense on the pro forma income statement.

D. The two important calculations on the pro forma balance sheet are for retained earnings and for the bank line of credit. Sunbird expects to pay a $20,000 dividend in the upcoming year. Adjusting the retained earnings for both projected income of $28,242 and the planned dividends payment results in a projected retained earnings level at $187,342.

E. Perhaps most importantly, the pro forma balance will determine whatever financing is needed to support the planned level of assets. Based on this analysis, Sunbird is projecting a $1,131,436 asset balance. Obviously, then, some combination of liabilities and equity must be in position to support the asset balance. Sunbird uses a line of credit at its bank as needed to support its balance of assets. The computation is

Total assets − Equity − Remaining liabilities = Balancing debt account
$1,131,436 − $718,000 − $187,342 − $13,283 − $18,828 = $193,983

Sunbird already has $100,000 on the line of credit, so management is projecting a $93,983 increase on the pro forma balance sheet.

IV. Building the Pro Forma Statement of Cash Flows

    A. The statement of cash flows is built largely based on changes in account balances on the balance sheets at the beginning and end of the year. Those two balance sheets and the changes in each account balance are listed below.

Current Balance Sheet		Pro Forma	Change
Current Assets			
Cash	$100,000	$115,115	15,115
Accounts receivable	60,000	68,943	8,943
Inventory	36,750	42,378	5,628
Long-term Assets			
Land	250,000	250,000	
Building and equipment	700,000	800,000	100,000
Less accum depreciation	(120,000)	(145,000)	(25,000)
Total Assets	**$1,026,750**	**$1,131,436**	
Current Liabilities			
Accounts payable	$11,650	$13,283	1,633
Income taxes payable	18,000	18,828	828
Bank line of credit	100,000	193,983	93,983
Stockholders' Equity			
Common stock	718,000	718,000	
Retained earnings	179,100	187,342	8,242
Total Liabilities & Equity	**$1,026,750**	**$1,131,436**	

    B. Computing the statement of cash flows follows two general rules. The first rule is the relationship of changes in balance sheet accounts with changes in the cash account. The relationship can be depicted in the following formula (note: = "change").

$$\Delta Cash = \Delta Debt + \Delta Equity - \Delta Assets$$

Increases in debt (liability) accounts or equity accounts result in increases in the cash account. Conversely, increases in asset accounts (all asset accounts other than cash) result in *decreases* in the cash account.

        1. Hence, since all asset accounts are expected to increase on the pro forma balance sheet for Sunbird, these changes will lead to decreases in cash on the statement of cash flows.

        2. Note that accumulated depreciation is a contra-asset, so the $25,000 increase in this contra-asset account leads to adjusting up the cash statement.

    C. The second rule of computing the statement of cash flows is the classification of cash flow changes across the three categories on this financial statement: cash from operating activities, cash from investing activities, cash from financing activities. Determining these classifications can often be resolved by the location of each account affecting cash flows on the balance sheet.

        1. Cash flows from operating activities are based on balance sheet accounts for current operating assets and current operating liabilities.

2. Cash flows from investing activities are based on balance sheet accounts for current non-operating assets and long-term assets.

3. Cash flows from financing activities are based on balance sheet accounts for current non-operating liabilities, long-term liabilities, and equity.

D. The Sunbird Boat Company uses the indirect method for its statement of cash flows (by far the most popular method to use). The indirect method affects only the section for operating activities. The other two sections (investing and financing) are unaffected by the choice to use either the indirect method or direct method. The indirect method begins the operating activities section by listing income and then adjusts income for changes in current operating assets and liabilities as well as non-cash expenses, losses, and gains.

E. Sunbird's pro forma statement of cash flows is presented below.

Pro Forma Statement of Cash Flows

Income	$28,242
Accounts receivable	(8,943)
Accounts payable	1,633
Income taxes payable	828
Inventory	(5,628)
Depreciation	25,000
Cash from Operating	**$41,132**
Purchase equipment	$(100,000)
Cash from Investing	**$(100,000)**
Bank loan increase	$93,983
Dividends payment	(20,000)
Cash from Financing	**$73,983**
Change in Cash	**$15,115**

1. Sunbird begins the section on cash flow from operating activities with its projected income of $28,242 and then adjusts that amount for changes in accounts receivable, accounts payable, income taxes payable, and inventory. Note that increases in assets lead to a decrease in cash flow while increases in liabilities lead to increases in cash flow. In addition, Sunbird's expectation for $25,000 in depreciation expense (a non-cash expense) is added back to income to determine cash flow from operating activities.

2. Sunbird's plan to purchase $100,000 in equipment will increase its long-term assets on the balance sheet. This leads to a decrease in cash flow resulting from investing activities.

3. Finally, Sunbird is projecting two events that will impact cash flows from financing activities. First, the $93,983 cash inflow due to the increase to the bank line of credit is a financing activity. Note that even though this is a current liability on the balance sheet, it is a non-operating liability. Hence, the change in this account is classified as a financing activity. Second, the dividend payment of $20,000 is a cash outflow in this section. Remember that the change in the retained earnings account on the balance sheet is based on both income and dividends. Only the dividends portion of that change is used in the financing section of the statement of cash flows.

V. Financial Ratio Analysis

A. Pro forma financial statements can help the organization's leadership team and budget committee to effectively "begin with the end in mind." Most organizations have very specific goals, as well as rigorous lender requirements and investor expectations, regarding financial statement performance as captured by various types of financial analysis ratios. Pro forma financial statements need to demonstrate that the organization is planning to achieve its financial performance objectives. Otherwise, adjustments need to be made to capital project plans and operational objectives.

B. Exhibited below are a number of traditional financial analysis ratios for Sunbird's current (actual) financial statements compared to its pro forma financial statements. Hopefully, most of these ratios are familiar to you.

Ratio Analysis[m]	Current	Pro Forma
Income Ratios		
Gross profit margin	28.0%	28.0%
Operating profit margin	8.0%	8.0%
Net profit margin	4.3%	4.5%
Interest coverage	20.0	14.3
Earnings per Share (50,000 shares)	$0.48	$0.56
Balance Sheet Ratios		
Quick ratio	1.23	0.81
Current ratio	1.52	1.00
Debt to assets ratio	12.6%	20.0%
Return Ratios		
Return on Assets	2.3%	2.5%
Return on Equity	2.7%	3.1%

[m] Note that these formulas are on the ICMA formula sheet.

1. The first three income ratios are margin ratios based on each profit item divided by sales revenue. The interest coverage ratio is the income before interest and taxes (i.e., operating profit) divided by interest expense. Earnings per share (EPS) is net income after tax divided by common shares outstanding. We're assuming that Sunbird has 50,000 shares outstanding.

2. The balance sheet ratios describe financial flexibility based on leverage. The quick ratio indicates how well Sunbird can pay its current liabilities using current assets that are liquid. For Sunbird, it is computed as cash plus accounts receivable divided by all current liabilities. The current ratio also allows for the use of inventory to help pay current liabilities (all current assets divided by all current liabilities). The debt to assets ratio is signaling long-term leverage as total liabilities divided by total assets.

3. The return ratios demonstrate value created using resources provided by lenders and investors. The return on assets (ROA) ratio is net income after tax divided by total liabilities and equity (i.e., total assets). The return on equity (ROE) ratio is net income after tax divided only by total equity. (Note that these return ratios are computed above using *ending* balance sheet values in the denominator. Alternatively, they can be computed using *average* balance sheet values.)

C. Based on the ratio analysis above for Sunbird, the leadership team can observe a planned performance pattern indicating somewhat improved net income performance, but a rather significant increase in leverage. If this pro forma result will be unacceptable to stakeholders in the Sunbird Boat Company, then the leadership team needs to reevaluate its strategy plan and master budget to determine what can be adjusted to position the organization better to meet its performance expectations.

D. Pro forma financial statements are the end result of the master budgeting process. However, remember that pro forma financial statements are often created by leadership to *guide* the master budgeting process. To that end, the diagram below demonstrates how pro forma financial statements can be built directly based on the organization's strategy, and then feed forward to help establish the operational budget and project budgets, as well as guide decisions regarding capital projects and operational objectives.

Guiding the Master Budget Process

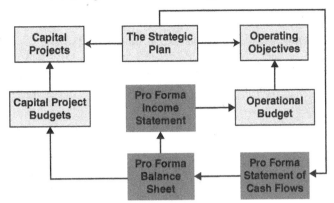

Practice Question

Larkin Styles Company, a specialty women's clothing retailer, is putting together a set of pro forma financial statements as an end goal to help guide its master budgeting process. Below is its current balance sheet.

Current Balance Sheet

Current Assets	
Cash	$135,000
Accounts receivable	105,000
Inventory	240,000
Total Current Assets	$480,000
Long-term Assets	
Building and equipment (net)	450,000
Land	400,000
Total Assets	**$1,330,000**
Liabilities	
Accounts payable	$210,000
Bank loan (long term)	345,000
Stockholders' Equity	
Common stock	450,000
Retained earnings	325,000
Total Liabilities & Equity	**$1,330,000**

Based on the strategy plan, the Larkin Styles management team is projecting sales next year at $1,400,000. The following expectations have been established.

- Cost of goods sold at 45% of sales revenue.
- Selling and administrative expense at 32% of sales revenue.
- Interest expense is incurred based on a 10% rate on the current bank loan balance.
- Tax expense is based on a 36% tax rate.
- Cash balance at 12% of sales revenue.
- Accounts receivable balance at 9% of sales revenue.
- Inventory balance at 19% of sales revenue.
- Accounts payable balance at 16% of sales revenue.

Continues...

- Equipment will be depreciated $15,000 (included in selling and administrative expense).

- A $50,000 equipment purchase is planned.

- Dividends of $63,000 will be paid on the 40,000 shares outstanding.

Build the pro forma income statement, balance sheet, and statement of cash flows for Larkin Styles Company. Based on the pro forma financial statements, compute the following ratios:

- Earnings per share

- Current ratio

- Debt to assets ratio

- Return on assets (based on ending balances on the pro forma balance sheet)

Answer

Pro Forma Income Statement

Sales revenue	**$1,400,000**	Given
Cost of goods sold	(630,000)	$1,400,000 × 45%
Gross margin	**$ 770,000**	
Selling & admin expense	(448,000)	$1,400,000 × 32%
Operating profit	**$ 322,000**	
Interest expense	(34,500)	$345,000 × 10%
Net income before tax	**$ 287,500**	
Income tax	(103,500)	$287,500 × 36%
Net income after tax	**$ 184,000**	

Pro Forma Balance Sheet

Current Assets		
Cash	$168,000	$1,400,000 × 12%
Accounts receivable	126,000	$1,400,000 × 9%
Inventory	266,000	$1,400,000 × 19%
Total Current Assets	$560,000	
Long-term Assets		
Building and equipment (net)	485,000	$450,000 + $50,000 − $15,000
Land	400,000	Unchanged
Total Assets	**$1,445,000**	
Liabilities		
Accounts payable	$224,000	$1,400,000 × 16%
Bank loan (long-term)	325,000	$1,445,000 − $450,00 − $446,000 − $224,000
Stockholders' Equity		
Common stock	450,000	Unchanged
Retained earnings	446,000	$325,000 + $184,000 − $63,000
Total Liabilities & Equity	**$1,445,000**	

Continues…

Pro Forma Statement of Cash Flows

Income	$ 184,000
Accounts receivable	(21,000)
Accounts payable	14,000
Inventory	(26,000)
Depreciation	15,000
Cash from Operating Activities	**$ 166,000**
Purchase equipment	$ (50,000)
Cash from Investing Activities	**$ (50,000)**
Bank loan payment	$ (20,000)
Dividends payment	(63,000)
Cash from Financing Activities	**$ (83,000)**
Change in Cash	**$ 33,000**

Pro Forma Ratio Analysis

Earnings per Share	$4.60	$184,000 ÷ 40,000 shares
Current ratio	2.50	$560,000 ÷ $224,000
Debt to assets ratio	38.0%	($224,000 + $325,000) ÷ $1,445,000
Return on Assets	12.7%	$184,000 ÷ $1,445,000

Summary

Pro forma financial statements are often built in advance by the organization's leadership team to help anticipate (and determine) where the operational budget and project budgets need to land. Using the strategy plan to determine the goal for sales, the pro forma income statement can be built using a percentage-of-sales approach to determine expenses that are a function of sales revenue. Then the pro forma balance sheet is built, again using a percentage-of-sales approach for those accounts that are assumed to adjust based on sales revenue, and forecasting the remaining balance sheet accounts based on management plans. Finally, with the pro forma income statement and balance sheet complete, the pro forma statement of cash flows is built based largely on changes to each of the balance sheet accounts. The organization can then assess planned performance based on various financial ratios to determine if expected results will be acceptable to stakeholders.

Section B Review Questions

aq.pc.bud.003_1802

1. Cut, Inc. (Cut) has developed the following production plan for its premium scissor line.

	September	October	November	December
Production Volume (scissors)	15,000	20,000	18,000	24,000

Each pair of scissors contains 0.5 pounds of stainless steel at a standard price of $1.25 per pound. The desired raw materials ending inventory is 35% of the next month's material needs for production plus an additional 150 pounds. September's beginning inventory meets this requirement. Using a direct materials purchases budget, determine direct material purchases for October and November.

A. $12,500.00 for October and $11,250.00 for November
B. $12,062.50 for October and $12,562.50 for November
C. $16,625.00 for October and $16,687.50 for November
D. $25,000.00 for October and $22,500.00 for November

aq.sp.bud.001_1802

2. Which of the following specific budgets is the key driving force of the overall operational budget?

A. The sales budget
B. The production budget
C. The capital projects budget
D. The pro forma income statement

aq.sp.bud.005_1802

3. Card & Co. (CC), a creator of popular card games such as "Tres" and "Go Hunt," is preparing a quarterly sales budget. CC predicts sales of 40,000 games in Q1 at $5.00 per game. CC predicts that game sales will grow by 4% each quarter and that game price will increase by 5% each quarter. Each game costs $3.00 to produce in Q1. Costs are expected to grow by 3% each quarter. Using a quarterly sales budget, calculate sales revenue for the year.

A. $800,000
B. $917,306
C. $169,859
D. $383,598

aq.lc.anal.001_0720

4. Wall, Corp. (Wall) is the leading manufacturer of sheetrock in the United States. Wall is trying to forecast direct material costs for next year. The cost of calcium sulfate dihydrate (gypsum) used in sheetrock production fluctuates from year to year. Below are Wall's estimates for the cost of a pound of gypsum next year.

Pound of Gypsum Price	Probability
$1.45	15%
$1.60	25%
$1.85	40%
$2.00	20%

Based on these estimates, what is the expected cost per pound of gypsum next year?

A. $1.45
B. $1.73
C. $1.85
D. $1.76

5. Which of the following is **not** a component of the selling and administrative expense budget?

A. The costs of advertising products
B. The transportation costs of delivering purchased products to customers
C. The production line manager
D. The depreciation of the administration building

6. Eight quarters of production data from Pear, Inc., a cell phone manufacturing company, are presented below. **Pear, Inc.**

Quarter	Phones	Cost
1	2,331	$3,245,874
2	2,657	$3,474,318
3	1,987	$2,883,675
4	2,412	$3,287,621
5	2,583	$3,354,966
6	2,497	$3,428,752
7	2,285	$3,152,347
8	2,645	$3,271,899

The regression analysis results on these data are displayed below.

	Coefficients	Standard Error	t Stat	P-value	Lower 95%	Upper 95%
Intercept	$1,473,119	$356,978	4.13	0.01	$599,625	$2,346,614
Phones	$738	$147	5.03	0.00	$379	$1,097

Regression Statistics	
Multiple R	0.90
R Square	0.81
Adjusted R Square	0.78
Standard Error	$87,127â
Observations	8

What is the regression equation (total cost equation) for the above information?

A. Total costs = $147(Phones) + $356,978
B. Total costs = $1,473,119(Phones) + 738
C. Total costs = $356,978(Phones) + $147
D. Total costs = $738(Phones) + $1,473,119

7. Nice Knives (Nice) is facing fierce competition in the cutlery industry. Nice's main competitors are stealing market share on certain knives by offering similar products at lower prices. Nice management believes that costs are not being allocated correctly across product lines of different knives. Nice would like to change its budgeting process to improve cost allocation assignment and better understand profitability

of knives. Which of the following budget tools and methods would be most helpful to Nice in this situation?

A. An activity-based budget
B. A continuous rolling budget
C. A zero-based budget
D. A flexible budget

aq.gen.strat.002_0720

8. Short-term objectives, tactics for achieving these objectives, and operational planning (master budget) must be congruent with what? Choose the best answer.

A. The organization's external environmental factors
B. The organization's internal environmental factors
C. The organization's performance evaluation and incentive compensation factors
D. The organization's strategic plan and long-term strategic goals

aq.gen.strat.005_1802

9. A cost leadership strategy, in addition to focusing on the company's ability to sell a large volume of low-cost products, is often aided by all of the following characteristics **except**:

A. Advanced production technology.
B. Access to low-cost production inputs (raw materials, labor, etc.).
C. More highly desirable product features.
D. Access to low-cost capital.

aq.wrap.ob.006_1802

10. Textbook Manufacturing (TM) is the leading textbook printing and binding company in the region. TM is starting a new line of Managerial Accounting textbooks this year and would like to calculate the budgeted total contribution margin for this line for 20X1. TM plans to sell every textbook they manufacture this year. The following information is available:

Sales Budget	Q1	Q2	Q3	Q4	Total
Sales Volume	1,300	1,600	1,900	1,500	6,300

Budgeted Sales Price per Unit	
Sales Price	$200.00

Standard Production Costs per Unit	
Variable Production Costs	$47.00 per book
Fixed Production Costs	19.00 per book
Total Production Costs	$66.00 per book

Standard Variable Selling & Admin Costs per Unit	
Standard Selling & Admin Costs	$25.00 per book
Fixed Selling & Admin Costs	35.00 per book
Total Selling & Admin Costs	$60.00 per book

Using a contribution margin statement, calculate TM's budgeted total contribution margin for the new line of Managerial Accounting textbooks for 20X1.

A. $74.00
B. $128.00
C. $806,400
D. $466,200

aq.sp.bud.009_1802

11. Card & Co. (CC), a creator of popular card games such as "Tres" and "Go Hunt," is preparing a quarterly production budget. CC predicts sales of 45,000 games in Q1 and predicts that game sales will grow 6% every quarter indefinitely. The company consistently follows a budget policy of maintaining an ending inventory of 20% of the next quarter's sales. Using a quarterly production budget, calculate production volume for the year.

    A. 199,220
    B. 208,220
    C. 196,858
    D. 207,806

aq.bud.stand.009_0720

12. How does budget slack affect the master budget?

    A. Budget slack hinders ease of communication of organizational goals.
    B. Presence of budget slack can lead to decreased commitment from the employees.
    C. Cumulative budget slack at each sublevel can result in an inaccurate master budget.
    D. Strategic goals do not receive priority in the budgetary process due to existence of budget slack.

aq.swot.009_0720

13. Which of the following is **not** an example of an external factor in SWOT analysis?

    A. The economy
    B. Financial resources
    C. Future technology trends
    D. Competitive forces

aq.lc.anal.003_0720

14. Which of the following is a benefit of expected value computations?

    A. The underlying probabilities used in the expected value formula are usually based on subjective judgments.
    B. The expected value computation reduces multiple outcomes down to a single value, which is easily understood and can be entered into a budget plan.
    C. The expected value computation is the most likely outcome in the future.
    D. Expected value computations incorporate multiple possibilities, making them more representative of a certain future.

aq.spec.tools.005_0720

15. Which of the following is **not** one of Porter's Five Forces?

    A. Threat of Regulation
    B. Threat of Substitute Products
    C. Intensity of Competition
    D. Threat of New Entrants

Section C. Performance Management

Topic 1. Cost and Variance Measures

Flexible Budgets and Performance Analysis

After studying this lesson, you should be able to:

- Analyze performance against operational goals using measures based on revenue, manufacturing costs, non-manufacturing costs, and profit depending on the type of center or unit being measured (1.C.1.a).

- Explain the reasons for variances within a performance monitoring system (1.C.1.b).

- Prepare a performance analysis by comparing actual results to the master budget, calculate favorable and unfavorable variances from the budget, and provide explanations for variances (1.C.1.c).

- Identify and describe the benefits and limitations of measuring performance by comparing actual results to the master budget (1.C.1.d).

- Analyze a flexible budget based on actual sales (output) volume (1.C.1.e).

- Calculate the flexible-budget variance by comparing actual results to the flexible budget (1.C.1.g).

- Investigate the flexible-budget variance to determine individual differences between actual and budgeted input prices and input quantities (1.C.1.h).

- Explain how budget variance reporting is utilized in a management-by-exception environment (1.C.1.i).

Organizations typically follow a management process of planning, controlling, and evaluating operations in order to achieve strategic objectives. Performance variance analysis is a key aspect of controlling and evaluating operations. Variances are computed as the difference between budgets and actual results. This lesson establishes a crucial difference between master budgets (sometimes called static budgets) that are built in advance of the operating period, and flexible budgets that are built after the operating period is concluded. Master budgets can be used to assess the *effectiveness* of the organization in achieving its goals regarding sales volumes, but these budgets are not useful to assess the *efficiency* of the organization with respect to how it manages sales prices and costs involved in operations. To assess performance on sales prices and costs, the organization needs to use a flexible budget that is adjusted for actual sales volumes.

I. Managing the Organization

    A. In Section B you studied planning and budgeting. Section C is focused on performance management. The performance management process begins with a master budget in place. Before stepping forward into the detailed work of performance management, it's important to first step back and see the big picture of decision making and management in organizations.

    B. Managers establish operational objectives and then work to achieve those objectives using a decision-making and management process that involves planning, controlling, and evaluating operations in the organization. This management process is a feedback loop that can be illustrated as shown.

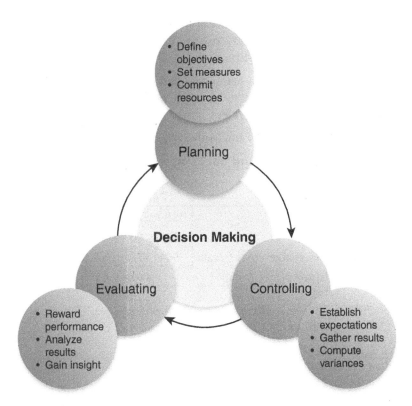

1. Operational planning is where the strategy is defined into operational objectives, performance measures are set, and resources are committed. This is the budgeting process for the organization.

2. Controlling operational processes requires that expectations are established and incentivized, and results are gathered and reported. It is in this process that management accountants capture and report variances.

3. Evaluating the operations involves rewarding performance, determining why objectives were met or not, and using the insight gained to complete the feedback loop and inform the planning stage for the upcoming operational cycle.

C. Performance analysis begins by capturing and reporting variances in operations (Controlling), and then determining causes for variances in order to incentivize employees (Evaluating).

II. Performance Analysis Using the Master (Static) Budget

A. The best way to understand variances is to work with the process of measuring variances. These first lessons in Section C will use Sunbird Boat Company, a hypothetical company that manufactures custom wood-built rowboats. (We also used the Sunbird Boat Company in Section B to explore the budgeting process.)

B. Assume that Sunbird Boat Company used the following standards to establish a master budget before the start of the upcoming operating year.

Sunbird Boat Company

Budget	Classic (Oak)	Deluxe (Teak)
Expected sales volume	156 boats	41 boats
Standard price per boat	$4,200	$9,400
Standard variable costs per boat	$2,785	$6,315
Budgeted fixed cost (total)	$183,600	

1. Note that Sunbird has two types of boats it sells. The Classic boat is made with a less expensive wood (oak), and the Deluxe boat is made with a more expensive wood (teak). In the upcoming year, Sunbird plans to sell 156 Classic boats and 41 Deluxe boats.

2. Before the year began, the standard prices and variable costs were established based on careful management analysis, and the budgeted fixed cost is determined based on expectations for the upcoming year.

C. At the end of the year, Sunbird had the following results.

Sunbird Boat Company

Actual	Classic (Oak)	Deluxe (Teak)
Actual sales volume	150 boats	45 boats
Actual price per boat (total)	$683,400	$403,875
Actual variable costs (total)	$443,772	$267,030
Actual fixed cost (total)	$192,450	

D. Clearly, Sunbird's results were different from the master budget. With the application of a little math, the following performance report can be established.

Sunbird Boat Company

	Actual Results	Master Budget	Variances
Classic sales volume	150 Boats	156 Boats	6 Boats U
Deluxe sales volume	45 Boats	41 Boats	4 Boats F
Classic revenue	$683,400	$655,200	$28,200 F
Deluxe revenue	403,875	385,400	18,475 F
Total revenue	$1,087,275	$1,040,600	$46,675 F
Classic variable costs	$(443,772)	$(434,460)	$9,312 U
Deluxe variable costs	(267,030)	(258,915)	8,115 U
Total variable costs	$(710,802)	$(693,375)	$17,427 U
Total fixed costs	(192,450)	(183,600)	8,850 U
Operating profit	$184,023	$163,625	$20,398 F

E. Even though Sunbird sold six fewer boats than expected, revenue on Classic boats was higher than expected, resulting in a $28,200 favorable (F) performance variance. What happened? Notice that you can compute the actual average selling price for Classic boats, which is $683,400 ÷ 150 boats = $4,556 per boat. Apparently, even though Sunbird sold fewer Classic boats, it did so at a higher price—a price high enough to make up the shortfall in volume and still have a favorable performance on revenue.

1. Go ahead and analyze the $18,475 F variance on Deluxe boats. Sunbird sold more boats (four more boats) than expected, but did it also sell them at a higher price? Take a moment and determine the selling price variance on Deluxe boats for Sunbird.

2. The solution for the selling price variance begins with $403,875 ÷ 45 boats = $8,975 actual price per Deluxe boat. The actual price is less than the standard price of $9,400 per Deluxe boat. Hence, there's a $9,400 − $8,975 = $425 U (unfavorable) performance variance on selling price for Sunbird.

F. Operating performance can be distinguished into goals related to effectiveness and goals related to efficiency. Sunbird is *effective* as an organization based on how well it achieves its *revenue (output) goals*. Sunbird is *efficient* based on how well it achieves its *cost (input) goals*. Based on the results above, Sunbird is effective overall in achieving its revenue goals for the year, even though it had an unfavorable sales volume variance on Classic boats and an unfavorable sales price variance on Deluxe boats.

G. How about Sunbird's efficiency performance, that is, how well did it perform with its costs for the year? This is actually a difficult analysis to perform using the Master Budget numbers above. The master budget is computing budgeted costs based on expected sales of 156 Classic boats and 41 Deluxe boats. However, the actual cost results are for actual sales of 150 Classic boats and 45 Deluxe boats. Hence, we'd expect that actual costs for Classic boats would be lower for Classic boats and higher for Deluxe boats. We need a different kind of budget in order to analyze the efficiency of cost performance for Sunbird.

III. Performance Analysis Using the Flexible Budget

A. Sunbird needs to be efficient with its costs. In order to assess efficiency at Sunbird for the last year of operations, the question to be answered is, "What level of costs would be efficient for the number of boats it *actually produced and sold?*" The master budget was built assuming 156 Classic boats and 41 Deluxe boats, but that didn't turn out to be the actual output level. Hence, Sunbird needs to establish a budget for costs based on what it actually produced and sold. This type of budget is called a "flexible budget."

B. What costs are expected to shift based on change in the output level? Only variable costs are expected to shift. Fixed costs should remain constant. Hence, a flexible budget needs to "flex" on the budgeted variable costs used to assess actual output. Budgeted fixed costs should not shift in the flexible budget (i.e., there is no flex in fixed costs!). Below is a flexible budget report for Sunbird's actual sales volume.

Sunbird Boat Company

	Actual Results	Flexible Budget	Variances
Classic sales volume	150 Boats	156 Boats	N/A
Deluxe sales volume	45 Boats	45 Boats	N/A
Classic revenue	$683,400	$630,000	$53,400 F
Deluxe revenue	403,875	423,000	19,125 U
Total revenue	$1,087,275	$1,053,000	$34,275 F
Classic variable costs	$(443,772)	$(417,750)	$26,022 U
Deluxe variable costs	(267,030)	(284,175)	17,145 F
Total variable costs	$(710,802)	$(701,925)	$8,877 U
Total fixed costs	(192,450)	(183,600)	8,850 U
Operating profit	$184,023	$167,475	$16,548 F

1. The most important factor in a flexible budget is that it is based on the actual outcome results (i.e., actual production and sales). This approach makes the costs in this budget relevant for analyzing the efficiency performance of the organization. That is, these are the input costs that *should have been used* to create the actual output.

2. The basic approach to building a flexible budget for costs is to use the following equation:

Total costs = Variable cost rate(Activity volume) + Total fixed costs

Note that Sunbird's standard variable cost rate is $2,785 for Classic boats and $6,315 for Deluxe boats. Total fixed costs are budgeted to be $183,600. These are the cost inputs used to establish the flexible budget above.

3. The budgeted variable costs in the flexible budget ($701,925) are different from the budgeted variable costs in the master budget ($693,375) due to the fact that the flexible budget is based on actual output (150 Classic boats and 45 Deluxe boats) while the master budget (sometimes called the static budget) is based on the original expectations for output (156 Classic boats and 41 Deluxe boats).

4. Again, there is no flex in the budgeted fixed costs. This part of the budget is the same for both the master (static) budget and the flexible budget ($183,600).

C. Now compare the variance analysis results using the master budget and the flexible budget. There are two basic differences.

1. First, the total revenue variance is different ($46,675 F versus $34,275 F). The $46,675 F variance in the master budget is due to the fact that sales volumes and sales prices were different than planned. Essentially, this variance number commingles these two results, making it difficult for managers to clearly control and evaluate issues involving sales volumes and sales prices. On the other hand, the $34,275 F variance in the flexible budget is based strictly on the difference between standard sales prices and actual sales prices. Hence, this variance isolates one issue for management, which is the issue of controlling and evaluating sales price performance for Sunbird. We'll talk more about sales price and sales volume variances in the next lesson.

2. Second, the total variable cost variance is also different ($17,427 U versus $8,877 U). The $17,427 U variance in the master budget is actually irrelevant for management use because it is comparing the budgeted costs to produce and sell 156 Classic boats and 41 Deluxe boats with the actual costs of 150 Classic boats and 45 Deluxe boats. These are not comparable costs. What about the $8,877 U variance in the flexible budget? This number is useful for managers at Sunbird because it is based on the variable costs that Sunbird *should have used* for its actual volume of boats. However, as we will study in subsequent lessons, cost variances are the consequence of two management issues, which are using more or less inputs (e.g., materials, labor, etc.), or paying more or less for those inputs. We need more information about Sunbird's costs before we can break down this $8,877 U variance into information useful for controlling and evaluating operations.

IV. Using Variance Reports to Manage

A. In this lesson we've used master budgets and flexible budgets to introduce you to the concept and computation of performance variances. Before we move forward into the next four lessons, we need to establish two important management concepts involving variances.

B. The first concept is that variance computations are based on the *ceteris paribus* principle, which is Latin for "all other things being equal." This means that a variance computation isolates the effect of a single issue in the organization and measures that effect on operating income. If the effect of the single issue is to increase operating income, then it is described as a "favorable" variance. And if the effect of the single issue decreases operating income, it is an "unfavorable" variance.

1. It is important to understand that "favorable" and "unfavorable" doesn't always mean "good" and "bad." Often management will make a decision leading to a particular unfavorable variance because the decision also leads to one or more favorable outcomes that when combined together have an overall positive effect on operating income.

2. One example of a good result from an unfavorable variance could be a decision to accept an unfavorable labor cost variance because it provides for a better product or service that leads to a favorable sales price variance.

C. The second key management concept involving variances is the concept of "management by exception." Variances provide a signal to management that indicates something in the organization is out of compliance with cost standards or budget expectations, regardless of whether the variance is favorable or unfavorable. If the variance is large enough, it calls attention to management. The value of this management-by-exception approach is it helps the organization focus on current processes that may need attention. It's important to note that variances do not inform management on what the actual problem is or what needs to be done. Variances are simply signals to management to investigate.

Practice Question

Faircloth & Company makes two types of products, Heather and Sage, and sells them for $20 and $25 per pound, respectively. Faircloth wants to analyze performance for the month. Originally, Faircloth planned to sell 30,000 pounds of Heather and 12,000 pounds of Sage in the upcoming month. Below are Heather's standard costs.

Cost Type	Cost Formula
Power:	$0.50 per direct labor hour (DLH)
Maintenance:	$1.25 per DLH + $134,500
Labor:	18.00 per DLH + $68,400
Rent:	$31,500

The Heather product requires 0.6 direct labor hours per pound and the Sage product requires 0.8 direct labor hours per pound.

Actual sales for the month were 32,000 pounds of Heather and 10,400 pounds of Sage at prices of $19.20 and $28.10, respectively. Below are Faircloth's actual costs for the month.

Heather variable costs:	$387,200
Sage variable costs:	$175,136
Total fixed costs:	$231,000

Build a variance report using Faircloth's original master budget. Then build a variance report using Faircloth's flexible budget.

Answer

Before building the budgets, first determine Faircloth's standard variable cost rates and expected total fixed costs as follows:

Variable cost per DLH = $0.50 + $1.25 + $18.00 = $19.75 per DLH

Heather standard variable cost rate = $19.75 per DLH × 0.6 DLH per pound = $11.85

Sage standard variable cost rate = $19.75 per DLH × 0.8 DLH per pound = $15.80

Expected total fixed costs = $134,500 + $68,400 + $31,500 = $234,400

Master Budget Variance Analysis

Faircloth & Company

Actual	Actual Results	Master Budget	Variances
Heather sales volume (lbs)	32,000	30,000	2,000 F
Sage sales volume (lbs)	10,400	12,000	1,600 U
Heather revenue	$614,400	$600,000	$14,400 F
Sage revenue	292,240	300,000	7,760 U
Total revenue	$906,640	$900,000	$6,640 F
Heather variable costs	$(387,200)	$(355,500)	$31,700 U
Sage variable costs	(175,136)	(189,600)	14,464 F
Total variable costs	$(562,336)	$(545,100)	$17,236 U
Total fixed costs	(231,000)	(234,400)	3,400 F
Operating profit	$113,304	$120,500	$7,196 U

Continues...

Flexible Budget Variance Analysis

Faircloth & Company

Actual	Actual Results	Flexible Budget	Variances
Heather sales volume (lbs)	32,000	32,000	N/A
Sage sales volume (lbs)	10,400	10,400	N/A
Heather revenue	$614,400	$640,000	$25,600 U
Sage revenue	292,240	260,000	32,240 F
Total revenue	$906,640	$900,000	$6,640 F
Heather variable costs	$(387,200)	$(379,200)	$8,000 U
Sage variable costs	(175,136)	(164,320)	10,816 U
Total variable costs	$(562,336)	$(543,520)	$18,816 U
Total fixed costs	(231,000)	(234,400)	3,400 F
Operating profit	$113,304	$122,080	$8,776 U

Summary

Beginning with the next lesson we will work on computing a number of specific variance computations that managers use to control and evaluate operations. As we work through these computations, it's important that you remember how the master budget compares to the flexible budget for computing variances. The master budget (also called the static budget) is based on the original expectations for production and sales volumes before the start of the operating period. In contrast, the flexible budget is built after the conclusion of the operating period and is based on actual production and sales volumes. The variance analysis using the master budget is useful only for evaluating the *effectiveness* of performance output involving sales volumes. The flexible budget, on the other hand, is focused on managing the *efficiency* of inputs used to produce and sell the organization's actual volume of products or services.

Sales Revenue Variances

After studying this lesson, you should be able to:

- Calculate the sales-volume variance and the sales-price variance by comparing the flexible budget to the master (static) budget (1.C.1.f).

- Calculate a sales-mix variance and explain its impact on revenue and contribution margin (1.C.1.n).

In this lesson we introduce the overall variance framework and begin working on computing specific variances. In particular, this lesson establishes the computations for the sales price variance, the sales volume variance, the sales mix variance, and the sales quantity variance.

I. Variance Frameworks and Variance Formulas

A. As described in the last lesson, it is crucial in the computation of variances to isolate on the factor creating the variance between budgeted and actual performance. There are two ways to approach the computation of variances—the framework approach and the formula approach. Either approach results in the same computation that isolates the factor causing the variance.

B. The framework approach is the more visual method of the two approaches. The most basic form of the variance framework is presented below.

The Variance Framework

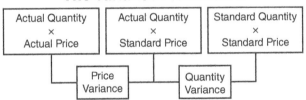

1. As you can see, the framework clearly distinguishes between quantities and prices. Revenue performance is the result of quantities sold and prices received, and cost performance is the result of quantities used and prices paid.

2. Moving from left to right, the framework approach begins by computing (or observing) the actual results based on actual quantity and prices. The next step is to compute how much should have been received (for revenues) or paid (for costs) based on the standard price. The difference between these two values (actual quantity at actual price versus actual quantity at standard price) isolates the effect of price on operating profits and is called the price variance.

3. The quantity variance is computed by continuing to move left to right. The third value in the framework is the standard quantity at the standard price.

- When working with revenue, the standard quantity represents how much quantity was expected to be sold (and is often referred to as the "expected quantity"). This quantity of expected output is represented in the organization's *master budget.*

- When working with costs, the standard quantity represents how much input (e.g., materials, labor, etc.) should have been used to produce the *actual volume of output* (and is often referred to as the "standard quantity allowed"). When computing cost variances, be sure to use the standard quantity allowed for the actual output, which comes from the organization's *flexible budget.*

4. As can be seen above, the quantity variance is computed by comparing the actual quantity at standard price with the standard quantity at standard price. This approach isolates the effect of the quantity variance on operating profit.

C. The formula approach to computing variances effectively shortcuts the visual framework approach by directly computing the variance.

    1. For the price variance, the formula is as follows:

$$\text{Actual quantity} \times (\text{Standard price} - \text{Actual price}) = \text{Price variance}$$

    2. For the quantity variance, the formula is as follows:

$$(\text{Standard quantity} - \text{Actual quantity}) \times \text{Standard price} = \text{Quantity variance}$$

        Note in the structure of these formulas that the source of the variance is contained with parentheses.

D. Finally, with respect to determining whether the variance is favorable (F) or unfavorable (U), it is best to make this determination *before* computing the variance. Remember from the last lesson that favorable and unfavorable doesn't necessarily mean "good" and "bad." Hence, don't worry about whether the computation results in a negative or positive number.

    1. For example, in the formula for the price variance above, note that if the actual price is higher than the standard price, the result will be a negative number. If this is a cost variance being computed, then the organization is actually paying a higher price (for materials or labor) than the standard, and that has an unfavorable (negative) effect on operating profit.

    2. On the other hand, what if the price variance formula above is used to compute a revenue variance? If the actual price is higher than the standard price (which results in a negative number in the formula structure above), the variance has a *favorable (positive) effect* on operating profit.

E. In the process of computing variances (using either the framework approach or formula approach), it's easy to become confused about whether the computational result is a favorable or unfavorable variance. Hence, don't wait to do the computation and then determine whether the variance is favorable or unfavorable. Instead, *before* computing the variance, consider the factor being isolated (price or quantity) and logically conclude if the relation between actual and standard has a favorable or unfavorable effect on operating profit. With the "U" or the "F" in place, *then* compute the size of the variance.

II. Sales Price Variance

A. Let's return now to our work with the Sunbird Boat Company. Below are some numbers you'll recognize from the last lesson.

Sunbird Boat Company

Budget	Classic (Oak)	Deluxe (Teak)
Expected sales volume	156 boats	41 boats
Standard price per boat	$4,200	$9,400

Actual	Classic (Oak)	Deluxe (Teak)
Actual sale volume	150 boats	45 boats
Actual price per boat	$4,556	$8,975

B. We can use the framework approach to compute the sales price variance for Sunbird. The specific framework for the sales price variance is below, followed by the computations.

The Sales Price Variance

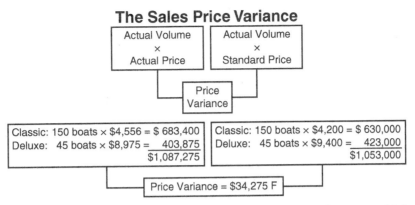

Because the left-side result of the framework with the actual sales price is higher than the right-side result with the standard sales price, this is a favorable (F) variance.

C. Alternatively, we can use the formula approach. Before computing the variance, note that the actual sales price for Classic boats ($4,556) is higher than the standard price ($4,200). Hence, the sales price variance for Classic boats is favorable. In contrast, the actual sales price for Deluxe boats ($8,975) is lower than its standard price ($9,400), which means the variance for Deluxe boats is unfavorable.

1. The formula approach for the sales price variance is as follows:

Actual volume $\times$ (Standard price $-$ Actual price)
Classic: 150 boats $\times$ ($4,200 $-$ $4,556) = $53,400 F
Deluxe: 45 boats $\times$ ($9,400 $-$ $8,975) = $19,125 U
Total sales price variance: $53,400 F $+$ $19,125 U = $34,275 F

2. Note that the computational solution for Classic boats is actually a negative value, but the result is reported as an absolute value (i.e., non-negative). Variances are not reported as negative or positive values, but as unfavorable (U) or favorable (F) values. Hence, even though the computation solution for Deluxe boats is a positive value, the variance is actually unfavorable as we determined before computing the size of the variances.

III. Sales Volume Variance—Measured by Price

A. In addition to actual sales prices being different from standard prices, Sunbird Boat Company also experienced sales volumes being different than expected (budgeted). Using the framework approach, the size and direction of Sunbird's sales volume variance is computed below.

The Sales Volume Variance

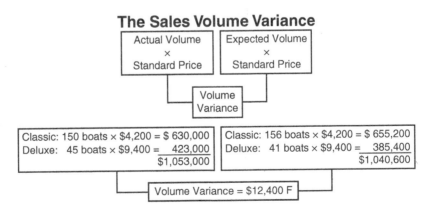

Again, because the left-side result of the framework with the actual sales volume is higher than the right-side result with the expected sales volume, this is a favorable (F) variance.

B. Using the formula approach, we can replicate the sales volume variance computation. But first let's determine if the results will be favorable or unfavorable. The actual sales volume for Classic boats (150 boats) is lower than expected (156 boats), which is an unfavorable result. On the other than, the actual volume for Deluxe boats (45 boats) is higher than expected (41 boats), which is a favorable result.

1. The formula approach for the sales volume variance is as follows:

(Expected volume − Actual volume) × Standard price
Classic: (156 boats − 150 boats) × $4,200 = $25,200 U
Deluxe: (41 boats − 45 boats) × $9,400 = $37,600 F
Total sales volume variance: $25,200 U + $37,600 F = $12,400 F

2. Again, remember that these computations are reported as absolute values. Hence, even though the Deluxe boats computational result is negative, it is reported as a favorable (F) value.

IV. Sales Volume Variance—Measured by Contribution Margin

A. When the volume of sales is different than expected, it affects both the revenue and the operating profit of the organization, but the dollar-size effect of the sales volume variance is different for revenue compared to the effect on operating profit.

B. With respect to the Sunbird Boat Company, we used the standard sales price to compute the sales volume variance as $12,400 F. The dollar value of this variance represents how much revenue will increase due to increased sales, but it doesn't represent how much the operating profit will increase for Sunbird. Why? Because increased sales volume not only increases revenue but also increases some costs—specifically, it increases the organization's variable costs.

C. Some organizations will use the standard sales price to understand how the sales volume variance affects revenues, but most organizations are focused on the "bottom-line effect" of the sales volume variance. In order to isolate the effect of the sales volume variance on operating profit, the organization needs to use the *standard contribution margin per unit* (rather than the standard sales price per unit) to measure the effect of the variance on profit.

D. We introduced Sunbird's standard variable costs per boat in the previous lesson. That information is provided below, along with the actual sales volume data needed to compute the sales volume variance measured in contribution margin dollars.

Sunbird Boat Company

Budget	Classic (Oak)	Deluxe (Teak)
Expected sales volume	156 boats	41 boats
Standard price per boat	$4,200	$9,400
Standard variable cost	(2,785)	(6,315)
Standard contribution margin	$1,415	$3,085

Actual sales volume	150 boats	45 boats

E. Using the framework approach, we can recompute Sunbird's sales volume variance measured in terms of contribution margin. The computations are below.

The Sales Volume Variance

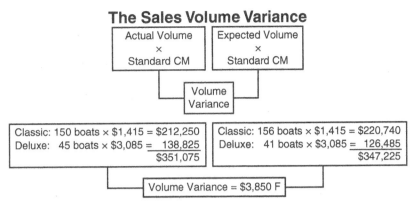

1. The total sales volume variance measured in standard contribution margin dollars is $3,850 F. Remember that we previously computed this volume variance measured in standard sales price dollars as $12,400 F. What these two values tells us is due to the volume of sales being different than planned, Sunbird's revenue will be $12,400 higher and its operating profit will be $3,850 higher.

2. Notice something interesting in these results. Sunbird actually sold a total of 195 boats (150 + 45). However, it expected to sell a total of 197 boats (156 + 41). Even though Sunbird total sales volume measured in boats was *less* than expected, the sales volume variance measured in dollars is *favorable*. Why? It has to do with selling more of the Deluxe boats, which have a higher standard contribution margin per boat. We'll explore this issue in the last part of this lesson.

F. Now let's use the formula approach to compute the sales volume variance measured in standard contribution margin (CM) dollars. We've already determined whether the computations will be favorable (F) or unfavorable (U). This determination is based strictly on comparing the volume of boats expected compared to actual volume. Using standard sales prices or standard contribution margins doesn't change the direction of the variances.

1. The formula approach is as follows:

(Expected volume − Actual volume) × Standard CM = Sales volume variance
Classic: (156 boats − 150 boats) × $1,415 = $8,490 U
Deluxe: (41 boats − 45 boats) × $3,085 = $12,340 F
Total sales volume variance: $8,490 U + $12,340 F = $3,850 F

2. Again, most organizations prefer to measure the sales volume variance in terms of standard contribution margin in order to understand the bottom line effect on operating profit. Hence, for the remainder of our work on variances, we're going to use standard contribution margin to measure all variances involving the sales volume. Be sure, though, to pay attention to whether the organization uses price or contribution margin to compute revenue variances.

V. Sales Mix and Quantity Variances

A. Before we wrap up our discussion on planning and controlling sales revenue using variance analysis, we need to work through one more management issue. Most organizations sell a mix of products or services, which means that the sales volume variance results not only from selling more or less total volume of goods and services, but also from selling *relatively more or less* of one type of product versus another. The financial size of the sales volume variance is affected by both of these issues.

B. For Sunbird Boat Company, note that Deluxe boats have a higher standard price and a higher standard contribution margin compared to Classic boats. When customers come to Sunbird to purchase a boat, they're choosing to buy either a Deluxe or Classic boat, and Sunbird certainly cares about which boat they buy! This means that Sunbird should work to sell more overall boats *and* sell more Deluxe boats compared to Classic boats. Performance on these two issues needs to be measured in order to control and evaluate sales volume operations at Sunbird Boat Company.

C. Variance analysis can break down the sales volume variance into two separate variances that distinguish the financial effect of selling more or less of one type of product or service relative to another, as well as the financial effect of selling more or less total products or services. The framework approach provides a visual method of seeing and computing these two variances.

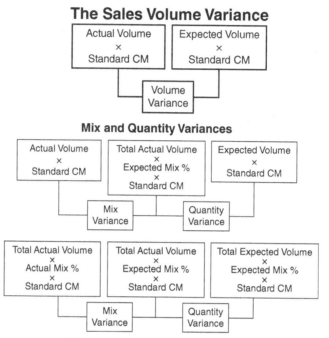

The Sales Volume Variance

Mix and Quantity Variances

1. As you can see above, the mix variance and the quantity variance are subsets of the volume variance. By inserting a middle box (total actual volume × expected mix percentage × standard contribution margin) between the two original boxes in the volume variance framework, we neatly split the volume variance into two parts—the mix variance and the quantity variance.

2. The logic of this middle box is seen by expanding the two original boxes as displayed in the bottom framework. Sunbird Boat Company is selling two different boat products, Classic and Deluxe. Each of those boat product lines has its own actual and expected level of sales volume. Combined, Sunbird actually sold 195 boats and expected to sell 197 boats, with an actual and expected mix percentage of each type of boat, as shown below.

Sunbird Boat Company

Master Budget	Classic (Oak)	Deluxe (Teak)	Total
Expected sales volume	156 boats	41 boats	197 boats
Expected mix percentage	79.19%	20.81%	100.00%
Standard contribution margin	$1,415	$3,085	

Actual	Classic (Oak)	Deluxe (Teak)	Total
Actual sales volume	150 boats	45 boats	195 boats
Actual mix percentage	76.92%	23.08%	100.00%

Note that the total expected sales volume (197 boats) multiplied by the expected mix percentage of Classic boats (79.19%) is equal to the expected volume of Classic boats (156 boats). Hence, we can compute the two original boxes in the sales volume framework using total quantities and product line mix percentages. This additional computational work doesn't change the results, but it does provide a way to see how the mix variance isolates the effect of selling more or less of one boat line compared to another boat line at Sunbird. This view also helps us see how the quantity variance is isolating the effect of Sunbird selling more or less *total* boats.

3. Using the framework approach, we compute the sales mix variance as shown below.

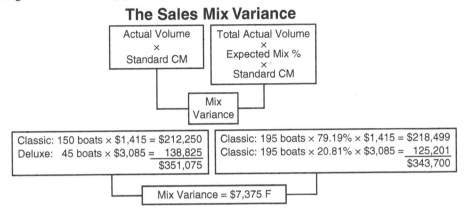

The Sales Mix Variance

When using mix percentages, it's very important to use the precise percentage number (don't round off the percentage). For example, the 79.19% in the formula above that calculates $218,499 must be used with its full precision (156 boats ÷ 197 boats = .791878).

4. This mix variance is favorable (F) because Sunbird's actual mix of Deluxe boats (23.08%) is higher than its expected mix percentage (20.81%) relative to the mix percentage of Classic boats. This has a favorable effect on operating profit because the standard contribution margin of Deluxe boats ($3,085) is higher than Classic boats ($1,415). In short, Sunbird was able to increase the percentage of sales to the product line with a higher contribution margin per unit.

5. Using the framework approach, we compute the sales quantity variance as shown below.

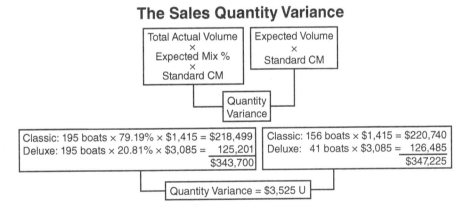

The Sales Quantity Variance

Again, be sure to use precise sales mix percentages when computing this variance. By doing so, the sales quantity variance combined with the sales mix variance will equal the sales volume variance ($7,375 F + $3,525 U = $3,850 F).

6. The sales quantity variance is unfavorable (U) because Sunbird sold fewer total boats (195 boats) than expected (197 boats). This computation isolates the effect of the total quantity variance by holding constant the standard sales mix in both boxes above.

D. The framework approach to computing the sales mix and sales quantity variances is rather involved, but it has the advantage of visually demonstrating how these two variances are subsets of the volume variance. Alternatively, we can compute these variances using the formula approach.

1. The formula approach for the sales mix variance is as follows:

   Total actual volume × (Expected mix % − Actual mix %) × Standard CM
   Classic: 195 boats × (79.19% − 76.92%) × $1,415 = $6,249 U
   Deluxe: 195 boats × (20.81% − 23.08%) × $3,085 = $13,624 F
   Total sales mix variance: $6,249 U + $13,624 F = $7,375 F

2. The formula approach for the sales quantity variance is as follows:

   (Total expected volume − Total actual volume) × Expected mix % × Standard CM
   Classic: (195 boats − 197 boats) × 79.19% × $1,415 = $2,241 U
   Deluxe: (195 boats − 197 boats) × 20.81% × $3,085 = $1,284 U
   Total sales quantity variance: $2,241 U + $1,284 U = $3,525 U

E. Note that the percentages used to compute the mix variance and the quantity variance are not rounded off in the computations above. For example, the expected sales percentage mix used for Classic boats is not exactly 79.19% but is closer to 79.1878173%. It's important to use a precise percentage mix in order to have the mix variance and the quantity variance sum up to the volume variance. By keeping the computations precise in the two variances (which are a subset of the volume variance), you can verify that you've handled the computations accurately if the sales mix variance and the sales quantity variance sum up precisely to the original sales volume variance ($7,375 F + $3,525 U = $3,850 F).

Practice Question

This question expands the Practice Question from the last lesson. Faircloth & Company makes two types of products, Heather and Sage, and sells them for $20 and $25 per pound, respectively. Originally, Faircloth planned to sell 30,000 pounds of Heather and 12,000 pounds of Sage in the upcoming month. Actual sales for the month were 32,000 pounds of Heather and 10,400 pounds of Sage at prices of $19.20 and $28.10, respectively. Heather's standard variable costs per pound are $11.85 for Heather and $15.80 for Sage.

Compute the following variances for Faircloth & Company.

a. Sales price variance

b. Sales volume variance measured by contribution margin

c. Sales mix variance measured by contribution margin

d. Sales quantity variance measured by contribution margin

Answer

a. Sales price variance

   Note first that Faircloth has an unfavorable (U) price variance for the Heather product (actual price < standard price) and a favorable (F) price variance for the Sage product (actual price > standard price).

   Sales price variance = Actual volume × (Standard price − Actual price)
   Heather: 32,000 pounds × ($20.00 − $19.20) = $25,600 U
   Sage: 10,400 pounds × ($25.00 − $28.10) = $32,240 F
   Total sales price variance: $25,600 U + $32,240 F = $6,640 F

b. Sales volume variance

   Faircloth has a favorable (F) volume variance for the Heather product (actual volume > expected volume) and an unfavorable (U) volume variance for the Sage product (actual volume < expected volume).

   Continues…

Standard contribution margin per pound for Heather: $20.00 − $11.85 = $8.15
Standard contribution margin per pound for Sage: $25.00 − $15.80 = $9.20
Sales volume variance = (Expected volume − Actual volume) × Standard price
Heather: (30,000 pounds − 32,000 pounds) × $8.15 = $16,300 F
Sage: (12,000 pounds − 10,400 pounds) × $9.20 = $14,720 U
Total sales volume variance: $16,300 F + $14,720 U = $1,580 F

c. Sales mix variance

Heather sales mix percentages (don't round off these percentages):

30,000 pounds ÷ 42,000 pounds = 71.43% *expected sales mix percentage*
32,000 pounds ÷ 42,400 pounds = 75.47% actual sales mix percentage (Favorable for Heather)

Sage sales mix percentages (don't round off these percentages):

12,000 pounds ÷ 42,000 pounds = 28.57% expected sales mix percentage
10,400 pounds ÷ 42,400 pounds = 24.53% actual sales mix percentage (Unfavorable for Sage)

Overall sales mix variance will be unfavorable (U) because Faircloth is selling relatively less of the product with the highest standard contribution margin (Sage).

Sales mix variance = Total actual volume × (Expected mix % − Actual mix %) × Standard CM
Heather: 42,400 pounds × (71.43% − 75.47%) × $8.15 = $13,971 F
Sage: 42,400 pounds × (28.57% − 24.53%) × $9.20 = $15,771 U
Total sales mix variance: $13,971 F + $15,771 U = $1,800 U

d. Sales quantity variance

Faircloth has a favorable (F) quantity variance because it sold more total pounds (42,400) than expected (42,000).

Sales quantity variance =
(Total expected volume − Total actual volume) × Expected mix % × Standard CM
Heather: (42,000 pounds − 42,400 pounds) × 71.43% × $8.15 = $2,329 F
Sage: (42,000 pounds − 42,400 pounds) × 28.57% × $9.20 = $1,051 F
Total sales quantity variance: $2,329 F + $1,051 F = $3,380 F

Summary
The overall variance framework is a useful way to visually work through the construction of specific variance formulas. Be sure to take note of this framework, which is the first exhibit in this lesson. Price variances are based on the difference between the actual price and standard price, multiplied by the actual quantity sold (or used). Quantity variances are based on the difference between actual quantity and standard quantity, multiplied by the standard price. When controlling and evaluating sales revenue, the quantity variance is usually referred to as the sales volume variance and is based on the difference between actual volume sold and the expected volume sold. The standard price used to determine the dollar size of the volume variance can be either the standard selling price or the standard contribution margin. Generally, most organizations use the standard contribution margin to establish the sales volume variance. The sales volume variance can be separated into the sales mix variance and the sales quantity variance. The sales mix variance is based on the difference between each product's expected and actual sales mix percentage of total sales, multiplied by the total actual volume of all products and the product's standard price or contribution margin. The sales quantity variance is based on the difference between the *total* expected sales volume of all products or service compared to the *total* actual volume, multiplied by each product's expected sales mix percentage and standard price or contribution margin.

Direct Material and Direct Labor Cost Variances

After studying this lesson, you should be able to:

- Define a standard cost system and identify the reasons for adopting a standard cost system (1.C.1.j).

- Demonstrate an understanding of price (rate) variances and calculate the price variances related to direct material and direct labor inputs (1.C.1.k).

- Demonstrate an understanding of efficiency (usage) variances and calculate the efficiency variances related to direct material and direct labor inputs (1.C.1.l).

- Calculate and explain a mix variance (1.C.1.o).

- Calculate and explain a yield variance (1.C.1.p).

In this lesson we will continue working with the overall variance framework to build computations for the directs materials price and usages variances, the direct labor rate and efficiency variances, and the mix and yield variances.

I. Standard Cost Systems

   A. Standard cost systems were thoroughly discussed in Section B. As a reminder, companies use cost standards throughout the management process of planning, controlling, and evaluating costs in the organization.

   B. A standard cost sheet functions like a "recipe card" that specifies standard prices and standard quantities to build and deliver a single product or service, as demonstrated below for the Sunbird Boat Company and its Classic boat product.

Sunbird Boat Company

Standard Cost Sheet—Classic Boat	Input Quantity	Cost per Input	Cost per Boat
Direct materials (oak wood)—square feet	80 ft^2	$10.00 per ft^2	$800.00
Direct labor (artisans)—direct labor hours	20 DLH	$47.50 per DLH	950.00
Direct labor (assistants)—direct labor hours	30 DLH	$15.00 per DLH	450.00
Variable manufacturing overhead—total DLH	50 DLH	$7.50 per DLH	375.00
Fixed manufacturing overhead—total DLH	50 DLH	$10.00 per DLH	500.00
Total Cost to Manufacture			**$3,075.00**
Variable selling overhead—boats	1 boat	$210 per boat	210.00
Total Cost to Deliver			**$3,285.00**

Note that the input quantity multiplied by the cost per input equals cost per boat. Also note in this example that manufacturing overhead (MOH) costs are being allocated on the basis of total direct labor hours (DLH).

II. Direct Materials Cost Variances

   A. Cost variances follow the same computational framework as revenue variances. The basic framework, which we introduced in the previous lesson, is presented below.

The Variance Framework

B. The approach we followed in the previous lesson to compute revenue variances works similarly for the cost variances used in controlling and evaluating direct materials costs. There are two important distinctions with direct materials cost variances, which are represented in the specific variance framework below for direct materials.

The Direct Materials Variance Framework

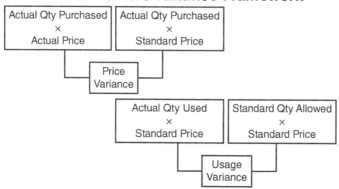

1. The best management approach to successfully control and evaluate costs is to identify the cost variance as soon as possible. When it comes to direct materials, rather than compute the price variance on the quantity used, best practice is to identify and report the price variance as soon as direct materials are purchased (i.e., quantity purchased). This means that the price variance should be computed for the quantity *purchased*, not for the quantity used subsequently in production.

2. To emphasize that the direct materials quantity variance is based on the quantity used in production, the variance is typically called the "usage variance." What's more important is to note that the variance isn't based on the standard quantity in the original master budget, but on the standard quantity in the flexible budget. This quantity is often referred to as the "standard quantity allowed" for the actual volume of production and sales.

C. Let's return now to our Sunbird Boat Company example. Sunbird produces and sells two types of boats, but for cost variance purposes in our lesson we'll focus just on cost management for the Classic boats using the standard costs provided at the beginning of this lesson, as well as the following actual information:

15,000 ft^2 of wood was purchased for $141,750 of which 13,290 ft^2 was used in production.

150 Classic boats were produced and sold during the year.

D. We can use the framework approach to compute the direct materials price variance for Sunbird as shown below.

The Direct Materials Price Framework

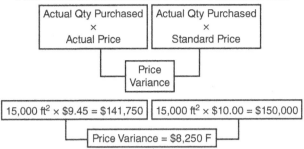

Note that we can compute the actual price paid per ft^2 of wood as $9.45 per ft^2 ($141,750 ÷ 15,000 ft^2). Since this actual price is less than the standard price, the direct materials price variance is favorable (F).

E. Alternatively, we can use the formula approach to compute direct material price variance.

1. The formula approach for this variance is as follows:

Actual quantity purchased × (Standard price − Actual price)

Direct materials price variance: 15,000 ft^2 × ($10.00 − $9.45) = $8,250 F

2. If Sunbird management chooses to compute the price variance on the direct materials quantity used, this is a simple adjustment in either the framework approach or the formula approach as follows:

Actual quantity used × (Standard price − Actual price)

Direct materials price variance: 13,290 ft^2 × ($10.00 − $9.45) = $7,309.50 F

F. To complete the direct material variance analysis for Sunbird Boat Company, we turn attention to how much material was actually used in production, and how much material should have been used to support the actual production output (i.e., standard quantity allowed). Based on the standard quantity of 80 ft^2 of oak wood per Classic boat and actual production and sales of 150 boats, Sunbird should have used 12,000 ft^2 of wood for its actual production (80 ft^2 × 150 boats).

G. Using the framework approach, we can compute the usage variance. Before doing so, note that this variance is clearly unfavorable (U) based on comparing the standard quantity allowed of 12,000 ft^2 against the actual quantity used reported above of 13,290 ft^2.

The Direct Materials Usage Framework

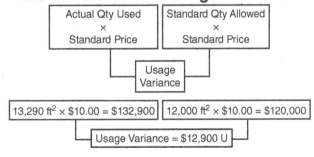

H. Using the formula approach, the direct materials usage variance can be computed quickly as follows:

(Standard quantity allowed − Actual quantity used) × Standard price

Direct materials usage variance: (12,000 ft^2 − 13,290 ft^2) × $10.00 = $12,900 U

III. Direct Labor Cost Variances

    A. Direct labor cost variances are quite similar to direct materials cost variances. Of course, most organizations don't purchase the direct labor in advance of actually using labor, so the variance framework for direct labor is very similar to the conceptual framework as shown below.

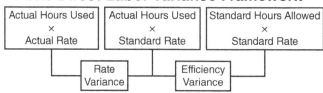

The Direct Labor Variance Framework

Note that there are two shifts in terminology for this framework that are specific to direct labor costs. First, "rate" is used in place of "price." Direct labor prices are often described as labor rates. Second, using more or less direct labor than budgeted is often an issue of managing the efficiency of labor usage. Hence, the quantity variance here is described as an efficiency variance.

    B. Assume the following actual direct labor results for Classic boats for the Sunbird Boat Company:

        Artisans were paid a total of $123,804 to work 2,715 hours, and assistants were paid a total of $87,135 to work 4,710 hours.

        150 Classic boats were produced and sold during the year.

    C. With the actual results above, and the standard inputs and costs provided earlier, we'll use the framework approach to compute the direct rate variance for Sunbird as shown below.

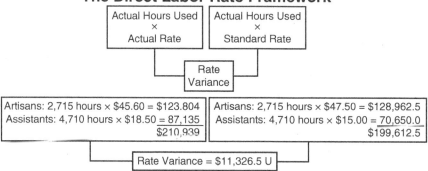

The Direct Labor Rate Framework

Since the left side of the framework, which is based on actual labor rates, is larger than the right side, this variance is unfavorable (U).

    D. Now we'll compute the labor rate variance using the formula approach. Note that the artisans' actual labor rate is lower than standard ($45.60 versus $47.50, respectively), which indicates a favorable (F) rate variance. The assistants' actual labor rate is higher than standard ($18.50 versus $15.00, respectively), which indicates an unfavorable (U) rate variance.

Actual quantity × (Standard rate – Actual rate)

Artisans: 2,715 hours × ($47.50 – $45.60) = $5,158.5 F

Assistants: 4,710 hours × ($15.00 – $18.50) = $16,485.0 U

Total labor rate variance: $5,158.5 F + $16,485.0 U= $11,326.5 U

    E. Let's now shift to the labor efficiency variance for Sunbird Boat Company. Remember that Sunbird produced and sold 150 Classic boats. Based on the standard number of direct labor hours provided in the standard cost sheet for Classic boats, the standard hours allowed for artisans is 3,000 hours (150 boats × 20 hours), and the standard hours allowed for assistants is

4,500 hours (150 boats × 30 hours). The framework approach delivers the direct labor efficiency variance as shown below.

The Direct Labor Efficiency Framework

```
┌─────────────────────┐  ┌──────────────────────┐
│ Actual Hours Used   │  │ Standard Hours Allowed│
│         ×           │  │          ×           │
│   Standard Rate     │  │    Standard Rate     │
└─────────────────────┘  └──────────────────────┘
            │     ┌──────────────┐    │
            └─────│  Efficiency  │────┘
                  │   Variance   │
                  └──────────────┘
```

| Artisans: 2,715 hours × $47.50 = $128,962.5
Assistants: 4,710 hours × $15.00 = 70,650.0
$199,612.5 | Artisans: 3,000 hours × $47.50 = $142,500
Assistants: 4,500 hours × $15.00 = 67,500
$210,000 |

Efficiency Variance = $10,387.5 F

The left side of the framework (representing the actual quantity of labor hours) is smaller than the right side, so this variance is favorable (F).

F. Using the formula approach, we can replicate the results above. Note that the artisans' actual total hours are lower than the standard hours allowed for actual production (2,715 hours versus 3,000 hours, respectively), which indicates a favorable (F) efficiency variance. And the assistants' actual hours are higher than standard allowed (4,710 hours versus 4,500 hours, respectively), which indicates an unfavorable (U) efficiency variance.

(Standard hours allowed – Actual hours used) × Standard rate

Artisans: (3,000 hours – 2,715 hours) × $47.50 = $13,537.5 F

Assistants: (4,500 hours – 4,710 hours) × $15.00 = $3,150.0 U

Direct labor efficiency variance: $13,537.5 F + $3,150.0 U = $10,387.5 F

IV. Mix and Yield Cost Variances

A. When it comes to controlling and evaluating labor costs, it's important that Sunbird measure and manage the relative proportions of its two types of labor (artisans and assistants) in the process of building boats. In fact, the sales mix and quantity variance we studied in the previous lesson are very similar to the direct labor mix and yield cost variances presented below as we close out this lesson.

B. Artisan labor hours cost substantially more than the labor hours of assistants. If artisan labor hours start increasing *relative* to assistant labor hours in the production process, that contributes to an unfavorable labor efficiency variance. In addition, if the *total* labor hours of both artisans and assistants are increasing, that also creates an unfavorable labor efficiency variance. This means that Sunbird management can (and should) separate the labor efficiency variance into a labor mix variance and a labor yield variance. (The term *yield* refers to how much total input was used to produce (or yield) the output.). We use the framework approach below to visualize and compute these two variances.

The Direct Labor Efficiency Framework

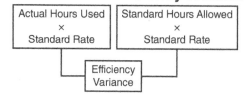

Mix and Yield Variances

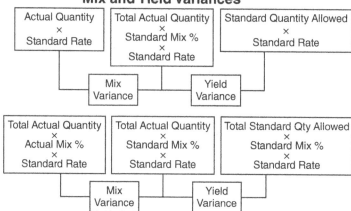

1. Similar to the sales volume variance relationship with sales mix and sales quantity, the mix variance and the yield variance are subsets of the labor efficiency variance. The middle box (total actual quantity × standard mix percentage × standard price) splits the efficiency variance into the mix variance and the yield variance.

2. The logic of this middle box is seen by expanding the two original boxes in the bottom part of the framework. Sunbird Boat Company uses two different types of labor to produce boats. Each of those types of labor has its own actual quantity and standard quantity allowed of hours for the boats produced. Combined, Sunbird used a total of 7,425 hours to build and sell 150 Classic boats, with an actual and standard mix percentage for each labor type as shown below.

Sunbird Boat Company

Flexible Budget	Artisans	Assistants	Total
Actual sales volume (Classic)	150 boats	150 boats	150 boats
Standard hours per boat	× 20 hours	× 30 hours	× 50 hours
Standard hours allowed	3,000 hours	4,500 hours	7,500 hours
Standard mix percentage	40.00%	60.00%	100.00%

Actual	Artisans	Assistants	Total
Actual quantity of hours	2,715 hrs	4,710 hrs	7,425 hrs
Actual mix percentage	36.57%	63.43%	100.00%

Note, for example, that the actual quantity of total hours (7,425 hours) multiplied by the actual mix percentage of artisan hours (36.57%) is equal to 2,715 hours, which is the actual quantity of artisan hours (be sure to not round off the mix percentage). Hence, we can compute the two original boxes in the direct labor efficiency framework using total total quantity and the labor mix percentages. This additional computational work doesn't change the results, but it does provide a way to seeing how the mix variance isolates the effect of using more or less of one labor type compared to another at Sunbird. This view also helps us see how the yield variance is isolating the effect of Sunbird using more or less *total* direct labor hours.

3. Using the framework approach, we compute the direct labor mix variance as shown below.

The Direct Labor Mix Variance

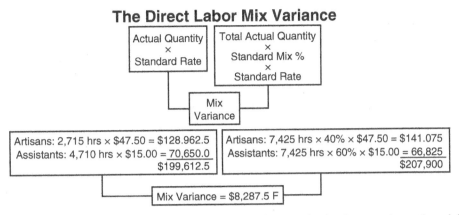

4. This mix variance is favorable (F) because Sunbird's actual mix of expensive artisan labor hours is lower than its standard mix percentage by 3.43% (40.00% − 36.75%). Of course, the mix percentage of the cheaper assistant hours has increased by the same 3.43%. This shift in relative labor inputs has a favorable effect on operating profit.

5. Using the framework approach, we compute the direct labor yield variance as shown below.

The Direct Labor Yield Variance

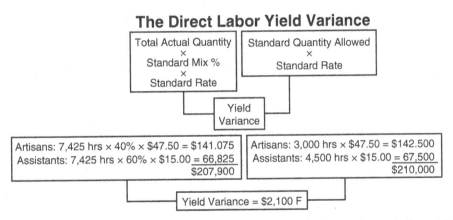

6. The direct labor yield variance is favorable (F) because Sunbird's total actual direct labor hours (7,425 hours) is fewer than total standard hours allowed (7,500 hours). This computation isolates the effect of the direct labor yield variance by holding constant each of the standard labor mix percentages in both boxes above.

7. Again, be sure to use precise mix percentages when computing this variance. By doing so, the yield variance combined with the mix variance will equal the efficiency variance ($8,287.5 F + $2,100 F = $10,387.5 F), which helps confirm that you've handled the computations correctly.

C. Alternatively, we can compute both of these variances using the formula approach.

1. The formula approach for the labor mix variance is as follows:

Total actual quantity × (Standard mix% − Actual mix%) × Standard rate

Artisans: 7,425 hours × (40.00% − 36.57%) × $47.50 = $12,112.5 F

Assistants: 7,425 hours × (60.00% − 63.43%) × $15.00 = $3,825.0 U

Total direct labor mix variance: $12,122.5 F + $3,825.0 U = $8,287.5 F

2. The formula approach for the labor yield variance is as follows:

(Total standard qty allowed– Total actual qty) × Standard mix% × Standard rate

Artisans: (7,500 hours – 7,425 hours) × 40.00% × $47.50= $1,425 F

Assistants: (7,500 hours – 7,425 hours) × 60.00% × $15.00= $675 F

Total direct labor yield variance: $1,425 F + $675 F = $2,100 F

D. Mix and yield variances can be computed for direct materials costs as well. That said, it is typically more realistic to consider the tradeoff of one type of labor versus another type of labor. Often employees are able to shift to other lines of work in the production process, and the organization should control and evaluate production processes to be sure the most efficient (cost-effective) employees are working each stage of the process. Certain products (e.g., some food products) can realistically shift the relative percentages of one type of direct material versus another, but for most products (e.g., cars, computers, etc.) it doesn't make sense to break down the direct materials usage variance into a mix and yield variance.

Practice Question

This question expands the Practice Question from previous lessons. Faircloth & Company makes two types of products. The standard cost sheet is provided below for one of those products, Sage. Actual sales on the Sage product last month were 10,400 lbs.

Faircloth & Company

Standard Cost Sheet—Sage Product	Input Quantity	Cost per Input	Cost per lb.
Direct materials (Zyph)—ounces	6 ounces	$2.00 per ounce	$12.00
Direct materials (Noosh)—ounces	12 ounces	$0.20 per ounce	2.40
Direct labor—direct labor minutes	2 DLM	$0.25 per DLM	.50
Variable manufacturing overhead—DLM	2 DLM	$0.45 per DLM	.90
Fixed manufacturing overhead—DLM	2 DLM	$5.00 per DLM	10.00
Total Product Cost			**$25.80**

Faircloth purchased 68,640 ounces of Zyph last month for $130,416 and purchased 108,160 ounces of Noosh for $27,040. All materials were completely used to produce and sell 10,400 pounds of Sage.

Faircloth also used 433.33 direct labor hours (26,000 direct labor minutes) at a cost of $6,760 to produce the 10,400 pounds of Sage that was sold last month.

Compute the following variances for the Sage product.

a. Direct materials price variance

b. Direct materials usage variance

c. Direct materials mix variance

d. Direct materials yield variance

e. Direct labor rate variance

f. Direct labor efficiency variance

Answer

a. Direct materials price variance

First, the actual price paid for Zyph was $1.90 per ounce ($130,416 ÷ 68,640 ounces). And the actual price paid for Zyph was $0.25 per ounce ($27,040 ÷ 108,160 ounces). Based on comparing actual prices to standard prices, Faircloth has a favorable (F) price variance for Zyph and an unfavorable price variance for Noosh.

Continues…

Direct materials price variance = Actual volume × (Standard price – Actual price)

Zyph: 68,640 ounces × ($2.00 – $1.90) = $6,864 F

Noosh: 108,160 ounces × ($0.20 – $0.25) = $5,408 U

Total direct materials price variance: $6,864 F + $5,408 U = $1,456 F

b. Direct materials usage variance

Based on the standard number of ounces reported in the standard cost sheet for the Sage product, the standard ounces allowed for Zyph is 62,400 ounces (10,400 pounds × 6.00 ounces), and the standard ounces allowed for Noosh is 124,800 ounces (10,400 pounds × 12.00 ounces). Faircloth has an unfavorable (U) usage variance for Zyph and a favorable (F) usage variance for Noosh.

Direct materials usage variance = (Standard quantity allowed – Actual quantity used) × Standard price

Zyph: (62,400 ounces – 68,640 ounces) × $2.00 = $12,480 U

Noosh: (124,800 ounces – 108,160 ounces) × $0.20 = $3,328 F

Total direct materials usage variance: $12,480 U + $3,328 F = $9,152 U

c. Direct materials mix variance

Faircloth purchased and used a total of 176,800 ounces of direct materials (68,640 ounces of Zyph + 108,160 ounces of Noosh). Faircloth should have used (the standard quantity allowed) a total of 187,200 ounces of direct materials, which is computed as (6.00 standard ounces + 12.00 standard ounces) × 10,400 actual pounds sold of Sage.

Zyph mix percentages (don't round off these percentages):

62,400 ounces ÷ 187,200 ounces = 33.33% standard sales mix percentage

68,640 ounces ÷ 176,800 ounces = 38.82% actual sales mix percentage (Unfavorable for Zyph)

Noosh mix percentages (don't round off these percentages):

124,800 ounces ÷ 187,200 ounces = 66.67% standard sales mix percentage

108,160 ounces ÷ 176,800 ounces = 61.18% actual sales mix percentage (Favorable for Noosh)

The overall direct materials mix variance on the Sage product will be unfavorable (U) because Faircloth is using relatively more of the direct material with the highest standard price (Zyph).

Direct materials mix variance = Total actual qty used × (Standard mix% – Actual mix%) × Standard price

Zyph: 176,800 ounces × (33.33% – 38.82%) × $2.00 = $19,413 U

Noosh: 176,800 ounces × (66.67% – 61.18%) × $0.20 = $1,941 F

Total direct materials mix variance: $19,413 U + $1,941 F = $17,472 U

d. Direct materials yield variance

Faircloth has a favorable (F) yield variance on the Sage product because its total ounces of direct materials used (176,800 ounces) to produce 10,400 pounds of Sage was less than the total standard quantity allowed (187,200 ounces).

Direct materials yield variance = (Total standard qty allowed – Total actual qty used) × Standard mix% × Standard price

Zyph: (187,200 ounces – 176,800 ounces) × 33.33% × $2.00 = $6,933 F

Noosh: (187,200 ounces – 176,800 ounces) × 66.67% × $0.20 = $1,387 F

Total direct materials yield variance: $6,933 F + $1,387 F = $8,320 F

Continues...

e. Direct labor rate variance

Faircloth paid $6,760 for 26,000 direct labor minutes (DLM). This works out to an actual rate of $0.26 per minute (or $15.60 per hour). Faircloth's standard labor rate to produce Sage is $0.25 per minute (or $15.00 per hour). Hence, Faircloth has an unfavorable direct labor rate variance, which can be computed as follows:

Actual quantity × (Standard rate − Actual rate) = 26,000 DLM × ($0.25 − $0.26) = $260 U

f. Direct labor efficiency variance

Faircloth used 26,000 direct labor minutes (DLM) to produce 10,400 pounds of Sage. The standard labor time to produce one pound of sage is 2.00 DLM. Hence, standard quantity allowed for the actual production of 10,400 pounds of sage is 20,800 DLM (10,400 pounds × 2.00 DLM). Since actual labor time is more than the standard quantity allowed, Faircloth has an unfavorable direct labor efficiency variance, which can be computed as follows:

(Standard qty allowed − Actual qty) × Standard rate = (20,800 DLM − 26,000 DLM) × $0.25 = $1,300 U

Summary

The computation of cost variances is quite similar to the computation of revenue variances. When computing any variances, be sure you can visualize the process with respect to the overall variance framework. By doing so, you'll see that the computation of cost variances is quite similar to the computation of revenue variances. Direct labor rate variances are based on the difference between the standard rate and the actual rate, multiplied by the actual quantity used. Computing direct materials prices variances is very similar except that many organizations will often multiply the difference between standard and actual prices by the actual quantity *purchased*. Quantity variances (called usage variances for materials and efficiency variances for labor) are computed based on the difference between the actual quantity and the standard quantity allowed for actual production, multiplied by the standard price per unit. For both direct materials and direct labor, when there is more than one type of input used in the product or service, the usage variance can be split into the mix variance and yield variance. The mix variance is based on the difference between each input's standard and actual mix percentage, multiplied by the total actual quantity of all inputs and multiplied by each input's standard price or rate. The yield variance is based on the difference between the *total* standard quantity allowed of all inputs compared to the *total* actual quantity, multiplied by each input's standard mix percentage and multiplied by each input's standard price or rate.

Factory Overhead Cost Variances

After studying this lesson, you should be able to:

- Demonstrate an understanding of spending and efficiency variances as they relate to fixed and variable overhead (1.C.1.m).

- Analyze factory overhead variances by calculating variable overhead spending variance, variable overhead efficiency variance, fixed overhead spending variance, and production volume variance (1.C.1.r).

> In this lesson we'll use the overall variance framework to build computations for overhead cost variances. Production overhead can be split into variable overhead and fixed overhead. Variable overhead variances include a spending variance and an efficiency variance. With respect to fixed overhead, we can compute a spending variance and a production volume variance.

I. Overhead Costs Application Systems

    A. In these lessons we've been computing variances to support the management process of controlling and evaluating revenues and costs. This lesson is focused on variance analysis of overhead costs. The challenge with overhead costs is they are "indirect," which means that these costs are not directly affected by the volume of production and sales.

        1. In contrast, the assumption in variance analysis of materials and labor costs is that those costs are "direct," which means the production and sales output volume of the organization's products or services will directly cause materials and labor input costs to shift in a way that is variable and measurable.

        2. Of course, it is not true in all organizations that materials and labor costs are tied directly to production output. Organizations with "indirect" materials and labor costs will need to control and evaluate these costs in a manner similar to overhead costs. The key management issue with indirect costs is that *these costs are applied* to production, and the reality of that cost application process changes the approach to variance analysis.

    B. Overhead costs are typically divided into variable overhead and fixed overhead. Variable overhead costs shift generally in the same direction as shifts in output volumes, but the cost movement does not coincide perfectly with output. For example, power costs in a manufacturing organization will move up and down with shifts in production, but that movement can't be perfectly predicted. Hence, the management accounting system is set up to apply VOH costs to production using an application basis such as machine hours, direct labor hours, or the production units themselves.

    C. Of course, fixed overhead costs do not shift at all as production and sales volumes change. Nevertheless, in order to track the "full costs" of its products or services, the organization needs to apply these costs as well. A very simplified approach to applying indirect overhead costs is to group all the costs into a single overhead cost application system. We will use a single cost application system for our ongoing work with the Sunbird Boat Company.

    D. The overhead cost application system is established as part of the master budgeting process (master budgeting was introduced in the first lesson of this section). Before the start of the year, Sunbird established an overhead cost budget for the Classic boat product line. Specifically, the management accountants budgeted for $58,500 in variable overhead costs and $78,000 in fixed overhead as part of the production plan to produce 156 Classic boats. The accountants then determined to apply these costs on the basis of direct labor hours. Recall that the production standard for each Classic boat requires 20 artisan hours and 30 hours from assistants for a total of 50 direct labor hours for each boat. As a result, the following overhead cost rates were established in the master budget:

- Planned production: 156 Classic boats

- Budgeted direct labor hours: 156 boats × 50 hours = 7,800 direct labor hours

- Variable overhead application rate: $58,500 ÷ 7,800 hours = $7.50 per direct labor hour

- Fixed overhead application rate: $78,000 ÷ 7,800 hours = $10.00 per direct labor hour

E. These overhead cost rates are included in the standard cost sheet presented below for Classic boats. In the last lesson we used these standard costs to establish variances for direct materials and direct labor. We'll also use standard costs from the standard cost sheet to compute variances for variable overhead and fixed overhead.

Sunbird Boat Company

Standard Cost Sheet - Classic Boat	Input Quantity	Cost per Input	Cost per Boat
Direct materials (oak wood) - square feet	80 ft²	$10.00 per ft²	$800.00
Direct labor (artisans) - direct labor hours	20 DLH	$47.50 per DLH	950.00
Direct labor (assistants) - direct labor hours	30 DLH	$15.00 per DLH	450.00
Variable manufacturing overhead - total DLH	50 DLH	$7.50 per DLH	375.00
Fixed manufacturing overhead - total DLH	50 DLH	$10.00 per DLH	500.00
Total Cost to Manufacture			**$3,075.00**
Variable selling overhead - boats	1 boat	$210 per boat	210.00
Total Cost to Deliver			**$3,285.00**

Note in the standard cost sheet above that there are actually two overhead rates that can be used to apply overhead. There is an overhead cost rate per direct labor hour (DLH) and an overhead cost rate per boat. For example, for every Classic boat produced Sunbird will use a standard number of 50 direct labor hours multiplied by $7.50 to apply variable overhead, or Sunbird can simply use $375 per boat to apply variable overhead. Either approach will apply the same amount of overhead cost.

II. Variable Manufacturing Overhead Variances

A. By the end of the year Sunbird Boat Company had the following actual results for the Classic boat product line:

- 150 Classic boats were produced and sold during the year.

- Artisans worked a total 2,715 hours, and assistants worked a total of 4,710 hours.

- Actual variable overhead costs were $74,992.50.

- Actual fixed overhead costs were $87,360.

B. Variable overhead costs follow the same variance framework as all other variances we've studied so far. The framework is provided below.

The Variance Framework

1. There are two important points to be made about variable overhead costs and the variance framework above. First, overhead costs (both variable and fixed) are an accumulation of specific types of costs. For example, variable overhead costs can include utilities, travel, supplies, etc. Hence, there's no "actual quantity" or "actual price" for overhead. Determining the actual overhead in the first box above is a matter of summing up all the overhead costs actually used during the period.

2. Second, because there isn't a specific "quantity" of overhead, how are the second and third boxes above computed? There is a quantity of the overhead application basis, often called the allocation activity basis. Sunbird used direct labor hours to apply overhead. Hence, the actual quantity of DLH is used in the second box, and the standard quantity allowed of DLH (based on actual boats produced) is used in the third box. The specific framework for variable overhead (VOH) costs is presented below.

The Variable Overhead Variance Framework

Total Actual Costs	Actual Activity Used × Standard VOH Rate	Standard Activity Allowed × Standard VOH Rate

| | Spending Variance | Efficiency Variance | |

C. With the variable overhead application rate and the actual results provided above, we can use the framework approach to compute the variable overhead spending variance below for Sunbird Boat Company.

The Variable Overhead Spending Variance

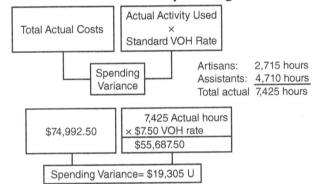

1. What is the meaning of the spending variance for variable overhead? Sunbird's management accountants chose to use direct labor hours to apply variable overhead costs. That choice should be based on some expectation that direct labor hours are correlated at least somewhat with variable overhead costs. If that is true, then we assume that actual direct labor hours can be used to "predict" actual variable overhead costs.

2. Artisans and assistants worked a total of 7,425 hours during the year. Based on a VOH rate of $7.50 per hour, we can predict that Sunbird would actually spend $55,687.50 for variable overhead. The difference between predicted and actual spending is unfavorable (U), which indicates that spending may be out of control and needs to be investigated. (Alternatively, this result might mean that direct labor hours are a poor predictor of variable overhead costs.)

D. We can also compute directly the variable overhead spending variance using the formula approach as follows:

(Actual activity used × Standard rate) − Actual costs
Variable overhead spending variance: (7,425 hours × $7.50) − $74,992.50 = $19,305 U

E. Moving on, we compute below the variable overhead efficiency variance using the framework approach.

The Variable Overhead Efficiency Variance

Actual Activity Used × Standard VOH Rate	Standard Activity Allowed × Standard VOH Rate

Efficiency Variance

Actual production: 150 boats
Standard hours: × 50 hours
Std hrs allowed   7,500 hours

7,425 Actual hours × $ 7.50 VOH rate $55,687.50	7,500 Standard hours × $ 7.50 VOH rate $56,250.00

Efficiency Variance = $562.50 F

1. Note that the $562.50 F variance is based entirely on the difference between actual direct labor hours and the standard labor hours allowed for actual production. What this means is that this variance really isn't about the efficient or inefficient use of variable overhead resources — it is about the efficiency of the underlying activity basis used to allocate variable overhead costs!

2. If you were to return back to the last lesson where we computed the direct labor efficiency variance, you'll see that the variance is $10,387.50 F. In the case of Sunbird Boat Company, the variable overhead efficiency variance here is actually providing the same management signal as the direct labor efficiency variance. Sunbird is efficient with its direct labor resources, but we actually don't know anything about the efficiency of variable overhead resources.

F. The formula approach for the variable overhead efficiency variance is displayed below. It should look familiar to you. It's the same formula as the direct labor efficiency variance formula. It simply uses a different rate to put a dollar size on the variance.

(Standard activity allowed − Actual activity used) × Standard rate
Standard activity allowed: 150 actual boats × 50 direct labor hours = 7,500 hours
VOH efficiency variance: (7,500 hours − 7,425 hours) × $7.50 = $562.50 F

III. Fixed Manufacturing Overhead Variances

A. Fixed manufacturing overhead variances follow a completely different approach from revenue, direct costs, and variable overhead costs. The reason for this difference is simply that these costs are fixed, and all other costs (and revenues) are expected to follow the movement of production volumes. Nevertheless, by establishing a fixed overhead rate and applying these costs to each unit of output, the overhead cost application process treats these fixed costs as if they are variable. That's a strange process for fixed manufacturing costs, but it creates an important management signal regarding how the actual production output compares to the expected production output. This is called the production volume variance, and it will be the last variance we study in this lesson.

B. Before we compute the production volume variance, we need to analyze fixed manufacturing costs to determine the fixed overhead spending variance (sometimes called the fixed overhead budget variance). This is a very simple variance. It's the difference between the original master budget for total fixed costs and the total amount of actual fixed costs spent, which you can see in the fixed overhead variance framework provided below.

The Fixed Overhead Variance Framework

Total Actual Costs	Master Budget Costs	Total Applied Costs

Spending Variance

Volume Variance

Budgeted Production Volume × Standard FOH Rate	Actual Production Volume × Standard FOH Rate

C. If the original master budget for fixed overhead costs isn't available, the master budget can be recreated using the fixed overhead (FOH) rate and the budgeted production volume. Remember that the FOH rate is $10.00 per direct labor hour or $500 per boat. The computation, which we performed above, is provided again below.

- Fixed manufacturing overhead budget: $78,000

- Planned production: 156 Classic boats

- Budgeted direct labor hours: 156 boats × 50 hours = 7,800 direct labor hours

- FOH rate: $78,000 ÷ 7,800 hours = $10.00 per DLH

- FOH rate: $78,000 ÷ 156 boats = $500.00 per boat

D. The framework approach for the fixed overhead spending variance is demonstrated below.

The Fixed Overhead Spending Variance

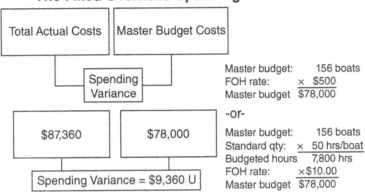

E. The formula approach for the fixed overhead spending variance is as follows:

Master budget − Actual costs spent

-or-

(Master budget production volume × FOH rate) − Actual costs spent
Fixed overhead spending variance: $78,000 − $87,360 = $9,360 U

F. The fixed overhead volume variance is often simply referred to as the production volume variance. This is because this variance results strictly from producing more or less output than originally planned in the master budget. It is important to note that because fixed selling and administrative costs are *not* allocated to production, *this variance involves only fixed manufacturing overhead costs*. The framework approach for the production volume variance is displayed below.

The Fixed Overhead Volume Variance

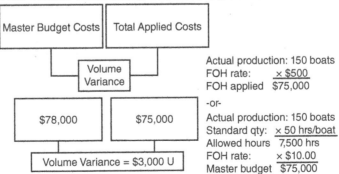

1. In order to see clearly how Sunbird's production volume variance works out to be $3,000 U, return back to the framework solution for the fixed overhead spending variance and observe the two alternative calculations for the master budget costs.

2. The difference between Sunbird's master budget for fixed production costs and applied fixed production costs is due to the difference in planned and actual production output. You can compute this difference by using the original production plan (156 boats) and the actual production by the year's end (150 boats). This difference is also seen in the master budget for 78,000 direct labor hours based on the original production plan compared to the standard 75,000 hours allowed based on actual production.

G. The formula approach for the production volume variance is perhaps the most straightforward method for computing the production volume variance. Before approaching the formula, first observe whether the variance will be favorable or unfavorable, which is done by comparing actual production output to the original master plan (i.e., budget). If actual exceeds budget, the production volume variance is favorable.

Applied costs − Master budget costs

-or-

(Actual production volume − Master budget volume) × FOH rate
Fixed overhead production volume variance: (150 boats − 156 boats) × $500 = $3,000 U

IV. Reconciling Overhead Variances to Over- or Under-Applied Overhead

A. Remember that variances for manufacturing overhead costs are complicated by the fact that these indirect costs are not directly related to production and so have to be applied using an overhead cost application system. This system actually presents a check figure for the four variance computations.

B. At the end of each reporting period, the organization must evaluate the Manufacturing Overhead account and reconcile the over- or under-applied overhead amount to subsequent inventory and cost of goods sold accounts. Computing the over- or under-applied overhead amount is straightforward for Sunbird Boat Company, as follows:

Total actual manufacturing overhead: $74,992.50 + $87,360 = $162,352.50
Total applied manufacturing overhead: 150 boats produced × $875 = $131,250
Under-applied manufacturing overhead: $162,352.50 − $131,250 = $31,102.50

C. This under-applied overhead number represents costs that have to be added to inventory and cost of goods sold accounts, which will reduce reported operating profit. This is an unhappy (i.e., unfavorable) situation for Sunbird. But this amount is a check figure for the four overhead variances, which should all add up to be $31,102.50 U (remember to *subtract* the favorable efficiency variance). As you can see below, the four overhead variances reconcile to the under-applied overhead amount for Sunbird.

Variable overhead spending variance:	$19,305.00 U
Variable overhead efficiency variance:	$562.50 F
Fixed overhead spending variance:	$9,360.00 U
Fixed overhead volume variance:	$3,000.00 U
Total	$31,102.50 U

Practice Question

This question expands the Practice Question from previous lessons. The standard cost sheet is provided below for one of Faircloth & Company's products, Sage. Actual sales on the Sage product last month were 10,400 lbs.

Faircloth & Company

Standard Cost Sheet—Sage Product	Input Quantity	Cost per Input	Cost per lb.
Direct materials (Zyph)—ounces	6 ounces	$2.00 per ounce	$12.00
Direct materials (Noosh)—ounces	12 ounces	$0.20 per ounce	2.40
Direct labor - direct labor minutes	2 DLM	$0.25 per DLM	.50
Variable manufacturing overhead—DLM	2 DLM	$0.45 per DLM	.90
Fixed manufacturing overhead—DLM	2 DLM	$5.00 per DLM	10.00
Total Product Cost			**$25.80**

In its master budget, Faircloth budgeted $10,800 for variable manufacturing overhead costs and $120,000 for fixed manufacturing overhead costs. Faircloth originally planned in its master budget to produce and sell 12,000 pounds of Sage, using 24,000 direct labor minutes (DLM).

Faircloth ultimately spent $10,920 and $115,500 for variable and fixed manufacturing overhead, respectively, and used 26,000 DLMs to produce and sell 10,400 pounds of Sage.

Compute the following variances for the Sage product:

a. Variable overhead spending variance

b. Variable overhead efficiency variance

c. Fixed overhead spending variance

d. Production volume variance

Answer

a. Variable overhead spending variance

> (Actual activity used × Standard rate) − Actual costs
> Variable overhead spending variance: (26,000 DLMs × $0.45) − $10,920 = $780 F

b. Variable overhead efficiency variance

> (Standard activity allowed − Actual activity used) × Standard rate
> Standard activity allowed: 10,400 pounds × 2 DLMs = 20,800 DLMs
> VOH efficiency variance: (20,800DLMs-26,000DLMs) × $0.45 = $2,340 U

c. Fixed overhead spending variance

> Master budget − Actual costs spent
> Fixed overhead spending variance: $120,000 − $115,500 = $4,500 F
> Note: 12,000 pounds of Sage × $10.00 FOH rate = $120,000 Master Budget

d. Production volume variance

> (Actual production volume − Master budget volume) ×FOH rate
> Fixed overhead production volume variance:(10,400 pounds − 12,000 pounds) × $10 = $16,000U
> Alternative: (20,800 standard allowed DLMs − 24,000 master budget DLMs) × $5 = $16,000 U

Summary

Variance analysis for overhead costs is complicated by the fact that overhead represents indirect costs, which means these costs must be applied using an overhead cost application system. Hence, variance analysis for overhead is different compared to variance analysis for direct materials and labor costs. The variable overhead spending variance compares actual overhead costs with the overhead costs that are "predicted" using the actual volume of the activity basis (such as machine hours or direct labor hours), multiplied by the variable overhead rate. The variable overhead efficiency variance is essentially the same computation as the labor efficiency variance, which is the difference between actual activity and the standard activity allowed for actual production, multiplied by the variable overhead rate. The fixed overhead spending variance is simply the difference between total actual costs and the original total master budget costs. Finally, the production volume variance, which is focused entirely on fixed manufacturing overhead costs, is the difference between the actual volume of production and the original master budget production volume, multiplied by the fixed overhead rate.

Management Work with Variance Analysis

After studying this lesson, you should be able to:

- Analyze variances, identify causes, and recommend corrective actions (1.C.1.s).

- Demonstrate how price, efficiency, spending, and mix variances can be applied in service companies as well as manufacturing companies (1.C.1.q).

Variance analysis is not used just for production costs, nor is its use limited to manufacturing companies. All types of organizations (manufacturing, service, and merchandising) need to plan, control, and evaluate costs. So long as a cost standard or budget can be established, the variance framework can be used to compute variances on actual costs. Managers can then use these variance reports to investigate and understand causes for both unfavorable and favorable variances.

I. Variance Analysis of Selling and Administrative Costs

    A. Let's return once more to the Sunbird Boat Company example that has been the focus of the lessons to this point in this section. Below is the standard cost card we've been using to compute all the variances for Sunbird.

Sunbird Boat Company

Standard Cost Sheet—Classic Boat	Input Quantity	Cost per Input	Cost per Boat
Direct materials (oak wood)—square feet	80 ft^2	$10.00 per ft^2	$800.00
Direct labor (artisans)—direct labor hours	20 DLH	$47.50 per DLH	950.00
Direct labor (assistants)—direct labor hours	30 DLH	$15.00 per DLH	450.00
Variable manufacturing overhead—total DLH	50 DLH	$7.50 per DLH	375.00
Fixed manufacturing overhead—total DLH	50 DLH	$10.00 per DLH	500.00
Total Cost to Manufacture			**$3,075.00**
Variable selling overhead—boats	1 boat	$210 per boat	210.00
Total Cost to Deliver			**$3,285.00**

    B. The focus of our variance computations has been on the product costs for Sunbird: direct materials, direct labor, and manufacturing overhead. But there's one cost above that isn't a production cost. Selling overhead is a sales and administration expense, and we've yet to compute a variance on this cost. Let's assume for Sunbird Boat Company that the standard cost of $210 per boat represents the budgeted costs of delivering a boat to a customer.

    C. Having worked through the previous lessons, computing a price or spending variance on sales and administrative (S&A) costs should not be difficult. Remember the variance framework (below), and assume the following for Sunbird's delivery costs on Classic boat sales:

        Actual total delivery costs: $31,766.70

        Actual sales volume: 150 boats

        Actual boats delivered: 147 boats (three boats did not have to be delivered because they were picked up by customers)

The Variance Framework

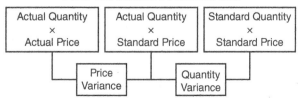

1. The actual delivery cost (price) on the 147 boats that were actually delivered can be computed as $216.10 per boat ($31,766.70 ÷ 147 boats). Clearly, Sunbird has an unfavorable variance compared to the standard cost of $210 per boat. Computing a price variance on this cost follows the standard formula.

Actual quantity delivered × (Standard price – Actual price) Selling overhead price variance: 147 boats × ($210 – $216.10) = $896.70 U

2. Assuming that Sunbird expects to deliver all boats sold to customers (i.e., its standard is to deliver each boat), we can compute a quantity variance that represents the efficiency of Sunbird's delivery work. Note that this is going to be a favorable variance since Sunbird didn't actually handle the delivery of all boats sold.

(Standard delivery events allowed – Actual boats delivered) × Standard rate Selling overhead efficiency variance: (150 boats – 147 boats) × $210 = $630.00 F

D. Variances can (and should) be computed on all costs that have a standard or budgeted level of performance. It doesn't really matter if the costs are part of a production process or not. If the S&A cost is variable (that is, the cost is a function of some activity), then both a price (or rate) and a quantity (or efficiency) variance can be computed. If the S&A cost is fixed, then typically only a spending (or budget) variance is computed, which would simply be the difference between the total budgeted cost and the total actual cost. Because fixed S&A costs in a standard cost system are not allocated to units sold using a predetermined rate, a fixed cost volume variance is rarely computed.

II. Variance Analysis in Service and Merchant Organizations

A. Generally, there are three types of organizations in the economy: manufacturing, service, and merchandising. In these lessons we've focused on a manufacturing organization—Sunbird Boat Company. But our example could have been a service organization or a merchant company. In any case, the same variance framework can be used to compute signals that management should investigate to determine why actual costs are different than expected costs.

B. Let's assume that Sunbird Boat Company is a small consulting firm that provides instruction and guidance to clients who want to build their own customized wooden rowboat. Sunbird has two different consulting services or "products." Clients can arrange for a Sunbird consultant to come to their home or personal woodshop and provide coaching and feedback on their boat design plan or construction process. Sunbird would charge by the hour for this service. Alternatively, clients can register for and attend a class wherein a Sunbird instructor teaches the attendees about the process of designing and building their own boat. Sunbird charges a flat registration fee for this course of instruction that has a set number of classroom hours.

1. Sunbird will want to manage revenues by planning and controlling the price of consulting hours and classroom events. In addition to sales price variances, Sunbird can use the variance framework to track sales volume variances and can break down the volume variance into the mix variance related to the tradeoff of consulting hours versus classroom hours, and sales quantity variance representing the revenue effect or more or less total hours of combined consulting and classroom hours.

2. While Sunbird may use supplies in the process of consulting or classroom teaching, the cost is likely not significant. Hence, Sunbird may not need to control and evaluate direct materials costs in its business. On the other hand, Sunbird has very significant costs in the direct labor of consulting and classroom teaching. Sunbird should establish standard labor rates and standard number of hours "allowed" for a client engagement or a classroom event, and track rate variances and efficiency variances.

3. Sunbird will also have overhead costs in the form of a building or buildings, equipment, vehicles, executive and staff salaries, etc. Some of these costs may increase or decrease based on the volume of consulting or classroom hours and should be controlled and evaluated using spending and efficiency variances.

4. Much of Sunbird's overhead may be fixed costs, and each category of fixed overhead costs should be tracked with simple spending variances (total budgeted costs less total actual costs). Will Sunbird have a production volume variance? It is possible, and perhaps advisable, for Sunbird to establish a normal capacity of consulting hours and classroom hours that its organization is set up to provide, and then compute a volume variance. Traditional accounting systems allocate fixed production costs only to tangible products that can be inventoried. Sunbird does not build "inventories" of consulting or classroom hours and so is not required to track the full cost of producing inventories by allocating fixed "production" costs to its service products. Nevertheless, by establishing a fixed overhead rate based on normal capacity of consulting and classroom, and then allocating that rate to actual consulting and classroom hours sold to clients, Sunbird can compute a favorable or unfavorable volume variance that provides a signal on its ability to use its consulting and teaching capacity.

C. Alternatively, assume that Sunbird Boat Company is a merchandising organization that purchases boats at wholesale prices and sells these boats at marked-up retail prices to customers who come to its product showroom or who place orders through its website.

1. Obviously, Sunbird will be tracking price variances in its retail business, as well as sales volume variances. And if Sunbird prices its showroom boats differently than boats sold through its website, then its management team should expand the volume variance into a mix variance and a quantity variance.

2. As a retailer, Sunbird has significant costs invested in its inventory of boats, which represent the "direct materials" cost of its business. It may or may not have an input quantity variance for boats sold. If every boat it purchases is sold, then a direct materials quantity variance will represent the same performance as the sales volume variance. However, Sunbird may not be able to sell all the boats it purchases, or it may experience some loss of inventory due to breakage or theft. In these circumstances, Sunbird should compute a type of direct materials quantity variance that represents unsold inventory or inventory shrinkage.

3. Sunbird as a merchant will have labor costs, but most of that labor may not be directly involved as an "input" in the process of acquiring and selling each boat. To the extent it has sales agents in the product showroom or perhaps telephone sales agents taking calls on website purchases, it may then compute direct labor variances. Otherwise, the rest of its labor costs will be managed and variances computed as part of its overhead cost structure.

III. Investigating Variances and Managing Operations

A. Remember that variances do not identify a problem in the organization. Variances provide a signal in the manage-by-exception system that something is different than expected and should be investigated. The variance may be signaling a problem to be rectified, or the variance could be part of a desirable result based on an operational goal (even if the variance itself is unfavorable). Sometimes the variance doesn't represent anything about actual results in the organization, but instead managers learn on investigating the variance that a standard price or standard quantity in the budget system is no longer relevant and needs to be adjusted.

B. Assuming that revenue and cost standards are up to date, what kinds of factors cause a variance to occur? Factors can be both internal (and largely controllable) or external (and largely uncontrollable) to the organization. Let's consider variances related to revenue.

1. The marketing department in the organization is often most responsible for evaluating the market and setting a sales price that represents the branding of the product or service and how the organization wants to compete in the market. Of course, it's the sales department that must actually generate desired sales volumes based on price.

2. However, price and volume of demand are not independent of each other in the market. Depending on the nature of the market and the type of product, an unfavorable volume variance that results from a favorable price variance could lead to either higher or lower overall revenue. Marketing and sales departments have more or less influence on prices and volumes of demand. Nevertheless, all revenue variances need to be carefully investigated in the important process of controlling and evaluating price and demand.

C. Causes for direct materials variances can also be spread across different parts of the organization.

1. In the case of direct materials price variances, which are typically the responsibility of the purchasing department in the organization, internal factors affecting price may include

decisions affecting the quantity and cash discounts available on each purchase, the quality of materials selected in the purchase, and the delivery method used to receive the purchase. However, the price variance may be beyond the control of the purchasing department due to external factors such as prices rising or falling based on economic events. Or perhaps the price variance is the result of unexpected demands by another department (such as the production department) that makes it necessary to expedite (speed up) a purchase and delivery, making it impossible to obtain standard pricing.

    2. The production department is often the area of the organization most responsible for direct materials usage variances. Depending on the experience, training, and motivation of the production crew, the usage variance could be better (favorable) or worse (unfavorable). How well production equipment is maintained or how well quality control processes are managed can lead to direct materials usage variances. Sometimes these variances are the result of decisions in other departments that can't be controlled by the production department. For example, the purchasing department may be acquiring direct materials at higher or lower quality standards, which lead to favorable or unfavorable usage variances.

D. Direct labor variances can interact with direct materials variances, as described above. In addition, the ability to control labor variances is spread across departments.

    1. Labor rates are a function of human resource (HR) goals and the availability of labor in the market (i.e., levels of unemployment in the economy). The HR department in the organization is responsible to find, hire, and initially train new employees. Achieving the standard labor rates for the organization is a key responsibility of the HR department, although achieving labor rate standards is impacted not only by the economy, but by demands of other departments for certain types of employees.

    2. While the initial ability of newly hired employees is a function of the HR process, the efficiency of that labor in the manufacturing or service process quickly becomes the responsibility of the production department (remember that organizations may be producing tangible manufactured products or may be "producing" intangible service products with their direct labor). Managers of manufacturing and service processes are responsible for the ongoing training and motivation of their team, which directly impacts labor efficiency variances.

E. Overhead costs are typically a compilation of many factors, which complicates the investigation and management process. That being said, in many organizations, the costs related to overhead exceed the costs of direct materials and the costs of direct labor, and in some organizations overhead costs *substantially* exceed the *combined* cost of direct materials and direct labor! As a result, many organizations with complicated overhead cost structures will often expand their system for tracing overhead cost variances to include many different types, prices, and inputs of overhead. Hence, the responsibility for overhead variances can spread across the entire organization, requiring careful control and evaluation by management processes.

F. As we wrap up our work on variances, it should be clear to you that variance analysis is a key aspect of management of revenues and costs in organizations. Variance computations are based on isolating causes and determining the monetary impact of each cause as a favorable or unfavorable result. However (and this is important!), it is not necessarily the goal of management to make sure that there are no unfavorable variances in the organization. Good management is about managing complexity across many factors with the intent to effectively achieve integrated, strategic goals.

    1. For example, managers may choose to pay more for direct materials (i.e., an unfavorable price variance) in order to reduce scrap and breakage in the production process (i.e., favorable materials usage and favorable labor efficiency variances).

    2. Another example of managing complexity across combinations of performance variances is the management choice to accept somewhat lower sales prices (i.e., unfavorable variance) as a result of substantially reducing materials and/or labor costs (i.e., favorable variances). Of course, this second example can also work profitably in the opposite direction.

Practice Question

Scranton Training, Inc. provides executive training seminars on time management skills. These seminars are sold as a training event to organizations, which then schedule to bring in their own employees. Seminars are held at hotels in a location that is convenient to the client organization. Scranton has a large number of certified seminar coaches that it contracts to travel to the event and provide the training. The standard price for a training seminar event is $30,000. Below are Scranton's standard variable costs for a seminar event.

Scranton Training, Inc.

Standard Price and Cost Sheet	Input Quantity	Cost per Input	Cost per Event
Printed packets—per attendee	50 attendees	$55 per attendee	$2,750
Coaches—per coach	2 coaches	$3,000 per coach	6,000
Travel reimbursement—per coach	2 coaches	$1,000 per coach	2,000
Hotel facility rent—per event	1 event	$15,000 per event	15,000
Total Product Cost			**$25,750**

In addition to the standard variable costs listed above, Scranton has budgeted $86,000 as an annual fixed cost for advertising.

For the year just completed Scranton had originally planned for 70 seminar events with 50 participants per event. Scranton actually held 68 seminar events for the year with an average of 54 participants at each event and collected $2,029,800 in revenue. Scranton's actual costs and activity volumes are listed below.

Printed materials: $251,288 for 4,040 packets

Coaches: $390,400 for 122 coach contract payments

Travel: $140,300 for 122 travel reimbursements

Hotels: $945,200 for 68 hotel bookings

Advertising: $92,200 total

Compute the following variances for the Scranton Training, Inc.:

a. Revenue price variance and volume variance

b. Printed materials price variance and usage variance

c. Coaches rate variance and efficiency variance

d. Travel rate variance and efficiency variance

e. Hotel spending variance

f. Advertising spending variance

Answer

a. Revenue price variance and volume variance (measured by price)

    Note that Scranton's average price per seminar event was actually $29,850 per event ($2,029,800 ÷ 68 events) and is unfavorable.

Revenue price variance = Actual volume × (Standard price – Actual price)

Revenue price variance = 68 events × ($30,000 – 29,850)= $10,200 U

Revenue volume variance = (Expected volume – Actual volume) × Standard price

Revenue volume variance = (70 seminars – 68 seminars) × $30,000 = $60,000 U

Continues…

b. Printed materials price variance and usage variance

Note that Scranton's average cost per packet was actually $62.20 per packet ($251,288 ÷ 4,040 packets) and is unfavorable. The standard packets allowed for the 68 actual events is 3,400 packets (50 standard packets per event × 68 actual events); compared to 4,040 actual packets, this results in an unfavorable variance.

(Remember that the flexible budget is based on the actual output the organization sells into the market. Scranton sells seminar events for groups with a standard expectation of 50 attendees. It doesn't sell individual registrations for attendees. Hence, the printed materials standard used by Scranton is 50 packets per event, not 1 packet per attendee.)

Materials price variance = Actual quantity × (Standard price – Actual price)

Materials price variance = 4,040 packets × ($55.00 – $62.20) = $29,088 U

Materials usage variance = (Standard quantity allowed – Actual quantity used) × Standard price

Materials usage variance = (3,400 packets – 4,040 packets) × $55 = $35,200 U

c. Coaches rate variance and efficiency variance

Scranton's average rate paid on coach contracts was actually $3,200 per contract ($390,400 ÷ 122 coach contracts) and is unfavorable. The standard coach contracts allowed for the 68 actual events is 136 contracts (2 contracts per event × 68 actual events); compared to 122 actual contracts, this results in a favorable variance (Scranton did not always have two coaches at every training event).

Coaches rate variance = Actual quantity × (Standard rate – Actual rate)

Coaches rate variance = 122 contracts × ($3,000 – $3,200) = $24,400 U

Coaches efficiency variance = (Standard quantity allowed – Actual quantity used) × Standard price

Coaches efficiency variance = (136 contracts – 122 contracts) × $3,000 = $42,000 F

d. Travel rate variance and efficiency variance

Scranton's average amount reimbursed on coach travel costs was actually $1,150 per reimbursement ($140,300 ÷ 122 reimbursements) and is unfavorable. The standard travel reimbursements allowed for the 68 actual events is 136 reimbursements (2 reimbursements per event × 68 actual events), which results in a favorable variance (again, Scranton did not always have two coaches at every training event).

Travel rate variance = Actual quantity × (Standard rate – Actual rate)

Travel rate variance = 122 contracts × ($1,000 – $1,150) = $18,300 U

Travel efficiency variance = (Standard quantity allowed – Actual quantity used) × Standard price

Travel efficiency variance = (136 reimbursements – 122 reimbursements) × $1,000 = $14,000 F

e. Hotel spending variance

Scranton's average booking cost on hotels is $13,900 per booking ($945,200 ÷ 68 events) and is favorable. Since this is the only source of hotel cost variance, this price variance represents the entire spending variance.

Hotel spending variance = (Actual activity used × Standard rate) – Actual cost

Hotel spending variance = (68 bookings × $15,000) – $945,200 = $74,800 F

f. Advertising spending variance

Because advertising is a fixed cost, the spending variance computation is very straightforward.

Advertising spending variance = Budgeted cost – Actual cost

Advertising spending variance = $86,000 – $92,200 = $6,200 U

Practice Question

The management team at Scranton Training, Inc. is meeting to analyze profit performance for the last year. A flexible budget has been prepared based on the 68 actual training events that Scranton delivered, and variances computed to provide the report below.

Scranton Training, Inc

Actual	Actual Results	Flexible Budget	Variances	Variance Type
Training events	68	68		
Events revenue	$2,029,800	$2,040,000	$10,200 U	Price variance
Printing costs	(251,288)	(187,000)	29,088 U	Price variance
			35,200 U	Usage variance
Coach costs	(390,400)	(408,000)	24,400 U	Rate variance
			42,000 F	Efficiency variance
Travel costs	(140,300)	(136,000)	18,300 U	Rate variance
			14,000 F	Efficiency variance
Hotel costs	(945,200)	(1,020,000)	74,800 F	Spending variance
Advertising costs	(92,200)	(86,000)	6,200 U	Spending variance
Operating profit	$210,412	$203,000	$7,412 F	Profit variance

Management is disappointed that the company was ineffective in achieving its sales goal of 70 training events for the year. However, apparently due to cost efficiencies, profits are $7,412 higher than expected based on the actual 68 training events that Scranton was able to sell.

What might the management team at Scranton Training, Inc. learn from this variance report, and what further questions should be asked and ascertained?

Answer

The unfavorable revenue price variance may be based on external economic realities in the market place. If the overall demand for executive training seminars is down in the market, Scranton may not be able to control this price variance. On the other hand, it may be true that the underlying cause for this price variance is internal due to a problem with how the marketing and sales department is managing client pricing.

Scranton paid $7.20 more per packet than planned. Further, there appears to be some inefficient waste in that 640 more packets were sent out to seminars than actually needed based on the number of total seminar attendees. It may be the case that packet copy prices are increasing in the market, or perhaps the purchasing department is not managing that cost. On the other hand, there is little question that the production team needs to better plan and control the number of packets being sent out.

Scranton paid on average $200 more for coaching contracts than budgeted. On the other hand, Scranton saved substantial costs based on using one coach (rather than two) at some seminar events. These two variances combined may indicate that Scranton is struggling to acquire coaches (based on paying more than expected and an inability to secure two coaches for every event). Further, if clients are unhappy about having one coach rather than two, this may explain why Scranton failed to book all the seminar events it had planned. This situation needs to be carefully examined.

Travel costs are increasing. Scranton reimbursed on average $150 more on each travel request than budgeted. Perhaps travel costs in the economy are increasing. More likely, coaches need some training and incentives to reduce their travel costs. On the other hand, the fact that Scranton is efficient in terms of how many coaches traveled to events is tied back to the earlier issue that Scranton isn't able to get two coaches for every seminar, which means the favorable efficiency variance on travel costs is not necessarily a good outcome.

Continues…

There were a number of unfavorable cost issues during Scranton's last year of operations. However, the substantial cost savings on hotels is the main reason Scranton was able to increase operating profit above expectation. Some of the cost savings on booking hotels may be due to better negotiations on pricing (which is good) or may be due to decisions to use cheaper hotels (which may or may not be good). Alternatively, if overall hotel booking prices are down in the market, perhaps Scranton should adjust this cost standard.

Finally, Scranton spent $6,200 more on advertising than expected. Although unfavorable, this variance may be the result of an important decision to increase the advertising effort in order to reduce the shortfall in the volume of seminar events. If in fact the volume of seminars would have been even lower had advertising costs not been increased, the question to be asked is if this actual cost should have been even higher in order to help Scranton achieve its sales volume goal of 70 seminars for the year.

Summary

So long as a standard (budgeted) price or quantity has been established by management, the variance framework can be used to analyze the actual results of any type of revenue or cost. Further, the variance framework is relevant to any type of organization structure, including manufacturing, service, and merchandising organizations. It's important to remember that variance computations by themselves do not communicate the problem in the organization, or even if a problem is actually occurring. Variances are signals (i.e., exceptions) that managers should investigate in order to determine the cause. The cause of most variances can potentially originate from more than one location or department in the organization, necessitating careful investigation in the controlling and evaluating management process. Finally, while each variance computation is focused on isolating a single cause, organizations should approach the management of variances as an integrated mix of conditions. It's often desirable to allow for some unfavorable variances in order to secure other more favorable variances, which then combine to generate overall higher profits.

Topic 2. Responsibility Centers and Reporting Segments

Business Units and Performance Evaluation

After studying this lesson, you should be able to:

- Identify and explain the different types of responsibility centers (1.C.2.a).

- Recommend appropriate responsibility centers given a business scenario (1.C.2.b).

- Calculate a contribution margin (1.C.2.c).

- Analyze a contribution margin report and evaluate performance (1.C.2.d).

- Identify segments that organizations evaluate, including product lines, geographical areas, or other meaningful segments (1.C.2.e).

- Explain why the allocation of common costs among segments can be an issue in performance evaluation (1.C.2.f).

- Identify methods for allocating common costs such as stand-alone cost allocation and incremental cost allocation (1.C.2.g).

This lesson defines the purpose of business units (or segments) in an organization's management structure. There are four types of responsibility centers in a management structure: cost centers, revenue centers, profit centers, and investment centers. While there are methods used to allocate indirect costs to business units (stand-alone methods and incremental methods), for control and evaluation purposes it is often unwise to allocate indirect costs.

I. ASC 280 (Segment Reporting) and IFRS 8 (Operating Segments)

   A. The fundamental GAAP (generally accepted accounting principles) concept underlying both ASC (Accounting Standards Codification) 280 and IFRS (International Financial Reporting Standards) 8 is that the company's segment disclosures should be consistent with the reporting structure used by executive management to plan, control, and evaluate the organization.

   B. Segments are defined as the business units that report directly to the chief operating decision maker (CODM). The CODM can be the company president, chief executive officer, chief operating officer, or even an executive committee.

   C. Operating segments can be organized in different ways, including by products and services, by geography, by type of customer, or by legal entity.

   D. Generally, companies must report segments with revenues, profits, or assets greater than 10% of the organization's combined revenues, profits, or assets, respectively. Companies must also report information about "major" customers (i.e., customers that represent 10% or more of the company's revenue).

   E. Segment financial reporting requirements include revenue and profit, as well as assets (if applicable). Segment profit is determined based on performance measures used to make decisions about allocating resources and assessing performance.

II. Responsibility Centers

   A. Companies generally minimize the number of segments they must report externally to the public. On the other hand, big organizations may internally organize themselves into hundreds of business units that report up through several layers of management. This type of organization is demonstrated in the organization chart below for IMC (a hypothetical organization).

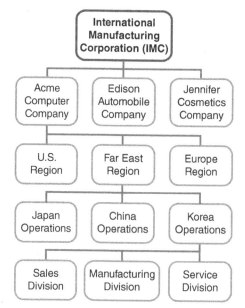

B. Effectively managing the organization's business processes requires clear stewardship responsibilities, coupled with appropriate measures and incentives. In order for performance measurement and performance incentives to be effective, business units should have the necessary decision rights to manage their performance.

C. Responsibility accounting is a system in which managers are assigned and held accountable for certain costs, revenues, and/or assets. There are two important behavioral considerations when assigning responsibilities to managers.

   1. The manager responsible for the business unit should be involved in developing the plan for the unit. People are more motivated to achieve a goal if they participate in setting it.

   2. The manager should be held accountable only for those costs, revenues, or assets for which the manager has "substantial control." For example, labor costs are generated within the business unit, but employee wages may be determined by a union scale controlled elsewhere inside or even outside of the organization. On the other hand, a manager given latitude to invest in marketing campaigns and adjust prices should be accountable for revenue performance in the business unit.

D. Responsibility centers are generally defined into four types. The performance measures and incentives used to manage responsibility centers should be aligned with the specific nature of each center being either a cost center, revenue center, profit center, or investment center of operations.

   1. *Cost centers.* As the name implies, a cost center is any organizational unit in which the manager of that unit has control only over the costs incurred. The manager of a cost center has no responsibility for revenues or assets, either because revenues are not generated in the center or because revenues and assets are under the control of someone else. The Manufacturing Division for the Korea Operations in the Far East Region of IMC's Acme Computer Company, for example, could be designated a cost center.

   2. *Revenue centers.* If a business unit is set up to focus exclusively on generating sales and revenue, without any responsibility for costs, that unit would be designated as a revenue center. This is not a very common type of business unit, but such a designation demonstrates the concept that a responsibility center should be held responsible only for the costs, revenues, and/or assets for which it has significant control. In our example with IMC, the Sales Division for Korea Operations could be treated as a revenue center assuming it does not have significant control over its costs.

   3. *Profit centers.* A profit center manager has responsibility for both costs and revenues. Profit centers are usually found at higher levels in an organization than are cost centers. The various country operations for IMC, such as China, Japan, and Korea operations within the Far East region of Acme, are likely to be profit centers, or perhaps even investment centers (described below).

4. *Investment centers.* The U.S., Far East, and Europe geographic regions at IMC are most likely to be treated as investment centers. The key responsibility that belongs solely to an investment center is the stewardship to manage the assets that generate revenue and consume costs for the business unit. If the manager has been delegated the responsibility to make decisions regarding the purchase, deployment, and retirement of the assets used in her or his business unit, then that unit is described as an investment center and investment-oriented performance measures are used accordingly.

III. Indirect Cost Allocation Methods

   A. Three of the four types of responsibility centers (cost centers, profit centers, and investment centers) are charged with management of costs. When assigning costs to a business unit for performance evaluation purposes, it is important to distinguish between controllable costs, direct costs, and indirect costs.

   1. Costs that managers of business units can significantly influence or control are considered to be the controllable costs of the business unit. These costs should be used to assess the performance of the manager or management team.

   2. The direct costs of a business unit include the costs controllable by the management team as well as any other costs that are directly connected to the operations of the unit. The key characteristic of direct costs is if the organization chooses to remove the business unit, the direct costs can be either removed or recovered by the organization. For example, direct costs that are *not* controllable by the business unit's management team might include occupancy costs (rent and property taxes) or the management team's own salaries.

   3. Indirect costs are costs allocated to the business unit that represent general administrative costs for the organization. Executive salaries, bank interest charges, and accounting and legal expenses are all possible examples of indirect costs. The key distinction is that if the organization removes the business unit, the allocated indirect costs cannot be removed or recovered; rather, they are reallocated to remaining business units. Other names used to describe indirect costs are common costs, allocated costs, and administrative burden costs.

   B. The Far East Region of IMC's Acme Computer Company is evaluating the profit performance of its three operations: China, Japan, and Korea. External reporting standards require that costs are fully allocated to subsidiary divisions.

   C. For external reporting purposes, IMC's cost allocation methods need to be applied consistently (year to year) using methods that are representative of general industry practices. Specific allocation methods are not mandated, but cost allocation practices generally follow either a stand-alone method or an incremental method.

   D. To demonstrate and compare a stand-alone cost allocation method and an incremental cost allocation method, let's assume that IMC's Far East Region in the Acme Computer Company needs to allocate 120,000,000 yen (¥120M) across its three operations in Japan, China, and Korea (yen is the functional reporting currency for IMC's Far East Region).

   1. Stand-alone cost allocations identify a common base of activity (e.g., revenue dollars, headcount, units produced, etc.) to proportionally allocate indirect costs. Using a stand-alone cost allocation method based on each business unit's revenue, the operating profit & loss report is provided below for last year's operations.

Far East Region — Profit & Loss Report (for the Acme Computer Company)

(in millions of yen)	Japan	China	Korea	Total
Revenue	**¥480**	**¥320**	**¥160**	**¥960**
Variable COGS	−170	−144	−61	−375
Variable S&A costs	−22	−18	−17	−57
Contribution margin	**¥288**	**¥158**	**¥82**	**¥528**
Fixed COGS	−160	−85	−56	−301
Fixed S&A costs	−45	−28	−21	−94
Allocated corporate costs*	−60	−40	−20	−120
Operating profit	**¥23**	**¥5**	**-¥15**	**¥13**
Allocation percent (based on revenue)	50.0%	33.3%	16.7%	100.0%

(COGS indicates Cost of Goods Sold, and S&A indicates Selling and Administrative)

Note that Japan Operations was allocated 50% of the ¥120M in corporate costs, with China Operations and Korea Operations receiving 33.3% and 16.7%, respectively.

2. Alternatively, IMC could have used each unit's contribution margin as the allocation basis, which would have resulted in the following assignment of indirect costs:

(in millions of yen)	Japan	China	Korea	Total
Contribution margin	**¥288**	**¥158**	**¥82**	**¥528**
Allocated corporate costs*	−65	−36	−19	−120
Operating profit	**¥18**	**¥9**	**-¥14**	**¥13**
Allocation percent (based on contrib. margin)	54.5%	29.9%	15.5%	100.0%

Note that using this basis would have allocated more costs to Japan Operations and less to the other two operations. You can imagine that the managers of each of these operations will have strong opinions about the appropriate cost basis, and that these managers will likely never fully agree on which basis to use!

3. Another approach to allocating indirect costs is to use an incremental method. The basic concept underlying incremental cost allocation methods is to identify the historical change in indirect (common) costs at the point in time that each business unit was established within the organization. Consider the operating profit & loss report below for the Far East Region, which is based on allocating corporate costs using an incremental method.

Far East Region — Profit & Loss Report (for the Acme Computer Company)

(in millions of yen)	Japan	China	Korea	Total
Revenue	**¥480**	**¥320**	**¥160**	**¥960**
Variable COGS	−170	−144	−61	−375
Variable S&A costs	−22	−18	−17	−57
Contribution margin	**¥288**	**¥158**	**¥82**	**¥528**
Fixed COGS	−160	−85	−56	−301
Fixed S&A costs	−45	−28	−21	−94
Allocated corporate costs[1]	−80	−35	−5	−120
Operating profit	**¥3**	**¥10**	**¥0**	**¥13**

*Based on corporate costs change when the business unit was added

4. The ¥80M in corporate costs allocated to Japan Operations is based on the approximate size of corporate costs when the Far East Region was established with Japan as the only center of operations. Subsequently, when China Operations were added, corporate costs increased another ¥35M. Recently, when Korea Operations began, Far East Region corporate costs

increased very little—approximately ¥5M. The problem with this method is that more recently added business units benefit from earlier units paying the majority of costs for shared corporate services—a result that may not represent the value of shared services that each business unit actually receives.

IV. Performance Evaluation and Common Costs

    A. External reporting requirements typically mandate that common corporate costs are allocated across all reporting segments. This is appropriate for external reporting needs, but the practice of allocating indirect (common) costs can interfere with effective performance evaluation decisions that are *internal* to the organization.

    B. When evaluating the performance of a manager for a cost, profit, or investment center, it is important to use only controllable costs. When evaluating the performance of the business unit itself, particularly for decisions regarding keeping or dropping the business unit from the organization, it is crucial to use only direct costs in the analysis.

    C. When making decisions regarding keeping or dropping the business unit from the organization, or even regarding distribution of investment resources to business units, analysis of profits computed with allocated indirect costs can lead to management decisions with *death spiral* results.

    D. To demonstrate a decision with potential *death spiral* results, let's return to the original operating profit & loss report for IMC's Far East Region with costs allocated on a stand-alone basis using revenue (be sure to review the first profit & loss report above).

        1. Note that Korea Operations is reporting a loss of -¥15M. Based on this performance report, Acme Computer Company managers or IMC executives may conclude that profits for the Far East Region would improve by ¥15M to ¥27M if Korea Operations were dropped from the business.

        2. However, if the ¥120M of corporate costs are actually indirect, then the business activities in the three operations (Japan, China, and Korea) will not directly affect these costs, and next year's performance report without the Korea business unit could look like the following (assuming all other revenues and costs remain the same as last year):

Far East Region — Profit & Loss Report (for the Acme Computer Company)

(in millions of yen)	Japan	China	Total
Revenue	¥480	¥320	¥800
Variable COGS	−170	−144	−314
Variable S&A costs	−22	−18	−40
Contribution margin	¥288	¥158	¥446
Fixed COGS	−160	−85	−245
Fixed S&A costs	−45	−28	−73
Allocated corporate costs*	−72	−48	−120
Operating profit	¥11	-¥3	¥8
Allocation percent (based on Revenue)	60.0%	40.0%	100.0%

        3. Note that corporate costs in the report above remain at ¥120M and continue to be allocated on the basis of revenue for the remaining operations. Also note that operating profit did not rise to ¥127M but fell by ¥5M to ¥8M!

        4. Most importantly, note that China Operations is now reporting a -¥3M loss. What if the management team now decides to drop China from the Far East Region? If allocated corporate costs continue to be indirect to these two business units, the results of dropping China would be disastrous (i.e., have a deadly effect) on profits for the Far East Region!

    E. The fundamental problem with allocating indirect costs is that by definition there is no direct relationship between these costs and the business units to which they're being assigned.

External regulations may require that allocations be made, but those regulations do *not* dictate *internal* accounting practices that support *internal* decision making.

F. Alternatively, IMC could determine to *not* allocate indirect costs to subsidiary business units when building performance reports for internal decision making. This management approach would result in the performance report below for Far East Region's three centers of operations.

Far East Region — Profit & Loss Report (for the Acme Computer Company)

(in millions of yen)	Japan	China	Korea	Total
Revenue	¥480	¥320	¥160	¥960
Variable COGS	−170	−144	−61	−375
Variable S&A costs	−22	−18	−17	−57
Contribution margin	¥288	¥158	¥82	¥528
Fixed COGS	−160	−85	−56	−301
Fixed S&A costs	−45	−28	−21	−94
Segment margin	¥83	¥45	¥5	¥133
Corporate costs				−120
Operating profit				¥13

1. Note that this operating profit & loss report highlights the financial value created directly by each center of operations. The ¥120M in corporate costs are not allocated to operations but are reported in the Total column for the Far East Region. This approach indicates that the ¥120M corporate costs are indirect to the three centers of operations *but are direct costs* for the Far East Region, i.e., these costs can only be removed if executive management decides to remove the Far East Region from the organization.

2. More importantly, this report solves the mystery of why profits are reduced by ¥5M if Korea Operations were to be dropped. A new reporting line has been added above, which is segment margin. This new number reports on the "true" profit (or loss) created directly by each business unit. Korea Operations is generating ¥5M of segment profit margin. That value is lost if this business unit is dropped.

Practice Question

Weston Company is composed of two separate business units. Common corporate costs include salary and wages of executive staff and office rent costs. These costs are allocated on the basis of each division's revenue. Weston's most recently monthly profit & loss report is provided below.

Weston Company Monthly Profit & Loss Report

	Division A	Division B	Total
Revenue	$35,000	$15,000	$50,000
Variable COGS	(20,000)	(4,000)	(24,000)
Variable S&A costs	(2,000)	(1,000)	(3,000)
Contribution margin	$13,000	$10,000	$23,000
Fixed COGS	(7,000)	(2,000)	(9,000)
Fixed S&A costs	(1,500)	(1,000)	(2,500)
Allocated corporate costs	(5,600)	(2,400)	(8,000)
Operating profit	($1,100)	$4,600	$3,500

Weston management is concerned that Division A regularly reports a loss similar to the $1,100 loss above. The management team has determined to drop Division A in order to improve company monthly profits by $1,100.

Continues…

What is likely to happen to company profits based on this decision?

What is a better way to report operating performance at Weston Company?

Answer

Assuming that allocated corporate costs are all indirect with respect to operations within each division, the $8,000 corporate cost is not going to be reduced by the removal of Division A. Instead, Weston Company will likely have the following performance in the near future.

Weston Company Monthly Profit & Loss Report

	Division B	Total
Revenue	$15,000	$15,000
Variable COGS	(4,000)	(4,000)
Variable S&A costs	(1,000)	(1,000)
Contribution margin	$10,000	$10,000
Fixed COGS	(2,000)	(2,000)
Fixed S&A costs	(1,000)	(1,000)
Allocated corporate costs	(8,000)	(8,000)
Operating profit	**($1,000)**	**($1,000)**

Answer

Weston should avoid allocating indirect corporate costs when assessing division performance—especially for decisions involving dropping divisions from the organization. An alternative (better) monthly profit & loss report would be as follows:

Weston Company Monthly Profit & Loss Report

	Division A	Division B	Total
Revenue	$35,000	$15,000	$50,000
Variable COGS	(20,000)	(4,000)	(24,000)
Variable S&A costs	(2,000)	(1,000)	(3,000)
Contribution margin	$13,000	$10,000	$23,000
Fixed COGS	(7,000)	(2,000)	(9,000)
Fixed S&A costs	(1,500)	(1,000)	(2,500)
Segment margin	$4,500	$7,000	$11,500
Corporate costs			(8,000)
Operating profit			$3,500

Note that Division A is reporting a segment margin of $4,500. This number explains why Weston profits went down by $4,500 when Division A was dropped.

Summary

External reporting regulations based on generally accepted accounting principles mandate that companies provide public financial reports identifying business segments that meet certain conditions. While most organizations desire to minimize the number of segments that they report publicly, for internal management reasons most organizations will define a reporting structure involving layers of many business units. For control and evaluation purposes, these business units should be identified as cost centers, revenue centers, profit centers, or investment centers. While external reporting regulations typically mandate that all costs are allocated across all reported business segments, this isn't true of cost assignment for internal management purposes. Costs should be identified as controllable, direct, or indirect. When allocating indirect costs, either stand-alone or incremental cost allocation methods can be used. Nevertheless, for internal performance reports, indirect costs should not be allocated at all, else decisions made using these performance reports can have *death spiral* results.

Transfer Pricing

After studying this lesson, you should be able to:

- Define transfer pricing and identify the objectives of transfer pricing (1.C.2.h).

- Identify the methods for determining transfer prices and list and explain the advantages and disadvantages of each method (1.C.2.i).

- Identify and calculate transfer prices using variable cost, full cost, market price, negotiated price, and dual-rate pricing (1.C.2.j).

- Explain how transfer pricing is affected by business issues such as the presence of outside suppliers and the opportunity costs associated with capacity usage (1.C.2.k).

- Describe how special issues such as tariffs, exchange rates, taxes, currency restrictions, expropriation risk, and the availability of materials and skills affect performance evaluation in multinational companies (1.C.2.l).

Transfer pricing is used to improve control and evaluation in organizations by setting up an "open market" system for business units within the organization to negotiate on goods and services that are transferred within the organization. This lesson will discuss the transfer pricing process and how prices are set between business units.

I. Need for Transfer Pricing

   A. Remember in our last lesson that business units can be set up as cost centers, revenue centers, profit centers, and investment centers. Cost centers and revenue centers often struggle with incentives that aren't aligned well with the overall organization.

      1. Cost centers are incentivized to reduce costs, but that incentive can motivate a cost center to minimize or delay support and services to other business units and damage overall company profitability.

      2. Revenue centers are incentivized to increase revenue without respect to costs. This kind of motivation can lead revenue centers to be very inefficient with resources of other business units, also leading to reduced overall profits in the company.

   B. As organizations increase in size and complexity, competitive internal pricing can be used to motivate performance and discipline processes in cost centers and revenue centers. Transfer pricing systems align cost centers and revenue centers with the organization's profit focus. Note, however, that a transfer price is essentially a budget transfer between business units that by itself doesn't actually change overall profits in the organization.

   C. Since the transfer price represents a revenue to the supplying business unit and a cost to the receiving business unit, managers of both business units will be focused on the maximizing the "profit" in this internal transaction. If the price is set correctly, the receiving business unit will expect quality and timeliness in the transaction, and the supply unit will be incentivized to provide the quality and timeliness. Setting the right transfer price is key for the transaction to take place.

II. Variable Cost Transfer Pricing

   A. Let's return to the International Manufacturing Corporation (IMC) example from the previous lesson. The organization chart for IMC is provided below.

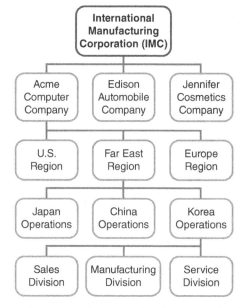

1. The U.S. Region in the Acme Computer Company has been purchasing monitor screens from an outside vendor that is assembled into the computers being manufactured and sold in the U.S. for $900 per computer. The U.S. Region business unit pays $110 per screen. Combined with $340 in other variable costs, this business unit has a $450 contribution margin on each computer sold on a monthly sales volume of 5,000 computers.

2. The China Operations business unit is selling monitor screens in its market at a $140 equivalent price (actual China Operations revenue is in Chinese yuan). The equivalent variable cost to manufacture each screen is $90, resulting in a $50 contribution margin. The China Operations monthly sales volume is 20,000 screens.

3. Data on both business units are provided below, including monthly fixed costs. Without any transfers taking place between the two business units, monthly performance combines to equal $950,000 in total profit for IMC.

Monthly Performance — No Transfer

	China Operations (Monitor Screens)	U.S. Region (Computers)	Total
Price per unit	$140	$900	
Variable costs per unit:			
Monitor screen costs		(110)	
Other variable costs	(90)	(340)	
Contribution margin	**$50**	**$450**	
Monthly volume (units)	20,000	5,000	
Total contribution margin	**$1,000,000**	**$2,250,000**	**$3,250,000**
Fixed costs	(600,000)	(1,700,000)	(2,300,000)
Operating profit	**$400,000**	**$550,000**	**$950,000**

   B. IMC, through its U.S. Region, is paying $110 to purchase computer monitor screens. But IMC can manufacture monitor screens at a variable cost of $90 in its China Operations. It makes sense for IMC if China Operations build and transfer screens to the U.S. Region, but at what transfer price? It turns out that for the overall IMC organization it doesn't matter what transfer price is used in the internal transaction.

C. Let's assume that the transfer takes place using China Operations' variable cost to produce a monitor screen. China Operations has the capacity to build the additional 5,000 screens needed in the U.S., and the cost to build these additional screens will be just the variable cost of $90. A transfer using the variable cost would result in the following combined monthly performance report.

Monthly Performance — Transfer at Variable Cost

	China Operations (Monitor Screens)	U.S. Region (Computers)	Total	
Price per unit	$140	$90	$900	
Variable costs per unit:				
Monitor screen costs			(90)	
Other variable costs	(90)	(90)	(340)	
Contribution margin	**$50**	**$0**	**$470**	
Monthly volume (units)	20,000	5,000	5,000	
Total contribution margin	**$1,000,000**	**$0**	**$2,350,000**	**$3,350,000**
Fixed costs	(600,000)		(1,700,000)	(2,300,000)
Operating profit	**$400,000**	**$0**	**$650,000**	**$1,050,000**
Improvement	*$0*	*$0*	*$100,000*	*$100,000*

The bottom highlighted line reports the increase or decrease in operating profit compared to the original combined monthly performance report with no transfer taking place between the business units. China Operations has no change in monthly profit, but the U.S. Region's profit will increase by $100,000, because it will save $20 per monitor screen ($110 – $90) by purchasing the screens internally ($20 × 5,000 computers = $100,000).

D. Setting the transfer price based on variable costs is often profitable for the receiving business unit, but the supplying business unit has no profit incentive to agree to the transfer at the variable cost price (except that it provides the means to give more employment for the business unit's employees).

III. Full Cost Transfer Pricing

A. Alternatively, organizations can set transfer prices based on full costs. This approach is often used by organizations since it represents a cost that is typically reported in accounting systems. A full cost transfer price provides a contribution margin to the supplying business unit to help cover its own costs, but it results in a higher price that the receiving business unit may not want to pay.

B. Returning to our example, let's assume that the transfer price is based on China Operation's full cost per unit. This business unit's total fixed costs are $600,000 (and are not expected to increase based on the additional 5,000 screens for the U.S. Region). The fixed cost per unit is computed as follows:

$600,000 ÷ (20,000 screens + 5,000 screens) = $24 per screen

C. A transfer using the full cost of $114 per monitor screen ($90 + $24) will provide the following combined monthly performance report

Monthly Performance — Transfer at Full Cost

	China Operations (Monitor Screens)	U.S. Region (Computers)	Total	
Price per unit	$140	$114	$900	
Variable costs per unit:				
Monitor screen costs			(114)	
Other variable costs	(90)	(90)	(340)	
Contribution margin	**$50**	**$24**	**$446**	
Monthly volume (units)	20,000	5,000	5,000	
Total contribution margin	**$1,000,000**	**$120,000**	**$2,230,000**	**$3,350,000**
Fixed costs	(600,000)		(1,700,000)	(2,300,000)
Operating profit	**$400,000**	**$120,000**	**$530,000**	**$1,050,000**
Improvement	$0	$120,000	($20,000)	$100,000

Note that China Operations has an increase in monthly profit of $120,000 but the U.S. Region's profit will decrease by $20,000 based on paying $4 more per monitor screen ($110 − $114).

D. Most importantly, note that IMC's overall profit will increase by the same $100,000 using either the variable cost or the full cost. The company's overall profit is unaffected by the transfer price. *The only thing that affects overall profit for IMC is whether or not the transfer takes place.*

IV. Managing Transfer Pricing

  A. There are two issues in transfer pricing that need to be clearly managed and separately evaluated. First, does the organization want the transfer to take place between the two business units? In other words, will a transfer increase or decrease overall profits for the organization?

    1. If there isn't an external supplier (vendor), then without an outside alternative the only option available is a transfer between the two business units.

    2. If the option to use an external supplier does exist, then the organization must determine if it is cheaper to buy externally or cheaper to internally produce and transfer the product or service. The method to determine the right solution is as follows:

      Is external market price > variable cost + opportunity cost + incremental fixed cost?

      If market price is higher, then the organization will be benefited by an internal transfer. (Opportunity costs and incremental fixed costs will be discussed later.)

  B. Assuming the organization wants the transfer to take place, the second issue to manage is setting the transfer price such that both business units will be incentivized to participate in the transfer.

    1. The supplying business unit needs to cover its variable costs plus any opportunity costs of making the transfer (i.e., lost profits in the open market) as well as any incremental fixed costs that may be required to provide the product to the receiving business unit. If the supplying business unit can make a profit on these costs, it will have incentive to do the transfer.

    2. The receiving business unit does not want to pay more than the price available in the external market. If there are any transaction savings by doing an internal transfer (for example, packaging or shipping that can be avoided), the receiving business unit may be willing to pay a higher price so long as the difference is offset by transaction savings. The key to incentivizing the receiving business unit is a transfer price that results in a net cost savings.

V. Market-Based Transfer Pricing and Opportunity Costs

  A. In determining the transfer price, the supplying business unit sets the floor (minimum) on that price and the receiving business unit sets the ceiling (maximum). When using costs to set price, the receiving business unit wants to pay the variable cost, and the supplying business unit wants to charge the full cost. How do these two business units resolve on the transfer price? If there is an outside market for the product or service, then most organizations will set the transfer price on the market price that the receiving business unit would normally pay.

B. The receiving unit's market price can create a competitive pressure (and opportunity) for the supplying business unit to reduce costs while improving the quality and timeliness of the product or service in order to compete effectively with the outside market for the transaction. This incentive aligns well with the organization's overall goals.

C. What about the outside market for the supplying business unit? If the supplying business unit is selling to an outside market, that situation is relevant *only if the supplying business unit is running out of production capacity*.

   1. If the supplying business unit has to give up any outside business in order to transfer product to the receiving business unit, then the lost contribution margin on that outside business is an opportunity cost that needs to be factored into the transfer price.

   2. In this case, the supplying business unit will set the minimal transfer price as follows:

(Total variable costs to supply units + total contribution margin lost) ÷ total units supplied

   3. And if there is an incremental fixed cost for the supplying business unit to produce and transfer product to the receiving business unit (e.g., special equipment or training), that fixed cost also needs to be factored into the minimal transfer price, as follows:

Total variable costs + contribution margin lost + incremental fixed costs) ÷ total units supplied

D. With the IMC example, let's assume that China Operations' production capacity limit is 24,000 monitor screens each month. If this is an all-or-nothing transfer situation, then China Operations must give up 1,000 units of the 20,000 units of outside sales in order to supply the U.S. Region with 5,000 screens. In addition, assume that China Operations must pay $10,000 each month for the shipping container to get the monitor screens to the U.S. Region.

   1. Remember that China Operations normally makes the equivalent of $50 on each monitor screen it sells into its market. Hence, it has an opportunity cost of $50,000 ($50 × 1,000 screens) in lost contribution margin by making the internal transfer.

   2. Combined with the $10,000 of incremental fixed costs, the minimal transfer price that China Operations will demand is:

$90 variable production cost per screen + ($50,000 + 10,000) ÷ 5,000 screens = $102

   3. The U.S. Region is currently paying $110 to an external vendor in its market to obtain monitor screens. Hence, these two business units should be incentivized to set the price between $102 and $110 and make the transfer. Assuming the transfer price is set at $106 per screen, the following combined monthly performance report would result:

Monthly Performance — Transfer at Negotiated Cost (Capacity limited to 24,000 monitor screens per month) (Incremental $10,000 fixed cost for transfer)

	China Operations (Monitor Screens)	U.S. Region (Computers)	Total	
Price per unit	$140	$106	$900	
Variable costs per unit:				
Monitor screen costs			(106)	
Other variable costs	(90)	(90)	(340)	
Contribution margin	**$50**	**$16**	**$454**	
Monthly volume (units)	19,000	5,000	5,000	
Total contribution margin	**$950,000**	**$80,000**	**$2,270,000**	**$3,300,000**
Fixed costs	(600,000)	(10,000)	(1,700,000)	(2,310,000)
Operating profit	**$350,000**	**$70,000**	**$570,000**	**$990,000**
Improvement	*($50,000)*	*$70,000*	*$20,000*	*$40,000*

4. The overall improvement in IMC profits ($40,000) is due to the difference in the total cost to provide monitor screens versus the cost to purchase from an external vendor, multiplied by the number of screens.

($110 − $102) × 5,000 screens = $40,000 total costs saved

5. It is important to understand that it doesn't matter to the IMC organization what transfer price is used between these two business units. Whatever transfer price is established will effectively divide the $40,000 in cost savings between the two business units. Hence, it's a negotiating process.

E. It is important to understand that the first issue in managing the transfer price process is to determine if the transfer takes place at all. In other words, will it improve overall profits for the organization to internally produce and transfer the product versus buy the product from an outside vendor? This is a straightforward make-or-buy decision.

1. To demonstrate, let's assume that production capacity at China Operations is actually 23,000 monitor screens per month, which means it will give up 2,000 units of outside sales to make the internal transfer.

2. These lost sales have an opportunity cost of $100,000 (= $50 contribution margin × 2,000 units). As a result, the cost to produce and transfer the 5,000 monitor screens (i.e., the minimum transfer price) is:

$90 variable production cost per screen + ($100,000 + 10,000) ÷ 5,000 screens = $112

3. This cost is higher than the $110 outside market price (i.e., the maximum transfer price), which means IMC will lose $10,000 if the internal transfer takes place.

($110 − $112) × 5,000 screens = $10,000 total cost increase

Clearly, the transfer should *not* take place.

VI. Negotiated Pricing and Dual-Rate Pricing

A. The intent of the transfer price computations we've been doing are to (1) determine if a transfer should in fact take place, and (2) identify the price range (floor and ceiling) within which the supplying (selling) business unit and receiving (buying) business unit will negotiate a transfer price. The decision tree below can be used to guide and summarize this process.

Managing Transfer Prices

B. A key aspect of successful management using transfer pricing is to create an "open market" within the organization wherein business units compete and negotiate with each other to set prices and make transfers. This approach creates positive competitive pressure to keep costs down and quality up on goods and services being delivered within the organization.

C. The challenge with an "open market" approach is that managers of business units don't always make the most optimal decision for the organization. For example, due to poor accounting information or misaligned incentives, managers of business units may choose to *not* transfer when it's actually optimal for the overall organization to have a transfer take place.

D. When managers of business units are making suboptimal decisions to engage in a transfer or not, it is tempting for the executive management team to step in and force the optimal decision. Generally, this is not advisable; otherwise, the benefits of important management objectives related to delegation, decision speed, and management training are lost.

E. A compromise approach to encourage managers of business units to make optimal decisions is to establish an accounting system that allows *dual pricing*.

1. For example, the accounting system could be designed to allow the supplying business to use a full cost-based price to recognize revenue into its profit performance report while allowing the receiving business unit to use a variable cost-based price to recognize costs into its profit performance report.

2. The difference between the two prices will have to be carried in the organization's overall accounting system and reconciled at the end of the reporting period.

VII. Managing International Issues

A. This lesson has emphasized the principle that the only transfer pricing factor affecting actual company profits at IMC is whether a transfer actually takes place between business units. The transfer price used in the transaction simply determines how the cost savings is split between each business unit. The transfer price itself doesn't affect *overall profits* for the organization.

B. However, this principle is only true when the organization conducts business within a single economic geography. When the organization's business units are spread across different economic zones, then issues such as tax rates, tariffs, exchange rates, and currency restrictions enter into the management decision on whether to conduct an internal transfer and what transfer price to use.

C. The transfer pricing example used in this lesson (IMC) is based on internal transactions between a business unit in China and a business unit in the U.S. Because transactions between these two business units cross international boundaries, a number of issues can complicate how IMC manages its transfer pricing processes.

1. For example, if the income tax rate in the U.S. is comparatively higher than in China, IMC may encourage transfer prices that result in most of the cost savings being split toward China Operations. In the choice between variable cost and full cost pricing, IMC will reduce its tax expense if full cost pricing is used to locate most of the cost savings in China.

2. As another example, trade tariffs are another form of a tax. If the U.S. places a high tariff rate on the value of computer technology goods coming into its country, then IMC is likely to encourage lower transfer prices on the monitor screens that China Operations ships to the U.S. Region. Hence, in the choice between variable costs or full costs, IMC will reduce the cost of tariffs by using variable costs to set transfer prices.

3. A final example: In order to manage the economic impact of large outflows of cash or assets from its country, governments can use currency restriction laws to limit how much cash a company can transfer out of the country's economy over a certain period of time. An organization can use transfer pricing to manage this risk (sometimes called "expropriation risk" or "policy risk") of having its cash retained in one country when it's needed in another country. If IMC is concerned that the U.S. is going to restrict the transfer of currency out of its country, it may encourage the use of full cost-based

transfer pricing to increase the amount of cash that the U.S. Region pays China Operations for monitor screens.

D. As a final note on international issues involved in transfer pricing policy, most country governments pay close attention to companies that use internal transfer prices primarily to reduce income tax expense, avoid paying tariffs, or work around currency restriction laws. To that end, there is significant government regulation involved in the process of setting transfer prices for international organizations like IMC.

Practice Question

Green River, Inc. sells fly-fishing equipment. One of its main products is a starter set for value-conscious consumers that includes a fishing rod, a reel, fishing line, and an assortment of flies, strike indicators, and other small supplies. Green River has a finished assembly operation that purchases various components from external supplies to compile the finished package.

Recently, Green River acquired a fishing reel manufacturing company. This fishing reel manufacturer is selling reels to external customers for $95 per unit. The variable cost to build the reels is $60 per reel. The manufacturer is currently selling 7,500 reels a month with a production capacity of 10,000 reels a month.

Green River's assembly operation is currently buying fishing reels from another external vendor for $85 per unit. The remaining variable costs (other components and direct labor) to assemble a finished package will total $650 per package. Green River is currently assembling and selling 5,000 packages each month, priced at $850 per package.

The Green River management team wants the fishing reel manufacturing unit to provide all the reels needed by the finished assembly business unit. To do this, the reel manufacturing operation will need to hire a part-time employee to handle special packaging and paperwork on the reels going to the package assembly operation. The fixed cost will be $2,500 per month.

If the transfer takes place between the two business units, what is the potential increase in total monthly profit for Green River, Inc.?

What is the range of the transfer price within which these two business units will negotiate to do the transfer?

Answer

Green River will save $25 per package by shifting purchases of the 5,000 reels from the external vendor to the variable costs in the fishing reel manufacturing operation. But due to capacity constraints in the reel manufacturing operation, 2,500 units of external sales will be forgone, which means the contribution margin on these lost sales will be an opportunity cost. In addition, another fixed cost will have to be added to the organization. This nets out to a $35,000 increase in total profits for Green River, Inc.

$125,000 cost savings in assembly = ($85 − $60) × 5,000 assembled packages

− 87,500 opportunity cost in manufacturing = ($95 − $60) × 2,500 reels not sold

−2,500 incremental fixed costs in manufacturing

$35,000 net increase in corporate profit

The minimum transfer price that the fishing reel manufacturing operation will accept is:

$60.00 to cover the variable cost per unit

+17.50 to cover the lost contribution margin = $87,500 ÷ 5,000 reels

+0.50 to cover the incremental fixed costs = $2,500 ÷ 5,000 reels

$78.00 total minimum price

The package assembly operation won't pay more than the $85 price it's paying on the open market for fishing reels. Hence, the price range for the negotiation between these two business units will be $78.00 to $85.00.

Summary

Transfer prices are simply budget transfers between different business units in an organization. However, transfer prices can be a powerful management mechanism to encourage better performance by establishing "competitive markets" between business units within the organization. If a business unit can supply a product or service to another business unit at a cheaper price and/or at a higher quality than an external vendor, a transfer price can be used to share (i.e., split) the cost savings or value created by the internal exchange. Transfer prices are based on a combination of internal costs and external market prices. Internal costs include the variable costs, any incremental fixed costs, and the opportunity cost of lost sales for the supplying business unit (i.e., the seller). These three potential internal costs for the seller serve as the floor price for the internal transfer. If the receiving business unit (i.e., the buyer) is able to obtain the product or service from an external vendor, then the market price that the buyer would have to pay the external vendor serves as the ceiling price for the internal transfer.

Topic 3. Performance Measures

Evaluating Product and Customer Profitability

After studying this lesson, you should be able to:

- Explain why performance evaluation measures should be directly related to strategic and operational goals and objectives; why timely feedback is critical; and why performance measures should be related to the factors that drive the element being measured, e.g., cost drivers and revenue drivers (1.C.3.a).

- Explain the issues involved in determining product profitability, business unit profitability, and customer profitability, including cost measurement, cost allocation, investment measurement, and valuation (1.C.3.b).

- Calculate product-line profitability, business unit profitability, and customer profitability (1.C.3.c).

- Evaluate customers and products on the basis of profitability and recommend ways to improve profitability and/or drop unprofitable customers and products (1.C.3.d).

In this lesson we explore a more complete and strategically focused view of profit measurement and management, including an effective approach to measuring and analyzing customer profitability.

I. Measuring Profits

   A. In the last lesson involving transfer pricing, the focus was on establishing a price on a particular product, whether it be a tangible product or a service product, in order to "sell" the product in an internal transfer between two business units within the same organization. The transfer pricing process establishes centers of operations within the organization as profit centers, each with its own internal revenue and costs. The result is an "open market" management system that incentivizes efficiency and value creation.

   B. The actual market in the economy, however, is more complicated and typically demands a more strategic approach to competition and profitability. This lesson explores a comprehensive (i.e., strategic) approach to defining and measuring profitability in the "real world" of a competitive economy.

   C. In the previous lesson we described centers of operations in an organization as a "business unit." The intent of that description is to emphasize the idea of internal business units functioning as profit centers. In this lesson we focus on "strategic business units" (SBUs). An SBU is a comparatively larger center of business that is responsible for an outward-facing product or product line that is being delivered into a specific market segment. A company with a focused product line functions as a single SBU. On the other hand, large corporations may be composed of multiple SBUs, each of which is responsible for its own profitability.

   D. The classic approach to measuring profitability is to establish what it costs to manufacture a product or provide a service compared to what the product or service can be sold for. This approach underscores the accounting definition of a product cost, which is composed of direct material costs, direct labor costs, and manufacturing (or production) overhead. On the income statement, these costs form the "cost of goods sold" that is used to determine a margin on sales revenue.

   E. The danger with this approach to product costs is the emphasis it places on profitability on each product or service sold into the marketplace. It is not always feasible, and sometimes it's not even wise, to be profitable on each product or product line. Most products (including services) follow a life cycle with an infant state, a mature state, and a declining state of existence. The typical unprofitability of a product in its infant state can very much support the SBU's long-term strategy of creating and deploying an evolving portfolio of products and services in the marketplace. Some products may never be individually profitable, but still fill an important complementary role in the SBU's product portfolio.

F. Do you remember the Boston Consulting Group (BCG) Growth-Share Matrix? The BCG Matrix is a strategy planning tool that visually represents an SBU's products or services across two market dimensions: the overall growth of the market, and the SBU's share of the market. Without going into much detail, the BCG Matrix describes four types of business or product lines: cash cows, rising stars, question marks, and dogs. Cash cow products provide the resources for the SBU to mature rising star products into profitability while exploring question mark products to determine if they can become rising star products or are dog products that need to be pruned from the business portfolio.

G. The competitive reality for most SBUs is the need to manage a mix of products and services that form a strategic portfolio. This portfolio represents an interrelated set of revenues and costs that needs to be managed well in order to establish *sustainable profitability* for the SBU. Profitability isn't sustainable if it isn't sufficient to do two things: (1) provide for an ongoing infrastructure of capital assets necessary to continue running the business, *and then* (2) provide a return to the investors in the business, whether that be the larger corporation that owns the SBU or actual shareholders who have purchased stock in the SBU.

H. This concept of sustainable profitability across a portfolio of products and services can be represented in the International Manufacturing Corporation (IMC) example used in previous lessons. IMC has three strategic business units (SBUs), each with its own focused strategy and defined market segments: Acme Computer Company, Edison Automobile Company, and Jennifer Cosmetics Company. The IMC organization chart is provided below.

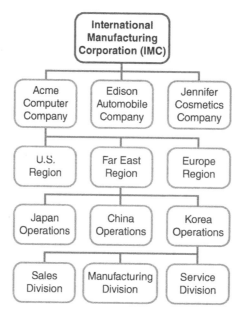

I. Acme Computer Company has three regions, each of which has three in-country operation centers. As a strategic business unit, Acme focuses its performance reports on geographic profit lines. As can be seen below, some operation centers are more profitable than others. Korea is a newly opened operations center. Both the France and Spain operation centers are struggling in a down economy, but Acme management hopes those economy sectors will be improving in the near future.

Acme Computer Company — Annual Performance Report

(in millions)	U.S. Region			Far East Region			Europe Region			Total
	East	West	South	Japan	China	Korea	UK	France	Spain	
Revenue	$100	$120	$55	$47	$54	$14	$33	$21	$23	$467
Cost of goods sold	(54)	(53)	(39)	(22)	(31)	(11)	(14)	(19)	(20)	(263)
Gross margin	$46	$67	$16	$25	$23	$3	$19	$2	$3	$204
Selling & admin exp	(20)	(49)	(14)	(10)	(18)	(8)	(7)	(9)	(8)	(155)
Operating profit	$26	$18	$2	$15	$5	($5)	$12	($7)	($5)	$49
Cost of capital										(38)
Residual income										$11

1. First, note that there is $12 M more in the selling and administrative expense total than is represented across the 12 in-country operations. This additional $12 M represents the annual costs of running the executive offices and staff for the management team at Acme.

2. Overall, Acme is running a profitable SBU representing a strategic mix of geographic profit lines. Korea is a question mark that Acme expects will become a rising star in its portfolio. Both France and Spain are also question marks that hopefully won't become dogs in the portfolio due to an ongoing sluggish economy.

3. The final point to be underscored in this performance report is the $38 M cost of capital near the bottom. This number represents the economic cost of maintaining all the capital assets necessary to maintain a business structure across so many countries. The remaining "residual" income is available to send back to IMC headquarters if needed for other purposes. We'll be discussing the residual income concept more in another lesson.

II. Customer Profitability

A. Acme Computer Company obviously sells computer products. As we've demonstrated, a successful SBU like Acme doesn't have to be profitable on every computer or line of computers it sells, nor does it have to be constantly profitable across all in-country operations. But it does need to track profit performance on all computer sales in order to plan, control, and evaluate its portfolio strategy.

B. In addition to tracking profits on computer sales, there is another strategic perspective that Acme can track in managing its strategy, and that is profitability of customers or customer groups. As you can see in the annual performance report above, much of Acme's total costs (approximately 37%) is tied up in selling and administrative expense. While these costs are not connected to computer production, many of these costs are tied directly to supporting the customer relationship process. Traditional accounting systems rarely track these "downstream costs" to customers.

C. Customer relationship management (CRM) is rich with a variety of activities and demand for downstream support costs, including:

1. Warehousing, showrooms, and online shopping
2. Ordering processes and change orders
3. Discounting, private labeling, and special packaging
4. Delivery, setup, and training
5. In-person, telephone, and online post-sales support
6. Returns, refunds, and restocking

D. Different customers demand different types and different levels of customer support in the process of purchasing the SBU's product or service. In that process, customers demonstrate different levels of overall profitability with respect to the costs of producing the product or service they purchase, combined with the costs of servicing their relationship demands on the SBU.

E. Most SBUs are quite effective at controlling and evaluating costs of goods sold (i.e., the product cost) in order to determine profitability of products and services. On the other hand, too many SBUs are not extending the same effort to break out the CRM costs that are often buried in the selling and administrative expense. As a result of not being able to clearly identify "high-quality" and "low-quality" customers (in terms of customer contribution to SBU profitability), these organizations are unable to focus on either removing unprofitable customers from their business or migrating those customers into profitable relationships.

F. The impact of not measuring and reporting customer profitability is demonstrated below in what's known as a whale curve chart. It's called a whale curve because the top of the potential profit shape resembles the back of a whale coming out of the water.

Customer Whale Curve Chart

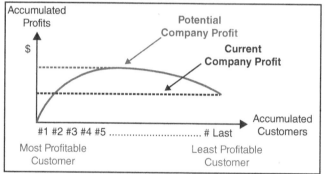

1. If organizations are able to track *all* the costs related to each of these customers (both costs of product purchased and costs to serve the customer relationship), they can then identify the profitability of each customer. The whale curve chart above demonstrates an analysis of customer profitability by organizing individual customers from most profitable to least profitable and comparing that relationship to total profits in the organization.

2. The top of the whale curve demonstrates a crossover point for individual customer profitability. Customers lined up to the right of the highest point on the whale curve are increasingly unprofitable customers that reduce overall profitability.

3. The message of the whale curve to management is that company profits could be much higher than current actual profit if the company were to do one of two things with unprofitable customers: either manage the costs to serve these customers in order to migrate them to profitability or, as necessary, raise prices on some customers to the point that they leave the company's business portfolio.

G. In most markets, the cost to acquire new customers is significant, which is why most SBUs are cautious about moving current customers out of their business portfolio. The migration of unprofitable customers toward profitability is twofold and is demonstrated in the migration chart below.

Customer Profit Migration Chart

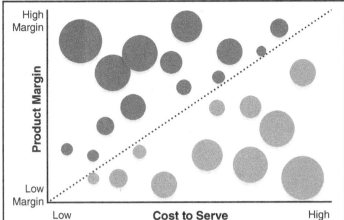

1. This chart represents the twofold relationship between the total margin on purchased goods and services that a customer generates and the total costs to serve that customer's relationship with the SBU. Customers that demand a lot of special support activities in the CRM process and yet don't produce much profit margin on product sales are the most unprofitable customers in the portfolio. On the other hand, customers who purchase a high volume of product or services or who select high-margin products *and* engage in customer support processes efficiently are the most profitable customers for the SBU.

2. The same crossover point in the whale curve is demonstrated in the migration chart above with the customers whose margin on purchases and offsetting use of support processes results in either a small profit or a small loss. These customers should likely be the priority focus to migrate toward more profitable relationships. On the other hand, customers with significant losses need to be closely (and quickly) evaluated to determine if the relationship is recoverable. Otherwise, these customers should likely be the priority focus to raise prices in order to remove them from the business portfolio.

III. Getting Performance Measurement Right

A. Before wrapping up this lesson on measuring performance on profitability, it's important to emphasize three key principles on performance measurement and management. These three key principles must be carefully balanced in the management process of planning, controlling, and evaluating.

1. The first principle is performance measures must be designed to represent the strategic objectives of the organization. This seems obvious, but it is actually challenging work. Strategy is constantly evolving and, therefore, performance measures in the organization need to constantly evolve as well if they are to be clearly tied to strategic outcomes.

2. Second, compensation and incentives need to be clearly tied to achieving performance measures; otherwise, employees will never be energized to accomplish work that is strategically critical to the organization. This also seems obvious but getting the incentives to function well is another challenging aspect of balancing performance measurement processes. Too much incentive on any one measure can result in hyperfocus, even potentially fraudulent behavior, in one area of the organization's strategy. And, of course, not enough incentive leaves other aspects of the strategy underachieved.

3. The third principle involves assigning the responsibility and decision rights necessary to accomplish the performance measure. The natural result of not delegating the proper authority to get the assigned job done is frustration. The complication in this principle is based in the reality of complex bureaucracy in large organizations. Strategic goals require multiple people and processes. It's difficult to identify and incentivize performance measures that are strategically aligned and that don't require the efforts of multiple teams. In that interrelated structure, it's difficult to identify individuals who are solely responsible for specific aspects of each performance target.

B. These three principles can be described as a three-legged stool, each necessary to supporting a balanced management structure involving performance measurement. This relationship is depicted below.

Management Structure

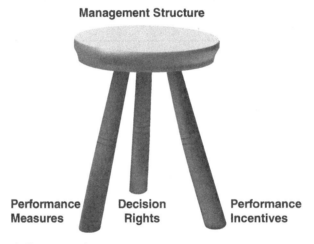

| Performance Measures | Decision Rights | Performance Incentives |

Source: BEPictured/Shutterstock

What is critical to remember in this relationship is that adjustments to any one aspect of this management structure must be followed by adjustments in the other two aspects. If a performance measure is changed, then new incentives must be evaluated and decision rights realigned.

C. Finally, watch out for measurement surrogation! Measures function as imperfect surrogates (or representatives) for the actual strategic objective in the organization. The measurement for operating profits on the income statement *represents* profitability as a strategic goal for the organization, but operating profits in any one operating period is not the actual strategic objective. If managers focus too much on this particular measure, they start making the mistake of making decisions strictly to move up that particular measure, regardless of possible negative effects on the long-term profitability of the organization, which is truly the strategic objective of the organization. This mistake is called measurement surrogation. Too much focus on reducing *reported* costs and increasing reported revenues can lead to a loss of focus on sustainable cost drivers and quality revenue drivers.

1. For example, operating costs can be reduced by cutting maintenance costs or firing employees needed for next year's operation. This isn't sustainable.

2. Another example is indiscriminately marketing for any kind of customer who will purchase the product and increase revenue without consideration for the impact that certain customers can have on selling and administrative expense. This leads to the accumulation of low-quality customers who drag down overall profitability.

Practice Question

The sales manager of Flying Carpets, a carpet manufacturer and wholesaler, is analyzing the profitability of two of the company's customers. One customer, a boutique store, purchases small orders for individual clients, and often wants a custom-run carpet. The other customer, a discount retailer, buys large lots of standard carpets. The sales manager is concerned that providing services for the boutique store is costing more than the contribution margin from its business. The accountant has gathered the following relevant information for the past year. All employees are guaranteed a 40-hour work week. Sales representatives are paid $20 per hour, and the production line supervisor is paid $18 per hour. Employee benefits and human resource services amount to approximately 50% of hourly wages. The discount retailer picks up large lots of carpets four times a year. Deliveries to customers of the boutique store must be made as the carpets are completed.

Relevant Information

	Boutique Store	Discount Retailer
Revenues	$135,000	$850,000
Direct product costs (DM and DL)	$80,000	$400,000
Sales representatives	60 hours	24 hours
Production line supervisor	90 hours	36 hours
Delivery costs	$20,000	$8,000

1. Compute profitability for each of these two customers.

2. Flying Carpets would like to retain the boutique store as a customer because its clients' homes are often featured in the local lifestyle magazine and the publicity is free advertisement. What suggestions can you make for negotiations with the customer about service costs?

3. If Flying Carpets can replace either customer with other business, what is your recommendation?

Answer

1. Computation of sales representative costs, including benefits and HR services:

   Boutique Store: 60 hours × $20 × 150% = $1,800

   Discount Retailer: 24 hours × $20 × 150% = $720

   Computation of production line supervisor costs, including benefits and HR services:

   Boutique Store: 90 hours × $18 × 150% = $2,430

   Discount Retailer: 36 hours × $18 × 150% = $972

Profitability Report

	Boutique Store	Discount Retailer
Revenues	$135,000	$850,000
Direct product costs (DM and DL)	(80,000)	(400,000)
Sales representatives	(1,800)	(720)
Production line supervisor	(2,430)	(972)
Delivery costs	(20,000)	(8,000)
Customer Profitability	**$30,770**	**$440,308**

2. Flying Carpet could ask that the Boutique Store pay for the additional customer service costs such as sales representative time, production line supervisor time, and delivery costs. Flying Carpet could also raise its Boutique Store prices to ensure that the total product and service costs as a percent of revenues are similar to the discount retailer.

Continues…

3. If there is another potential customer who can provide more total profit than the Boutique Store, it's possible that it should be replaced. However, managers at Flying Carpets do not know whether sales at the discount retailer are affected by the featured homes in the local lifestyle magazine. Without data about potential losses in sales, it may be risky for Flying Carpet's strategy to stop serving the Boutique Store.

Summary

Planning, controlling, and evaluating profitability in the open market for a strategic business unit (SBU) is complicated. The process involves more than simply being profitable on every product or service sold. SBUs often pursue strategies that involve maturing products or services that are initially unprofitable, and may also include unprofitable products or services in their business portfolio because of the complementary nature of these loss leaders. In addition, SBUs should consider the full cost of their customers. Including costs to serve customers along with the costs of products or services purchased allows SBUs to compute customer profitability, and work to effectively manage the emerging profitability of customers or customer groups. When establishing performance measures on profits (or on any other strategic objective), SBUs need to be sure that the management structure in the organization balances accurate deployment of strategically connected measures, appropriate levels of incentives, and effective delegation of decision rights.

Return on Investment and Residual Income

After studying this lesson, you should be able to:

- Define and calculate return on investment (ROI) (1.C.3.e).

- Analyze and interpret ROI calculations (1.C.3.f).

- Define and calculate residual income (RI) (1.C.3.g).

- Analyze and interpret RI calculations (1.C.3.h).

- Compare and contrast the benefits and limitations of ROI and RI as measures of performance (1.C.3.i).

- Explain how revenue and expense recognition policies may affect the measurement of income and reduce comparability among business units (1.C.3.j).

- Explain how inventory measurement policies, joint asset sharing, and overall asset measurement policies may affect the measurement of investment and reduce comparability among business units (1.C.3.k).

Investment centers are assigned the responsibility to manage costs, revenues, and assets. As a result, the measures used to evaluate performance of investment centers need to incorporate all three business aspects. In this lesson we explore two of the most common measures used to evaluate investment centers: return on investment and residual income.

I. Return on Investment (ROI)

A. Remember that responsibility centers include cost centers, revenue centers, profit centers, and investment centers. In this lesson we discuss classic performance measures on investment centers. Investment centers are responsible for the efficient use of capital assets to effectively manage costs and revenues, which results in profit. The fact that investment centers are responsible for costs, revenues, and assets means that their management focus is largely aligned with the strategic focus of the organization, which is why investment centers are typically classified as strategic business units (SBUs).

B. The most common performance measure for an organization or SBU is return on investment or ROI. This measure has been around for a long time and there are a number of specific versions of this measure. The basic ROI computation, as suggested by its name, is as follows:

Income ÷ Investment = Return on investment (ROI)

C. Starting with the numerator, there are many ways to define *income* when measuring ROI. After-tax net income, as *the* bottom line of the income statement, is certainly a valid definition of the ROI numerator. Alternatively, pre-tax income could be used in the ROI numerator, or operating profit, gross margin, or even cash flow from operations. Hence, it's important to carefully define exactly what version of "income" is used in the ROI measure. It all depends on what strategic performance is being measured for management purposes.

D. Similarly, *investment* in the denominator has multiple definitions. Typically, total assets are used in this computation. However, remember that assets = debt + equity. If the strategic issue is to manage total assets in order to *create value* that achieves a particular goal, then return on total assets is the right formulation. On this basis, the ROI formula is computed as follows:

Income ÷ Total assets = Return on assets (ROA)

(If you're preparing for the CMA© exam, you should note that this formula is on the ICMA formula sheet. Note this ROA version of the ROI formula uses the same terminology of the ICMA formula.)

1. Alternatively, based on an assumption that generally only long-term debt and equity require a return on the money employed (i.e., short-term operating liabilities usually don't carry

explicit interest rates), the ROI formula can be focused on creating value to cover the costs of the long-term capital employed by the business, and is computed as follows:

Income ÷ (Long-term debt + Equity) = Return on capital employed (ROCE)

Or

Income ÷ (Total assets – Short-term debt) = Return on capital employed (ROCE)

2. Another version of ROI is focused on the fact that the true investors in the organization are the shareholders who have provided equity and expect a return on their equity investment. If the ROI formula is focused on measuring the ability of management to *capture value* after paying all obligations in order to provide that value to shareholders, then the formula is computed as follows:

Income ÷ Equity = Return on equity (ROE)

Or

Income ÷ (Total assets – Total debt) = Return on equity (ROE)

E. The DuPont Corporation is credited with creating the ROI formula, which is why it is often called the DuPont Equation. However, in the 1920s when the formula was first employed, DuPont managers didn't limit the formula to a single measure. The formula was expanded to form what's still known as the DuPont Model or DuPont Analysis. Consider below an ROI formula based on total assets (ROA) that demonstrates a DuPont analysis. Note that the ROA formula is separated into two important components: Profit Margin and Asset Turnover.

$$\boxed{\textbf{Dupont Analysis for ROA}}$$

$$\frac{\text{Profit}}{\text{Assets}} = \frac{\text{Profit}}{\text{Sales}} \times \frac{\text{Sales}}{\text{Assets}}$$

Return on Assets = Profit Margin × Asset Turnover

1. Of the two components, profit margin is likely the most familiar. This component of ROA measures the percentage of sales revenue that is captured as profit. While a large profit margin is certainly good for ROA, generating a significant profit margin is not necessarily the strategic focus of all organizations. Some organizations engage the market and their competition on very thin profit margins. Nevertheless, these organizations can still generate a healthy ROI performance.

2. Asset turnover is determined above as sales ÷ assets. This ROA component is based on an assumption that the primary purpose of assets is to create a volume of business for the organization (i.e., to generate sales). This component of ROA reports on the number of sales dollars generated by each dollar invested into assets. Of course, each sales dollar is then used by the profit margin measure to determine the percentage of that dollar captured as profit. This means that an organization that can efficiently churn out (i.e., turn over) a lot of sales dollars from its assets can still accumulate a significant amount of total profit despite competing on a thin profit margin percentage.

F. Let's take a look at how a DuPont analysis works with the International Manufacturing Corporation (IMC) example we've been using in our lessons to this point. Remember that IMC has three SBUs, which are reported in the DuPont analysis below. Consider the ROA measures provided in this report and how they combine to illustrate the investment center performance for each SBU.

International Manufacturing Corporation Subsidiary Report

(in millions)	Acme Computer Company	Edison Automobile Company	Jennifer Cosmetics Company	Total for IMC
Sales revenue	$467	$441	$355	$1,263
Operating profit	$49	$30	$34	$113
Beginning of year assets	$595	$368	$169	$1,132
End of year assets	$578	$355	$173	$1,106
Average assets	$586.5	$361.5	$171.0	$1,119.0
Profit margin	10.49%	6.80%	9.58%	8.95%
× Asset turnover	0.796	1.220	2.076	1.129
Return on Assets	**8.35%**	**8.30%**	**19.88%**	**10.10%**

1. Before starting the analysis, note the use of average assets in the performance report above. Remember that revenue and profit are totals that accumulate over a period of time while balance sheet numbers represent a financial position at a single point in time. In order to bring together numbers from the income statement and the balance sheet, it is good practice to use the beginning and ending balances from the balance sheet and create an average balance that (hopefully) represents a reasonable approximation of the assets available for use throughout the operating period.

2. It is important not to round off results on profit margin and asset turnover when using these intermediate numbers to compute ROA.

3. Note that Acme Computer Company and Edison Automobile Company both provide fairly similar ROA measures (8.35% and 8.30%, respectively). Yet these two SBUs generated their investment returns following different performance paths. Compared to Edison, Acme has a larger profit margin (10.49%), but less turnover on assets ($0.796 in revenue for every $1.00 invested in assets). On the other hand, Edison with its lower profit margin is more efficient with the capital investment in assets compared to Acme, generating $1.220 in revenue for every $1.00 in assets. Depending on its strategic objectives, its capital structure, and the nature of its market competition, each of these two SBUs could improve ROA performance by focusing on either profit margin (reduce costs or increase sales) or asset turnover (reduce assets or increase sales).

4. The best of the three SBUs is the Jennifer Cosmetics Company with an ROA of 19.88%, which is based on comparatively strong performance in both profit margin (9.58%) and asset turnover ($2.076 per asset dollar). Clearly, Jennifer is doing very well as an SBU within the IMC organization.

II. Residual Income

A. Using an ROI measure as a performance evaluation tool can occasionally lead to decisions by some SBUs that are suboptimal for the overall organization. Let's take a look at Jennifer Cosmetics Company and consider a scenario wherein Jennifer management is considering a significant capital investment to expand the business. The new business will need $52M in additional capital investment (assets) and is expected to generate $8M in annual profit. This means that the expansion generates a 15.38% ROA (= $8M ÷ $52M).

1. This 15.38% ROA is a good rate of return for IMC, especially compared to the returns generated by Acme and Edison SBUs. But the Jennifer management team may hesitate to take on this new business because its ROI will dilute the SBU's overall ROA.

2. This dilution effect can be computed. Note that Jennifer's original ROA is 19.88% based on its current income and assets ($34M ÷ $171M = 19.88%). However, when the new business is added to the Jennifer Cosmetics Company portfolio, the result for the SBU is as follows:

Profit ÷ Assets = ($34M + $8M) ÷ ($171M + $52M) = 18.83% ROA

3. If IMC assesses SBU performance based on ROA, the Jennifer management team is not likely to take on a 15.38% project that would boost IMC's overall 10.10% rate of return while diluting their own 19.88% rate of return. In short, the ROI approach to performance assessment creates a misalignment in the management structure for high-performing SBUs with particular investment decisions. This misalignment is illustrated below.

4. If an SBU's current ROI performance is higher than the minimum expected ROI for the organization, that SBU will avoid investments desired by the organization if the ROI is below (i.e., will dilute) the SBU's current ROI performance. This is an inherent limitation of ROI as a performance measure within an organization. Let's explore an alternative measure that avoids this limitation.

B. In the last lesson we briefly mentioned the concept of cost of capital and residual income. This can be a rather involved financial issue. The basic concept is that assets are obtained using debt and equity. Debt financing requires regular payments based on effective interest rates, and equity financing results in capital commitments and opportunity costs in the market to satisfy shareholder demands. These cost commitments can be represented as a combined rate of return required to cover financing costs.

1. Until an organization earns enough income to pay the costs of its debt and equity financing structure, it is not really making an economic profit. This view, representing an economic breakeven concept, can be used to establish a "hurdle rate" that an SBU, functioning as an investment center, must clear in order to create economic value (over and above its cost of capital) for the organization.

2. This hurdle rate is a benchmark for ROI performance and represents the organization's minimum required ROI. If we assume that IMC has an economic hurdle rate of 6.5%, then all three of its SBUs are clearing that hurdle and providing economic value to the organization. However, the difference between this hurdle rate and each SBU's current ROI represents a potential misalignment zone.

C. An alternative to the ROI measure is the "residual income" measure, which is computed as follows (using total assets to represent the capital investment):

Assets × Hurdle rate = Required income

Current income − Required income = Residual income

(Note: "Income" means "Operating profit" unless specified otherwise)

(If you're preparing for the CMA© exam, you should note that this formula is on the ICMA formula sheet. Note this ROA version of the ROI formula uses the same terminology of the ICMA formula.)

D. Returning to IMC, let's compute the residual income for each of its SBUs.

International Manufacturing Corporation Subsidiary Report

(in millions)	Acme Computer Company	Edison Automobile Company	Jennifer Cosmetics Company	Total for IMC
Average assets	$586.5	$361.5	$171.0	$1,119.0
× Hurdle rate	6.5%	6.5%	6.5%	6.5%
Required income	$38.1	$23.5	$11.1	$72.7
Current operating profit	$49.0	$30.0	$34.0	$113.0
Residual income	**$10.9**	**$6.5**	**$22.9**	**$40.3**

In terms of evaluating each SBU's performance, the residual income measure is consistent with the ROA measure. The Jennifer Cosmetics Company is significantly outperforming the other two strategic business units.

E. The real value of using residual income to assess performance is the alignment of all SBUs with the organization's objective to maximize residual income. Let's return to the business opportunity being considered by Jennifer Cosmetics Company and observe that using residual income to assess SBU performance will encourage Jennifer to take on a project that is good for IMC. Remember that the expansion available to Jennifer will require $52M in additional assets and will generate $8M in additional annual profit.

   1. First, note that Jennifer's current performance is $22.9M in residual income. The new business opportunity will generate the following residual income:

      $52M × 6.5% = $3.4M Required income

      $8.0M − $3.4M = $4.6 Residual income

   2. This $4.6 of additional residual income will improve Jennifer's performance to $27.5M (= $22.9M + $4.6M). Hence, the Jennifer management team is motivated to take on this business opportunity that is good overall for IMC.

III. Comparing ROI and Residual Income

   A. Which measure is best to use when controlling and evaluating the performance of investment centers? Organizations should consider the benefits and limitations of each measure in the design of their management structure.

   B. Return on investment (ROI) measures (including ROA, ROIC, and ROE) are easily understood by managers and widely used in practice. These types of measures make it easy to compare performance across different business units. However, as described above, ROI measures will discourage SBU managers from investing in certain business projects that are good for the organization if the project ROI will dilute the SBU's current ROI.

   C. Residual income measures avoid the ROI incentive problem on projects with desirable rates of return that are below the high-performing SBUs' current rate of return. However, the concept of capital costs and economic income is a bit more difficult to understand and communicate than is the ROI concept. In addition, residual income measures can cause a bias when comparing performance between different SBUs that are dramatically different in size because larger SBUs will typically have an inherent advantage in generating more residual income dollars compared to smaller SBUs.

   D. Both ROI and residual income measures are focused on performance involving costs, revenues, and assets. This focus makes these measures useful for evaluating the performance of investment centers in organizations. However, this overall focus also leads to three fundamental concerns with using either ROI or residual income as the core performance measure on SBUs.

      1. First, both of these measures are based on the assumption that costs, revenues, and assets can be clearly distinguished between business units in the organization. However, when assets are jointly shared by different business units or revenues of one business unit are

affected by performance in another business unit or common costs are shared and allocated across business units, it can become difficult to clearly distinguish performance of one business unit from another.

2. Second, accounting policies occasionally shift within organizations and across economic zones. When this happens, ROI and residual income measures are affected by modifications in revenue and expense recognition policies, as well as by adjustments in asset measurement policies. The result is performance measures that change due to accounting policy rather than due to actual performance.

3. Finally, financial performance measures such as ROI or residual income do not provide a full strategic view of business performance. These measures tend to focus on short-term operating results and are obviously limited to financial objectives. Management of strategy involves much more than financial performance indicators. Strategy is a long-term process of integrating multifaceted objectives involving quality, timeliness, innovation, service, positioning, throughput, safety, etc. When performance is focused solely or largely on financial measures, the imbalance in that limited perspective creates blind spots in management and limits the organization's success and viability. In the next lesson, we will explore a larger and more integrative model of performance measures that better supports the management process of planning, controlling, and evaluating.

Practice Question

Trenton Industries evaluates SBU managers on the basis of ROI. Since the cost of capital for Trenton is 14%, managers are evaluated on their ability to exceed an ROI of 14%. At the close of the last quarter, the Sandy Manufacturing Plant had operating income of $1.35 million on total assets of $7.5 million. The Sandy manager is considering a potential plant investment of $1.5 million that is expected to generate additional income of $240,000.

What does Trenton Industries want the Sandy manager to do with this investment decision?

What will the Sandy manager most likely do with this investment decision?

Answer

Currently, the Sandy Manufacturing Plant ROI = $1,350,000 ÷ $7,500,000 = 18%. The ROI on the new plant investment = $240,000 ÷ $1,500,000 = 16%. Because the cost of capital for Trenton is 14%, any return greater than 14% is valuable (optimal) to the company. Trenton Industries will want the Sandy manager to make this investment.

However, because this investment will dilute Sandy's current ROI performance to 17.67% (see computation below), the manager will *not* be inclined to make this investment, which is a suboptimal decision overall for Trenton Industries.

Sandy's diluted ROI = ($1,350,000 + $240,000) ÷ ($7,500,000 + $1,500,000) = 17.67%

Practice Question

Continuing with Trenton Industries, assume now that Trenton Industries evaluates SBU managers on the basis of residual income. Since the cost of capital for Trenton is 14%, managers are evaluated on their ability to generate income that exceeds the 14% required income level. Again, the Sandy Manufacturing Plant had operating income of $1.35 million on total assets of $7.5 million, and the Sandy manager is considering a potential plant investment of $1.5 million that is expected to generate additional income of $240,000. Based on the residual income measure, what will the Sandy manager do with this investment decision?

Answer

Currently, the Sandy Manufacturing Plant residual income = $1,350,000 − ($7,500,000 × 14%) = $300,000. The residual income on the new plant investment = $240,000 − ($1,500,000 × 14%) = $30,000. Because this investment will increase Sandy's residual income to $330,000, the manager will be inclined to make this investment, which is an optimal decision overall for Trenton Industries.

Summary

Investment centers are assigned the responsibility to manage costs, revenues, and assets. These types of business units are often referred to as strategic business units (SBUs). Performance measures such as return on investment (ROI) and residual income represent the work by SBUs to improve profits (revenues and costs) while efficiently using assets. The basic ROI measure is income ÷ investment. The basic ROI measure can be expanded further to (income ÷ sales) × (sales ÷ assets) in order to evaluate profit margin and asset turnover. Residual income is measured as current income − (assets × hurdle rate). Each measure has benefits and limitations that need to be understood by management in order to effectively use these tools in planning, controlling, and evaluating the financial performance of SBUs.

The Balanced Scorecard

After studying this lesson, you should be able to:

- Define key performance indicators (KPIs) and discuss the importance of these indicators in evaluating a firm (1.C.3.l).

- Define the concept of a balanced scorecard and identify its components (1.C.3.m).

- Identify and describe the perspectives of a balanced scorecard, including financial, customer, internal process, and learning and growth (1.C.3.n).

- Identify and describe the characteristics of successful implementation and use of a balanced scorecard (1.C.3.o).

- Demonstrate an understanding of a strategy map and the role it plays (1.C.3.p).

- Analyze and interpret a balanced scorecard and evaluate performance on the basis of the analysis (1.C.3.q).

- Recommend performance measures and a periodic reporting methodology given operational goals and actual results (1.C.3.r).

Key performance indicators (KPIs) are an essential component of strategy design and implementation. This lesson focuses on the Balanced Scorecard as an effective model for designing and deploying KPIs within an organization.

I. Key Performance Indicators (KPIs)

    A. A good way to get a quick sense of an organization's strategy is to look at the key performance indicators (KPIs) being used to guide decision making and track progress within the organization. KPIs are not just another term to describe measures at the organization. Many companies will track thousands of measures in the process of running the business. KPIs, as the name implies, are a small set of critical data points that indicate to the executive team and other stakeholders whether the organization is on track to accomplishing its strategic objectives.

    B. Each strategic objective established by company leaders should be identified by one to three KPIs. For example, if customer satisfaction is a strategic objective for the company, then below is a list of possible KPIs to represent customer satisfaction:

- Survey scores submitted by customers

- Type of comments gathered from social media platforms

- Likelihood of customers to recommend the company to friends

- Complaint resolution rates at support centers

- Number of returning customers

    C. As you consider the list of possible measures above, you might wonder which measure should actually be used to represent customer satisfaction, or you may consider that all of these measures should be used. Alternatively, you may take a position that some of these measures don't actually represent customer satisfaction, or that none of these measures can perfectly represent customer satisfaction. The questions or concerns you have about the list represent some of the challenges with designing strategic objectives and selecting KPIs to use in managing strategy. Company leaders and executive teams run into a number of challenges in the process of designing and deploying KPIs, including the following:

       1. Accurately representing a strategic objective with one or more KPIs

       2. Essentially abandoning a strategic objective by failing to establish a KPI for it

3. Creating "orphan" KPIs that are not tied to a strategic objective.

4. Not adjusting KPIs as the strategy evolves

5. Having so many KPIs in the organization that it creates confusion

6. Struggling to determine which KPIs are most important in the organization

For the remainder of this lesson, we'll focus on a strategic measurement model that helps to address these kinds of challenges with KPIs.

II. The Balanced Scorecard Model

A. The Balanced Scorecard (BSC) is a strategic performance measurement model that came into practice in the 1990s. The initial design of the BSC is to support for-profit organizations based on four connected strategy perspectives or themes (BSC models have been subsequently developed to effectively support not-for-profit and government organizations). These four themes are illustrated in the BSC model presented below. Note that at the center of the BSC is the organization's strategic vision and strategic mission. In an earlier section of this learning series, we defined the organization's vision as a statement of what it intends *to be or become* while the mission is the core statement of what the organization intends *to do*.

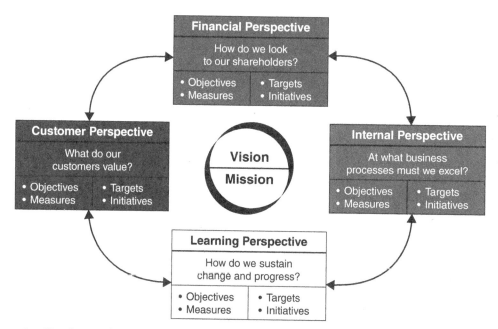

1. The financial perspective in the BSC is where the organization's vision and mission are translated into financial performance. Identifying how financial performance should be tied to an organization's vision and mission is a matter of answering the question: "How do we look to our shareholders?" The organization needs to identify why exactly their particular shareholders have invested in the company. For example, are they looking for diversification, market share and revenue growth, earnings, or dividend payments? Identifying what the shareholders are expecting from their investment will define the types of financial KPIs that should be established for the organization.

2. The customer perspective is focused on answering the question: "What do our customers value?" The competitive concept here is often described as delivering "value-added" products and services to customers. If asked, customers generally respond that they're interested in receiving all kinds of value, such as low price, high quality, innovative design, timely delivery, excellent post-sale support, etc. However, the key to understanding what customers truly value is *identifying what value customers are willing to pay for*. Clearly defining and focusing on the value that customers will pay for establishes a sustainable relationship with customers and provides a key connection between the customer perspective and the financial perspective in the organization's BSC.

3. The internal perspective in the BSC is also known as the internal process perspective. Successfully answering the strategic question, "At what business processes must we excel?" depends on how the organization's internal processes are tied to successfully delivering on the customer perspective. Generally, there are three types of internal processes that can potentially establish value that customers will pay for: research and development (or innovation), production and delivery, and post-sale service or support. Think about various companies where you spend money. You should be able to easily define the internal process that you value at each company. Is it the innovation of the product (or service) design? Is it the quality and/or price of the product delivered to you? Or is it the dependability of the company's support of the product once you've received it?

4. The most foundational perspective in the BSC is the learning perspective, also known as the learning and growth perspective. However, compared to the financial, customer, and internal process perspectives, the learning and growth perspective is often the least developed aspect of the organization's strategic performance measurement model. Answering the question: "How do we sustain change and progress?" is about identifying the key areas to be improving in order to support key internal processes and key customer values. One obvious area of learning and growth is employees, but this perspective isn't limited to employee development. The other two traditional areas for learning and growth are systems (computers, communication, security, etc.) and management structure (measures, incentives, decision rights, etc.).

B. Before moving on, we need to emphasize one other aspect of the BSC model. Note within each perspective is a deployment list that includes objectives, measures, targets, and initiatives. The order here is intentional. Within each perspective the organization must first establish a clear set of actionable strategic objectives that answers the key strategic question for each perspective. With the strategic objectives in place, the organization then designs one or more measures (i.e., KPIs) to capture progress on each objective. Before the start of each operating period, the target or goal for each measure is determined. Finally, initiatives are put in place (i.e., resources are committed) to accomplish the target. Using these four steps, the organization's strategy is operationalized through the BSC.

III. The Balanced Scorecard Strategy Map

A. Perhaps the most important aspect of a successful BSC is establishing links between strategic objectives through interconnected strategic measures. The "balance" in a good BSC model is the idea that no single strategic objective or strategic measure (KPI) is more important than another. Each objective and measure is designed to follow from and/or lead to another objective and measure. Designing and deploying a successful strategy is very much about "hypothesis testing." That is, management determines that success in a particular financial objective requires effective deployment of core customer objectives that are dependent upon implementation of critical internal processes that are sustained by ongoing learning and growth initiatives. If management is right about the strategic linkages they establish in the BSC, the organization should be in a position to succeed.

B. It is difficult to demonstrate these critical linkages between strategic objectives and between KPIs using the classic BSC model illustrated above. Therefore, a different perspective is needed—the BSC strategy map. Let's return once more to the IMC example and look at a possible BSC strategy map for the Acme Computer Company (below).

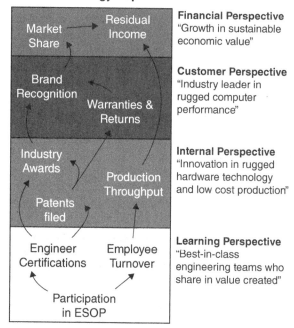

**Acme Computer Company
BSC Strategy Map**

Market Share → Residual Income

Financial Perspective
"Growth in sustainable economic value"

Brand Recognition

Warranties & Returns

Customer Perspective
"Industry leader in rugged computer performance"

Industry Awards

Production Throughput

Patents filed

Internal Perspective
"Innovation in rugged hardware technology and low cost production"

Engineer Certifications

Employee Turnover

Learning Perspective
"Best-in-class engineering teams who share in value created"

Participation in ESOP

1. First of all, note how Acme Computer Company has stated a response to each of the questions that define each of the four BSC perspectives. These statements represent the strategic objective for each perspective.

2. Next, observe that two or three KPIs have been established to represent each objective in the management structure at Acme. For example, the three measures in the Internal Perspective should clarify how Acme intends to accomplish its objective to achieve innovation in rugged hardware technology and low cost production.

3. Finally, and perhaps most importantly, you can see arrows linking measures together that represent hypotheses about cause-and-effect relationships in the Acme strategic plan. For example, one set of connected relationships represent the Acme belief that increasing the number of employees who participate in the ESOP (employee stock ownership plan) will reduce employee turnover. This is important because experienced employees are better positioned to find and deliver improvements in production throughput, which reduces production costs and increases residual income. These connections are rigorously tested by gathering performance data and observing whether relationships between strategic objectives and KPIs are demonstrated.

IV. Implementing a Balanced Scorecard

   A. The process of implementing a BSC can be (and should be) an elaborate process, especially if the effort also involves designing and implementing the organization's strategy. The BSC implementation process starts with the leadership team working to clarify the organization's vision and mission into a strategy that can be communicated *as an actionable statement(s)* to all key stakeholders (employees, investors, suppliers, etc.).

   B. Next, the leadership team drafts out a balanced scorecard and strategy map to introduce to middle management supervisors. This is a key communication process that is focused on generating feedback to refine the BSC and obtain buy-in from the managers who will be working daily with operations and employees to accomplish the strategic objectives.

C. When ready, an implementation team is established composed of a cross-functional representation of key leaders, managers, and front-line employees. This team handles the front-line issues involved in a significant change management process for the organization. Specifically, the implementation team works to further refine the BSC as needed to accommodate implementation, design and deploy the marketing campaign through the organization, and execute and guide training events.

D. While the implementation team is engaged in rolling out the change process, the leadership team takes on the particularly sticky challenge of identifying and eliminating nonstrategic investments (product lines, business units, customer groups, etc.) in the organization. This realistic task represents the truth that strategy is as much about determining what to *stop doing* as it is deciding what to start or keep doing.

E. While eliminating nonstrategic investments, the leadership team also works to realign the organization to tightly focus on the strategic objectives and KPIs represented in the BSC. This effort involves identifying how each business unit, department, team, and individual in the organization relates to one key aspect or another of the BSC. Of course, this realignment effort is done in concert with the implementation team's campaign and training events.

F. If eliminating nonstrategic investments in the organization is the hardest aspect of implementing a new strategy and BSC, the second hardest aspect is adjusting incentives and compensation. Remember from a previous lesson that management structure is a three-legged stool composed of measures, incentives, and decision rights. If one leg of the stool is adjusted, the other two must be adjusted as well. A BSC realignment certainly requires new performance measures as well as new responsibility and reporting structures. That being said, until compensation and incentives are adjusted to support the new strategic focus, little will actually change in the organization. Significant changes to compensation systems almost always encounter significant resistance at all levels in the organization. Leadership will need to establish compensation transition processes while the implementation team educates everyone on the new incentive system.

G. Remember that designing strategic objectives and KPIs is very much about hypothesis testing. Objectives, measures, and linkages between measures will never be perfect. Data gathering, feedback, and refining is an ongoing process. Implementing a balanced scorecard must be viewed as a learning process. Hence, the last step of implementation is a commitment to constantly test strategic assertions with data while gathering feedback from employees and working to better design and deploy a scorecard that effectively guides decision making and operation processes in a constantly evolving business environment.

Practice Question

Eastern Ensign Bank is a community bank that focuses on small business commercial loans. Its vision is to be the most valued banking partner in the local business community. Its mission statement is "Creating lending solutions that work for individual needs." The bank partners at Eastern Ensign are committed to creating a balanced scorecard solution to guide strategy and have worked through the four BSC perspectives to craft an answer for each key question. These questions and answers are below:

Financial Perspective

Question: How do we look to our partners? Answer: Growth in returns on partner investments.

Customer Perspective

Question: What do our customers value? Answer: Personalized service and excellent results that earn client loyalty.

Internal Process Perspective

Question: At what business processes must we excel? Answer: Fast lending solutions that are the *beginning* of a client relationship.

Learning and Growth Perspective

Question: How do we sustain change and progress? Answer: Continuous professional development that leads to happy employees.

Continues...

Working with their management team, the partners have identified the following ten KPIs:

- Return on Partner Equity (ROE)

- Lending Income (monthly)

- Loan Portfolio Growth (quarterly percentage growth)

- Client Promotion Score (survey on likelihood of clients to recommend bank to colleagues)

- Client Loan Satisfaction (survey score)

- Number of Customer Solutions (created for clients)

- Number of Client Touch Points (personally connecting with client to acknowledge business events, family celebrations, etc.)

- Loan Processing Speed and Accuracy (a combined score based on days to fund loan and loan errors)

- Employee Satisfaction (survey score)

- Number of Employee Training Events

Guided by the partners' question and answer for each BSC perspective, consider the KPIs listed above and decide where to locate each KPI within the BSC perspectives. Then build a BSC strategy map that demonstrates linkages between KPIs. (*Note:* This is a subjective exercise. Make your best assumptions about where to locate each KPI and how it links to other KPIs, and then compare your solution to the solution below.)

Answer

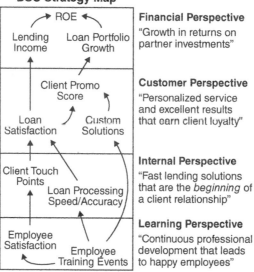

Remember that this is a subjective solution. For example, the KPI "Custom Solutions" could be located within the Internal Process perspective rather than within the Customer perspective. Be sure to review through each KPI's position in the BSC Strategy Map and how it is being linked from and to other KPIs to determine if the choices in this solution make sense to you.

Summary

Key performance indicators (KPIs) are an essential tool in designing and deploying strategy within an organization. The Balanced Scorecard (BSC) model provides an effective approach to guide the development and use of KPIs. The BSC model is generally based on four strategic perspectives: financial, customer, internal process, and learning and growth. KPIs should be associated with a specific BSC perspective. Just as importantly, managers need to carefully consider and map out how KPIs are related to each other as a set of strategic linkages (i.e., cause-and-effect relationships). Implementing a BSC model and strategy map across an organization is an involved process that requires careful development, organization realignment, cross-functional participation, employee training and buy-in, compensation restructuring, and continuous feedback and refinement.

aq.dirmat.dlcv.001_1807

1. Data on Goodman Company's direct labor costs are given below:

Standard direct labor hours	30,000
Actual direct labor hours	29,000
Direct labor usage (efficiency) variance	$4,000 Favorable
Direct labor rate variance	$5,800 Favorable
Total payroll	$110,200

What was Goodman's standard direct labor rate?

A. $3.60
B. $3.80
C. $3.67
D. $4.00

aq.manw.va.009_0820

2. Fake Flowers (FF) paid more property tax on their manufacturing facility this year than they were expecting. This would most likely cause an:

A. unfavorable fixed overhead volume variance.
B. unfavorable fixed overhead spending variance.
C. unfavorable variable overhead efficiency variance.
D. unfavorable variable overhead spending variance.

aq.balscore.004_1807

3. What perspective of the Balanced Scorecard (BSC) is focused on the question: "At what business process must we excel?"

A. Internal perspective
B. Learning perspective
C. Customer perspective
D. Financial perspective

aq.tran.pri.006_0820

4. Business Unit A produces a widget product that can be sold either to external customers or internally to Business Unit B. Business Unit B is currently purchasing 15,000 widgets from an external supplier for $42 per unit. Both Business Unit A and Business Unit B are evaluated as profit centers. Production and sales data for Business Unit A are provided below. Assuming that variable costs of $4 per widget can be avoided by Business Unit A if an internal transfer takes place, should Business Unit A transfer widgets to Business Unit B? If so, what should the transfer price be?

Business Unit A:	
Capacity in units	80,000
Number of units being sold to external customers	80,000
Selling price per unit to external customers	$45
Variable costs per widget	$20
Fixed costs per unit (based on capacity)	$10

A. No transfer should take place.
B. A transfer should take place; the transfer price should be $45.
C. A transfer should take place; the transfer price should be between $20 and $45.
D. A transfer should take place; the transfer price should be between $41 and $42.

aq.perev.bs.001_0820

5. Any organizational unit in which the manager of that unit has control only over the costs incurred best describes what type of responsibility center?

A. Investment center
B. Revenue center
C. Profit center
D. Cost center

aq.retinv.ri.006_1807

6. The Pacific Line in the U&P Railroad operates as a profit center. In the last quarter, the Pacific Line generated $200,000 in operating income on $1,000,000 in total assets. The Pacific Line has $250,000 in current liabilities. Assuming that the U&P required rate of return is 12%, what is the residual income for the Pacific Line?

A. $320,000
B. $200,000
C. $120,000
D. $80,000

aq.flex.bpa.007_1807

7. Given the following information, what is the flexible budget variance on operating profit for Trendy Technology (TT)?

	Actual Results	Flexible Budget
Total Sales Revenue	$325,000	$350,000
Total Variable Costs	$135,000	$120,000
Total Fixed Costs	$44,000	$42,000

A. $188,000 Favorable
B. $42,000 Favorable
C. $42,000 Unfavorable
D. $188,000 Unfavorable

aq.retinv.ri.005_0820

8. Frigid Fridges Co. (FFC) is a refrigerator manufacturer and wholesaler. For the month of July, FFC had the following operating statistics:

Sales	$600,000
Operating Income	40,000
Net Profit	10,000
Total Assets	700,000
Shareholders' Equity	300,000
Cost of Capital	5%

Based on the above information, what is FFC's residual income (RI)?

A. $5,000
B. ($25,000)
C. $25,000
D. $10,000

aq.perev.bs.004_0820

9. The following information from the prior year was provided by Comfortable Sofas & Couches, Inc. (CSCI):

   - The company produced 1,900 units and sold 1,800 units, as expected.

   - There was no beginning or ending work-in-process inventories and no beginning finished goods inventory.

   - Budgeted and actual fixed costs were equal, all variable manufacturing costs were affected by production volume only, and all variable selling costs were affected by sales volume only.

   - Budgeted per unit revenues and costs were as follows:

	Per Unit
Sales price	$120
Direct materials	$25
Direct labor	$20
Other variable manufacturing costs	$15
Fixed manufacturing costs	$12
Variable selling costs	$8
Fixed selling costs	$6
Fixed administrative costs	$5

What is the contribution margin earned by CSCI for the prior year?

A. $72,000
B. $108,000
C. $93,600
D. $86,400

aq.flex.bpa.009_0820

10. Which of the following correctly represents the management-by-exception concept in variance analysis?

   A. Only favorable variances provide a signal to management indicating that something in the organization is out of compliance with budget standards or performance expectations.
   B. Only unfavorable variances provide a signal to management indicating that something in the organization is out of compliance with budget standards or budget performance.
   C. Both favorable and unfavorable variances provide a signal to management indicating that something in the organization is out of compliance with budget standards or performance expectations.
   D. Variances by themselves *do not* provide a signal to management that something in the organization is out of compliance with budget standards or performance expectations.

aq.facov.cv.004_0820

11. The following information relates to one particular department of the Herman Company for the fourth quarter:

Actual variable overhead	$68,500
Variable overhead application rate	$0.50 per hour
Total overhead application rate	$1.50 per hour
Spending variance	$8,000 unfavorable
Volume variance	$5,000 favorable

What were the actual hours worked in this department during the quarter?

A. 137,000
B. 121,000
C. 127,000
D. 119,000

aq.balscore.001_1807

12. All of the following describe key performance indicators (KPIs) **except**:

A. a small set of critical data points.
B. a term describing all the measures used in an organization in the process of running the business.
C. measures that indicate to the executive team and other stakeholders whether the organization is on track to accomplishing its strategic objectives.
D. a good way to get a quick sense of an organization's strategy.

aq.perev.bs.007_0820

13. Quick Microwaves, Inc. (QMI) is preparing for external reporting and performance evaluation at the end of the year. QMI is split up into two companies: Microwave Company and Microwave Oven Company. Each company is split up into geographical regions with those regions being split up into different operations. Each operation has a sales division, manufacturing division, and service division. Based on the organizational structure of QMI, identify business units that QMI should evaluate each year based on performance.

A. Companies, regions, operations, and divisions
B. Companies, regions, and operations
C. Operations and divisions
D. Companies and regions

aq.tran.pri.007_1807

14. Business Unit A produces a widget product that can be sold either to external customers or internally to Business Unit B. Business Unit B is currently purchasing 15,000 widgets from an external supplier for $25 per unit. Both Business Unit A and Business Unit B are evaluated as profit centers. Production and sales data for Business Unit A are provided below. Assuming that no costs can be avoided if an internal transfer takes place, should Business Unit A transfer widgets to Business Unit B? If so, what should the transfer price be?

Business Unit A:	
Capacity in units	90,000
Number of units being sold to external customers	75,000
Selling price per unit to external customers	$29
Variable costs per widget	$26
Fixed costs per unit (based on capacity)	$2

A. No transfer should take place.
B. A transfer should take place; the transfer price should be $25.
C. A transfer should take place; the transfer price should be between $26 and $29.
D. A transfer should take place; the transfer price should be between $25 and $29.

15. Classy Purses, Inc. (CPI) is an international manufacturer of stylish shoulder bags. CPI is split up into three regions: Europe Region, Asia Eastern Region, U.S. Region. The Europe region is split into three operating units: England Operations, France Operations, Germany Operations. The France operating unit is split up into the Sales Division and Manufacturing Division. The France sales division is set up to focus exclusively on generating sales and revenue, without responsibility for cost. Which of the following most accurately identifies the responsibility center for the Sales Division, Manufacturing Division, and France Operations of CPI?

   A. Sales Division: cost center; Manufacturing Division: revenue center; France Operations: profit center.
   B. Sales Division: revenue center; Manufacturing Division: cost center; France Operations: profit center.
   C. Sales Division: profit center; Manufacturing Division: cost center; France Operations: cost center.
   D. Sales Division: profit center; Manufacturing Division: revenue center; France Operations: revenue center.

Section D: Cost Management

Topic 1. Measurement Concepts

Cost Drivers and Cost Flows

After studying this lesson, you should be able to:

- Calculate fixed, variable, and mixed costs and demonstrate an understanding of the behavior of each in the long and short term and how a change in assumptions regarding cost type or relevant range affects these costs (1.D.1.a).

- Distinguish between fixed and variable overhead expenses (1.D.3.a).

- Determine the appropriate time frame for classifying both variable and fixed overhead expenses (1.D.3.b).

- Identify cost objects and cost pools and assign costs to appropriate activities (1.D.1.b).

- Demonstrate an understanding of the nature and types of cost drivers and the causal relationship that exists between cost drivers and costs incurred (1.D.1.c).

- Demonstrate an understanding of the various methods for measuring costs and accumulating work-in-process and finished goods inventories (1.D.1.d).

- Identify and define cost measurement techniques such as actual costing, normal costing, and standard costing; calculate costs using each of these techniques; identify the appropriate use of each technique; and describe the benefits and limitations of each technique (1.D.1.e).

There are a number of cost accounting systems and models available for organizations to use in the management process of planning, controlling, and evaluating. This lesson establishes some critical concepts and basic accounting issues that must be understood before we explore different systems and models.

I. The Behavior of Costs

    A. Cost assignment systems are at the core of accounting performance reports. Understanding how to effectively assign costs begins with a clear view of cost behavior.

    B. Cost behavior is typically classified as either variable or fixed. This seems to be a straightforward distinction, but it's complicated by several important realities. First, many costs in organizations are not strictly variable or fixed but exhibit both variable and fixed characteristics. For most decisions, these "mixed" costs need to be split out into a variable cost component and a fixed cost component. In other lessons we've worked with a variety of methods that are used to split out these costs (e.g., high–low method, visual fit method, and regression analysis method). However, it's usually not possible to *precisely* split a mixed cost into its variable cost and fixed cost components. The methods used to split out these costs provide at best an approximation.

    C. The second complication is fixed costs can shift in total as the organization moves between significant cost structures. As the volume of business increases or decreases, there are "step-up" or "step-down" points when a fixed cost is dramatically increased or decreased (e.g., investments or reductions in property, plant, and equipment). Similarly, the variable cost rate can increase or decrease as the organization moves dramatically up or down its volume of business (e.g., changes in labor cost rates or utility cost rates as the business expands or contracts). This reality is described by the key concept "relevant range." Within a particular (i.e., relevant) range of business volume, fixed costs are constant in total and variable costs are constant as a variable cost rate. Outside of the relevant range of volume, total fixed costs and variable cost rates start shifting.

    D. The third complication is the time horizon for the performance report or decision analysis. In very short horizons (e.g., over the next week or perhaps even over the next 24 hours), most costs are fixed. In contrast, over very long horizons (e.g., over the next two to ten years), most costs are variable. Hence, identifying variable costs as the costs that can be expected to increase or decrease with changes to business volume must be based on a clear view of the time horizon involved. So, for example, if the performance report is focused on the next week in the organization's business (a very short time horizon), few costs will actually behave as variable. If the performance report is focused on the next five years of business (a longer horizon), it can be expected that many costs will behave as variable across a wide span of time.

E. Finally, and perhaps most importantly, the distinction on cost behavior as variable or fixed is based on the *cost object*. Traditionally, variable costs are defined as the costs that shift as the volume of *production output* changes. But production output is only one type of cost object in the organization. What if the cost object was the headcount of employees, or the square footage of building space, or the number of customers, or the frequency of internal training events? Each of these occurrences are possible cost objects (along with many others in the organization). Some costs that are variable based on, for example, the number of customers would be unaffected and fixed based on the frequency of internal training events. Hence, when determining variable versus fixed costs, it's critical to be clear about what cost object is being used in the analysis.

II. Cost Pools, Cost Drivers, and Cost Objects

A. In the next several lessons we will explore a number of different models and systems for assigning or allocating costs in organizations. All cost allocations follow the same basic conceptual model shown below.

1. Cost pools are sets of costs that are related together, both functionally and behaviorally. That is, costs that are pooled together for cost assignment should represent a distinct function in the organization. Further, these costs should also move together (i.e., behave similarly in terms of being variable or fixed).

2. Cost objects are the target of the cost assignment system. Typically, cost objects are tied to the organization's income statement and can also represent the revenue objects (i.e., what creates revenue) for the organization.

3. The most key aspect of this basic conceptual model is the identification of cost drivers that establish a relationship between cost pools and cost objects. If the cost is variable with respect to the cost object, the cost driver represents a *consumption relationship*, which is to say the cost driver is how the cost object consumes the resources for which the cost pool is being spent. If the cost is fixed with respect to the cost object, then the cost driver represents an *allocation method* that is used to assign a *burden* of costs to a cost object.

B. More complex organizations will have several levels of cost pools and cost drivers that eventually cascade to the cost object. Hence, costs can move through several cost pools before eventually arriving at the cost object. This complexity is represented below.

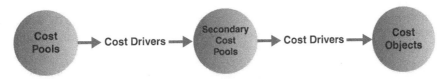

C. Cost drivers are used to establish cost driver rates, and these cost driver rates are used to track or allocate costs to the cost object. This is a two-step process as illustrated below.

$$\text{Step 1:} \quad \frac{\text{Cost Pool Total}}{\text{Cost Driver Volume}} = \frac{\text{Cost}}{\text{Driver Rate}}$$

$$\text{Step 2:} \quad \frac{\text{Cost}}{\text{Driver Rate}} \times \frac{\text{Cost}}{\text{Object Activity}} = \frac{\text{Assigned}}{\text{Cost}}$$

If there is a direct consumption relationship between the cost pool and the cost object, then the cost driver is **tracking** direct costs to the cost object. Conversely, if there isn't a direct consumption relationship (i.e., the cost pool is fixed with respect to activity in the cost object), then the cost driver rate is **allocating** indirect costs to the cost object. It's critical to be very clear about the nature of the relationship when using rates to assign costs in cost systems.

III. Accounting for Cost Flows

A. It is important to understand that costs are *not* the same thing as expenses. Costs represent spending by the organization. These costs may initially represent investments in assets or spending on other resources made available for the organization to use. When the purpose of the spending is used up, only then do the costs become expenses.

B. The cost of goods sold, which is an expense on the income statement, begins as costs spent to establish assets on the balance sheet and other collections of value for the organization to use. Remember that there are three types of product costs that eventually become cost of goods sold: direct materials, direct labor, and manufacturing overhead. These three costs flow into the work-in-process inventory account, which may then flow into the finished goods inventory account, and will eventually flow into the cost of goods sold account on the income statement. Accounting for these costs in the accounting system can be represented as a "flow" in the illustration below.

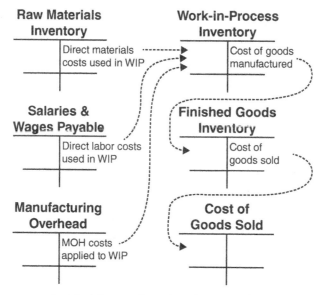

1. As you can see, materials, labor, and overhead costs each are represented by an account on the balance sheet. As these costs are used (i.e., "spent"), they flow out of their respective account and into the work-in-process inventory account. You should think of this account as the "production area" for the organization where organizations create the final cost object(s) that will be sold to customers or clients.

2. When the product is completed, it flows out of the work-in-process inventory account into the finished goods inventory account.

3. When the product is sold, it flows out of the finished goods inventory account (and off of the balance sheet) into the cost of goods sold account on the income statement. At this point, the cost transforms from an asset (an unexpired cost) to an expense (an expired cost).

C. Other lessons in this learning series have described how the three product costs are represented in manufacturing, service, and merchandising organizations. In the case of manufacturing organizations, the costs and cost flows are depicted in the exhibit above. However, the cost and cost flows for service and merchandising organizations are very similar to the exhibit above.

D. In the case of most service organizations, the direct materials cost is described as supplies used in the process of producing the service and is not tracked directly into the work-in-process inventory account. Instead, these costs are combined with the overhead costs that are applied to the production area.

   1. Further, the work-in-process inventory account is typically described as an "open invoice" or "unbilled services" account on the balance sheet. Nevertheless, it represents the production area for the service organization and it functions as an inventory asset.

   2. Finally, once the service product is completed, it doesn't go into some kind of finished goods inventory account. As the service production process goes forward, the completed service product is delivered simultaneously to the client. Hence, costs will flow from the unbilled services account directly to the cost of services account on the income statement.

E. In the case of most merchandising organizations, the direct materials cost is the most substantial product cost. Labor costs that support the acquisition and delivery of product to the customer are not directly tracked to the product but are combined with the overhead costs. And, since the product is not "produced," there is no work-in-process inventory account. Instead, the costs of acquiring products to sell are carried in a merchandise inventory account before flowing to the cost of goods sold account on the income statement. Overall, merchandising and service organizations have similar accounting cost flows as manufacturing organizations.

IV. Actual, Normal, and Standard Cost Accounting Systems

A. Go back to the last exhibit and look at the arrows flowing into the work-in-process inventory account (which would be the unbilled services inventory for a service organization or the merchandise inventory account for a merchandising organization). These costs of direct materials, direct labor, and overhead flowing into the work-in-process inventory account can be either actual costs or budgeted costs. The definition of *actual, normal,* and *standard cost accounting systems* is based on the choice organizations make about using either actual or budgeted costs in these three flows.

B. Actual cost accounting systems are the simplest cost accounting approach, yet these kinds of cost accounting systems are rarely used. As the name implies, actual cost accounting systems are based on using actual cost inputs coming into the work-in-process inventory account. The cost of goods sold that is finally reported on the income statement must be actual costs, so you may wonder why organizations would use anything other than actual cost flows in the accounting system. The problem with actual cost systems is the challenge that actual overhead costs don't "flow" very well.

C. Normal cost accounting systems are quite common in smaller and newer companies that have yet to make a serious investment in using cost systems to plan, control, and evaluate operational processes. These systems use actual costs to account for direct material and direct labor flowing into work-in-process accounts and (unlike actual cost systems) use *budgeted costs to account for overhead* flowing into work-in-process accounts. Normal cost systems address the fact that spending on overhead costs is not a constant (daily) flow throughout the year.

   1. For example, spending on overhead costs such as property taxes and insurance for the facility takes place periodically (quarterly or perhaps annually). There is no consumption relationship between the spending on these costs and the day-to-day production of products and services (in contrast to spending on costs of direct materials and direct labor). Most overhead costs (utilities, supervision, training, security, information technology, etc.) demonstrate a periodic and disconnected spending pattern compared to the flow of production volume. Hence, how can these actual overhead costs be tracked to daily production output in order to support decisions involving product pricing and profit analysis? The answer takes us back to our earlier discussion regarding cost driver rates.

2. Organizations using normal cost accounting systems deal with the disconnect between actual overhead costs and actual production output by building and applying overhead cost rates using the two-step process that we illustrated earlier. Before the year begins, overhead costs are budgeted as a cost pool and then divided by a cost driver in order to establish an *overhead cost rate*. Then throughout the year as products are manufactured or services are produced, the overhead cost rate is used to *apply* overhead costs to products in the work-in-process inventory account or to services in the "unbilled services" account.

3. Organizations using normal cost accounting systems also track spending on actual overhead costs throughout the year. At the end of the year, the spending on actual overhead costs is compared to the overhead costs applied to production. The difference between these two numbers is an underapplied or overapplied amount of overhead costs. That difference must then be reconciled across the accounting system in order to adjust the amount of cost of goods sold on the income statement to represent actual overhead costs.

4. The amount of underapplied or overapplied overhead costs is a cost variance in the accounting system. By effectively building an overhead cost budget into the accounting system, normal cost accounting systems provide organizations with cost performance data that are very helpful in the management process of planning, controlling, and evaluating overhead costs.

D. Standard cost accounting systems use budgeted costs for all three cost flows (direct materials, direct labor, and overhead) going into work-in-process accounts. Organizations with standard cost accounting systems recognize the value of using budget cost flows throughout the accounting system while separately tracking spending on actual costs. The reconciliation of budgeted to actual costs in the process of building income statements *generates valuable cost variance data for all product costs* (cost variances are discussed thoroughly in other lessons in this learning series). Standard cost accounting systems are quite common in large, advanced organizations that have made significant investments in planning, control, and evaluation systems.

Practice Question

Allied Tax Services, LLC is a small accounting firm that provides personal tax return services. Allied uses a normal cost accounting system to track product costs to the income statement, and has the following summary cost information for the month of March:

Unbilled tax services, beginning balance (March 1):	$16,000
Unbilled tax services, ending balance (March 31):	$21,000
Actual direct labor cost of accountants in March:	$46,000
Actual office overhead costs in March:	$51,000
Applied office overhead costs in March:	$63,000

Using the information above, determine the amount of costs transferred to the cost of services account (on the income statement) for March.

Answer

Allied uses a normal cost accounting system, which means applied overhead costs are transferred into the unbilled tax services (i.e., work-in-process) account. Cost of services in March is computed as:

Unbilled tax services, beginning balance (March 1):	$16,000
Actual direct labor cost of accountants in March:	46,000
Applied office overhead costs in March:	63,000
Unbilled tax services, ending balance (March 31):	(21,000)
Cost of services in March:	$104,000

Continues...

The cost flows through Allied's accounting system can be demonstrated below:

	Unbilled Tax Services	
Beginning balance	16,000	
Actual direct labor costs ┈▶	46,000	104,000 ┈▶ Cost of services
Applied overhead costs ┈▶	63,000	
Ending balance	21,000	

Summary

Cost behavior can be described as either variable or fixed, but that description must be established carefully according to the relevant range, time horizon, and cost object involved in the decision context. Cost pools are connected to cost objects based on cost drivers that are used to institute cost driver rates. If the size of the cost pool varies with the activity in the cost object due to a consumption relationship, then the cost driver is *tracking* direct costs to the cost object. Otherwise, the cost driver is *allocating* indirect costs to the cost object. Cost accounting systems flow the three product costs (direct materials, direct labor, and overhead) to cost objects in the work-in-process inventory account. Actual cost accounting systems use actual costs in this flow. Normal cost accounting systems use budgeted overhead costs and actual direct materials and direct labor costs in this flow. Standard cost accounting systems use budgeted costs for overhead, direct materials, and direct labor cost flows.

Variable Costing versus Absorption Costing

After studying this lesson, you should be able to:

- Demonstrate an understanding of variable (direct) costing and absorption (full) costing and the benefits and limitations of these measurement concepts (1.D.1.f).

- Calculate inventory costs, cost of goods sold, and operating profit using both variable costing and absorption costing (1.D.1.g).

- Demonstrate an understanding of how the use of variable costing or absorption costing affects the value of inventory, cost of goods sold, and operating income (1.D.1.h).

- Prepare summary income statements using variable costing and absorption costing (1.D.1.i).

When fixed costs are allocated to production, management incentives can be biased to make decisions about production and inventory that are not aligned with the organization's best interest. In this lesson we explore the difference between absorption costing systems that allocate fixed costs and variable costing systems that do not.

I. Fixed Costs and Inventory Production

    A. Cost behavior can be variable or fixed in the production process. When product costs are reported on the balance sheet, the *full cost* of the inventory should be conveyed. Hence, inventory costs include fixed production costs such as salaries, depreciation, property tax, etc.

    B. While it is appropriate to include fixed production costs in the value of inventory on the balance sheet, these fixed production costs present a particular problem on the income statement. Shifts in production volume or sales volume result in changing inventory levels. As inventory levels adjust, prior period fixed costs are released from the balance sheet and current period fixed costs are retained (absorbed) onto the balance sheet. This release and retention of fixed production costs creates income effects that can lead to confusion in the organization when income is used as a performance measure.

    C. Remember from the last lesson that the production of services often results in significant inventory costs on the balance sheet in the unbilled services (i.e., work-in-process) account. Hence, the "fixed cost absorption" issue happens in both service organizations and manufacturing organizations.

II. Inventory Effects on Income

    A. In the last lesson we learned that costs are assigned with the following two-step process:

$$\textbf{Step 1} : \frac{\text{Cost Pool Total}}{\text{Cost Driver Volume}} = \text{Cost Driver Rate}$$

$$\textbf{Step 2} : \text{Cost Driver Rate} \times \text{Cost Object Activity} = \text{Assigned Cost}$$

When the cost pool is fixed with respect to activity in the cost object, then the cost driver rate is *allocating* indirect costs (rather than *tracking* direct costs) to the cost object. Using this process, fixed production costs are allocated to products and services being produced using a fixed cost rate.

    B. Assuming that production flows in a FIFO (first-in-first-out) pattern, beginning inventory levels represent production from the previous period and have been allocated fixed costs using the fixed cost rate from the previous period. Conversely, ending inventory levels represent production from the current period and have been allocated fixed costs using the current period fixed cost rate.

C. The fixed cost absorption issue on the income statement can be represented as a set of computations involving beginning and ending inventory levels, as well as prior period and current period fixed production cost rates.

Computations When Fixed Cost Rates are Changing					
Released Costs:	(Beginning Inventory)	×	Prior Period Fixed Production Cost Rate	=	**(Decrease to Income)**
					+
Absorbed Costs:	Ending Inventory	×	Current Period Fixed Production Cost Rate	=	**Increase to Income**

1. Because beginning inventory is the first production cost to flow from the balance sheet onto the income statement where it becomes an expense (cost of goods sold or cost of sales), all of the production costs (including the fixed production costs) from the prior period are effectively being "released" from the balance sheet, which has a *decreasing* effect on operating income.

2. On the other hand, ending inventory is "absorbing" current period production costs (including fixed production costs), keeping these costs from becoming expenses on the income statement in the current period. This has the effect of *increasing* operating income.

3. The combined effect of released fixed costs and absorbed fixed costs results in a net increase or a net decrease in operating profits and net income. Be sure to note that whether income goes up or down is a function of the size of beginning versus ending inventory *and* the size of the prior period fixed product cost rate versus the current period rate.

D. Some organizations don't need to adjust their fixed production cost rates every year. When the fixed production cost rate is the same this year as it was last year, a shortcut computation can be used instead of separately computing and adding up the effects of beginning inventory and ending inventory on income. The shortcut is demonstrated below.

Shortcut When Fixed Cost Rates are Constant					
Released Costs:	Inventory Decrease	×	Fixed Production Cost Rate	=	**Net Decreased Income**
or					**or**
Absorbed Costs:	Inventory Increase	×	Fixed Production Cost Rate	=	**Net Increased Income**

Note that *either* the first or the second computation in this shortcut is performed based on whether the inventory level has decreased or increased (respectively) during the year.

III. Absorption Costing Income Statements versus Variable Costing Income Statements

A. The formats of both the absorption costing income statement and the variable costing income statement should be familiar to you (see below).

Absorption Costing Income Statement	Variable Costing Income Statement
Sales Revenue (Cost of Goods Sold)	Sales Revenue (Variable Costs)
Gross Margin (Selling & Admin Expense)	Contribution Margin (Fixed Costs)
Operating Income	Operating Income

1. Absorption costing income statement is the traditional statement required for external financial reporting. This approach tracks the full production cost of inventory to the balance sheet and onto the income statement. As a result, this approach results in a "full cost" valuation of inventory on the balance sheet, which is essential for accurate balance sheet presentation. But absorption costing income statements create a troublesome incentive in the management system.

2. Variable costing income statements are often referred to as contribution margin income statements. The variable costing income statement approach is used to separate fixed costs from variable costs, and does *not* use cost rates to assign fixed production costs to each unit of the organization's production and sales output. Instead, total fixed production costs are fully expensed to the variable costing income statement in the period in which they occur. The only production costs used to value the inventory on the balance sheet are the variable costs of production. As a result, variable costing income statements are *not* allowed for external financial reporting, but they avoid the troublesome incentive that we'll discuss below.

B. Consider the following scenario. Below are listed the sales price and production costs for Quigley Ladders, Inc. To keep the example simple, we'll assume that sales price and production costs are both budgeted and actual. Quigley then experienced the following sales and production volumes in its first two years of business.

Quigley Ladders, Inc. (Original Data)

Sales price per ladder	$200
Variable production cost per ladder	$100
Annual fixed production costs	$360,000

	Units Sold	Units Produced	Beginning Inventory	Ending Inventory	Fixed Rate per Unit
Year 1	9,000	10,000	0	1,000	$36.00
Year 2	9,000	8,000	1,000	0	$45.00

1. Note that the price, production costs, and sales volume were the same for each year. To further simplify this example, we'll assume that Quigley has no selling and administrative expenses.

2. Note also that Quigley produced more ladders than it needed in Year 1 and then scaled back production in Year 2 to reduce inventory to zero. As a result, its fixed cost rate per ladder was different in Year 1 ($360,000 ÷ 10,000 = $36) compared to Year 2 ($360,000 ÷ 8,000 = $45).

C. Quigley's absorption costing income statement is presented below.

Quigley Ladders, Inc. (Absorption Costing)

	Year 1	Year 2	Total
Sales revenue	$1,800,000	$1,800,000	$3,600,000
Variable cost of goods sold	(900,000)	(900,000)	(1,800,000)
Fixed costs of goods sold	(324,000)	(396,000)	(720,000)
Operating income	**$576,000**	**$504,000**	**$1,080,000**

1. Prices and sales volumes are constant each year, resulting in $1,800,000 in annual revenue ($200 × 9,000 units). Variable cost of goods sold is also constant each year at $900,000 ($100 × 9,000 units).

2. Remember, due to a different production volume of ladders in each year, that the fixed production cost per ladder varies ($36 in Year 1 and $45 in Year 2). Fixed costs of goods sold in Year 1 is computed as $36 × 9,000 units = $324,000. However, not all the ladders produced in Year 1 were sold in Year 1. In Year 2 Quigley had 1,000 ladders in beginning inventory from Year 1 and sold those ladders first. Quigley then produced another 8,000 ladders to support sales for the rest of Year 2. Hence, fixed costs of goods sold in Year 2 is computed as ($36 × 1,000 units) + ($45 × 8,000 units) = $396,000.

3. It's important to see that fixed costs of goods sold on the absorption costing income statement are treated as if fixed production costs are variable. As a result, despite the fact that spending on fixed production costs is constant each year at $360,000 and sales volume is constant each year at 9,000 ladders, the fixed cost of goods sold is different each year, resulting in different operating incomes.

4. From a management perspective, it doesn't make sense that Quigley's operating income in Year 1 is more than in Year 2. Sales prices and sales volumes are unchanged each year, and production costs are constant at $100 per ladder (variable) plus $360,000 (total fixed). The only factor affecting the change in Quigley's annual income is the difference in production volume.

D. Alternatively, Quigley's variable costing (contribution margin) income statement is presented below.

Quigley Ladders, Inc. (Variable Costing)

	Year 1	Year 2	Total
Sales revenue	$1,800,000	$1,800,000	$3,600,000
Variable cost of goods sold	(900,000)	(900,000)	(1,800,000)
Contribution margin	$900,000	$900,000	$1,800,000
Fixed costs of production	(360,000)	(360,000)	(720,000)
Operating income	**$540,000**	**$540,000**	**$1,080,000**

1. Sales revenue and variable cost of goods sold are consistent with Quigley's absorption costing income statement. However, a fixed rate isn't used to assign fixed production costs to the ladders produced and sold. Instead, total fixed costs are fully expensed each year to the income statement.

2. Total operating profit for both years is $1,080,000, which is the same total operating profit reported in Quigley's absorption costing income statement. However, as a result of using the variable costing approach, Quigley's operating profit is constant year to year at $540,000, which is appropriate since sales prices and volumes and production costs are the same in each year.

E. We can reconcile the difference in Quigley's annual operating profits using the beginning and ending inventory levels coupled with fixed production cost rates, as demonstrated below.

	Year 1 Income Effect	Year 2 Income Effect
Fixed costs released (beg. inv.)	0 units = $0	1,000 units × $36 = ($36,000)
Fixed costs absorbed (end. inv.)	1,000 units × $36 = $36,000	0 units = $0
Net effect on operating income	$36,000	($36,000)

1. In Year 1, Quigley's absorption costing income is $36,000 *higher* than its variable costing income ($576,000 − $540,000). This is due to the fact that ending inventory in Year 1 absorbed $36,000 in fixed production costs onto the balance sheet, which reduced the fixed costs that were expensed as cost of goods sold on the Year 1 absorption costing income statement.

2. In Year 2, Quigley's absorption costing income is $36,000 *lower* than its variable costing income ($504,000 − $540,000), which is explained by the fact that the fixed production costs absorbed in Year 1 ending inventory are released as Year 2's beginning inventory, which is sold and reported on the Year 2 absorption costing income statement.

F. The situation described above, resulting in a $36,000 difference in income in each of Quigley's two years, may not appear to be a very significant issue. Total income across both years

($1,080,000) is the same in either case. The issue is simply a matter of timing from year to year, and so you may be wondering how the "troubling incentive" mentioned earlier is a factor in managing performance at Quigley Ladders, Inc.

1. It turns out that timing is quite important in performance measurement and incentives. If the income statement used to measure and incentivize performance at Quigley is based on absorption costing, then the reward on operating income performance will be higher in Year 1 compared to the variable costing approach, and the reason will be because management produced more inventory than the company sold. For most competitive organizations, spending money to produce more than can be sold is generally *not* a desirable outcome.

2. Coming into Year 2, it makes sense that management should reduce production in order to reduce inventory. This is generally good management practice. However, reducing inventory (i.e., producing less than is sold) is *not* rewarded on the absorption costing income statement compared to the variable costing income statement. The performance signal coming from the absorption costing income statement doesn't appear to align management with the best interests of the organization.

IV. Troubling Incentives with Absorption Costing Income Statements

A. To demonstrate how troubling the management incentive can be with absorption costing income statements, let's think about the pressure on management to increase operating income in Year 2. If Quigley managers want to increase income, they obviously need to do one (or more) of three things: increase sales price, increase sales volume, or decrease costs. But the absorption costing income statement presents a fourth option to increase income, *and that is to increase production!*

B. Holding everything else constant (sales price, sales volume, and production costs), consider what would happen if Quigley management chose to produce 12,000 ladders in Year 2 instead of 8,000 ladders. First, note below the effect on inventory and the fixed cost rate per ladder in Year 2 (differences from the original example are highlighted in yellow).

Quigley Ladders, Inc. (Changed Data)

Sales price per ladder	$200
Variable production cost per ladder	$100
Annual fixed production costs	$360,000

	Units Sold	Units Produced	Beginning Inventory	Ending Inventory	Fixed Rate per Unit
Year 1	9,000	10,000	0	1,000	$36.00
Year 2	9,000	12,000	1,000	4,000	$30.00

C. Using the change in the fixed cost rate for Year 2, the absorption costing income statement is presented below along with the variable costing income statement (which is unaffected by the fixed cost rate).

Quigley Ladders, Inc. (Absorption Costing)

	Year 1	Year 2	Total
Sales revenue	$1,800,000	$1,800,000	$3,600,000
Variable cost of goods sold	(900,000)	(900,000)	(1,800,000)
Fixed costs of goods sold	(324,000)	(276,000)	(600,000)
Operating income	$ 576,000	$624,000	$1,200,000

Quigley Ladders, Inc. (Variable Costing)

	Year 1	Year 2	Total
Sales revenue	$1,800,000	$1,800,000	$3,600,000
Variable cost of goods sold	(900,000)	(900,000)	(1,800,000)
Contribution margin	$ 900,000	$ 900,000	$1,800,000
Fixed costs of production	(360,000)	(360,000)	(720,000)
Operating income	$ 540,000	$ 540,000	$1,080,000

D. By increasing (rather than decreasing) production and inventory by 2,000 ladders in Year 2, managers are able to avoid a decrease in operating profit on the absorption costing income statement. In fact, the combined income for both years will increase $120,000 on the absorption costing income statement compared to the variable costing income statement ($1,200,000 – $1,080,000). Again, we can reconcile this difference using beginning and ending inventory levels coupled with the fixed production cost rates, as demonstrated below.

	Year 1 Income Effect	Year 2 Income Effect
Fixed costs released (beg. inv.)	0 units = $0	1,000 units × $36 = ($36,000)
Fixed costs absorbed (end. inv.)	1,000 units × $36 = $36,000	4,000 units × $30 = $120,000
Net effect on operating income	$36,000	$84,000

E. As you can see in the highlighted numbers above, the $120,000 difference in combined income represents the Year 2 fixed production cost that has been absorbed to inventory on the balance sheet at the end of Year 2. What happens when Quigley eventually reduces the 4,000 ladders in its inventory? The absorbed costs will be released to the absorption costing income statement and the reported operating income will be dramatically reduced. You can see that Quigley managers are now "stuck" with inventory that they will be reluctant to reduce. This is the troubling incentive with using absorption costing income statements to plan, control, and evaluate operations within organizations.

V. Other Computational Issues

A. There are two remaining computational issues with absorption costing income statements. First, as illustrated earlier, there is a shortcut available to compute the effect of using absorption costing when building income statements. This shortcut works when the fixed production cost rate per unit is constant from year to year. We'll explore this shortcut in the practice problem at the end of this lesson.

B. The other computational issue involves reconciling actual and applied manufacturing overhead in the accounting system for absorption costing income statements. Most, if not all, of the fixed production costs are found in the manufacturing overhead for the organization. Remember from the previous lesson in both normal and standard cost accounting systems that manufacturing overhead (MOH) is *applied* to the work-in-process inventory account. *Actual* fixed MOH costs do not flow through the balance sheet, as demonstrated below.

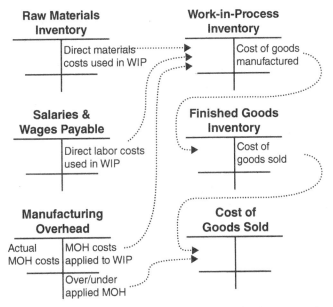

1. Note that if applied MOH costs are more than actual MOH costs, then overhead has been over-applied during the year and cost of goods sold will be too high on the income statement. Conversely, if applied MOH is less than actual MOH, then overhead has been under-applied and costs of goods sold will be too low.

2. To rectify the over-/under-applied overhead and adjust the income statement to report actual costs, the difference in the manufacturing overhead account is closed out to the cost of goods sold account (or is closed out proportionally to the inventory accounts and the cost of goods sold account). The example used in this lesson did not have over-/under-applied overhead. We'll explore this accounting process in the practice problem at the end of the lesson.

VI. Benefits and Limitations of Each System

A. Much of this lesson has focused on the limitations of using absorption costing income statements to plan, control, and evaluate operations in organizations. However, both absorption costing and variable costing have benefits and limitations.

B. As clearly demonstrated in this lesson, the absorption costing system creates a troubling incentive in managers to overproduce and build inventory. On the other hand, by allocating fixed costs to production, managers have a more complete measure of the full costs (i.e., full value) of inventory. Financial reporting standards require a full cost valuation of inventory on the balance sheet, which means absorption costing systems are necessary for external financial reporting.

C. Variable costing systems avoid the troubling incentive to overproduce and build inventory by not accounting for fixed production costs as if they behave like variable costs. On the other hand, by expensing all fixed cost spending to the income statement, inventory is undervalued on the balance sheet. Managers need to be mindful of this undervaluation if inventory costs are used in decisions such as pricing. Further, variable costing systems do not comply with external financial reporting standards. Hence, organizations using variable costing systems for internal management purposes will still need to use an absorption costing system for external financial reports.

Practice Question

Return to the lesson example involving Quigley Ladders, Inc. Below are listed the sales price and production costs for Quigley (price and costs are both budgeted and actual). Variable production costs are all direct materials and direct labor. Fixed production costs are all manufacturing overhead (MOH). Assume that normal production capacity for Quigley is 9,600 ladders per year and that Quigley uses this normal production capacity to establish its fixed overhead rate at $37.50 per ladder (as shown below). Quigley then experienced the following sales and production volumes in its first two years of business.

Quigley Ladders, Inc.

Sales price per ladder	$200
Variable production cost per ladder	$100
Annual fixed production costs	$360,000
Normal production capacity	9,600 units
Fixed production rate per ladder	$37.50

	Units Sold	Units Produced	Beginning Inventory	Ending Inventory
Year 1	9,000	10,000	0	1,000
Year 2	9,000	12,000	1,000	4,000

Quigley adjusts all of its over-/under-applied manufacturing overhead to cost of goods sold.

Compute Quigley's absorption costing income statement and variable costing income statement. Provide a reconciliation between the two statements.

Answer

First, determine the over-/under-applied overhead that needs to be adjusted to cost of goods sold for each year. Note that the actual annual MOH in both Year 1 and Year 2 was $360,000 (all fixed costs). In Year 1 applied MOH was $375,000 (10,000 × $37.50), and in Year 2 applied MOH was $450,000 (12,000 × $37.50). Hence, Year 1 MOH was over-applied by $15,000 (375,000 – $360,000) and Year 2 MOH was over-applied by $90,000 ($450,000 – $360,000). As a result, cost of goods sold in Year 1 and Year 2 will be adjusted at the end of the year by $15,000 and $90,000, respectively. These cost flows can be illustrated in the accounting system as shown below.

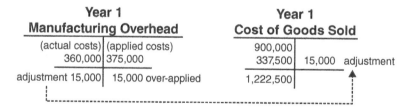

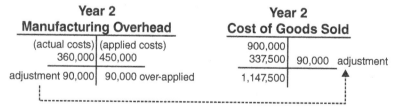

Quigley's absorption costing and variable costing income statements for Year 1 and Year 2 are provided below.

Continues...

Quigley Ladders, Inc. (Absorption Costing)

	Year 1	Year 2	Total
Sales revenue	$1,800,000	$1,800,000	$3,600,000
Variable cost of goods sold	(900,000)	(900,000)	(1,800,000)
Fixed costs of goods sold	(337,500)	(337,500)	(675,000)
Adjustment to COGS	15,000	90,000	105,000
Operating income	**$577,500**	**$652,500**	**$1,230,000**

Quigley Ladders, Inc. (Variable Costing)

	Year 1	Year 2	Total
Sales revenue	$1,800,000	$1,800,000	$3,600,000
Variable cost of goods sold	(900,000)	(900,000)	(1,800,000)
Contribution margin	$900,000	$900,000	$1,800,000
Fixed costs of production	(360,000)	(360,000)	(720,000)
Operating income	**$540,000**	**$540,000**	**$1,080,000**

Because Quigley uses the same fixed production rate per ladder to apply MOH each year, the reconciliation between the two types of income statements can be performed with the net change in inventory multiplied by the fixed cost rate. Note that inventory is increasing in each of the two years. Hence, absorption costing income will be higher in each year compared to variable costing income.

	Year 1 Income Effect	Year 2 Income Effect
Inventory increase (absorbed costs)	1,000 unit × $37.50 = $37,500	3,000 unit × $37.50 = $112,500

Quigley's combined operating income for both years is $150,000 higher using absorption costing compared to variable costing ($1,230,000 – $1,080,000). This total difference is explained by the fact that the 4,000 ladders in inventory at the end of the two years has absorbed $150,000 in fixed production costs (4,000 × $37.50).

Summary
Cost drivers are used to assign costs. It is important to understand the implications of using cost drivers to track variable costs compared to using cost drivers to allocate fixed costs. Absorption costing systems allocate fixed production costs to units produced, which leads to fixed costs being included in inventory on the balance sheet. Variable costing systems do not allocate fixed costs to production but expense all fixed costs to the income statement. Absorption costing systems create a troubling incentive for managers to build unnecessary inventory on the balance sheet in order to absorb fixed costs and keep these costs from flowing immediately to the income statement. Nevertheless, absorption costing income statements are required by external financial reporting. Hence, organizations need to understand and reconcile the differences in income reported by these two systems. The reconciliation is based on beginning and ending inventory levels combined with prior period and current period fixed cost rates.

Joint Product Costing

After studying this lesson, you should be able to:

- Determine the appropriate use of joint product and by-product costing (1.D.1.j).

- Demonstrate an understanding of concepts such as split-off point and separable costs (1.D.1.k).

- Determine the allocation of joint product and by-product costs using the physical measure method, the sales value at split-off method, constant gross profit (gross margin) method, and the net realizable value method; describe the benefits and limitations of each method (1.D.1.l).

Many organizations establish joint production processes and shared facilities to process multiple products and services for sale. While working through the joint process, products are indistinguishable. Nevertheless, external financial reporting guidelines require that these common (fixed) costs be allocated to participating products. This lesson explores four optional allocation methods available for this purpose.

I. Joint Production Processes

   A. Joint products and services share a common value-added joint process in the organization. The way these products and services participate in the joint process makes them indistinguishable from each other in terms of how they each consume the joint process costs.

   B. The following are examples of joint production processes:

      1. An oil refinery processes crude oil to the point where distinguishable products begin to emerge, such as gasoline, motor oil, and kerosene. Each of these products then requires additional specific processing to be complete.

      2. A dairy production plant processes raw milk to the point where the product separates into pasteurized milk, butter, and cheese. Further processing takes place to finish each type of diary product.

      3. The training facility for a large consulting firm provides four weeks of initial onboarding for all new consultants before moving on to being trained in the specific technical work they will perform for the firm's clients.

   C. It's important to distinguish between joint products and by-products. Joint products are the main purpose for the value-added joint process in the organization. Organizations invest in the joint process to create the main joint products that are the focus of the organization's profit plan. Therefore, the accounting system is designed to allocate the joint process costs to the main joint projects.

   D. In addition to the main joint products, many joint production processes result in "by-products." These by-products will have some commercial value, but the value is not significant to the organization. Since the purpose of the joint process is not to create by-products, the accounting system doesn't allocate joint process costs to by-products.

   E. The following are examples of by-products:

      1. In the joint process of producing gasoline, motor oil, and kerosene, oil refinery processes can also result in an asphalt by-product that can be used as tar or blacktop for paving roads.

      2. Whey is the liquid remaining after milk has been curdled and strained and is a by-product of the manufacture of cheese. It has several possible commercial uses such as a protein supplement for athletic training or as an animal feed enhancement.

      3. Available space and staff time in a training facility for a large consulting firm may be scheduled for lease to outside organizations. Since the core commercial purpose of the

facility is onboarding new consultants, any extra value created from using "slack" in the training system is a by-product of the facility.

F. Joint costs are part of the absorption costing system studied in the last lesson, which means that these costs are allocated in order to comply with external financial reporting rules. There is no "optimal" method for allocating joint costs. Joint costs are fixed with respect to the individual activity in each joint product. In fact, the process of allocating these joint costs may suggest to management that these costs are affected by individual project lines—they are not! Therefore, managers need to be careful when using joint cost allocations in the process of planning, controlling, and evaluating operations.

II. Setting Up the Joint Cost Allocation Example

A. For the remainder of this lesson we'll use Muddyboys Cement Company to explore a joint process to manufacture cement construction products from a single raw material. There are two main construction products (Product A and Product B), and a by-product (Product Z) that come out of the joint process. The weekly production flow and price/cost data are presented below.

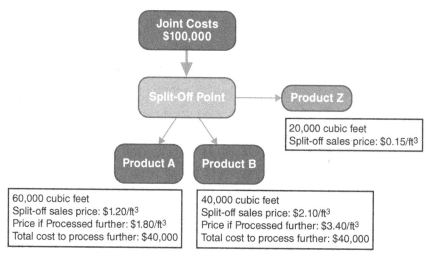

1. The Muddyboys joint process requires $100,000 in weekly costs. After moving common materials through the joint process, an output of production volume can be identified for each product.

2. The split-off point is the point when the joint process is complete and the products are identifiable. Each of the three products can be sold at the split-off point. The split-off price is provided.

3. The main products A and B can be processed further and sold at a higher price per cubic foot. The price if further processed, as well as the total cost to process further, is provided for each of the main products. The by-product Z cannot be processed past the split-off point for more value.

B. Before we work through four traditional methods used to allocate joint costs, remember the standard two-step model for assigning costs that was introduced in our first lesson.

$$\text{Step 1}: \frac{\text{Cost Pool Total}}{\text{Cost Driver Volume}} = \text{Cost Driver Rate}$$

$$\text{Step 2}: \text{Cost Driver Rate} \times \text{Cost Object Activity} = \text{Assigned Cost}$$

1. Three of the four joint cost allocation methods follow this model quite closely.

2. The final method (constant gross margin method) also uses this basic approach but sets a profit margin target and then works backwards through the model to determine the joint cost allocation.

3. Remember that the by-product does not receive any joint cost allocation.

III. Cost Allocation Using the Physical Units Method

A. The physical units method for allocating joint costs is straightforward and is based on a simple logic that as more of a product is produced, it should bear more of the joint process costs.

B. Muddyboys' joint process generates a total of 100,000 cubic feet of main product composed of 60,000 cubic feet (ft^3) for Product A and 40,000 cubic feet (ft^3) for Product B. The physical units allocation works as follows:

1. Cost driver rate = Cost pool ÷ Total driver volume = $100,000 ÷ 100,000 ft^3 = $1.00/$ft^3$

2. Product A allocation = $1.00/$ft^3$ × 60,000 ft^3 = $60,000;

Product B allocation = $1.00/$ft^3$ × 40,000 ft^3 = $40,000

C. Note that the cost driver in this method is the physical units *produced* (not the physical units *sold*).

IV. Cost Allocation Using the Sales Value at Split-Off Method

A. The sales value at split-off method is based on the logic that the joint process adds value to the main products, so the value established at the point the products are identifiable and ready for sale should be the basis for the allocation.

B. The joint process for Muddyboys generates $72,000 in split-off value for Product A ($1.20 × 60,000 ft^3) and $84,000 in split-off value for Product B ($2.10 × 40,000 ft^3) for a total of $156,000. The sales value at split-off allocation works as follows:

1. Cost driver rate = Cost pool ÷ Total driver volume = $100,000 ÷ $156,000 = $0.641/$1.00

2. Product A allocation = $0.641/$1.00 × $72,000 = $46,154;

Product B allocation = $0.641/$1.00 × $84,000 = $53,846

(In order for allocation results to sum up exactly to the $100,000 joint costs, do not round off the cost driver rate.)

C. Note that the cost driver in this method uses the amount of product produced and saleable at the split-off point, *not* the amount of product actually sold at the split-off point. Of course, this allocation method is available only if products are saleable at the split-off point.

V. Cost Allocation Using the Net Realizable Value (NRV) Method

A. Net realizable value (NRV) is defined in this third allocation method as the final sales value of the product less any additional processing and distribution costs necessary to get the product to the final sales position. The logic of the NRV method is that joint costs should be allocated based on the product's ability to pay the costs, defined as the product's NRV.

B. One important note is that NRV is not always based on the sales value available assuming the product is further processed to the final extent possible. In this method we assume that the organization makes an optimal decision for each product in order to maximize its total value. In short, the NRV method is based on allocating joint costs using the highest value that each product can provide the organization.

1. Remember that Product A's sales value at split-off is $72,000 ($1.20 × 60,000 ft^3). However, its NRV if processed to the end of its potential is $68,000 ($1.80 × 60,000 ft^3 – $40,000 additional costs). Hence, Muddyboys will *not* further process Product A, and the NRV method will use the $72,000 split-off value.

2. On the other hand, the optimal decision for Muddyboys is to further process Product B for the higher $3.40 price. This decision is based on comparing the split-off value of $84,000 ($2.10 × 40,000 ft^3) with the NRV value of $96,000 ($3.40 × 40,000 ft^3 − $40,000). Hence, the NRV method will use the $96,000 net realizable value.

C. Overall, by making optimal decisions Muddyboys generates a total value of $168,000 ($72,000 + $96,000) to pay the joint cost and generate overall profit. The NRV allocation works as follows:

1. Cost driver rate = Cost pool ÷ Total driver volume = $100,000 ÷ $168,000 = $0.595/$1.00

2. Product A allocation = $0.595/$1.00 × $72,000 = $42,857;

3. Product B allocation = $0.595/$1.00 × $96,000 = $57,143

(Again, in order for allocation results to sum up exactly to the $100,000 joint costs, do not round off the cost driver rate.)

VI. Cost Allocation Using the Constant Gross Profit (Gross Margin) Method

A. One of the problems in choosing an allocation method to use with joint costs (or any other fixed costs) is that any method used results in a zero-sum game within the organization. That is, each of the product line managers at Muddyboys is concerned about the amount of joint cost being assigned by the accounting system, and that concern is complicated by the fact that any reduction in allocated cost to one product line is exactly offset by an increase in allocation to another product line.

B. To demonstrate the zero-sum game problem with choosing a joint cost allocation method, consider below the results with the three methods we've explored so far.

Muddyboys Cement Company – Comparing Methods

	Physical Units Method	Sales Value at Split-Off Method	Net Realizable Value Method
Allocation to Product A	$60,000	$46,154	$42,857
Allocation to Product B	$40,000	$53.846	$57,143
Total joint cost allocated	$100,000	$100,000	$100,000

1. Each method is based on a certain business logic, and all three methods are acceptable for external financial reports reporting. However, if the product managers are evaluated on profit performance using an allocation of joint costs, they will certainly be concerned about which allocation method is used.

2. The Product A manager will strongly favor the NRV method since it results in the lowest allocation for his product division, but the Product B manager will argue for the physical units method because it generates the lowest cost allocation for her division.

3. In this particular situation, the sales value at split-off method happens to be in-between the extremes of the other two methods. The managers may be able to compromise to accept this method, but it doesn't really address their concerns about how the joint cost affects their profit performance.

C. The constant gross profit method is an effort to neutralize the effects of the joint cost allocation decision on managers' profit-based performance measures. In fact, if managers are evaluated on the gross profit (i.e., gross margin) as a percentage of sales, then this method is neutral in its effect on the performance evaluation.

D. The allocation approach in the constant gross profit allocation method is to start with the overall gross profit percentage for the organization, and then mathematically work backwards to ensure that the cost allocation in each product line results in the same gross profit percentage. The allocation for Muddyboys works as follows:

1. Like the NRV method, first determine the most optimal profit solution for the main products. For Muddyboys the most optimal profit solution is to sell Product A at the split-off point and process further Product B to sell at the higher sales price.

2. Assuming all products produced are sold, determine the overall gross profit percentage for Muddyboys, which is 32.69% as computed below.

Muddyboys Cement Company

	Total
Sales revenue	$208,000
Dirct processing cost (Product B)	(40,000)
Indirect joint cost allocated	(100,000)
Gross profit	$68,000
Gross profit percentage (divide by Sales)	32.69%

3. Use the overall gross profit percentage for Muddyboys to compute the cost allowed for each product line in order to generate the same gross profit percentage as shown below.

Product A: $72,000 revenue × (1 – 32.69%) = $48,462 allowed costs

Product B: $136,000 revenue × (1 – 32.69%) = $91,538 allowed costs

(Once again, in order for allocation results to sum up exactly to the $100,000 joint costs, do not round off the gross profit percentage rate.)

4. Finally, for relevant product lines, remove any direct processing costs that are used to optimize company profit. The remaining costs represent the joint cost allocation as shown below.

Product A: $48,462 allowed costs – $0 processing costs = $48,462 allocated costs

Product B: $91,538 allowed costs – $40,000 processing costs = $51,538 allocated costs

E. The constant gross profit allocation results in the following potential profit report for Muddyboys and should help avoid conflict generated by the zero-sum game effects of the other three joint cost allocation approaches. (Remember that this approach assumes all products produced are sold.)

Muddyboys Cement Company — Profit Report
(based on constant gross margin allocation)

	Product A	Product B	Total
Sales revenue	$72,000	$136,000	$208,000
Direct processing cost		(40,000)	(40,000)
Indirect joint cost allocated	(48,462)	(51,538)	(100,000)
Gross profit	$23,538	$44,462	$68,000
Gross profit percentage	32.69%	32.69%	32.69%

VII. Accounting for By-Products

A. We have yet to handle the Product Z by-product for Muddyboys. Remember that it is not the purpose of the joint process to produce by-products. For that reason, we don't allocate joint process costs to by-products.

B. Product Z is generating a small revenue of $3,000 (= $0.15 × 20,000 ft^3). How should this revenue be reported? Regardless of which joint cost allocation method is used for the main products, Muddyboys has two choices to handle the reporting of its by-product. We'll use the physical units method to demonstrate these two choices.

1. The first reporting choice is to establish a separate product line in the organization's profit report. This is shown below.

Muddyboys Cement Company — Profit Report

(based on physical units allocation)

	Product A	Product B	Product Z	Total
Sales revenue	$72,000	$136,000	$3,000	$211,000
Direct processing cost		(40,000)		(40,000)
Indirect joint cost allocated	(60,000)	(40,000)		(100,000)
Gross profit	$12,000	$56,000	$3,000	$71,000

Notice how the relatively lower performance of Product Z stands out in this overall report. It looks a bit strange.

2. The second reporting choice is to offset the joint process cost with the by-product revenue before computing the joint cost allocation. The result of this approach is shown below.

Muddyboys Cement Company — Profit Report

(based on physical units allocation)

	Product A	Product B	Total
Sales revenue	$72,000	$136,000	$208,000
Direct processing cost		(40,000)	(40,000)
Indirect joint cost allocated	(58,200)	(38,800)	(97,000)
Gross profit	**$13,800**	**$57,200**	**$71,000**

Note that the original $100,000 joint cost has been reduced by $3,000 to $97,000. This lower cost is then allocated to Products A and B based on their physical units (60,000 ft^3 and 40,000 ft^3, respectively). This reporting choice is generally used by most organizations.

Practice Question

Altamont Company manufactures pet food from a joint production process and has four main products: Yelp, Wiggs, Mew, and Ranz. Joint costs for one batch are as follows:

At the split-off point, one joint process batch yields 1,200 bags of Yelp, 1,800 bags of Wiggs, 3,000 bags of Mew, and 3,600 bags of Ranz. If all products are sold at the split-off point, prices are $60 per bag for Yelp, $75 per bag for Wiggs, $20 per bag for Mew, and $30 per bag for Ranz.

Direct materials	$84,450
Direct labor	42,000
Overhead	23,550
Total joint costs	$150,000

Altamont has the option of further processing all products into premium brands with the following added costs and premium prices:

Continues…

	Added Cost	Premium Price
Yelp	$30,000	$90 per bag
Wiggs	$25,000	$95 per bag
Mew	$20,000	$25 per bag
Ranz	$44,000	$40 per bag

Allocate the joint cost using the following methods:

Physical units

Sales value at split-off

Net realizable value (NRV)

Constant gross profit

Answer

Physical units method

Total bags of product = 1,200 + 1,800 + 3,000 + 3,600 = 9,600 bags

Cost driver rate = $150,000 ÷ 9,600 bags = $15.625 per bag

Yelp allocation = $15.625 × 1,200 bags = $18,750

Wiggs allocation = $15.625 × 1,800 bags = $28,125

Mew allocation = $15.625 × 3,000 bags = $46,875

Ranz allocation = $15.625 × 3,600 bags = $56,250

Sales value at split-off method

Total split-off dollars = ($60 × 1,200) + ($75 × 1,800) + ($20 × 3,000) + ($30 × 3,600) = 375,000

Cost driver rate = $150,000 ÷ $375,000 = $0.40 per split-off dollar

Yelp allocation = $0.40 × $72,000 = $28,800

Wiggs allocation = $0.40 × $135,000 = $54,000

Mew allocation = $0.40 × $60,000 = $24,000

Ranz allocation = $0.40 × $108,000 = $43,200

NRV method

First, determine the optimal production and sales solution for Altamont by comparing additional revenue to additional cost.

Yelp: ($90 – $60) × 1,200 bags = $36,000 is greater than $30,000 → Process further!

Wiggs: ($95 – $75) × 1,800 bags = $36,000 is greater than $25,000 → Process further!

Mew: ($25 – $20) × 3,000 bags $15,000 is NOT greater than $20,000 → Do not process further!

Ranz: ($40 – $30) × 3,600 bags = $36,000 is NOT greater than $44,000 → Do not process further!

Total NRV = ($90 × 1,200 – $30,000) + ($95 × 1,800 – $25,000) + ($20 × 3,000) + ($30 × 3,600) = 392,000

Cost driver rate = $150,000 ÷ $392,000 = $0.3827 per NRV (don't round off this number)

Yelp allocation = $0.3827 × $78,000 = $29,847

Wiggs allocation = $0.3827 × $146,000 = $55,867

Continues...

Mew allocation = $0.3827 × $60,000 = $22,959

Ranz allocation = $0.3827 × $108,000 = $41,327

Constant gross profit method

Based on the optimal production and sales solution determined above, Altmamont's overall gross profit percentage is 54.14% as determined below.

Altamont Company

	Total
Sales revenue	$447,000
Direct cost (Yelp + Wiggs)	(55,000)
Indirect joint cost	(150,000)
Gross profit	$242,000
Gross profit percentage	54.14%

Using this gross profit percentage (don't round it off), the allowed costs for each product are as follows:

Yelp = $108,000 × (1 − 54.14%) = $49,530 allowed cost

Wiggs = $171,000 × (1 − 54.14%) = $78,423 allowed cost

Mew = $60,000 × (1 − 54.14%) = $27,517 allowed cost

Ranz = $108,000 × (1 − 54.14%) = $49,530 allowed cost

After removing relevant direct processing costs, the remaining costs represent the allocated joint costs.

Yelp allocation = $49,530 − $30,000 = $19,530

Wiggs allocation = $78,423 − $25,000 = $53,423

Mew allocation = $27,517 − $0 = $27,517

Ranz allocation = $49,530 − $0 = $49,530

The report below summarizes the results of all four allocation methods for Altamont Company.

Altamont Company – Comparing Methods

	Physical Units Method	Sales Value at Split-off Method	Net Realizable Value Method	Constant Gross Profit Method
Allocation to Yelp	$18,750	$28,800	$29,847	$19,530
Allocation to Wiggs	$28,125	$54,000	$55,867	$53,423
Allocation to Mew	$46,875	$24,000	$22,959	$27,517
Allocation to Ranz	$56,250	$43,200	$41,327	$49,530
Total cost Allocation	**$150,000**	**$150,000**	**$150,000**	**$150,000**

Summary

Allocating joint process costs is necessary for external financial reporting. There are four methods available. The physical units method is based on the quantity of production output for each of the main products. The sales value at split-off method is based on using the total sales revenue available at the point the products split from the joint process and are identifiable. The net realizable value (NRV) method uses the optimal net value (final revenue − additional processing costs) created by each product. The constant gross profit method helps settle disputes between product lines by mathematically solving the allocation such that all product lines can report the same gross profit percentage. Finally, by-products do not receive an allocation of joint process costs.

Topic 2. Costing Systems

Job Order Costing

After studying this lesson, you should be able to:

- Define the nature of different cost systems, understand the cost flows of each system, and identify its appropriate use (1.D.2.a).
- Calculate inventory values and cost of goods sold in a job order costing system (1.D.2.b).
- Discuss the strategic value of cost information regarding products and services, pricing, overhead allocations, and other issues (1.D.2.d).

> There are a number of cost models used to track costs through the organization's cost accounting system. Two of the most common cost models are job order costing and process costing. In this lesson we'll study the job order costing model and review the accounting for overhead in the cost accounting system.

I. Job Order Costing versus Process Costing

    A. Do you recognize this kind of invoice? It's the invoice a car mechanic shop might "assemble" as your car undergoes a major repair.

Certified Mechanics Shop

Date: May 17 **Owner:** Joe Smith **Phone:** 321-456-0987

Make: Ford **Model:** Trundy **Year:** 2008 **Miles:** 176,541

Symptoms: Engine sputtering, low gas mileage

Diagnosis: Cracked exhaust manifold, worn gaskets

Parts		List Price
Exhaust manifold		$785.34
EGR valve		$435.79
Gasket kit		$138.50
Total Parts		$1,359.63

Labor Hours	Shop Rate	Total
7.50	$95.00	$712.50

Shop supplies		$38.00

Total cost		$2,110.13
Sales tax @ 5.5%		$116.06
Total Invoice		$2,226.19

    Can you identify the direct materials costs in this invoice? How about the direct labor costs? Do you see overhead being applied? Actually, you've got to look a little more closely to find the applied overhead. The $95 per hour "shop rate" certainly isn't just the cost that the shop pays for direct labor (i.e., the mechanics). That rate also includes a significant application of overhead that represents the costs of facility maintenance, equipment, tools, supervision, insurance, property taxes, etc. And of course, a profit margin has been factored into all the costs on this invoice.

    B. This example represents a job order cost accounting model. Anytime a product or service is built for a specific customer or client, the costs on that job are assembled together as the work is done and the costs move through the organization's accounting system as a "group." The contrast to job order costing is process costing. The nature of the organization's work determines which costing system to use.

1. If the customer or client receiving the product can be identified before the process begins (whether it be a manufacturing process or a service process) and the job and its costs are tracked together throughout the process, then a job order costing model is used.

2. Conversely, if the organization is building similar products without separately identifying each product during the process and can only identify the buyer during the selling process, then a process costing model is used to track costs through the balance sheet and onto the income statement.

C. For example, let's assume a clothing company produces men's and women's professional suits. If these suits are custom ordered and fitted to clients before assembly, then the company will use a job order costing model. Alternatively, if similar suits are produced in various sizes and subsequently sold "off the rack" as customers come to a digital or physical storefront, then the company will use a process costing model. Notice that the product is the same in either system—professional suits—and notice that the nature of costs is the same as well—materials, labor, and overhead. The difference is the existence of an identified customer that provides the means to track production costs to a specific job as the costs flow through the accounting system.

II. Accounting Cost Flows in Organizations

A. In previous lessons we've discussed accounting flows in the three basic types of organizations: manufacturing, service, and merchandising. The exhibit below summarizes the overall differences in these flows.

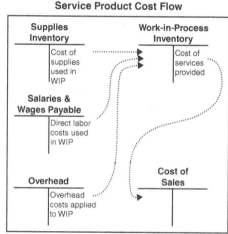
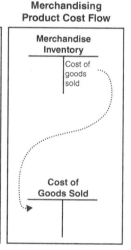

B. It is important that you see that there is very little difference between manufacturing product cost flows through the accounting system compared to service "product" cost flows. Other than some modifications in naming conventions, the only significant difference is that most manufacturing organizations have a finished goods inventory account, and service organizations generally do not have this account.

C. Alternatively, the product cost flow through a merchants account system is quite different from the other two types of organizations. Conceptually, merchant product costs are handled with a fairly simple accounting structure. We won't spend time here discussing merchandising product cost flows.

D. The other important observation for this and the next lesson is that both job order costs and process costs flow in and out of work-in-process accounts in a very similar manner. The only difference is that job costs of materials, labor, and overhead flowing in and out of the work-in-process account are organized into a job cost invoice. On the other hand, process costs of materials, labor, and overhead flowing in and out of the work-in-process account are organized into periods of time (e.g., daily, weekly, or monthly production reports).

III. Disposing of Over-/Under-Applied Manufacturing Overhead

    A. As we've discussed in a previous lesson, it's important to understand how overhead accounting works in manufacturing and service organizations. Effectively, it can be described as a three-step process.

        1. Typically, the reporting period for most organizations is a year. Before the start of the year, an overhead application rate is established by determining the overhead cost budget (i.e., cost pool) and an overhead application basis (i.e., cost driver). Dividing the cost budget by the application basis results in an overhead application rate that will be used throughout the year. This first step is illustrated below for manufacturing overhead (MOH).

$$\frac{\text{Budgeted MOH Costs}}{\text{Budgeted Application Basis}} = \text{MOH Application Rate}$$

        2. During the year, the overhead application rate is used to apply costs to actual job or service invoices as the work takes place. This process represents the flow of applied overhead costs out of the overhead account and into the work-in-process account. Also during the year, actual overhead costs are recorded and tracked in the same overhead account. This flow of *actual* costs into the overhead account and *applied* costs out of the overhead account is illustrated below.

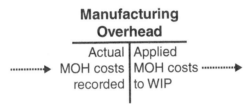

        3. At the conclusion of the year, the overhead account is reconciled to determine if overhead costs have been over-applied or under-applied during the year. The imbalance in the overhead account (i.e., the over-/under-applied overhead) is used to adjust the cost of goods sold account. If the imbalance is large, it is used to proportionally adjust the inventory accounts and the cost of goods sold account.

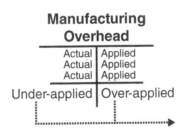

    B. Be sure to work through the practice questions in this lesson to be comfortable with the flow of job order costs through the accounting system.

IV. The Strategic Value of Cost Information

    A. Accurately tracking costs within the organization is challenging. That challenge becomes more difficult and more crucial to manage successfully as organizations become larger and more complex, and as competition becomes faster and more aggressive.

    B. Tracking costs is often about much more than knowing how to properly set prices. In fact, most organizations in most markets don't actually have the opportunity to set prices. Typically, the nature of competition puts most organizations in a "price taker" rather than a "price maker" position in the economy. Nevertheless, to compete effectively, the organization's ability to accurately track costs is critical in two ways:

        1. Without a clear and confident view of costs, organizations will struggle to *efficiently* manage costs and incentivize employees in order to reduce costs and improve quality.

2. Organizations that have a clear and confident view of costs can then use that information to *effectively* manage their market positions by emphasizing and deemphasizing (or even exiting) certain products or customers available in the organizations' portfolio in order to establish the most strategically successful market position.

Practice Question

The following information is available for a particular consulting contract performance by Newton Business Consultants:

Newton applies overhead on the basis of client consulting hours. The estimated total overhead for the year was $8.25 million and the estimated total consulting hours was 150,000. Newton pays its consultants $40 per hour.

Consulting labor costs	$6,500.00
Supplies	850.50
Overhead	?
Total Cost	?

Compute the predetermined overhead application rate. What is the allocated cost and total cost of this particular contract?

Answer

The overhead application rate is $8,250,000 ÷ 150,000 hours = $55.00 per hour. Based on the $40 pay rate, Newton used 162.5 hours ($6,500.00 ÷ $40) on this client job. The total cost of the job is presented below.

Consulting labor costs	$6,500.00
Supplies	850.50
Overhead $55 × 162.5	8,937.50
Total cost	$16,288.00

Practice Question

Allister Furniture Company manufactures custom furniture and uses job order costing to track cost. Allister uses a normal cost accounting system. The following information is available in Allister's cost accounting system.

Beginning raw materials inventory	$ 30,000
Raw materials used in production	95,000
Ending raw materials inventory	55,000
Actual manufacturing overhead (MOH)	250,000
Beginning work-in-process inventory	130,000
Ending work-in-process inventory	145,000
Direct labor costs	100,000
Beginning finished goods inventory	65,000
Ending finished goods inventory	80,000
Underapplied MOH	25,000

The accounts below have been set up with accounting balances provided above. Use these accounts to flow job order costs through the accounting system, and then compute the following:

Continues...

Raw materials purchased

Cost of goods manufactured (COGM) that flow into the finished goods inventory account

Cost of goods sold (COGS) after adjusting for under-applied manufacturing overhead

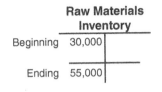

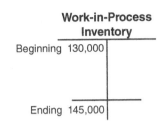

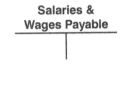

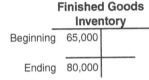

Answer

The job order costs flow through the accounting system as shown below.

Raw Materials Inventory

Beginning	30,000	95,000	Transferred to WIP
Purchased	120,000		
Ending	55,000		

Work-in-Process Inventory

Beginning	130,000	405,000	COGM
Direct materials	95,000		
Direct labor	100,000		
Applied MOH	225,000		
Ending	145,000		

Salaries & Wages Payable

	100,000	Transferred to WIP

Finished Goals Inventory

Beginning	65,000	390,000	COGS
Cost of goods manf.	405,000		
Ending	80,000		

Manufacturing Overhead

Actual	250,000	225,000	Transferred to WIP
Under-applied	25,000	25,000	Transferred to COGS

Cost of Goods Sold

COGS 390,000	
Adjustment 25,000	
Adjusted COGS 415,000	

Raw materials purchased = $95,000 + $55,000 – $30,000 = $120,000

COGM = $130,000 + $95,000 + $100,000 + $225,000* – $145,000 = $405,000

Adjusted COGS = $65,000 + $405,000 – $80,000 + $25,000 = $415,000

(*Note: Applied MOH = Actual MOH $250,000 – Under-applied MOH $25,000)

Summary

Costs can flow through the accounting system using either a job order cost model or a process cost model. Job order costing is used by organizations that can identify (and even customize) the product or cost in advance for a specific customer or client. The three product costs (direct materials, direct labor, and overhead) are then tracked to a job cost invoice that is used to flow the costs through the accounting system until they are expensed to the income statement as cost of goods sold. In both job order and process costing, be sure to follow a three-step approach for applying overhead. The process is (1) build the predetermined application rate, (2) apply overhead with the predetermined rate while tracking actual overhead costs, and (3) reconcile the overhead account and use the over-/under-applied overhead to adjust the cost of goods sold account.

Process Costing

After studying this lesson, you should be able to:

- Demonstrate an understanding of the concept of equivalent units in process costing and calculate the value of equivalent units (1.D.2.f).

- Calculate inventory values and cost of goods sold in a process costing system (1.D.2.b).

- Demonstrate an understanding of the proper accounting for normal and abnormal spoilage (1.D.2.c).

In this lesson we'll study the process costing model. A key aspect of process costing is the computation of equivalent units of production, which are necessary to track costs between periods of production time as they move through work-in-process inventory accounts.

I. Process Costing and Equivalent Units

    A. In our last lesson we learned that job order and process costing are different approaches to tracking costs through the accounting system. Both approaches track material, labor, and overhead costs in and out of the work-in-process account. Job order costing is able to use a customer focus as the means to track production costs to a specific job as the costs flow through the accounting system.

    B. On the other hand, process costing is used by organizations that can't identify the customer before building the product or service. Instead, these organizations build inventory now that is sold later when customers purchase completed products. Determining the cost of producing a product or service basically involves summing up the costs going into the production process and dividing by the number of units that complete the process. Since organizations using process costing can't track production costs and production output to a particular job or customer, the costs and outputs are tracked to a period of time (a day, a week, a month, etc.).

    C. The challenge with using a period of time to track costs is the problem of partially complete units of work. Organizations with process costing systems need to solve this problem before production costs can be divided by output in order to create cost-per-unit measures needed in accounting and management processes. The challenge of partially complete units of work is handled by using "equivalent units" of production.

    D. It's best to illustrate the concept and computation of equivalent units of production with an example. We'll use Morning Mills, a company that produces specialized flour in a continuous manufacturing process. The flour is mixed in one step and then transferred to the finished goods warehouse. The company tracks production costs as a set of monthly reports.

        1. At the beginning of July, Morning Mills had 1,600 bags of flour in process and estimated that the flour was 20% complete in terms of direct materials and 60% complete in terms of labor. Since Morning Mills allocates manufacturing overhead on the basis of labor, then this beginning inventory was also 60% complete in terms of overhead.

        2. During July, Morning Mills started another 20,000 bags of flour into production.

        3. By the end of the month, 2,000 bags remained in process. These bags were estimated to be 100% complete in terms of direct materials and 70% complete in terms of labor and overhead. (*Note:* When overhead is allocated on the basis of labor, these costs then move together and are referred to as "conversion costs.")

    E. In terms of bags of flour, can we determine how much production activity took place in July for Morning Mills? We can, using the concept of equivalent units.

        1. Starting with beginning inventory in the work-in-process account, how much production on those 1,600 bags took place in July? With respect to direct materials, the bags are 20% complete based on work done in June. That means the last 80% of the direct materials

"work" will happen in July before the finished bags are transferred to the finished goods warehouse. Completing the direct materials investment in July's beginning inventory is the equivalent of producing 1,280 bags from scratch (1,600 bags × 80%). Similarly, completing these bags that are 60% done in terms of conversion costs is the equivalent of starting and completing the labor and overhead work on 640 bags (1,600 bags × 40%).

2. Of the 20,000 bags that were started in July, we know that 2,000 of these bags remain in production and form the ending balance of the work-in-process inventory. Therefore, we know that Morning Mills thoroughly completed and transferred 18,000 of these bags to the warehouse. Hence, in terms of work completed in July, we know that Morning Mills started and completed 100% of 18,000 bags of flour.

3. Now, how much work was done on the remaining 2,000 bags in ending working-in-process inventory? All of the direct materials cost (100%) is complete, which is the equivalent of 2,000 bags of direct materials "work." Additionally, 70% of the conversion work is done on these 2,000 bags, which is the equivalent of 1,400 bags (2,000 bags × 70%).

4. All of the computations for equivalent units described above are listed below in the equivalent units report for Morning Mills. As can be seen, in terms of direct materials costs, Morning Mills completed the equivalent of 21,280 bags of flour. In terms of conversion costs (direct labor and manufacturing overhead), Morning Mills completed 20,040 equivalent bags of flour in July.

Morning Mills — Equivalent Units

	Physical Units	% Done in July	Direct Materials	% Done in July	Conversion Costs
Beginning work-in-process	1,600	80%	1,280	40%	640
Started and completed	18,000	100%	18,000	100%	18,000
Ending work-in-process	2,000	100%	2,000	70%	1,400
Equivalent units in July			**21,280**		**20,040**

II. Cost Flows in the Process Costing System

A. Now that we know how much "work" (in equivalent units) was done in July at Morning Mills, we're ready to start tracking process costs through Morning Mills accounting system. First of all, we need to know the beginning balance of costs in Morning Mill's work-in-process inventory. We'll assume that the beginning balance is $7,056 and that it is composed of $1,200 in direct materials cost and $5,856 in conversion costs.

B. Next, we need to know how much direct materials costs were used in July by Morning Mills, as well as how much labor was spent and how much overhead was applied. We will assume that Morning Mills transferred $80,864 from the raw materials inventory account into production during July. And we'll assume during July that the combined cost spent on direct labor and applied in manufacturing overhead was $120,240. With these July costs and July equivalent units, we can easily compute the average cost per bag for direct materials and conversion costs in July (as shown below).

Morning Mills — Cost per Unit

	Direct Materials	Conversion Costs
Costs in July	$80,864	$120,240
Equivalent units in July	÷ 21,280	÷ 20,040
Cost per unit in July	**$3.80**	**$6.00**

1. These costs per unit are very helpful for both Morning Mills' management team and accounting staff. The management team will use these numbers to plan, control, and evaluate production and cost performance at Morning Mills.

2. The accounting team will use these numbers to compute the costs transferred to the finished goods warehouse (costs of goods manufactured), as well as compute the ending balance in the work-in-process inventory account.

C. Remember that the percentage of work done on Morning Mills' beginning and ending work-in-process inventory is different for direct materials costs than it is for conversion costs. As a result, accounting for the costs of goods manufactured and transferred to the warehouse in July must be handled separately for direct materials costs and for conversion costs. These computations for July are presented below.

Morning Mills — Transferred Materials Costs

	Equivalent Units	Cost per Unit	Direct Materials
June costs			$1,200
Beginning work-in-process	1,280	$3.80	$4,864
Started and completed	18,000	$3.80	$68,400
Total costs transferred out			**$74,464**

Morning Mills — Transferred Conversion Costs

	Equivalent Units	Cost per Unit	Conversion Costs
June costs			$5,856
Beginning work-in-process	640	$6.00	$3,840
Started and completed	18,000	$6.00	$108,000
Total costs transferred out			**$117,696**

1. As you can see, there are three steps to computing cost of goods manufactured for Morning Mills. First, the costs in beginning inventory represent June production costs to get beginning inventory partially completed. Since we assume that the beginning inventory is the first production that Morning Mills will complete in July, these costs are simply included with the July production costs that are transferred to the warehouse as cost of goods manufactured.

2. Next, Morning Mills needs to account for the production costs to complete the beginning work-in-process inventory. The equivalent units used to compute costs per unit for July are also used to measure the costs to complete this inventory. Remember this completion work was done in July. Therefore, the July unit costs for direct materials and conversion costs are used in the computations.

3. With the 1,600 bags from beginning inventory accounted for, the Morning Mills accounting staff now turn their attention to the remaining units of work transferred out to the warehouse, which will be the 18,000 bags that were started and completed in July. Since these bags are 100% done in July, the equivalent units are equal to the physical units, and are multiplied by July unit costs.

4. The approach used above separately tracks the direct materials costs and the conversion costs. Combined, the total cost of goods manufactured in July is $192,160 ($74,464 + $117,696). This cost is transferred out with the 19,600 completed bags of flour (1,600 bags in beginning inventory + 18,000 bags started and completed).

D. With the costs of goods manufactured now transferred out of the work-in-process inventory account and into the finished goods inventory account, we conclude the cost accounting for July by computing the ending balance in the work-in-process inventory account. One way to compute the ending balance is the traditional accounting approach, which is to simply subtract the costs transferred out from the beginning costs plus the costs transferred in. This approach is demonstrated in the accounts below.

Work-in-Process Inventory (units)			
Beginning	1,600	19,600	Transferred
Started	20,000		
Ending	2,000		

Work-in-Process Inventory ($)			
Beginning	7,056	192,160	COGM
Direct materials	80,864		
Conversion	120,240		
Ending	16,000		

1. First, notice that the first work-in-process account is tracking the flow of *physical units* (not costs) in July for Morning Mills. This can be helpful to be sure that the production process is fully accounted for.

2. The second account is tracking working-in-process costs. Assuming that the beginning balance, transferred in, and transferred out costs are correct, then the ending balance is easily computed as $16,000 ($7,056 + $80,864 + $120,240 − $192,160).

E. Alternatively, Morning Mills can directly compute the ending balance in this account using an approach similar to the computations for cost of goods manufactured. That computation is presented below.

Morning Mills — Ending Work-in-Process Inventory

	Equivalent Units	Cost per Unit	Total Cost
Direct materials	2,000	$3.80	$7,600
Direct labor and overhead	1,400	$6.00	$8,400
Total ending work-in-process			**$16,000**

III. Normal and Abnormal Spoilage

A. Spoilage in the production process is unavoidable for many manufacturing organizations, and managers work hard to minimize the costs of spoilage. A key aspect of that management process is identifying and separating "normal" from "abnormal" spoilage. Normal spoilage is an accepted cost of production while abnormal spoilage represents an unacceptable loss in the production process.

B. Even though all spoilage represents units of work that are lost in the production process and cannot be transferred forward to the next department, the *costs* of normal spoilage actually are transferred forward to the finished goods inventory account (or to the next department's work-in-process inventory account). Conversely, the *costs* of abnormal spoilage are transferred into a loss account that is immediately recognized on the income statement.

C. Returning to our example with Morning Mills, we will assume that it is acceptable (normal) for as many as 100 bags to be spoiled in the production process during the month. And let's assume that Morning Mills had 300 bags spoiled during the July production process, which means that Morning Mills could transfer only 19,300 bags (not 19,600 bags) to the warehouse.

1. The costs of 200 abnormal spoiled bags will be transferred immediately to a loss account and reported on the income statement. The costs of the 100 normal spoiled bags will be included with the rest of the costs of goods manufactured that are transferred to the finished goods inventory account. This accounting is represented below.

Work-in-Process Inventory (units)				Work-in-Process Inventory ($)			
Beginning	1,600	19,300	Transferred	Beginning	7,056	190,200	COGM
Started	20,000	300	Spoiled	Direct materials	80,864	1,960	Loss
Ending	2,000			Conversion	120,240		
				Ending	16,000		

2. Be sure to note that *300 bags* are coming out of the work-in-process inventory account, but these spoiled bags will not be transferred forward to the next balance sheet account.

3. More importantly, note that $1,960 have been removed from the costs of goods manufactured. These costs represent the *200 bags* that constitute abnormal spoilage. The costs of these bags are based on the costs per unit for July. The computation on the loss is 200 bags × ($3.80 + $6.00) = $1,960. The cost of the 100 bags representing normal spoilage remain in the cost of goods manufactured and transferred to the finished goods inventory account.

IV. Weighted-Average Process Costing

A. This lesson assumes that Morning Mills' manufacturing process is first-in-first-out (FIFO). That is, the work in beginning inventory is completed before production on new bags of flour will commence. This is the nature of most manufacturing and service processes.

B. There are, in fact, two methods available to use when performing process cost accounting. We've been using the FIFO method in this lesson. This method most accurately represents the actual flow of costs and production at Morning Mills. The alternative method is the weighted-average (W/A) method.

C. The W/A method saves a few mathematical steps by aggregating costs spent and work done in the previous period on beginning inventory with costs spent and work done in the current period. However, this approach can be a little confusing since it doesn't really represent how costs and work actually flow in most organizations. In the past this *was* a compelling approach to use when accounting was done largely by hand. With the advent of computer technology, there is little reason for the W/A method. Nevertheless, this method is still used in some organizations.

D. The basic computational difference from the FIFO method is to assume that the beginning balance in the work-in-process account is 0% complete at the beginning of the period (regardless of its actual level of completion). In other words, all units transferred out are assumed to have been started and completed in the current period. The W/A method also treats all costs actually spent during the previous period on beginning inventory as part of the costs spent in the current period.

E. Below are the reports we originally generated for Morning Mills using the FIFO method, but restated with new computations based on the W/A method.

Morning Mills — Equivalent Units (W/A)

	Physical Units	% Done in July	Direct Materials	% Done in July	Conversion Costs
Transferred out	19,600	100%	19,600	100%	19,600
Ending work-in-process	2,000	100%	2,000	70%	1,400
Equivalent units in July			**21,600**		**21,000**

Morning Mills — Cost per Unit (W/A)

	Direct Materials	Conversion Costs
Costs from June	$1,200	$5,856
Costs in July	$80,864	$120,240
Total costs	$82,064	$126,096
Equivalent units in July	÷ 21,600	÷ 21,000
Cost per unit in July	$3.7993	$6.0046

Morning Mills — Transferred Costs (W/A)

	Physical Units	Cost per Unit	Direct Materials
Direct material costs transferred out	19,600	$3.7993	$74,466
Conversion costs transferred out	19,600	$6.0046	$117,690
Total costs transferred out			$192,156

Morning Mills — Ending WIP Inventory (W/A)

	Equivalent Units	Cost per Unit	Total Cost
Direct materials	2,000	$3.7993	$7,599
Direct labor and overhead	1,400	$6.0046	$8,406
Total ending work-in-process			$16,005

Practice Question

Union Center, Inc. is a loan processing center for several regional banks. Loans move through two processing centers at Union —prequalification and document preparation. The data that follow show the production and cost results for the prequalification center for the month of March:

Prequalification Production Data:	
Loan files in process, March 1 (80% complete)	50
Loan files started in production	2,500
Loan files in process, March 31 (60% complete)	55

Prequalification Cost Data:	
Costs of loan files in process, March 1	$3,500
Costs for March	$238,848

Costs of direct materials (paper, staples, etc.) are immaterial for Union. Hence, all production costs are conversion costs (labor and overhead).

Using both the first-in-first-out (FIFO) method and the weighted-average (W/A) method, compute for March the cost of prequalification services completed and transferred out to the documentation preparation process, and compute the value of ending work-in-process inventory for the prequalification process.

Continues…

Answer

Prequalification Process (FIFO)

	Physical Files	% Done in March	Conversion Costs
Beginning work-in-process	50	20%	10
Started and completed	2,445	100%	2,445
Ending work-in-process	55	60%	33
Equivalent files in March			**2,488**

(Note: 2,445 files started and completed = 2,500 files — 55 files)

	Conversion Costs
Costs in March	$238,848
Equivalent files in March	÷ 2,488
Cost per file in March	**$96.00**

	Equivalent Files	Cost per File	Conversion Costs
February costs			$3,500
Beginning work-in-process	10	$96.00	$960
Started and completed	2,445	$96.00	$234,720
Total costs transferred out			**$239,180**

	Equivalent Files	Cost per File	Total Cost
Total ending work-in-process	33	$96.00	**$3,168**

Prequalification Process (W/A)

	Physical Files	% Done in March	Conversion Costs
Transferred out	2,495	100%	2,495
Ending work-in-process	55	60%	33
Equivalent files in March			**2,528**

(Note: 2,495 files transferred out = 50 files + 2,500 files – 55 files)

	Conversion Costs
Costs from February	$3,500
Costs in March	$238,848
Total costs	$242,348
Equivalent files in March	÷2,528
Cost per file in March	**$95.866**

	Physical Files	Cost per File	Conversion Costs
Costs transferred out	2,495	$95.866	**$239,186**

	Equivalent Files	Cost per File	Total Cost
Total ending work-in-process	33	$95.866	**$3,164**

Summary

Process costing is used by organizations with production processes that make it impractical to identify the customer's product or cost as a "job" during the process. Without a potential customer to target costs moving through the accounting system, the process costing method uses a production period of time to group together costs and output until they are eventually transferred to the finished goods inventory. The challenge in this approach is that there tends to be partially complete products or services at the beginning and/or end of a production period. Dealing with this challenge requires the computation of equivalent units of production. Cost are then tracked on these equivalent units as they move through the production process. This lesson worked through a series of computations to track costs of goods manufactured and transferred forward, and computations to measure the value of the ending balance in the work-in-process inventory account. Both the first-in-first-out (FIFO) and weighted-average (W/A) methods of process costing were demonstrated.

Activity-Based Costing (ABC) and Life Cycle Costing

After studying this lesson, you should be able to:

- Define the elements of activity-based costing such as cost pool, cost driver, resource driver, activity driver, and value-added activity (1.D.2.g).

- Calculate product cost using an activity-based system and compare and analyze the results with costs calculated using a traditional system (1.D.2.h).

- Explain how activity-based costing can be utilized in service firms (1.D.2.i).

- Compare and contrast traditional overhead allocation with activity-based overhead allocation (1.D.3.l).

- Calculate overhead expense in an activity-based costing setting (1.D.3.m).

- Identify and describe the benefits derived from activity-based overhead allocation (1.D.3.n).

- Identify and describe the benefits and limitations of each cost accumulation system (1.D.2.e).

- Demonstrate an understanding of the concept of life-cycle costing and the strategic value of including upstream costs, manufacturing costs, and downstream costs (1.D.2.j).

Traditional job order and process costing methods may be appropriate for organizations with simple processes and similar products, but larger, more complex organizations with a diversified product mix need a better costing method. Otherwise, these more complex organizations are at risk of serious decision errors regarding their product management. This lesson explores a more complete view of product cost flows using the activity-based costing (ABC) method. This lesson also describes life cycle costing.

I. Problems with Traditional Costing Methods

   A. Job order and process costing are traditional methods used to track and allocate costs through the accounting system. These methods are usually adequate for small and fairly simple organizations. However, as the organization becomes larger and its products and process more complex, these traditional costing methods are not adequate—in fact, these methods can lead to dangerous management decisions based on two potential errors in the cost accounting system.

   B. Remember that cost assignment is a "zero-sum game" within the organization. That is, there is rarely any confusion about total cost spending by the organization. The confusion is in knowing how costs are actually being consumed specifically by customers, products, or whatever cost objects are being evaluated by management. For example, if costs being consumed by one type of customer are being allocated in error to another type of customer, the organization is led to believe that the first customer type is more profitable *and* the second customer type is less profitable than in fact they are. This is a *cross-subsidization error* since the costs in one part of the organization are being effectively subsidized by another part of the organization.

      1. The danger of cross-subsidization is that managers are prone to overpromote certain products or customers, believing that profit will result when in fact the profits will not actually materialize, or worse if losses are actually generated.

      2. Simultaneously, managers will underemphasize or drop other products or customers, believing them to be less profitable or even unprofitable when in fact these products or customers are profitable. The dual nature of management errors due to cross-subsidization can significantly harm the organization's total profit.

   C. The second type of error due to poor cost accounting is the allocation of common fixed costs that are not actually consumed by any customer or product lines within the organization. These kinds of costs tend to be high-level administrative costs such as property taxes and insurance, executive salaries, depreciation on administrative buildings and offices, etc. The issue with these costs is not which customer or product lines should be allocated the costs, but whether the cost should even be allocated at all! The costs are unrelated to any activities taking place at the level of customers, services, or product lines. Hence, any cost driver used to allocate these common fixed costs can only "spread" the costs using some kind of uniform mathematical approach.

1. The result of allocating common fixed costs is an overall cost burden that serves to dampen profit performance for all business units, leading to the possibility that the reported profit of a particular customer or product is pushed into a loss.

2. The danger of pushing down reported profits with unrelated cost allocations is the risk that managers will make decisions to drop a customer or product that is reporting a loss but which is actually generating profit for the organization. Once this happens, the cost driver rate increases in order to allocate the same level of common fixed costs across a smaller group of customer or product lines, likely leading to more loss reporting by remaining customer or product lines. If the pattern of irrelevant allocating continues to be followed by dropping profitable business units in error, the actual profit loss across the organization can become irreparable, which is why this error is described as a *death spiral effect*.

II. The ABC Model

A. Activity-based costing (ABC) is focused on breaking down and identifying how costs are actually consumed in an organization, and then fully costing product lines or customer lines using activities as the cost assignment base. At this point, the lessons in this section have identified cost relationships as variable or fixed, and that definition of cost behavior has largely been based on volume of output in units of products or individual customers. This is actually a limited view of variable cost behavior.

B. Fixed overhead costs can represent the largest group of costs in an organization. Poor allocations of these costs are the source of cross-subsidization errors and death spiral effects in most companies. The major contribution of activity-based costing is an approach to breaking down fixed overhead costs into cost pools that relate to product or customer lines using activities other than volumes of output in units. ABC uses a hierarchy of types of activities to identify the variable nature of cost consumption. The illustration below demonstrates how the traditional view of product costing (with its unit-based emphasis on volume of output) relates to the ABC hierarchy.

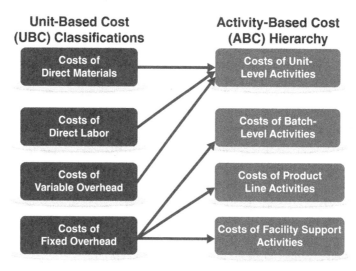

1. The traditional unit-based cost (UBC) approach to analyzing cost behavior typically focuses on the classification of direct materials, direct labor, and some overhead as variable costs. This classification is based on an analysis of cost consumption as the volume of production output increases or decreases. In the ABC hierarchy, these costs are related to (consumed by) unit-level activities. For example, the direct materials and direct labor involved in the production of a single product are unit-level activities. With respect to overhead, unit-level activities that consume overhead costs could include machine maintenance and certain depreciation methods (such as "units of production"), as well as electricity and other utility costs.

2. Batch-level activities have an important consumption relationship with many types of costs that are not actually related to the volume of production output. For example, if production inspection activities are handled by sampling some amount of each batch of production, then that cost is driven by the volume of batches and not by the volume of units within each batch. Other examples of batch-level activities that result in a variable cost based on the volume of batches include machine setups, movement of materials for production, and production scheduling.

3. Other types of overhead traditionally considered fixed with respect to the volume of units are variable with respect to number of various product lines within the organization. Production line activities are necessary for organizations to support an expanded product mix. Examples of product line activities can include engineering product design and support, training of production personnel, and product marketing campaigns.

4. Poor cost assignment of batch-level and product line activity costs are the cause of cross-subsidization errors in the organization. But it is the allocation of facility support costs that leads to death spiral effects. Remember from our discussion above that there is no type of cost driver available to somehow represent a consumption of common fixed costs (e.g., shared structure costs and executive administration costs). In the ABC hierarchy, these activities and their associated costs are represented as facility support activities. For decisions involving profitability analysis, facility support costs should *not* be allocated.

C. By tracking the consumption of costs related to unit activities, batch activities, and product line activities, managers can establish a better measure of the actual profitability of product lines and product business units. The ABC hierarchy can also be used to evaluate the profitability of customers and customer categories.

1. Customer unit-level activities are tied to the resources consumed for each unit sold to a customer. Examples of activity costs that are tied to the volume of units handled for a customer include shipping costs, restocking costs, and sales commissions.

2. Customer batch-level activities represent the resources required to support a sales transaction to a customer. Examples of sales transaction activities that consume costs in a batch pattern include order processing, invoicing, and recording product returns. These costs are not affected by the number of units purchased by the customer.

3. Customer-sustaining activities are similar to product-line activities and represent the resources consumed to service a customer relationship regardless of the number of units sold to or the volume of sales transactions handled for the customer. Examples of customer-sustaining activities include monthly statement processing, travel expense by sales personnel, and customer training and support.

III. Cost Assignment Using the ABC Model

    A. The ABC hierarchy is helpful to organizations in the process of identifying and grouping various activities in order to establish cost drivers used to accurately assign costs. The identification of activities relevant to the assignment of costs is at the center of the ABC cost assignment model. In the first lesson in this section we introduced the basic conceptual model and a two-step process for assigning costs. The model and the process are illustrated below.

$$\text{Step 1: } \frac{\text{Cost Pool Total}}{\text{Cost Driver Volume}} = \text{Cost Driver Rate}$$

Step 2: Cost Driver Rate × Cost Object Activity = Assigned Cost

        1. The conceptual focus of a cost assignment centers on a cost driver that connects a pool of costs to a cost object.

        2. Subsequently, every cost assignment process we've explored in these lessons then follows the two steps of (1) identifying a cost pool and cost driver to compute a cost driver rate, and (2) using that cost driver rate to assign cost to a cost object. The ABC cost assignment model follows a similar pattern.

    B. The specific ABC cost assignment model is laid out below.

Activity-Based Costing (ABC)

        1. Without regard to costs being located in support departments or production departments, all costs that can be identified as related to unit-level, batch-level, or product line (or customer-sustaining) activities are identified for cost assignment. These costs are described as "resources" in order to emphasize that these costs should represent value-added resources in the organization.

        2. With unit-level, batch-level, and product line (customer sustaining) activities identified, resource-based cost drivers are established to assign costs to activities in order to form activity cost pools.

        3. Once the organization defines its cost objects (products, customers, sales agents, business units, market regions, etc.), the relationship between cost objects and activity cost pools is established as a cost consumption relationship using activity-based cost rates. In other words, the activity cost pools are treated as "variable" costs and tracked (not allocated) to cost objectives based on how the cost object uses (consumes) the relevant activity.

    C. To demonstrate the ABC model, we'll use Smeltz & Sons, Inc., a company that makes two types of products: Product X and Product Z.

1. The following production and sales data have been accumulated for the previous month.

Smeltz & Sons — Production Cost Data

	Product X	Product Z	Total
Production and sales volume (units)	1,000	500	
Selling price per unit	$190.00	$220.00	
Direct materials cost per unit	$10.00	$15.00	
Direct labor cost per hour	$12.00	$16.00	
Direct labor hours per unit	3	2	
Manufacturing overhead costs			**$242,000**

2. The management team at Smeltz has traditionally allocated the manufacturing overhead using direct labor hours. Following that approach, a $60.50 manufacturing overhead (MOH) allocation rate was established and used to develop the following monthly profit & loss report for management decision making.

Smeltz & Sons — Overhead Cost Allocation Rate

	Product X	Product Z	Compute
Total manufacturing overhead costs			$242,000
Product and sales volume (units)	1,000	500	
Direct labor hours per unit	× 3	× 2	
Total direct labor hours	3,000	1,000	÷ 4,000
Manufacturing overhead allocation rate			**$60.50**

Smeltz & Sons — Traditional Cost Allocation

	Product X	Product Z	Total
Sales revenue (units × price)	$190,000	$110,000	$300,000
Direct materials costs (units × DM rate)	(10,000)	(7,500)	(17,500)
Direct labor costs (units × hours × DL rate)	(36,000)	(16,000)	(52,000)
Manufacturing overhead (units × MOH rate)	(181,500)	(60,500)	(242,000)
Gross profit	**$(37,500)**	**$26,000**	**$(11,500)**

3. Based on this performance report, the Smeltz management team is considering dropping the Product X business line.

D. It is clear to Smeltz managers that the cost of manufacturing overhead is the problem for the Product X line. However, they are concerned about product cost cross-subsidization and possible death spiral effects in the current approach to allocating overhead costs. Hence, activity-based costing will be applied before making any significant management decisions.

1. As a first step toward ABC, managers determine to remove any common fixed costs that are unaffected by activity taking place within each product line. It is clear that administrative salaries (supervision, accounting, and security) and occupancy costs (rent and insurance) would be unaffected if either product line was dropped. These monthly costs total up to $62,000 and are identified as a facility support common cost that should *not* be allocated. A new MOH allocation rate is established without including these common costs, and new profit and loss report is created (shown below).

Smeltz & Sons — Overhead Rate Without Common Costs

	Product X	Product Z	Compute
Total manufacturing overhead costs			$180,000
Product and sales volume (units)	1,000	500	
Direct labor hours per unit	× 3	× 2	
Total direct labor hours	3,000	1,000	÷ 4,000
Manufacturing overhead allocation rate			**$45.00**

Smeltz & Sons — Allocation Without Common Costs

	Product X	Product Z	Total
Sales revenue (units × price)	$ 190,000	$ 110,000	$ 300,000
Direct materials costs (units × DM rate)	(10,000)	(7,500)	(17,500)
Direct labor costs (units × hours × DL rate)	(36,000)	(16,000)	(52,000)
Manufacturing overhead (units × MOH rate)	(135,000)	(45,000)	(180,000)
Product line gross profit	**$9,000**	**$41,500**	**$50,500**
Administrative costs (facility support)			(62,000)
Gross profit			**$(11,500)**

2. The report above removes the cost burden of factory administrative salaries and occupancy costs from the profit performance of each product line. Of course, last month's overall gross profit for the company (a $11,500 loss) is unaffected by this change to the cost allocation approach. Nevertheless, the results suggest strongly that management should not be too quick to drop the Product X business line.

E. The Smeltz management team is still concerned that cost allocations are cross-subsidizing the profit performance of the two product lines. The remaining $180,000 in overhead costs is being spent largely to support three core production activities: utilities, quality, and engineering. With analysis and discussion, Smeltz managers work with the company accountants and determine that the manufacturing overhead costs can be separated into the following three activity cost pools.

Smeltz & Sons — Activity Cost Pools

	Total
Cost of manufacturing utilities	$30,000
Cost of quality	90,000
Cost of engineering	60,000
Total overhead activity costs	**$180,000**

F. Note that it is fairly typical in early ABC adoptions to not initially build resource-based cost rates to determine activity cost pools. In the effort to move quickly to an ABC solution, management estimates are often used to break down overhead costs into activity cost pools.

1. With activity cost pools established, managers and accountants work together to identify an appropriate activity driver for each cost pool. Manufacturing utilities is classified as a unit-level activity cost that is driven by the number of direct labor hours involved in the volume of units produced. Quality is classified as a batch-level activity cost that varies based on the number of quality inspections taking place on production runs. Engineering is classified as a product line activity cost that depends on the number of engineering changes that typically takes place for each product line during the month. The transaction volume of each of these activities for last month is reported below.

Smeltz & Sons — Activity Transactions

	Product X	Product Z
Production volume (unit level)	1,000	500
Quality inspections (batch level)	22	18
Engineering changes (product line level)	4	8

2. Using these activity cost pools and volume of activity transactions, activity-based cost rates are computed (shown below).

Smeltz & Sons — Activity Cost Tracking Rates

	Product X	Product Z	Compute
Manufacturing utility cost pool			$ 30,000
Total direct labor hours	3,000	1,000	÷ 4,000
Utility cost rate (unit level)			**$7.50**
Quality inspection cost pool			$ 90,000
Production batches	22	18	÷ 40
Inspection cost rate (batch level)			**$2,250**
Engineering cost pool	4	8	$ 60,000
Engineering changes			÷ 12
Engineer cost rate (product line level)			**$5,000**

3. These new activity-based cost rates represent how overhead costs are actually consumed (in a variable cost behavior pattern) in the production of the two product lines at Smeltz & Sons. What this means is that rather than *allocating* costs, Smeltz managers and accountants are able to *track* costs to each product line using these activity-based cost rates. The results of the ABC analysis are shown below with a new profit & loss performance report.

Smeltz & Sons — Activity-Based Cost Tracking

	Product X	Product Z	Total
Sales revenue (units × price)	$190,000	$110,000	$300,000
Direct materials costs (units × DM rate)	(10,000)	(7,500)	(17,500)
Direct labor costs (units × hours × DL rate)	(36,000)	(16,000)	(52,000)
Utility costs (labor hours × utility rate)	(22,500)	(7,500)	(30,000)
Quality costs (batches × inspection rate)	(49,500)	(40,500)	(90,000)
Engineering costs (changes × engineer rate)	(20,000)	(40,000)	(60,000)
Product line gross profit	**$ 52,000**	**$ (1,500)**	**$ 50,500**
Administrative costs (facility support)			(62,000)
Company gross profit			**$(11,500)**

G. What has the Smeltz management team learned about the two product lines? Obviously, they've learned that Product X is not a profit problem for the company, and that Product Z is a profit problem. The managers are probably not very surprised by this insight. Based on the low output volume and high demand for quality processes and engineering support, they likely expect to see a low profit performance for Product Z. The cost allocation system using a single cost rate based on the volume of production units is creating a cross-subsidization effect at Smeltz. Due to this traditional cost accounting approach, Product X is subsidizing costs that are actually being consumed by Product Z.

H. The ABC method of tracking costs based on activity consumption is particularly adept at identifying cost cross-subsidization in organizations with high volume standard products being produced alongside low volume complex products. Similarly, ABC methods can identify and resolve cross-subsidization of customer costs when there is significant variance in how customers use different service processes in the organization.

IV. Benefits and Limitations of Activity-Based Costing

   A. ABC methods have a number of advantages compared to traditional methods such as job-order costing and process costing. Advantages of ABC methods include the following:

   1. ABC methods provide more accurate measures of costs of products, customers, sales agents, business units, market regions, etc.

   2. ABC methods can be used to identify value-added and non-value-added activities and costs.

   3. ABC methods support a more strategic view of cost management and product mix decisions.

   B. There are also disadvantages and limitations with ABC methods. Compared to traditional costing methods, limitations of ABC can include the following:

   1. ABC methods are more costly and time intensive to design, implement, and maintain.

   2. ABC cost consumption relationships are based on a longer time horizon than traditional systems, which means that it takes substantial time and effort to adjust spending on many of the activities used in the ABC solution.

   3. Profit and loss reports based on ABC methods may or may not conform to external reporting requirements, which means that organizations may need to maintain more than one version of their cost system.

V. Life-Cycle Costing

   A. Compared to traditional costing methods with the focus on unit-based analyses, activity-based costing is a more complete view of costs that organizations need to manage in manufacturing products or serving customers. However, ABC methods tend to be focused only on measuring and reporting costs involved in production and service processes. A more complete view of the costs of establishing and sustaining a product or customer is called life-cycle costing.

   B. The life cycle for a product begins in the research and development (R&D) stage. While most external reporting requirements require R&D costs to be expensed in the period in which they are spent, the life-cycle costing method seeks to track those costs forward as part of a product's life cycle in the organization.

   C. At the other end of the product's life cycle are the costs required to support the product after it has been manufactured. These costs include delivery, customer training, support and service, product warranty, and potential product liability costs.

   D. By tracking these *upstream costs* prior to the manufacture of the product and *downstream costs* subsequent to the manufacture of the product, organizations are able to establish a more strategic view of managing all three core product stages: R&D, production, and post-sale support. For example, with life-cycle costing, organizations are better able to identify and justify valuable investments in product design that are more than offset in production savings, product quality, or robust performance that avoids unnecessary post-sale support.

Practice Question

Big Mike's Crane Company manufacturers three different crane engines with 150 horsepower (hp), 225 hp, and 300 hp, respectively. Relevant sales and production for each engine product line is below.

Big Mike's Crane Company — Production Cost Data

	150 hp		225 hp		300 hp	
	Per Unit	Total	Per Unit	Total	Per Unit	Total
Units produced and sold		250		200		150
Sales price	$8,500	$2,125,000	$11,400	$2,280,000	$14,300	$2,145,000
Direct materials cost	$1,700	$425,000	$1,850	$370,000	$2,400	$360,000
Direct labor cost	$2,380	$595,000	$2,550	$510,000	$3,150	$472,500

Big Mike's manufacturing overheads costs is displayed here.

Manufacturing Overhead Costs

	Total
Machine maintenance costs	$162,000
Purchasing costs	196,800
Quality control costs	884,000
Engineering costs	1,024,000
Factory occupancy costs	750,000
Total overhead costs	$3,016,800

Big Mike's manufacturing overhead allocation rate is based on the volume of units produced. Compute the manufacturing overhead allocation rate and compute the gross profit for each product line and the overall company gross profit.

Answer

Big Mike's Crane Company — Traditional Cost Allocation

	150 hp	225 hp	300 hp	Compute
Total manufacturing overhead				$3,016,800
Units produced	250	200	150	÷ 600
Manufacturing overhead rate				$5,028
	150 hp	**225 hp**	**300 hp**	**Total**
Sales revenue	$2,125,000	$2,280,000	$2,145,000	$6,550,000
Direct materials costs	(425,000)	(370,000)	(360,000)	(1,155,000)
Direct labor costs	(595,000)	(510,000)	(472,500)	(1,577,500)
Manufacturing overhead	(1,257,000)	(1,005,600)	(754,200)	(3,016,800)
Gross profit	**$ (152,000)**	**$394,400**	**$ 558,300**	**$800,700**

Practice Question

Continuing with the analysis at Big Mike's Crane Company, the management team is concerned that overhead allocation is creating a false signal on product line profitability, and has determined to use activity-based costing (ABC) to reperform the company profit and loss analysis. The following activities and activity volumes for each product line were identified.

Continues...

331

Overhead Activities

	150 hp	225 hp	300 hp	Total
Production volume (unit level)	250	200	150	600
Purchasing events (batch level)	44	52	54	150
Machine setups (batch level)	60	68	80	208
Engineering change orders (product line level)	52	84	120	256

Machine maintenance costs are tracked using production volume as the activity basis. Purchasing costs are tracked using purchasing events that take place to support a batch production run. Similarly, quality control takes place each time machine setups take place at the start of a batch production run. Engineering costs are tied to engineer change orders that support each product line. Finally, the management team at Big Mike's has determined that factory occupancy costs are not related to any particular activity that takes place to support a product line.

Use the overhead activities to compute activity-based cost rates, then use these rates to establish the gross profit for each product line and the overall company gross profit.

Answer

Activity Cost Tracking Rates

	150 hp	225 hp	300 hp	Compute
Machine maintenance cost pool				$ 162,000
Total units produced	250	200	150	÷ 600
Maintenance cost rate				**$270**
Purchasing cost pool				$ 196,800
Total purchasing events	44	52	54	÷ 150
Purchasing cost rate				**$1,312**
Quality control cost pool				$ 884,000
Total machine setups	60	68	80	÷ 208
Quality cost rate				**$4,250**
Engineering cost pool				$1,024,000
Total engineering change orders	52	84	120	÷ 256
Engineering cost rate				**$4,000**

Big Mike's Crane Company — Activity-Based Cost Tracking

	150 hp	225 hp	300 hp	Total
Sales revenue	$2,125,000	$2,280,000	$2,145,000	$6,550,000
Direct materials costs	(425,000)	(370,000)	(360,000)	(1 51 55,000)
Direct labor costs	(595,000)	(51 0,000)	(472,500)	(1,577,500)
Maintenance costs	(67,500)	(54,000)	(40,500)	(162,000)
Purchasing costs	(57,728)	(68,224)	(70,848)	(196,800)
Quality costs	(255,000)	(289,000)	(340,000)	(884,000)
Engineering costs	(208,000)	(336,000)	(480,000)	(1,024,000)
Product line gross profit	**$ 516,772**	**$ 652,776**	**$ 381,152**	$1,550,700
Factory occupancy costs				(750,000)
Company gross profit				**$800,700**

Summary

Activity-based costing (ABC) methods provide a more complete view of product and customer cost consumption in the organization. An ABC solution begins by identifying activities across a hierarchy of unit-level, batch-level, or product line activity groupings. Activities that don't fall within these categories typically represent the common costs of facility support activities that should *not* be assigned to specific products or customers. The ABC cost model is Resources → Activities → Cost Objects. Resources should represent value-added costs that can be reorganized into activity cost pools. Some appropriate measure of activity consumption is then identified for each activity cost pool, and activity-based cost rates are formed to accurately *track* (not allocate) costs to cost objects (i.e., products, customers, etc.). ABC methods provide a more accurate view of costs flowing through production processes. Life-cycle costing methods further expand the ABC view to include an analysis of upstream product costs in the research and development (R&D) stage, as well as downstream product costs that take place in the process of delivery and supporting products after the sale has taken place.

Topic 3. Overhead Costs

Support Department Costing

After studying this lesson, you should be able to:

- Explain why companies allocate the cost of service departments such as Human Resources or Information Technology to divisions, departments, or activities (1.D.3.o).

- Calculate service or support department cost allocations using the direct method, the reciprocal method, the step-down method, and the dual allocation method (1.D.3.p).

> There are three methods available to use in the process of assigning support department costs to production departments. This lesson provides a walkthrough of the direct method, step-down method, and reciprocal method of assigning support department costs.

I. Why Allocate Costs of Shared Services?

    A. As organizations grow in size and complexity, various business units within the organization are established to focus on specific stewardships of responsibility. Initially, organizations will establish business units to focus on distinct segments of their business model, such as specific product lines or customer groups.

    B. Once organizations begin instituting a structure of business units focused on the creation of products (goods and services) to be sold to customers, organizations will often begin consolidating shared services into departments that support the production departments.

    C. For example, rather than have each production department establish and manage its own HR (human resource) process and IT (information technology) process, the organization can typically save costs while improving processes by establishing a separate HR department and IT department, each of which is tasked to support all production departments.

    D. The issue is how to track or allocate the pools of support department costs to production departments. Remember from your work in previous lessons that if the cost assignment taking place between a cost pool and a cost object is based on a cost consumption driver, then we describe the relationship as a *cost tracking process*. Alternatively, if the cost pool is fixed with respect to activity in the cost object, then assigning the costs is described as a *cost allocation process*. Regardless of whether the process is based on cost tracking or cost allocation, organizations generally work to accomplish four management objectives in the assignment of support department costs to production departments. Choices regarding cost assignment processes will affect the accomplishment of each of these goals.

        1. First, the cost assignment process needs to be *transparent* to all departments involved. Confusion, and even frustration, emerges naturally when managers don't understand the process used to assign costs to their unit.

        2. Second, the cost assignment process should emphasize *equity* in results of the cost assignment. Equity doesn't mean that every production department should receive the same amount of support department costs. It does mean that whenever possible the cost assignment represents actual consumption of a variable cost, or at least that it represents an accurate measure of the use of a fixed cost resource.

        3. Third, the method(s) used to assign support department costs to production departments should be *relevant* to the types of decisions being made based on those costs. If the organization is making decisions regarding adding or dropping product lines, it is important to avoid allocating fixed costs that are unaffected, for example, by the decision to close out a product line.

4. Finally, cost assignment systems are most effective when they establish *accountability* within the organization. If the costs are *tracked* to production departments based on consumption of variable cost resources, then production departments are effectively held accountable for their impact on support department costs. When fixed costs of support departments are *allocated* to production departments, it provides an opportunity for support departments to be held accountable to production departments for spending decisions on the costs being allocated.

E. The rest of this lesson describes different methods used to assign or allocate support department costs to production departments. Each of these methods can be used more or less effectively to accomplish the management goals of transparency, equity, relevancy, and accountability.

II. The Direct Method

A. When assigning support department costs to production departments, the simplest approach is to use the direct method. We'll use an example for a CPA firm known as Dennis Bain, LLC. Bain has a Janitor support department and an HR support department with two production departments —Audit and Tax. Both of these support departments provide services to the Audit Department and to the Tax Department. Of course, these support departments provide janitorial and HR support to each other. However, the direct method avoids the reality of support departments serving each other and instead makes the cost assignments directly to the production departments using the traditional two-step process by (1) building a cost assignment rate and then (2) using the rate to assign costs to the cost object. The direct method approach for the firm is illustrated below.

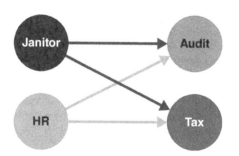

B. Total quarterly costs for the Janitor Department are $118,800. These costs are assigned based on the occupancy of square footage in the office space. The quarterly costs for the HR Department are $252,000 and are assigned using headcount of personnel. The direct method solution for Bain is presented below.

Dennis Brain, LLC — Direct Assignment Method

	Janitor Dept	HR Dept	Audit Dept	Tax Dept	Relevant Total
Support Dept Costs	$118,800	$252,000			$370,800
Square feet (Janitor base)	1,600	1,200	2,800	6,000	8,800
Head count (HR base)	10	8	48	42	90
Janitor rate & assignment	$13.50		$37,800	$81,000	$118,800
HR rate & assignment		$2,800	$134,400	$117,600	$252,000
Total Assignment			$172,200	$198,600	$370,800

1. Using the direct method, the Janitor Department will assign its costs on the combined basis of 2,800 square feet in Audit Department office space and 6,000 square feet in the Tax Department (2,800 + 6,000 = 8,800 total square feet). The cost assignment rate is $13.50 ($118,800 ÷ 8,800 ft^2). The Audit Department will receive $37,800 in Janitor costs ($13.50 × 2,800 ft^2) and the Tax Department will receive $81,000 ($13.50 × 6,000 ft^2). As a check figure, note that the costs assigned sum up to the original costs in the Janitor Department.

2. Check yourself on the HR Department by (1) building the $2,800 rate per head and (2) using headcount in the two producing departments to assign HR costs. Make sure your cost assignment computations sum back up to the original $252,000 in the HR Department.

3. Finally, note that the direct method began with a total of $370,800 in support department costs ($118,800 + $252,000), and concludes with $370,800 costs assigned to the two producing departments ($172,200 + $198,600).

III. The Step-Down Method

A. The direct method is a straightforward approach to assigning support department costs to production departments, but that approach avoids an important reality—support departments also provide support to each other! Using a similar computational approach as the direct method, the step-down method pays *some* attention to the fact that support departments provide support to each other, although the step-down method is far from a perfect solution on this issue. Nevertheless, it is a popular cost assignment method used by many organizations.

B. The key characteristic (and limitation) of the step-down method is the order of service departments selected by management for the computation. This order is often based on identifying the department that provides the most support to the other departments, followed by the department that provides the second most support, and so forth. For the Bain firm, we'll assume that management determines the Janitor Department will be first in the step-down method process. Based on that decision, the step-down method for Bain is illustrated below.

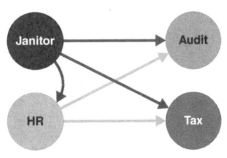

C. Using the same costs and activity bases, the step-down method solution for Bain is provided here.

Dennis Brain, LLC — Step-Down Assignment Method

	Janitor Dept	HR Dept	Audit Dept	Tax Dept	Relevant Total
Support Dept Costs	$118,800	$252,000			$370,800
Square feet (Janitor base)	1,600	1,200	2,800	6,000	10,000
Head count (HR base)	10	8	48	42	90
Janitor rate & assignment	**$11.88**	$14,256	$33,264	$71,280	$118,800
HR Dept costs to allocate		$266,256			
HR rate & assignment		**$2,958.40**	$142,003	$124,253	$266,256
Total Assignment			$175,267	$195,533	$370,800

1. First, the basis used to compute the cost assignment rate for the Janitor Department *includes the square feet in the HR Department*, as well as the square feet in Audit and Tax Departments. This works out to a total basis of 10,000 square feet (1,200 + 2,800 + 6,000) and results in a cost assignment rate of $11.88 ($118,800 ÷ 10,000 ft^2).

2. Next, using this rate, the Janitor Department directly assigns its costs to all three "downstream" departments (HR, Audit, and Tax). The HR Department now has a new and higher amount of costs ($252,000 + $14,256 = $266,256) that it subsequently needs to assign to Audit and Tax.

3. HR's combined costs results in a $2,958.40 per-head rate ($266,256 ÷ 90 headcount). Using this rate, HR directly assigns its costs to the production departments.

4. The final cost assignments to Audit and Tax sum up to the original support departments' total costs of $370,800. Be sure to see, though, that the costs assigned to each of these production departments are different using the step-down method compared to the direct method. For example, costs assigned to Audit are $172,200 using the direct method, and are $175,267 using this step-down method.

D. The decision about the order used in the step-down method is subjective. For example, there are likely several ways an organization can define what it means for one department to provide comparatively more support than another department. This ordering decision is important because it affects the costs finally assigned to production departments.

1. For example, assume that Bain chooses instead to prioritize the HR Department first in the approach it uses for the step-down cost assignment method, as illustrated below.

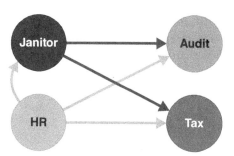

2. The impact on costs assigned to Audit and Tax is substantial. The effect of changing the order in the step-down method reduces the Audit Department's assigned cost from $175,267 to $166,778. And the Tax Department's assigned costs increase from $195,533 to $204,022. (This solution is provided below as a practice problem, but first you should attempt to solve this step-down cost assignment yourself.)

IV. The Reciprocal Method

A. The step-down method comes closer than the direct method to representing the reality of support departments providing service to other support departments, but it is limited in its computational approach. It forces a one-way flow of cost assignments through a subjective order of support departments.

B. In our example with the Bain firm, the Janitor and HR departments obviously provide services to each other while serving the needs of the two production departments. The actual flow of resources in and out of the two support departments is better represented in the diagram below.

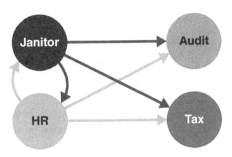

C. The reciprocal cost assignment method can create a two-step solution that represents (1) a simultaneous assignment of costs between the two support departments followed by (2) a direct assignment of costs to the production departments. In the Bain firm example with two support departments, we can establish a simultaneous cost assignment using a fairly basic algebraic approach sometimes called "the substitution method for two unknowns."

D. To create a simultaneous solution to that assigns costs back and forth between the two support departments, first set up an equation for each department that represents its total cost after receiving an assignment of costs from the other department.

   1. For example, the Janitor Department has $118,800 of its own costs and it should be assigned 10% of the costs coming from the HR Department. The 10% is computed by the 10 employees (headcount) in the Janitor Department divided by the combined 100 employees in Janitor, Audit, and Tax (10 + 48 + 42). Hence, letting J represent the Janitor Department and H represent the HR Department, the total cost equation for the Janitor Department is:

   $$J = \$118,800 + .10(H)$$

   2. Similarly, the HR Department has $252,000 of its own costs, plus a 12% assignment of costs from the Janitor Department, which is computed as 1,200 ft^2 ÷ (1,200 ft^2 + 2,800 ft^2 + 6,000 ft^2). The total cost equation for the HR Department is:

   $$H = \$252,000 + .12(J)$$

E. With the cost equations established for each support department, the substitution method for two unknowns takes place in three steps.

   1. Select either of the two equations to solve first. We'll start with the equation for the Janitor Department.

   2. Solve the first equation by substituting the second equation into the first equation. This is done below.

   $$J = \$118,800 + .10(H)$$

   $$J = \$118,800 + .10(\$252,000 + .12(J))$$

   $$J = \$118,800 + \$25,200 + .012(J)$$

   $$1(J) - 0.12(J) = \$118,800 + \$25,200$$

   $$.988(J) = \$144,000$$

   $$J = \$145,748.99$$

   (or $145,749 rounded)

   Now solve the second equation using the solution from the first equation, as is done below.

$$H = \$252{,}000 + .12(J)$$

$$H = \$252{,}000 + .12(\$145{,}748.99)$$

$$H = \$252{,}000 + \$17{,}489.88$$

$$H = \$269{,}489.88$$

(or $269,490 rounded)

These simultaneous solutions for each department would be the same if the three-step process began with the HR Department. (This alternative solution approach beginning with the HR Department is provided below as a practice problem, which you should first attempt to solve yourself.)

F. The simultaneous solution for each support department represents how much cost each department now needs to assign to *all* other departments (both support and production departments). Note that the $145,749 cost that the Janitor Department will assign is $26,949 more than the $118,800 in costs that it actually has. However, simultaneous with the $145,749 that it will assign, the Janitor Department will receive $26,949 cost assignment from the HR Department, which leaves the Janitor Department with exactly zero costs remaining to be assigned. A similar offsetting cost assignment will go from the Janitor Department to the HR Department. The full reciprocal cost assignment solution for Bain is shown below.

Dennis Brain, LLC — Reciprocal Assignment Method

	Janitor Dept	HR Dept	Audit Dept	Tax Dept	Relevant Total
Support Dept Costs	$118,800	$252,000			$370,800
Square feet (Janitor base)	1,600	1,200	2,800	6,000	10,000
Head count (HR base)	10	8	48	42	100
Reciprocal Cost Solution[1]	$145,749	$269,490			
Janitor rate & assignment	**$14.57**	$17,490	$40,810	$87,449	$145,749
HR rate & assignment	$26,949	**$2,694.90**	$129,355	$113,186	$269,490
Total Assignment			**$170,165**	**$200,635**	**$370,800**

*Support department costs after reciprocal (simultaneous) cost assignment.

G. The reciprocal method is reasonably simple to solve when it involves only two support departments. However, when more than two support departments are involved, the simultaneous equations are based on a much more involved mathematical solution using matrix algebra, and is typically handled using computer technology.

H. Once again, a different method used to assign the support department costs results in a different amount of total support costs landing on the Audit Department and the Tax Department. For comparison, the results of all three methods we worked through are presented below.

Dennis Brain, LLC — Cost Assignment Comparison

	Audit Dept	Tax Dept	Total Costs Assigned
Direct Method	$172,200	$198,600	$370,800
Step-Down Method	$175,267	$195,533	$370,800
Recirocal Method	$170,165	$200,635	$370,800

V. Using Dual Rates

A. If you look back at the Dennis Bain, LLC example above, the discussion is careful to use the generic word *assign* when describing the movement of costs from support departments to production departments. Are these support costs being *tracked* to the production departments, or are they being *allocated* to the production departments?

1. For example, if there is a consumption relationship between the pool of Janitor Departments costs and the square feet of space being used by the organization (that is, if Janitor Department costs are variable with respect to Bain having more or less square feet in each of its departments), then the methods above are *tracking* costs to the Audit and Tax departments. Alternatively, if the janitorial costs are fixed (and they likely are fixed) with respect to square footage space (because square footage space itself is fixed for Bain), then these support costs are being *allocated* to the production departments.

2. While janitorial costs are probably fixed with respect to square footage of space, it may be that HR costs are largely variable with respect to the headcount at Bain increasing and decreasing within each department from quarter to quarter throughout the year. If this is the case at Bain, then the process of assigning HR Department costs to Audit and Tax can be described as *tracking* costs to these production departments.

B. This distinction between fixed cost allocation and variable cost tracking is important since many organizations will use a *dual rate approach* to assign costs. In the case of assigning support department costs, the dual rate approach splits costs into fixed and variable, then allocates fixed costs using a fixed cost rate and tracks variable costs using a variable cost rate. In the traditional two-step cost assignment process (compute a cost driver rate and then use the rate to assign the cost), the key difference is the basis used to compute the cost driver rates.

1. For fixed cost allocation rates, the basis is established on the *normal capacity* of the activity. For example, Bain's Janitor Department is likely set up to provide maintenance on all the square feet of space that the firm occupies, regardless of whether every square foot of space will be used in the upcoming quarter. The Janitor Department represents a fixed cost commitment to the capacity to serve and maintain all the square feet available for Bain's use in its normal course of business. The result of using a fixed cost allocation rate is relatively consistent assignments of support department costs over time.

2. Conversely, for variable cost tracking rate, the basis is established on the *budgeted use* of the activity, with an expectation that spending on the variable costs being assigned will be adjusted depending on expected increases and decreases in the budgeted activity that uses the support costs. In the case of Bain's HR Department, if spending in this department will fluctuate quarter to quarter depending on the expected headcount in the organization, then a variable cost tracking rate will be computed and multiplied by the various levels of expected headcount in each department being assigned HR costs. Using a variable cost tracking rate, costs assigned are expected to fluctuate over time based on changes in spending and usage.

Practice Question

Return to the study guide example for Dennis Bain, LLC. What are the computations for the step-down method using the HR Department as the first support department costs to assign?

Answer

Dennis Brain, LLC — Step-Down Assignment Method

	Janitor Dept	HR Dept	Audit Dept	Tax Dept	Relevant Total
Support Dept Costs	$118,800	$252,000			$370,800
Square feet (Janitor base)	1,600	1,200	2,800	6,000	8,800
Head count (HR base)	10	8	48	42	100
HR rate & assignment	$25,200	$2,520.00	$120,960	$105,840	$252,000
Janitor Dept costs to allocate	$144,000				
Janitor rate & assignment	$16.36		$45,818	$98,182	$144,000
Total Assignment			$166,778	$204,022	$370,800

Practice Question

Return again to the study guide example for Dennis Bain, LLC. What are the simultaneous equation solutions for the reciprocal method, assuming that the equation for the HR Department is solved before the equation for the Janitor Department?

Answer

Solve the HR equation by substituting in the Janitor equation.

$H = \$252{,}000 + .12(J)$

$H = \$252{,}000 + .12(\$118{,}800 + .10(H))$

$H = \$252{,}000 + \$14{,}256 + .012(H)$

$1(H) - .012(H) = \$252{,}000 + \$14{,}256$

$.988(H) = \$266{,}256$

$H = \$269{,}489.88$

(or \$269,490 rounded)

Now solve the Janitor equation using the HR solution.

$J = \$118{,}800 + .10(H)$

$J = \$118{,}800 + .10(\$269{,}489.88)$

$J = \$118{,}800 + \$26{,}948.98$

$J = \$145{,}748.99$

(or \$145,749 rounded)

Practice Question

Donaldson Company has two service departments (Personnel and Finance) that provide services for one another as well as for two production departments, Assembly and Finishing. Data for the month follow:

	Personnel	Finance	Assembly	Finishing
Employees	6	8	20	15
Costs to run payroll	$15,000	$14,000	$30,000	$27,000

Personnel Department costs for the month were \$86,000, and Finance Department costs were \$41,000. Donaldson uses employees as the assignment base for Personnel Department costs and uses costs to run the payroll process as the assignment base for Finance Department costs.

1. Assign support costs using the direct method.

2. Assign support costs using the step-down method, with personnel costs assigned first.

Continues…

Answer

1. Using the direct method.

Donaldson Company — Direct Assignment Method

	Personal Dept	Finance Dept	Assembly Dept	Finishing Dept	Relevant Total
Support Dept Costs	**$86,000**	**$41,000**			**$127,000**
Employees	6	8	20	15	35
Payroll costs	$15,000	$14,000	$30,000	$27,000	$57,000
Personnel rate & assignment	**$2,457.14**		$49,143	$36,857	$86,000
Finance rate & assignment		**$0.72**	$21,579	$19,421	$41,000
Total Assignment			**$70,722**	**$56,278**	**$127,000**

(Be careful to *not* round the cost assignment rates)

2. Using the step-down method, with personnel costs assigned first.

Donaldson Company — Step-Down Assignment Method

	Personal Dept	Finance Dept	Assembly Dept	Finishing Dept	Relevant Total
Support Dept Costs	**$86,000**	**$41,000**			**$127,000**
Employees	6	8	20	15	43
Payroll costs	$15,000	$14,000	$30,000	$27,000	57,000
Personnel rate & assignment	**$2,000.00**	$16,000	$40,000	$30,000	$86,000
Finance Dept costs to allocate		**$57,000**			
Finance rate & assignment		**$1.00**	$30,000	$27,000	$57,000
Total Assignment			**$70,000**	**$57,000**	**$127,000**

Used with permission from Cost Management: Measuring, Monitoring, and Motivating Performance, 3rd Canadian Edition *(Wiley) by Leslie G. Eldenburg, Susan K. Wolcott, Liang-Hsuan Chen, and Gail Cook.*

Summary

Organizations strive for transparency, equity, relevancy, and accountability in the process of assigning costs from one part of the organization to another. These characteristics may be more or less achieved as organizations assign support department costs to production departments. There are three methods available for the assignment of support department costs. The direct method assigns support department costs directly to production departments without consideration of how support departments employ resources to support each other. The step-down method provides some representation of interdepartmental support by effectively cascading cost assignments through a subjectively ordered set of support departments. The reciprocal method uses simultaneous algebraic solutions to objectively assign costs between support departments before ultimately assigning costs to production departments. To the extent that support department costs can be separated into fixed costs and variable costs, a dual rate approach can be used to allocate fixed costs and track variable costs.

Variable and Fixed Overhead Costs

After studying this lesson, you should be able to:

- Demonstrate an understanding of the different methods of determining overhead rates (e.g., plant-wide rates, departmental rates, and individual cost driver rates) (1.D.3.c).

- Describe the benefits and limitations of each of the methods used to determine overhead rates (1.D.3.d).

- Estimate fixed costs using the high–low method and demonstrate an understanding of how regression can be used to estimate fixed costs (1.D.3.q).

- Identify the components of variable overhead expense (1.D.3.e).

- Determine the appropriate allocation base for variable overhead expenses (1.D.3.f).

- Calculate the per-unit variable overhead expense (1.D.3.g).

- Identify the components of fixed overhead expense (1.D.3.h).

- Identify the appropriate allocation base for fixed overhead expense (1.D.3.i).

- Calculate the fixed overhead application rate (1.D.3.j).

- Describe how fixed overhead can be over- or under-applied and how this difference should be accounted for in the cost of goods sold, work-in-process, and finished goods accounts (1.D.3.k).

This lesson provides a "big picture" review of the accounting process for overhead costs in organizations. We'll focus particularly on differences in accounting for variable versus fixed overhead costs, and describe analytical methods for breaking out and estimating variable and fixed costs.

I. Four Stages of Cost Accounting in Organizations

    A. One major objective of cost accounting in organizations is assigning costs to the organization's products (goods and services) in order to plan, control, and evaluate profitability. For many organizations this often means that most or all costs are allocated and tracked to the product based on a four-stage approach that results in a fully costed product which complies with absorption costing standards. This approach is depicted below.

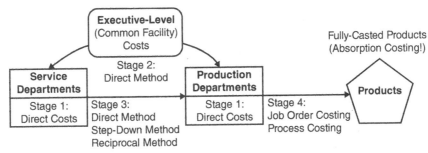

      1. In Stage 1 of this approach, conceptually the easiest stage, the direct costs of all departments are accurately located and reported by the cost accounting system within each business unit.

      2. Stage 2 typically involves a direct allocation of executive-level administrative costs across the whole organization. This allocation is often done with plant-wide allocation rates based on one or two factors such as headcount or floorspace. Allocating these common costs creates some challenges with performance evaluation and decision making in the organization, which we've discussed in a previous lesson.

3. With the executive-level costs allocated across all departments in the organization, Stage 3 is the point where the costs in support departments (including the allocated executive costs) are assigned to production departments using departmental rates based on cost assigment methods such as direct, step-down, or reciprocal.

4. Finally, with all costs "fully loaded" in production departments, costs can be assigned individually to the products sold into the marketplace. Traditional cost systems, such as job order costing or process costing, are used here to build rates and deploy costs depending on the nature of the product and production process.

B. Activity-based costing (ABC) methodology can be employed through the organization to better establish consumption relationships between cost pools and cost objects. At a minimum, organizations will work to separate costs into variable and fixed groups, and use dual-rate cost allocation methods to separately track variable costs and allocate fixed costs.

II. Estimating Variable and Fixed Overhead Costs

A. There are several analytic methods available to support the effort of separating costs into variable and fixed groups. Consider the data set below representing production output and total production costs over eight quarters for a company (Seabreeze, Inc.) that produces windsurfing boards.

Seabreeze, Inc.

Quarter	Boards	Cost
1	108	$101,300
2	128	$168,750
3	185	$189,000
4	245	$200,145
5	311	$276,200
6	352	$255,250
7	389	$305,700
8	428	$376,500

B. One method available to separate these data into variable costs per unit and total fixed costs is the high–low method. The method focuses solely on the highest and lowest activity level (i.e., production volume). These high and low points are highlighted in the data set above.

1. By comparing the change in production costs to the change in activity level at these two points, a variable cost per board can be established as follows.

$$\frac{\$376,500 - \$101,300}{428 \text{ boards} - 108 \text{ boards}} = \frac{\$275,200}{320 \text{ boards}} = \$860 \text{ variable cost per board}$$

2. Isolating the total fixed cost requires using the formula for total cost. Specifically, use the variable cost per board to solve for the unknown fixed cost term in the total cost formula. This solution is demonstrated below using the high point in the data set.

Total cost = (Variable cost per unit × Total units) + Total fixed costs

$376,500 = ($860 × 428 boards) + Total fixed costs

$376,500 = $368,080 + Total fixed costs

$376,500 – $368,080 = Total fixed costs = $8,420

C. Based on the high–low method, Seabreeze costs are separated into $860 variable cost per board and $8,420 total fixed costs. Note that the solution above for total fixed costs can also be achieved using the low point in the data set. However, none of the data points other than the high and low point can be used in this method. This, in fact, is the major limitation of the high–low method. This method is focused strictly on using just two data points and essentially ignores the rest of the data.

D. Compared to the high–low method, regression analysis is a much more comprehensive approach to analyzing cost patterns in order to identify variable and fixed costs. Computer technology is often used to perform regression analysis. Below is a more comprehensive analysis on the Seabreeze data set using the line charting tool and the regression data analysis tool in Excel™.

Seabreeze, Inc.

Quarter	Boards	Cost
1	108	$101,300
2	128	$168,750
3	185	$189,000
4	245	$200,145
5	311	$276,200
6	352	$255,250
7	389	$305,700
8	428	$376,500

Simple Regression Analysis

	Coefficients	Standard Error	t Stat	P-value	Lower 95%	Upper 95%	Lower 80%	Upper 80%
Intercept	$49,701.29	$25,333	1.96	0.10	($12,286)	$111,689	$13,228	$86,175
Boards	$687.43	$87	7.90	0.00	$474	$900	$562	$813

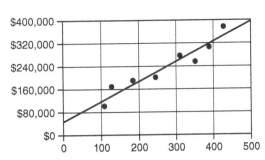

1. This analysis is based on *all of the data* provided in the report involving eight quarters of production. The line chart plots all eight data points and demonstrates a relationship between total production costs and production output.

2. Using Excel™, a line has been fitted as tightly as possible to the data points. The slope of this line (rise over run) represents the variable cost per boat. The intercept point of the line to the y-axis represents the total fixed costs.

3. The simple regression analysis provides a lot of information. First, note the two coefficients in the first column. The intercept coefficient estimates the total fixed costs at $49,701. The coefficient for Boards estimates the variable cost per board at $687. The rest of the regression analysis report describes the fact that there is a lot of potential variance (standard error) surrounding these estimates. Each of these statistics is fully discussed in another section of this learning system.

4. Perhaps the most useful description of variance in the regression analysis estimates of variable and fixed costs is in the "Lower 80%" and "Upper 80%" columns. These are confidence intervals that essentially describe the uncertainty surrounding the cost estimates. Specifically, the regression analysis determines with 80% confidence that actual total fixed costs at Seabreeze are between $13,228 and $86,175 per quarter. Similarly, with 80% (not 100%!) confidence, the actual variable cost per board is expected to be between $562 and $813 per windsurfing board. (Be sure to note that there's a 20% probability that the actual fixed costs and variable costs are outside of these ranges.) At 95% confidence, the estimate range for actual costs is even wider. In order to confidently estimate variable and fixed costs with more precision, Seabreeze needs more data and likely needs to use better cost drivers than boards produced.

III. Determining an Allocation Base for Overhead Costs

A. The first step assigning overhead costs is establishing the cost assignment or allocation rate. Whether the costs are variable or fixed, the basic approach is the same, which is to (1) identify the overhead cost pool and establish a budgeted cost for the upcoming period, (2) identify the basis on which to assign the costs and establish an expected activity level for the upcoming period, and then (3) divide budgeted cost by expected activity to form the cost assignment rate.

B. Because many fixed overhead costs such as taxes, insurance, leases, and utilities follow a yearly cycle of spending intended to support a yearly cycle of production activity, fixed cost rates are usually established at the beginning of the year, used throughout the year, and then evaluated at the end of the year and adjusted if needed for the next year.

C. Fixed overhead cost allocation rates should be based on how the resource is used or how value is provided by the resource, though it is often difficult to establish a clear relationship between fixed cost pools and cost objects. Typical activities used to set fixed cost allocation rates include production output, machine hours, direct labor hours, headcount, revenue dollars, etc. Activity-based costing methods can be used to break down some fixed overhead costs to identify consumption relationships.

D. The relationship between variable overhead cost pools and products or production departments is often much easier to establish with relevant cost drivers that track costs accurately. Nevertheless, cost relationships are never perfect, and both variable and fixed overhead costs are often over-applied or under-applied by some amount as the year concludes. Accounting systems need to be adjusted by these over-/under-applied amounts.

IV. Overhead Cost Flows in the Accounting System

A. In an earlier lesson in this section we discussed the flow of overhead costs in accounting systems. In this lesson, as we're wrapping up our discussion of overhead cost accounting, it's valuable to come back once more to the accounting system and visualize the flow of overhead costs through the system.

B. In the diagram below for a manufacturing company, actual manufacturing overhead (MOH) costs are recorded in the MOH account. Using variable and fixed overhead allocation rates, costs are applied to the work-in-process inventory accounts during the year, subsequently flowing through finished goods inventory accounts and finally ending up in the cost of goods sold account. This flow is depicted by the blue lines.

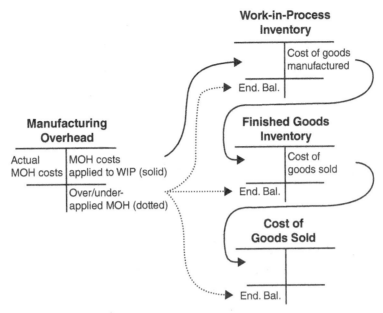

C. At the end of the year, the MOH account is usually under-applied or over-applied by some amount. This amount, representing a cost variance, must be reconciled into the accounting system. There are two approaches to take in this reconciliation.

1. One choice, which is represented by the red lines in the diagram above, is to proportionally adjust the ending balance in all "downstream" accounts. This is the most accurate approach, and is particularly important to use when the under-/over-applied amount is significant.

2. The other choice is to simply adjust the cost variance in the MOH account by flowing the under-/over-applied amount directly to the cost of goods sold account. While often acceptable for external financial reporting, this approach will over-adjust the cost of goods sold account and leave inaccuracies in the ending balance of the inventory accounts.

Practice Question
The following table shows the manufacturing overhead costs of Denon Plastic, Inc. for six months of operations.

Month	Units Produced	Total Manufacturing Overhead Costs
January	1,150	$41,850
February	1,020	$39,380
March	1,250	$43,750
April	1,400	$46,600
May	1,350	$45,650
June	1,280	$44,320

Use the high–low method to estimate the variable cost per unit and total fixed cost per month.

Answer

High and low production volumes are in April and February, respectively. Comparing the change in overhead costs with the change in production volume results in a $19 estimate for variable overhead cost per unit that is computed as follows:

Continues...

$$\frac{\$46,600 - \$39,380}{1,400 \text{ units} - 1,020 \text{ units}} = \frac{\$7,220}{380 \text{ units}} = \$19 \text{ variable cost per unit}$$

Using the $19 variable cost and either the high or low point data, the estimated total monthly fixed costs can be computed. Based on the low point data in February, the monthly fixed costs are computed as follows:

$39,380 = ($19 × 1,020 units) + Total fixed costs

$39,380 = $19,380 + Total fixed costs

$39,380 − $19,380 = Total fixed costs = $20,000

Practice Question

At the beginning of the accounting period, the accountant for ABC Industries estimated that total overhead would be $80,000. Overhead is allocated to jobs on the basis of direct labor cost. Direct labor was budgeted to cost $200,000 this period. Only three jobs were worked on during the year. The following summarizes the direct materials and labor costs for each job.

	Job 1231	Job 1232	Job 1233
Direct materials	$45,000	$70,000	$30,000
Direct labor	$70,000	$90,000	$50,000

Job 1231 was finished and sold, Job 1232 was finished but is waiting to be sold, and Job 1233 is still in process. Actual overhead for the period was $82,000.

1. Calculate the total cost of each job.

2. Calculate the cost of goods sold for ABC Industries.

3. Calculate the amount of over-applied or under-applied overhead that will be prorated to the ending balances in work in process, finished goods, and cost of goods sold.

Answer

1. The overhead allocation rate is $80,000 ÷ $200,000 = $0.40 per dollar of labor cost. The total cost of each job is established as follows:

	Job 1231	Job 1232	Job 1233	Total
Direct materials	$45,000	$70,000	$30,000	$145,000
Direct labor	70,000	90,000	50,000	210,000
Applied overhead	28,000	36,000	20,000	84,000
Total	**$143,000**	**$196,000**	**$100,000**	**$439,000**

2. Cost of goods sold for ABC Industries is represented by Job 1231 = $143,000.

3. The manufacturing overhead is over-applied, computed as follows:

Applied overhead − Actual overhead = $84,000 − $82,000 = $2,000

Continues…

The work-in-process (WIP), finished goods (FG), and cost of goods sold (COGS) accounts will be *decreased* by a proportional share of the over-applied overhead cost based on their ending balances as follows:

	Ending Balances	Weights	× $2,000
WIP: Job 1233	$100,000	22.78%	$ 456
FG: Job 1232	196,000	44.65%	893
COGS: Job 1231	143,000	32.57%	651
Total	**$439,000**	**100.00%**	**$2,000**

Used with permission from Cost Management: Measuring, Monitoring, and Motivating Performance, 3rd Canadian Edition *(Wiley) by Leslie G. Eldenburg, Susan K. Wolcott, Liang-Hsuan Chen, and Gail Cook.*

Summary

Overhead costs are typically assigned throughout organizations in a cascading pattern of allocation rates for fixed costs and tracking rates for variable costs. The end goal is to establish a fully loaded cost on the goods and services being sold. To establish fixed and variable cost assignment rates, overhead costs must first be separated into fixed and variable groups. A number of analytical tools are available to help separate costs into fixed and variable, including the high–low method and regression analysis. Both fixed and variable overhead rates are then set up using budgeted overhead cost pools divided by appropriate cost assignment bases. Using these rates, overhead costs are applied during the year. At the end of the year, there is often an over-applied or under-applied amount that must be reconciled in the accounting system. This amount, representing a cost variance, can be either proportionally adjusted to all inventory accounts and the cost of goods sold account, or simply adjusted directly to the cost of goods sold account.

Topic 4. Supply Chain Management

Inventory Management and Production Systems

After studying this lesson, you should be able to:

- Explain supply chain management (1.D.4.a).
- Explain the concept of outsourcing and identify the benefits and limitations of choosing this option (1.D.4.g).
- Define lean resource management techniques (1.D.4.b).
- Identify and describe the operational benefits of implementing lean resource management techniques (1.D.4.c).
- Define material requirements planning (MRP) (1.D.4.d).
- Identify and describe the operational benefits of implementing a just-in-time (JIT) system (1.D.4.e).
- Identify and describe the operational benefits of enterprise resource planning (ERP) (1.D.4.f).

This lesson introduces (briefly) a number of key management systems and concepts involving effective inventory management. These management models include outsourcing, supply chain management (SCM), enterprise resource planning (ERP), materials requirement planning (MRP), just-in-time (JIT), and Lean.

I. Outsourcing

   A. Business in a fast-moving economy is complex, and organizations need to focus on their strengths to succeed. Outsourcing processes that are not mission critical can be an important part of a company's strategy.

   B. For example, the choice to outsource the weekly payroll processing function to a third-party vendor can provide a lot of benefits. In addition to freeing up internal resources to focus on the core business, other benefits of outsourcing include greater flexibility to expand or contract the outsourced process as needed, better process quality and efficiency assuming the third-party vendor has comparatively more expertise, and risk reduction depending on how much of the risk in the process can be shifted to the vendor based on the contract. Outsourcing to international vendors can also provide significant cost reductions and tax breaks for the organization.

   C. Outsourcing has its limitations as well, particularly new kinds of risks since organizations must now trust a process that they no longer control. For example, sensitive proprietary information may need to be trusted with the vendor. If the vendor goes out of business or has legal problems, those failures affect the organization.

   D. One key aspect of a high-quality outsourcing process is visibility. Risks are increased when the organization is largely blind to how the vendor handles the outsourced process. Shared information systems, regular reporting, and clear performance standards increase visibility in the outsourced process.

II. Supply Chain Management (SCM) and Enterprise Resource Planning (ERP) Systems

   A. Supply chain management (SCM) signifies a core focus on operations management for an organization, and outsourcing is only one aspect of that process. SCM also involves much more than handling logistics in a complex and fast-moving world economy. SCM is an expansive and complex management approach to understanding and establishing partnerships involving suppliers, distributors, other producers, wholesale/retail merchants, and even the consumer across a network of relationships as depicted below.

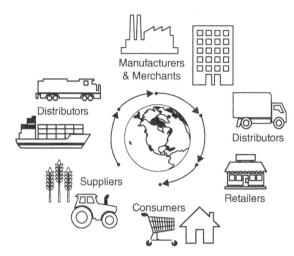

B. Operating in this ecosystem of a worldwide economy requires effective alignment and communication between all entities involved in a supply chain, which may also include governments, communities, and other nonprofit organizations. The concept of "sustainability" in a SCM management model demands a responsible approach to environmental, social, and legal issues in the conduct of business.

C. Planning, controlling, and evaluating operations and processes in a complex supply chain model requires very effective systems and technology. Enterprise resource planning (ERP) systems are evolving to manage core business processes needed to effectively run a supply management solution for the organization. Core business processes include finance, HR, manufacturing, supply chain, services, procurement, and others. The goal of an ERP system is to integrate these core processes into a single system solution in order to provide the organization with the intelligence, visibility, analytics, and efficiency needed to run the business well. ERP systems require significant investments in design, implementation, and maintenance in order to successfully support the organization.

III. Material Requirements Planning (MRP)

A. A subset of ERP is material requirements planning (MRP), which is a planning and control system for inventory, production, and scheduling. Developed in the 1960s, this management model is focused on launching a master production schedule into a series of detailed daily schedules that determine raw material and work-in-process inventory levels based on the scheduling of purchases and release events in order to have components arrive as needed in the production process.

B. MRP systems help manage complex organizations and production processes to reduce inventory and workflow interruptions. Because integrated manufacturing operations tend to be extremely codependent, designing an MRP system that creates effective production schedules can be a mathematically intense solution.

C. MRP views inventory based on independent (outside) demand and dependent (internal) demand. The timing and quantity needed to support the dependent demand for internal inventory (i.e., purchased parts and work-in-process components) is based on identifying timing and quantity demands for finished goods inventory. Key input variables in the design of an MRP solution include expected lead times based on movement, queuing, and production stages, as well as bills of material (BOM) that detail the quantities of the raw materials, assemblies, and components that make up each finished product.

D. MRP systems have been effective at improving production output while decreasing time and costs. However, these systems are described as "push" systems that are based on anticipating inventory needs and then scheduling inventory arrivals to satisfy needs. Unforeseen interruptions in production, which are common in many organizations, can create serious disruptions in MRP schedules that result in inventory spikes and production slowdowns.

IV. Just-in-Time (JIT)

    A. Just-in-time (JIT) systems have similar management objectives as MRP systems, but take a very different approach to reducing inventory and increasing production output. JIT (sometimes known as the Toyota Production System) involves ordering and receiving inventory for production and customer sales only as it is needed to produce goods, and not before.

    B. Like MRP, JIT bases the management solution on the finished goods inventory needed to support sales. However, JIT does not preplan the inventory needs to design a purchase and release schedule. Instead, JIT establishes a carefully coordinated system based on signals (called *kanban*) from downstream processes to initiate the release of inventory from upstream processes. This is a reactive production model that "pulls" inventory (raw materials, work-in-process, finished goods) into the system only when needed to support production and sales.

    C. The initial objective of JIT systems is to reduce all inventory in the organization to extreme low or zero levels. Because inventory serves as a buffer against breakdowns and disruptions in the production system, JIT subsequently demands well-controlled processes with high-quality parts and a very low tolerance for errors. Partnerships in the organization's supply chain must be tight due to a high level of codependent trust needed to work without inventory levels.

    D. Although the initial focus is on reducing inventory, *zero inventory levels is not the true objective of JIT systems*. The true objective, similar to MRP systems, is to improve quality, increase speed, and grow output. However, as described above, JIT takes a very different approach to this objective compared to MRP.

V. Lean Manufacturing

    A. The term *Lean* was coined to describe Toyota's business during the late 1980s by a U.S. research team. The core idea of Lean is to maximize customer value while minimizing waste. Hence, Lean simply means creating more value for customers using fewer resources.

    B. Lean changes the focus of management from optimizing separate technologies, processes, and assets to optimizing the flow of products and services through the entire organization with a perspective that is "horizontal" and targeted on end results rather than "vertical" and focused on individual departments and business units.

    C. The concept of eliminating waste in Lean is much more encompassing than one might initially assume. Not only is Lean focused on eliminating excess inventory and production scrap and spoilage, it is also about reducing time spent waiting in the production process, eliminating unnecessary movement of inventory and people, and reducing processing that isn't desired by the customer.

    D. While Lean was originally designed as a management tool for manufacturing organizations, many of the Lean principles involving horizontal realignment of processes and aggressive commitments to eliminate waste also apply very well to service and merchandising organizations.

Practice Question

Carly Brown owns a small retail shop. Historically, her annual sales have been about $250,000, with 60% of that coming in the November and December holiday season. This year, on a buying trip to southern China, Carly discovered an item that she is certain will be in huge demand. It's a mechanical cricket powered by a photovoltaic cell—the cricket automatically silences at night when it gets dark and then starts chirping in the morning when the sun's rays hit it. Carly can buy the crickets from her supplier for $1.00 each, and she plans to sell them for $9.95 each. Carly is trying to decide how many of the crickets she should order. If she orders 30,000 or more, she can get a volume discount and pay just $0.80 each. However, she does not have room to store that many crickets and will have to rent storage space. Also, Carly does not have very good credit, so she will have to pay 17% annual interest on the money needed for this purchase. Finally, Carly hasn't purchased and received shipping out of southern China before, and isn't sure what the best shipment solution may be.

Continues...

Carly has come to you for advice about whether she should buy this large quantity of crickets or play it safe and order just 10,000. What are the supply chain management opportunities and risks potentially present in this decision for Carly?

Answer

Of course, the bigger the purchase order, the more Carly's holiday season business is at risk, but risk goes both ways. A big order could be very good for Carly's business. The following are some upside opportunities in this transaction for Carly.

- The most obvious opportunity is a safe purchase that arrives on time and in good condition, coupled with strong holiday buying demand.

- The bigger opportunity may be that Carly uses this purchase to establish an ongoing relationship with the Chinese supplier.

- It is likely that the supplier has other good connections in that region, including connections that can help with partial shipments that might couple with shipments other buyers are receiving. This can help Carly with shipping costs and storage concerns if she's able to break down the order to smaller amounts.

- The supplier is likely very interested in the transaction, and may offer credit. Alternatively, the supplier may be able to help Carly identify potential purchase lending relationships in that region that could help with this purchase, as well as with future purchases.

On the downside, Carly needs to manage the exposure she has in a major purchase commitment for the most important part of her business year. Carly needs to consider a number of ways to mitigate risk, including the following risks and possible solutions.

- References are important to use to verify the ability of the supplier to deliver. Can Carly obtain independent verification of the supplier's past performance as a business partner?

- How binding will the agreement or contract be in this deal? What does Carly need to do to confirm that she has the ability to follow up on or enforce the agreement?

- Can the shipping be insured in case of loss or delay? Will the supplier act as an insurer?

- How confident is she in the projection of sales demand? Can she identify a backup market in the event she can't sell the product in her current market?

- More importantly, what can be done to increase visibility as the transaction takes place? The more information that can be shared along each step of this supply chain transaction, the more it will help Carly to manage or reduce many of these risks.

Practice Question

Describe the difference between independent and dependent demand in the management of inventory. [Source: Russell and Taylor, *Operations and Supply Chain Management*, 9 ed.]

Answer

In general, independent demand items are final or finished products that are not dependent upon internal production activity; that is, the demand is usually external and beyond the direct control of the organization. Alternatively, dependent demand is usually a component part or material used to produce a final product. An example of independent demand for a pizza restaurant would be a final product such as a pizza, whereas dependent demand would be any of the ingredients (cheese, tomato sauce, dough, etc.) and perhaps complementary items such as drinks.

Practice Question
What is the difference between a "push" production inventory management system and a "pull" production and inventory system?

Answer

In a push system that uses materials resource planning (MRP), a schedule is prepared in advance for the entire production process, and each department or workstation in that process is expected to purchase and/or complete work-in-process inventory and "push" it forward to the next station at the right time for the next station to receive it. With a pull system such as JIT (just-in-time), a signaling process begins with the most downstream department (likely, the sales department) to request the receipt of inventory. With that signal, each department or operation in turn sends upstream its own signal and the inventory production moves forward on demand.

Summary
Many organizations use outsourcing to shift nonstrategic processes to outside suppliers and third-party vendors in order to increase flexibility and improve quality on the outsourced processes. Outsourcing reduces some risks for organizations, but increases other risks due to interdependency on outside suppliers. In a complex and fast-moving economy, organizations need to be fully engaged in effective partnerships up and down their supply chain. Effective supply chain management (SCM) requires significant investments in shared complex processes and schedules that extend beyond the organization. Enterprise resource planning (ERP) systems can provide critical support to operate successfully in a complex supply chain ecosystem. Materials requirement planning (MRP) systems are an early version of ERP. MRP systems are used to internally manage production processes with careful scheduling of inventory movement. In contrast to using a top-down master schedule MRP solution, just-in-time (JIT) production systems establish a signal at downstream operations that "pulls" production through from upstream operations. The primary mechanism to create the "pull" is the elimination of inventory as a buffer in the operation process. JIT is an example of a broader concept of aligned horizontal processes that is known as Lean Manufacturing, or more simply as "Lean." Along with horizontal realignment of processes, Lean is focused on absolute elimination of any kind of waste in the organization.

The Theory of Constraints

After studying this lesson, you should be able to:

- Demonstrate a general understanding of the Theory of Constraints (1.D.4.h).

- Identify the five steps involved in Theory of Constraints analysis (1.D.4.i).

- Define throughput costing (super-variable costing) and calculate inventory costs using throughput costing (1.D.4.j).

- Define and calculate throughput contribution (1.D.4.k).

The theory of constraints (TOC) is similar to the just-in-time (JIT) management model, but differs on one very important principle, which is the need to focus the production process around the bottleneck operation. Further, in contrast to JIT, TOC does emphasize the use of inventory as a buffer in front of the bottleneck. This lesson provides an overview of TOC and the throughput accounting system that supports TOC.

I. The Theory of Constraints (TOC) Concept

    A. The theory of constraints (TOC) and just-in-time (JIT) management systems are both based on the same basic perspective of inventory, which is that inventory is not really an asset in the production process, but is often a barrier to achieving the organization's main goals. Assuming the organization is a for-profit company, then its main operational goal is to make money, that is, to decrease costs, increase revenues, and increase the speed of production and sales. Inventory gets in the way of all three of these operational objectives.

        1. First, unneeded inventory is a costly investment that doesn't generate an income return. In addition to this economic holding cost, inventory also creates out-of-pocket costs to move, store, and secure. Finally, inventory has a shrinkage cost as it is lost, damaged, or becomes obsolete.

        2. Second, inventory hides problems with quality. If there are quality problems with raw materials purchased or if the production process creates quality problems in work-in-process inventory, those quality problems are hidden within the inventory "pile" until discovered when the inventory eventually moves into the next process. Until discovered, the quality problem continues in the organization, leading to needless rework and scrap. Even worse, quality problems in the hands of customers reduce future revenue.

        3. Third, inventory slows down the production process, leading to delayed or even lost sales. Each point in the production process where inventory exists is effectively a nonproductive queue where the product is simply waiting in line for its turn to move through the next process. More inventory represents a longer line.

    B. TOC and JIT both recognize these three problems with inventory (cost, quality, timeliness). Further, in contrast to management systems that seek to optimize each operation by maximizing its individual production capacity, both TOC and JIT focus on a horizontal process view that emphasizes optimizing each operation as a coordinated system to produce only what is needed.

    C. The core difference between TOC and JIT is that TOC identifies the bottleneck in the organization and uses it as the focus to coordinate the whole system. Hence, for TOC, optimizing the system is a function of optimizing the bottleneck. Put another way, any production lost at the bottleneck operation represents a permanent loss in the entire organization. In contrast, all other operations have by definition more capacity than the bottleneck operation. Hence, not only should non-bottleneck operations be controlled to produce only at the capacity level of the bottleneck, non-bottleneck operations should use their excess capacity to do everything possible to facilitate the bottleneck's ability to *always* operate at its full capacity.

D. The focus of the TOC management model is to optimize the bottleneck's capacity, which then optimizes the organization's actual capacity. The TOC model is described as a *drum-buffer-rope system* (also referenced as a D-B-R system). Understanding the drum-buffer-rope system requires first conceptualizing every non-bottleneck operation as being either an upstream operation (i.e., sending production to the bottleneck) or a downstream operation (i.e., receiving production from the bottleneck and moving it forward).

1. The *drum* in the TOC management model is a scheduling and signaling process for downstream operations. The objective for downstream operations is to move forward work-in-process inventory coming out of the bottleneck operation as quickly as possible and without damaging or wasting the bottleneck's output. The drum indicates to downstream processes the current pace of the bottleneck so that output from the bottleneck is absolutely anticipated and handled as perfectly as possible.

2. The *buffer* represents the one place in the organization where work-in-process inventory is valuable, which is directly in front of the bottleneck operation. The objective of buffer inventory is never to let the bottleneck "starve" (i.e., stand idle waiting for upstream operations to catch up and deliver work-in-process inventory).

3. The *rope* represents constraints placed on upstream operations in order to not overwhelm the bottleneck operation with so much inventory that cost, quality, and timeliness problems start becoming an issue. Upstream operations need to deliver just enough in-process inventory to the bottleneck buffer to ensure that the bottleneck is never idle based on problems upstream in the organization.

II. The Five Steps of TOC

A. Managing the bottleneck to optimize the organization's true capacity to create value is a five-step process.

1. *Step 1. Identify the constraint* (i.e., the bottleneck). Constraints can be either internal within the organization or external to the organization. *Internal process constraints* occur when a given process or operation has insufficient capacity to meet market demand. *Internal policy constraints* happen, for example, when management or employee unions enforce a rule that limits an operation's output or flexibility. *External material constraints* represent a restricted supplier source of materials or other needed resources. *External market constraints* are the bottleneck when there is inadequate market demand to fully utilize the organization's capacity.

2. *Step 2. Determine how to exploit the constraint.* Once the bottleneck is identified, the organization must maximize the moneymaking capacity of the bottleneck. This step is only important when there are multiple possible uses of the bottleneck to create value for the organization. In TOC, value is defined as throughput, which is revenue less "extremely variable costs" such as raw materials (more on throughput later in this lesson). To exploit the constraint means the organization doesn't emphasize the product with the highest profit per product unit. Instead, the organization is most benefited when it emphasizes the product(s) with the highest throughput per bottleneck unit (e.g., per hour on the bottleneck or per pound manufactured by the bottleneck). This is what it means to exploit the constraint for maximum throughput.

3. *Step 3. Subordinate all other operations to the constraint.* Once the organization determines how the constraint is to be exploited to maximize throughput for the organization, all other operations and their capacities become secondary to the needs of the bottleneck. The purpose of the drum-buffer-rope TOC system is to support this step of the TOC process, which is a coordinated effort to keep the constraint operating at full capacity.

4. *Step 4. Elevate the constraint.* It may seem that once the constraint is identified, the next step should be to elevate the constraint. However, it doesn't make sense to immediately increase the capacity of the constraint until the maximum value of the current capacity has been realized. Hence, only after Steps 2 and 3 are accomplished does the organization begin exploring the means to increase the capacity of the constraint. Typical methods of elevating the constraint (i.e., the bottleneck) include adding more shifts or employees to the

bottleneck operation, scheduling overtime, acquiring more equipment for the bottleneck, outsourcing some of the bottleneck work, scheduling longer bottleneck production runs to reduce time spent with setups, etc. What's critical to understand is working to increase the capacity of *non-bottleneck* operations is a waste of the organization's resources and management effort!

5. *Step 5. When the constraint is broken, go back to Step 1*. As the organization works on elevating the capacity of the constraint, eventually the bottleneck will shift to a new constraint, which can be either internal or external to the organization. It should be clear at this point that TOC views the bottleneck not as an impediment but as the means to focus the organization on an optimizing program of continuous improvement in its operations.

III. Throughput Costs and Inventory Valuation

A. Throughput accounting establishes the accounting systems, reports, and performance measures needed to implement TOC in the organization. Throughput accounting does not replace traditional management accounting or financial reporting methods. Throughput accounting supports a very specific and extremely short-term managerial view of an operation—the incremental value from a more effective employment of a constrained resource.

B. Throughput accounting defines and emphasizes three critical accounting terms: throughput, inventory, and operational expense.

1. *Throughput*, often called throughput margin, is computed as revenue minus extremely variable costs, which typically are the cost of raw materials and perhaps other extremely variable costs such as selling commissions. All other costs, including direct and indirect labor, are considered fixed and are not included in the computation of throughput margin. This definition is based on a very short-term view of costs, perhaps as short as a few weeks to a few days.

2. *Inventory*, also called investment in throughput accounting, represents all the money tied up in the production system, including purchased inventory, machines, buildings, and other assets. In throughput accounting, labor and overhead costs are *not* allocated to inventory but are immediately expensed to the income statement.

3. *Operational expense* represents all costs other than raw materials used to convert inventory into throughput. These costs, including direct labor, are treated as fixed expenses and are, as noted above, immediately expensed to the income statement.

C. Note that throughput margin has some similarities to contribution margin. However, throughput accounting takes a much more extreme view of what constitutes a variable cost in its computation of "margin." Again, this choice is based on the timeline view. Contribution margin computations tend to take a three-to-twelve-month perspective in defining variable costs while throughput margin computations are based on an operating perspective that has a much shorter timeline.

IV. Throughput Accounting Demonstration

A. We'll use the example of Excel Sports Company to demonstrate throughput margin analysis. Excel Sports builds sports equipment. One of its plant locations is dedicated to hockey sticks and baseball bats for youth leagues. The plant has three machines that are used in the production of both hockey sticks and baseball bats. The production process, along with selling and cost data, is depicted below.

Excel Sports Company

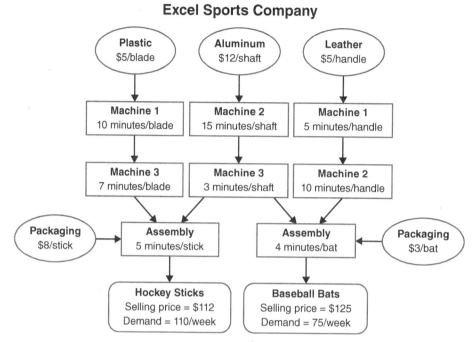

1. The diagram serves as a map of the production process for both the hockey stick and the baseball bat products. Specifically, the shaft in both products is built using an aluminum material. Plastic is used to build the blade that comes together with a shaft to form a hockey stick. Similarly, leather is prepared and wrapped on an aluminum shaft to form a baseball bat. Finally, each product is packaged.

2. Aluminum, plastic, leather, and packaging are the raw materials used to produce hockey sticks and baseball bats. These raw materials are the extremely variable costs used to compute the throughput margin. Hence, the throughput margin on hockey sticks is $87 per unit ($112 – $12 – $5 – $8). And the throughput margin on baseball bats is $105 ($125 – $12 – $5 – $3).

3. Not shown are the operating expenses, which are treated as fixed expenses in throughput accounting. The total of all other costs at Excel Sports (labor, overhead, sales, and administration) equal $10,500 per week. These costs must be covered by throughput margin generated in the operation above before Excel Sports can make an operating profit.

B. Which product is most valuable to Excel Sports? This determination is *not* based on the throughput margin per unit. It is based on the constraint, which still needs to be identified. This is Step 1 in the TOC process. Reviewing the production process for Excel Sports, the constraint probably appears to be Machine 2, but this needs to be determined computationally as follows.

Excel Sports Company: Constraint Analysis

Operation	Minutes Per Stick	(110 sticks sales volume) Total Minutes Needed	Minutes Per Bat	(75 bats sales volume) Total Minutes Needed	(2,400 available minutes) Capacity Use
Machine 1	10	1,100	5	375	61.5%
Machine 2	**15**	**1,650**	**25**	**1,875**	**146.9%**
Machine 3	10	1,100	3	225	55.2%
Assembly	5	550	4	300	35.4%

1. Excel Sports employees work 40 hours a week and are currently operating with a freeze on overtime. This means that each machine can be operated at a maximum of 2,400 minutes per week (40 hours × 60 minutes per hour).

2. Based on the weekly sales volume demand of 110 hockey sticks and 75 baseball bats, the number of minutes required on each machine to satisfy market demand can be computed. For example, Machine 1 spends 10 minutes of production on each hockey stick, which means 1,100 production minutes are needed on Machine 1 to satisfy demand for hockey sticks (10 minutes × 110 sticks). Another 375 minutes are needed on Machine 1 to satisfy demand for baseball bats (5 minutes × 75 bats). This means that Machine 1 will be operating at 61.5% capacity to satisfy market demand for both products ((1,100 minutes + 375 minutes) ÷2,400 minutes).

3. Working through similar computations for the remaining three operations (Machine 2, Machine 3, and Assembly) indicates that Machine 2 is a bottleneck at 146.9% capacity use. There is not enough time available on this machine to satisfy market demand. However, before increasing this constraint, Machine 2 needs to be exploited to its full potential to create throughput margin (Step 2). Using the drum-buffer-rope system, all other operations need to be subordinated to Machine 2 to be sure it is operating at its full capacity (Step 3).

4. Note that if all four operations were able to satisfy market demand, then Excel Sports would have an external constraint, which would be the market demand for units produced. Step 2 (exploiting market demand to its full throughput value) and Step 3 (subordinating all operations to maximize sales to the market) would still apply to a market demand constraint.

C. Step 2 in the TOC process involves determining how to best use (i.e., exploit) the constraint to maximize throughput for the organization. Since Machine 2 can't meet all the market demand for hockey sticks and baseball bats, Excel Sports needs to determine which product to prioritize based on the throughput created for every bottleneck minute used for each product.

1. This priority is determined by dividing the throughput per product by the product's use of the constraint. Hockey sticks, which have a throughput margin of $87 per stick, require 15 minutes on the bottleneck machine (Machine 2). This means that Excel Sports generates $5.80 throughput per minute on Machine 2 when it produces hockey sticks ($87 ÷ 15 minutes).

2. In contrast, Baseball bats with a throughput margin of $105 per bat only generate $4.20 throughput per minute on Machine 2 ($105 ÷ 25 minutes). Therefore, Machine 2 is exploited for its fullest throughput value when it is used to produce all of the hockey sticks needed for market demand, and then uses its remaining capacity to produce baseball bats.

D. Using Machine 2 as the constraint, Excel Sports can compute the result on operating profit of prioritizing hockey sticks rather than baseball bats.

1. First, Excel Sports determines how many bottleneck minutes are required to produce all of the hockey sticks needed to meet market demand for 110 hockey sticks. This number is 1,650 minutes (110 sticks × 15 minutes per stick), leaving 750 minutes on Machine 2 to produce baseball bats (2,400 minutes − 1,650 minutes). Then Excel Sports determines how

many baseball bats it can produce with the remaining capacity on the bottleneck, which is 30 bats (750 minutes ÷ 25 minutes per bat). Producing and selling 110 hockey sticks and 30 baseball bats will provide $2,220 in weekly operating profit for Excel Sports as demonstrated in the throughput accounting report below.

Excel Sports Company: Priority on Hockey Sticks

	110 Hockey Sticks		30 Baseball Bats		Company
	Per stick	Total	Per bat	Total	Total
Revenue	$112.00	$12,320	$125.00	$3,750	$16,070
Raw materials	(25.00)	(2,750)	(20.00)	(600)	(3,350)
Throughput margin	$87.00	$9,570	$105.00	$3,150	$12,720
Operating expense					(10,500)
Operating profit					$2,220

2. In contrast, should Excel Sports choose to prioritize baseball bats in its operation (perhaps because baseball bats have a higher margin per unit), then it will use 1,875 minutes (75 bats × 25 minutes per bat) on the bottleneck (Machine 2) to produce the bats needed to meet market demand. This means 525 minutes (2,400 minutes – 1,875 minutes) remain on Machine 2 to produce 35 hockey sticks (525 minutes ÷ 15 minutes per stick). Producing and selling 35 hockey sticks and 75 baseball bats will provide only $420 in weekly operating profit for Excel Sports as demonstrated in the throughput accounting report below.

Excel Sports Company: Priority on Baseball Bats

	35 Hockey Sticks		75 Baseball Bats		Company
	Per stick	Total	Per bat	Total	Total
Revenue	$112.00	$3,920	$125.00	$9,375	$13,295
Raw materials	(25.00)	(875)	(20.00)	(1,500)	(2,375)
Throughput margin	$87.00	$3,045	$105.00	$7,875	$10,920
Operating expense					(10,500)
Operating profit					$420

E. Excel Sports now knows that optimal weekly operating profit ($2,220) can only be achieved by working Machine 2 to its full capacity to emphasize the production of hockey sticks and using only its remaining capacity to produce baseball bats. Therefore, all other operations need to be subordinated to Machine 2 using the drum-buffer-rope system (Step 3 in the TOC process).

1. Machine 3 and Assembly for baseball bats are downstream from Machine 2. The "drum" at Excel Sports should establish a schedule and signaling system so that these two operations know how to pace themselves to move forward Machine 2 output as quickly as possible.

2. A buffer inventory of aluminum raw materials and Machine 1 work-in-process leather handles should be established to ensure that Machine 2 never has to wait for materials or parts.

3. Aluminum purchasing and Machine 1 represent upstream operations that need to be managed so that they don't overwhelm Machine 2 with unnecessary inventory; otherwise, cost, quality, and timeliness problems will ensue. Just as importantly, these operations need to be sure that there is enough inventory in front of Machine 2 to serve as a buffer against any problems or unanticipated events. Excel Sports managers can then work with these upstream operations to improve processes in order to reduce the buffer inventory over time.

F. Before Excel Sports invests to raise the production capacity of Machine 2 (Step 4 in the TOC process), it must first be sure it can use all of its current capacity to create throughput for the organization. This means that Excel Sports won't elevate the constraint at Machine 2 until it has successfully established a fully subordinated drum-buffer-rope production system around Machine 2.

G. When ready, Excel Sports can start lifting the production capacity of Machine 2 while maintaining an effective drum-buffer-rope system. Eventually, Excel Sports will come to Step 5 in the TOC process when the bottleneck shifts to another constraint (perhaps Machine 1 or perhaps market demand for hockey sticks or baseball bats). Throughout this improvement process, Excel Sports will be steadily increasing its weekly operating profit.

Practice Question

Excel Sports Company has another plant that focuses on manufacturing gloves for hockey and baseball. Hockey gloves are sold as a set of two gloves for $95 and baseball gloves are sold individually for $65. Leather is the only raw material in both products. Hockey glove sets require $40 in leather and baseball gloves require $25 in leather. The gloves are largely built by hand using four employees. The employee names and their production times per product are provided below.

	Hockey Glove Sets	Baseball Gloves
Nicole	10 minutes	10 minutes
Brandon	8 minutes	15 minutes
Jessica	10 minutes	15 minutes
Stuart	16 minutes	20 minutes

Excel Sports maintains a zero overtime policy at this plant. Hence, each employee has the capacity to work 40 hours (2,400 minutes) per week. Currently, the market demand for hockey glove sets is 80 sets per week. Similarly, the demand for baseball gloves is 80 gloves per week.

Use market demand to compute each employee's current production capacity, and identify which employee represents the operation constraint. Determine the optimal product mix to exploit the constrained operation, and then build a throughput accounting report for weekly operating profit based on the optimal production mix. Assume operational expense totals $5,000 each week.

Answer

Excel Sports Company: Constraint Analysis

Time (Minutes)	Minutes Per Hockey Glove Set	(80 sets sales volume) Total Minutes Needed	Minutes Per Baseball Glove	(80 gloves sales volume) Total Minutes Needed	(2,400 available minutes) Capacity Use
Nicole	10	800	10	800	66.7%
Brandon	8	640	15	1,200	76.7%
Jessica	10	800	15	1,200	83.3%
Stuart	**16**	**1,280**	**20**	**1,600**	**120.0%**

Based on market demand and required production times, Stuart is clearly the operation constraint (i.e., the bottleneck).

To exploit the bottleneck, Excel sports should emphasize the production of hockey glove sets based on the analysis below using throughput margin per unit divided by time required on the bottleneck.

Hockey glove sets: ($95 − $40) ÷ 16 minutes = $3.44 (rounded) throughput per bottleneck minute

Baseball gloves: ($65 − $25) ÷ 20 minutes = $2.00 throughput per bottleneck minute

Continues…

Stuart will use 1,280 minutes (16 minutes × 80 sets) to produce 80 sets of hockey gloves, leaving him with 1,120 minutes (2,400 minutes − 1,280 minutes) remaining to produce 56 baseball gloves (1,120 minutes ÷ 20 minutes per glove). A production and sales mix of 80 hockey glove sets and 56 baseball gloves will fully exploit the constraint and maximize throughput for Excel Sports at this production facility. The optimal throughput accounting report is below.

Excel Sports Company: Priority on Hockey Glove Sets

	80 Hockey Glove Sets		56 Baseball Gloves		Company
	Per stick	Total	Per Glove	Total	Total
Revenue	$95.00	$7,600	$65.00	$3,640	$11,240
Raw materials	(40.00)	(3,200)	(25.00)	(1,400)	(4,600)
Throughput margin	$55.00	$4,400	$40.00	$2,240	$6,640
Operating expense					(5,000)
Operating profit					$1,640

Summary

The theory of constraints (TOC) shares a number of management concepts similar to the just-in-time (JIT) management model. However, TOC differs significantly from JIT in how it uses the constraint (also known as the bottleneck) in the organization to manage processes and optimize operating output. TOC operating processes follow a drum-buffer-rope approach that organizes and focuses operations downstream and upstream from the operations. TOC then uses a buffer inventory in front of the bottleneck to ensure its full production capacity. Throughput accounting is used to support TOC management. It defines throughput margin as revenue less extremely variable costs. All other costs are defined as operational expense, are considered to be fixed, and are immediately expensed to the income statement (i.e., not used to value assets on the balance sheet). The five steps in the TOC process are (1) identify the constraint, (2) determine how to exploit the constraint, (3) subordinate all other operations to the constraint, (4) elevate the constraint, and (5) when the constraint is broken, go back to Step 1.

Managing Capacity

After studying this lesson, you should be able to:

- Describe how capacity level affects product costing, capacity management, pricing decisions, and financial statements (1.D.4.l).

- Explain how using practical capacity as the denominator for the fixed cost allocation rate enhances capacity management (1.D.4.m).

- Calculate the financial impact of implementing the above-mentioned methods (1.D.4.n).

Many fixed costs in the organization represent its capacity to produce goods and services at a certain level of scale and efficiency. This lesson focuses on accounting for the costs of capacity, particularly the costs of idle capacity (sometimes called unused or excess capacity).

I. Capacity Costs

    A. As an organization grows in size and expands its set of goods and services, significant investments are made in the organization's capacity to increase the scale and cost efficiency of production output. These investments are made in buildings, equipment, information technology, and support staff.

        1. These kinds of capital investments mean the organization is making long-term commitments to fixed costs. Often, these fixed cost commitments reduce the proportion of variable costs in the organization as the operational leverage in the cost structure increases. (*Note:* The operating leverage concept is explored in a different section of this learning system.)

        2. Many fixed costs can be described as *costs of capacity*. A particular challenge of capacity costs is the organization rarely uses all of its capacity. This is in contrast to variable costs (like materials, direct labor, utilities, etc.), which are by definition fully used as the spending on the costs takes place. The main issue with fixed capacity costs is determining how to handle costs of idle capacity (sometimes called unused or excess capacity) as part of the management process of planning, controlling, and evaluating costs in the organization.

    B. Most of the lessons you've worked through at this point in this section have involved different methods for assigning costs to products. Many of these methods allocate fixed costs to products using the traditional two-step approach to (1) build a cost allocation rate and then (2) use the rate to apply costs to the product.

        1. Methods that allocate fixed costs to products include job order costing, process costing, activity-based costing, joint process costing, and service department costing. These are absorption costing methods that track fixed costs through the inventory accounts on the balance sheet.

        2. Some costing methods, such as contribution margin costing and throughput costing, don't allocate fixed costs to products but instead expense all fixed costs in a lump sum to the income statement.

    C. None of the product systems studied so far in these lessons explicitly considers the issue of how to track and report the fixed costs of idle capacity in the organization's production process. When unused capacity costs are not clearly identified and managed, product costs are unintentionally inflated, leading to pricing decisions that can damage the organization's market share. In addition, without an accounting system that transparently reports capacity costs, it becomes difficult to effectively plan, control, and evaluate excess capacity in the organization.

II. Choosing the Capacity Denominator

    A. Determining the basis used to allocate fixed capacity costs is perhaps the most critical issue in accounting for these costs. Capacity costs are by definition a category of overhead costs. When a predetermined overhead rate is established at the beginning of the year, a measure of output, such as units produced, is used in the denominator for the overhead cost rate. However, the *actual* volume of output is not available to use in the predetermined allocation rate. Since the predetermined rate is allocating budgeted costs, one obvious denominator to use for the predetermined rate seems to be the budgeted volume of output.

    B. Some organizations may choose to use the budgeted volume of output as the denominator for the overhead cost rate but this approach has a problem if the organization uses product costs to establish or evaluate prices in the market place.

        1. If the cost of a particular product or service is high compared to the market price, the organization may either seek to raise the price or choose to reduce promotion on the product compared to other products it offers to the market.

        2. In either case, the likely result is that the expected (budgeted) volume for the following production period will be reduced, *which serves to increase the predetermined cost allocation rate*. Now the organization is in a type of product pricing death spiral. Allocated costs are increased, which results in decisions that further decreases the volume of production and sales, which further increases the cost allocation rate used to assign fixed capacity costs to the product.

    C. A popular alternative to using a budgeted volume of output as the basis for capacity cost allocation rates is to use the practical (sometimes called the normal) capacity level. The advantage of using practical capacity to set the predetermined allocation rate is costs assigned during the year are unaffected by expected increases or decreases in the denominator used to set the allocation rate. Practical (normal) production capacity represents the level of output that can be realistically achieved based on current management policies, as well as based on machine and labor scheduling expectations. Practical capacity also allows for unavoidable productivity losses due to machine breakdowns, production errors, employee vacations, maintenance, and so on. Using practical capacity to set overhead allocation rates has the benefit of minimizing risk due to product price death spiral.

        1. By the end of the year, actual production volume often turns out to be less than practical production capacity. This difference may be due to higher-than-normal production problems in the facility. More often, though, the difference is simply due to the fact that actual production output and sales were less than the practical capacity of the organization. As a result of this difference, fixed capacity costs will be under-applied at the end of the year, and an accounting entry will be made to adjust inventory and cost of goods sold accounts in order to "catch up" the under-applied costs.

        2. Sometimes the actual production volume turns out to be higher than practical production capacity. Improvements in production processes result in better output than expected, or perhaps increased sales put a temporary demand increase on the production facility that was handled using overtime work with equipment and employees. The accounting result will then be over-applied capacity costs that will need to be adjusted out of the ending inventory and cost of goods sold accounts.

        3. Basing cost allocation rates on practical capacity has the advantage of avoiding increases in allocated per-unit costs when expected production and sales volumes decline, potentially leading to death spiral effects in management pricing decisions. However, practical capacity can be a "moving target." For example, as the organization makes changes in production policies or processes, practical capacity levels will shift. Perhaps more importantly, organizations using practical capacity denominators do not have a clear focus on the *potential* capacity imbedded in their capital investment.

D. The third option to use as the basis for capacity cost allocation rates is a theoretical (or ideal) level of capacity. A theoretical capacity level assumes that all policy constraints and scheduling limitations are removed, and it also assumes that no productivity is ever lost due to breakdowns, errors, etc. This is an ideal world that is never actually achieved.

    1. Using a theoretical capacity level has two advantages. First, it never needs adjusting. Second, it can highlight to the organization what is possible in terms of achieving a higher level of practical capacity.

    2. The challenge with using a theoretically ideal capacity level on which to base the cost allocation rate is that a significant amount of capacity costs will not be allocated to products during the year, resulting in capacity costs being significantly under-applied by the end of the year. If pricing decisions are based on product costs, the organization may let prices slip too low to cover the under-applied costs that are adjusted back into the accounting system at the end of the year. However, if organizations are careful not to let prices slip and employ a specific expense account to report idle theoretical capacity costs, then a theoretical capacity approach can be used.

III. Demonstrating Capacity Management

    A. To demonstrate how capacity management can work using different types of cost allocation bases, we'll work with a healthcare provider example. Prescott Imaging Clinic provides x-ray, MRI, and ultrasound imaging services. Each of these three processes requires significant investments in specialized equipment and staff. We'll focus on the MRI (magnetic resonance imaging) service process.

    B. We'll assume for this example that last year Prescott budgeted $501,600 in fixed capacity costs for its MRI process. These capacity costs are completely fixed regardless of how much the MRI facility is used, and include costs such as building lease, equipment depreciation, personnel training, and site security.

    C. Prescott allocates capacity costs on MRI scans, and budgeted for 2,200 scans last year. The Prescott management team has determined practical capacity at 2,400 MRI scans a year based on the ability to perform approximately one scan per hour, working eight hours a day and six days a week while operating 50 weeks of the year (1 scan per hour × 8 hours × 6 days × 50 weeks). Based on last year's budgeted volume, Prescott planned for an idle capacity of 200 scans (2,400 scans − 2,200 scans).

        1. Prescott actually performed 2,150 MRI scans by the end of last year, which is 50 scans less than budgeted (2,200). This variance represents an *unplanned* idle capacity that is due either to problems in the MRI process or to MRI "sales" being less than planned for the year.

        2. Finally, Prescott management recognizes 8,736 scans as an absolutely ideal standard for capacity use of the MRI facilities. This theoretically ideal capacity level is based on using the MRI facility non-stop throughout the year, which means 24 hours a day for seven days a week while operating 52 weeks of the year (8,736 scans = 1 scan per hour × 24 hours × 7 days × 52 weeks). Approaching this theoretical capacity level would require significantly more operating costs in the form of salaries, utilities, supplies, etc., but would not require more capacity costs. Compared to current practical limitations (8 hours a day, six days a week, 50 weeks a year), this theoretical capacity level signals to Prescott management that the *potential* capacity in the MRI facility is significant. This theoretical capacity also indicates that planned idle capacity is much higher than 200 scans (2,400 scans practical capacity − 2,200 scans currently budgeted). Perhaps Prescott management should recognize that planned idle capacity is potentially as high as 6,536 scans (8,736 scans theoretically possible − 2,200 scans currently budgeted).

        3. Comparing these three capacity levels (budgeted, practical, and theoretical) to the actual volume of scans is visually represented below.

Prescott Imaging Clinic

D. Prescott could choose to establish the capacity cost allocation rate based on the budgeted volume, practical capacity, or theoretical capacity. The budgeted cost would be the same at $501,600. However, the predetermined rate would be different based on which denominator is used. Below is a capacity analysis report on the MRI scan facility for Prescott Imaging Clinic.

Prescott Imaging Clinic: Capacity Analysis for MRI Scanner

Actual Volume	MRI Scan Activity	Budgeted Volume	Practical Capacity	Theoretical Capacity
2,150	Volume of scans	2,200	2,400	8,736
	Unplanned idle capacity	50	50	50
	Planned idle capacity	N/A	200	6,536

Budgeted Fixed Costs	MRI Fixed Capacity Costs	Budgeted Volume	Practical Capacity	Theoretical Capacity
$501,600	Allocation rate per scan	$228.00	$209.00	$57.4176
	Allocation fixed costs	$490,200	$449,350	$123,448
	Unplanned idle capacity	$ 11,400	$10,450	$ 2,871
	Planned idle capacity	N/A	$ 41,800	$375,281
	Total costs allocated	$501,600	$501,600	$501,600

1. The top part of the report is focused on the volume and capacity levels of MRI scans, which we've already discussed. The second part of the report is focused on accounting for the capacity costs in the MRI facility. It begins by computing three possible capacity cost allocation rates based on dividing the budgeted fixed capacity costs of $501,600 by the 2,200 scans budgeted volume, the 2,400 scans practical capacity, and the 8,736 scans theoretical capacity.

2. Next, the budgeted capacity costs are allocated using each of these three rates. Using the budgeted allocation rate of $228.00 per scan, most of the fixed costs are allocated to scans during the year ($228 per scan × 2,150 actual scans = $490,200). At the end of the year the $11,400 cost of unplanned idle capacity ($228 per scan × 50 scans) will be adjusted to the cost of sales for the MRI facility. The concern with this approach is that it doesn't report the cost of *planning to not use* 200 scans that are reasonably (practically) available. Instead, these planned idle costs are included with the capacity used during the year, resulting in a higher cost per scan that may lead Prescott management to make poor decisions about pricing or promotion of MRI services.

3. Based on a practical capacity of 2,400 scans, the capacity cost allocation rate is somewhat lower at $209.00 per scan. Prescott's actual performance of 2,150 scans during the year results in an allocation of $449,350 ($209 per scan × 2,150 scans). The unplanned idle capacity costs of $10,450 ($209 per scan × 50 scans) will continue to be adjusted to the cost of sales at the end of the year. The important part of this report is the $41,800 of planned idle capacity costs ($209 per scan × 200 scans) that will *not* be reported as a cost of sales. Instead, this cost will be separately tracked and reported as exactly what it is—the cost of planned idle capacity. This cost should not be included in cost of sales, but reported lower on the income statement so that it can be observed and consciously managed in the future.

4. Basing capacity cost allocations on the practical capacity level has a lot of measurement and management advantages for Prescott. Alternatively, the company could choose to allocate capacity costs using the theoretical capacity level. This allocation would be done using a significantly lower cost allocation rate of $57.4176 per scan ($501,600 ÷ 8,736 scans). The result of this approach would allocate $123,448 to scans during the year ($57.4176 per scan × 2,150 scans), leading to a $2,871 adjustment to cost of sales at the end of the year ($57.4176 × 50 scans). The very large cost of planned (potential) idle capacity at $375,281 ($57.4176 × 6,536 scans) is a strong signal to management that Prescott Imaging Clinic may be sitting on significant untapped capacity resources to do a lot more MRI scans.

Practice Question

Three Hour University (THU) has designed an education product crafted as a three-hour course of online instruction in a live classroom that is taught by a content expert. THU has created courses for a large variety of professional skills and academic topics. Customers sign up for an engaging and effective learning experience that is limited to 30 students in order to facilitate discussion and feedback in the learning community. Capacity costs required for the learning facility are significant and include the annual costs of Internet bandwidth and servers, depreciation on technology hardware, and occupancy cost on the teaching classroom. Total annual capacity costs are budgeted at $1,182,720.

The THU measure for production output is students in session (SiS). Annual practical capacity is established based on an average of 28 students per session and operating the teaching room facility 12 hours a day. At four sessions per day, working six days per week, and operating 50 weeks for the year, this works out to a 33,600 SiS practical capacity level (28 students × 4 sessions × 6 days × 50 weeks). Theoretically, THU has an 87,360 SiS capacity based on ideally filling every session with 30 students, operating worldwide on a 24-hour basis, and working seven days a week for 52 weeks of the year (30 students × 8 sessions × 7 days × 52 weeks). Last year THU set its budgeted SiS volume at 33,000 and actually enrolled and taught 33,200 students in session.

Continues...

Perform a capacity analysis for THU's online classroom and determine costs of unplanned and planned idle capacity.

Answer

The capacity volume analysis is provided below. THU actually did better than expected on its volume of students in session based on budgeting for 33,000 SiS and actually having 33,200 SiS. This production performance results in unplanned excess use of idle capacity that reported below as −200 SiS.

Three Hour University: Capacity Volume Analysis

Actual SiS Volume	MRI Scan Activity	Budgeted Volume	Practical Capacity	Theoretical Capacity
33,200	SiS volume	33,000	33,600	87,360
	Unplanned idle capacity	−200	−200	−200
	Planned idle capacity	N/A	600	54,360

The capacity cost analysis is presented below. Based on the unplanned excess use of idle capacity and depending on which capacity cost allocation rate is used, THU will be adjusting *down* its cost of sales at the end of the year between $7,168 and $2,708. Perhaps the most interesting report in the analysis is the estimation of $735,951 in potential capacity available for THU to use if it chooses to aggressively expand its volume of business.

Three Hour University: Capacity Cost Analysis

Budgeted Fixed Costs	MRI Fixed Capacity Costs	Budgeted Volume	Practical Capacity	Theoretical Capacity
$1,182,720	Allocation rate per Sis	$35.84	$35.20	$13.53846
	Allocation fixed costs	$ 1,189,888	$ 1,168,640	$ 449,477
	Unplanned idle capacity	$ (7,168)	$ (7,040)	$ (2,708)
	Planned idle capacity	N/A	$ 21,120	$ 735,951
	Total costs allocated	$ 1,182,720	$ 1,182,720	$ 1,182,720

Summary
Capacity costs (which are fixed) represent costs the organization has invested in the long run to increase production scale and cost efficiencies. Most organizations allocate these capacity costs to goods and services being produced in the facility. Organizations need to be careful when making pricing and promotion decisions on products that have been allocated these fixed capacity costs. There are three types of denominator bases available to set capacity cost allocation rates: budgeted volume level, practical capacity level, and theoretical capacity level. Most of the problems with allocating capacity costs involve using the budget volume level to set the cost allocation rate. When cost allocation rates are based on the practical capacity level, organizations are able to separately track planned and unplanned idle capacity costs, and avoid pricing death spiral problems that occur when using budgeted volume levels to set allocation rates. Alternatively, some organizations will base cost allocation rates on the theoretical capacity level, which can result in important cost signals regarding potential capacity available for use in the future.

Topic 5. Business Process Improvement

Creating and Capturing Value

After studying this lesson, you should be able to:

- Define value chain analysis (1.D.5.a).

- Identify the steps in value chain analysis (1.D.5.b).

- Explain how value chain analysis is used to better understand a firm's competitive advantage (1.D.5.c).

- Define, identify, and provide examples of a value-added activity and explain how the value-added concept is related to improving performance (1.D.5.d).

- Demonstrate an understanding of process analysis and business process reengineering, and calculate the resulting savings (1.D.5.e).

- Define best practice analysis and discuss how it can be used by an organization to improve performance (1.D.5.f).

- Demonstrate an understanding of benchmarking process performance (1.D.5.g).

- Identify the benefits of benchmarking in creating a competitive advantage (1.D.5.h).

Creating and capturing value is at the core of what every successful organization does. This lesson explores three tools that can be used to guide an organization in the effort to build value for its customers and for itself. These tools are value chain analysis, business process reengineering, and benchmarking.

I. Value Chain Analysis

    A. Strategy and business success can largely be boiled down to two fundamental challenges: *creating* value and then *capturing* value.

        1. First, organizations need to identify what is valued in the marketplace in terms of what customers or potential customers are willing to pay (i.e., give value) to receive. Michael Porter describes three basic strategic approaches that organizations can take to create value that customers are willing to pay to receive. In another lesson in this series we've studied the specifics of these three strategy models. To summarize, one approach is to provide a low-cost product across the market that satisfies the customers' needs. Another approach is to provide a differentiated (i.e., innovative) product across the market that customers can't obtain otherwise. The third approach is to target a subset of the market (i.e., a niche market) that is being underserved and provide either a low-cost or differentiated product into that niche market.

        2. A strategy that focuses solely on *creating* value that the market wants or needs is not enough to be successful. The organization must also *capture* and retain some of the value created. In other words, the price on the product must be high enough and the cost to provide the product must be low enough for the organization to sustain profits.

    B. Value chain analysis is an approach used by an organization to evaluate its internal activities and identify how each is involved in creating and capturing value in the marketplace. The classic value chain analysis view is illustrated below.

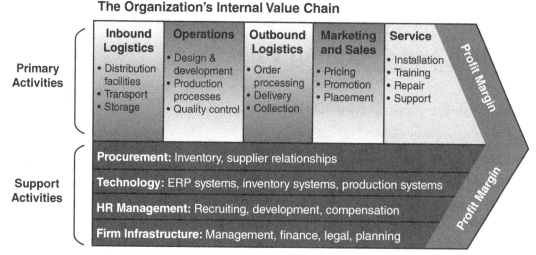

The Organization's Internal Value Chain

1. The organization's primary activities are focused on the logistics of receiving inputs, converting inputs into goods and services, delivering the finished product to customers, marketing the product, and supporting the product with service after the sale. If organization strategy is focused on low-cost products, efficiencies in the primary activities are crucial. Alternatively, the primary activities can be focused on a product differentiation strategy.

2. Equally important are the organization's activities that form the core support functions. Primary activities add value directly to the production process, but a differentiated advantage derives mainly from technological improvements or innovations in business models or processes. Therefore, such support activities as information systems, human resource processes, or general management can be the most important source of the organization's differentiation strategy.

C. Value chain analysis involves a careful review of all primary and support activities to determine how each activity relates to the organization's strategy and how it contributes to the organization's profit margin. Activities that are identified as central to the organization's strategy (whether it be a low cost, differentiation, or niche strategy) become the focus of the organization's investment and improvement efforts. Activities that are secondary to the organization's strategy are candidates for outsourcing to a third-party vendor.

II. Benchmarking

A. Benchmarking against the best practices of competitors and noncompetitors both inside and outside of the industry can be a valuable aspect of process analysis and improvement. Benchmarking is not simply about gathering data or insight about the business practices of other organizations. Like all process improvement programs, successful benchmarking is a dedicated management method that follows specific steps.

B. The steps involved in a benchmarking process are depicted below.

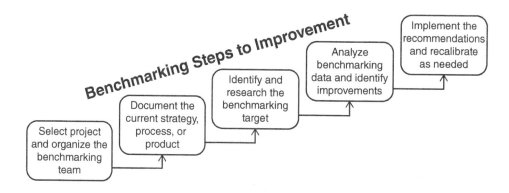

1. The first step is to identify and prioritize the areas of the organization to be improved through benchmarking, and then establish the benchmarking team who will perform the research and design the implementation.

2. Before investigating the benchmarking target, perform a thorough review and document the current organization practice to be improved using benchmarking data. This is the first input to establishing what is sometimes called a "gap analysis."

3. The team is now ready to identify possible organizations (targets) that currently demonstrate business practices that should be studied. Determine the data gathering method(s) to be used and collect benchmark performance data.

4. Analyze the benchmark data in comparison to the organization's current business practice and establish the performance gap to be addressed using the data. Identify causes for the gap and determine future attainable performance.

5. Finally, with management support, establish the new business practice and implement goals and incentives. Track progress and evaluate when the benchmark data and standards for performance should be recalibrated to encourage continual improvement.

C. Benchmarking targets do not have to be competitors or even organizations within the same industry. Innovative solutions for breakthrough performance are sometimes found by identifying benchmarking targets in completely different industries or geographies. Alternatively, benchmarking targets do not have to be found in external organizations. Management should look within their own company to identify quality business practices that can be studied and scaled across the entire organization.

D. Organizations can benchmark both processes and products for improvement. Generally, there are three possible aspects for improvement: costs, quality, and timeliness. The need to improve any or all of these three aspects of processes and products can inspire a benchmarking study.

E. Benchmarking studies are not only used to improve operations, but can also serve to strengthen the strategic focus of the organization. Studying the strategy design and implementation of other organizations can help directors and officers guide the organization forward to identify and build core competencies, develop new business lines, enter new markets, and establish better risk management systems.

III. Business Process Reengineering

A. Business process reengineering (BPR) represents a total review and reconstruction of the organization's core processes in order to better support the organization's strategy and to reduce costs. This approach goes way beyond simply fine-tuning operations and adjusting teams and processes. The focus in BPR is to obliterate unproductive management layers, wipe out redundancies, and radically remodel processes. It is not a management solution for the faint of heart.

B. BPR starts with a high-level assessment of the organization's mission, strategic goals, and customer needs. Fundamental questions to ask in the assessment might include: "Does our mission need to be redefined?" "Are our strategic goals aligned with our mission?" "Who are our customers?" "How do we add value?"

C. With a clear focus on mission, strategy, customers, and value, the organization goes forward to evaluate every process, activity, and employee role in the organization using the BPR cycle (depicted below).

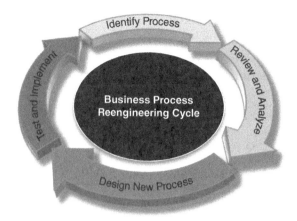

1. A current process is identified for evaluation and restructuring.

2. The process is carefully reviewed and analyzed for alignment with the organization's strategy and for efficiency.

3. The process is then updated, redesigned, or entirely replaced.

4. Testing and implementation of the updated or new process provides feedback to the BRP cycle and helps identify the next process to be reengineered.

D. Because the evaluation and restructuring process is very costly, it must be emphasized that real BPR has risks. The pain in the organization can be profound and everyone needs to be prepared for change. BPR is not always successful. Some organizations don't survive the experience. But there are many success stories of organizations transformed as a result of this intense approach to process analysis and improvement.

Practice Question

Health Systems International (HSI) provides and supports data management systems for family care physicians, dental professionals, and eye care specialists. HSI has been in business for more than 20 years and has a strong market reputation. Lately, though, the company has been struggling with increasing costs and is concerned about a growing trend of complaints from key client groups. You have been approached as a consultant to help HSI focus on improving its processes to be sure that it can continue to provide a valued data solution for its clients while remaining profitable.

Provide a brief overview of how HSI can use value chain analysis to assess processes in order to continue creating and capturing value in its competitive space. Then describe how benchmarking and business process reengineering (BPR) might be applied to improve processes at HSI.

Answer

If it hasn't already, HSI needs to first clearly determine its strategic approach to creating and capturing value. Does it provide a low-cost data management system for its clients, or has HSI innovated a data management solution that is differentiated from alternatives in the marketplace? HSI is providing data management systems to three different types of healthcare providers. Is this a niche market approach?

Next HSI should identify the primary activities that have been established to develop and design data management systems, deliver and install each system, market its data management systems, and provide post-sale support to its clients. HSI also needs to recognize the core activities in place to support the primary activities. These support activities should largely focus around procurement of resources needed for its business, technology used to support the business, the HR management

Continues…

approach that creates the employee team, and the overall infrastructure of leadership, planning, finance, legal, etc. Each of these primary and support activities is then carefully evaluated to determine its relationship to the HSI strategy. Investments are made to further develop and strengthen activities deemed crucial to the strategy. Secondary activities are evaluated to ascertain how to streamline them for efficiency and identify which secondary activities to outsource.

HSI can use benchmarking studies to target other successful organizations and learn what HSI can do to improve specific activities in order to create more value for customers or capture more value through efficiencies. If HSI determines that dramatic change is required across the whole organization in order to survive and be successful in the future, BPR could be considered as the means to aggressively review and restructure every activity and employee role in the organization. However, HSI should not enter into a BPR approach without carefully considering the time and cost required in this process.

Summary

Creating and capturing value is at the core of a successful strategy and business practice. An organization working to build value for its customers and for itself can start with a value chain analysis, which involves a careful review of primary and support activities to identify which are essential to its value creation and capture strategy. Investments are then made to focus and strengthen strategically essential activities. Benchmarking is a valuable tool in the effort to improve business practices. Benchmarking studies can target a wide variety of organizations available for research. Using insights from the benchmarking study, management performs a gap analysis of current business practices, and then designs and implements new processes. If managers determine that extensive change across the entire organization may be needed, business process reengineering (BPR) is a powerful tool used to guide organizations through what can be a painful rebuilding of most or all processes.

Managing Quality

After studying this lesson, you should be able to:

- Apply activity-based management principles to recommend process performance improvements (1.D.5.i).

- Explain the relationship among continuous improvement techniques, activity-based management, and quality performance (1.D.5.j).

- Explain the concept of continuous improvement and how it relates to implementing ideal standards and quality improvements (1.D.5.k).

- Describe and identify the components of the costs of quality, commonly referred to as prevention costs, appraisal costs, internal failure costs, and external failure costs (1.D.5.l).

- Calculate the financial impact of implementing the above-mentioned processes (1.D.5.m).

- Identify and discuss ways to make accounting operations more efficient, including process walk-throughs, process training, identification of waste and overcapacity, identifying the root cause of errors, reducing the accounting close cycle (fast close), and shared services (1.D.5.n).

This lesson focuses on managing the quality of operations in the organization. Activity-based management (ABM), a framework for managing activities, can be used as a structured template for tracking total quality management data. *Kaizen* is a total quality management (TQM) concept that emphasizes making small improvements continuously throughout the organization. Costs of quality (COQ) represent four categories of quality costs in the organization that need to be intelligently balanced against each other. Accounting, as its own operation in the organization, can and should benefit from TQM and other management concepts.

I. Activity-Based Management (ABM)

    A. In an earlier lesson you learned about activity-based costing (ABC). The ABC method centers on using activities to assign costs. Specifically, ABC begins by identifying activities that consume resources and assigning resource costs to those activities based on resource cost rates. Then ABC uses activity rates to assign activity cost pools to cost objects such as products, services, customers, etc.

    B. It requires significant effort to identify core activities for the ABC cost assignment process. The ABC model describes costs assigned to activities as "resources" in order to emphasize the view that costs should be invested in activities in order to add value to the organization. Activity-based management (ABM) is an expansion of the ABC model that emphasizes the view that organizations should be oriented around value-added activities and should focus the management process on these activities. A combined ABC/ABM model is presented below.

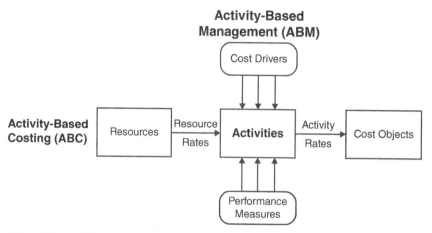

C. The ABC model is depicted above as a *horizontal* relationship with activities in the organization. Activities function as a vehicle to accurately carry costs spent on resources in the organization and assign those costs to the organization's cost objects.

D. The ABM model above is demonstrated to have a *vertical* relationship with activities. ABM goes beyond using activities as a cost assignment vehicle by establishing activities as the focus of management. ABM is focused on reporting cost drivers and performance measures to help manage each activity.

    1. Once an activity is defined for activity-based costing purposes, then the costs consumed by that activity can be tracked and reported to support the management process of planning, controlling, and evaluating. Management accountants will identify cost drivers that cause the activity to consume more or fewer resources.

    2. But costs are not the only performance factor in the organization. Remember from previous lessons that management of operations emphasizes a balanced view of costs, quality, and timeliness. Hence, other performance measures related to quality and timeliness are also identified for each activity, and these non–cost performance measures (illustrated above with the red box) form the rest of the vertical view on managing activities.

E. To demonstrate, below is an ABC/ABM model for the raw materials purchasing activity at SeatJoy, Inc., a furniture manufacturing company.

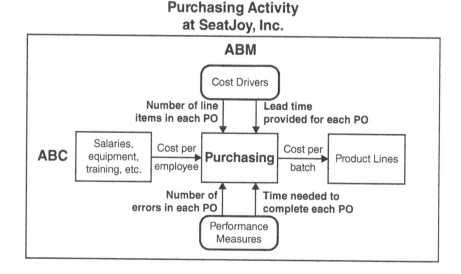

1. The horizontal ABC view shows that the cost rate used to assign SeatJoy's resources to the purchasing activity is cost per employee involved in the purchasing activity. Purchasing is viewed as a batch-level activity since every time SeatJoy sets up for a production run, a number of purchase orders are initiated to obtain raw materials. Hence, this activity cost is assigned to product lines using a per-batch rate.

2. The vertical ABM view captures the main factors that drive costs up or down on this activity. The management accountants at SeatJoy have determined that the primary cost drivers are the complexity of the purchase order (PO), which is defined as the number of line items in the PO, and the lead time provided to initiate the PO. More line items and shorter lead times drive up the cost of purchase orders at SeatJoy.

3. The vertical ABM view is also focused on the performance of the purchasing activity. Quality in this activity is based on the number of errors that are identified in a purchase event that can be traced back to a PO. Further, SeatJoy values the ability of the purchasing group to put together a PO quickly, and so the company tracks the amount of time from the PO request to the completion of the PO.

F. It is important to understand that the ABM model is not itself a management concept. ABM is an integrated framework that management can use to establish and maintain a reporting structure to support the management objectives of the organization. For example, if total quality management is the organization's objective, then management will identify activities that represent a quality-focused organization, and track costs and performance measures on those activities (as well as use those activities to assign costs to cost objects). Since the remainder of this lesson is focused on quality management, be sure to envision how ABM might be used to capture and report on the quality management objectives we discuss.

II. Continuous Improvement (Kaizen)

A. The management process to increase quality in an organization is often described using a single Japanese word, *kaizen*, which means "improvement" or "good improvement." In the context of total quality management (TQM), the kaizen concept is more typically thought of as "continuous improvement that takes place in a constant series of small steps." This continual process of improvement by small steps is in contrast to more radical business process improvement concepts such as business process reengineering (BPR), which is an approach that seeks for large, dramatic, and often painful transformations in the organization.

B. Because kaizen is focused on taking small steps doesn't mean that kaizen management has small goals. In fact, the typical practice of total quality management using kaizen is based on ideal standards of performance.

1. For example, in an earlier lesson on managing capacity we discussed practical (normal) capacity measures versus theoretical (ideal) capacity measures to tracking costs of idle capacity. It may have seemed extreme to use the expectation of absolutely perfect utilization of the organization's capacity as a basis for tracking costs. Using a theoretical capacity base typically results in a very large number of fixed costs being tracked as an unacceptable cost of idle capacity rather than as an acceptable cost of production.

2. Kaizen would establish the basis for capacity using a theoretically ideal standard. To measure variances on cost inputs, it would use an ideal cost standard with zero expectation of error, downtime, scrap, etc. To track performance on quality or timeliness, the goal would be absolutely perfect quality and absolutely no time lost on any function that wasn't necessary to add value to the process.

C. The key kaizen concept in using ideal standards is to *not* focus on measuring the variance (i.e., the distance) from the standard as the performance measure. Rather, the kaizen performance measure is based on *tracking progress toward the ideal standard*. The management objective is to keep progressing forward in a focused and disciplined manner. The expectation in kaizen is continual small improvements targeting ideal standards that will eventually yield large results in terms of overall improvement in productivity.

D. The kaizen activity cycle often follows a Plan → Do → Check → Act approach (PDCA).

   1. The Plan phase of the PDCA cycle is about assessing a current or proposed process and establishing a plan to improve it.

   2. In the Do phase, small changes are put in place and data are gathered that will be used to determine if the changes made are effective and results are as expected.

   3. The Check phase is where the evaluation on the research data takes place, decisions regarding adjustments are made, and additional "doing" and data gathering takes place until it becomes clear what improvements will best provide the desired results.

   4. Finally, the Act phase is effectively the go/no go decision in the kaizen cycle. Assuming the organization determines the process can and should be improved, then the new process is rolled out, new performance standards are set, and the organization "acts" on the change.

III. Costs of Quality

   A. TQM is an investment of management effort, and it is often evaluated in terms of costs versus benefits. Costs are invested to increase quality with the anticipation that the benefits will offset the costs. Managers will then target an optimal level of investment in costs. Before talking about optimizing the costs of quality, we must first define the four types of costs of quality.

   1. *Prevention costs* are costs incurred to ensure that tasks are performed correctly the first time and that the product or service meets customer requirements. Examples of prevention costs include costs of process or product design, employee training, education of suppliers, preventive maintenance, and quality improvement meetings and projects.

   2. *Appraisal costs* represent what the organization spends on inspection, testing, and sampling of raw materials, work in process, and finished goods and services. These costs include overhead expenses for quality inspectors, costs to adjust measuring and test equipment, and costs of associated supplies and materials.

   3. *Internal failure costs* are all the scrap and rework costs that are incurred to dispose of or fix defective products before they are shipped to the customer. Costs of downtime or reduced yield due to production of defective parts or services are also included in this cost category.

   4. Internal failure costs can be very expensive for the organization, but *external failure costs* are generally the highest costs of a low-quality process. Some examples of external failure costs are the costs of processing complaints, customer returns, warranty claims, product recalls, field service, and product liability. The most serious type of external failure cost likely results from unhappy customers. Because bad news travels fast, defects found by a customer can lead to a serious decline in market share and future profits. The significant challenge of measuring external failure costs is estimating the *future cost* of a bad reputation due to *quality problems today*. Too often these reputation costs are either undermeasured or not measured at all!

B. Investments in prevention costs and appraisal costs should reduce quality problems that lead to internal and external failure costs. The goal in measuring and managing costs of quality is to determine the optimal level of quality performance where the total costs of quality are minimized. A Cost of Quality (COQ) chart that represents trade-off and optimization of quality costs is presented below.

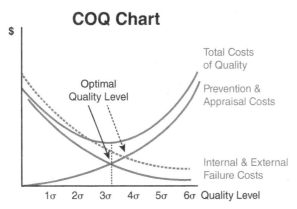

COQ Chart

1. In the chart above, the green line represents the total costs invested in prevention and appraisal activities. The increasing slope of this line indicates that increasing the level of quality requires an increasingly higher investment in these costs. In mathematical terms, these costs have an exponential and positive relationship with the level of quality.

2. The solid red line represents the current measure of internal and external failure costs for the organization. Initial improvements in quality result in significant reductions of internal and external failure of the product or service, but further quality improvements demonstrate smaller reductions in failure costs. In other words, the mathematical slope of this line represents cost savings that have an exponential and negative relationship with the level of quality.

3. The blue line represents the sum of the other two lines and is the total cost of quality for the organization. The lowest point of this line, which is also the point where the other two lines intersect, is the optimal level of quality that minimizes total quality costs.

C. In the practice of total quality management, the level of quality is often described in terms of variance from perfect quality. In statistical terms, variance is described using the Greek term *sigma*, which is represented by the Greek symbol σ. A one-sigma (1σ) quality level means that 69% of the output can be expected to have quality problems (a 31% yield rate on quality). That's a terrible result for any organization. As the level of process quality improves, the outcome gets exponentially better. A 2σ quality level reverses the results with 31% of the output expected to have quality problems, or in other words, a 69% yield rate on quality. A 3σ quality level, which is about where the organization in the chart above is performing, means only 6.7% output will have quality problems (93.3% quality yield).

D. You probably wouldn't want to do business with a 3σ company that expects nearly 7% of its results to have quality problems, although you've likely experienced these kinds or organizations! Yet the chart above suggests to this organization that 3σ is its optimal level of quality. However, do you remember the point made earlier regarding external failure costs and the challenge organizations have to accurately estimate these kinds of costs? Most organizations that struggle to invest in quality are not fully estimating the cost of poor quality experienced by their customers (an external failure cost).

1. There is a dotted red line in the chart above. This dotted red line represents failure costs that include a more complete measure of the costs of reputation lost and its future effects on sales and profits. Including the full value of reputation costs in this COQ chart shifts the failure costs line to the right, which shifts the optimal cost of quality to be much closer to a 4σ quality level (imagine a new blue line in the chart that represents the new total cost of quality). A 4σ quality level has just 0.62% output with quality problems (a 99.38% quality yield).

2. You may have heard of a quality standard referred to as "six-sigma" (6σ) performance. Organizations that set a standard to perform at six-sigma quality expect to have a 99.9997% quality yield rate on their products or services. That's the kind of organization you want to do business with!

IV. Quality and Accounting

A. All the lessons in this section have focused on using accounting systems and accounting information to help management improve the operations of the organization. As we wrap up this last lesson, let's consider that TQM and other management concepts can be applied to improving the accounting operation.

B. Remember that the objective of improving processes is to decrease costs while increasing quality and timeliness. Along with managing all other processes in the organization, managers should also expect to improve the cost, quality, and time performance of accounting operations.

C. The "lean" concept we studied in an earlier lesson emphasizes the absolute elimination of waste in the process; in other words, to eliminate anything that does not add value for the customer. The customers of accounting are managers and decision makers who use the accounting information. Applying the lean concept to accounting includes eliminating reports that have little management use, eliminating the time a report waits for another accounting operation before it's ready for managers, and eliminating the effort and process required for managers to request or receive accounting reports (typically by facilitating managers with direct access to accounting data). Eliminating waste in accounting can significantly reduce the cost and increase the value of accounting processes.

D. A performance measure on timeliness that is often applied to accounting is the speed of the accounting cycle at the end of a reporting period. The issue is how fast the accounting team is able to close out the books at the end of each period and provide a report on operations. The "fast close" performance measure can often experience dramatic improvement with clear investments In training of accounting staff based on coordinated walkthroughs of the close process.

E. One performance measure of quality in accounting is focused on reducing errors in reports. Applying the kaizen management process to accounting involves setting an ideal standard of zero errors. Continual improvements in accounting processes must then become a constant and well-structured process. One specific tool of kaizen and quality management involves identifying the root cause of errors using a series of five *why* questions. Far too often when an error is discovered in accounting (or any other process in the organization), the first answer to the question "Why did this accounting error happen?" is not actually the root cause of the error. Root cause analysis involves asking a penetrating series of *why* questions until the root (real) cause of the error is identified and corrected.

F. Another performance measure of quality in accounting, and for most organizations the most important quality, is relevance. Accounting must have high relevance in the management process of planning, controlling, and evaluating operations. When it doesn't have relevance, when accounting is not a key input to decisions involving operations and strategy, then accountants need to carefully consider many of the lessons in this section and how these lessons should apply to themselves and their own operations. Accounting is a core activity. When it's done well, the organization is greatly strengthened.

Practice Question

Alandra García is preparing to open her own CPA firm. Alandra is a smart businessperson and wants to maximize her profits. She is working on designing the structure of her firm's approach to audit quality and has analyzed the costs of quality related to operating a CPA firm. She has developed the following analysis:

- *Prevention costs:* The best way to ensure the quality of the audit is to increase the quality of the staff hired and increase the time that the staff spends on each audit. Alandra knows that hiring higher-quality staff will cost more money.

- *Appraisal costs:* Alandra plans to inspect the work of staff auditors by having audit managers review the work. The average salary rate for an audit manager (including all fringe benefits) is $50 per hour.

- *Internal failure costs:* Sometimes the audit team will do such a poor job that an audit partner will have to personally supervise the completion of the audit work. The average salary rate for an audit partner is $100 per hour.

- *External failure costs:* If investors or creditors rely on financial statements that later prove to be false, the audit firm that approved those financial statements will probably be sued. The expected frequency and cost of being sued is different depending on the quality of the audit. Note that Alandra expects a premium quality audit practice will engage better-established clients. The downside is that, in the event of an audit failure, these kinds of clients tend to sue for larger amounts.

Alandra estimates the following costs of quality related to the quality level of audits performed in the size of CPA firm that she is planning to build:

	Low Quality	Average Quality	Premium Quality
Prevention costs:			
Staff hours spent on audit	20 hours	40 hours	100 hours
Staff salary rate	$20/hour	$25/hour	$40/hour
Appraisal costs:			
Manager review of audit work	3 hours	8 hours	20 hours
Internal failure costs:			
Frequency of bad audits	1 in 3 audits	1 in 10 audits	1 in 50 audits
Partner time to fix a bad audit	10 hours	5 hours	4 hours
External failure costs:			
Frequency of a lawsuit	1 in 5 audits	1 in 40 audits	1 in 100 audits
Expected loss on each lawsuit	$200,000	$200,000	$1,000,000

Alandra expects that the audit fee will be the same regardless of the inherent quality of the audit. Hence, in order to maximize firm profit, compute the optimal costs of quality level. Do Alandra's assumptions regarding expected quality costs appear to be appropriate?

Continues…

Answer

Analysis of Expected Costs of Audit Quality

	Low Quality	Average Quality	Premium Quality
Prevention costs:			
Staff hours spent on audit	20 hours	40 hours	100 hours
Staff salary rate per hour	× $20	× $25	× $40
Total prevention costs	**$400**	**$1,000**	**$4,000**
Appraisal costs:			
Manager review of audit work	3 hours	8 hours	20 hours
Manager salary rate per hour	× $50	× $50	× $50
Total appraisal costs	**$150**	**$400**	**$1,000**
Internal failure costs:			
Frequency of a bad audit	1 in 3 audits	1 in 10 audits	1 in 50 audits
Partner time to fix a bad audit	10 hours	5 hours	4 hours
Partner salary rate per hour	× $100	× $100	× $100
Total internal failure costs	**$333**	**$50**	**$8**
External failure costs:			
Frequency of a lawsuit	1 in 5 audits	1 in 40 audits	1 in 100 audits
Expected lawsuit cost	× $200,000	× $200,000	× $1,000,000
Total external failure costs	**$40,000**	**$5,000**	**$10,000**
Total Costs of Quality	**$40,883**	**$6,450**	**$15,008**

The analysis indicates that the quality level is optimal for Alandra's new firm based on performing average-quality audits. However, Alandra assumes that revenue from an audit is the same no matter the quality of her firm's audit work. In reality, a higher-quality firm can probably charge more for an audit. In addition, a higher-quality firm may find it easier to attract clients. If true, then both of these factors should be considered as additional external failure costs for a low-quality or average-quality firm. As a result, Alandra may be missing some external failure costs, which could lead her to conclude that premium-quality audits represent the most optimal costs of quality.

Summary
Activity-based management (ABM) is an extension of activity-based costing (ABC). ABM is a system of management for each of the activities identified and used in the ABC process that involves establishing cost drivers for each activity along with performance measures on the quality and timeliness of the activity. The principle of kaizen in total quality management describes a focus on continuous improvement throughout the organization based on ongoing small steps using a Plan→Do→Check→Act cycle of improvement. Costs related to quality in the organization can be categorized as prevention costs, appraisal costs, internal failure costs, and external failure costs. Increased investments in prevention and appraisal costs are offset by decreases in internal and external failure costs. Managers seek for an optimal level of combined costs of quality. Finally, quality management tools can and should be applied to accounting operations. As accountants eliminate waste in the accounting process while increasing the quality and speed of their accounting reports, they contribute significantly to the performance of management throughout the organization.

Section D Review Questions

aq.proc.c.009_0820

1. Which of the following is true regarding normal and abnormal spoilage?

   A. Normal spoilage is an accepted cost of production while abnormal spoilage represents an unacceptable loss in the production process.
   B. The costs of abnormal spoilage are transferred forward to the finished goods inventory account or to the next department's work-in-process inventory account.
   C. Spoilage in the production process is completely avoidable for many manufacturing organizations if managers work hard to eliminate the costs of spoilage.
   D. The costs of normal and abnormal spoilage are transferred into a loss account that is immediately recognized on the income statement.

aq.concept.cd.002_0820

2. The Ramirez Company makes leather jackets that sell for $175 each. The total cost in May of manufacturing 1,000 jackets is $114,860. The variable cost for each jacket is $57. What are Ramirez's fixed costs for the month?

   A. $57,000
   B. $114,860
   C. $60,140
   D. $57,860

aq.v.fc.006_0820

3. A manufacturer of wooden furniture has identified two models for analysis under activity-based costing. Each model is associated with two activity pools: Cutting and Assembly. Model A requires 25 cuts and 5 direct labor hours per unit, while Model B requires 30 cuts and 7.5 direct labor hours per unit. Total factory overhead of $375,000 is split such that 70% is assigned to the Cutting cost pool and 30% is assigned to the Assembly cost pool. The cost driver for Cutting is the number of cuts, and the cost driver for Assembly is direct labor hours. Furthermore, $125,000 of product design overhead is allocated to these two product lines and split equally between them. What is the factory overhead cost per driver unit for Cutting if the company manufactures 25,000 pieces of furniture, 60% of which are Model A?

   A. $0.875 per cut
   B. $0.1667 per cut
   C. $0.389 per cut
   D. $0.70 per cut

aq.v.fc.010_0820

4. Keystone Company applies overhead on the basis of machine hours, and reported the following data.

Estimated annual overhead cost	$2,250,000
Actual annual overhead cost	$2,227,500
Estimated machine hours	300,000
Actual machine hours	295,000

Compute the amount of overhead that is under-applied or over-applied for the period.

   A. $22,500 under-applied
   B. $15,000 over-applied
   C. $15,000 under-applied
   D. $22,500 over-applied

aq.man.cap.006_1809

5. Which of the following correctly describes theoretical capacity?

   A. Theoretical capacity is the level of output that the organization actually achieves in a period.
   B. Theoretical capacity is the amount of capacity that management predicts the organization will produce in the period.
   C. Theoretical capacity represents the level of output if all policy constraints and scheduling limitations are removed. It also assumes that no productivity is lost due to breakdowns, errors, etc.
   D. Theoretical capacity represents the level of output that can be realistically achieved based on current management policies, as well as based on machine and labor scheduling expectations.

aq.costflows.vac.005_0820

6. Oak Products produced and sold 5,000 units during its most recent fiscal year. Direct materials were $9 per unit, direct labor costs were $4 per unit, and variable overhead costs were 110% of direct labor costs. Fixed overhead was $50,000, fixed selling and administrative expenses totaled $50,000, and variable selling and administrative expenses were a combined $8 per unit. Calculate inventory costs based on using the absorption (full) costing method.

   A. $87,000
   B. $137,000
   C. $227,000
   D. $127,000

ac.job.oc.001_0820

7. Which of the following correctly depicts the flow of inventory costs in a job order cost system?

   A. Raw Materials Inventory, Work-in-Process Inventory, Finished Goods Inventory, Cost of Goods Sold
   B. Finished Goods Inventory, Work-in-Process Inventory, Cost of Goods Sold
   C. Work-in-Process Inventory, Raw Materials Inventory, Finished Goods Inventory, Cost of Goods Sold
   D. Cost of Goods Sold, Work-in-Process Inventory, Raw Materials Inventory, Finished Goods Inventory

aq.val.ca.001_0820

8. Which of the following most accurately defines value chain analysis?

   A. An approach used by an organization to allocate capacity costs while tracking and reporting the fixed costs of idle capacity in the organization's production process
   B. An approach used by an organization to evaluate its internal activities determine how essential each activity is strategically creating and capturing value for the organization's customers
   C. A system based on the idea that Inventory is not really an asset in the production process, but is often a barrier to achieving the organization's main goals
   D. A system that supports a very specific and extremely short-term managerial view of an operation —the incremental value from a more effective employment of a constrained resource

aq.v.fc.008_0820

9. Leigh M. is working with her production supervisor to compute a predetermined fixed overhead rate for the coming year. Leigh and her production supervisor have put together a budget of 1,600 direct labor hours for the coming year. During the same period, they plan for 2,000 machine hours in the production process. Leigh has assembled the following information for the upcoming year:

Direct materials	$100,000
Direct labor cost	140,000
Salaries for factory janitors	70,000
Sales supervisor salary	102,000
Rent on factory building	24,000
Advertising expense	10,000

If Leigh decides to use a predetermined manufacturing overhead rate based on direct labor hours, what will be the predetermined manufacturing overhead rate?

A. $58.75 per direct labor hour
B. $47.00 per machine hour
C. $128.75 per direct labor hour
D. $103.00 per machine hour

aq.ab.cost.003_0820

10. Mandy Appliances manufactures toaster ovens. Each oven contains 15 parts totaling $35 in direct materials. Each oven requires 3 hours of machine time and 1.5 hours for inspection. The company has the following information regarding activities, activity drivers, and cost per driver units:

Activity	Activity Driver	Cost per Driver Unit
Machining	Machine hours	$3.75/machine hour
Materials handling	Number of parts	$1.20/part
Assembly	Number of parts	$0.85/part
Inspection	Inspection hours	$11.80/inspection hour

What is the cost of machining per toaster oven?

A. $18.00
B. $12.75
C. $11.25
D. $17.70

aq.costflows.vac.007_0820

11. Last year, Welk Company had 16,000 units in its beginning inventory. During the year, the company's variable production costs were $6 per unit and its fixed manufacturing overhead costs were $4 per unit. The company's net income for the year was $24,000 higher under absorption costing than it was under variable costing. Given these facts, what was the number of units in the ending inventory?

A. 16,000 units
B. 20,000 units
C. 22,000 units
D. 6,000 units

aq.proc.c.005_0820

12. A department adds raw materials to a process at the beginning of the process and incurs conversion costs uniformly throughout the process. For the month of January, there were 10,000 units in the Beginning Work-in-Process Inventory that were 80% complete; 90,000 units were started into production in January; and 20,000 units that were 40% complete in the Ending Work-in-Process Inventory at the end of January. Using the FIFO method of process costing, what are the equivalent units of production for materials for the month of January?

A. 70,000 equivalent units
B. 100,000 equivalent units
C. 90,000 equivalent units
D. 80,000 equivalent units

aq.concept.cd.003_0820

13. A product currently sells for $50 per unit and has variable manufacturing costs of $15 per unit, and variable selling and administrative costs of $6 per unit. How will the total contribution margin change when output is increased from 8,000 to 9,000 units?

A. Decrease of $15,000
B. Increase of $29,000
C. Decrease of $6,000
D. Increase of $50,000

14. A processing department produces joint products Ajac and Bjac, each of which incurs separable production costs after split-off. Information concerning a batch of these products produced with a $60,000 joint cost follows:

Product	Separable Costs	Final Sales Value
Ajac	$8,000	$80,000
Bjac	22,000	40,000
Total	$30,000	$120,000

What amount of the joint cost would be allocated to Ajac if joint costs are allocated to products using the net realizable value method?

A. $56,000
B. $12,000
C. $48,000
D. $40,000

15. Dana's real estate agency has increased its listings by offering an extensive advertising program, but Dana is concerned about her advertising costs. She is not sure how much she spends on advertising per listing because her advertising costs have both variable and fixed components.

Month	Number of Listings	Advertising Cost
March	35	$23,145
April	23	$15,025
May	22	$15,280
June	42	$27,205
July	48	$30,565
August	51	$32,485
September	50	$31,835
October	56	$36,020
November	54	$36,920

Based on the information above and the high-low method, what is Dana's fixed cost for advertising?

A. $1,860
B. $1,213
C. $863
D. $2,230

Section E: Internal Controls

Topic 1. Governance, Risk, and Compliance

Internal Control Structure and Management Philosophy

After studying this lesson, you should be able to:

- Identify and describe internal control objectives (1.E.1.b).

- Explain how a company's organizational structure, policies, objectives, and goals, as well as its management philosophy and style, influence the scope and effectiveness of the control environment (1.E.1.c).

- Identify and describe the major internal control provisions of the Foreign Corrupt Practices Act (1.E.1.t).

- Identify and describe the five major components of COSO's Internal Control - Integrated Framework (2013)(1.E.1.u).

When a company is small, an owner can be very involved in every aspect of its business. However, as it grows, this becomes very difficult. Internal controls help to ensure that a business runs as an owner intends. This lesson will use the COSO Internal Control Framework to discuss how to implement effective internal controls. Included in this lesson will be the *why*, *what*, and *where* of internal controls.

I. Internal Control

   A. When organizations are very small, an owner of a company can be intimately involved in all aspects of the business. As a company grows, this level of oversight quickly becomes difficult or even impossible! Thus, internal controls must be put in place to ensure that organizations run as the owner intends.

   B. Because each business is different, internal control systems must be able to cater to different management styles, industries, and regulatory environments. Nevertheless, effective internal control systems follow the same basic guidelines.

II. COSO Internal Control Framework

   A. The Committee of Sponsoring Organizations (COSO) was formed in 1985 to guide efforts to articulate and improve accounting controls. COSO is made up of five organizations: the American Institute of Certified Public Accountants, the Institute of Internal Auditors, the Institute of Management Accountants, the American Accounting Association, and the Financial Executives Institute. This committee established a helpful framework for understanding internal controls known as the COSO Internal Control Framework.

   B. The COSO Internal Control Framework is often portrayed as a cube.

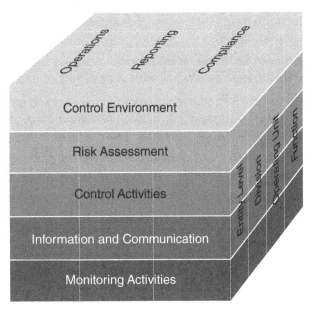

Source: Graham, Lynford. *Internal Control Audit and Compliance: Documentation and Testing Under the New COSO Framework*. Wiley Corporate F&A, 2015. Reproduced with permission of John Wiley & Sons.

C. The COSO Internal Control Framework helps companies visualize three dimensions of internal controls. These three dimensions address the following three questions: (1) Why does a company have internal controls? (2) What is internal control? and (3) Where should a company have various internal controls? These issues are next discussed in greater detail.

   1. *Why does a company have internal controls?* Recall that the purpose of an internal control system is to ensure that organizations run as the owner intends. A functioning system of internal control is a process which provides reasonable assurance that an entity is achieving three objectives:

      a. *Operations:* Internal controls are designed to make sure the business runs effectively and efficiently. Internal controls safeguard assets and help facilitate business growth.

      b. *Reporting:* Internal controls are designed to ensure that financial and nonfinancial reports generated by the business are reliable, timely, and transparent. Reliable reporting allows the owner to analyze performance and business strategies without being involved in every function of the business, and provides useful information to other parties such as managers, regulators, and lenders.

      c. *Compliance:* Internal controls are designed to ensure that businesses are compliant with applicable laws and regulations. Failure to follow laws and regulations can lead to devastating consequences to the business, the environment, and society.

         i. Companies that have international operations must be particularly mindful of complying with the Foreign Corrupt Practices Act (FCPA), which prohibits companies from paying bribes to foreign government officials to obtain a public contract. Firms or employees who violate the FCPA are subject to substantial criminal and civil penalties. Companies' internal controls must be sufficient to provide reasonable assurances that:

            ● Access to assets can only be permitted with management's authorization.

            ● The companies' records accurately reflect transactions and the disposition of assets in accordance with GAAP or other relevant accounting standards.

   2. *What are internal controls?* An effective control system has five components that work together to ensure that internal control objectives are being met. They are:

      a. *Control Environment:* This component relates to a company's attitude and culture toward internal control. Leadership is key—effective and ethical leaders set the tone for the rest of the organization. Companies should also ensure that employees are competent and able to perform their functions and that individuals are held accountable for internal control responsibilities.

    b. *Risk Assessment:* Companies must periodically review their processes and business environment to identify risks to ensure they can stay competitive.

    c. *Control Activities:* This component relates to the nuts and bolts of internal controls. Companies must put accounting systems and information technology in place to safeguard assets and ensure the proper recording of business transactions.

    d. *Information and Communication:* Businesses with effective internal controls are able to identify, capture, and communicate information accurately, efficiently, and securely.

    e. *Monitoring Activities:* Businesses should monitor their internal controls to ensure that they are working properly. As the business environment changes, proper monitoring allows companies to see when and how controls should change to address business changes.

3. *Where should a company have various internal controls?* Today's companies are often large and complex. Different parts of the organization require different controls. Thus, companies should consider appropriate controls at each of the following levels:

    a. Organization-wide

    b. Division level

    c. Operating unit

    d. Function (for example, accounting, marketing, information technology)

Summary

The Committee of Sponsoring Organizations (COSO) was formed in order to guide efforts to articulate and improve accounting controls. COSO has developed the Internal Control Framework in order to help businesses visualize the three aspects of internal controls. Under the COSO framework, a functioning control system provides reasonable assurance that a company is running effectively and efficiently, has reliable financial and nonfinancial reports, and is compliant with applicable laws and regulations. Additionally, the framework defines the five components of an effective control system and defines the key places where a company should have internal controls.

Internal Control Policies for Safeguarding and Assurance

After studying this lesson, you should be able to:

- Describe how internal controls are designed to provide reasonable (but not absolute) assurance regarding achievement of an entity's objectives involving (i) effectiveness and efficiency of operations, (ii) reliability of financial reporting, and (iii) compliance with applicable laws and regulations (1.E.1.g).

- Explain why personnel policies and procedures are integral to an efficient control environment (1.E.1.h).

- Define and give examples of segregation of duties (1.E.1.i).

- Explain why the following four types of functional responsibilities should be performed by different departments or different people within the same function: (i) authority to execute transactions, (ii) recording transactions, (iii) custody of assets involved in the transactions, and (iv) periodic reconciliations of the existing assets to recorded amounts (1.E.1.j).

- Demonstrate an understanding of the importance of independent checks and verification (1.E.1.k).

- Identify examples of safeguarding controls (1.E.1.l).

- Explain how the use of prenumbered forms, as well as specific policies and procedures detailing who is authorized to receive specific documents, is a means of control (1.E.1.m).

The purpose of internal controls is to ensure that companies are running effectively and efficiently, have reliable financial and nonfinancial reports, and are compliant with applicable laws and regulations. However, designing and implementing an effective control system can be very challenging. This lesson will explore some of the design principles that can be used to create and maintain effective controls as well as discuss a few specific controls related to personnel and safeguarding of assets.

I. Designing Internal Controls

   A. Recall that the purpose of internal controls is to ensure that companies can meet their objectives, including running effective and efficient operations, having reliable financial reporting, and complying with laws and regulations. However, no internal control system is perfect. For instance, internal control systems cannot completely protect an organization from collusion (i.e., when multiple employees work together to defraud the company). Furthermore, even if an organization has good policies and procedures in place, these policies and procedures are only effective if employees follow them. Finally, if internal controls do not change as the business changes, good controls can become obsolete! Thus, designing an effective control system can be challenging.

   B. Incorporating the following design principles can greatly help a company institute and maintain effective controls:

   1. *Control:* Internal control systems should safeguard a firm's assets and ensure that data generated by the accounting system are reliable.

   2. *Compatibility:* Internal control systems must fit the company. Internal controls are often specific to an industry or business unit, and to a certain extent can be customized to be compatible with each company.

   3. *Flexibility:* Internal controls need to be able to accommodate the growth of the organization. For instance, a small company may require that the CFO approve all large capital expenditures. As the company grows, this internal control may become too cumbersome for the CFO, and other individuals will need to be given authority to approve expenditures.

4. *Cost-benefit:* This principle is critical! There is always a tradeoff between internal control effectiveness and the cost that such controls have in an organization. For instance, the accuracy of financial reports could be improved if every transaction were entered into the accounting system by two individuals. However, while this control may slightly improve financial reporting quality, the increased reporting quality probably would not justify doubling the cost of the company's accounting staff!

II. Personnel Controls

   A. **Hiring:** There are several personnel controls that companies implement to make sure they have trustworthy, well-qualified employees. After all, internal controls are often only as effective as the employees who use them. The first personnel control relates to hiring. Organizations must screen potential employees to ensure that they have the skills, education, or certifications necessary to perform the job well. Background and reference checks can also help organizations avoid hiring unqualified employees.

   B. **Training:** Once qualified individuals are hired, organizations should devote adequate resources to training and developing employees. Organizations should also track employee performance in order to coach employees and help them improve. Employee expectations and performance feedback should be timely and informative.

   C. **Job Rotation and Mandatory Vacations:** There are a couple of reasons why companies should require that employees temporarily leave their post. First, cross-training employees increases employee knowledge of the company and ensures that operations can continue in the event of employee absence. Second, certain fraud schemes require employees to have complete control over an aspect of a business. Thus, when another employee temporarily takes over, fraud is often discovered.

III. Safeguarding Assets

   A. One of greatest benefits of internal controls is the increased protection of a firm's assets. Some of the controls designed to safeguard assets are general and apply to all employees. These include locked doors, security systems, electronic key cards, and computer passwords. These general controls reduce the risk that assets are stolen, misused, or damaged. As companies' assets become increasingly digital (e.g., intellectual property and customer information), a company must alter controls to address changing risks. However, the underlying principles of safeguarding assets remain unchanged.

      1. The following are examples of safeguarding controls:

         a. Petty cash is in a locked container with the key held by the controller.

         b. Computer systems are in a locked room with access restricted to appropriate personnel.

         c. Prenumbered forms allow for proper review of exceptions or missing documents. If a check number is missing, the accounting department can research why the check is missing.

         d. Prenumbered purchase orders allow the purchasing department to identify missing purchase order numbers and develop an approach for identifying causes of a missing purchase order.

   B. *Segregation of duties* refers to separating responsibilities for key business transactions such as making sales, shipping products, and paying invoices. The purpose of segregation of duties is to reduce the risk of fraud and errors. Accounting frauds are often the result of improper segregation of duties (e.g., WorldCom). If a company has proper segregation of duties, it's highly unlikely that fraud will occur (though segregation of duties cannot prevent collusion). For key business transactions, the following responsibilities should be separated.

      1. Authorization or approving transactions

      2. Recording transactions

      3. Custody of assets

4. Periodic reconciliation (Ideally, a distinct party verifies processes to ensure that segregation of duties is functioning properly.)

   a. *Segregation of Duties Example:* Different employees perform the duties of creating a vendor record, creating a purchase order, receiving goods, and paying invoices. If a single employee performed all these duties, then that employee could create a fictional vendor, create a purchase order to that fictitious vendor for inventory, and then pay that vendor without anyone noticing that the company's money is being diverted to illegitimate vendors.

   b. *Segregation of Duties Example:* Different employees receive cash, make deposits, and reconcile the bank account so a single employee cannot steal cash and cover the theft with improper deposit entries.

C. Segregation of duties is often impossible for small companies, as they may not have enough employees to separate all necessary functions. Thus, owners must be particularly vigilant when performing periodic reconciliations to ensure that policies related to these transactions are being followed. Large companies can and should separate these responsibilities.

Summary

No internal control system is perfect nor can it completely protect an organization. However, there are many factors that can help create and maintain an effective control system. Four basic principles for designing effective controls are to ensure that controls: safeguard assets, are compatible with a company's industry/environment, accommodate growth, and provide enough benefit to justify their cost. Personnel controls are critical to a company and should encompass hiring, training, job rotation, and mandatory vacations. One of the greatest benefits of internal controls is safeguarding a firm's assets. There are many controls that help to safeguard assets but one of the most important ones to protect against fraud is the segregation of duties.

Internal Control Risk

After studying this lesson, you should be able to:

- Demonstrate an understanding of internal control risk and the management of internal control risk (1.E.1.a).

- Define and distinguish between preventive controls and detective controls (1.E.1.o).

- Assess the level of internal control risk within an organization and recommend risk mitigation strategies (1.E.1.v).

Internal controls help to ensure a company achieves its objectives of running effectively and efficiently, has reliable financial and nonfinancial reports, and complies with applicable laws and regulations. The risk that an organization fails to achieve one of these objectives is called internal control risk. This lesson will define the inherent risks of internal controls as well as preventive, detective, and corrective controls. In addition, it will discuss risk assessment and mitigation strategies for internal control.

I. Internal Control Risk

A. Internal controls are designed to ensure that an organization meets its objectives (i.e., effective and efficient operations, reliable financial reporting, and compliance with applicable laws and regulations). Thus, internal control risk refers to the risk that an organization will fail to achieve one of its objectives.

B. The likelihood of an internal control failure is a function of inherent risks and the effectiveness of various types of controls. While controls can be categorized in a number of ways, a simple categorization divides them into: (1) preventive controls, (2) detective controls, and (3) corrective controls. The risk of an internal control failure can be modeled as follows:

Likelihood of Internal Control Failure
$$= \text{Inherent Risk} \times \text{Control Effectiveness}(\text{Preventive, Detective, and Corrective})$$

where:

1. **Inherent risks** represent risks that control failures would occur in the absence of any controls. Inherent risks are those risks that occur because of the industry in which a company operates or the business decisions that a company chooses to make. For instance, restaurants face a much higher risk of employees skimming cash than hospitals. It's a natural consequence of working in the restaurant industry, which entails many small cash transactions. This inherent risk can be addressed using a combination of several types of controls.

2. **Preventive controls** are designed to prevent control failures from occurring. In the case of restaurants attempting to keep employees from skimming cash, management could simply decide not to accept cash. While this would certainly prevent skimming, it would likely hurt the business in the form of lost sales.

3. **Detective controls** are designed to detect control failures after they occur. For instance, a restaurant may use security cameras to review previous days' transactions and attempt to identify employee skimming. Detective controls tend to be much more costly than preventive controls.

4. **Corrective controls** reverse or reduce the errors found through detective controls. For instance, a restaurant may use analytics to inform management about which employees are most likely to steal based on historical cash sales. Resources could then be deployed to monitor certain employees.

    C. Inherent risks can originate from inside (e.g., employee fraud, inventory spoilage) or outside of the company (e.g., increased business competition or government regulation).

    D. Companies should use an efficient combination of preventive, detective, and corrective controls that effectively address inherent risks. Effective controls of one type may lower or even eliminate the need for other types of controls.

II. Risk Assessment and Mitigation Strategies

    A. While the previous model provides a way to assess the *likelihood* of an internal control failure, internal control risk is a function of likelihood *and* the potential for loss. Thus, companies must also consider how costly an internal control failure will be when determining how many resources should be devoted to addressing inherent risks.

    B. The following risk matrix can be used when determining how to mitigate internal control risk:

	Low Potential Loss	High Potential Loss
Low Likelihood	Accept Risk	Insurance
High Likelihood	Controls	Avoid Risk

        1. When the likelihood and potential loss of an internal control failure are low, companies should generally accept the risk. In this case, the cost of implementing controls will probably outweigh the benefit of lower risk. For instance, hardware stores may be susceptible to customers stealing individual nuts and bolts, but the cost and likelihood are so low that it may be best to consider the associated loss as a cost of doing business.

        2. When the potential loss of an internal control failure is low but the likelihood is high, companies should implement internal controls that prevent or detect and correct the internal control failure. For instance, the likelihood of employees stealing cash at a register may be high even if they don't steal much on average. In this case, restaurants may wish to implement internal controls over cash transactions.

        3. When the potential loss from an internal control failure is high but the likelihood is low, companies should purchase insurance to help mitigate the internal control risk. For instance, hurricanes and other natural disasters are highly unlikely but very costly when they occur. Most companies purchase insurance to address the risk of natural disasters.

        4. When both the potential loss and likelihood from an internal control failure is high, companies may decide to alter their business strategy in order to avoid the risk. This should explain why banks are unwilling to loan large amounts of money to people with terrible credit scores!

Summary

Internal control risk is the risk that a company will fail to achieve one of its objectives. The likelihood of an internal control failure is a function of inherent risks and the effectiveness of various types of controls. Inherent risks are risks that would occur in the absence of any controls. The three main categories of controls are preventive (used to prevent control failures from occurring), detective (used to detect control failures after they occur), and corrective (used to reverse or reduce errors found). A risk matrix can be used to help companies determine whether to accept or prevent particular inherent risks based upon the likelihood and the potential loss of the risk.

Corporate Governance

After studying this lesson, you should be able to:

- Identify the board of directors' responsibilities with respect to ensuring that the company is operated in the best interest of shareholders (1.E.1.d).

- Identify the hierarchy of corporate governance; i.e., articles of incorporation, bylaws, policies, and procedures (1.E.1.e).

- Demonstrate an understanding of corporate governance, including rights and responsibilities of the CEO, the board of directors, the audit committee, managers and other stakeholders; and the procedures for making corporate decisions (1.E.1.f).

- Describe the major internal control provisions of the Sarbanes-Oxley Act (Sections 201, 203, 204, 302, 404, and 407) (1.E.1.p).

One of a company's objectives is to be compliant with applicable laws and regulations. The system of rules and regulations by which a corporation is directed and controlled is referred to as corporate governance. This lesson will discuss the governance structure a corporation must put in place before it can become a corporation, the responsibilities of the board of directors and the audit committee, and the corporate governance provisions mandated by the Sarbanes-Oxley Act of 2002.

I. Corporate Governance

    A. Corporate governance refers to the system of rules and procedures by which a corporation is directed and controlled. The governance structure must meet certain requirements set forth by federal and state regulators. Before a corporation is formed, it must submit several documents such as articles of incorporation which legally document its formation. These documents provide a detailed outline of the corporation's planned governance structure.

    B. An organization's governance structure details the rights and responsibilities of various company stakeholders, including the board of directors, various executives, the internal audit function, and other parties.

    C. The governance structure also specifies the rules and policies for addressing various business functions. For example, company bylaws may dictate when and how often the board of directors meets, as well as describe the rules for governing how shareholders can vote on various issues.

    D. Corporate governance ultimately provides the owners (i.e., shareholders) with the ability to direct the affairs of the organization. Since businesses often have thousands of owners, it isn't possible for each individual shareholder to be involved in the day-to-day operations of the business. Thus, shareholders elect a board of directors to oversee and monitor the operation of the company.

II. Board of Director and Audit Committee Responsibilities

    A. The board of directors' primary responsibility is to ensure that the company operates in the best interest of shareholders. Generally, this means that the board is responsible for business practices and results. In addition to generating a profit for shareholders, boards of directors often encourage good *corporate social responsibility* (CSR) activities that address the needs of other corporate stakeholders. If shareholders are unsatisfied with the results, they can replace board members.

    B. The board is responsible for establishing corporate policies and appointing senior management of the company. This includes the chief executive officer (CEO), who is responsible for managing the corporation on a day-to-day basis, and the chief financial officer (CFO), who has responsibility for the financial affairs of the company. These hiring decisions are critical because top management has a strong influence on the culture and philosophy of a company, which impacts the effectiveness of internal controls.

C. Board members are often part of various committees within the board. One such committee is the audit committee, which is responsible for the oversight of the financial reporting process. For companies that have an internal audit function, the internal auditors should report directly to the audit committee. The audit committee is also responsible for hiring independent external auditors.

III. Sarbanes-Oxley Act of 2002 (SOX) and Corporate Governance

    A. Several large corporate frauds and failures, such as WorldCom and Enron, occurred in part because of poor corporate governance. Ineffective audit committees were partly to blame because some committees lacked independence and were therefore unwilling to challenge unethical or questionable practices. Other audit committees did not have sufficient financial expertise to uncover financial reporting failures. As a result, SOX required several new corporate governance standards.

        1. Section 301 requires audit committee independence. Specifically, audit committee members cannot accept any consulting, advisory, or other fees from their company.

        2. Section 407 requires audit committees to have at least one member who qualifies as a financial expert. Companies that fail to have a financial expert on the audit committee must explain why they have no such expert.

        3. Section 404 requires public companies to establish and maintain a system of internal controls, which must be audited by external auditors.

        4. Section 201 prohibits accounting firms from providing some non-audit services (such as bookkeeping and accounting systems design) to audit clients to help maintain the independence of the audit firm.

        5. Section 203 requires lead audit partners to rotate off engagements every five years to help maintain the independence of the audit partner.

        6. Section 302 puts management on the hook for internal control failures. As part of the annual reporting process, key executives (usually the CEO and CFO) must attest, under penalty of law, that:

            a. They have reviewed the financial statements.

            b. To their knowledge, the financial statements do not contain material inaccuracies and fairly present the financial position of the company.

            c. They are responsible for internal controls.

            d. They have designed internal controls that are adequate to ensure financial reporting integrity.

            e. They have evaluated and given their opinion regarding the effectiveness of internal control effectiveness within 90 days of the report.

            f. They have disclosed to the auditors and audit committee significant changes in internal controls, all known frauds, and significant internal control deficiencies and weaknesses.

Summary

The system of rules and regulations by which a corporation is directed and controlled is referred to as corporate governance. Before a corporation can even be formed, it must submit a detailed outline of its planned governance structure, including the right and responsibilities of various stakeholders and the rules and policies for addressing various business functions. The shareholders of corporations elect a board of directors to ensure the company operates in the best interest of its shareholders as well as to serve on various committees, including the audit committee. Corporate governance today is heavily influenced by the 2002 Sarbanes-Oxley Act, which improved corporate governance standards.

External Audit Requirements

After studying this lesson, you should be able to:

- Define inherent risk, control risk, and detection risk (1.E.1.n).

- Identify the role of the PCAOB in providing guidance on the auditing of internal controls (1.E.1.q).

- Differentiate between a top-down (risk-based) approach and a bottom-up approach to auditing internal controls (1.E.1.r).

- Identify the PCAOB preferred approach to auditing internal controls as outlined in Auditing Standard #5 (1.E.1.s).

- Demonstrate an understanding of external auditor responsibilities, including the types of audit opinions the external auditors issue (1.E.1.w).

As learned in the previous lesson, the Sarbanes-Oxley Act was created in 2002 as a result of corporate frauds and failures. As part of this Act, the Public Company Accounting Oversight Board was created to issue audit standards for audit firms that audit public companies and to periodically review for quality and compliance with these audit standards. This lesson will explore some facets of the external audit, including the audit risk model, auditing of internal controls, and audit opinions.

I. The Public Company Accounting Oversight Board (PCAOB)

    A. The PCAOB was created by the Sarbanes-Oxley Act of 2002 (SOX) and oversees audit firms that audit "issuers," which are defined as public companies that are required to file with the SEC. The PCAOB is responsible for issuing auditing standards and periodically reviewing auditors for quality and compliance with those standards.

II. Audit Risk Model

    A. The auditor's primary job is to provide assurance of the reliability of a company's financial statements to financial statement users. The audit consists of a series of steps designed to provide auditors with enough evidence to substantiate their opinion about whether the financial statements are free from material misstatement.

    B. Audit risk is the likelihood that a company's financial statements are materially misstated *and* the auditor expresses an inappropriate audit opinion. In other words, audit risk is the risk that auditors make the wrong call. An inappropriate audit opinion can be extremely costly to an audit firm. Auditors are often sued for incorrect opinions. In addition, some firms, such as Arthur Andersen, have gone out of business because the public did not trust the audit firm to perform a good audit.

    C. The Audit Risk Model: Auditors often use the audit risk model to assess risk and plan the audit:

$$\text{Audit Risk} = \text{Inherent Risk} \times \text{Control Risk} \times \text{Detection Risk}$$

where:

    1. **Audit risk** is the risk that the auditor expresses an unqualified opinion and the financial statements are materially misstated. Audit risk is chosen by the auditor and can vary between firms. Some firms are willing to take a higher risk of expressing an incorrect opinion, so long as the additional risk corresponds with increased audit fees from the client.

    2. **Inherent risk** is the likelihood that the financial statements contain a material misstatement in the absence of controls. These risks are related to the business decisions, culture, and environment of the audit client.

    3. **Control risk** is the likelihood that the client's internal control systems will fail to either prevent, or detect and correct, a material misstatement in the financial statements.

4. **Detection risk** is the likelihood that the auditor's procedures will fail to detect a material misstatement in the financial statements. It is important to note that this is the only element of the audit risk model that can be influenced by the amount of work an auditor plans to do during the audit. In other words, once acceptable audit risk is determined by the audit firm, the only mechanism that auditors have at their disposal to adjust audit risk to the predetermined level is by altering detection risk through increased or decreased audit work. These risks (Inherent, Control, and Detection risks) are interactive. Thus, if the client's internal controls are effective, the auditor may determine that less audit testing is necessary to perform the financial statement audit (i.e., a higher detection risk is planned).

III. Auditing Internal Controls

A. Section 404 of SOX requires that external auditors attest to and report on the adequacy of public companies' internal controls over financial reporting.

B. Auditing Standard No. 5 provides guidance for how the auditors are to comply with Section 404. (*Note: the PCAOB has since reorganized/renumbered the Auditing Standards, but these standards are still in force.*) Specifically, the standard requires auditors to perform a top-down, risk-based approach to auditing internal controls over financial reporting. To do so, auditors identify accounts and disclosures that are significant to the financial statements, and then determine the risk of material misstatement in these accounts and disclosures. Auditors then examine client's controls that reduce the risk of material misstatement in these accounts and disclosures. Finally, the auditors plan their own tests needed to gather evidence on the client's internal controls. Auditors alter the nature, timing, and extent of their testing to reduce audit risk to an acceptable level.

C. In contrast to the top-down approach required by Auditing Standard No. 5, a bottom-up approach entails testing internal controls and examining how inadequate internal controls may lead to material misstatements in the financial statements. Such an approach typically requires more work and is less flexible than the top-down, risk-based approach.

IV. Audit Opinions

A. At the conclusion of the audit, the auditor must provide an opinion about the client's financial statements. The types of audit opinions an auditor may issue include:

1. **An unqualified opinion**, which is issued when auditors have examined a complete set of financial statements and have gained sufficient appropriate evidence that the financial statements are free from material misstatement.

2. **An unqualified opinion with an emphasis-of matter or other-matter paragraph.** This occurs when the auditors have gained sufficient appropriate evidence that the financial statements are free from material misstatement, and feel there is a minor issue that should be brought to the attention of financial statement users such as:

   a. Inconsistent application of accounting principles.

   b. Going-concern doubts, meaning that the auditor is unsure whether the client will be able to continue doing business.

   c. Uncertainty about significant future events, such as the outcome of pending litigation.

   d. There is a change in opinion for a prior period that is included in the current financial statements or the predecessor auditor's report for a prior period that is not presented in the current financial statements.

3. **A qualified opinion** may be issued for several reasons. For instance, this may occur if auditors believe the financial statements are materially (but not pervasively) misstated (i.e., modified opinion due to a specific departure from GAAP), or if the auditor was prevented from obtaining sufficient audit evidence for some area of the audit (i.e., modified opinion due to scope limitation).

4. **An adverse opinion** is issued when the auditors have evidence that the financial statements are materially and pervasively misstated.

5. **A disclaimer of opinion** is issued when the auditor is unable to obtain sufficient audit evidence to make an opinion regarding the reliability of the financial statements.

B. For public companies, the auditor's report also includes an opinion about whether the company has effective internal control over financial reporting.

Summary

The PCAOB is responsible for issuing auditing standards for and overseeing audit firms that audit public companies. An auditor's primary responsibility is to provide an opinion about whether a firm's financial statements are free from material misstatement. Audit risk is the risk that auditors state the wrong opinion and is a product of three different risks: inherent risk, control risk, and detection risk. External auditors are also required to attest to and report on public firms' internal controls over financial reporting primarily using a top-down, risk-based approach. At the conclusion of the audit, the external auditor will issue an opinion which may include an unqualified opinion, an unqualified opinion with an emphasis-of matter or other-matter paragraph, a qualified opinion, an adverse opinion, or a disclaimer of opinion.

Topic 2. Systems Controls and Security Measures

Information System General Controls

After studying this lesson, you should be able to:

- Describe how the segregation of accounting duties can enhance systems security (1.E.2.a).

- Identify threats to information systems, including input manipulation, program alteration, direct file alteration, data theft, sabotage, viruses, Trojan horses, theft, and phishing (1.E.2.b).

- Demonstrate an understanding of how systems development controls are used to enhance the accuracy, validity, safety, security, and adaptability of systems input, processing, output, and storage functions (1.E.2.c).

- Identify procedures to limit access to physical hardware (1.E.2.d).

- Identify means by which management can protect programs and databases from unauthorized use (1.E.2.e).

- Identify and describe the types of storage controls and demonstrate an understanding of when and why they are used (1.E.2.g).

- Identify and describe the inherent risks of using the Internet as compared to data transmissions over secured transmission lines (1.E.2.h).

- Define data encryption and describe why there is a much greater need for data encryption methods when using the Internet (1.E.2.i).

- Identify a firewall and its uses (1.E.2.j).

- Explain the importance of backing up all program and data files regularly, and storing the backups at a secure remote site (1.E.3.l).

- Define business continuity planning (1.E.2.m).

- Define the objective of a disaster recovery plan and identify the components of such a plan including hot, warm, and cold sites (1.E.2.n).

> Businesses' reliance on information systems to collect, process, organize, and summarize data is dramatically increasing. With this increased use of information systems, businesses face increased risks. As a result of these increased risks, businesses must implement controls into their internal control system that specifically address information systems. This lesson will discuss the risks that businesses face due to the use of information systems, and the general (or pervasive) controls that are used to address these risks.

I. The Purpose of Information Systems

    A. Companies depend on their information systems to collect, process, organize, and summarize data and information.

    B. As businesses generate more and more data, it is increasingly important for companies to have the capabilities to make sense of that data, as well as to protect that data from third parties.

II. Information System Risks

    A. The increased use of information systems in today's businesses has introduced a number of risks to companies. These risks include the following:

- Information systems do not leave a paper trail of documents. Organizations must ensure controls are in place to identify who entered a transaction and the time of the transaction to replace paper-based source documents.

- Reduced manual intervention increases the possibility of errors not being detected by employees.

- Individuals may use computers to bypass internal controls and access information systems.

- Sabotage, or intentional alteration or destruction of applications and/or data.

- Unauthorized employees or external hackers may alter, delete, or manipulate, or steal data.

- Phishing, which is the use of electronic communication to obtain sensitive information from the organization.

- Software bugs.

- Computer viruses and other threats, such as Trojan horses.

- Hardware, software, or Internet connections may malfunction, leaving an organization's employees unable to access the systems required to perform their duties.

B. To address these risks, an organization's internal control system must include the proper design, execution, and monitoring of information systems to protect data, produce accurate financial information, and help the organization achieve its goals and objectives. This is accomplished through the use of *General Controls* (also known as Pervasive Controls) and *Application Controls*. General controls are discussed in the next section while application controls are discussed in the following lesson.

III. Information Systems General Controls

   A. *Organizational, personnel, and operations controls* relate to how information system responsibilities and access are divided among employees.

      1. Segregation of duties must be maintained to reduce the risk of fraud and error within the information system. To effectively segregate duties:

         a. The information technology (IT) section should remain independent of the organization because it serves all departments.

         b. Within the IT function, the organization should segregate these IT duties:

            i. Systems development—IT analysts and application developers accountable for creating the systems

            ii. IT operations—The computer operators, data library custodian, and those responsible for managing the input and output of the information systems

            iii. Technical support—Administrators of network security, databases, and network utilities designed to keep the IT function running smoothly

         c. An effective use of IT can help facilitate segregation of duties by:

            i. Ensuring that transactions originate and are authorized by individuals outside of the IT function.

            ii. Ensuring the accounting department authorizes all changes to the master file or related transaction files.

      2. Organizations should implement a mandatory vacation policy to reduce the probability of fraud by a single employee.

         a. The 2012 Dixon, IL, fraud case illustrates the importance of mandatory vacation time.

      i. The comptroller of Dixon, IL, was sentenced to prison in 2012 for embezzling over $50 million from the city.

      ii. Over many years, the comptroller never took lengthy vacations. The fraud was uncovered only after an employee performing the comptroller's duties uncovered secret bank accounts used in the embezzlement.

    b. Employees committing fraudulent acts often can continue the fraud only by maintaining control over systems and financial information.

  3. Only approved users should be able to access information systems.

    a. Administrators can use passwords and other controls to limit access to information systems.

    b. Authorizations also allow administrators to determine if employees are using the system properly.

B. At times, companies must update their information systems. *Systems development controls* refer to the standards and processes that should be followed when systems are updated or when new systems are implemented. The purpose of controls is to enhance system accuracy, validity, safety, security, and adaptability. Examples of systems development controls include:

  1. Thoroughly documenting all changes.

  2. Following a standardized process for updating systems.

  3. Adequately testing all systems to ensure they function as designed.

  4. Ensuring that updated systems comply with applicable laws and regulations.

C. *Network, hardware, and facility controls* protect the company's information and data.

  1. Network controls restrict access to the appropriate company personnel.

    a. Local area networks (LANs), wide area networks (WANs), and virtual private networks (VPNs) allow an organization to network systems together to process information in a secure manner.

    b. The Internet presents new threats with risks of unauthorized hacking, malware, and viruses.

  2. Facility controls protect key hardware from the threat of damage and unauthorized access.

    a. Key computer equipment should be placed in a locked room with access granted only to specific personnel.

    b. Computer hardware should be in rooms with protection from natural disasters, such as fire, and from power surges.

    c. Organizations also should have duplicate systems to protect data and continue operations if one piece of hardware malfunctions.

    d. Facility controls are important to protect the devices organizations use to store important company data, such as:

      i. Individual personal computers (not recommended, but some confidential information may be on users' personal computers)

      ii. Network servers

      iii. Storage area networks (SANs), which are networked devices specifically designed to provide a central storage location for key company data

      iv. Cloud-based storage networks, such as Dropbox or Box.com

      v. Dedicated remote servers storing company data offsite and accessed through the Internet

3. Data traveling through an organization's network should have the appropriate data encryption to avoid hacking.

   a. Data encryption converts data into an unreadable format to reduce the possibility of unauthorized interception.

   b. Routing verification ensures transactions are directed to the correct computer.

   c. Message acknowledgment verifies to the receiving computer that the entire data transmission was received.

   d. The increased use of cloud-based IT storage networks, such as Dropbox, and remote servers increases the Internet traffic of sensitive company information.

      i. Data encryption becomes even more important when data is transmitted over public Internet data lines rather than private company data networks.

      ii. Companies must encrypt data traveling over the Internet to protect proprietary business information and private customer or supplier information.

      iii. Data encryption is particularly important when consumer health information is transmitted over the Internet instead of secure company networks.

4. Antivirus software and firewalls protect networks from unauthorized access and malicious software.

   a. Firewalls are hardware, software, or a combination of both designed to prevent unauthorized external use of a company network and to limit the access of internal users to designated sites.

   b. Firewalls keep hackers, viruses, and other malicious users and users of a company's network from accessing a company's network.

   c. Firewalls can also keep internal users from accessing social networks, sports sites, and other time wasters as well as sites where sensitive company information could be communicated.

D. *Disaster recovery and backup controls* protect information systems from natural disasters, such as fires, earthquakes, and floods.

   1. Businesses must develop plans to secure company data, quickly restart operations, and continue serving customers after a natural disaster or unexpected event, such as a loss of company data.

   2. The primary objectives of a disaster recovery/business continuity plan are to:

      a. Protect the well-being of employees and others in business facilities.

      b. Ensure company data is not lost and that it is adequately protected.

      c. Return to normal business operations as quickly as possible.

      d. Secure temporary or permanent alternative office/facility space.

      e. Develop alternative offsite working arrangements, such as remote working or temporary office space.

      f. Protect the company legally.

      g. Properly protect electronic and hardcopy records.

   3. The rise of IT makes the proper backup and retrieval of data essential to protect a company's reputation, legal standing, and information needs.

   4. Data backup requires some method of offsite storage to ensure data is secure and available for use.

   5. Many organizations back up their data daily using the grandfather-father-son method to store three copies of data.

a. The "son" is the most recent daily backup of data. This is the fastest method of data retrieval.

b. The "father" is a weekly backup method of data securing the past week's worth of data.

c. The "grandfather" is a monthly backup, which is often stored in a fireproof safe or in an offsite location to reduce the risk of loss from a natural disaster striking the facility.

d. The rise of cloud-based storage and remote servers has changed the nature of this backup method, but many organizations still use the grandfather-father-son backup methodology.

6. Backup data should be stored at an offsite location.

a. Many organizations use third-party suppliers to store data offsite, reducing the possibility of data loss in the event of a disaster at the primary place of business.

b. Organizations should back up systems configurations in addition to data.

7. Companies can configure alternative sites to quickly restart operations in the event of damage or destruction to the primary facility.

a. "Hot" sites have hardware and software that are configured and ready to be used immediately in case of an emergency.

b. "Warm" sites have hardware and networking ready for an organization to continue operations in a short amount of time.

c. "Cold" sites do not have network or hardware capabilities, but the organization can create a new operations location there somewhat quickly in the event of a disaster.

Summary
The use of information systems in business has created a number of new risks. In order to address these risks, an organization's control system must include specific information system controls. The first type of information system controls are General (or Pervasive) Controls. There are several types of General Controls. Organizational, personnel, and operations controls relate to how information system responsibilities and access are divided among employees. Systems development controls ensure that updated systems continue to meet a company's objectives. Network, hardware, and facility controls protect the company's information and data. Finally, disaster recovery and backup controls protect information systems from natural disasters, such as fires, earthquakes, and floods.

Information System Application Controls

As discussed in the previous lesson, information system controls are an important piece of a company's internal control system. General or pervasive controls were discussed in the previous lesson. This lesson will cover information system application controls, including input controls, processing controls, and output controls. It will also discuss the use of flowcharts to map an organization's control system.

I. Information Systems Application Controls

    A. An effective accounting information system (AIS) must have a series of application and transaction controls to prevent, detect, and correct mistakes and intentional misstatements in the system. Application controls can be categorized as input controls, processing controls, and output controls.

    B. *Input controls* help an organization prevent and detect errors and irregularities related to the input of data into the AIS.

        1. Supervisors should confirm the accuracy of source data before employees input data into the AIS.

        2. The organization should have appropriate approval procedures.

        3. There should be dual observation/review of data before it is input into the AIS.

        4. Where employees manually enter long strings of numbers (for example, a bar code or an account number) a check digit serves as a redundancy check to help ensure that that the number was entered correctly. A check digit is calculated by using the string of numbers and an algorithm. A typo will likely change the calculation, and the algorithm output will no longer match the check digit.

        5. Manually calculated totals of various fields of the documents should be batched. Batch totals are compared to computer-calculated totals and are used to ensure the accuracy and completeness of data entry.

            a. Examples of batch controls include:

                i. Record counts—Counting the number of records in a batch or lines in a document to determine the completeness of processing.

                ii. Control totals—Totaling fields, such as the amount field or another financially meaningful field as a check figure.

                iii. Hash totals—Totals of a field, usually an account code field, for which the total has no logical meaning, such as a total of customer account numbers in a batch of invoices.

        6. Source documents should be well designed so it is easy to input data. This will reduce the probability of input errors.

        7. Interactive edits—This control ensures that data entered into the system meet certain requirements such as:

            a. Character checks—requiring that certain fields contain only alphabetic or numeric texts.

            b. Completeness checks—ensuring that there are no missing data fields.

            c. Limit or reasonable checks—comparing entered text with certain requirements. For example, an issued paycheck or a customer's age should be below a certain level.

          d. Validity checks–comparing entered text with pre-specified data stored within the company's information system. For example, the vendor on a purchase order would be flagged if it did not appear on a company's list of approved vendors.

   C. *Processing controls* cover how the accounting information system turns input data into information output for managers and others in the organization. These controls include the following:

      1. Using standard and consistent procedures for processing—Performing the same process the same way every time will reduce the possibility of errors from incorrectly performing the procedure.

      2. Automating as much processing as possible to reduce human error and increase employee efficiency.

      3. Using predefined values as appropriate, such as a default of 40 hours per week for labor, to reduce or eliminate repetitive entry of information.

      4. Balancing the processing totals against the source documentation batch total to ensure that all records have been processed and recorded accurately.

      5. Confirming that the balance of subsidiary ledgers equals the general ledger control account, such as customer accounts receivable balances.

      6. Matching source documentation to the processing records, such as the traditional three-way match of an inventory receiving report, supplier invoice, and purchase order. Properly recorded and authorized source documentation shows the approval of transactions and proper valuation of transactions.

      7. Implementing redundant processing of data for quality control, such as two payroll employees processing payroll and comparing answers. Independent processing and data review may reduce the possibility of data error or fraudulent activity.

   D. *Output controls* help an organization determine if the input and processing activities result in valid output for decision making.

      1. The accounting information system should have password protection and security of key forms to prevent unauthorized transactions from occurring or unauthorized people from accessing the system.

      2. Master file changes should be tracked and logged to match against scheduled changes in the accounting information system.

      3. Where review of every entry is impossible, exception reports can show significant changes to master files for review and monitoring.

      4. Other output controls can identify problems after processing is complete.

         a. Organizations should reconcile key balance sheet accounts, such as cash, accounts receivable, and fixed assets, to verify financial totals match control totals.

         b. Aging reports can identify accounts with no recent activity.

         c. Suspense files and accounts show unprocessed or partially complete transactions for further review.

         d. Independent parties should audit files, processes, or accounts periodically to detect internal control issues. An external confirmation of a receivables account is one example of an independent verification.

         e. Discrepancy reports list items that violate normal procedures and require additional investigation.

II. Flowcharts

   A. Organizations can use flowcharts to map how their control systems should operate when processing various transactions.

      1. Flowcharts provide a visual representation of how the system works for auditors and management to identify potential control weaknesses. See example below:

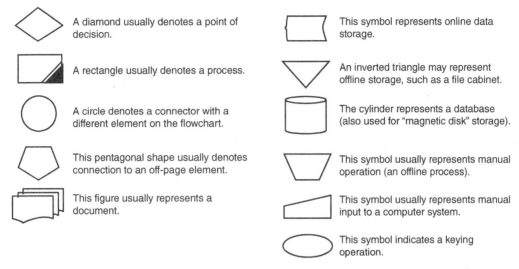

A diamond usually denotes a point of decision.	This symbol represents online data storage.
A rectangle usually denotes a process.	An inverted triangle may represent offline storage, such as a file cabinet.
A circle denotes a connector with a different element on the flowchart.	The cylinder represents a database (also used for "magnetic disk" storage).
This pentagonal shape usually denotes connection to an off-page element.	This symbol usually represents manual operation (an offline process).
This figure usually represents a document.	This symbol usually represents manual input to a computer system.
	This symbol indicates a keying operation.

2. Different actions and activities in a flowchart are indicated through the use of various symbols. See the following table for a list of commonly used symbols:

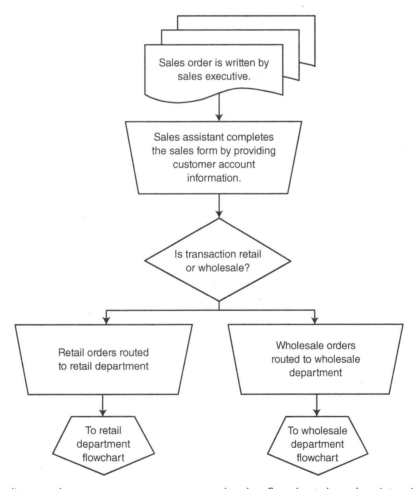

3. Auditors and company management can develop flowcharts based on interviews with company personnel and then test the system to determine if the system works as described.

4. Flowcharts also can identify resource constraints or inefficient procedures. Improvements would then allow the organization to run more efficiently.

5. Flowcharts also can depict any process in the organization, describe relationships between processes or data elements, and track the movement of a document through a given process.

Summary

Application controls are used to prevent, detect, and correct mistakes and intentional misstatements in an information system. There are three main types of application controls: input, processing, and output. Input controls help an organization prevent and detect errors and irregularities related to the input of data into the AIS. Processing controls cover how the accounting information system turns input data into information output to managers and others in the organization. Output controls help an organization determine if the input and processing activities result in valid output for decision making. Flowcharts are often used by an organization in order to map how their control systems should operate.

aq.ic.policies.008_1802

1. The safeguarding of inventory **most likely** includes:

    A. Comparison of the information contained on the purchase requisitions, purchase orders, receiving reports, and vendor invoices.
    B. Analytical procedures for raw materials, work-in-process, and finished goods that identify unusual transactions, theft, and obsolescence.
    C. Application of established overhead rates based on direct labor hours or direct labor costs.
    D. Periodic reconciliation of detailed inventory records with the actual inventory on hand by taking a physical count.

aq.ext.aud.req.003_1802

2. Inherent risk and control risk differ from detection risk in that they:

    A. Arise from the misapplication of auditing procedures.
    B. May be assessed in only quantitative terms.
    C. Exist independently of the financial statement audit.
    D. Can be changed at the auditor's discretion.

aq.corp.gov.002_1802

3. Which of the following is **not** an attribute required by the Sarbanes Oxley Act for the financial expert who serves on the board of directors and the board's audit committee?

    A. An understanding of internal controls
    B. The individual must be a CPA or CFA
    C. An understanding of audit committee functions
    D. The ability to assess the accounting for accruals, estimates, and reserves

aq.gen.c.006_1802

4. What is the backup facility that can be up and running at a short notice called?

    A. VAN
    B. Hot site
    C. Remote site
    D. Cold site

aq.ext.aud.req.004_1802

5. An auditor uses the assessed level of control risk to:

    A. Evaluate the effectiveness of the entity's internal control policies and procedures.
    B. Identify transactions and account balances where inherent risk is at the maximum.
    C. Indicate whether materiality thresholds for planning and evaluation purposes are sufficiently high.
    D. Determine the acceptable level of detection risk for financial statement assertions.

aq.ic.policies.010_1802

6. Proper segregation of duties reduces the opportunities to allow individuals to be in positions to both:

    A. Journalize entries and prepare financial statements.
    B. Authorize transactions and record cash disbursements.
    C. Record cash receipts and cash disbursements.
    D. Establish internal controls and authorize transactions.

aq.corp.gov.006_1802

7. Which of the following correctly describes the Sarbanes-Oxley Act requirements with respect to auditor rotation?

   A. The audit firm must rotate the lead audit partner every five years.
   B. The company being audited must rotate the audit firm every five years.
   C. The audit firm must rotate the audit staff every five years.
   D. The company being audited must rotate the audit committee every five years.

aq.sys.app.c.001_1802

8. Which of the following is an example of a validity check?

   A. The computer flags any transmission for which the control field value did not match that of an existing file record.
   B. The computer ensures that a numerical amount in a record does not exceed some predetermined amount.
   C. As the computer corrects errors and data are successfully resubmitted to the system, the causes of the errors are printed out.
   D. After data for a transaction are entered, the computer sends certain data back to the terminal for comparison with data originally sent.

aq.ext.aud.req.001_1802

9. According to the PCAOB auditing standards (AS), the auditor of a company that issues securities must audit the company's internal control, as well as its financial statements. What is the recommended timing of these two audits?

   A. The two audits should be integrated.
   B. The internal control audit should be performed first and be immediately followed by the audit of the company's financial statements.
   C. The financial statement audit should be performed first and be immediately followed by the audit of the company's internal control.
   D. The internal control audit should be performed first, unless there is an adequate reason for first performing the financial statement audit.

aq.corp.gov.007_1802

10. The Sarbanes-Oxley Act disallows each of the following services for auditors of a publicly traded company except for:

    A. Human resource services.
    B. Financial information systems design.
    C. Tax preparation services.
    D. Actuarial services.

aq.corp.gov.003_1802

11. Which board of directors committee is charged with overseeing the financial reporting process?

    A. The audit committee
    B. The compensation committee
    C. The financial committee
    D. The governance committee

aq.ic.phil.003_1802

12. The Committee of Sponsoring Organizations (COSO) internal control framework consists of five interrelated components. Which of the following is **not** one of these components?

    A. Risk assessment
    B. Information and communication
    C. Management risk
    D. Monitoring

aq.ic.policies.009_1802

13. How would the use of pre-numbered forms be a means of control?

    A. Pre-numbered forms allow for proper review of exceptions or missing documents.
    B. Pre-numbered forms are no longer a useful means of control because companies' assets and procedures are becoming increasingly digital.
    C. Pre-numbered forms allow a company to know when it needs to reorder new forms.
    D. Pre-numbered forms are not a useful means of control because they do not increase protection of a firm's assets.

aq.ic.phil.007_1802

14. Companies with international operations must comply with the Foreign Corrupt Practices Act (FCPA). In order to comply with FCPA, a company's internal controls must provide reasonable assurance that:

    A. Management must authorize all access to assets.
    B. The company's financial records are in accordance with applicable accounting standards.
    C. Management must authorize all access to assets and that the company's financial records are in accordance with applicable accounting standards.
    D. Management does not need to authorize all access to assets and the company's financial records are not required to be in accordance with applicable accounting standards.

aq.ic.risk.002_1802

15. An auditor uses the knowledge provided by the understanding of internal controls and the assessed level of control risk primarily to:

    A. Determine whether the control procedures and supporting records concerning the safeguarding of assets are reliable.
    B. Determine the nature, timing, and extent of further audit procedures.
    C. Modify the preliminary judgments about materiality levels.
    D. Modify the initial assessments of inherent risk.

Section F: Technology and Analytics

Topic 1: Information Systems

Accounting Information Systems

After studying this lesson, you should be able to:

- Identify the role of the accounting information system (AIS) in the value chain (1.F.1.a).

- Demonstrate an understanding of the accounting information system cycles, including revenue to cash, expenditures, production, human resources and payroll, financing, and property, plant, and equipment, as well as the general ledger (GL) and reporting system (1.F.1.b).

- Identify and explain the challenges of having separate financial and nonfinancial systems (1.F.1.c).

> Businesses depend on accounting information systems to make good business decisions. This lesson discusses what accounting information systems are, what they do, and how technology enhances these systems.

I. What are accounting information systems?

    A. An accounting information system (AIS) is a formalized process to collect, store, and process accounting information. Historically, a company's AIS was maintained through physical books (i.e., journals and ledgers). Today, an AIS is typically an electronic system made of a software, computers, and servers.

    B. An AIS captures the pertinent information and recordkeeping needed in order to produce financial statements (e.g., balance sheet, income statement, statement of cash flows, statement of owner's equity) and performance reports (e.g., budgets, project profitability, product cost, etc.). This information is critical to understanding an organization's business activities. AIS adds value to an organization by providing information needed for analysis, evaluation, and strategic decision making.

    C. A primary function of an AIS is to report information. Many stakeholders rely on information produced by an organization's AIS. These include but are not limited to the following: executives, accountants, managers, analysts, auditors, regulators, and tax authorities. Producing accurate and timely information is a critical feature of an effective AIS.

II. The role of the AIS in the value chain.

    A. A value chain is a business model that describes the activities undertaken by an organization to provide value to customers. The primary activities of the value chain are inbound logistics, operations, outbound logistics, marketing and sales, and service. To be successful, a company must ensure that customer value exceeds production costs. In other words, customers must be willing to pay more a product or service than an organization spends to produce that product or service.

    B. An AIS is integral part of the value chain. It forms part of the infrastructure that supports value chain activities. For starters, an AIS provides the information necessary for management to analyze performance in various steps of the value chain, and to make decisions to increase efficiency and effectiveness. This is critical for companies as they adopt and maintain their strategy. For example, the AIS not only enables marketing expenses, but also provides information necessary to analyze whether marketing effectively increases sales. An AIS can also tracks the flow of inbound raw materials and outbound products, which enables organizations to focus on effective production and improving the customer experience. Better information equates to better decisions. An AIS can become more effective when it is linked to the value chains of other organizations, creating an efficient supply chain.

III. AIS Cycles

An AIS can be broken down into several cycles, or sets of related business transactions. The AIS collects and stores information about the activities of an organization related to the following:

A. The *Revenue to Cash Cycle* is the process of taking orders, shipping products or delivering services, billing customers, and collecting cash from sales.

B. The *Expenditure Cycle* is the process of placing orders, receiving shipment of products or delivery of services, approving invoices, and making cash payments.

C. The *Production Cycle* is the process by which raw materials are converted into finished goods.

D. The *Human Resources and Payroll Cycle* is the process of recruiting, interviewing, and hiring personnel, paying employees for their work, promoting employees, and finalizing employees' status from retirements, firings, or voluntary terminations.

E. The *Financing Cycle* is the process of obtaining funding, through debt or equity, to run an organizations' activities and to purchase PPE, servicing the financing, and ultimate repayment of financial obligations.

F. The *Property, Plant, and Equipment Cycle* is the process of acquiring resources (e.g., land, buildings, and machinery) needed to enable an organization's business activities.

G. The *General Ledger and Reporting System* is the process of recording, classifying, and categorizing an organization's economic transactions and producing summary financial reports.

IV. Information Systems for Financial and Nonfinancial Data

A. Historically, financial information was the primary, and often only, information recorded in an AIS. This limitation was primarily a result of technological limitations. Separate systems for tracking nonfinancial information, such as inventory tracking systems, customer sales logs, or human resource information, were maintained as stand-alone systems. The primary challenge of separate systems for financial and nonfinancial data is data maintenance. Because companies maintained separate systems, updates in one system would not automatically flow through to other systems. Manually updating multiple systems can take substantial amounts of time and result in errors. As a result, companies must take great care to ensure that any changes in product price, customer contracts, etc. were reflected in all relevant systems to ensure proper reconciliation.

Modern AIS have greater computing capabilities and larger storage capacity than previous AIS. This has facilitated an integrated approach wherein financial and nonfinancial information can be linked within a single information system, which is known as an Enterprise Resource Planning (ERP) system. ERP systems will be discussed in the next lesson.

B. A Customer Relationship management (CRM) system is a good example of a system that runs in parallel with an AIS. Within an overarching ERP system, the CRM and AIS are linked. However, while the AIS process financial data, the CRM processes nonfinancial data specific to customers. This includes information about sales calls, shipment tracking, and customer profiles. Linking these sytems together reduces potential errors and increases the usefulness of an organization's data.

Summary
Companies use accounting information systems to collect, store, and process financial information. Accounting information systems are usually broken down into types of transactions, such as revenue, expenditure, and production cycles. A well-functioning accounting information system allows for the compilation of financial statements and helps business leaders make good decisions.

Enterprise Resource Planning Systems

After studying this lesson, you should be able to:

- Define enterprise resource planning (ERP) and its characteristics (1.F.1.d).

- Explain how ERP helps overcome the challenges of separate financial and nonfinancial systems, integrating all aspects of an organization's activities (1.F.1.e).

- Demonstrate an understanding of a database management system and describe its characteristics (1.F.1.f).

- Define data warehouse and data mart (1.F.1.g).

Businesses are capitalizing on the power of information to improve their operations. An Enterprise Resource Planning System (ERP) is a tool to that allows employees throughout a company to make the most of company data. In this lesson, we discuss Enterprise Resource Planning Systems, Database Management Systems, and Data Warehouses.

I. What is Enterprise Resource Planning?

    A. *Enterprise Resource Planning* is the integrated management of core business processes. ERP brings together business functions such as inventory management, accounting, finance, human resources, supply chain management; and integrates these functions into a single, overaching system. ERP systems are modular so that they can be adapted to companies of varying sizes and industries. As systems grow and become more complex, the benefits of adding modules increase. This resulting shared database that underlies the ERP system allows employees in one business function to view and access data generated in other business functions.

    B. The shared database structure of an ERP allows greater synchronization of information across business functions. Employees can interact with a single system rather than with separate systems in siloed business functions. Updates made to any system flow through to other business functions because all functions use the same underlying data. Improved data allows companies to effectively improve the value chain by cutting costs and focusing on value-added activities.

    C. ERP has many benefits:

        1. Employees have access to information in real time rather than having to wait for data to be shared across business functions.

        2. Increased standardization of business processes.

        3. Increased regulatory compliance.

        4. Improved financial reporting.

        5. Improved customer experience and satisfaction.

        6. Collaboration and teamwork are encouraged because information is widely distributed.

        7. Employees only need to learn how to use a single system rather than multiple.

        8. Although initially very expensive, ERP can lower long-term operational costs by eliminating redundant systems and simplifying system maintenance.

        9. Improved organizational outcomes such as improved financial reporting and improved customer experience.

II. Database Management System (DBMS)

    A. A *database management system* is the interface or program between a company's databases and the application programs that access these databases. The DBMS defines, reads, manipulates, updates, and deletes data in a database. It controls access to the data and maps each user's view of the data (i.e., the DBMS can be programmed to present data in a way that makes sense for each user).

B. The information about various business functions provided to users of ERP systems is generated from company data that is accessed by a DBMS. The ERP makes the data more accessible to the average employee. In companies without ERP systems, employees can access the data through the DBMS using query languages such as SQL. Companies often use relational databases because they present data in a table format that are easy to visualize, understand, and manipulate.

C. A database management system optimizes how data in databases are stored and retrieved. The database management system facilitates an organization's administrative operations related to disaster recovery, regulatory and legal compliance, and performance monitoring.

D. In addition to providing access to data, a DBMS protects a company's data by ensuring data integrity, confidentiality, and availability. Passwords and data encryption help ensure integrity and confidentiality. A recovery plan and backup copies help ensure that data are available when needed.

III. What is a data warehouse?

A. A *data warehouse* is used to aggregate data from multiple sources into a central integrated data repository. Data warehouses are used to analyze business activities and operations.

B. Whereas databases are typically focused on processing transactions, a data warehouse does not process data. A data warehouse is the storage of historical summary data from disparate sources that are aggregated in order to facilitate data analysis.

Summary

Traditionally, companies have used separate systems to process financial and nonfinancial information. Enterprise resource planning integrates both types of information and improves the usability of information within a company. Database management systems allow users convenient access to information and ensure that company data is safeguarded and complies with various regulatory and legal requirements. Companies use data warehouses as an integrated repository for data.

Enterprise Performance Management Systems

After studying this lesson, you should be able to:

- Define enterprise performance management (EPM) (also known as corporate performance management or CPM and business performance management or BPM) (1.F.1.h).

- Discuss how EPM can facilitate business planning and performance management (1.F.1.i).

> Companies use Enterprise Performance Management Systems to link strategic objectives with employee actions. EPM systems leverage technology to improve communication within a company as well as allow employees to spend more time on high-value tasks such as analysis that are likely to help companies achieve their strategic goals.

I. Enterprise Performance Management

    A. Today's companies have more data available than ever before, and this data can drive strategy and other business decisions. However, companies have so much data that it is often difficult to focus on which data are most important to a company's success. In addition, it's difficult to communicate strategy and performance effectively throughout large and complex organizations. *Enterprise Performance Management* (EPM) is the process of using data to link an organization's strategies to specific plans and actions.

    B. EPM is sometimes known as Corporate Performance Management (CPM) or Business Performance Management (BPM).

    C. Companies most often use EPM for several key sub-processes including the following:

        1. Planning, budgeting, and forecasting

        2. Performance reporting

        3. Profitability and cost analysis

    D. Many companies use some form of a plan-do-check-act (PDCA) process when implementing strategy. These steps include

        1. Plan. Management designs or revises business strategies.

        2. Do. The company implements these strategies.

        3. Check. The company assesses and reports performance.

        4. Act. Determine how strategies can be changed or maintained in the future.

    E. EPM facilitates strategy implementation. For instance, a company may determine that a key part of their strategy for increasing sales by 10% is to increase traffic to the company's website using targeted advertising. EPM would link this strategy to plans and actions in the following ways.

        1. The EPM system would communicate this strategic goal to employees. The goal would be reflected in employees' action plans. EPM is not only a performance tracking system, but also a communication tool.

        2. As the company improves advertising, The EPM software allows management to easily collect real-time key performance indicators (KPI). In this case, the EPM would track and make available statistics on web-traffic or unique website visitors, as well as sales information.

        3. The EPM would generate reports, which may take the form of dashboards updated in real time, to report web traffic and sales figures to decision makers.

        4. The EPM would make use of historical data analytics models to determine how KPI indicators affect performance. In this case, management has likely identified how web traffic influences sales through the use of predictive analytic models. These models are updated or changed, and insights garnered from this process influence changes to company strategy.

F. EPM makes use of all information systems and data sources. Ideally, these data are automatically consolidated to create a set of performance metrics against which company goals can be compared.

G. EPM requires reviews and updates on a periodic basis. The timing and frequency of these reviews can be adapted to serve the needs of the organization. For example, companies with a shorter operating cycle, such as retail, may need more frequent review than some manufacturing companies with longer operating cycles.

H. EPM software packages can improve efficiencies in planning, budgeting, and reporting processes by relying on a centralized database and workflow, similar to an ERP system. An ERP system focuses on automating transactional processes and is just one component or subset of a comprehensive EPM system that is intended to communicate and carryout strategy.

I. EPM provides a more holistic view of an organization's performance by linking its financial and operational data and metrics. This helps facilitate the analysis and reporting of the organization's activities.

Summary

Enterprise performance management is the process of using company strategies to set goals, monitor and analyze performance, and improve operations. Communication is key to successful enterprise performance management, and companies must determine how to best correspond with employees to ensure that effort aligns with company strategy and objectives are being met. Accounting information systems and enterprise resource management complement enterprise performance management by providing easier access to higher-quality information.

Topic 2: Data Governance

Data Policies and Procedures

After studying this lesson, you should be able to:

- Define data governance; i.e., managing the availability, usability, integrity, and security of data (1.F.2.a).

- Demonstrate a general understanding of data governance frameworks, COSO's Internal Control framework and ISACA's COBIT (Control Objectives for Information and Related Technologies) (1.F.2.b).

> This lesson defines data governance and discusses various practical frameworks that companies can use to develop policies and procedures to manage data governance.

I. What Is Data Governance?

    A. Data governance is a set of defined procedures, policies, rules, and processes that oversee the following attributes of an organization's data:

        1. *Availability* refers to the ability to make data accessible when it is needed and where it is needed. Data that is available can be easily accessed in a timely manner. Policies and procedures related to data availability can also cover how data is accessed when disruptions occur within an organization's IT system.

        2. *Usability* refers to data being delivered to end-users in formats and structures that allow the completion of desired business activities, analysis, and operations. Usable data can be successfully integrated and processed in software and applications desired by end-users.

        3. *Integrity* of data refers to the accuracy and consistency of data. Data must be reliable in order for proper inferences and decisions. Data governance policies should provide specific safeguards and protections to ensure that data is accurate and valid.

        4. *Security* of data governs how data is protected from unauthorized access and from possible data corruption. Examples of data security techniques include data encryption and physical barriers. Secure data are protected against accidental or intentional modifications, removals, or disclosures. Data security includes both electronic and physical safeguards to protect data. The increase in cyber theft over the past several years has made data security an important concern for organizations.

    B. Good data governance ensures that companies consistently and properly use and safeguard an organization's data.

II. Data Governance Frameworks

    A. Data governance frameworks have several objectives designed to improve the use and security of data. These include:

        1. Enable management to make informed decisions about how to manage data.

        2. Realize value from data

        3. Minimize cost and complexity of data collection, use, and storage.

        4. Manage data-related risks

        5. Ensure compliance with relevant regulations. These can include laws about the protection of financial- or health-related information.

B. COSO's Internal Control-Integrated Framework

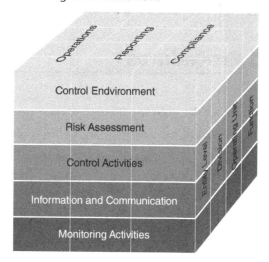

The COSO internal control framework helps companies visualize various dimensions of internal control. Internal controls must be implemented to ensure proper data governance. The framework does not provide specific policies that should be implemented. Rather, it provides guidelines to help companies consider which internal controls make sense for their organization.

1. The top face of the cube illustrates *why* we internal controls are needed. Internal controls over data governance are necessary for operations, reporting, and compliance with applicable laws and regulations.

2. The right face of the cube illustrates where we need internal control. Internal controls over data governance should be implemented at all levels of the organization, including the entity, divisions, operating units, and individual functions.

3. The front face of the cube illustrates *how* organizations can have good internal controls, or what components must be in place. According to the framework, there are five components of internal controls, each of which is built on guiding principles or goals necessary to implement effective internal controls. The five components are:

  i. Control environment – internal control over data governance depends on good leadership and culture. This is often referred to as "tone at the top."

  ii. Risk assessment – companies must identify risks to data governance. This allows companies to use controls strategically to address these risks.

  iii. Control activities – these are the specific policies and procedures put in place to ensure data governance.

  iv. Information and communication – ensuring proper internal controls over data governance improves information quality throughout the company.

  v. Monitoring activities – companies need to monitor and adapt controls to respond to changes in the environment.

C. ISACA's COBIT

  1. ISACA (the organization formerly known as Information Systems Audit and Control Association) created a best-practice framework called the Control Objectives for Information and Related Technologies (COBIT) to guide information technology (IT) governance and management.

    i. Governance has to do with evaluating stakeholder needs, setting objectives based on organizational priority, and monitoring performance to determine if those objectives are met. Governance is typically the responsibility of the board of directors or those charged with overseeing the organization.

    ii. Management is where the rubber meets the road. Management entails planning, using, and monitoring activities that alight and support governance objectives. Management is typically the responsibility of executive management who are tasked with carrying out the directives of the board.

2. COBIT is primarily concerned with security, risk management, and information governance.

3. The 5 key principles of COBIT are:

    i. Meeting stakeholder needs

    ii. Covering the enterprise end-to-end

    iii. Applying a single, integrated framework

    iv. Enabling a holistic approach

    v. Separating governance from management

Summary

Companies' success depends on good data. Data governance is a set of procedures, policies, rules, and processes to ensure that data can be relied upon. Data governance frameworks help companies envision the steps that must be taken to protect and safeguard data.

Life Cycle of Data

After studying this lesson, you should be able to:

- Identify the stages of the data life cycle; i.e., data capture, data maintenance, data synthesis, data usage, data analytics, data publication, data archiving, and data purging (1.F.2.c).

- Demonstrate an understanding of data preprocessing and the steps to convert data for further analysis, including data consolidation, data cleaning (cleansing), data transformation, and data reduction (1.F.2.d).

- Discuss the importance of having a documented record retention (or records management) policy (1.F.2.e).

This lesson defines and discusses the various phases of the data life cycle, and the importance of data retention policies. In addition, the lesson discusses the preprocessing of data, which consists of a series of steps to make data ready for analysis.

I. The data life cycle is a representation of the stages that data pass through from initial generation to eventual archival or deletion. The stages of the data life cycle are:

   A. *Data capture* is the initial stage of data wherein data is collected. Data can be captured through a variety of means such as manual data entry, automated data entry, or acquisition of existing data from an external source. Data capture brings data into an organization that previously it did not have.

   B. *Data maintenance* is a process by which data is put into useful forms. Data maintenance does not provide evaluations or analysis, but rather is focused on cleaning up data and putting it into structures to make it user-friendly for an organization's system, software, and end-users. Many forms of data, such as handwriting or video, are difficult to analyze without making them useful through sophisticated software.

   C. *Data synthesis* creates new data by using existing data and deriving logic outputs. Data synthesis involves combining experience, judgments, or opinions to provide logical interpretations of existing data points. For example, credit scores are a result of data synthesis wherein various data points are used alongside prescribed metrics to arrive at a credit score.

   D. *Data usage* is simply employing data within the business activities and processes of an organization. Data usage may be affected by permissions and authorizations within an organization along with outside legal and regulatory requirements. Although data may exist, accessing and using the data is typically subject to data governance policies and rules.

   E. *Data analytics* is a specialized stage wherein data is used in models to facilitate pattern recognition and evaluation of correlations and associations. Data analysis can take many forms such as regression analysis, cluster analysis, trend analysis, and more.

   F. *Data publication* involves making data available outside of an organization. Not all data will pass through this stage if the data is not needed to be transferred to third-parties. Data that is published cannot itself be changed by the organization and would need to be revised and resent if errors are discovered. Data publication does not necessarily need to be the willful act of an organization.

   G. *Data archiving* is the stage wherein data is set aside from active usage. Data that is archived is stored for future use. Archived data remains as is and is not involved with data maintenance, data usage, data analysis, or data publication until it is restored to active usage.

   H. *Data purging* is the final stage for data and involves data being deleted or removed from existence. Data purging is meant to be permanent erasure or removal of data. For example, on a personal computer deleted files are first held in a temporary deletion folder, the Recycle Bin.

These files could still be restored if desired. Once the contents of the Recycle Bin is emptied, it is effectively a data purge whereby the files are permanently removed, freeing up space on the computer's hard drive, without the possibility of the files being restored.

II. Data preprocessing

    A. Preparing data from its raw form to a form that is understandable for analysis often takes far more time and effort than data analysis. This process is known as data preprocessing and includes the following steps:

        i. Data consolidation: Data often come from a variety of sources. Consolidation is the process of bringing this data together so that it can be more easily analyzed.

        ii. Data cleaning (cleansing): Data must be "cleaned" before analysis. Raw data often include missing data and outliers, which can substantially change the results of data analysis. Cleaning data includes identifying and either excluding or altering missing data and outliers.

        iii. Data transformation: This step involves changing the nature of the data for analysis purposes. For instance, data can be normalized to ensure all values fall within a certain range. For instance, a company may have customers fill out a number of surveys with various scales. These data can be standardized such that all values fall between 1 and 5, or simply changed to a 0 or 1 to indicate whether they are higher or lower than the survey median. Data can also be aggregated to reduce variability in the data. For example, daily sales can be transformed to monthly data.

        iv. Data reduction: As the amount of data collected by companies increase, it may be useful to reduce the data to require less memory and processing time. This step may entail excluding irrelevant data. Companies may also use principal component analysis (PCA), which is a statistical technique that creates a new variable by combining several related variables. For example, an indicator of customer satisfaction can be assessed by combining customer attitudes towards a company, its products, its reputation, and customer service.

III. Record Retention

    A. A documented record retention policy is an important control to ensure data are secure. The policy provides a framework by which data are created, recorded, maintained, accessed, deleted, and stored. The policy provides clear guidance on how information may be used and which employees can perform data-related functions.

    B. A records management policy can make sure that an organization complies with applicable legal and regulatory requirements. Data storage requirements may vary in length and detail across business functions such as accounting, human resources, and operations.

    C. A records management policy can also safeguard the organization against the loss of key strategic information. Operational data can provide a history of an organization's business activities and be a valuable resource for evaluating business processes, outcomes of decisions, and financial performance.

Summary

Data are the lifeblood of an organization. To ensure that data are useful to an organization, data must be properly captured, organized, and analyzed. Data preprocessing is often necessary before data can be used and analyzed. The steps of the data life cycle detail how data is properly handled by organizations. Companies must also ensure that data are maintained for certain lengths of time to comply with regulatory requirements.

Controls Against Security Breaches

After studying this lesson, you should be able to:

- Identify and explain controls and tools to detect and thwart cyberattacks, such as penetration and vulnerability testing, biometrics, advanced firewalls, and access controls (1.F.2.f).

This lesson discusses various types of cyberattacks, as well as methods for protecting against such attacks.

I. Preventing and Detecting Cyberattacks

    A. Information security is critical in today's business environment. Proper information security is ensured by adhering too the following principles:

        1. *Confidentiality.* Data should only be accessed by authorized individuals.

        2. *Integrity.* Data must be protected from unauthorized changes.

        3. *Availability.* Data should be accessible as needed.

    B. A *cyberattack* is an attempt by unauthorized users to gain access to the information system or computer of another individual or organization. A cyberattack is a malicious or deliberate action taken in order to inflict harm on another by altering, disabling, destroying, or stealing electronic information. A few examples of the many cyberattack techniques include:

        1. Malware breaches a system or computer through a vulnerability. Malware can block access to computer or server functions (ransomware), it can be used to gather and transmit data (spyware), and it can disrupt system processing (viruses).

        2. Phishing is the false presentation or fraudulent communication of information from a reputable source with the goal of installing malware or stealing valuable personal information.

        3. A denial-of-service attack overloads a network or computer with requests to process information. The requests exhaust the computational processing power or bandwidth of the computer or network and thereby makes them unable to process legitimate requests.

    C. Organizations can put in place security controls to prevent and detect cyberattacks. Controls can be classified as preventive, (prevents an attack before it occurs), detective (detects an attack as it occurs), or corrective/recovery (repairs damage done after an attack). In some literature you'll see another category of control: compensating controls, which are controls used to augment one or more existing controls. For instance, a compensating control may require that a user log in multiple times or systems that use multiple layers of encryption. Examples of controls against cyberattacks include but are not limited to the following:

        1. *Vulnerability testing* is used to identify existing vulnerabilities. It does not, however, attempt to assess if and how the vulnerability could be exploited. In contrast, *penetration testing* is undertaken to actively exploit potential weaknesses in a system. Penetration tests assess the possibility of breaches and their potential severity. The penetration tests help determine if a vulnerability is genuine and what could be the potential resulting damages.

        2. *Biometrics* are the use of physical features and measurements for identity verification. Biometrics can include using fingerprints, facial recognition, and even stride pattern to verify individuals. Based on the identity of the individual accessing the system, access and authorizations can be granted or denied. Biometrics help ensure that only authorized personnel are allowed to physically be in certain locations, to access and alter data, and/or perform specified business functions. Biometric authentication can safeguard data by preventing its unauthorized access. Biometrics are generally more secure than passwords because they assess "what you are" or "what you do" rather than "what you know."

Information security is especially effective when biometrics are used in conjunction with passwords, and explains why dual-factor authentication is increasingly popular.

3. *Firewalls* are used in computer networks to prevent unauthorized users from gaining access to a network. Firewalls monitor the incoming and outgoing traffic on a network and place a barrier around network systems and databases. Simple firewalls examine a packet's source address and its destination address and port. They don't examine the contents of packets, so if harmful content comes from a trusted source, simple firewalls won't stop it. Advanced firewalls can look at a packet's contents instead of just examining the source and destination addresses and port, and thus provide a higher level of security. Firewalls can take the form of hardware, software, or a combination of both. Advanced firewalls can do more than filter packets - they can filter applications and the data they use.

4. *Access controls* place limits on who can access a place or a resource. Access controls primarily address data confidentiality and integrity, and can be physical or logical. Physical access controls restrict who can enter into geographic areas, buildings, and/or rooms. Logical access controls restrict which individuals can connect to computer networks, system files, and data. In both cases, the access control might take the form of passwords, personal identification numbers (PINs), credentials, or other authorization and authentication forms.

Summary

Cyberattacks are enormously expensive to firms, both in terms of financial costs, as well as reputation costs. As cyberattacks become more sophisticated, companies must ensure that adequate resources are used to lower the risk of cyberattacks to an acceptable level.

Topic 3: Technology-Enabled Finance Transformation

System Development Life Cycle

After studying this lesson, you should be able to:

- Define the systems development life cycle (SDLC), including systems analysis, conceptual design, physical design, implementation and conversion, and operations and maintenance (1.F.3.a).

- Explain the role of business process analysis in improving system performance (1.F.3.b).

> Developing an information system is a multistep process called the Systems Development Life Cycle. This lesson will describe the steps of systems development life cycle as well as discuss the improvement of system performance.

I. Systems Development Life Cycle

   A. The development of an information system typically is a multistep process. The steps can include the following:

      1. *System analysis* is an evaluative process to assess user needs, resource requirements, benefits, and costs. Gathering pertinent information may require surveys of employees, in-depth interviews with system users, documentation of best practices, and data analysis. Understanding the end goals and uses of the system is important to ensure its proper design and to assess system feasibility.

      2. *Conceptual design* is the process of creating plans for meeting the needs of the organization. Detailed specifications are created to provide instruction on how to achieve the desired system. Often, several designs will be considered at this stage. Organizations will weigh the costs and benefits of each design before selecting the one that best meets the organizations' needs.

      3. *Physical design* is the process of identifying the features, specifications, and equipment needed in order to make the system operational. At this point in the SDLC, Specific database schema objects, or blueprints, are defined and specified. Consideration is given both to the end-user experience of interacting with system and to the backend computational and processing power needed. The system structure may also involve networking if desired.

      4. *Implementation and conversion* is the process of making the system design a reality. This step takes consider amounts of time, as software must be written, installed and tested. Hardware must also be installed and tested to ensure proper functionality. If the new system is replacing an older system, data must be transferred and integrated in the processes and procedures of the new system. Testing can be extensive with the new system to identify processing errors or design flaws. It is important to verify the system functions as expected and produces valid output.

      5. *Operations and maintenance* is the process of fine-tuning and refining the system as users explore functionalities and place demands on the system processing. One important component of this step is to identify and authorize users that will have access to various components of the system. New capabilities may be required as users identify needs. Despite earlier testing, flaws are frequently identified and reported during this phase. Hardware may also need replacement over time due to wear and tear and/or obsolescence. Software may also be updated to improve processing or to add functional options.

B. Deviations from the SDLC

    1. The SDLC framework increases the quality and auditability of the system development process. However, the methodical approach prescribed by the SDLC framework takes time. As a result, some organizations allow for emergency deviations from the standard process. Such "break the glass" procedures allow developers to bypass safeguards and quickly make changes to the system. Developers usually get formal approval for these changes after they are made

II. Improving System Performance

    A. *Business process analysis* is used to evaluate and improve core business processes. It takes a fresh view of the process and asks how it could be done differently with greater speed or with greater effectiveness. The analysis involves gathering information about the current process and understanding what its objectives are. Diagrams and flowcharts might be used to document the logical flow of how the business process functions, and these visualizations sometimes show steps that are unnecessary or duplicative. New ideas and alternatives are then identified and evaluated on whether the process can be altered while still achieving the same objectives.

    B. Examples of practices used during business process analysis include:

        1. Hands-on observation of how a process is performed.

        2. In-depth interviews with employees closely involved with a process or who perform key parts of a process.

        3. Identifying value-added components of the process and evaluating whether non-value-adding activities can be changed or removed.

        4. Conducting time-and-motion studies to assess the efficiency of a process.

        5. Mapping, diagraming, and flowcharting processes to understand and evaluate workflow and critical decision points.

Summary

An information system is developed through a process called the systems development life cycle. This life cycle has multiple steps, including system analysis, physical design, implementation and conversion, and operations and maintenance. Another important aspect of information systems is improving system performance. This is typically done through business process analysis, which is used to evaluate and improve core business processes.

Process Automation

After studying this lesson, you should be able to:

- Define robotic process automation (RPA) and its benefits (1.F.3.c).

- Evaluate where technologies can improve efficiency and effectiveness of processing accounting data and information (e.g., artificial intelligence (AI)) (1.F.3.d).

In many instances, automated processes are being developed to replace human labor in performing certain functions. This lesson will discuss a few of these types of processes.

I. Robotic Process Automation

    A. *Robotic process automation* (RPA) is the use of software to complete routine, repetitive tasks. RPA is typically used in settings with high volumes of routinized actions. Rather than employing human labor to perform these functions, robots can be employed to manipulate data, record transactions, process information, and perform many other business and IT processes.

    B. RPA can bring many benefits to organizations.

        1. RPA greatly increases efficiency. Computers are much faster than humans, and they can work 24 hours a day. Companies that have adopted RPA have reported high returns on their RPA investment because of efficiency gains.

        2. RPA increases the consistency of operations since computers are not prone to human error.

        3. RPA can lead to cost savings in certain industries where computers are able to replace or assist human workers. This is especially important in industries that have difficulty finding a sufficient number of workers.

        4. RPA is generally used for routine tasks - tasks that employees often find boring. In many industries where RPA has been adopted, employees report higher satisfaction as they are able to focus on more challenging tasks.

    C. Drawbacks of RPA:

        1. The initial investment to develop a rule-based system that automates workplace tasks can be costly. It requires significant time and understanding to define procedures and processes, and further time and resources to test, verify, and/or audit the process to ensure accurate completion of the task. RPA can lower companies' costs by increasing throughput and reducing errors, yet that benefit must be weighed against the cost of designing and implementing the automated process.

        2. Some tasks are not good candidates for RPA. Tasks that are performed with irregularity may not merit the development costs of RPA. In addition, tasks that have high levels of variability are not good candidates for RPA, because RPA is ideal for tasks that perform the same actions time and time again. Finally, tasks that require human judgment cannot be replaced with RPA.

        3. If rules or processes change, then the RPA system requires updating. This can require significant time and energy if changes are significant.

    D. An example of a task that could be automated with RPA is inventory reordering. Consider a grocery store that manually reorders inventory when stock hits a predefined threshold, such as 10%. RPA can follow these predefined rules to automatically reorder inventory without human intervention.

II. Artificial Intelligence

   A. *Artificial intelligence* is different from RPA because rather than a prescribed, rule-based system, artificial intelligence involves computers performing tasks requiring critical analysis and pattern recognition. For example, artificial intelligence can be used to recognize speech or textual patterns. It can be used to analyze various inputs and provide a recommended decision.

   B. Artificial intelligence (AI) also involves a learning aspect. That is, the computer can learn from prior information processing experiences and revise and update future processing, much like a human would do. Rather than simply following a set of rules as in RPA, AI is adaptive.

   C. AI can augment human analysis and decision making by processing information more quickly and in larger quantities than the human mind can. AI can thereby help discover patterns and trends. AI also does not suffer computational fatigue, but can perform analyses in high volume and high frequency that might otherwise cause fatigue and strain for a human.

   D. Grocery stores use AI to know when to reorder groceries. This is different than using RPA, which follows predefined rules to order inventory (such as when stock hits 10% of capacity). Instead, AI can analyze how much inventory must be discarded due to spoilage and alter order size and frequency to improve the freshness of items and decrease waste. With increased data input, AI can also incorporate data such as seasonality, weather, and changing consumer preferences to further optimize order quantities. What's more — AI can be programmed to perform these analyses for each individual sku in the store!

   E. AI can have specific applications and uses in accounting. AI can be used to classify or categorize transactions into appropriate accounts. AI can be used to identify potential errors or irregularities in accounting data, which could be used to improve financial reporting or by auditors to detect misstatements and/or fraudulent activities. AI can be used to analyze cost data and create reports on cost behaviors and patterns. While a skilled accountant is needed to help define the parameters and metrics of interest, AI can be trained through repetitive data processing to perform many accounting functions.

Summary

Companies employ different means to use automated processes to replace human labor. Robotic process automation is typically used to perform high volumes of repetitive and routine tasks. Artificial intelligence is able to perform tasks that require critical analysis and pattern recognition.

Innovative Applications

After studying this lesson, you should be able to:

- Define cloud computing and describe how it can improve efficiency (1.F.3.e).

- Define software as a service (SaaS) and explain its advantages and disadvantages (1.F.3.f).

- Recognize potential applications of blockchain, distributed ledger, and smart contracts (1.F.3.g).

With the high use of technology to perform business functions, companies utilize many different functionalities in order to manage data and perform tasks. This lesson will specifically discuss cloud computing, software as a service (SaaS), blockchain, and smart contracts.

I. Cloud Computing

   A. Cloud computing is a shared resource setup that allows for improved processing of electronic information. Cloud computing is a network of remote servers that are connected by the Internet. Companies run virtual machines from anywhere in the word which are connect to remote servers. The remote servers are used to store, manage, and process data. Rather than performing these functions on a local server or a personal computer, cloud computing joins numerous servers and computers. Cloud computing can provide access to larger data storage, processing speeds, and software applications.

   B. Cloud computing can help avoid data loss due to localized hardware failures and malfunctions because of networked backups and redundancies. The "cloud" or network of servers provides a safeguard by storing information on multiple servers at multiple geographic locations. While cloud computing does rely on the Internet in order to function, it alleviates the reliance on individual servers and computers to store and process information.

II. Software as a Service

   A. Cloud computing can reduce information technology (IT) costs. While cloud computing is a distributed, remote network of servers and computers, it can act like a centralized system that enables local users to have more computing power and more software availabilities. Rather than building up local computing capabilities and installing software on each local PC, a cloud-based system can make these features available system-wide to each local PC without repetitive installments and equipment. This can reduce IT costs for local servers and computers. This type of setup is referred to as *Software as a Service*. It is based upon delivering and licensing software through online applications, in an "on-demand format," rather than installations on individual computers.

   B. *Software as a Service* (SaaS) often shifts the responsibility for software maintenance and troubleshooting to the software provider, thereby allowing firms to outsource typical IT responsibilities. Many firms may still find it advisable to have local backups of critical business data.

   C. SaaS can face limitations on functionality and offerings compared to localized installation of software on individual computers. For instance, because software is stored on remote servers, it typically will not function as quickly as on-premises applications. More specialized and customized software may not be a good fit for SaaS; however, advancements in technology are quickly making this less of an issue.

III. Innovative Applications

   A. *Blockchain* is a distributed, digital ledger of economic transactions. It is distributed in that it is a decentralized, public database. The ledger keeps track of all transactions within a peer-to-peer network. This is primarily due to increased transparency of Blockchain over traditional systems. The database is not stored in a single location, making it not only publicly available, but also difficult to be hacked or corrupted. The data is stored across thousands of computers and servers simultaneously.

B. *Blockchain* improves the validity of data. The digital record of transactions is widely distributed, but cannot be copied. The digital record cannot be altered once recorded and therefore requires new transactions to update or change information.

C. A popular use of *Blockchain* is for cryptocurrencies such as Bitcoin. Cryptocurrencies facilitate economic exchange based on a public, digital ledger to record and verify transactions. Blockchain works well for this purpose because a distributed, digital ledger makes it easy to see changes in asset ownership.

D. *Block chain* has been used to develop a new type of contractual agreement called *smart contracts*. *Smart contracts* based on blockchain technology allow for contractual terms to be completed without involving third parties. That is, agreed-upon terms can be verified and carried out using a distributed digital ledger whereby the transactions are trackable and unalterable and are executed and enforced based on computerized protocols. These self-executed contractual agreements can eliminate the need for third-party involvement and oversight in order to initiate and complete contractual clauses.

Summary

Cloud computing is utilized by many individuals and companies by using a network of remote servers connected to the Internet in order to provide a place to store information on multiple servers at multiple geographic locations. SaaS uses a cloud-based system to provide software to multiple computers at a time rather than having to install software on each local PC. Blockchain is a decentralized, public database that keeps track of all transactions within a peer-to-peer network.

Topic 4: Data Analytics

Business Intelligence

After studying this lesson, you should be able to:

- Define *big data*, explain the four *V*'s (volume, velocity, variety, and veracity), and describe the opportunities and challenges of leveraging insight from this data (1.F.4.a).

- Explain how structured (spreadsheet), semi-structured, and unstructured data is used by a business enterprise (1.F.4.b).

- Describe the progression of data, from data to information to knowledge to insight to action (1.F.4.c).

- Describe the opportunities and challenges of managing data analytics (1.F.4.d).

- Explain why data and data science capability are strategic assets (1.F.4.e).

- Define business intelligence (BI), i.e., the collection of applications, tools, and best practices that transform data into actionable information in order to make better decisions and optimize performance (1.F.4.f).

Many companies use *big data* to gain important insights and improve decision making. This lesson discusses what big data is, some of the challenges of managing the data, and how this data is transformed into knowledge and action.

I. Big Data

   A. *Big data* refers to datasets which are extremely large and/or complex. Big data is too large to be analyzed by traditional data-analysis software and requires special software and computational power to be processed and analyzed. Big data is used to gain insight into relationships and associations to improve decision making and strategy. The advancement of computer processing has enabled organizations to record, store, and analyze large volumes of data which were previously unavailable.

   B. *Big data* is broken down into four dimensions:

   1. *Volume* refers to the scale of the data. Big data is just that, BIG. Enormous amounts of data are stored in databases with information on thousands, millions, or even billions of observational units. Because so much data are available, companies should pay close attention to data sources to ensure that data are of high quality.

   2. *Velocity* refers to the speed by which big data is generated and analyzed. Big data can involve the analysis of a constant stream of new data. For example, the New York Stock Exchange captures over 1 terabyte of trade information during each trading session. This huge amount of data is instantly incorporated into analyses.

   3. *Variety* means that big data comes in many different forms. Big data can refer to traditional relational databases, videos, social media exchanges, emails, health monitors, and more. Variety is the most valuable of the 4 Vs. The ability to analyze data from many different sources makes it possible to learn more from data than ever before.

   4. *Veracity* refers to the truthfulness or accuracy of data. Poor-quality data can make business decision making more difficult.

II. Data Structure

   A. Data can be structured or organized in several ways.

   1. *Structured data* has fixed fields, such as data organized in a spreadsheet with column or row identifiers. Structured data is easily searchable because it is organized and identifiable,

typically in a relational database form with unique identifiers easily linking databases together.

2. *Semi-structured data* does not have neat, organized fixed fields like structured data, but may still contain organizing features such as tags or markers. While it does not have the formal structure of a relational database, semi-structured data does have features which allow it to have classifications and groupings. XML, Extensible Markup Language, which is used to encode documents in human and machine readable formats, and email are forms of semi-structured data.

3. *Unstructured data* is unorganized and is not easily searchable. Unstructured data is often text-based, like human speech, rendering it difficult to categorize and organize into predefined, set data fields. Information from a Twitter feed, text messages, photos, or videos are examples of unstructured data.

III. From Data to Action

A. *Business intelligence* is all of the applications, tools, and best practices that transform data into actionable information in order to make better decisions and optimize performance. Business intelligence supports better decision making.

B. *Data* by itself has very limited meaning. It is simply facts, statistics, symbols, numbers, texts, or characters that may lack structure or form. Data are raw and unorganized. When structures or organizations are used, data are transformed into information. *Information* is different from data because information carries meaning and understanding. Knowledge is defined and created from information. *Knowledge* is what we know and how we understand the way things are. From knowledge, critical analysis can be done through logical thinking to understand situations and generate insight. Insight leads companies to undertake actions.

C. Data analytics is a critical step in the progression of data to actions. Data analytics processes data into information by organizing data and using analysis techniques to identify and understand relationships, patterns, trends, and causes. Data analytics can help individuals develop and refine information into knowledge, which requires human understanding. Increased understanding may lead to insight or judgment as individuals recognize connections that are not readily apparent.

D. Data analytics can be challenging for a variety of reasons. Big data requires the compilation of disparate data sources into a unified, structured database. In addition to the computational processing needs, gathering and combining databases can be time consuming and intellectually challenging. Cleaning data for analysis can be enormously time consuming. Procedures and processes must be put in place to validate data sources and verify that proper processing has taken place. Often, specialized training in computer sciences, information systems, and statistics is needed in order to have the requisite skillset to conduct data analyses. Furthermore, new technologies are being developed that require training and education.

E. When done properly, data analytics can become a strategic asset. Data analytics not only can help identify new opportunities, but it can also be used to evaluate and verify the efficacy of a company's business practices and philosophies. Data analytics can help increase the value of a company by improving the understanding of a company's operations and providing information to guide the evaluation of company performance and strategic options.

F. Business Intelligence solutions usually provide visual analytics of consolidated data in dashboard form. These dashboards allow companies to quickly assess the health of the organization and take actions to improve operations.

Summary
Big data refers to very large and/or complex datasets that can help companies gain insight into relationships and associations to improve decision making and strategy. Business intelligence and data analytics assist the organization in transforming raw data into information, information into knowledge, and knowledge into actions. This process is challenging for multiple reasons, but big data and data analytics can become an important strategic asset for an organization.

Data Mining

After studying this lesson, you should be able to:

- Define data mining (1.F.4.g).

- Describe the challenges of data mining (1.F.4.h).

- Explain why data mining is an iterative process and both an art and a science (1.F.4.i).

- Explain how query tools (e.g., Structured Query Language (SQL)) are used to retrieve information (1.F.4.j).

- Describe how an analyst would mine large data sets to reveal patterns and provide insights (1.F.4.k).

> Data mining is a process used to extract information from data. This lesson will describe this process and discuss some of the challenges of data mining.

I. Data Mining

   A. Data mining is used to reveal patterns and insights, typically from large data sets. Data mining involves statistical methods, computer learning, artificial intelligence, and large-scale computing power to analyze large amounts of data in order to extract useful information about relationships, trends, patterns, and anomalies. The primary goal is to provide useful information for decision making and anticipating future outcomes.

   B. Data mining can be challenging for many reasons.

      1. Data quality—if data has missing values, errors, or insufficient sample size, it can limit the ability to conduct statistical tests and draw inferences. If there is bias in how the data is collected, such as a non-response bias to a survey, it can limit how broadly the results of the data can be generalized. It may also not represent the targeted population, such as when only disgruntled customers respond to a customer satisfaction survey, and can thereby limit its usefulness due to lack of a representative sample.

      2. Data mining often involves coalescing and combining data distributed across multiple sources. This data may come in a variety of formats, making it difficult to match observations. Companies are legally prohibited from using some data, such as health data or facial recognition data in certain locales due to privacy laws. It may also be difficult to transform the data into a common format to use for analysis.

      3. Data mining can involve enormous datasets. Analyzing large datasets can require computational power beyond the capabilities of standard computers. This can lead to inefficient processing, sometimes even making computations inoperable without the use of a specialized computer with greater processing capabilities. Furthermore, special software, servers, and storage might be needed in order to conduct data mining analyses. This software and hardware can be expensive.

      4. Data mining techniques can produce large quantities of output. Sifting through the output to identify useful information can demand significant time and effort. It can also require specialized knowledge about the data context in order to properly interpret data output.

   C. Data mining is an iterative process. It requires skill to conduct computational algorithms and statistical tests to process data, and then further requires understanding and knowledge to interpret the output. Data mining is a mix of both science and art that can require many iterations and analyses in order to identify patterns, trends, and associations.

   D. Data mining involves the use of specific tools to manipulate and extract information from a database. SQL, that is, Structured Query Language, is the standard programming language used to communicate with a database. SQL can be used to perform various functions with databases such as manipulating data, defining data, and accessing data.

E. Data mining has many uses in business settings. For example, it can be used to identify sales trends or predict customer purchases habits. One of the most common analyses is association rules or market basket analysis, which provides companies with information on which items are purchased together. It could also be used to better understand a firm's cost structure and identify cost drivers. Possible techniques could include looking for groupings or clustering of data, identifying associations to help classify and categorize information, or using regression analysis to estimate statistical associations and effect sizes.

Summary

Data mining is a process that involves the use of tools such as SQL to provide useful information for decision making and anticipating future outcomes. Among other reasons, data mining can be challenging because of the quality of the data, the process of combining data from multiple sources, the amount of computational power that is required, and the time and effort required to identify the useful information that results from the process.

Analytic Tools

After studying this lesson, you should be able to:

- Explain the challenge of fitting an analytic model to the data (1.F.4.l).

- Define the different types of data analytics, including descriptive, diagnostic, predictive, and prescriptive (1.F.4.m).

- Define the following analytic models: clustering, classification, and regression; determine when each would be the appropriate tool to use (1.F.4.n).

- Identify the elements of both simple and multiple regression equations (1.F.4.o).

- Calculate the result of regression equations as applied to a specific situation (1.F.4.p).

- Demonstrate an understanding of the coefficient of determination (R-squared) and the correlation coefficient (R) (1.F.4.q).

- Demonstrate an understanding of time series analyses, including trend, cyclical, seasonal, and irregular patterns (1.F.4.r).

- Identify and explain the benefits and limitations of regression analysis and time series analysis (1.F.4.s).

- Define standard error of the estimate, goodness of fit, and confidence interval (1.F.4.t).

- Explain how to use predictive analytic techniques to draw insights and make recommendations (1.F.4.u).

- Describe exploratory data analysis and how it is used to reveal patterns and discover insights (1.F.4.v).

- Define sensitivity analysis and identify when it would be the appropriate tool to use (1.F.4.w).

- Demonstrate an understanding of the uses of simulation models, including the Monte Carlo technique (1.F.4.x).

- Identify the benefits and limitations of sensitivity analysis and simulation models (1.F.4.y).

- Demonstrate an understanding of what-if (or goal-seeking) analysis (1.F.4.z).

- Identify and explain the limitations of data analytics (1.F.4.aa).

Companies are increasingly using data analytics to better understand how one factor is connected to another so they can better understand and predict future outcomes. This lesson defines the types of data analytics and describes various types of data analytic techniques.

I. Fitting Analytic Models

    A. Analytic models are an empirical or data-driven approach to understanding connections, effects, and outcomes. Underlying an analytic model is a question about how one factor is affecting another. Is the relationship positive or negative? Do two factors (variables) have a significant statistical association? Part of the challenge when analyzing data is developing explanations, otherwise known as theories, and/or hypotheses (expectations) about empirical relationships. Analytic models can provide insight by validating with statistical techniques that effects do exist and by providing estimates of effect sizes. Analytic models can also help with the discovery of potentially unexpected relationships.

    B. Companies have several inexpensive software options available for analyses that require little or no need to write software code. Despite the availability of software, the value of data analytics can be limited by:

        1. Not asking the right questions

        2. An inability to interpret results

3. Poor quality data

4. Models that are overly complex or that don't allow for natural variation in data

5. Over-reliance on models to the exclusion of experience and common sense.

C. Types of Data Analytics

1. *Descriptive*—this form of data analytics aims to answer the question "What is or what was?" Descriptive data analysis is observational and reports the characteristics of historical data. It describes statistical properties such as the mean, median, range, or standard deviation. Descriptive data analysis is beneficial because it provides understanding of what has actually taken place.

2. *Diagnostic*—this form of data analytics aims to answer the question "Why did this happen?" Diagnostic data analysis looks at correlations, the size and strength of statistical associations. Data are explored to identify meaningful empirical relationships - some of which may be unknown or uncertain. Diagnostic data analysis tries to uncover and understand why certain outcomes take place and what could be important factors causing those outcomes.

3. *Predictive*—this form of data analytics aims to answer the question "What will happen?" Predictive analysis builds upon descriptive and diagnostic analytics to make predictions about future events. It can take the form of what-if analysis where sets of possible facts, their likelihoods, and ranges are used to formulate potential future outcomes. Predictive analysis considers risk assessments, usually taking the form of outcome likelihoods and uncertainties, to guide the prediction of future outcomes and trends.

4. *Prescriptive*—this form of data analytics aims to answer the question "What should happen?" Prescriptive analytics draws upon the other forms of data analytics to infer or recommend the best course of action. Prescriptive analysis can take the form of optimization or simulation analyses to identify and prescribe the actions to undertake to realize the best or most desired result.

D. When to Use Analytic Models

1. *Clustering* is a data analysis technique that involves grouping similar objects together. Clustering is focused on the discovery and identification of patterns of similarity and dissimilarity. Clustering is an exploratory technique that provides insight into common properties or characteristics. It typically does not start with predefined groupings or categories, but rather explores whether a set of items has a relationship. Results of cluster analysis are often presented graphically to aid in the identification of groupings.

2. *Classification* is a data analysis technique which attempts to predict which category or class an item belongs to. Classification typically begins with predefined categories and then attempts to sort an item into one of those categories.

3. *Regression* is a data analysis method of analyzing the correlation of an outcome (dependent variable) with explanatory or independent variables. Regression can be performed with only one independent variable (i.e., simple regression) or with many independent variables (i.e., multiple regression). Regression takes into account all of the observed values and provides estimates of the correlation between dependent and independent variables.

A regression equation typically uses the following format: $y = \beta 0 + \beta 1x + \varepsilon$. In this case, y is the dependent variable. The intercept is represented by $\beta 0$. The slope is represented by $\beta 1$. X is the independent variable. In multiple regression, more independent variables are added. For example, $y = \beta 0 + \beta 1x + \beta 2w + \beta 3z + \varepsilon$.

In accounting, cost equations are often estimated using regression analysis. A cost equation could look like the following: Total Cost = Fixed Cost + Variable Cost × Units. If the regression output estimated the fixed cost (intercept) to be $1,000 and the variable cost (slope) to be $20, then the total cost equation would look like this: Total Cost = $1,000 + $20 × Units. This equation could then be used to predict a total cost based on the output level. If output was 100 units, then the total cost would be estimated to be $3,000 = $1,000 + ($20 × 100 units).

Linear regression should be used when the desired output (Y) is quantitative, such as in the previous example that examines total cost. Logistic regression is a useful derivation that should be used when the desired output is categorical. For example, banks may use a logistic regression to determine whether a client will or will not default on a loan.

How well a regression line fits the observed data is measured by the coefficient of determination, commonly referred to as R^2. R^2 can be interpreted as the percent of variation in the dependent variable that is explained by variation in the independent variables. That is, if R^2 is equal to 0.73, it means that 73% of the variation in the dependent variable is explained by variation in the independent variables.

Another commonly used statistical measure is the correlation coefficient, commonly referred to as R. R is a measure of how two variables are related. It provides both the direction, positive or negative, and the strength of the relationship between two variables. R ranges between −1 and 1.

Regression analysis provides other useful statistical measures. The *standard error of the estimate* measures the accuracy of predictions. The regression analysis provides a prediction line, and the standard error of the estimate tells how far away a data point is from the predict point. The *goodness of fit* is a measure of how well the observed data fit a statistical model. That is, it is a summary of the discrepancy between observed values and what the model would predict the value to be. Finally, a *confidence interval* is a range of values in which the true value lies. Regression models only provide estimates of effect sizes and relationships. A confidence interval provides a range rather than point estimate over which the true value is likely to be.

Regression modeling provides many useful benefits, but does face limitations. For example, regression models should only be used to make predictions within what is called the relevant range. The relevant range refers to a set of observed values. If a desired prediction is outside of the set of observed values, there is a possibility that the estimated relationship from the regression model will not be the same outside of the observed values. Doing so is referred to as extrapolation whereby predictions about an unknown observational range are inferred from a known observation range. Regression analysis can also be affected by outliers, extreme values that are unlike other observations.

4. *Time series* is a data analysis method that considers data points over time. The temporal ordering of data points allows for patterns to be identified, aiding the prediction of future values.

   It should be noted that regression analysis is often done on cross-sectional data; that is, data that takes place within the same time period. It is possible to combine cross-sectional data with time-series data to observe the same phenomena over multiple periods of time. Combined cross-sectional and time-series data is referred to as panel data.

   Time-series analysis can identify patterns in observed data. Trends provide useful information to help predict future outcomes based on what has happened in the past. Common trends include systematic trends (such as prolonged upward or downward movements), cyclical trends (such as macroeconomic cycles that rise and fall), seasonal trends (such as periodic spikes in retail shopping around holidays), and irregular trends (such as erratic fluctuations due to unforeseen events like natural disasters).

5. Other Data Analysis Techniques:

   a. *Exploratory data analysis* is used to summarize the characteristics of a dataset. This technique often involves using visual methods to examine the data for patterns or anomalies. Summary statistics and graphical representations aid in understanding what the data is and what possible questions the data can help address. Rather than focusing on hypothesis testing, exploratory data analysis is used to help identify and discover what hypotheses to test. Exploratory data analysis is the initial step that is used to inform future data collections and statistical tests.

b. *Sensitivity analysis* recognizes that predicted outcomes from analytic models have uncertainties and assumptions. Sensitivity analysis is the exploration of how a dependent variable might be affected given different possible sets of independent variables. For example, when predicting a company's net income in future years, an assumption is likely made about how fast sales will grow. Will sales grow at 5%, 10%, or 2%? Sensitivity analysis examines how results might change if assumptions about a model or prediction are changed. This type of analysis can be referred to as *what-if* analysis. One type of what-if analysis is a goal-seeking analysis which asks what assumptions must hold true in order for a particular outcome to occur.

c. *Simulation models* are based on computational algorithms that follow specified assumptions to model possible outcomes. Monte Carlo simulations are a specific type of simulation that generates the probability that an outcome will occur. Monte Carlo simulations aid in the assessment of risk and uncertainty and are commonly used for prediction and forecasting. They are based on random sampling done repeatedly in order to form probability distributions for the outcome of interest. That is, a Monte Carlo simulation randomly draws values for variables of interest, each with specified possible ranges and probability distributions, and then provides the realized outcome. This is done thousands, even tens of thousands of times and results in a probability distribution of the outcome of interest. That probability distribution can then be used to help assess the risk and uncertainty related to the outcome variable.

Summary
Analytic models help organizations understand the question of how one factor affects another. Data analytics can be broken down into four forms (descriptive, diagnostic, predictive, and prescriptive) that build on each other to recommend the best course of action. Various techniques such as clustering, classification, regression, and time series are used to analyze the data to determine patterns and relationships among the data. Other data analysis techniques such as exploratory data analysis, sensitivity analysis, and simulation models can also be used to test hypotheses under different scenarios and forecast future results.

Data Visualization

- Utilize table and graph design best practices to avoid distortion in the communication of complex information (1.F.4.bb).

- Evaluate data visualization options and select the best presentation approach (e.g., histograms, boxplots, scatterplots, dot plots, tables, dashboards, bar charts, pie charts, line charts, bubble charts) (1.F.4.cc).

- Understand the benefits and limitations of visualization techniques (1.F.4.dd).

- Determine the most effective channel to communicate results (1.F.4.ee).

- Communicate results, conclusions, and recommendations in an impactful manner using effective visualization techniques (1.F.4.ff).

> Companies can present data in many ways. One way to present data clearly is through data visualization, which is simply using visual forms to analyze, evaluate, and present data. This lesson describes some of the options for data visualization and how to effectively communicate conclusions and gives recommendations using these techniques.

I. Data Visualization

    A. Data visualization is the creation, analysis, and evaluation of data presented in visual forms. These forms can include but are not limited to the following: charts, graphs, diagrams, pictures, dashboards, infographics, tables, or maps.

    B. Data visualization helps identify patterns, trends, and outliers. It can provide understanding about correlations and relationships among critical success factors for an organization's activities or for industry and market behaviors. Data visualization can be particularly useful with *big data* to help make sense of thousands, even millions of observations. Data visualization aims to make data more understandable and memorable. It can be used to augment rigorous statistical and analytical techniques as well as to convey summary ideas and findings.

    C. Determining how to present data involves exploration and trial-and-error. Data analysis and visualization software come with automated visual options. These can include the following:

        1. Histograms show the distribution of numerical data.

        2. Boxplots show the distribution of data by displaying the quartiles in which data occur.

        3. Scatterplots show how two variables are related.

        4. Dot plots are similar to histograms and are used when values fall into discrete categories. Values are typically represented by small circles stacked onto each other in each category.

        5. Tables list information in rows and columns.

        6. Dashboards are a quick summary view of key performance indicators.

        7. Bar charts are used with categorical data to show the proportion of data in each category with horizontal or vertical bars.

        8. Pie charts are used with categorical data to show the proportion of data in each category with slices in a circle.

        9. Line charts are used to show a series of data points for one variable. Multiple lines may be stacked onto the same chart to show multiple variables.

       10. Bubble charts are an enhancement of a scatter chart wherein an additional dimension of the data is shown by the size of the circle.

D. How to communicate:

1. Remember that there are many different ways to communicate. Make sure the medium "matches" the message. For example, the richness of face-to-face communication is probably more appropriate for bad news such as company layoffs than an email. Data visualization can help others understand the message, but is not a substitute for careful, thoughtful communication.

2. Keeping graphs clear and concise is vital for effective visualization. Avoid including irrelevant information so that users of the visuals focus on what matters most.

3. Be sure to provide context to the data you are sharing. Often, the individuals who are tasked with creating visual aids are more familiar with the topic than others. Visual aids should be created such that anyone in the audience can quickly grasp the significance of the presented information.

4. Revisit visual aids frequently and make incremental improvements where possible.

E. Companies should be careful not to become too dependent on visualizations. Visualizes have the potential to oversimplify results and ignore nuance that can provide insight and improved decision making. Remember that good information leads to good decisions. If visualization distracts from or distracts from good information, poor decisions will eventually follow.

Summary

Data visualization presents the analysis and evaluation of data in visual forms. This can be useful to provide understanding about the relationships and correlations of critical success factors for an organization's activities or industry and market behaviors. Data can be visualized in many ways; therefore, it is important to understand the benefits and limitations of each visualization technique. Just as it is important to choose a proper method to visualize the data, it is important to determine the most effective channel to use and then communicate the results and recommendations in an impactful manner.

Section F Review Questions

AQ.sec.brch.002_1904

1. Which of the following **best** describes the purpose of an advanced firewall?

    A. This security device is limited to stateful inspection of network traffic but can allow the addition of other features to discourage access into the corporate network.
    B. It allows communication between two trusted networks.
    C. It allows communication between two unknown networks.
    D. It is a network security component that monitors, regulates, and provides a barrier for incoming and outgoing network traffic between a trusted and untrusted network by using features such as application filtering.

AQ.sec.brch.004_1904

2. Regarding cyberattacks, which of the following uses only approved and qualified testers to conduct real-world attacks against a computer system or network?

    A. Proxy testing
    B. Penetration testing
    C. Alpha testing
    D. Fault-injection testing

aq.ana.too.004_1905

3. All of the following are types of time series analysis **except**:

    A. Trend analysis
    B. Seasonal analysis
    C. Cyclical analysis
    D. Sensitivity analysis

aq.dat.min.001_1905

4. Which of the following can uncover hidden patterns, trends, correlations, outliers, anomalies, and subtle relationships in data and help to infer rules that allow for the prediction of future results and outcomes?

    A. Web scraping
    B. Data mining
    C. Web mining
    D. Social mining

aq.er.plan.sys.005_1906

5. Which answer BEST describes a data warehouse?

    A. A location where document hard copies can be aggregated and analyzed
    B. A term to associate multiple sites used for disaster recovery
    C. A storage of large amounts of data from various databases used for specialized analysis
    D. A storage commonly used for critical data such as system relationships, data types, formats, and sources

AQ.data.proc.004_1904

6. All of the following are one of the identified COSO (Committee of Sponsoring Organizations of the Treadway Commission) Internal Control-Integrated Framework components **except**:

    A. Risk Assessment
    B. Monitoring Activities
    C. Control Activities
    D. Vulnerability Assessment

aq.ana.too.002_1905
7. A **major** difference between a simple regression analysis and multiple regression analysis is which of the following?

    A. Number of dependent variables
    B. Number of mathematical equations
    C. Number of independent variables
    D. Number of design experiments

aq.proc.au.001_1904
8. Which of the following can be described by the possibility for machines to learn from experience, adjust to new inputs, and perform human-like tasks?

    A. Robotic process automation
    B. Artificial intelligence
    C. Cloud computing
    D. Business intelligence

aq.er.plan.sys.002_1906
9. Which of the following items is an advantage of an ERP (Enterprise Resource Planning) System?

    A. Scalability
    B. Low cost of implementation and maintenance
    C. Lack of complexity
    D. Affordable software

aq.bus.int.002_1905
10. Which of the following is an example of unstructured data?

    A. Data in disconnected computer systems
    B. Data in data warehouses
    C. Data in databases
    D. Web pages on the Internet

aq.ana.too.005_1905
11. Which use case represents an ideal scenario to utilize sensitivity analysis?

    A. An analyst wants a method for predicting the outcome of a decision if a situation turns out to be different compared to the key predictions.
    B. An analyst wants to assess relative variables for bond price, inflation, and market interest rates.
    C. An analyst wants to reduce assumptions.
    D. An analyst wants an objective assessment of data.

aq.life.data.002_1904
12. Which of the following functions of the data life cycle is involved with the removal of every copy of a data item from the enterprise?

    A. Data purging
    B. Data archiving
    C. Data maintenance
    D. Data synthesis

AQ.data.proc.003_1904

13. Identify which of the following BEST describes ISACA's COBIT key principles?

    A. Meeting Stakeholder Needs, Covering the Enterprise End-to-End, Applying a Single-Integrated Framework, Enabling a Holistic Approach, and Separating Governance from Management
    B. Integrity, Confidentiality, Redundancy, Availability, Governing Policies
    C. Identification, Authentication, Authorization, Auditing, and Accounting
    D. Trust Boundaries, Data Flow Paths, Input Points, Privileged Operations, Details about Security Stance and Approach

aq.ana.too.001_1905

14. All of the following are defining characteristics of predictive analytics **except**:

    A. Historical patterns are utilized to output specific outcomes using algorithms.
    B. Decisions are automated using trend data and industry insights.
    C. The variability of the component data will have a relationship with what is likely to happen.
    D. Analytical output provides specific recommendations to take action on.

aq.er.plan.sys.004_1906

15. All of the following are a function of a database management system (DBMS) **except**:

    A. Backup and recovery
    B. Encryption
    C. Data integrity
    D. Malware detection

Review Questions and Answers

Section A. External Financial Reporting Decisions

aq.rec.002_1802

1. When the allowance method of recognizing bad debt expense is used, the allowance for doubtful accounts would decrease when a(n):

   A. Specific account receivable is collected.
   B. Bad Debt Expense is recorded using the balance sheet approach.
   C. Bad Debt Expense is recorded using the income statement approach.
   D. Specific uncollectible account is written off.

Answer: D

When the allowance method of recognizing bad debts is used, the entry to establish the allowance account is:

Bad Debt Expense	xx	
Allowance for bad debts		xx

The entry to write off a specific uncollectible account is

Allowance for bad debts	xx	
Accounts Receivable		xx

Thus, the allowance is decreased when the account is written off.

aq.gen.liab.001_1802

2. A company has the following liabilities at year-end:

Mortgage note payable; $16,000 due within 12 months	$355,000
Short-term debt that the company has refinanced with long-term debt shortly after year-end but prior to the issuance of the financial statements	$175,000
Deferred tax liability arising from book and tax differences in depreciation	$25,000

   What amount should the company include in the current liability section of the balance sheet?

   A. $0
   B. $ 16,000
   C. $ 41,000
   D. $191,000

Answer: B

Determine the amount to be included in the current liability section of the balance sheet. Although the mortgage note payable is a long-term liability, the amount due within the next 12 months, $16,000, should be reclassified to the current liability section of the balance sheet. The short-term debt that the company is refinancing with long-term debt is reclassified as a long-term liability because the company has completed the refinancing prior to the issuance of the financial statements. Deferred tax assets and liabilities are classified as noncurrent by definition. Therefore, the only item that should be included in the current liability section of the balance sheet is the $16,000 of long-term debt that is due within the next 12 months.

aq.cf.fsa.002_1802

3. In its cash flow statement for the current year, Ness Co. reported cash paid for interest of $70,000. Ness did not capitalize any interest during the current year. Changes occurred in several balance sheet accounts as follows:

Accrued interest payable	17,000 decrease
Prepaid interest	23,000 decrease

In its income statement for the current year, what amount would Ness have reported as interest expense?

A. $ 76,000
B. $ 30,000
C. $ 64,000
D. $110,000

Answer: A

The amount is calculated as cash paid for interest minus the decrease in accrued interest payable and plus the amount of decrease in prepaid interest, or $76,000 = $70,000 − $17,000 + $23,000.

aq.inv.oe.008_1802

4. If a company uses the equity method to account for an investment in another company, which of the following is true?

A. Income to the investing company consists only of actual dividends, interest, or capital gains.
B. All of the investee's income is included in the investor's income except for income relating to intra-entity transactions.
C. A proportionate share of the investee's net income is included in the investor's income statement.
D. Income of the investee is included in the investor's income but reduced by any dividends paid to the investor.

Answer: C

With the equity method, only the proportional share of the investee's income (% ownership × investee earnings) is reported on the investor's income statement.

aq.leases.002_1904

5. Lease A does not contain a bargain purchase option, but the lease term is for a major part of the remaining economic life of the underlying asset. Lease B does not transfer ownership of the property to the lessee by the end of the lease term, but the present value of the minimum lease payments exceeds substantially all of the fair value of the underlying asset. How should the lessee classify these leases? (Answers are in form of: Lease A, Lease B)

A. Finance lease, Finance lease
B. Finance lease, Operating lease
C. Operating lease, Finance lease
D. Operating lease, Operating lease

Answer: A

Since each lease has either a lease term for a major part of the remaining economic life of the underlying asset or a present value of the minimum lease payments that exceeds substantially all of the fair value of the underlying asset, each is classified as a finance lease.

6. In a company's statement of cash flows, interest paid is:

    A. part of the investing section
    B. part of the financing section
    C. part of the operating section
    D. part of the debt service section

Answer: C

Interest paid out is part of the operating section, as it is considered an operating expense.

7. Zulu Corp.'s (Zulu) comparative balance sheet at December 31, Year 6 and Year 5, reported accumulated depreciation balances of $800,000 and $600,000, respectively. Property with a cost of $50,000 and a carrying amount of $40,000 was the only property sold in Year 6. How much depreciation was charged to Zulu's operations in Year 6?

    A. $190,000
    B. $200,000
    C. $220,000
    D. $210,000

Answer: D

Accumulated depreciation began the year at $600,000. The property with a $50,000 cost and $40,000 carrying amount must have had accumulated depreciation of $10,000 ($50,000 – $40,000). When the property was sold, the accumulated depreciation would have been reduced from $600,000 to $590,000. Because accumulated depreciation ended the year at $800,000, depreciation must have been recorded in the amount of $800,000 – $590,000 = $210,000.

8. This information pertains to equipment owned by Brigade Company.

    - Cost of equipment: $10,000

    - Estimated residual value: $2,000

    - Estimated useful life: 5 years

    - Depreciation method: Straight-line

The accumulated depreciation at the end of year 3 is:

    A. $4,800.
    B. $1,600.
    C. $6,000.
    D. $5,200.

Answer: A

Accumulated depreciation at the end of year 3 = [($10,000 – $2,000) ÷ 5] × 3 = $4,800.

aq.acc.inc.tax.009_1802

9. Sandy Inc. prepares financial statements under IFRS. At December 31, Year 4, Sandy's income for financial (book) purposes equaled $100,000 and Sandy's only temporary difference related to depreciation. For financial (book) purposes, depreciation equaled $10,000 and for tax purposes, depreciation equaled $15,000. The difference is expected to reverse evenly over the next two years. The enacted tax rate for the current year, Year 4, is 30% and the enacted tax rate for all future years is 40%. In its year-end balance sheet, what amount should Sandy report as a deferred tax asset (liability)?

   A. $1,500 deferred tax asset
   B. $1,500 deferred tax liability
   C. $2,000 deferred tax asset
   D. $2,000 deferred tax liability

Answer: D

A timing difference where, in the future, taxable income will be greater than financial (book) income is reported as a deferred tax liability. The amount to be recorded as the deferred tax liability is the temporary difference multiplied by the future enacted tax rate ($5,000 × 40% = $2,000).

aq.inv.oe.003_1802

10. Shelton Devin Corp. has two stock investments in which they own 30% of the outstanding stock. The CEO of the company is not in favor of presenting consolidated financial statements. Based on the information, which of the following is **most likely** true?

   A. The decision of the CEO is correct as companies are required to issue consolidated statements only when the ownership exceeds 50%.
   B. The decision of the CEO is wrong as companies are required to issue consolidated statements when the ownership exceeds 20%.
   C. The decision of the CEO is wrong as companies are required to issue consolidated statements only if they hold more than ten subsidiaries.
   D. The decision of the CEO is correct as companies are required to issue consolidated statements only when they have three or more subsidiaries.

Answer: A

As required by ASC 810 Consolidation, all companies with subsidiaries are required to issue consolidated statements including each subsidiary they control, usually meaning 50% or more ownership.

aq.ifrs.001_1802

11. Simply Pharmaceutical (SP) is a company that specializes in (1) research and development of new medications and (2) acquisition of patents for new medications. SP follows IFRS accounting standards. In SP's situation, which of the following statements about the treatment of intangible assets is correct?

   A. Intangible assets must be measured using the cost model.
   B. Intangible assets with indefinite lives must be amortized annually.
   C. Intangible assets may be revalued to fair value if there is an active market for the asset.
   D. Research and development costs are expensed as incurred, except for software development.

Answer: C

Intangible assets may be revalued to fair value if there is an active market for the asset is true under IFRS.

aq.rev.rec.014_1809

12. All of the following are steps of the five recognition steps to recognizing revenue **except**:

A. Select an output method for estimating stand-alone selling price.
B. Identify the contract with a customer.
C. Determine the transaction price.
D. Identify separate performance obligations in the contract.

Answer: A

This is not one of the revenue recognition steps. Stand-alone selling prices may be estimated as part of step four, allocate the transaction price to the performance obligations. However, output methods are not used for this purpose.

aq.rec.003_1802

13. A method of estimating bad debts that focuses on the income statement rather than the balance sheet is the allowance method based on:

A. Direct write-off.
B. Aging the trade receivable accounts.
C. Credit sales.
D. The balance in the trade receivable accounts.

Answer: C

Estimating bad debts based on credit sales of the period is the income statement approach in that bad debts are treated as a function of sales.

AQ.int.repo.003_1904

14. Manufactured capital, as defined under Integrated Reporting, includes all of the following items **except**:

A. Work-in-process inventory
B. Patents and trademarks
C. Custom-made tools and patterns used in the manufacturing process
D. Roads and bridges

Answer: B

Patents and trademarks are intellectual capital.

aq.rev.rec.001_1809

15. In November and December Year 1, Dorr Co., a newly organized magazine publisher, received $72,000 for 1,000 3-year subscriptions at $24 per year, starting with the January Year 2 issue. Dorr elected to include the entire $72,000 in its Year 1 income tax return. What amount should Dorr report in its Year 1 income statement for subscriptions revenue?

A. $0
B. $ 4,000
C. $24,000
D. $72,000

Answer: A

Revenue should be recognized as performance obligations are fulfilled using an output method based on units delivered. Because the magazines are not delivered until Year 2, no revenue should be recognized in Year 1, as no performance obligation has been fulfilled.

Section B. Planning, Budgeting and Forecasting

aq.pc.bud.003_1802

1. Cut, Inc. (Cut) has developed the following production plan for its premium scissor line.

	September	October	November	December
Production Volume (scissors)	15,000	20,000	18,000	24,000

Each pair of scissors contains 0.5 pounds of stainless steel at a standard price of $1.25 per pound. The desired raw materials ending inventory is 35% of the next month's material needs for production plus an additional 150 pounds. September's beginning inventory meets this requirement. Using a direct materials purchases budget, determine direct material purchases for October and November.

A. $12,500.00 for October and $11,250.00 for November
B. $12,062.50 for October and $12,562.50 for November
C. $16,625.00 for October and $16,687.50 for November
D. $25,000.00 for October and $22,500.00 for November

Answer: B

The following is Cut's direct material purchases budget for October and November.

	October	November	December
Production Volume	20,000 pairs	18,000 pairs	24,000 pairs
× Standard Pounds per Pair	0.5 lbs	0.5 lbs	0.5 lbs
Material Needs for Production	10,000 lbs	9,000 lbs	12,000 lbs
Planned Ending Inventory	3,300 lbs	4,350 lbs	
Total Material Needed	13,300 lbs	13,350 lbs	
Less Beginning Inventory	(3,650) lbs	(3,300) lbs	
Total Material to Purchase	9,650 lbs	10,050 lbs	
× Standard Price per Pound	$1.25	$1.25	
Direct Material Purchases	$12,062.50	$12,562.50	

Note that October beginning inventory = 10,000 lbs × 35% + 150 lbs = 3,650 lbs.

aq.sp.bud.001_1802

2. Which of the following specific budgets is the key driving force of the overall operational budget?

A. The sales budget
B. The production budget
C. The capital projects budget
D. The pro forma income statement

Answer: A

The sales budget is the key driving force of the operational budget.

aq.sp.bud.005_1802

3. Card & Co. (CC), a creator of popular card games such as "Tres" and "Go Hunt," is preparing a quarterly sales budget. CC predicts sales of 40,000 games in Q1 at $5.00 per game. CC predicts that game sales will grow by 4% each quarter and that game price will increase by 5% each quarter. Each game costs $3.00 to produce in Q1. Costs are expected to grow by 3% each quarter. Using a quarterly sales budget, calculate sales revenue for the year.

A. $800,000
B. $917,306
C. $169,859
D. $383,598

Answer: B

Below is CC's quarterly sales budget for the year. (Note: prices are rounded to the penny each quarter.)

	Q1	Q2	Q3	Q4	Total
Sales Volume	40,000	41,600	43,264	44,995	169,859
× Price	$5.00	$5.25	$5.51	$5.79	
Revenue	$200,000	$218,400	$238,385	$260,521	$917,306

aq.lc.anal.001_0720

4. Wall, Corp. (Wall) is the leading manufacturer of sheetrock in the United States. Wall is trying to forecast direct material costs for next year. The cost of calcium sulfate dihydrate (gypsum) used in sheetrock production fluctuates from year to year. Below are Wall's estimates for the cost of a pound of gypsum next year.

Pound of Gypsum Price	Probability
$1.45	15%
$1.60	25%
$1.85	40%
$2.00	20%

Based on these estimates, what is the expected cost per pound of gypsum next year?

A. $1.45
B. $1.73
C. $1.85
D. $1.76

Answer: D

The expected cost per pound of gypsum is calculated as follows:

Pound of Gypsum Price	Probability	Weighted Value
$1.45	15%	$0.22
$1.60	25%	$0.40
$1.85	40%	$0.74
$2.00	20%	$0.40
Expected Value	100%	$1.76

aq.wrap.ob.004_0720

5. Which of the following is **not** a component of the selling and administrative expense budget?

A. The costs of advertising products
B. The transportation costs of delivering purchased products to customers
C. The production line manager
D. The depreciation of the administration building

Answer: C

This is a manufacturing overhead expense, not a selling and administrative expense.

6. Eight quarters of production data from Pear, Inc., a cell phone manufacturing company, are presented below.

Pear, Inc.

Quarter	Phones	Cost
1	2,331	$3,245,874
2	2,657	$3,474,318
3	1,987	$2,883,675
4	2,412	$3,287,621
5	2,583	$3,354,966
6	2,497	$3,428,752
7	2,285	$3,152,347
8	2,645	$3,271,899

The regression analysis results on these data are displayed below.

	Coefficients	Standard Error	t Stat	P-value	Lower 95%	Upper 95%
Intercept	$1,473,119	$356,978	4.13	0.01	$599,625	$2,346,614
Phones	$738	$147	5.03	0.00	$379	$1,097

Regression Statistics	
Multiple R	0.90
R Square	0.81
Adjusted R Square	0.78
Standard Error	$87,127
Observations	8

What is the regression equation (total cost equation) for the above information?

A. Total costs = $147(Phones) + $356,978
B. Total costs = $1,473,119(Phones) + 738
C. Total costs = $356,978(Phones) + $147
D. Total costs = $738(Phones) + $1,473,119

Answer: D

This is the correct regression equation (total cost equation) for the above information.

7. Nice Knives (Nice) is facing fierce competition in the cutlery industry. Nice's main competitors are stealing market share on certain knives by offering similar products at lower prices. Nice management believes that costs are not being allocated correctly across product lines of different knives. Nice would like to change its budgeting process to improve cost allocation assignment and better understand profitability of knives.

Which of the following budget tools and methods would be most helpful to Nice in this situation?

A. An activity-based budget
B. A continuous rolling budget
C. A zero-based budget
D. A flexible budget

Answer: A

Activity-based budgeting methods focus on identifying and using core activities throughout the organization to establish activity cost rates in order to assign costs to products, customers, and other business targets based on actual consumption relationships. This process will give the management team the information they seek by making the cost allocation process more accurate.

aq.gen.strat.002_0720

8. Short-term objectives, tactics for achieving these objectives, and operational planning (master budget) must be congruent with what? Choose the best answer.

   A. The organization's external environmental factors
   B. The organization's internal environmental factors
   C. The organization's performance evaluation and incentive compensation factors
   D. The organization's strategic plan and long-term strategic goals

Answer: D

Short-term objectives, tactics for achieving these objectives, and operational planning (master budget) must be congruent with the strategic plan and contribute to the achievement of long-term strategic goals. The external and internal environmental factors will have an influence on the strategic plan and long-term strategic goals. Performance evaluation and incentive compensation factors are then based on the the organization's strategic objectives and tactics.

aq.gen.strat.005_1802

9. A cost leadership strategy, in addition to focusing on the company's ability to sell a large volume of low-cost products, is often aided by all of the following characteristics **except**:

   A. Advanced production technology.
   B. Access to low-cost production inputs (raw materials, labor, etc.).
   C. More highly desirable product features.
   D. Access to low-cost capital.

Answer: C

Having more highly desirable product features is a characteristic of a differentiation strategy, not a cost leadership strategy.

aq.wrap.ob.006_1802

10. Textbook Manufacturing (TM) is the leading textbook printing and binding company in the region. TM is starting a new line of Managerial Accounting textbooks this year and would like to calculate the budgeted total contribution margin for this line for 20X1. TM plans to sell every textbook they manufacture this year. The following information is available:

Sales Budget	Q1	Q2	Q3	Q4	Total
Sales Volume	1,300	1,600	1,900	1,500	6,300

Budgeted Sales Price per Unit	
Sales Price	$200.00

Standard Production Costs per Unit		
Variable Production Costs	$47.00	per book
Fixed Production Costs	19.00	per book
Total Production Costs	$66.00	per book

Standard Variable Selling & Admin Costs per Unit		
Standard Selling & Admin Costs	$25.00	per book
Fixed Selling & Admin Costs	35.00	per book
Total Selling & Admin Costs	$60.00	per book

Using a contribution margin statement, calculate TM's budgeted total contribution margin for the new line of Managerial Accounting textbooks for 20X1.

A. $74.00
B. $128.00
C. $806,400
D. $466,200

Answer: C

The following is TM's contribution margin statement.

Budgeted Constribution Margin Statement		
Sales Price per Unit	$200.00	per book
Variable Costs per Unit	(72.00)	per book
Contribution Margin	$128.00	per book
× Budgeted Sales Volume	6,300	books
Total Contribution Margin	$806,400	

aq.sp.bud.009_1802

11. Card & Co. (CC), a creator of popular card games such as "Tres" and "Go Hunt," is preparing a quarterly production budget. CC predicts sales of 45,000 games in Q1 and predicts that game sales will grow 6% every quarter indefinitely. The company consistently follows a budget policy of maintaining an ending inventory of 20% of the next quarter's sales. Using a quarterly production budget, calculate production volume for the year.

A. 199,220
B. 208,220
C. 196,858
D. 207,806

Answer: A

The following is CC's quarterly production budget for the year.

	Q1	Q2	Q3	Q4	Total
Sales Volume	45,000	47,700	50,562	53,596	196,858
Planned End. Inventory	9,540	10,112	10,719	11,362	11,362
Units Needed	54,540	57,812	61,281	64,958	208,220
Less Beg. Inventory	(9,000)	(9,540)	(10,112)	(10,719)	(9,000)
Production Volume	45,540	48,272	51,169	54,239	199,220

Q1 Planned Ending Inventory is calculated as 47,700 Q2 Sales Volume × 20% = 9,540. Q2 Sales Volume is calculated as 45,000 Q1 Sales Volume × 1.06 = 47,700.

Q1 Beginning Inventory is the ending inventory from last year's Q4. Even though this number is not provided, it can be calculated because CC constantly follows the budget policy of maintaining an ending inventory of 20% of the next quarter's sales. Q1 Beginning Inventory is calculated based on Q1 sales as 45,000 × 20% = 9,000.

Follow this same pattern for all quarters.

Note: Sales volume in Q1 of the following year, necessary for computing ending inventory in Q4, will be 53,596 units × 1.06 = 56,812 units, based on the same assumption of 6% growth in game sales.

aq.bud.stand.009_0720

12. How does budget slack affect the master budget?

   A. Budget slack hinders ease of communication of organizational goals.
   B. Presence of budget slack can lead to decreased commitment from the employees.
   C. Cumulative budget slack at each sublevel can result in an inaccurate master budget.
   D. Strategic goals do not receive priority in the budgetary process due to existence of budget slack.

   Answer: C

   Budget slack occurs when budgeted performance differs from actual performance because managers tend to build in some extra money for their budget to deal with the unexpected. Budget slack is built-in freedom to fail, and cumulative budget slack at each sublevel can result in a very inaccurate master budget.

aq.swot.009_0720

13. Which of the following is **not** an example of an external factor in SWOT analysis?

   A. The economy
   B. Financial resources
   C. Future technology trends
   D. Competitive forces

   Answer: B

   This is not an example of an external factor in SWOT analysis. It is an internal factor that could be considered as a strength or a weakness for the organization.

aq.lc.anal.003_0720

14. Which of the following is a benefit of expected value computations?

   A. The underlying probabilities used in the expected value formula are usually based on subjective judgments.
   B. The expected value computation reduces multiple outcomes down to a single value, which is easily understood and can be entered into a budget plan.
   C. The expected value computation is the most likely outcome in the future.
   D. Expected value computations incorporate multiple possibilities, making them more representative of a certain future.

   Answer: B

   This is a benefit of expected value computations.

aq.spec.tools.005_0720

15. Which of the following is **not** one of Porter's Five Forces?

   A. Threat of Regulation
   B. Threat of Substitute Products
   C. Intensity of Competition
   D. Threat of New Entrants

   Answer: A

   This is not one of Porter's Five Forces.

Section C. Performance Management

aq.dirmat.dlcv.001_1807

1. Data on Goodman Company's direct labor costs are given below:

Standard direct labor hours	30,000
Actual direct labor hours	29,000
Direct labor usage (efficiency) variance	$4,000 Favorable
Direct labor rate variance	$5,800 Favorable
Total payroll	$110,200

What was Goodman's standard direct labor rate?

A. $3.60
B. $3.80
C. $3.67
D. $4.00

Answer: D

The standard direct labor rate is calculated as follows:
Labor rate variance = actual hours × the difference between the standard and actual labor rates, designated as "D".

$5,800 = 29,000(D)
D = $0.20 per hour

Because the rate variance is favorable, the standard rate must be $0.20 more than the actual rate of

$3.80 ($110,200 ÷ 29,000).

$3.80 + $0.20 = $4.00

aq.manw.va.009_0820

2. Fake Flowers (FF) paid more property tax on their manufacturing facility this year than they were expecting. This would most likely cause an:

A. unfavorable fixed overhead volume variance.
B. unfavorable fixed overhead spending variance.
C. unfavorable variable overhead efficiency variance.
D. unfavorable variable overhead spending variance.

Answer: B

Manufacturing facility property tax is most often considered a fixed cost. The fixed overhead spending variance is the difference between total actual fixed costs and master budget costs. The property tax would cause total actual costs to exceed master budget costs, leading to an unfavorable fixed overhead spending variance.

aq.balscore.004_1807

3. What perspective of the Balanced Scorecard (BSC) is focused on the question: "At what business process must we excel?"

A. Internal perspective
B. Learning perspective
C. Customer perspective
D. Financial perspective

Answer: A

The internal perspective is focused on the question: "At what business processes must we excel?" This depends on how the organization's internal processes are tied to successfully delivering on the customer perspective. The three types of internal processes are innovation, production and delivery, and post-sale service or support.

aq.tran.pri.006_0820

4. Business Unit A produces a widget product that can be sold either to external customers or internally to Business Unit B. Business Unit B is currently purchasing 15,000 widgets from an external supplier for $42 per unit. Both Business Unit A and Business Unit B are evaluated as profit centers. Production and sales data for Business Unit A are provided below. Assuming that variable costs of $4 per widget can be avoided by Business Unit A if an internal transfer takes place, should Business Unit A transfer widgets to Business Unit B? If so, what should the transfer price be?

Business Unit A:	
Capacity in units	80,000
Number of units being sold to external customers	80,000
Selling price per unit to external customers	$45
Variable costs per widget	$20
Fixed costs per unit (based on capacity)	$10

A. No transfer should take place.
B. A transfer should take place; the transfer price should be $45.
C. A transfer should take place; the transfer price should be between $20 and $45.
D. A transfer should take place; the transfer price should be between $41 and $42.

Answer: D

A transfer should take place. Unit A will spend $16 in variable costs ($20 – $4) to produce the widgets to transfer. In addition, due to lack of capacity, Unit A will lose a $25 contribution margin ($45 – $20) due to lost external sales. Hence, Unit A will demand at minimum a $41 price ($16 + $25) to transfer, and Unit B will pay no more than $42 (equal to the current price it is paying to an external supplier).

aq.perev.bs.001_0820

5. Any organizational unit in which the manager of that unit has control only over the costs incurred best describes what type of responsibility center?

A. Investment center
B. Revenue center
C. Profit center
D. Cost center

Answer: D

A cost center is any organizational unit in which the manager of that unit has control only over the costs incurred. The manager of a cost center has no responsibility for revenues or assets, either because revenues are not generated in the center or because revenues and assets are controlled somewhere else in the organization.

aq.retinv.ri.006_1807

6. The Pacific Line in the U&P Railroad operates as a profit center. In the last quarter, the Pacific Line generated $200,000 in operating income on $1,000,000 in total assets. The Pacific Line has $250,000 in current liabilities. Assuming that the U&P required rate of return is 12%, what is the residual income for the Pacific Line?

   A. $320,000
   B. $200,000
   C. $120,000
   D. $80,000

Answer: D

Residual income is calculated as follows:Residual Income = Actual Income - (Assets × Required Rate of Return)$200,000 - ($1,000,000 × 12%) = $80,000

aq.flex.bpa.007_1807

7. Given the following information, what is the flexible budget variance on operating profit for Trendy Technology (TT)?

	Actual Results	Flexible Budget
Total Sales Revenue	$325,000	$350,000
Total Variable Costs	$135,000	$120,000
Total Fixed Costs	$44,000	$42,000

   A. $188,000 Favorable
   B. $42,000 Favorable
   C. $42,000 Unfavorable
   D. $188,000 Unfavorable

Answer: C

The flexible budget variance on operating profit for TT is calculated as follows:

	Actual Results	Flexible Budget	Variances
Total Sales Revenue	$325,000	$350,000	$25,000 U
Total Variable Costs	135,000	120,000	15,000 U
Contribution Margin	$190,000	$230,000	$40,000 U
Total Fixed Costs	44,000	42,000	2,000 U
Operating Profit	$146,000	$188,000	$42,000 U

aq.retinv.ri.005_0820

8. Frigid Fridges Co. (FFC) is a refrigerator manufacturer and wholesaler. For the month of July, FFC had the following operating statistics:

Sales	$600,000
Operating Income	40,000
Net Profit	10,000
Total Assets	700,000
Shareholders' Equity	300,000
Cost of Capital	5%

Based on the above information, what is FFC's residual income (RI)?

A. $5,000
B. ($25,000)
C. $25,000
D. $10,000

Answer: A

The formula for RI = Division's Income – (Total Assets × Cost of Capital). The investment base is defined by the Total Assets figure provided. FFC's required income on this investment is $35,000, which is computed by taking $700,000 total assets × 5% cost of capital. Operating income is $40,000, representing the return on investment. Therefore, $40,000 Operating Income – $35,000 Required Income = $5,000 RI.

aq.perev.bs.004_0820

9. The following information from the prior year was provided by Comfortable Sofas & Couches, Inc. (CSCI):

   ○ The company produced 1,900 units and sold 1,800 units, as expected.

   ○ There was no beginning or ending work-in-process inventories and no beginning finished goods inventory.

   ○ Budgeted and actual fixed costs were equal, all variable manufacturing costs were affected by production volume only, and all variable selling costs were affected by sales volume only.

   ○ Budgeted per unit revenues and costs were as follows:

	Per Unit
Sales price	$120
Direct materials	$25
Direct labor	$20
Other variable manufacturing costs	$15
Fixed manufacturing costs	$12
Variable selling costs	$8
Fixed selling costs	$6
Fixed administrative costs	$5

What is the contribution margin earned by CSCI for the prior year?

A. $72,000
B. $108,000
C. $93,600
D. $86,400

Answer: C

The contribution margin equals total sales minus all variable costs expensed. Provided that there was no work-in-process and no beginning finished goods, the contribution margin is $93,600 = 1,800 × ($120 – $25 – $20 – $15 – $8).

aq.flex.bpa.009_0820

10. Which of the following correctly represents the management-by-exception concept in variance analysis?

   A. Only favorable variances provide a signal to management indicating that something in the organization is out of compliance with budget standards or performance expectations.
   B. Only unfavorable variances provide a signal to management indicating that something in the organization is out of compliance with budget standards or budget performance.

C. Both favorable and unfavorable variances provide a signal to management indicating that something in the organization is out of compliance with budget standards or performance expectations.

D. Variances by themselves *do not* provide a signal to management that something in the organization is out of compliance with budget standards or performance expectations.

Answer: C

Variances provide a signal to management indicating that something in the organization is out of compliance with budget standards or performance expectations, regardless of whether the variance is favorable or unfavorable. If the variance is large enough, it calls attention to management. The value of this management-by-exception approach is it helps the organization focus on current processes that may need attention. It's important to note that variances do not inform management on what the actual problem is or what needs to be done. Variances are simply "signals" to managers to investigate.

aq.facov.cv.004_0820

11. The following information relates to one particular department of the Herman Company for the fourth quarter:

Actual variable overhead	$68,500
Variable overhead application rate	$0.50 per hour
Total overhead application rate	$1.50 per hour
Spending variance	$8,000 unfavorable
Volume variance	$5,000 favorable

What were the actual hours worked in this department during the quarter?

A. 137,000
B. 121,000
C. 127,000
D. 119,000

Answer: B

The actual hours worked in the given department during the quarter is calculated as follows:

Actual variable overhead	$68,500	
Less: spending variance	8,000	Unfavorable
Predicted variable costs	$ 60,500	
Variable overhead rate	÷ $0.50	
Actual hours worked	121,000	Hours

aq.balscore.001_1807

12. All of the following describe key performance indicators (KPIs) **except**:

A. a small set of critical data points.
B. a term describing all the measures used in an organization in the process of running the business.
C. measures that indicate to the executive team and other stakeholders whether the organization is on track to accomplishing its strategic objectives.
D. a good way to get a quick sense of an organization's strategy.

Answer: B

KPIs are not just another term to describe measures at the organization. Many companies will track thousands of measures in the process of running the business. KPIs, as the name implies, are a small set of critical data points that indicate to the executive team and other stakeholders whether the organization is on track to accomplishing its strategic objectives.

13. Quick Microwaves, Inc. (QMI) is preparing for external reporting and performance evaluation at the end of the year. QMI is split up into two companies: Microwave Company and Microwave Oven Company. Each company is split up into geographical regions with those regions being split up into different operations. Each operation has a sales division, manufacturing division, and service division. Based on the organizational structure of QMI, identify business units that QMI should evaluate each year based on performance.

   A. Companies, regions, operations, and divisions
   B. Companies, regions, and operations
   C. Operations and divisions
   D. Companies and regions

Answer: A

QMI should evaluate all companies, regions, operations, and divisions during the end-of-year performance evaluation. When evaluating the performance of a manager for a cost, profit, or investment center, it is important to use only controllable costs. When evaluating the performance of the business unit itself, particularly for decisions regarding keeping or dropping the business unit from the organization, it is crucial to use only direct costs in the analysis.

14. Business Unit A produces a widget product that can be sold either to external customers or internally to Business Unit B. Business Unit B is currently purchasing 15,000 widgets from an external supplier for $25 per unit. Both Business Unit A and Business Unit B are evaluated as profit centers. Production and sales data for Business Unit A are provided below. Assuming that no costs can be avoided if an internal transfer takes place, should Business Unit A transfer widgets to Business Unit B? If so, what should the transfer price be?

Business Unit A:	
Capacity in units	90,000
Number of units being sold to external customers	75,000
Selling price per unit to external customers	$29
Variable costs per widget	$26
Fixed costs per unit (based on capacity)	$2

   A. No transfer should take place.
   B. A transfer should take place; the transfer price should be $25.
   C. A transfer should take place; the transfer price should be between $26 and $29.
   D. A transfer should take place; the transfer price should be between $25 and $29.

Answer: A

No transfer should take place. Business Unit A has the capacity to supply widgets to Business Unit B without losing any external sales. However, the incremental cost to supply the widgets is $26. Since Business Unit B can purchase widgets for $25 from an external supplier, no transfer should take place.

aq.perev.bs.003_1807

15. Classy Purses, Inc. (CPI) is an international manufacturer of stylish shoulder bags. CPI is split up into three regions: Europe Region, Asia Eastern Region, U.S. Region. The Europe region is split into three operating units: England Operations, France Operations, Germany Operations. The France operating unit is split up into the Sales Division and Manufacturing Division. The France sales division is set up to focus exclusively on generating sales and revenue, without responsibility for cost. Which of the following most accurately identifies the responsibility center for the Sales Division, Manufacturing Division, and France Operations of CPI?

A. Sales Division: cost center; Manufacturing Division: revenue center; France Operations: profit center.
B. Sales Division: revenue center; Manufacturing Division: cost center; France Operations: profit center.
C. Sales Division: profit center; Manufacturing Division: cost center; France Operations: cost center.
D. Sales Division: profit center; Manufacturing Division: revenue center; France Operations: revenue center.

Answer: B

Because the Sales Division is set up to focus exclusively on generating sales and revenue, without responsibility for cost, it is a revenue center, not a profit center. The Manufacturing Division does not generate any revenue, but it does generate costs, making it a cost center. France Operations generates both revenue and expenses, making it a profit center.

Section D: Cost Management

aq.proc.c.009_0820

1. Which of the following is true regarding normal and abnormal spoilage?

   A. Normal spoilage is an accepted cost of production while abnormal spoilage represents an unacceptable loss in the production process.
   B. The costs of abnormal spoilage are transferred forward to the finished goods inventory account or to the next department's work-in-process inventory account.
   C. Spoilage in the production process is completely avoidable for many manufacturing organizations if managers work hard to eliminate the costs of spoilage.
   D. The costs of normal and abnormal spoilage are transferred into a loss account that is immediately recognized on the income statement.

   Answer: A

   Some amount of spoilage in the production process is unavoidable for many manufacturing organizations, and managers work hard to minimize the costs of spoilage. A key aspect of that management process is identifying and separating "normal" from "abnormal" spoilage. Normal spoilage is an accepted cost of production while abnormal spoilage represents an unacceptable loss in the production process.

aq.concept.cd.002_0820

2. The Ramirez Company makes leather jackets that sell for $175 each. The total cost in May of manufacturing 1,000 jackets is $114,860. The variable cost for each jacket is $57. What are Ramirez's fixed costs for the month?

   A. $57,000
   B. $114,860
   C. $60,140
   D. $57,860

   Answer: D

   The fixed cost equals the total cost of manufacturing minus the variable cost. Therefore, the fixed cost equals $57,860 ($114,860 − (1,000 × $57)).

aq.v.fc.006_0820

3. A manufacturer of wooden furniture has identified two models for analysis under activity-based costing. Each model is associated with two activity pools: Cutting and Assembly. Model A requires 25 cuts and 5 direct labor hours per unit, while Model B requires 30 cuts and 7.5 direct labor hours per unit. Total factory overhead of $375,000 is split such that 70% is assigned to the Cutting cost pool and 30% is assigned to the Assembly cost pool. The cost driver for Cutting is the number of cuts, and the cost driver for Assembly is direct labor hours. Furthermore, $125,000 of product design overhead is allocated to these two product lines and split equally between them. What is the factory overhead cost per driver unit for Cutting if the company manufactures 25,000 pieces of furniture, 60% of which are Model A?

   A. $0.875 per cut
   B. $0.1667 per cut
   C. $0.389 per cut
   D. $0.70 per cut

Answer: C

There are 15,000 pieces of Model A (25,000 × 60%), and 10,000 pieces of Model B (25,000 × 40%). To produce this many units of each model, 375,000 cuts are required for Model A (15,000 × 25), and 300,000 cuts are required for Model B (10,000 × 30), resulting in 675,000 total cuts (375,000 + 300,000). The cost allocated to cutting equals $262,500 ($375,000 × 70%). The cost per cut equals $0.389 ($262,500 ÷ 675,000).

aq.v.fc.010_0820

4. Keystone Company applies overhead on the basis of machine hours, and reported the following data.

Estimated annual overhead cost	$2,250,000
Actual annual overhead cost	$2,227,500
Estimated machine hours	300,000
Actual machine hours	295,000

Compute the amount of overhead that is under-applied or over-applied for the period.

A. $22,500 under-applied
B. $15,000 over-applied
C. $15,000 under-applied
D. $22,500 over-applied

Answer: C

The overhead application rate equals estimated overhead divided by estimated machine hours. The overhead application rate in this example is $7.50 per machine hour ($2,250,000 ÷ 300,000). The overhead applied equals the overhead application rate multiplied by the actual machine hours. The overhead applied equals $2,212,500 ($7.50 per machine hour × 295,000 actual machine hours). Overhead is under-applied because applied overhead ($2,212,500) is less than (or "under") actual overhead ($2,227,500). The amount under-applied is the difference between actual and applied overhead, which equals $15,000 ($2,227,500 – $2,212,500).

aq.man.cap.006_1809

5. Which of the following correctly describes theoretical capacity?

A. Theoretical capacity is the level of output that the organization actually achieves in a period.
B. Theoretical capacity is the amount of capacity that management predicts the organization will produce in the period.
C. Theoretical capacity represents the level of output if all policy constraints and scheduling limitations are removed. It also assumes that no productivity is lost due to breakdowns, errors, etc.
D. Theoretical capacity represents the level of output that can be realistically achieved based on current management policies, as well as based on machine and labor scheduling expectations.

Answer: C

A theoretical capacity level assumes that all policy constraints and scheduling limitations are removed. It also assumes that no productivity is lost due to breakdowns, errors, etc. This is an ideal world that is never actually achieved.

aq.costflows.vac.005_0820

6. Oak Products produced and sold 5,000 units during its most recent fiscal year. Direct materials were $9 per unit, direct labor costs were $4 per unit, and variable overhead costs were 110% of direct labor costs. Fixed overhead was $50,000, fixed selling and administrative expenses totaled $50,000, and variable selling and administrative expenses were a combined $8 per unit. Calculate inventory costs based on using the absorption (full) costing method.

A. $87,000
B. $137,000
C. $227,000
D. $127,000

Answer: B

Inventory costs under absorption (full) costing consist of direct materials, direct labor, and variable and fixed overhead.

Inventory costs = $(5,000 \times \$9) + (5,000 \times \$4) + (5,000 \times \$4 \times 110\%) + \$50,000$
Inventory costs = $\$45,000 + \$20,000 + \$22,000 + \$50,000$
Inventory costs = $\$137,000$

ac.job.oc.001_0820

7. Which of the following correctly depicts the flow of inventory costs in a job order cost system?

A. Raw Materials Inventory, Work-in-Process Inventory, Finished Goods Inventory, Cost of Goods Sold
B. Finished Goods Inventory, Work-in-Process Inventory, Cost of Goods Sold
C. Work-in-Process Inventory, Raw Materials Inventory, Finished Goods Inventory, Cost of Goods Sold
D. Cost of Goods Sold, Work-in-Process Inventory, Raw Materials Inventory, Finished Goods Inventory

Answer: A

A business would first purchase and store raw materials in Raw Materials Inventory. The raw materials would then be requisitioned into Work-in-Process Inventory where labor and overhead are applied. When the goods are finished, they are transferred from Work-in-Process Inventory to Finished Goods Inventory. Goods that are sold are transferred from Finished Goods Inventory to Cost of Goods Sold.

aq.val.ca.001_0820

8. Which of the following most accurately defines value chain analysis?

A. An approach used by an organization to allocate capacity costs while tracking and reporting the fixed costs of idle capacity in the organization's production process
B. An approach used by an organization to evaluate its internal activities determine how essential each activity is strategically creating and capturing value for the organization's customers
C. A system based on the idea that inventory is not really an asset in the production process, but is often a barrier to achieving the organization's main goals
D. A system that supports a very specific and extremely short-term managerial view of an operation —the incremental value from a more effective employment of a constrained resource

Answer: B

Value chain analysis is an approach used by an organization to evaluate its internal activities and identify how each is involved in creating and capturing value for the organization's customers.

aq.v.fc.008_0820

9. Leigh M. is working with her production supervisor to compute a predetermined fixed overhead rate for the coming year. Leigh and her production supervisor have put together a budget of 1,600 direct labor hours for the coming year. During the same period, they plan for 2,000 machine hours in the production process. Leigh has assembled the following information for the upcoming year:

Direct materials	$100,000
Direct labor cost	140,000
Salaries for factory janitors	70,000
Sales supervisor salary	102,000
Rent on factory building	24,000
Advertising expense	10,000

If Leigh decides to use a predetermined manufacturing overhead rate based on direct labor hours, what will be the predetermined manufacturing overhead rate?

A. $58.75 per direct labor hour
B. $47.00 per machine hour
C. $128.75 per direct labor hour
D. $103.00 per machine hour

Answer: A

Total overhead equals factory janitors' salaries plus factory building rent, which adds up to $94,000 ($70,000 + $24,000). Note that the salary for the sales supervisor and the advertising expense is not a manufacturing overhead cost. The predetermined overhead rate based on direct labor hours equals total overhead divided by direct labor hours. Therefore, the predetermined overhead rate equals $58.75 per direct labor hour ($94,000 ÷ 1,600).

aq.ab.cost.003_0820

10. Mandy Appliances manufactures toaster ovens. Each oven contains 15 parts totaling $35 in direct materials. Each oven requires 3 hours of machine time and 1.5 hours for inspection. The company has the following information regarding activities, activity drivers, and cost per driver units:

Activity	Activity Driver	Cost per Driver Unit
Machining	Machine hours	$3.75/machine hour
Materials handling	Number of parts	$1.20/part
Assembly	Number of parts	$0.85/part
Inspection	Inspection hours	$11.80/inspection hour

What is the cost of machining per toaster oven?

A. $18.00
B. $12.75
C. $11.25
D. $17.70

Answer: C

The cost per driver unit for machining is $3.75 per machine hour. Each oven requires 3 hours of machine time. Therefore, the cost of machining per toaster oven is $11.25 ($3.75 × 3 hours).

aq.costflows.vac.007_0820

11. Last year, Welk Company had 16,000 units in its beginning inventory. During the year, the company's variable production costs were $6 per unit and its fixed manufacturing overhead costs were $4 per unit. The company's net income for the year was $24,000 higher under absorption costing than it was under variable costing. Given these facts, what was the number of units in the ending inventory?

A. 16,000 units
B. 20,000 units
C. 22,000 units
D. 6,000 units

Answer: C

Because net income under absorption costing is higher than net income under variable costing, more units were produced than sold. To find how many more units were produced than sold, divide the difference in incomes by the fixed manufacturing overhead costs per unit: $24,000 ÷ $4 = 6,000 units. Remember that there are 16,000 units in beginning inventory. Add 6,000 to the beginning inventory to determine the ending inventory: 16,000 + 6,000 = 22,000 units.

12. A department adds raw materials to a process at the beginning of the process and incurs conversion costs uniformly throughout the process. For the month of January, there were 10,000 units in the Beginning Work-in-Process Inventory that were 80% complete; 90,000 units were started into production in January; and 20,000 units that were 40% complete in the Ending Work-in-Process Inventory at the end of January. Using the FIFO method of process costing, what are the equivalent units of production for materials for the month of January?

A. 70,000 equivalent units
B. 100,000 equivalent units
C. 90,000 equivalent units
D. 80,000 equivalent units

Answer: C

Remember that materials are added to the production process at the beginning of the production process. Therefore, the 10,000 units in the Beginning Work-in-Process Inventory already had all materials added last month and no more will be added this month. Similarly, the 20,000 units in the Ending Work-in-Process Inventory had all materials added at the beginning of the process this month. Equivalent units are calculated as follows:

	Physical Units	**% Done in Jan.**	**Equivalent Units**
Beginning work-in-process	10,000	0%	0
Started and completed	70,000	100%	70,000
Ending work-in-process	20,000	100%	20,000
Equivalent units in January			**90,000**

(*Note:* 70,000 units started and completed = 90,000 units started – 20,000 units in ending work-in-process.)

13. A product currently sells for $50 per unit and has variable manufacturing costs of $15 per unit, and variable selling and administrative costs of $6 per unit. How will the total contribution margin change when output is increased from 8,000 to 9,000 units?

A. Decrease of $15,000
B. Increase of $29,000
C. Decrease of $6,000
D. Increase of $50,000

Answer: B

The unit contribution margin equals $29 per unit ($50 – $15 – $6). The increase in output increases by 1,000 units (9,000 – 8,000). The increase in total contribution margin equals $29,000 (1,000 units × $29 per unit).

14. A processing department produces joint products Ajac and Bjac, each of which incurs separable production costs after split-off. Information concerning a batch of these products produced with a $60,000 joint cost follows:

Product	Separable Costs	Final Sales Value
Ajac	$8,000	$80,000
Bjac	22,000	40,000
Total	$30,000	$120,000

What amount of the joint cost would be allocated to Ajac if joint costs are allocated to products using the net realizable value method?

A. $56,000
B. $12,000
C. $48,000
D. $40,000

Answer: C

The amount of joint costs allocated to Ajac are calculated as follows:

Product	Sales Value	– Sep. Cost	= NRV	Relative NRV	Joint Cost Allocation
Ajac	$80,000	$8,000	$72,000	72,000 ÷ 90,000 = 80%	80% × $60,000 = $48,000
Bjac	40,000	22,000	18,000	18,000 ÷ 90,000 = 20%	20% × $60,000 = $12,000
Total	$120,000	$30,000	$90,000	100%	$60,000

aq.v.fc.003_1809

15. Dana's real estate agency has increased its listings by offering an extensive advertising program, but Dana is concerned about her advertising costs. She is not sure how much she spends on advertising per listing because her advertising costs have both variable and fixed components.

Month	Number of Listings	Advertising Cost
March	35	$23,145
April	23	$15,025
May	22	$15,280
June	42	$27,205
July	48	$30,565
August	51	$32,485
September	50	$31,835
October	56	$36,020
November	54	$36,920

Based on the information above and the high–low method, what is Dana's fixed cost for advertising?

A. $1,860
B. $1,213
C. $863
D. $2,230

Answer: A

The month with the highest number of listings is October, and the month with the lowest number of listings is May, so use the data for those months for the high–low method. The variable cost is $610 per listing (($36,020 – $15,280) ÷ (56 – 22)). The fixed cost equals the total cost minus the variable cost. Using May's data, the fixed cost is $1,860 ($36,020 – (56 × $610)).

Section E: Internal Controls

aq.ic.policies.008_1802

1. The safeguarding of inventory **most likely** includes:

    A. Comparison of the information contained on the purchase requisitions, purchase orders, receiving reports, and vendor invoices.
    B. Analytical procedures for raw materials, work-in-process, and finished goods that identify unusual transactions, theft, and obsolescence.
    C. Application of established overhead rates based on direct labor hours or direct labor costs.
    D. Periodic reconciliation of detailed inventory records with the actual inventory on hand by taking a physical count.

    Answer: D

    Periodic reconciliation of the recorded amounts to a physical count of inventory is necessary to identify inventory accuracy and potential spoilage, obsolescence, and shortages.

aq.ext.aud.req.003_1802

2. Inherent risk and control risk differ from detection risk in that they:

    A. Arise from the misapplication of auditing procedures.
    B. May be assessed in only quantitative terms.
    C. Exist independently of the financial statement audit.
    D. Can be changed at the auditor's discretion.

    Answer: C

    AU 312 states that inherent risk and control risk exist independently of the audit, whereas detection risk relates to the auditor's procedures and can be changed at his discretion.

aq.corp.gov.002_1802

3. Which of the following is **not** an attribute required by the Sarbanes Oxley Act for the financial expert who serves on the board of directors and the board's audit committee?

    A. An understanding of internal controls
    B. The individual must be a CPA or CFA
    C. An understanding of audit committee functions
    D. The ability to assess the accounting for accruals, estimates, and reserves

    Answer: B

    There is no requirement that an individual who is the financial expert is either a CPA or CFA.

aq.gen.c.006_1802

4. What is the backup facility that can be up and running at a short notice called?

    A. VAN
    B. Hot site
    C. Remote site
    D. Cold site

    Answer: B

    A hot site is a backup facility that can be up and running with short notice.

aq.ext.aud.req.004_1802

5. An auditor uses the assessed level of control risk to:

    A. Evaluate the effectiveness of the entity's internal control policies and procedures.
    B. Identify transactions and account balances where inherent risk is at the maximum.
    C. Indicate whether materiality thresholds for planning and evaluation purposes are sufficiently high.
    D. Determine the acceptable level of detection risk for financial statement assertions.

    Answer: D

    According to the audit risk model, acceptable detection risk is a function of allowable audit risk, inherent risk, and control risk.

aq.ic.policies.010_1802

6. Proper segregation of duties reduces the opportunities to allow individuals to be in positions to both:

    A. Journalize entries and prepare financial statements.
    B. Authorize transactions and record cash disbursements.
    C. Record cash receipts and cash disbursements.
    D. Establish internal controls and authorize transactions.

    Answer: B

    The responsibilities of authorization and recording transactions should be segregated to reduce the risk of fraud and errors.

aq.corp.gov.006_1802

7. Which of the following correctly describes the Sarbanes-Oxley Act requirements with respect to auditor rotation?

    A. The audit firm must rotate the lead audit partner every five years.
    B. The company being audited must rotate the audit firm every five years.
    C. The audit firm must rotate the audit staff every five years.
    D. The company being audited must rotate the audit committee every five years.

    Answer: A

    This requirement is described in Section 201 of the Sarbanes-Oxley Act.

aq.sys.app.c.001_1802

8. Which of the following is an example of a validity check?

    A. The computer flags any transmission for which the control field value did not match that of an existing file record.
    B. The computer ensures that a numerical amount in a record does not exceed some predetermined amount.
    C. As the computer corrects errors and data are successfully resubmitted to the system, the causes of the errors are printed out.
    D. After data for a transaction are entered, the computer sends certain data back to the terminal for comparison with data originally sent.

    Answer: A

    Validity checks are computer-programmed routines that determine whether a character is legitimate. This option is an example of a validity check.

aq.ext.aud.req.001_1802

9. According to the PCAOB auditing standards (AS), the auditor of a company that issues securities must audit the company's internal control, as well as its financial statements. What is the recommended timing of these two audits?

    A. The two audits should be integrated.
    B. The internal control audit should be performed first and be immediately followed by the audit of the company's financial statements.
    C. The financial statement audit should be performed first and be immediately followed by the audit of the company's internal control.
    D. The internal control audit should be performed first, unless there is an adequate reason for first performing the financial statement audit.

    Answer: A

    The PCAOB has recommended that the two audits should be integrated as much as possible, in part to reduce both time and cost.

aq.corp.gov.007_1802

10. The Sarbanes-Oxley Act disallows each of the following services for auditors of a publicly traded company except for:

    A. Human resource services.
    B. Financial information systems design.
    C. Tax preparation services.
    D. Actuarial services.

    Answer: C

    Tax preparation services are not prohibited under the services that the Sarbanes-Oxley Act disallows to be provided to an audit client.

aq.corp.gov.003_1802

11. Which board of directors committee is charged with overseeing the financial reporting process?

    A. The audit committee
    B. The compensation committee
    C. The financial committee
    D. The governance committee

    Answer: A

    The audit committee is charged with overseeing the financial reporting process.

aq.ic.phil.003_1802

12. The Committee of Sponsoring Organizations (COSO) internal control framework consists of five interrelated components. Which of the following is **not** one of these components?

    A. Risk assessment
    B. Information and communication
    C. Management risk
    D. Monitoring

    Answer: C

    The five interrelated components are the control environment, risk assessment, control activities, information and communication, and monitoring.

aq.ic.policies.009_1802

13. How would the use of pre-numbered forms be a means of control?

    A. Pre-numbered forms allow for proper review of exceptions or missing documents.
    B. Pre-numbered forms are no longer a useful means of control because companies' assets and procedures are becoming increasingly digital.
    C. Pre-numbered forms allow a company to know when it needs to reorder new forms.
    D. Pre-numbered forms are not a useful means of control because they do not increase protection of a firm's assets.

Answer: A

Pre-numbered forms allow for proper review of exceptions or missing documents.

aq.ic.phil.007_1802

14. Companies with international operations must comply with the Foreign Corrupt Practices Act (FCPA). In order to comply with FCPA, a company's internal controls must provide reasonable assurance that:

    A. Management must authorize all access to assets.
    B. The company's financial records are in accordance with applicable accounting standards.
    C. Management must authorize all access to assets and that the company's financial records are in accordance with applicable accounting standards.
    D. Management does not need to authorize all access to assets and the company's financial records are not required to be in accordance with applicable accounting standards.

Answer: C

Companies with international operations that must comply with the FCPA must have internal controls that provide reasonable assurance that management must authorize all access to assets and that the company's financial records are in accordance with applicable accounting standards.

aq.ic.risk.002_1802

15. An auditor uses the knowledge provided by the understanding of internal controls and the assessed level of control risk primarily to:

    A. Determine whether the control procedures and supporting records concerning the safeguarding of assets are reliable.
    B. Determine the nature, timing, and extent of further audit procedures.
    C. Modify the preliminary judgments about materiality levels.
    D. Modify the initial assessments of inherent risk.

Answer: B

An auditor uses the knowledge provided by the understanding of internal controls and the assessed level of control risk primarily for the reasons mentioned here.

Section F: Technology and Analytics

AQ.sec.brch.002_1904

1. Which of the following **best** describes the purpose of an advanced firewall?

   A. This security device is limited to stateful inspection of network traffic but can allow the addition of other features to discourage access into the corporate network.
   B. It allows communication between two trusted networks.
   C. It allows communication between two unknown networks.
   D. It is a network security component that monitors, regulates, and provides a barrier for incoming and outgoing network traffic between a trusted and untrusted network by using features such as application filtering.

   Answer: D

   This best explains an advanced firewall from the aspect of application filtering, the ability to determine whether the application traversing the firewall is actually as advertised.

AQ.sec.brch.004_1904

2. Regarding cyberattacks, which of the following uses only approved and qualified testers to conduct real-world attacks against a computer system or network?

   A. Proxy testing
   B. Penetration testing
   C. Alpha testing
   D. Fault-injection testing

   Answer: B

   Penetration testing is the process of using approved personnel to conduct real-world attacks against a computer system or network to identify and correct security weaknesses or flaws (security holes) before they are discovered and exploited by others such as outsiders (hackers) and insiders (disgruntled employees).

aq.ana.too.004_1905

3. All of the following are types of time series analysis **except**:

   A. Trend analysis
   B. Seasonal analysis
   C. Cyclical analysis
   D. Sensitivity analysis

   Answer: D

   Sensitivity analysis is not a type of time series analysis. Sensitivity analysis is a process of varying input parameters of a model within the allowed area and observing the resulting changes in the model solution. The purpose of sensitivity analysis is to indicate the sensitivity of simulation to uncertainties in the values of input data in the model.

aq.dat.min.001_1905

4. Which of the following can uncover hidden patterns, trends, correlations, outliers, anomalies, and subtle relationships in data and help to infer rules that allow for the prediction of future results and outcomes?

   A. Web scraping
   B. Data mining
   C. Web mining
   D. Social mining

Answer: B

This is the definition of data mining. Data mining is the application of database technologies and advanced data-analytics programs to uncover hidden patterns, trends, correlations, outliers, anomalies, and subtle relationships in data and to help infer rules that allow for the prediction of future results and outcomes. Data mining analyzes data for relationships that have not previously been discovered and other insights not suggested by a priori hypotheses or explicit assumptions. Big data is often used as input into data mining applications due to its vast amounts of data, meaning the more the data available, the more it can be applied to. This means that a data analyst can mine large amounts of data (big data) to reveal patterns and to provide insights. Note that data mining drives web scraping, web mining, and social mining as it is a common factor in them.

aq.er.plan.sys.005_1906

5. Which answer BEST describes a data warehouse?

A. A location where document hard copies can be aggregated and analyzed
B. A term to associate multiple sites used for disaster recovery
C. A storage of large amounts of data from various databases used for specialized analysis
D. A storage commonly used for critical data such as system relationships, data types, formats, and sources

Answer: C

A data warehouse is a collection of multiple databases usually containing historical information not usually saved in production systems.

AQ.data.proc.004_1904

6. All of the following are one of the identified COSO (Committee of Sponsoring Organizations of the Treadway Commission) Internal Control-Integrated Framework components **except**:

A. Risk Assessment
B. Monitoring Activities
C. Control Activities
D. Vulnerability Assessment

Answer: D

This is an important aspect of Data Governance but not specifically defined as part of the COSO Internal Framework.

aq.ana.too.002_1905

7. A **major** difference between a simple regression analysis and multiple regression analysis is which of the following?

A. Number of dependent variables
B. Number of mathematical equations
C. Number of independent variables
D. Number of design experiments

Answer: C

Two types of regression analysis are simple regression and multiple regression. In simple regression, there will be only two variables: one dependent variable and one independent variable. In multiple regression, there will be more than two variables: one dependent variable and more than one independent variable. Hence, the number of independent variables is the major difference between multiple regression analysis and simple regression analysis.

8. Which of the following can be described by the possibility for machines to learn from experience, adjust to new inputs, and perform human-like tasks?

    A. Robotic process automation
    B. Artificial intelligence
    C. Cloud computing
    D. Business intelligence

Answer: B

Artificial intelligence relies heavily on deep learning and natural language processing. Using these technologies, computers can be trained to accomplish specific tasks by processing large amounts of data and recognizing patterns in the data.

9. Which of the following items is an advantage of an ERP (Enterprise Resource Planning) System?

    A. Scalability
    B. Low cost of implementation and maintenance
    C. Lack of complexity
    D. Affordable software

Answer: A

Most ERP systems can grow with a business, adding modules or customizations as the company grows.

10. Which of the following is an example of unstructured data?

    A. Data in disconnected computer systems
    B. Data in data warehouses
    C. Data in databases
    D. Web pages on the Internet

Answer: A

Data in disconnected computer systems is unstructured due to multiple and dissimilar systems collecting data with different data formats and with different data structures. Unstructured data consists of external data sources with free-form format.

11. Which use case represents an ideal scenario to utilize sensitivity analysis?

    A. An analyst wants a method for predicting the outcome of a decision if a situation turns out to be different compared to the key predictions.
    B. An analyst wants to assess relative variables for bond price, inflation, and market interest rates.
    C. An analyst wants to reduce assumptions.
    D. An analyst wants an objective assessment of data.

Answer: A

Sensitivity analysis helps in analyzing how sensitive the output is by the changes in one input while keeping the other inputs constant. Sensitivity analysis works on the simple principle of "change the model and observe the behavior."

aq.life.data.002_1904

12. Which of the following functions of the data life cycle is involved with the removal of every copy of a data item from the enterprise?

    A. Data purging
    B. Data archiving
    C. Data maintenance
    D. Data synthesis

Answer: A

Possibly due to a retention policy, where a data item is removed forever from the enterprise, this is data purging.

AQ.data.proc.003_1904

13. Identify which of the following BEST describes ISACA's COBIT key principles?

    A. Meeting Stakeholder Needs, Covering the Enterprise End-to-End, Applying a Single-Integrated Framework, Enabling a Holistic Approach, and Separating Governance from Management
    B. Integrity, Confidentiality, Redundancy, Availability, Governing Policies
    C. Identification, Authentication, Authorization, Auditing, and Accounting
    D. Trust Boundaries, Data Flow Paths, Input Points, Privileged Operations, Details about Security Stance and Approach

Answer: A

These are the five key principles that ISACA's COBIT are based on.

aq.ana.too.001_1905

14. All of the following are defining characteristics of predictive analytics **except**:

    A. Historical patterns are utilized to output specific outcomes using algorithms.
    B. Decisions are automated using trend data and industry insights.
    C. The variability of the component data will have a relationship with what is likely to happen.
    D. Analytical output provides specific recommendations to take action on.

Answer: D

Specific recommendations are an output of prescriptive analytics versus predictive analytics. Prescriptive analytics provide the user with actions to take in order to experience a desired outcome (i.e., based on known traffic patterns at this time, take this route to work/home).

aq.er.plan.sys.004_1906

15. All of the following are a function of a database management system (DBMS) **except**:

    A. Backup and recovery
    B. Encryption
    C. Data integrity
    D. Malware detection

Answer: D

This is an important security control but not a function of a DBMS.

Appendixes

Content Specification Outlines

CMA® (Certified Management Accountant) Examinations

The Content Specification Outlines presented below represent the body of knowledge that will be covered on the CMA examinations. The outlines may be changed in the future when new subject matter becomes part of the common body of knowledge.

Candidates for the CMA designation are required to take and pass Parts 1 and 2.

Candidates are responsible for being informed about the most recent developments in the areas covered in the outlines. This includes understanding public pronouncements issued by accounting organizations as well as being up-to-date on recent developments reported in current accounting, financial, and business periodicals.

The Content Specification Outlines serve several purposes. The outlines are intended to:

- Establish the foundation from which each examination will be developed.

- Provide a basis for consistent coverage on each examination.

- Communicate to interested parties more detail as to the content of each examination part.

- Assist candidates in their preparation for each examination.

- Provide information to those who offer courses designed to aid candidates in preparing for the examinations.

Important additional information about the Content Specification Outlines and the examinations is listed below.

1. The coverage percentage given for each major topic within each examination part represents the relative weight given to that topic in an examination part. The number of questions presented in each major topic area approximates this percentage.

2. Each examination will sample from the subject areas contained within each major topic area to meet the relative weight specifications. No relative weights have been assigned to the subject areas within each major topic. No inference should be made from the order in which the subject areas are listed or from the number of subject areas as to the relative weight or importance of any of the subjects.

3. Each major topic within each examination part has been assigned a coverage level designating the depth and breadth of topic coverage, ranging from an introductory knowledge of a subject area (Level A) to a thorough understanding of and ability to apply the essentials of a subject area (Level C). Detailed explanations of the coverage levels and the skills expected of candidates are presented below.

4. The topics for Parts 1 and 2 have been selected to minimize the overlapping of subject areas among the examination parts. The topics within an examination part and the subject areas within the topics may be combined in individual questions.

5. With regard to U.S. federal income taxation issues, candidates will be expected to understand the impact of income taxes when reporting and analyzing financial results. In addition, the tax code provisions that impact decisions (e.g., depreciation, interest, etc.) will be tested.

6. Candidates for the CMA designation are assumed to have knowledge of the following: preparation of financial statements, business economics, time value of money concepts, statistics, and probability.

7. Parts 1 and 2 are four-hour exams and each contains 100 multiple-choice questions and two essay questions. Candidates will have three hours to complete the multiple-choice questions and one hour to complete the essay section. A small number of the multiple-choice questions on each exam are being validated for future use and will not count in the final score.

8. For the essay questions, both written and quantitative responses will be required. Candidates will be expected to present written answers that are responsive to the question asked, presented in a logical manner, and demonstrate an appropriate understanding of the subject matter.

In order to more clearly define the topical knowledge required by a candidate, varying levels of coverage for the treatment of major topics of the Content Specification Outlines have been identified and defined. The cognitive skills that a successful candidate should possess and that should be tested on the examinations can be defined as follows:

Knowledge: Ability to remember previously learned material such as specific facts, criteria, techniques, principles, and procedures (i.e., identify, define, list).

Comprehension: Ability to grasp and interpret the meaning of material (i.e., classify, explain, distinguish between).

Application: Ability to use learned material in new and concrete situations (i.e., demonstrate, predict, solve, modify, relate).

Analysis: Ability to break down material into its component parts so that its organizational structure can be understood; ability to recognize causal relationships, discriminate between behaviors, and identify elements that are relevant to the validation of a judgment (i.e., differentiate, estimate, order).

Synthesis: Ability to put parts together to form a new whole or proposed set of operations; ability to relate ideas and formulate hypotheses (i.e., combine, formulate, revise).

Evaluation: Ability to judge the value of material for a given purpose on the basis of consistency, logical accuracy, and comparison to standards; ability to appraise judgments involved in the selection of a course of action (i.e., criticize, justify, conclude).

The three levels of coverage can be defined as follows:

Level A: Requiring the skill levels of knowledge and comprehension.

Level B: Requiring the skill levels of knowledge, comprehension, application, and analysis.

Level C: Requiring all six skill levels of knowledge, comprehension, application, analysis, synthesis, and evaluation.

The levels of coverage as they apply to each of the major topics of the Content Specification Outlines are shown on the following pages with each topic listing. The levels represent the manner in which topic areas are to be treated and represent ceilings, i.e., a topic area designated as Level C may contain requirements at the "A," "B," or "C" level, but a topic designated as Level B will not contain requirements at the "C" level.

CMA Content Specification Overview

Part 1 - Financial Planning, Performance, and Analytics
(4 hours – 100 questions and 2 essay questions)

External Financial Reporting Decisions	15%	Level C
Planning, Budgeting, and Forecasting	20%	Level C
Performance Management	20%	Level C
Cost Management	15%	Level C
Internal Controls	15%	Level C
Technology and Analytics	15%	Level C

Part 2 - Strategic Financial Management
(4 hours – 100 questions and 2 essay questions)

Financial Statement Analysis	20%	Level C
Corporate Finance	20%	Level C
Decision Analysis	25%	Level C
Risk Management	10%	Level C
Investment Decisions	10%	Level C
Professional Ethics	15%	Level C

Part 1 - Financial Planning, Performance, and Analytics

A. External Financial Reporting Decisions (15% - Levels A, B, and C)

1. *Financial statements*

    a. Balance sheet

    b. Income statement

    c. Statement of changes in equity

    d. Statement of cash flows

    e. Integrated reporting

2. *Recognition, measurement, valuation, and disclosure*

    a. Asset valuation

    b. Valuation of liabilities

    c. Equity transactions

    d. Revenue recognition

    e. Income measurement

    f. Major differences between U.S. GAAP and IFRS

B. Planning, Budgeting, and Forecasting (20% - Levels A, B, and C)

1. *Strategic planning*

    a. Analysis of external and internal factors affecting strategy

    b. Long-term mission and goals

    c. Alignment of tactics with long-term strategic goals

    d. Strategic planning models and analytical techniques

    e. Characteristics of a successful strategic planning process

2. *Budgeting concepts*

    a. Operations and performance goals

    b. Characteristics of a successful budget process

    c. Resource allocation

    d. Other budgeting concepts

3. *Forecasting techniques*

    a. Regression analysis

    b. Learning curve analysis

    c. Expected value

4. *Budgeting methodologies*

   a. Annual business plans (master budgets)

   b. Project budgeting

   c. Activity-based budgeting

   d. Zero-based budgeting

   e. Continuous (rolling) budgets

   f. Flexible budgeting

5. *Annual profit plan and supporting schedules*

   a. Operational budgets

   b. Financial budgets

   c. Capital budgets

6. *Top-level planning and analysis*

   a. Pro forma income

   b. Financial statement projections

   c. Cash flow projections

C. Performance Management (20% - Levels A, B, and C)

1. *Cost and variance measures*

   a. Comparison of actual to planned results

   b. Use of flexible budgets to analyze performance

   c. Management by exception

   d. Use of standard cost systems

   e. Analysis of variation from standard cost expectations

2. *Responsibility centers and reporting segments*

   a. Types of responsibility centers

   b. Transfer pricing

   c. Reporting of organizational segments

3. *Performance measures*

   a. Product profitability analysis

   b. Business unit profitability analysis

   c. Customer profitability analysis

   d. Return on investment

   e. Residual income

   f. Investment base issues

   g. Key performance indicators (KPIs)

   h. Balanced scorecard

D. Cost Management (15% - Levels A, B, and C)

1. *Measurement concepts*

    a. Cost behavior and cost objects

    b. Actual and normal costs

    c. Standard costs

    d. Absorption (full) costing

    e. Variable (direct) costing

    f. Joint and by-product costing

2. *Costing systems*

    a. Job order costing

    b. Process costing

    c. Activity-based costing

    d. Life-cycle costing

3. *Overhead costs*

    a. Fixed and variable overhead expenses

    b. Plant-wide vs. departmental overhead

    c. Determination of allocation base

    d. Allocation of service department costs

4. *Supply chain management*

    a. Lean resource management techniques

    b. Enterprise resource planning (ERP)

    c. Theory of Constraints

    d. Capacity management and analysis

5. *Business process improvement*

    a. Value chain analysis

    b. Value-added concepts

    c. Process analysis, redesign, and standardization

    d. Activity-based management

    e. Continuous improvement concepts

    f. Best practice analysis

    g. Cost of quality analysis

    h. Efficient accounting processes

E. Internal Controls (15% - Levels A, B, and C)

1. Governance, risk, and compliance

    a. Internal control structure and management philosophy

    b. Internal control policies for safeguarding and assurance

    c. Internal control risk

    d. Corporate governance

    e. External audit requirements

2. System controls and security measures

    a. General accounting system controls

    b. Application and transaction controls

    c. Network controls

    d. Backup controls

    e. Business continuity planning

F. Technology and Analytics (15% - Levels A, B, and C)

1. Information systems

    a. Accounting information systems

    b. Enterprise resource planning systems

    c. Enterprise performance management systems

2. Data governance

    a. Data policies and procedures

    b. Life cycle of data

    c. Controls against security breaches

3. Technology-enabled finance transformation

    a. System development life cycle

    b. Process automation

    c. Innovative applications

4. Data analytics

    a. Business intelligence

    b. Data mining

    c. Analytic tools

    d. Data visualization

Learning Outcome Statements

Part 1 – Financial Planning, Performance, and Analytics

Section A. External Financial Reporting Decisions (15% - Levels A, B, and C)

Part 1 - Section A.1. Financial statements

For the balance sheet, income statement, statement of changes in equity, and the statement of cash flows, the candidate should be able to:

    a. identify the users of these financial statements and their needs

    b. demonstrate an understanding of the purposes and uses of each statement

    c. identify the major components and classifications of each statement

    d. identify the limitations of each financial statement

    e. identify how various financial transactions affect the elements of each of the financial statements and determine the proper classification of the transaction

    f. demonstrate an understanding of the relationship among the financial statements

    g. demonstrate an understanding of how a balance sheet, an income statement, a statement of changes in equity, and a statement of cash flows (indirect method) are prepared

With respect to integrated reporting, the candidate should be able to:

    h. define integrated reporting (IR), integrated thinking, and the integrated report and demonstrate an understanding of the relationship between them

    i. identify the primary purpose of IR

    j. explain the fundamental concepts of value creation, the six capitals, and the value creation process

    k. identify elements of an Integrated report; i.e., organizational overview and external environment, governance, business model, risks and opportunities, strategy and resource allocation, performance, outlook, and basis of preparation and presentation

    l. identify and explain the benefits and challenges of adopting IR

Part 1 - Section A.2. Recognition, measurement, valuation, and disclosure

The candidate should be able to:

Asset valuation

    a. identify issues related to the valuation of accounts receivable, including timing of recognition and estimation of the allowance for credit losses

    b. distinguish between receivables sold (factoring) on a with-recourse basis and those sold on a without-recourse basis, and determine the effect on the balance sheet

    c. identify issues in inventory valuation, including which goods to include, what costs to include, and which cost assumption to use

    d. identify and compare cost flow assumptions used in accounting for inventories

e. demonstrate an understanding of the lower of cost or market rule for LIFO and the retail inventory method and the lower of cost and net realizable value rule for all other inventory methods

f. calculate the effect on income and on assets of using different inventory methods

g. analyze the effects of inventory errors

h. identify advantages and disadvantages of the different inventory methods

i. recommend the inventory method and cost flow assumption that should be used for a firm given a set of facts

j. demonstrate an understanding of the following debt security types: trading, available-for-sale, and held-to-maturity

k. demonstrate an understanding of the valuation of debt and equity securities

l. determine the effect on the financial statements of using different depreciation methods

m. recommend a depreciation method for a given set of data

n. demonstrate an understanding of the accounting for impairment of long-term assets and intangible assets, including goodwill

Valuation of liabilities

o. identify the classification issues of short-term debt expected to be refinanced

p. compare the effect on financial statements when using either the assurance warranty approach or the service warranty approach for accounting for warranties

Income taxes (applies to Assets and Liabilities subtopics)

q. demonstrate an understanding of interperiod tax allocation/deferred income taxes

r. distinguish between deferred tax liabilities and deferred tax assets

s. differentiate between temporary differences and permanent differences and identify examples of each

Leases (applies to Assets and Liabilities subtopics)

t. distinguish between operating and finance leases

u. recognize the correct financial statement presentation of operating and finance leases

Equity transactions

v. identify transactions that affect paid-in capital and those that affect retained earnings

w. determine the effect on shareholders' equity of large and small stock dividends, and stock splits

Revenue recognition

x. apply revenue recognition principles to various types of transactions

y. demonstrate an understanding of revenue recognition for contracts with customers using the five steps required to recognize revenue

z. demonstrate an understanding of the matching principle with respect to revenues and expenses and be able to apply it to a specific situation

Income measurement

    aa.   define gains and losses and indicate the proper financial statement presentation

    bb.   demonstrate an understanding of the treatment of gain or loss on the disposal of fixed assets

    cc.   demonstrate an understanding of expense recognition practices

    dd.   define and calculate comprehensive income

    ee.   identify the correct treatment of discontinued operations

GAAP – IFRS differences

Major differences in reported financial results when using GAAP vs. IFRS and the impact on analysis

    ff.   identify and describe the following differences between U.S. GAAP and IFRS: (i) expense recognition, with respect to share-based payments and employee benefits; (ii) intangible assets, with respect to development costs and revaluation; (iii) inventories, with respect to costing methods, valuation, and write-downs (e.g., LIFO); (iv) leases, with respect to lessee operating and finance leases; (v) long-lived assets, with respect to revaluation, depreciation, and capitalization of borrowing costs; and (vi) impairment of assets, with respect to determination, calculation, and reversal of loss

Section B. Planning, Budgeting, and Forecasting (20% - Levels A, B, and C)

Part 1 - Section B.1. Strategic planning

The candidate should be able to:

    a.   discuss how strategic planning determines the path an organization chooses for attaining its long-term goals, vision, and mission, and distinguish between vision and mission

    b.   identify the time frame appropriate for a strategic plan

    c.   identify the external factors that should be analyzed during the strategic planning process and understand how this analysis leads to recognition of organizational opportunities, limitations, and threats

    d.   identify the internal factors that should be analyzed during the strategic planning process and explain how this analysis leads to recognition of organizational strengths, weaknesses, and competitive advantages

    e.   demonstrate an understanding of how the mission leads to the formulation of long-term business objectives such as business diversification, the addition or deletion of product lines, or the penetration of new markets

    f.   explain why short-term objectives, tactics for achieving these objectives, and operational planning (master budget) must be congruent with the strategic plan and contribute to the achievement of long-term strategic goals

    g.   identify the characteristics of successful strategic plans

    h.   describe Porter's generic strategies, including cost leadership, differentiation, and focus

    i.   demonstrate an understanding of the following planning tools and techniques: SWOT analysis, Porter's 5 forces, situational analysis, PEST analysis, scenario planning, competitive analysis, contingency planning, and the BCG Growth-Share Matrix

Part 1 - Section B.2. Budgeting concepts

The candidate should be able to:

  a. describe the role that budgeting plays in the overall planning and performance evaluation process of an organization

  b. explain the interrelationships between economic conditions, industry situation, and a firm's plans and budgets

  c. identify the role that budgeting plays in formulating short-term objectives and planning and controlling operations to meet those objectives

  d. demonstrate an understanding of the role that budgets play in measuring performance against established goals

  e. identify the characteristics that define successful budgeting processes

  f. explain how the budgeting process facilitates communication among organizational units and enhances coordination of organizational activities

  g. describe the concept of a controllable cost as it relates to both budgeting and performance evaluation

  h. explain how the efficient allocation of organizational resources are planned during the budgeting process

  i. identify the appropriate time frame for various types of budgets

  j. identify who should participate in the budgeting process for optimum success

  k. describe the role of top management in successful budgeting

  l. demonstrate an understanding of the use of cost standards in budgeting

  m. differentiate between ideal (theoretical) standards and currently attainable (practical) standards

  n. differentiate between authoritative standards and participative standards

  o. identify the steps to be taken in developing standards for both direct material and direct labor

  p. demonstrate an understanding of the techniques that are used to develop standards such as activity analysis and the use of historical data

  q. discuss the importance of a policy that allows budget revisions that accommodate the impact of significant changes in budget assumptions

  r. explain the role of budgets in monitoring and controlling expenditures to meet strategic objectives

  s. define budgetary slack and discuss its impact on goal congruence

Part 1 - Section B.3. Forecasting techniques

The candidate should be able to:

  a. demonstrate an understanding of a simple regression equation

  b. define a multiple regression equation and recognize when multiple regression is an appropriate tool to use for forecasting

  c. calculate the result of a simple regression equation

  d. demonstrate an understanding of learning curve analysis

  e. calculate the results under a cumulative average-time learning model

  f. list the benefits and shortcomings of regression analysis and learning curve analysis

g. calculate the expected value of random variables

h. identify the benefits and shortcomings of expected value techniques

i. use probability values to estimate future cash flows

Part 1 - Section B.4. Budget methodologies

For each of the budget systems identified [annual/master budgets, project budgeting, activity-based budgeting, zero-based budgeting, continuous (rolling) budgets, and flexible budgeting], the candidate should be able to:

a. define its purpose, appropriate use, and time frame

b. identify the budget components and explain the interrelationships among the components

c. demonstrate an understanding of how the budget is developed

d. compare and contrast the benefits and limitations of the budget system

e. evaluate a business situation and recommend the appropriate budget solution

f. prepare budgets on the basis of information presented

g. calculate the impact of incremental changes to budgets

Part 1 - Section B.5. Annual profit plan and supporting schedules

The candidate should be able to:

a. explain the role of the sales budget in the development of an annual profit plan

b. identify the factors that should be considered when preparing a sales forecast

c. identify the components of a sales budget and prepare a sales budget

d. explain the relationship between the sales budget and the production budget

e. identify the role that inventory levels play in the preparation of a production budget and define other factors that should be considered when preparing a production budget

f. prepare a production budget

g. demonstrate an understanding of the relationship between the direct materials budget, the direct labor budget, and the production budget

h. explain how inventory levels and procurement policies affect the direct materials budget

i. prepare direct materials and direct labor budgets based on relevant information and evaluate the feasibility of achieving production goals on the basis of these budgets

j. demonstrate an understanding of the relationship between the overhead budget and the production budget

k. separate costs into their fixed and variable components

l. prepare an overhead budget

m. identify the components of the cost of goods sold budget and prepare a cost of goods sold budget

n. demonstrate an understanding of contribution margin per unit and total contribution margin, identify the appropriate use of these concepts, and calculate both unit and total contribution margin

o. identify the components of the selling and administrative expense budget

p. explain how specific components of the selling and administrative expense budget may affect the contribution margin

q. prepare an operational (operating) budget

r. prepare a capital expenditure budget

s. demonstrate an understanding of the relationship between the capital expenditure budget, the cash budget, and the pro forma financial statements

t. define the purposes of the cash budget and describe the relationship between the cash budget and all other budgets

u. demonstrate an understanding of the relationship between credit policies and purchasing (payables) policies and the cash budget

v. prepare a cash budget

Part 1 - Section B.6. Top-level planning and analysis

The candidate should be able to:

a. define the purpose of a pro forma income statement, a pro forma balance sheet, and a pro forma statement of cash flows, and demonstrate an understanding of the relationship among these statements and all other budgets

b. prepare pro forma income statements based on several revenue and cost assumptions

c. evaluate whether a company has achieved strategic objectives based on pro forma income statements

d. use financial projections to prepare a pro forma balance sheet and a pro forma statement of cash flows

e. identify the factors required to prepare medium- and long-term cash forecasts

f. use financial projections to determine required outside financing and dividend policy

Section C. Performance Management (20% - Levels A, B, and C)
Part 1 - Section C.1. Cost and variance measures

The candidate should be able to:

a. analyze performance against operational goals using measures based on revenue, manufacturing costs, nonmanufacturing costs, and profit depending on the type of center or unit being measured

b. explain the reasons for variances within a performance monitoring system

c. prepare a performance analysis by comparing actual results to the master budget, calculate favorable and unfavorable variances from the budget, and provide explanations for variances

d. identify and describe the benefits and limitations of measuring performance by comparing actual results to the master budget

e. analyze a flexible budget based on actual sales (output) volume

f. calculate the sales-volume variance and the sales-price variance by comparing the flexible budget to the master (static) budget

g. calculate the flexible-budget variance by comparing actual results to the flexible budget

h. investigate the flexible-budget variance to determine individual differences between actual and budgeted input prices and input quantities

i. explain how budget variance reporting is utilized in a management by exception environment

j. define a standard cost system and identify the reasons for adopting a standard cost system

k. demonstrate an understanding of price (rate) variances and calculate the price variances related to direct material and direct labor inputs

l. demonstrate an understanding of efficiency (usage) variances and calculate the efficiency variances related to direct material and direct labor inputs

m. demonstrate an understanding of spending and efficiency variances as they relate to fixed and variable overhead

n. calculate a sales-mix variance and explain its impact on revenue and contribution margin

o. calculate and explain a mix variance

p. calculate and explain a yield variance

q. demonstrate how price, efficiency, spending, and mix variances can be applied in service companies as well as manufacturing companies

r. analyze factory overhead variances by calculating variable overhead spending variance, variable overhead efficiency variance, fixed overhead spending variance, and production volume variance

s. analyze variances, identify causes, and recommend corrective actions

Part 1 - Section C.2. Responsibility centers and reporting segments

The candidate should be able to:

a. identify and explain the different types of responsibility centers

b. recommend appropriate responsibility centers given a business scenario

c. calculate a contribution margin

d. analyze a contribution margin report and evaluate performance

e. identify segments that organizations evaluate, including product lines, geographical areas, or other meaningful segments

f. explain why the allocation of common costs among segments can be an issue in performance evaluation

g. identify methods for allocating common costs such as stand-alone cost allocation and incremental cost allocation

h. define transfer pricing and identify the objectives of transfer pricing

i. identify the methods for determining transfer prices and list and explain the advantages and disadvantages of each method

j. identify and calculate transfer prices using variable cost, full cost, market price, negotiated price, and dual-rate pricing

k. explain how transfer pricing is affected by business issues such as the presence of outside suppliers and the opportunity costs associated with capacity usage

l. describe how special issues such as tariffs, exchange rates, taxes, currency restrictions, expropriation risk, and the availability of materials and skills affect performance evaluation in multinational companies

Part 1 - Section C.3. Performance measures

The candidate should be able to:

   a. explain why performance evaluation measures should be directly related to strategic and operational goals and objectives; why timely feedback is critical; and why performance measures should be related to the factors that drive the element being measured, e.g., cost drivers and revenue drivers

   b. explain the issues involved in determining product profitability, business unit profitability, and customer profitability, including cost measurement, cost allocation, investment measurement, and valuation

   c. calculate product-line profitability, business unit profitability, and customer profitability

   d. evaluate customers and products on the basis of profitability and recommend ways to improve profitability and/or drop unprofitable customers and products

   e. define and calculate return on investment (ROI)

   f. analyze and interpret ROI calculations

   g. define and calculate residual income (RI)

   h. analyze and interpret RI calculations

   i. compare and contrast the benefits and limitations of ROI and RI as measures of performance

   j. explain how revenue and expense recognition policies may affect the measurement of income and reduce comparability among business units

   k. explain how inventory measurement policies, joint asset sharing, and overall asset measurement policies may affect the measurement of investment and reduce comparability among business units

   l. define key performance indicators (KPIs) and discuss the importance of these indicators in evaluating a firm

   m. define the concept of a balanced scorecard and identify its components

   n. identify and describe the perspectives of a balanced scorecard, including financial, customer, internal process, and learning and growth

   o. identify and describe the characteristics of successful implementation and use of a balanced scorecard

   p. demonstrate an understanding of a strategy map and the role it plays

   q. analyze and interpret a balanced scorecard and evaluate performance on the basis of the analysis

   r. recommend performance measures and a periodic reporting methodology given operational goals and actual results

Section D. Cost Management (15% - Levels A, B, and C)

Part 1 - Section D.1. Measurement concepts

The candidate should be able to:

   a. calculate fixed, variable, and mixed costs and demonstrate an understanding of the behavior of each in the long and short term and how a change in assumptions regarding cost type or relevant range affects these costs

b. identify cost objects and cost pools and assign costs to appropriate activities

c. demonstrate an understanding of the nature and types of cost drivers and the causal relationship that exists between cost drivers and costs incurred

d. demonstrate an understanding of the various methods for measuring costs and accumulating work-in-process and finished goods inventories

e. identify and define cost measurement techniques such as actual costing, normal costing, and standard costing; calculate costs using each of these techniques; identify the appropriate use of each technique; and describe the benefits and limitations of each technique

f. demonstrate an understanding of variable (direct) costing and absorption (full) costing and the benefits and limitations of these measurement concepts

g. calculate inventory costs, cost of goods sold, and operating profit using both variable costing and absorption costing

h. demonstrate an understanding of how the use of variable costing or absorption costing affects the value of inventory, cost of goods sold, and operating income

i. prepare summary income statements using variable costing and absorption costing

j. determine the appropriate use of joint product and by-product costing

k. demonstrate an understanding of concepts such as split-off point and separable costs

l. determine the allocation of joint product and by-product costs using the physical measure method, the sales value at split-off method, constant gross profit (gross margin) method, and the net realizable value method; describe the benefits and limitations of each method

Part 1 - Section D.2. Costing systems

For each cost accumulation system identified (job order costing, process costing, activity-based costing, life-cycle costing), the candidate should be able to:

a. define the nature of the system, understand the cost flows of the system, and identify its appropriate use

b. calculate inventory values and cost of goods sold

c. demonstrate an understanding of the proper accounting for normal and abnormal spoilage

d. discuss the strategic value of cost information regarding products and services, pricing, overhead allocations, and other issues

e. identify and describe the benefits and limitations of each cost accumulation system

f. demonstrate an understanding of the concept of equivalent units in process costing and calculate the value of equivalent units

g. define the elements of activity-based costing such as cost pool, cost driver, resource driver, activity driver, and value-added activity

h. calculate product cost using an activity-based system and compare and analyze the results with costs calculated using a traditional system

i. explain how activity-based costing can be utilized in service firms

j. demonstrate an understanding of the concept of life-cycle costing and the strategic value of including upstream costs, manufacturing costs, and downstream costs

Part 1 - Section D.3. Overhead costs

The candidate should be able to:

a. distinguish between fixed and variable overhead expenses

b. determine the appropriate time frame for classifying both variable and fixed overhead expenses

c. demonstrate an understanding of the different methods of determining overhead rates, e.g., plant-wide rates, departmental rates, and individual cost driver rates

d. describe the benefits and limitations of each of the methods used to determine overhead rates

e. identify the components of variable overhead expense

f. determine the appropriate allocation base for variable overhead expenses

g. calculate the per unit variable overhead expense

h. identify the components of fixed overhead expense

i. identify the appropriate allocation base for fixed overhead expense

j. calculate the fixed overhead application rate

k. describe how fixed overhead can be over- or under-applied and how this difference should be accounted for in the cost of goods sold, work-in-process, and finished goods accounts

l. compare and contrast traditional overhead allocation with activity-based overhead allocation

m. calculate overhead expense in an activity-based costing setting

n. identify and describe the benefits derived from activity-based overhead allocation

o. explain why companies allocate the cost of service departments such as Human Resources or Information Technology to divisions, departments, or activities

p. calculate service or support department cost allocations using the direct method, the reciprocal method, the step-down method, and the dual allocation method

q. estimate fixed costs using the high-low method and demonstrate an understanding of how regression can be used to estimate fixed costs

Part 1 - Section D.4. Supply chain management

The candidate should be able to:

a. explain supply chain management

b. define lean resource management techniques

c. identify and describe the operational benefits of implementing lean resource management techniques

d. define material requirements planning (MRP)

e. identify and describe the operational benefits of implementing a just-in-time (JIT) system

f. identify and describe the operational benefits of enterprise resource planning (ERP)

g. explain the concept of outsourcing and identify the benefits and limitations of choosing this option

h. demonstrate a general understanding of the Theory of Constraints

i. identify the five steps involved in Theory of Constraints analysis

j. define throughput costing (super-variable costing) and calculate inventory costs using throughput costing

  k. define and calculate throughput contribution

  l. describe how capacity level affects product costing, capacity management, pricing decisions, and financial statements

  m. explain how using practical capacity as the denominator for the fixed cost allocation rate enhances capacity management

  n. calculate the financial impact of implementing the above-mentioned methods

Part 1 - Section D.5. Business process improvement

The candidate should be able to:

  a. define value chain analysis

  b. identify the steps in value chain analysis

  c. explain how value chain analysis is used to better understand a firm's competitive advantage

  d. define, identify, and provide examples of a value-added activity and explain how the value-added concept is related to improving performance

  e. demonstrate an understanding of process analysis and business process reengineering, and calculate the resulting savings

  f. define best practice analysis and discuss how it can be used by an organization to improve performance

  g. demonstrate an understanding of benchmarking process performance

  h. identify the benefits of benchmarking in creating a competitive advantage

  i. apply activity-based management principles to recommend process performance improvements

  j. explain the relationship among continuous improvement techniques, activity-based management, and quality performance

  k. explain the concept of continuous improvement and how it relates to implementing ideal standards and quality improvements

  l. describe and identify the components of the costs of quality, commonly referred to as prevention costs, appraisal costs, internal failure costs, and external failure costs

  m. calculate the financial impact of implementing the above-mentioned processes

  n. identify and discuss ways to make accounting operations more efficient, including process walk-throughs, process training, identification of waste and overcapacity, identifying the root cause of errors, reducing the accounting close cycle (fast close), and shared services

Section E. Internal Controls (15% - Levels A, B, and C)

Part 1 - Section E.1. Governance, risk, and compliance

The candidate should be able to:

  a. demonstrate an understanding of internal control risk and the management of internal control risk

  b. identify and describe internal control objectives

  c. explain how a company's organizational structure, policies, objectives, and goals, as well as its management philosophy and style, influence the scope and effectiveness of the control environment

d. identify the board of directors' responsibilities with respect to ensuring that the company is operated in the best interest of shareholders

e. identify the hierarchy of corporate governance; i.e., articles of incorporation, bylaws, policies, and procedures

f. demonstrate an understanding of corporate governance, including rights and responsibilities of the CEO, the board of directors, the audit committee, managers and other stakeholders; and the procedures for making corporate decisions

g. describe how internal controls are designed to provide reasonable (but not absolute) assurance regarding achievement of an entity's objectives involving (i) effectiveness and efficiency of operations; (ii) reliability of financial reporting; and (iii) compliance with applicable laws and regulations

h. explain why personnel policies and procedures are integral to an efficient control environment

i. define and give examples of segregation of duties

j. explain why the following four types of functional responsibilities should be performed by different departments or different people within the same function: (i) authority to execute transactions, (ii) recording transactions, (iii) custody of assets involved in the transactions, and (iv) periodic reconciliations of the existing assets to recorded amounts

k. demonstrate an understanding of the importance of independent checks and verification

l. identify examples of safeguarding controls

m. explain how the use of pre-numbered forms, as well as specific policies and procedures detailing who is authorized to receive specific documents, is a means of control

n. define inherent risk, control risk, and detection risk

o. define and distinguish between preventive controls and detective controls

p. describe the major internal control provisions of the Sarbanes-Oxley Act (Sections 201, 203, 204, 302, 404, and 407)

q. identify the role of the PCAOB in providing guidance on the auditing of internal controls

r. differentiate between a top-down (risk-based) approach and a bottom-up approach to auditing internal controls

s. identify the PCAOB preferred approach to auditing internal controls as outlined in Auditing Standard #5

t. identify and describe the major internal control provisions of the Foreign Corrupt Practices Act

u. identify and describe the five major components of COSO's Internal Control - Integrated Framework (2013)

v. assess the level of internal control risk within an organization and recommend risk mitigation strategies

w. demonstrate an understanding of external auditor responsibilities, including the types of audit opinions the external auditors issue

Part 1 - Section E.2. System controls and security measures

The candidate should be able to:

a. describe how the segregation of accounting duties can enhance systems security

b. identify threats to information systems, including input manipulation, program alteration, direct file alteration, data theft, sabotage, viruses, Trojan horses, theft, and phishing

c. demonstrate an understanding of how systems development controls are used to enhance the accuracy, validity, safety, security, and adaptability of systems input, processing, output, and storage functions

d. identify procedures to limit access to physical hardware

e. identify means by which management can protect programs and databases from unauthorized use

f. identify input controls, processing controls, and output controls and describe why each of these controls is necessary

g. identify and describe the types of storage controls and demonstrate an understanding of when and why they are used

h. identify and describe the inherent risks of using the internet as compared to data transmissions over secured transmission lines

i. define data encryption and describe why there is a much greater need for data encryption methods when using the internet

j. identify a firewall and its uses

k. demonstrate an understanding of how flowcharts of activities are used to assess controls

l. explain the importance of backing up all program and data files regularly, and storing the backups at a secure remote site

m. define business continuity planning

n. define the objective of a disaster recovery plan and identify the components of such a plan including hot, warm, and cold sites

Section F. Technology and Analytics (15% - Levels A, B, and C)

As indicated in the Content Specification Outlines, candidates are assumed to have an understanding of basic statistics, including measures of central tendency and dispersion.

Part 1 - Section F.1. Information systems

The candidate should be able to:

a. identify the role of the accounting information system (AIS) in the value chain

b. demonstrate an understanding of the accounting information system cycles, including revenue to cash, expenditures, production, human resources and payroll, financing, and property, plant, and equipment, as well as the general ledger (GL) and reporting system

c. identify and explain the challenges of having separate financial and nonfinancial systems

d. define enterprise resource planning (ERP) and identify and explain the advantages and disadvantages of ERP

e. explain how ERP helps overcome the challenges of separate financial and nonfinancial systems, integrating all aspects of an organization's activities

f. define relational database and demonstrate an understanding of a database management system

g. define data warehouse and a data mart

h. define enterprise performance management (EPM) [also known as corporate performance management (CPM) or business performance management (BPM)]

i. discuss how EPM can facilitate business planning and performance management

Part 1 - Section F.2. Data governance

The candidate should be able to:

j. define data governance; i.e., managing the availability, usability, integrity, and security of data

k. demonstrate a general understanding of data governance frameworks, COSO's Internal Control framework and ISACA's COBIT (Control Objectives for Information and Related Technologies)

l. identify the stages of the data life cycle; i.e., data capture, data maintenance, data synthesis, data usage, data analytics, data publication, data archival, and data purging

m. demonstrate an understanding of data preprocessing and the steps to convert data for further analysis, including data consolidation, data cleaning (cleansing), data transformation, and data reduction

n. discuss the importance of having a documented record retention (or records management) policy

o. identify and explain controls and tools to detect and thwart cyberattacks, such as penetration and vulnerability testing, biometrics, advanced firewalls, and access controls

Part 1 - Section F.3. Technology-enabled finance transformation

The candidate should be able to:

a. define the systems development life cycle (SDLC), including systems analysis, conceptual design, physical design, implementation and conversion, and operations and maintenance

b. explain the role of business process analysis in improving system performance

c. define robotic process automation (RPA) and its benefits

d. evaluate where technologies can improve efficiency and effectiveness of processing accounting data and information [e.g., artificial intelligence (AI)]

e. define cloud computing and describe how it can improve efficiency

f. define software as a service (SaaS) and explain its advantages and disadvantages

g. recognize potential applications of blockchain, distributed ledger, and smart contracts

Part 1 - Section F.4. Data analytics

The candidate should be able to:

Business intelligence

a. define Big Data, explain the four Vs: volume, velocity, variety, and veracity, and describe the opportunities and challenges of leveraging insight from this data

b. explain how structured, semi-structured, and unstructured data is used by a business enterprise

c. describe the progression of data, from data to information to knowledge to insight to action

d. describe the opportunities and challenges of managing data analytics

e. explain why data and data science capability are strategic assets

f. define business intelligence (BI); i.e., the collection of applications, tools, and best practices that transform data into actionable information in order to make better decisions and optimize performance

Data mining

    g. define data mining

    h. describe the challenges of data mining

    i. explain why data mining is an iterative process and both an art and a science

    j. explain how query tools [e.g., Structured Query Language (SQL)] are used to retrieve information

    k. describe how an analyst would mine large data sets to reveal patterns and provide insights

Analytic tools

    l. explain the challenge of fitting an analytic model to the data

    m. define the different types of data analytics, including descriptive, diagnostic, predictive, and prescriptive

    n. define the following analytic models: clustering, classification, and regression; determine when each would be the appropriate tool to use

    o. identify the elements of both simple and multiple regression equations

    p. calculate the result of regression equations as applied to a specific situation

    q. demonstrate an understanding of the coefficient of determination (R squared) and the correlation coefficient (R)

    r. demonstrate an understanding of time series analyses, including trend, cyclical, seasonal, and irregular patterns

    s. identify and explain the benefits and limitations of regression analysis and time series analysis

    t. define standard error of the estimate, goodness of fit, and confidence interval

    u. explain how to use predictive analytic techniques to draw insights and make recommendations

    v. describe exploratory data analysis and how it is used to reveal patterns and discover insights

    w. define sensitivity analysis and identify when it would be the appropriate tool to use

    x. demonstrate an understanding of the uses of simulation models, including the Monte Carlo technique

    y. identify the benefits and limitations of sensitivity analysis and simulation models

    z. demonstrate an understanding of what-if (or goal-seeking) analysis

    aa. identify and explain the limitations of data analytics

Visualization

    bb. utilize table and graph design best practices to avoid distortion in the communication of complex information

    cc. evaluate data visualization options and select the best presentation approach (e.g., histograms, box-plots, scatter plots, dot plots, tables, dashboards, bar charts, pie charts, line charts, bubble charts)

    dd. understand the benefits and limitations of visualization techniques

    ee. determine the most effective channel to communicate results

    ff. communicate results, conclusions, and recommendations in an impactful manner using effective visualization techniques

Time-Value of Money Tables

Present Value of $1

n	1%	2%	3%	4%	5%	6%	8%	10%	12%
1	0.99010	0.98039	0.97087	0.96154	0.95238	0.94340	0.92593	0.90909	0.89286
2	0.98030	0.96117	0.94260	0.92456	0.90703	0.89000	0.85734	0.82645	0.79719
3	0.97059	0.94232	0.91514	0.88900	0.86384	0.83962	0.79383	0.75131	0.71178
4	0.96098	0.92385	0.88849	0.85480	0.82270	0.79209	0.73503	0.68301	0.63552
5	0.95147	0.90573	0.86261	0.82193	0.78353	0.74726	0.68058	0.62092	0.56743
6	0.94205	0.88797	0.83748	0.79031	0.74622	0.70496	0.63017	0.56447	0.50663
7	0.93272	0.87056	0.81309	0.75992	0.71068	0.66506	0.58349	0.51316	0.45235
8	0.92348	0.85349	0.78941	0.73069	0.67684	0.62741	0.54027	0.46651	0.40388
9	0.91434	0.83676	0.76642	0.70259	0.64461	0.59190	0.50025	0.42410	0.36061
10	0.90529	0.82035	0.74409	0.67556	0.61391	0.55839	0.46319	0.38554	0.32197
11	0.89632	0.80426	0.72242	0.64958	0.58468	0.52679	0.42888	0.35049	0.28748
12	0.88745	0.78849	0.70138	0.62460	0.55684	0.49697	0.39711	0.31863	0.25668
13	0.87866	0.77303	0.68095	0.60057	0.53032	0.46884	0.36770	0.28966	0.22917
14	0.86996	0.75788	0.66112	0.57748	0.50507	0.44230	0.34046	0.26333	0.20462
15	0.86135	0.74301	0.64186	0.55526	0.48102	0.41727	0.31524	0.23939	0.18270
16	0.85282	0.72845	0.62317	0.53391	0.45811	0.39365	0.29189	0.21763	0.16312
17	0.84438	0.71416	0.60502	0.51337	0.43630	0.37136	0.27027	0.19784	0.14564
18	0.83602	0.70016	0.58739	0.49363	0.41552	0.35034	0.25025	0.17986	0.13004
19	0.82774	0.68643	0.57029	0.47464	0.39573	0.33051	0.23171	0.16351	0.11611
20	0.81954	0.67297	0.5537	0.45639	0.37689	0.31180	0.21455	0.14864	0.10367

Present Value of Ordinary Annuity

n	1%	2%	3%	4%	5%	6%	8%	10%	12%
1	0.99010	0.98039	0.97087	0.96154	0.95238	0.94340	0.92593	0.90909	0.89286
2	1.97040	1.94156	1.91347	1.88609	1.85941	1.83339	1.78326	1.73554	1.69005
3	2.94099	2.88388	2.82861	2.77509	2.72325	2.67301	2.50771	2.48685	2.40183
4	3.90197	3.80773	3.71710	3.62990	3.546595	3.46511	3.31213	3.16987	3.03735
5	4.85343	4.71346	4.57971	4.45182	4.32948	4.21236	3.99271	3.79079	3.60478
6	5.79548	5.60143	5.41719	5.24214	5.07569	4.91732	4.62288	4.35526	4.11141
7	6.72819	6.47199	6.23028	6.00205	5.78637	5.58238	5.20637	4.86842	4.56376
8	7.65168	7.32548	7.01969	6.73274	6.46321	6.20979	5.74664	5.33493	4.96764
9	8.56602	8.16224	7.78611	7.43533	7.10782	6.80169	6.24689	5.75902	5.32825
10	9.47130	8.98259	8.53020	8.11090	7.72173	7.36009	6.71008	6.14457	5.65022
11	10.36763	9.78685	9.25262	8.76048	8.30641	7.88687	7.13896	6.49506	5.93770
12	11.25508	10.57534	9.95400	9.38507	8.86325	8.38384	7.53608	6.81369	6.19437
13	12.13374	11.34837	10.63496	9.98565	9.39357	8.85268	7.90378	7.10336	6.42355
14	13.00370	12.10625	11.29607	10.56312	9.89864	9.29498	8.24424	7.36669	6.62817
15	13.86505	12.84926	11.93794	11.11839	10.37966	9.71225	8.55948	7.60608	6.81086
16	14.71787	13.57771	12.56110	11.65230	10.83777	10.10590	8.85137	7.82371	6.97399
17	15.56225	14.29187	13.16612	12.16567	11.27407	10.47726	9.12164	8.02155	7.11963
18	16.39827	14.99203	13.75351	12.65930	11.68959	10.82760	9.37189	8.20141	7.24967
19	17.22601	15.67846	14.32380	13.13394	12.08532	11.15812	9.60360	8.36492	7.36578
20	18.04555	16.35143	14.87747	13.59033	12.46221	11.46992	9.81815	8.51356	7.46944

Present Value of Annuity Due

n	1%	2%	3%	4%	5%	6%	8%	10%	12%
1	1.00000	1.00000	1.00000	1.00000	1.00000	1.00000	1.00000	1.00000	1.00000
2	1.99010	1.98039	1.97087	1.96154	1.95238	1.94340	1.92593	1.90909	1.89286
3	2.97040	2.94156	2.91347	2.88609	2.85941	2.83339	2.78326	2.73554	2.69005
4	3.94099	3.88388	3.82861	3.77509	3.72325	3.67301	3.57710	3.48685	3.40183
5	4.90197	4.80773	4.71710	4.62990	4.54595	4.46511	4.31321	4.16987	4.03735
6	5.85343	5.71346	5.57971	5.45182	5.32948	5.21236	4.99271	4.79079	4.60478
7	6.79548	6.60143	6.41719	6.24214	6.07569	5.91732	5.62288	5.35526	5.11141
8	7.72819	7.47199	7.23028	7.00205	6.78637	6.58238	6.20637	5.86842	5.56376
9	8.65168	8.32548	8.01969	7.73274	7.46321	7.20979	6.74664	6.33493	5.96764
10	9.56602	9.16224	8.78611	8.43533	8.10782	7.80169	7.24689	6.75902	6.32825
11	10.47130	9.98259	9.53020	9.11090	8.72173	8.36009	7.71008	7.14457	6.65022
12	11.36763	10.78685	10.25262	9.76048	9.30641	8.88687	8.13896	7.49506	6.93770
13	12.25508	11.57534	10.95400	10.38507	9.86325	9.38384	8.53608	7.81369	7.19437
14	13.13374	12.34837	11.63496	10.98565	10.39357	9.85268	8.90378	8.10336	7.42355
15	14.00370	13.10625	12.29607	11.56312	10.89864	10.29498	9.24424	8.36669	7.62817
16	14.86505	13.84926	12.93794	12.11839	11.37966	10.71225	9.55948	8.60608	7.81086
17	15.71787	14.57771	13.56110	12.65230	11.83777	11.10590	9.85137	8.82371	7.97399
18	16.56225	15.29187	14.16612	13.16567	12.27407	11.47726	10.12164	9.02155	8.11963
19	17.39827	15.99203	14.75351	13.65930	12.68959	11.82760	10.37189	9.20141	8.24967
20	18.22601	16.67846	15.32380	14.13394	13.08532	12.15812	10.60360	9.36492	8.36578

Time-Value of Money Tables

Future Value of $1

period	1%	2%	3%	4%	5%	6%	8%	10%	12%
1	1.01000	1.02000	1.03000	1.04000	1.05000	1.06000	1.08000	1.10000	1.12000
2	1.02010	1.0400	1.06090	1.08160	1.10250	1.12360	1.16640	1.21000	1.24550
3	1.03030	1.06121	1.09273	1.12486	1.15763	1.19102	1.25971	1.33100	1.40493
4	1.04060	1.08243	1.12551	1.16986	1.21551	1.26248	1.36049	1.46410	1.57352
5	1.05101	1.10408	1.15927	1.21665	1.27628	1.33823	1.46933	1.61051	1.76234
6	1.06152	1.12616	1.19405	1.26532	1.34010	1.41852	1.58687	1.77156	1.97382
7	1.07214	1.14869	1.22987	1.31593	1.40710	1.50363	1.71382	1.94872	2.21068
8	1.08286	1.17166	1.26677	1.36857	1.47746	1.59385	1.85093	2.14359	2.47596
9	1.09369	1.19509	1.30477	1.42331	1.55133	1.68948	1.99900	2.35795	2.77308
10	1.10462	1.21899	1.34392	1.48024	1.62889	1.79085	2.15892	2.59374	3.10585
11	1.11567	1.24337	1.38423	1.53945	1.71034	1.89830	2.33164	2.85312	3.47855
12	1.12683	1.26824	1.42576	1.60103	1.79586	2.01220	2.51817	3.13843	3.89598
13	1.13809	1.29361	1.46853	1.66507	1.88565	2.13293	2.71962	3.45227	4.36349
14	1.14947	1.31948	1.51259	1.73168	1.97993	2.26090	2.93719	3.79750	4.88711
15	1.16097	1.34587	1.55797	1.80094	2.07893	2.39656	3.17217	4.17725	5.47357
16	1.17258	1.37279	1.60471	1.87298	2.18287	2.54035	3.42594	4.59497	6.13039
17	1.18430	1.40024	1.65285	1.94790	2.29202	2.69277	3.70002	5.05447	6.86604
18	1.19615	1.42825	1.70243	2.02582	2.40662	2.95434	3.99602	5.55992	7.68997
19	1.20811	1.45681	1.75351	2.10685	2.52695	3.02560	4.31570	6.11591	8.61276
20	1.22019	1.48595	1.80611	2.19112	2.65330	3.20714	4.66096	6.72750	9.64629

516

Future Value of Ordinary Annuity

n	1%	2%	3%	4%	5%	6%	8%	10%	12%
1	1.00000	1.00000	1.00000	1.00000	1.00000	1.00000	1.00000	1.00000	1.00000
2	2.01000	2.02000	2.03000	2.04000	2.05000	2.06000	2.08000	2.10000	2.12000
3	3.03010	3.06040	3.09090	3.12160	3.15250	3.18360	3.24640	3.31000	3.37440
4	4.06040	4.12161	4.18363	4.24646	4.31013	4.37462	4.50611	4.64100	4.77933
5	5.10101	5.20404	5.30914	5.41632	5.52563	5.63709	5.86660	6.10510	6.35285
6	6.15202	6.30812	6.46841	6.63298	6.80191	6.97532	7.33593	7.71561	8.11519
7	7.21354	7.43428	7.66246	7.89829	8.14201	8.39384	8.92280	9.48717	10.08901
8	8.28567	8.58297	8.89234	9.21423	9.54911	9.89747	10.63663	11.43589	12.29969
9	9.36853	9.75463	10.15911	10.58280	11.02656	11.49132	12.48756	13.57948	14.77566
10	10.46221	10.94972	11.46388	12.00611	12.57789	13.18079	14.48656	15.93742	17.54874
11	11.56683	12.16872	12.80780	13.48635	14.20679	14.97164	16.64549	18.53117	20.65458
12	12.68250	13.41209	14.19203	15.02581	15.91713	16.86994	18.97713	21.38428	24.13313
13	13.80933	14.68033	15.61779	16.62684	17.71298	18.88214	21.49530	24.52271	28.02911
14	14.94742	15.97394	17.08632	18.29191	19.59863	21.01507	24.21492	27.97496	32.39260
15	16.09690	17.29342	18.59891	20.02359	21.57856	23.27597	27.15211	31.77248	37.27971
16	17.25786	18.63929	20.15688	21.82453	23.65749	25.67253	30.32429	35.94973	42.75328
17	18.43044	20.01207	21.76159	23.69751	25.84037	28.21288	33.75023	40.54470	48.88367
18	19.61475	21.41231	23.41444	25.64541	28.13238	30.90565	37.45024	45.59917	55.74971
19	20.81090	22.84056	25.11687	27.67123	30.53900	33.75999	41.44626	51.15909	63.43968
20	22.01900	24.29737	26.87037	29.77808	33.06595	36.78559	45.76196	57.27500	72.05244

Essay Tips

I. Writing CMA Essay Questions

    A. Overview of CMA Exam Essay Questions

        1. Each part of the CMA exam will have two essay questions to let you demonstrate a deep understanding of the subject matter tested.

        2. The essay questions follow the 100 multiple-choice questions portion.

        3. Exam takers have a maximum time of four hours to complete the entire exam.

            a. 3 hours of multiple-choice questions (approximately 75% of the exam).

            b. 1 hour of essay questions or 30 minutes each (approximately 25% of the exam).

        4. At least 50% on multiple-choice questions must be earned in order to advance to essays and once advanced to essays, candidates cannot return to the multiple-choice portion.

        5. Expect 3–6 questions for each essay scenario.

        6. There is no spreadsheet application for computational problems on the exam.

            a. Candidates will be expected to write supporting work in the essay word-processing application.

            b. Candidates can use pencils and scratch paper provided at the test site to develop computations before writing them in the word-processing application.

    B. How to Prepare an Essay Question Response

        1. Each question should take 30 minutes of time.

        2. Quickly scroll through both scenarios and determine which one is easier to answer.

        3. Also scroll through each question within the scenario to determine how much time you will need for each question.

        4. Answer the easier or more familiar question first.

            a. This helps ensure not spending excessive time on the harder question, leaving little time for the easier question.

            b. This gives candidates confidence to answer the more challenging question.

        5. Follow these guidelines for budgeting time to complete an essay question in 30 minutes:

            a. Spend the first 2 to 5 minutes reading the question and creating an outline.

                1. Read the entire question to ensure understanding of all requirements.

                2. The outline will allow you to collect your thoughts and structure a framework for answering the question.

                3. If time is short, type your outline as your answer to secure at least partial credit on the essay question.

            b. Spend the next 20 to 25 minutes answering the question.

                1. Use the action verbs in the question to determine how to answer the question.

                    a. If the question asks you to compare and contrast two approaches, then list the benefits and costs of each approach and describe how one approach differs from another.

                    b. If the question asks to define a term, provide a definition of the term and demonstrate that you understand how to apply the definition.

                2. Rephrase the question's key words and phrases to make it easier for the grader.

    3. Use bullet points to organize your answers. Show sufficient detail to allow the grader to understand your knowledge of the subject matter.

    4. Write one to two sentences at the start of the question to introduce the topic and one to two sentences at the end of the topic to summarize key points.

  c. Spend the final 3 to 5 minutes proofreading your answer.

    1. Ensure your answer has addressed the key action words in the questions.

    2. Review the organization, structure, and clarity of your answers.

    3. Review basic grammar and writing skills.

    4. Compare your answer to your initial outline to ensure you have addressed the points you wanted to cover.

6. Monitor your time. Do not spend too much time on one question.

7. Be brief and to the point; it is okay to use bullet points.

8. Do not leave a question blank.

  a. If you do not have the time to write a full answer, at least use your outline of the main points to demonstrate your understanding of the topic.

9. The goal of the exam grader is to give you points, not take them away.

  a. Essay grading rubrics (grade sheets) provide more possible answers than what is necessary to obtain maximum points.

  b. Include as much detail as possible to add more points to your score.

  c. You cannot score higher than the maximum number of points for the question. (e.g., If the question is 15 points and you provide enough detail for 18 points, you will only score 15 points).

II. CMA™ Exam Review Course Essay Questions

  A. Practice essay questions are available as part of the test bank. Select "Question Type: Essay" when taking a quiz through the test bank to access these questions.

  B. The practice essay questions are original questions and are not released ICMA questions.

CMA Exam Ratio Definitions

Abbreviations

EBIT = Earnings before interest and taxes

EBITDA = Earnings before interest, taxes, depreciation and amortization

EBT = Earnings before taxes

EPS = Earnings per share

ROA = Return on assets

ROE = Return on equity

Part 1: Financial Reporting, Planning, Performance, and Control Section C Performance Management

Section C Decision Analysis

Section C.3 Performance measures

e.* ROI = Income of business unit / Assets of business unit

g. Residual Income (RI) = Income of business unit – (Assets of business unit × required rate of return

   Note: "Income" means operating income unless otherwise noted.

   * Letter references refer to subtopics in Learning Outcome Statements.

Part 2: Financial Decision Making

Section A Financial Statement Analysis

Section A.1 Basic Financial Statement Analysis

   a. Common size statement = line items on income statement and statement of cash flows presented as a percent of sales; line items on balance sheet presented as a percent of total assets

   b. Common base year statements = (new line item amount / base year line item amount) × 100

   c. Annual growth rate of line items = (new line item amount / old line item amount) – 1

Section A.2 Financial Ratios

   Unless otherwise indicated, end of year data is used for balance sheet items; full year data is used for income statement and statement of cash flow items.

Liquidity

a(1). Current ratio = current assets / current liabilities

a(2). Quick ratio or acid test ratio = (cash + marketable securities + accounts receivable) / current liabilities

a(3). Cash ratio = (cash + marketable securities) / current liabilities

a(4). Cash flow ratio = operating cash flow / current liabilities

a(5). Net working capital ratio = net working capital / total assets

Leverage

f(1). Degree of financial leverage = % change in net income / % change in EBIT, or

= EBIT / EBT

f(2). Degree of operating leverage = % change in EBIT / % change in sales, or = contribution margin / EBIT

h. Financial leverage ratio = assets / equity

i(1). Debt to equity ratio = total debt / equity

I(2). Long-term debt to equity ratio = (total debt – current liabilities) / equity

I(3). Debt to total assets ratio = total debt / total assets

j(1). Fixed charge coverage = earnings before fixed charges and taxes / fixed charges

Fixed charges include interest, required principal repayment, and leases

j(2). Interest coverage (times interest earned) = EBIT / interest expense

j(3). Cash flow to fixed charges = (cash from operations + fixed charges + tax payments) / fixed charges. Note: cash from operations is after-tax.

Activity

l(1). Accounts receivable turnover = credit sales / average gross accounts receivables

l(2). Inventory turnover = cost of goods sold / average inventory

l(3). Accounts payable turnover = credit purchases / average accounts payable

m(1). Days sales in receivables = average accounts receivable / (credit sales / 365), or = 365 / accounts receivable turnover

m(2). Days sales in inventory = average inventory / (cost of sales / 365), or = 365 / inventory turnover

m(3). Days purchases in payables = average payables / (purchase / 365), or =365 / payables turnover

n(1). Operating cycle = days sales in receivables + days sales in inventory

n(2). Cash cycle = Operating cycle – days purchases in payables

o(1). Total asset turnover = sales / average total assets

o(2). Fixed asset turnover = sales / average net plant, property and equipment

Profitability

p(1). Gross profit margin percentage = gross profit / sales

p(2). Operating profit margin percentage = operating income / sales

p(3). Net profit margin percentage = net income / sales

p(4). EBITDA margin = EBITDA / sales

q(1). ROA = net income / average total assets

q(2). ROE = net income / average equity

Market

r(1). Market-to-book ratio = current stock price / book value per share

r(2). Price earnings ratio = market price per share / EPS

s. Book value per share = (total stockholders' equity – preferred equity) / number of common shares outstanding

u(1). Basic EPS = (net income − preferred dividends) / weighted average common shares outstanding

(Number of shares outstanding is weighted by the number of months shares are outstanding)

u(2). Diluted EPS = (net income − preferred dividends) / diluted weighted average common shares outstanding

(Diluted EPS adjusts common shares by adding shares that may be issued for convertible securities and options)

v(1). Earnings yield = EPS / current market price per common share

v(2). Dividend yield = annual dividends per share / market price per share

v(3). Dividend payout ratio = common dividend / earnings available to common shareholders

v(4). Shareholder return = (ending stock price − beginning stock price + annual dividends per share) / beginning stock price

Section A.3 Profitability Analysis

a(1). ROA = Net profit margin × total asset turnover; (net income / sales) × (sales / average total assets) = net income / average total assets

b(2). ROE = ROA × financial leverage; (net income / average total assets) × (average total assets / average equity) = net income / average equity

g(1). Operating profit margin percentage = operating income / sales

g(2). Net profit margin percentage = net income / sales

j. Sustainable growth rate = (1− dividend payout ratio) × ROE

Section B Corporate Finance

Section B.4 Working capital management

b. Net working capital = current assets − current liabilities

Section C Decision Analysis

Section C.1 Cost/volume/profit analysis

f(1). Breakeven point in units = fixed costs / unit contribution margin

f(2). Breakeven point in dollars = fixed costs / (unit contribution margin / selling price)

i(1). Margin of safety = planned sales − breakeven sales

i(2). Margin of safety ratio = margin of safety / planned sales

Section C.3 Pricing

n. Elasticity is calculated using the midpoint formula. For price elasticity of demand

E = [change in quantity / (average of quantities)] / [change in price / (average of prices)]

Index

P

PCAOB (Public Company Accounting Oversight Board), 403

Performance analysis:
  and managing organizations, 190–191
  using flexible budget, 193–194
  using master budget, 191–193

Performance evaluation:
  and business units, 233–240
  and common costs, 237–239

Performance management, 189–279
  cost and variance measures, 190–232
  performance measures, 251–273
  practice questions, 275–279, 470–476
  responsibility centers and reporting segments, 233–249

Performance measures, 251–273
  Balanced Scorecard, 267–273
  evaluating product and customer profitability, 251–258
  return on investment and residual income, 259–265

Performance obligations:
  revenue recognition for, 83–85
  transaction price allocated to, 82–83

Periodicity, on financial statements, 3

Periodic method, 37–38

Perpetual method, 38

Personnel controls, 396, 408

PEST analysis, 106–107

PESTLE model, 106–107

Phishing, 435

Physical design (in SDLC), 437

Physical units method, 301

Planning, budgeting, and forecasting, 95–188
  annual profit plan and supporting schedules, 135–163
  budgeting concepts, 111–122
  budget methodologies, 165–173
  forecasting techniques, 123–134
  practice questions, 185–188, 464–469
  strategic planning, 96–109
  top-level planning and analysis, 175–183

Porter's five forces, 107

Porter's generic planning strategies, 101–102

Practical significance, 125–126

Predictive data analytics, 448

Preferred stock, 4, 11

Prescriptive data analytics, 448

Prevention costs, 382

Preventive controls, 399

Price variance, 197, 198
  direct materials, 208–209
  and sales volume variance, 199–200

Probability, in forecasting, 129

Process automation, 439–440

Process costing, 315–322
  cost flows in, 316–318
  and equivalent units, 315–316
  job order costing vs., 309–310
  normal and abnormal spoilage in, 318–319
  weighted-average process costing, 319–320

Processing controls, 414

Production budget, 137–138

Production costs, 141–147

Production cycle (accounting information system), 423

Product profitability, 251–258

Profits:
  evaluating product and customer profitability, 251–258
  measuring, 251–253

Profit centers, 234–235

Pro forma financial statements, 175–183
  balance sheet, 176–178
  closing strategic loop, 175
  financial ratio analysis, 179–181
  income statement, 176
  statement of cash flows, 178–179

Project budgets, 171

Property, plant, and equipment cycle (accounting information system), 423

Public Company Accounting Oversight Board (PCAOB), 403

Q

Qualified opinions, 404

Quality, management of, 379–386

Quantity variances, 197, 198, 201–204

R

Receivables, 31–36
  credit losses (bad debts), 31–34
  credit (default) risk, 31
  factoring, 35–36
  non-cash sales, 31

Reciprocal method, 338–340

Recognition, measurement, valuation and disclosure – liabilities, 63–72

Record retention, 434

Regression (data analysis technique), 448–449

Regression analysis:
  multiple, 126–127
  simple, 123–125

Reporting, 393. *See also* External financial reporting decisions; Integrated reporting

Reporting segments, 233–249
  business units and performance evaluation, 233–240
  transfer pricing, 241–249

Repurchase of treasury stock, 12

Resale of treasury stock, 12

Residual income, 261–264

Responsibility centers, 233–237

Responsive budgeting, 111–112

Retained earnings, 4, 12

Return on investment (ROI), 259–261, 263–264

Revenue centers, 234

Revenue recognition, 79–85
  allocating transaction price to performance obligations, 82–83
  determining transaction price, 81–82
  for each performance obligations, 83–85
  FASB and IASB converged standard for, 79
  identifying contracts with customers, 79–80
  identifying separate performance obligation in contracts, 80–81

Revenue to cash cycle (accounting information system), 422